Burning the veil

MANCHESTER
1824
Manchester University Press

Burning the veil

The Algerian war and the 'emancipation' of Muslim women, 1954–62

NEIL MACMASTER

Manchester
University Press

Manchester and New York

distributed in the United States exclusively
by Palgrave Macmillan

Copyright © Neil MacMaster 2009

The right of Neil MacMaster to be identified as the author of this work has been asserted by him in accordance with the Copyright, Designs and Patents Act 1988.

Published by Manchester University Press
Oxford Road, Manchester M13 9NR, UK
and Room 400, 175 Fifth Avenue, New York, NY 10010, USA
www.manchesteruniversitypress.co.uk

Distributed in the United States exclusively by
Palgrave Macmillan, 175 Fifth Avenue, New York,
NY 10010, USA

Distributed in Canada exclusively by
UBC Press, University of British Columbia, 2029 West Mall,
Vancouver, BC, Canada V6T 1Z2

British Library Cataloguing-in-Publication Data
A catalogue record for this book is available from the British Library

Library of Congress Cataloging-in-Publication Data applied for

ISBN   978 0 7190 7473 8   hardback

First published 2009

18 17 16 15 14 13 12 11 10 09   10 9 8 7 6 5 4 3 2 1

The publisher has no responsibility for the persistence or accuracy of URLs for any external or third-party internet websites referred to in this book, and does not guarantee that any content on such websites is, or will remain, accurate or appropriate.

Typeset in Sabon
by Servis Filmsetting Ltd, Stockport, Cheshire
Printed in Great Britain
by CPI Antony Rowe, Chippenham, Wiltshire

For my mother Lisa
who can also put up a good fight

Contents

Illustrations and tables

Tables

Acknowledgements

I would like to thank the Leverhulme Trust for the award of a Leverhulme Emeritus Fellowship in 2004 that made possible much of the research carried out in Paris and Aix-en-Provence. Also to the individuals who were generous with their time and support in forwarding the project, especially Marc Garanger, Jean-Louis Gérard, Monique Hervo, Jim House, Michel Launay, Mary MacMaster and Ryme Seferdjeli.

List of abbreviations

AFMA	Association des femmes musulmanes algériennes
AI	Affaires indigènes
ALN	Armée de libération nationale
AMG	Aide médicale gratuite
ANAS	Association nationale des assistants sociales
APC	Assemblées populaires communales
APP	Archives de la Préfecture de police (Paris)
ASSRA	Adjointes sanitaires et sociales rurales auxiliaires
AUMA	Association des ulema musulmans algériens
CAA	Corps d'armée d'Alger
CAC	Centre des archives contemporaines (Fontainbleau)
CAOM	Centre des archives d'outre-mer (Aix-en-Provence)
CAS	Comité d'action sociale
CASD	Comité d'action scientifiques de défense nationale
CEP	Certificat d'étude primaire
CHPT	Compagnie de haute-parleurs et de tracts
CM	commune mixte
CNFF	Conseil national des femmes françaises
CNRA	Conseil national de la Révolution algérienne
CPE	commune de plein exercice
CSP	Comité de salut public
CSW	Commission on the Status of Women (UN)
DPU	Dispositive de protection urbaine
ECPAD	Établissement de communicaion et de production audiovis- uelle de la défense (Fort-Ivry, Paris)
EMSI	Équipes medico-sociale itinérantes
ENA	Étoile nord-africaine
FLN	Front de libération nationale
FSNA	Français de souche nord-africaine
GCR	Groupement des contrôles radioélectriques
GG	Gouvernement générale

GPRA	Gouvernement provisoire de la République algérienne
IGAME	Inspecteur général de l'administration en mission extraordinaire
JFMA	Jeunes filles musulmanes algérienne
JUDMA	Jeunesse de l'union démocratique du manifeste algérien
LSSHA	Laboratoire des sciences humaines appliquées
MNA	Mouvement national algérien
MRP	Mouvement républicaines populaires
MSF	Mouvement de solidarité féminine
MTLD	Mouvement pour le triomphe des libertés démocratique
OAC	Organisation de l'action civique
OAS	Organisation armée secrète
OPA	Organisation politico-administrative
OR	Officier de renseignement
OS	Organisation spéciale
PCA	Parti communiste algérien
PCF	Parti communiste français
PDT	Political Development Theory
PFAT	Personnel féminine de l'armée de terre
PPA	Parti du peuple algérien
RG	Renseignements généraux
SAS	Section administrative spécialisée
SAU	Section administrative urbaine
SCA	Service cinématographiques des armées
SCI	Service civil international
SDECE	Service de documentation extérieure et de contre-espionnage
SHAT	Service historique de l'armée de terre (Vincennes)
UDMA	Union démocratique du manifeste algérien
UFA	Union des femmes d'Algérie
UFSF	Union française pour le suffrage des femmes
UGEMA	Union générale des étudiants musulmans algériens
UNAF	Union nationale des associations familiales
UNFA	Union nationale des femmes algériennes
WIDF	Women's International Democratic Federation
ZAA	Zone autonome d'Alger
ZCO	Zone centre oranais
ZEO	Zone est oranais
ZNE	Zone nord oranais
ZOC	Zone ouest constantinois
ZOO	Zone ouest oranais

Glossary

adjouzat	an elderly woman, head of the female household
Algérie française	the political slogan of those wishing to keep Algeria as a French colony
amilate	rural women recruited by the ALN to carry out domestic support tasks
arrondissement	local administrative area, corresponding to a sub-prefecture
attentisme	concealment of individual support for any one side in the conflict
ayala	the patriarchal, extended-family unit
bachadel	legal official in Islamic court
bachaga	honorific title of a 'traditional' leader appointed by the government
bakchich	bribes, often demanded by local Algerian leaders or *caïds*
bidonvilles	shantytowns
bled	the isolated rural interior
burnus	a hooded thick woollen cloak
cadi	a Muslim magistrate or judge
caïd	Chief or Algerian leader, appointed by the government with local administrative powers.
Centres sociaux	the educational and training centres for adults and juveniles established by Germaine Tillion
chéchia	a turban-like head-scarf
chicaya	the settlement of local disputes by army officer
colon	European settler, usually a land-owner
commando de chasse	small commando units trained to track ALN guerrilla bands
commune de pleine exercice	urban or small-town communes control led by European councillors

commune mixte	vast rural communes inhabited mainly by Algerians and administered by government appointees
corvée de bois	literally 'wood collecting fatigue': euphemism for summary execution in an isolated location
dechra	small village
délégués spéciaux	municipal councillors appointed under the *loi cadre* reform
djebel	mountains or sierra
djellaba	long over-gown
djemâa	traditional village council of elders
djounoud	soldiers
douar	village or rural commune
état civil	state civil register of births, marriages, deaths
évolué	educated and westernised Muslim person
fatiha	invocation or reading of Koran, for example to solemnise a marriage
fellagha	rebel fighter
fidayate	women urban fighters
fidayine	male commando fighters
fiqh	Islamic jurisprudence, doctrine
goum	an indigenous military unit
gourbis	a hut or shack
grande famille	influential family holding military, religious or political functions and exercising quasi-feudal power
hadj	pilgrimage to Mecca
hadjar	small, triangular face veil
haïk	long over-gown of light material used to provide total body cover and veiling
harka	common name for an indigenous unit attached to the French army
harki	common name for member of an indigenous unit attached to the French army
idda	three-month period of maintenance following repudiation
ijtihad	independent reasoning, a source of Muslim law
îlots	literally 'island': a block of urban housing
imam	religious leader of mosque
jebr	right in Islamic law for father or male guardian to choose the marriage partner

jihad	holy war
kanoun	customary laws
khammès	peasant share-cropper, usually taking one fifth of the yield
livret de famille	official family registration book
loi cadre	reform of local government law introduced by the Lacoste government
maghzen	indigenous armed unit attached to the SAS
mahakma	jurisdiction or court
majlis	assembly or council
marabout	holy man, descended from a saintly lineage and often possessing magical powers
mechta	farmhouse or hamlet
médersa	a religious school often attached to a mosque
Mintaqa	ALN military zone, subdivision of Wilaya
morchida	women political propagandist with the ALN
moudjahidate	women fighters attached to ALN units in the interior
moudjahidine	male ALN combatants in the interior
moussebilate	women militants, mainly peasants engaged in domestic support for ALN units
muphti	an expert in Islamic law
nachid	nationalist hymn or song
nahia	subdivision of Mintaqa in ALN organisation
ouvroir	sewing circle
pieds-noirs	common name for European settlers
ralliement	collective act of surrender or allegiance to French side
regroupement	military relocation of peasantry into a resettlement camp
roumi	European 'infidel'
salafiyya	return to pure scriptural sources
sharia	the holy law of Islam
sheikh	an elder or chief, head of a tribe or religious order
statut personnel	legal status of being under Islamic law
supplétifs	general term for all categories of indigenous auxiliaries with French army
talaq	the Islamic act of repudiation
taleb	Muslim teacher or scholar
tariqa	Sufi mystical confraternity or a method of spiritual discipline

ulema	religious scholar, or a member of the AUMA (Association des ulema musulmans algériens)
umma	the global community of all Muslims
village nègre	poor Arab quarter, usually on the outskirts of European urban settlements
walî	legal guardian
Wilaya	the largest military and administrative zone of the FLN
zaouia	monastic-type religious centre of the confraternities, often a place of pilgrimage and Islamic study
zone interdit	French military free-fire zone in mountainous interior

Introduction

There is . . . a lot of work that needs to be done on the role of women in
the Revolution. The woman in the town, in the mountains, in the enemy
administration, the prostitute and the intelligence that she obtains, the
woman in prison, under torture, in the face of death, and before the
tribunals.

Frantz Fanon, *L'An V de la révolution algérienne* (1959)

From 1926 onwards, the date of the foundation of the Algerian pro-
independence movement the *Étoile nord-africaine* (ENA), the forces of
nationalism began to gain a mass popular base and to place enormous
pressure for change on a colonial regime that was intent on preserving the social, political and economic domination of European settler
society. The tensions between the two communities reached breaking point at the end of the Second World War. The declaration of the
Atlantic Charter (14 August 1941) in which Churchill and Roosevelt
offered a vision of a post-war world in which all peoples would have
the right to self-determination; the Anglo-American landings in North
Africa in November 1942; the fall of the Algerian pro-Pétainist regime;
coupled with expectations that the massive involvement and sacrifice
of Algerian soldiers in the European campaigns against fascism would
receive political recompense, generated an intense expectation of change
among the nationalists. However, the right-wing settler political elites
were determined to respond to this challenge not by carrying out long-
overdue reform and by accepting Algerian equal rights, but rather by
trying to reassert the pre-war status quo that was based on a system of
military power, repressive laws, policing and state violence. The tensions
finally came to a head on VE day, 8 May 1945, when the nationalists
participated in mass demonstrations to celebrate the defeat of the Nazi
regime. At Sétif the Algerians paraded the illegal flag of the independence movement, and this was met with police gunfire that in turn triggered off a small-scale peasant revolt in which a hundred settlers were
killed.

This presented the opportunity that reactionary colonials had been waiting for, and the whole of the North Constantine region was subjected to a huge and disproportionate repression by the French army, navy and air-force and by settler civilian militias, which slaughtered tens of thousands of Algerians. The aim of this massive repression was to teach the Algerians a lesson, to reassert colonial hegemony and to stop in its tracks the dynamic expansion of the nationalist movement by arresting, torturing and killing its political cadres.[1] The murderous wave of colonial repression assumed its clearest logic in the provincial town of Guelma where, under the guidance of the Sub-Prefect André Achiary, impromptu militias arrested the most educated and promising of local Algerian youth, condemned them to death before 'revolutionary' tribunals of Public Safety, and dispatched them by lorry to isolated killing fields.[2] A prime target for Achiary was the cultured Reggui family, upwardly mobile entrepreneurs who enjoyed a rich intellectual life that was rooted in both Arab and Francophone language and culture. The logic of the situation dictated that the Reggui, a local symbol of integration between the Algerian and European communities that offered a beacon of hope for the future, had to be destroyed by settlers who were blindly intent on asserting their domination and on wrecking any chance of a peaceful inter-ethnic resolution to the deepening crisis of colonialism.

After the brutal elimination of two of the five Reggui sons, the only daughter Zohra, with enormous courage, directly confronted Achiary about the fate of her brothers only to be arrested and shot in turn. Zohra Reggui was an exceptional young woman by the standards of provincial Algeria: highly educated and 'westernised', she did not wear the veil and personified the rare example of the emancipated Muslim woman. As a symbol of modernity and Franco-Algerian integration Zohra also had to be eliminated by the die hard reactionaries, and among the many hundreds of executions carried out by the Guelma militias she, the most independent and Francophile, was the only woman.[3]

Thirteen years later in May 1958, and four years into the Algerian War of Independence, the revolt led by generals Salan and Massu again appropriated the revolutionary and republican symbolism of the French Revolution by seizing power through a Committee of Public Safety. But, in a reversal of the events of May 1945, the rebels orchestrated ceremonies of mass unveiling by Muslim women and quickly promulgated a raft of 'emancipation' policies. One of the questions that this book explores is how and why this U-turn came about. Why was it that a repressive colonial system that had for over a century maintained the material and intellectual backwardness of Algerian women now, in the

midst of a bloody war of decolonisation, turned to an extensive programme of 'emancipation', which included reform of the personal status
law, granting of the franchise, health and social security programmes,
educational provision and unveiling?

The principal aim of this introduction is to provide a general con-
textualisation and interpretive framework to set the scene for the more
detailed investigation that follows. Firstly, the term 'emancipation',
which is retained throughout, is not used in the sense of contemporary
or 'second-wave' feminism since this would be evidently anachronistic,
but rather in the sense that it was used constantly during the Algerian
War by the colonial government and military. This meaning will
become increasingly evident as the book progresses, but underlying it
was a reformist agenda that sought to extend citizenship and equality of rights to Algerian Muslim women so that they could 'catch up'
with their European sisters in metropolitan France and Algeria with
regard to voting rights, education, professional training, employment
opportunities, health care and welfare.[4] But it should be kept in mind
that the yard-stick or model of progress being applied by the colonial
authorities was that of contemporary French society, which during this
period (1954–62) saw women relegated to a highly conservative position marked by a Catholic and natalist ambiance, and repressive laws
in relation to marriage, divorce and birth-control. Implicit within the
drive to 'emancipation' was a Eurocentric and assimilationist model
that sought to transform Algerian women into 'civilised' and westernised beings who would share the essential cultural features of bourgeois
French women in relation to everything from dress style to consumerism
and an idealised model of the nuclear family and the conjugal married
couple bound by mutual affection.[5]

The emancipation programme of the French army, like the overall
strategy of counter-insurgency, had a dual reformist and repressive
purpose that generated constant and ultimately irresolvable tensions.[6]
This contradiction arose from the fact that emancipation was initiated
as part of a repressive and intelligence gathering process and, simultaneously, as a reformist endeavour to win Algerian hearts and minds to
the French cause. The policy on women that first appeared in late 1956
coincided with, and was engineered by, psychological warfare specialists
of the Fifth Bureau, which rose to gain extraordinary levels of political
power in the army between late 1956 and early 1960. The Fifth Bureau
was inspired by the idea that attempts to win over the Algerian population to the French side could not afford to neglect women, one half of
the population. Moreover, good or accurate intelligence – which was
regarded as the key to any successful counter-insurgency programme

– was crucially dependent on building close contacts with informers and local populations in general,[7] and women in particular. One anonymous general told the journalist Jacques Perrier, 'Algerian women constitute a third force between us and the *Front de libération nationale* (FLN). When, in certain regions that are infested with rebels, the women come over to our side then pacification is not far off'.[8]

In this drive to bring Algerian women on side, the military had come to share one of the key ideological beliefs of Algerian nationalism, the view that women and the family constituted the last remaining bastion of religious, cultural and social identity. This mythical structure or *topos* reflected or was grounded in some kind of reality in the sense that French colonialism had, during over a century of penetration, subjugated and fragmented the basic economic and social structures of indigenous society, but had hesitated to encroach on the 'private' reserve of the family which remained subject to Muslim law and custom. One line of enquiry in this study is to see how the French, under the umbrella of emancipation, attempted through a 'strategy of contact', particularly through female army social workers, to breach the defence-works of secluded Muslim women and build bridges to the wives and daughters of fighters and militants of the FLN.

While many French colonels and officers regarded intelligence gathering as primary, others placed economic development at the heart of the overall emancipation strategy. A key assumption of the French government and army was that victory in modern guerrilla warfare was not dependent on the strength of advanced technology or conventional forces, but on winning over the allegiance of the masses so that insurgent forces would be deprived of their support base. In the famous Maoist dictum, guerrillas flourished among the people like fish in water, unless the enemy succeeded in draining away the lake. Algerian women would be won over to the French side by a raft of measures that included combating the endemic poverty and misery of peasants and slum-dwellers who had been systematically marginalised and discriminated against by the colonial system, measures that included free medical and food aid, primary education, job creation and better housing.

From one angle there seems to be nothing particularly surprising about the French agenda: pragmatic common-sense would seem to dictate that Algerians would side with *Algérie française* if they became convinced that France offered the prospect of a higher standard of living under the financial and technical umbrella of an advanced European state, as opposed to the risky endeavour of 'going it alone', trapped in the dire poverty of a Third World country led by 'communist' or 'pan-Arab' terrorists.[9] The agenda could be seen as a fairly standard developmental programme, one that was symbolised by de Gaulle's announcement of the industrial and agrarian investment of the 1958 Constantine Plan. Such a programme did not necessarily have to be addressed to women in particular: indeed, during the first two years of the war, notably under the Governor Jacques Soustelle, there was little specific mention of women or gender, largely because women were tacitly assumed to be the 'trickle-down' beneficiaries of an overall economic transformation and progress. There was little discussion during 1954–56 regarding Algerian women *as* women: rather their 'backwardness' would be abolished along with the improvement in living standards of the whole population.

However, from late 1956 onwards the colonial government began to shift its attention towards a quite specific gendered policy of development that was targeted at women. What began to emerge was a programme that moved far beyond any technical or economic logic and which sought to 'modernise' Algerian women, to liberate them from what was perceived to be the ignorance and the benighted horrors of Muslim patriarchy and seclusion, and to transform them via a European model of womanhood. The prison of domestic seclusion would be battered down, and the degrading practices of child-marriage, polygamy and repudiation, of love-less arranged marriage, would be exchanged for a western model of the nuclear family and conjugal relations founded on mutual attraction and equality. One of the themes of this study is an examination of the structure of this model and of the propaganda techniques deployed by the army, from cinema and radio to village assemblies, to try and diffuse western concepts of emancipation. While, as will be seen, this initiative appeared from late 1956 in response to quite specific events and contingencies in the development of the war, it was far from unique and can be better understood when placed within a wider historical and comparative perspective of similar authoritarian and largely male-driven state reform programmes throughout the Middle East.

During the late nineteenth century and early twentieth century bourgeois nationalist intellectuals throughout the major urban centres of the Middle East and North Africa were preoccupied by the vital question of the backwardness of their own societies, and why they were so economically and militarily weak compared to European powers that invaded both through armed force and a dynamic capitalism. One emergent school of thought, well represented by the Egyptian lawyer Qasim Amin in *The Liberation of Women* (1899), was that national regeneration could only be achieved through the emancipation of women.[10] Male intellectuals and politicians in the Middle East, through contact with

western society and travels in Europe, were impressed by the relative
state of freedom enjoyed by western women and their contribution to
social and economic progress. It took about two decades for such an
ideological position to impact significantly on political practice, particularly through the radical initiatives of Mustapha Kemal ('Atatürk')
in Turkey. Kemal promulgated the 'top-down' emancipation of women,
symbolised by unveiling and the introduction in 1926 of a modern,
secular family code based on Swiss law, as part of a broader package
of measures to create a strong state.[11] The Kemalist 'revolution', particularly in relation to women, had a significant impact on a number
of neighbouring militarised and authoritarian regimes, including that
of Riza Shah Pahlavi in Iran (1925–41),[12] King Amanullah (1919–29)
in Afghanistan, and, most dramatically of all, Bolshevik colonialism
in Central Asia.[13] The key feature of the inter-war period was that
women's organisations were given a considerable boost as an integral
part of nationalist movements, but at the same time such an alliance
served to harness the energy of women to the needs of 'state feminism'
that had little interest in facilitating the basic rights and autonomy of
such organisations.[14]

There are a number of shared features of these inter-war movements,
that can be characterised as an 'autocratic secular nationalism',[15] that
help to throw light on French policy during the Algerian War. Forced
emancipation tended to create deep divisions between pro-western modernisers and conservative, religious forces that regarded the penetration
of European culture as a dangerous subversion and corruption of Islam
and an authentic religio-national identity. Battle lines over radically
opposed visions of the nation were invariably formulated by reference
to the 'woman question', dress codes and the veil. The centrality of the
veil arose from the fact that it provided a readily identifiable symbol, a
public and visible marker, of support or opposition to Islamic values,
gender segregation, familial honour and the socio-political domination
of the male lineage. For the leaders of authoritarian, modernising states
who were keen to carry out a cultural revolution, dress codes provided
a ready mechanism for the policing of society, the public exposure
of degrees of inner resistance or of levels of support for the official
agenda of national construction. Such strategies have a long history: for
example, the Enlightened despot Peter the Great (1682–1725), in his
attempts to force a backward Russia to catch up with western Europe,
had compelled his courtiers to cut off their beards (or pay a special tax)
and to dress in a European style.

The instrumental purpose of such dress codes is shown by the
fact that in Turkey and Iran in the 1920s they were directed as much

towards males as towards women through the official banning of the fez and turban for a European-style hat.[16] Iranian policemen and soldiers publicly tore off and trampled turbans, to which riotous crowds led by conservative clerics responded by making bonfires of the 'Pahlavi hat'.[17] Long before the orchestration of mass unveiling ceremonies by the French army in Algeria during May 1958 (examined in chapter 3) such spectacles had occurred in Egypt (1923), Uzbekistan (1927) Syria (1942) and Lebanon (1944).[18] Resistance to such campaigns or general processes of cultural westernisation took the form of physical assault by male (and sometimes female) Islamist vigilante groups on women who were accused of dressing like 'whores', wearing make-up, drinking alcohol, smoking or displaying themselves in public spaces, especially cafés and cinemas which were regarded as places of debauchery.

The veil, as the key symbol of the subordination of women, always referred to far more than tensions over the relatively trivial question of dress design: it was a marker of the total form of society to which bitterly opposed camps aspired. In particular the widespread battles over the veil throughout the Middle East, Soviet Central Asia and the Maghreb after 1919 were intimately linked to processes of state-building. In western Europe the modern state had developed over many centuries through processes of centrifugal expansion from geographical heartlands (the courts of London, Paris, Madrid and elsewhere), and the gradual extension of power over the periphery, by destroying regional particularism or alternative foci of loyalty or identity. The centre imposed homogenous and 'universal' systems of governance across the national space through the bureaucratic maintenance of uniform systems of law, language, coinage, taxation, education and conscription.[19]

The emerging nations of the Middle East were attempting to 'catch up' with the west by accelerating, often within the space of a few years or decades, processes that had taken many centuries in Europe. The Kemalist model of modernisation that was influential in Iran, Afghanistan, Egypt and elsewhere was much like a contemporary form of enlightened despotism: many reformers saw the best chance for the rapid transformation of the nation not through slow processes of democratisation, but via highly militarised regimes, backed by powerful reformed armies, which could impose 'revolutionary' change from above without being deterred by the fear of mass resistance by religious or conservative populist revolt, particularisms that could be crushed by soldiers and police forces. Typical of such autocratic reformism was Riza Shah Pahlavi who, much impressed by Kemal during his state visit to Turkey in 1934, sought to impose western dress as just one component of a much vaster programme to create a strong state through a centralising drive that included census registration, conscription, judicial reform and radical secularisation.[20] As Zehra Arat points out, the reform programme of Kemal was to provide Turkish women with education and skills as instruments of the economic development of the *nation*, but this was certainly not feminism in the sense of liberation that would promote women's individual or collective consciousness 'for themselves'. Turkish women, through modernisation, were to improve their skills *as* wives and mothers.[21]

Authoritarian regimes, in the drive to emancipate women as part of the modernising process, invariably met diffuse but dogged resistance at the level of the most fundamental social unit, the family. Historians have explored in detail how the modern European state gradually penetrated and transformed the private autonomy of feudalism, the clans, kin and extended family networks that as units of localised production, economic autarky and primary loyalty long provided an alternative core of identity.[22] In the Middle East and North Africa however, 'tribal' and extended family groups, underpinned by a religiously sanctioned ideology of patriarchy, remained a strong and dynamic force well into the late twentieth century. Authoritarian reformism was confronted with the almost insuperable problem of trying to erode or transform the very bedrock of society; a problem of particular importance to the Algerian situation, to which we return below. A number of specialists on women in the Middle East, notably Deniz Kandiyoti, Suad Joseph and Mounira Charrad, have argued that the changing position of women in Muslim societies can be best understood through linking it to state-building processes.[23] It was precisely because family structure carried within it a blueprint for the global society, everything from property relations to political power, that it was the focus of bitter struggle. While veiling, as a symbol of this wider field, generated much passion, the most crucial way in which opposing forces attempted to steer or shape the internal logic of the family was through conservative defence of Islamic law (*sharia*) or through reform of the personal status laws relating to marriage.[24]

After this digression into the broader processes at work throughout the Middle East, we are in a better position to understand the nature of French emancipation during the Algeria War of Independence. Firstly, French policy towards Algerian women after 1956 was directly influenced and, to some extent, modelled on the earlier programmes introduced in Turkey, Syria, Lebanon, Egypt, Tunisia and elsewhere. Many colonial cadres in Algeria, both military and civilian, had had a direct experience of the more advanced Arab women's organisations in other French colonies, protectorates or mandates, particularly interwar Lebanon and Syria.[25] The colonial government was inspired by a

Kemalist approach in its modernisation of Algerian society, a reform programme that recognised that a developmental project could not work unless it included women. Secondly, the emancipation was also very much part of a highly militarised agenda, in which a huge army through the policy of *quadrillage*, the occupation and control of the entire geographical space of the colony, possessed the bureaucratic and armed power to impose a radical 'top-down' reform on a recalcitrant periphery. Finally, and most crucially, the French army – not unlike the quasi-dictatorial regimes in inter-war Turkey, Iran, Iraq and Afghanistan – aimed at a 'forced march' modernisation programme. In the French case the urgency arose from the need to win over the population as a condition of victory in a violent and costly colonial war that needed to be terminated as quickly as possible. Significantly both Atatürk and the French colonels found inspiration in the Jacobin Revolution, the primary symbol of a radical secularisation and process of state-formation that depended on a programme of forced centralisation, populist élan, and the crushing of priestly and provincial obscurantism.[26] It was no mere coincidence that the generals' revolt of May 1958 led to the establishment of a Committee of Public Safety that, among its very first acts, orchestrated mass unveiling parades.

It may seem surprising to characterise the French occupation and repression of 1954–62 as a project of state-building, particularly as France has been so widely interpreted by historians as an exemplar of the advanced bureaucratic and centralised nation. However, the colonels saw their revolt as an attempt to regenerate the weak and effete government of the Fourth Republic from the colonial periphery, but also to weld Algeria, a literal extension of French soil, into a strong and integrated economic power.[27] Under the official slogan of 'l'Algérie nouvelle', the colonels set out to create a dynamic nation-state through a process of 'integration' that would completely transform the identity and mind-set of both the *colons*, who were regarded by them as a prime cause of the colonial crisis through their egotistic racism and unbending refusal to accept Algerians into the *cité*, as well as of the impoverished Algerians. The foundation myth of this new imperial nation was established during the ecstatic and theatrical 'fraternisation' parades of May 1958 when both settler and Algerian women embraced each other in the Algiers Forum. Muslim women, claimed the army, expressed their 'spontaneous' wish to meld into the new nation by unveiling and declaring their deep wish to become identical to their European sisters in dress, freedom from seclusion and basic rights.

The apparent conundrum of France, one of the most highly developed nations in the world, engaging in a process of accelerated state-building at such a late stage as the mid-twentieth century, can be resolved by the fact that it showed simultaneously the features of both a 'strong' and a 'weak' state. As Matthew Connelly has noted, the geography or 'frontier' of a 'North–South' divide between an advanced western economy (metropolitan France) and an impoverished 'Third World' colonial Algeria did not lie along the barrier of the Mediterranean Sea, but rather ran east–west some two hundred miles south of the Algeria coast separating the advanced urban and European dominated societies of the northern literal from the underdeveloped interior in which 70 per cent of Algerians lived in abject poverty as peasants and nomads.[28]

The difference between the two Algerias was the consequence of long-term and complex processes by which *colons* had ensured a monopoly of state investment in their own settlements, the *commune de pleine exercice* (CPE), in the form of roads, electrification, water supply, schools, hospitals and other infrastructures, and the withholding of modernisation for the native zones, the *commune mixte* (CM), that were left in endemic poverty.[29] However, as Claudine Chaulet and others have argued, the dualism of Algerian space did not mean that the isolated interior (*bled*) was simply 'abandoned' to its fate by the European settlers, since the rural and mountainous interior, as with the Bantustan system of apartheid in South Africa, offered a reserve of cheap, mobile labour for the *colon* estates, docks, construction sites and industries to the north.[30] Colonial capitalism thus had an interest in actively retaining the 'breeding' capacity of Algeria's rural population, and this system carried major implications for women who paid the heavy costs of reproducing and sustaining labour-power.[31] However, the civilian and military heads of the Algerian government after 1954, most of them without previous experience of the colony, were shocked to discover the extent of the 'Third World' backwardness of the *bled*, precisely the interior, mountainous and forested zones in which the *Armée de libération nationale* (ALN) guerrilla army established a support base among the local population. It seemed crucial to the generals to win the battle for hearts and minds in rural Algeria, but the attempt to carry out a crash modernisation programme faced the almost insuperable problem of trying to reverse the accumulated effect of what was euphemistically referred to as under-administration (*sous administration*), over a century of under-investment, neglect and weak government

The biggest challenge facing the colonial government in its project of emancipation was the endemic poverty, illiteracy and ignorance of women in the *bled*. But in the periphery the modern state was historically weak (lack of local administrators, of courts, an accurate civil register, schools, doctors, roads) while the potential foci of resistance to

state encroachment, such as 'traditional' tribal, kin and religious organisations, were at their strongest. A key part of our overall argument is
that the colonial economic and political system had for over a century,
until the insurrection of 1954, worked to ensure the 'protection' of the
extended family group, and the ideology of patriarchy that underpinned
it, thus reinforcing the domestic structures that would radically impede
modernisation of the family by the French (1956–62), and then by the
post-independence FLN government. After 1956 the heavily militarised
colonial government, in its attempt to force through an accelerated
'revolutionary' transformation of women's position, faced problems of
breaking down the opposition of patriarchal authority and conservative religious leaders that was very similar to the difficulties faced by
authoritarian and militarised regimes engaged in state-building processes in Soviet Central Asia, Turkey, Iran and Afghanistan in the 1920s.
If anything French interventionism in Algeria was even more forceful
in the context of the Cold War since US and European 'political development theory' and counter-insurgency doctrine, upholding a need to
aid weak colonial states that were exposed to communist insurgency,
often saw modern armies as bureaucratic organisations that were best
able to guide 'archaic' societies towards modernity.[32] But one of the big
questions facing the French after 1954, as for the 1920s regimes, was
whether reform might be pushed too far and too fast so as to generate
revolt and public opposition on a scale to threaten the survival of government, as occurred with the Afghan tribal revolts that brought down
King Amanullah in 1929.

The French emancipation agenda, far from accepting full equality between European and Algerian women, a process of integration
founded on pluralism and multiculturalism before the letter, was built
on a Eurocentric cultural model of domesticity through which Muslim
women would reach true freedom by a modernisation process that
would 'westernise' them in every respect. Underlying French policy
and discourse on Algerian women was a fundamental, and perhaps
fatal assumption of an inevitable global progress by which all societies
would, sooner or later, move from simple or primitive forms of organisation to a 'higher' phase of civilisation, a stage that was overtly or implicitly always imagined by reference to contemporary western models.
According to this teleology Algerian women would, through economic
change, urbanisation, education and entry into a modern world of
consumerism, eventually come to share an identical lifestyle to that of
European women. As will be seen, the vision of a golden future held
out by army propagandists to Algerian women was essentially a petit-
bourgeois dream of gleaming Formica kitchens, washing machines, the

nuclear family and the conjugal couple bound together by sentiment.[33] A considerable part was played in the promulgation of this model of domesticity, as in many other colonial contexts, by European women, the wives and daughters of senior army officers or the women recruited into mobile welfare teams, the *Équipes médico-sociale itinérantes* (EMSI). The great, and unforeseen, danger of this *civilising mission* was that the French wrongly assumed the inevitable and necessary triumph of their own culture: it was, to them, so unquestionably superior and right, that they could not imagine Algerian women (and men), once educated and rational actors, choosing to adhere to an 'inferior' and backward way of life. This model, which was shared by developmental policy-makers, meant that the French were overly optimistic about the way in which the emancipation agenda would sweep all before it and, more importantly, they were blind to the enormous resilience and power of Algerian extended family structures that worked according to a radically different logic from the European nuclear family. The French emancipation programme, like that of Algerian post-independence modernisation, was broken on the invisible rocks and reefs of patriarchy.

The FLN, nationalism and the marginalisation of women

While the centre of gravity of this study lies in the history of French emancipation as an instrument of counter-insurgency and modernisation (chapters 2 to 8), it is also concerned with the impact of this strategy on the FLN. As will be seen, it is not easy to establish whether the 'liberation' policy and practices of the FLN originated in response to French innovations, or vice versa. Once the emancipation agenda had taken off on both sides during 1956 it is evident that the opposed forces entered into a constant struggle to command the support of Muslim women and developed techniques or programmes that mimicked or were modelled on the other. But in general, it is argued that the French army had a much stronger motivation to deploy a discourse and practice of liberation than the FLN, which assumed a more reactive position. This nationalist discourse was to carry long-term conservative implications for Algerian policies on Muslim women both during and after the war (chapters 9 to 11).

During the Algerian War and the first years of independence the liberation struggle of Algerian women was held up across the globe as a shining beacon by socialist, Third World and anti-colonial movements. The predominant media image was of maquis heroines and urban terrorists, strong and determined women who, it was assumed, would claim a full and equal place in the future independent society. This was the message conveyed by Gillo Pontecorvo's powerful film, *The Battle of Algiers* (1965), in which female freedom fighters broke through the constraints of traditional Muslim gender roles, and also by the thesis of Frantz Fanon's influential essays in *L'An V de la révolution algérienne* (1959).[34] This heroic myth, which entered the main stream of western culture and for long obscured the reality of Algerian policy on women, is itself a testimony to the efficacy of FLN propaganda. However, in particular after the conservative and *sharia*-based legislation on women and the family formulated during c. 1980–84, feminists have widely accepted the fact that the post-independence Algerian state assumed a highly regressive position on women's rights, one that was more reactionary than that of many comparable modern states in the Middle East, and in particular of neighbouring Tunisia.

For long there was a tendency to explain this failure as the result of an authoritarian, single-party regime that through a quasi-military coup at the point of independence shattered the revolutionary optimism generated during the war. The idea of a key break in 1962 has been more recently revised by historians, following in the steps of Mohammed Harbi's innovative work,[35] who instead of operating in terms of a binary colonial/post-colonial opposition have begun to trace the long-term origins and continuities of the contemporary Algerian state in the early history of the nationalist movement from the 1920s onwards.[36] Since the 1990s this approach has been facilitated by historians' access to a wealth of previously unavailable 'inside' information about the war-time FLN. Firstly, the Algerian political crisis after 1988 shattered the ideological hegemony of the single-party, authoritarian FLN-led state, the attempt to impose an official version of the history of the 'revolution' and to exercise a tight control over access to Algerian archival sources. For example, the ground-breaking research of Djamila Amrane (née Danièle Minne), a former FLN militant who was imprisoned by the French, was based on oral sources as well as access to the official registers of the veterans' organisation (*Ministère des Moudjahidine*) relating to 10,949 women combatants.[37] Secondly, since the 1990s the systematic cataloguing of, and more open access provided to, the immense military and civilian archives 'repatriated' in 1962 and deposited in Paris and Aix-en-Provence have facilitated a remarkable change in the character and volume of research on the Algerian War.[38] While the archives provide a vast amount of information on the internal and often secretive workings of the war-time military and civilian government – the key source used for mapping our main theme of French emancipation – they provide information that extends well beyond the mind-set and practices of the dominant colonial power. The French army and police captured a mass of internal FLN reports, which allow the organisation to be interpreted through its own documents rather than being refracted through the prism of the French army. This material is now facilitating a major shift in the historical understanding of the FLN,[39] and has provided the basis for a wave of new research relating to Algerian women.[40]

In the light of these sources, which relate primarily to the opposing male-led agendas of the French government and the FLN, it should be emphasised that this study is *not* concerned with an attempt to try and unlock the extremely difficult and contested field of subaltern studies, to reconstruct the subjective experience and universe of Algerian women. Such a project remains problematic for the period of the Algerian War, in part because some 96 per cent of all women were illiterate and left very little in the way of written evidence, but also because it has proved particularly difficult to gather and interpret oral evidence.[41] However, while Algerian women often appear to be silent victims that were caught or crushed between the masculine agendas of power, of colonial occupiers and resisters, the archive still provides a considerable amount of valuable information (as long as it is interpreted with care as an expression of the male voice) about the organisation and role of Algerian women. For example, confidential or secret reports provide almost daily information about the difficulties faced by army teams working to build contact with women in rural locations, including, for example, incidents involving women sabotaging generators or the electricity supply during the showing of propaganda films. The reports of police spies and informers between 1944 and 1954 provide invaluable information about what was happening inside the meetings of the early nationalist women's organisations (chapter 1). The colonial government and army also employed specialist colonial officers, mainly from the *services des affaires indigènes* as well as ethnographers like Germaine Tillion and Jean Servier, who were proficient in Arabic and Berber dialect and had a close knowledge of Islamic and customary law, to investigate the situation of Algerian women. The archive thus contains a considerable volume of sophisticated commentary on women, and employed social scientific methodology, including, for example, a 1959 report on Algerian attitudes towards French emancipation that was based on 15,000 questionnaire returns. One advantage of this extensive material is that it enables a more detailed picture to be built up of the situation of the great mass of women in the interior, the heartland of the rebellion, who tend to have been under-researched.[42] The wealth of sociological and intelligence data has been further enriched by utilising the extensive archive of photographs of women taken by professional photojournalists and rank-and-file soldiers.[43] In particular the photographs of

Marc Garanger have served as the starting point of a detailed case-study approach (chapter 6) to the situation of peasant women within the context of military violence and 'reform' in the isolated village of Bordj Okhriss.

In chapter 1 it is argued that an organised Algerian women's movement appeared much later than in many other states in the Maghreb and Middle East. During the decade 1944–54 a militant and dynamic organisation first appeared in the major urban centres as an integral component of the wider nationalist movement. While under normal peacetime conditions this infant organisation might have been expected to expand and lay the basis for a strong, post-independence feminist movement, in reality this promising current was arrested, if not 'broken', by the War of Independence. While this set-back can be partly ascribed to the repressive violence of the French army and the dislocation of family life, equally important was the way in which any movement which represented the specific demands of women was voluntarily dissolved for the duration of the war into the urgent and higher priority of the struggle for independence. FLN propaganda, which made skilful use of the heroic symbol of female warriors while superficially appearing to international opinion to champion the position of women, did no such thing: rather it was able to draw upon a long oral and written tradition within Muslim societies that, in an Islamic version of the myth of Joan of Arc as national saviour, referred back to historic or mythic female warriors who during moments of mortal danger to the community *temporarily* assumed the martial role of men.[44] In the deployment of the traditional myth of the heroine fighters the assumption was that, once victory was gained, women would revert to their allotted domestic and maternal functions.[45] Algeria followed in a path that was shared by many other nationalist movements: a common but contradictory pattern was that while resistance and independence movements played a major role in providing an impetus to women's organisations, once victory was assured and constitutional or independence goals achieved, governments proceeded to renege on or dampen female militancy or reformist demands.[46]

However, in a fast changing world in which women's rights as citizens were being rapidly extended and built into UN and other international conventions, the FLN, which laid claim to being a modernising force for the liberation of a subject people, could not afford to be seen to neglect the issue of women's rights. In the decade between 1944 and 1954 the emerging women's movement was not split by a simple binary opposition between modernisers and 'traditionalists', but revealed a complex pattern of internal tensions and contradictions. For example, many progressive women did not view Islam as incompatible with women's interests,[47] but what the deadly divisions of war achieved was to halt the complex and potentially fertile debate emerging in the women's movement before 1954 and to channel it into deeply entrenched positions. As in Iran where Riza Shah's autocratic intervention on veiling caused 'an unbridgeable chasm' among women,[48] so did the French army drive to emancipation, a strategy that was designed precisely to outflank the nationalists by the pre-emptive occupation of this ideological terrain.

With the outbreak of the war for independence a significant strata of educated Algerian women (*évoluées*) found themselves moving into the French camp, which appeared to them to offer the best hopes of a progressive, modernising agenda, so draining away part of the potential support base for a unified women's movement. Facing them were nationalist and communist women activists whose movements were virtually dissolved into the FLN organisation where they became subsidiary to, or locked into, a male-led agenda. The FLN hierarchy throughout the war was riven by numerous internal divisions, one of them being between a current of more secular intellectuals who favoured a Kemalist or socialist model of women's rights based on a separation of civil and religious powers, and a more conservative 'Islamo-Arabic' current that ultimately triumphed in the battle for political power. In general women on the FLN side began to share a religious nationalism that emphasised Islamic cultural resistance to dangerous western subversion of the *sharia*, Arab language and identity, an authentic nationhood that was constructed by a highly gendered ideology that placed women as the mothers of the people, the guardians of the sacred space of the family/household, and the educators of a future generation of male warriors and citizens.

The ideological formulation of the 'family-as-cultural-fortress' can be found in nationalist movements throughout the Middle East and North Africa in the twentieth century, and it served to internally fracture and weaken women's organisations.[49] However, the balance of forces between 'modernising' and 'traditionalist' agendas varied considerably from one country to another, depending on the specific historical and political context. Elizabeth Thompson has suggested that in independent states like Turkey or Egypt (after 1922), it was politically possible for governments to support a modernising agenda for women by opposing or eroding the position of the conservative religious establishment: a degree of westernisation or secularism was seen as compatible with nationalism.[50] Under Kemal the élan of nationalism and modernisation of women drove in the same direction. Similarly, in the remarkable instance of Tunisia, Bourguiba was able to make good use of the popular prestige that he enjoyed at independence as leader of

[handwritten margin note: useful counter-example of Tunisia after independence]

a successful liberation struggle, to legislate immediately the progressive
1956 reform of the personal status law.

In the colonial context, the dynamic could be quite different. As
Douglas Northrop notes, historically most imperial powers had not
sought to assimilate indigenous peoples through extension of equal
legal, political or citizenship rights, but had preserved a dualistic system
that locked 'native' masses of the periphery into an inferior subject
status. Soviet colonial policy in Central Asia was unusual in the extent
to which it sought complete integration such that Muslim women 'were
to be remade into fully modern Soviet citizens'.[51] However, French
policy on Algerian women after 1956 went through an abrupt U-turn
from a dualistic system of domination to one of integration that was
remarkably similar to the Soviet model. This had considerable implications for the reinforcement of conservative Islamist ideology at the core
of nationalism.

In some post-1945 colonial contexts, such as Nigeria, where the transition to independence was relatively peaceful, it was possible for the
British government to invest in development aid and reform for women,
from extension of education to health and welfare programmes, with
the tacit support of nationalists. Post-independence government openly
acknowledged its debt to the positive side of planned decolonisation.[52] But in the Algerian instance, emancipation was embedded in an
extremely violent liberation war and in these circumstances any Algerian
women siding with westernisation could be viewed as traitors. While in
many nationalist struggles we can find traces of currents or tendencies
that associated female support for western forms of emancipation with
treason,[53] perhaps nowhere was this more damaging than in Algeria
where the association was welded in the crucible of a long and bloody
war, and in which the occupying army championed European forms
of female modernity and liberation with particular force. This linkage
was to have extremely negative, long-term implications for Algerian
women.

The ideological formulation of the 'family-as-cultural-fortress' provided FLN ideologues during the war with a powerful means to counter
French emancipation as a dangerous Fifth-column agenda to penetrate
and subvert the very life-force of the nation. Conversely, Algerian women
who favoured the advancement of women's rights could be marginalised
as colonialist lackeys. That this conservative, rather than progressive
and secular, position on women won out within the FLN can also be
linked to the roots of Algerian populist nationalism. The internal FLN
documents captured by the French army show that in general militants,
guerrilla fighters and the wider population in which they found support,

were far less 'revolutionary' than has often been imagined, particularly
by left-wing commentators in the past. To the mass of illiterate peasants
the battle against the French had little if anything to do with Marxist
or socialist forms of transformative liberation, but rather with removal
of the oppressor *tout court*. This is not to deny the enormous potency
of the utopian faith which inspired the huge sacrifices that were made,
but this was formulated more in terms of a messianic vision constructed
on the restoration of a 'true' Islamic society that lay nascent beneath
centuries of colonial destruction, rather than with relation to a secularist
blue-print. The FLN, instead of opposing or marginalising the ideological position represented by Islamic clerics, and in particular the influential *Association des ulema musulmans algériens* (AUMA) founded
by Ben Badis, absorbed the Islamist leaders and their doctrine into the
core of the nationalist movement. As in Lebanon the nationalists forged
a 'gender pact' with Islamic populism which operated in two stages.
Firstly, during the phase of armed conflict, nationalist women would
agree to postpone their demands *as* women until independence was
won. But with victory assured the pact between male nationalists and
clerics would ensure that masculine authority would be firmly reasserted
over women who in the chaos of war might have challenged seclusion,
veiling and patriarchal controls.[54] The infant, but dynamic women's
movement that had appeared during 1944–54 was thus 'mothballed' for
the duration of the long struggle (1954–62), but did not exit from the
war with the expected new-found energy, but was radically smothered
for another two decades.

Finally, it is argued, the FLN did not only enter into a pact with
Islamic forces because of the strength of religion in society, but also
because Islam provided the ideological expression and legitimation for
patriarchy. The term 'patriarchy' is not used here in the radical feminist sense of a universal and a-historical male domination, but refers
to complex kinship systems and modes of inheritance that sought to
enhance the long-term chances of survival of family groups through
strategies that controlled access to land, resources and reproduction
(labour power and male descent). In the 'classic patriarchy' prevalent
throughout the Middle East, girls were given away to their husband's
family group, where they were subordinate to both males and senior
women.[55] Marriage strategies, which ideally aimed to prevent subdivi-
sion of land and property through endogamy, were crucially dependent
on alliances built through arranged marriages that were 'rationally'
controlled by elders, not by the romantic choice of youth. The 'market-
ability' of women, the negotiation of the 'good marriage', was crucially
dependent on the group's ability to guard sexual honour and status

through rigorous gender segregation (seclusion, veiling). Women, in particular the older matriarchs, were not (as often perceived from the 'west'), subjugated and passive victims but actively colluded in the reproduction of the system and its values. Conversely women who fell outside the stability and protection offered by the family (widows, divorcees, refugees and victims of disrupted groups) were condemned to a life of harsh poverty, toil, marginalisation and dishonour.

Deniz Kandiyoti, Mounira Charrad and Suad Joseph note that the patriarchal system varied from one state or region to another in the Middle East and North Africa, but that in order to understand such differences it is important to make an analytic distinction between Islam and the underlying social, economic and political logic of kinship.[56] Geographically Islam made various accommodations to the complex mosaic of societies it encountered on the ground. However, since Islam provided the crucial ideological formulation, the sacred and encoded doctrinal base for family regulation (notably through the *sharia* and customary law), most Algerians *believed* that the defence of patriarchy was a religious obligation. Unlike the earlier historiography of the Algerian War that portrayed it as a revolutionary movement, access to the FLN archive reveals the extent to which the *moudjahidine* and population in general were motivated by a diffuse, but very real religious or *jihadist* sentiment. The conservative FLN nationalist discourse on women's rights reflected a certain *real politik*, a pragmatic recognition of the strength of patriarchy in Algerian society. In the mortal struggle with the French for popular support it proved wiser not to alienate the conservative religious leaders (*imams*, the *Ulema*, *cadis*, *caïds*) that held such influence over the masses, nor to challenge existing structures of familial and clan power that subjugated women. It was the French who, through a risky emancipation agenda, ran the greater danger of inciting resistance and reinforcing support for the FLN. The Algerian extended patriarchal family group (the *ayala*) showed extraordinary adaptability and powers of resistance to the threat posed by the chaos of war, social and economic dislocation, mass uprooting and the centralised planning initiatives of post-independence governments. It is argued (chapters 10–11) that it was the recognition by the state of the inner strength of the *ayala* that led FLN political elites after 1962, as they manoeuvred for political power in a situation of civil war, instability and conflicting clientele systems, to quietly acquiesce in the subordination of women and the retention of highly conservative personal status or family laws.

The vitality of a patriarchy that adapted well to provide economic security in a rapidly changing society carried some negative implications for the extension of full civic rights to women. As Suad Joseph notes, there exists a deep contradiction between the western liberal theory of rights, an individualism that treats the citizen in an abstract way as an autonomous being who enters into a contract with the sovereign state, and the patriarchal family system in which the 'relational rights' of the collectivity is primary.[57] The newly independent Algerian state did, on paper, in various constitutional and legal statements, announce the full and equal rights of women. However, there existed an enormous gap between such principles of universal rights and the reality of the continuing subordination of women to male control. For example, many women failed to exercise voting rights or to participate in political associations because male members of the family exercised the vote 'on their behalf' or imposed strict seclusion. It was FLN recognition of patriarchy both during and after the War of Independence that prevented any move by nationalists to counter the French project on women by offering its own emancipation agenda. In the long term it is possible to trace a link between this fatal pact with conservative Islamist forces and the bloody civil war after 1992 during which extreme levels of male aggression and violence were directed specifically against 'modern' women who were perceived as a threat to patriarchy.

Notes

1 On the context of the killings of May–June 1945, often referred to as the 'Sétif massacre', see Radouane Aïnad Tabet, *Le Mouvement du 8 mai 1945 en Algérie* (Algiers: OPU, 1987 edn); Boucif Mekhaled, *Chroniques d'un massacre. 8 Mai 1945: Sétif, Guelma, Kherrata* (Paris: Syros/Au nom de la mémoire, 1995); Yves Benot, *Massacres coloniaux 1944–1950: La IVe République et la mise au pas des colonies françaises* (Paris: La Découverte, 1994); Annie Rey-Goldzeiguer, *Aux origines de la guerre d'Algérie, 1940–1945: De Mers-el-Kebir aux massacres du Nord-Constantinois* (Paris: La Découverte, 2002); Jean-Louis Planche, *Sétif 1945. Histoire d'un Massacre Annoncé* (Paris: Perrin, 2006).
2 Marcel Reggui with Preface by Jean-Pierre Peyroulou, *Les Massacres de Guelma. Algérie, Mai 1945: une enquête inédite sur la furie des milices coloniales* (Paris: La Découverte, 2006).
3 Reggui, *Guelma*, 121–2, describes Zohra as a 'symbol of the new Algeria'.
4 The population of Algeria was divided by contemporaries into three religious or 'racial' categories: Europeans, Jews and Muslim Algerians. By 1954 there were 984,000 settlers of European descent (who were often referred to as *pieds noirs*), an official category that included indigenous Jews who under the Crémieux Decree of 1870 held full French citizenship; and 8,546,000 Arab-Berbers, officially designated *français musulmanes*, who as 'subjects' came under the jurisdiction of Islamic family law. I have used the term 'Algerian' and 'Muslim' interchangeably throughout for the latter: on

the changing demographic structure see especially, Kamel Kateb, *Européens, 'Indigènes' et Juifs en Algérie (1830–1962)* (Paris: INED/PUF, 2001). While the term 'Muslim' may seem to essentialise Algerian personality in religious terms, it does reflect the contemporary self-identification of the vast majority, even those who were highly secularised, as belonging to a community that defined itself by social and cultural affiliation to Islam. Only a tiny number of elite, francophone Algerians opted for 'naturalisation', which gave full citizenship on condition of renouncing personal status, an act that was widely viewed as a form of apostasy verging on political treason.

5 Throughout the book 'emancipation' is used in this sense and for convenience the use of 'scare-quotes' will be omitted hereafter.

6 Such a contradiction has been recognised to lie at the heart of many, if not most, post-Second World War counter-insurgency operations from Vietnam to contemporary Iraq: see for example Michael D. Schafer, *Deadly Paradigms: The Failure of US Counterinsurgency Policy* (Princeton, N.J: Princeton University Press, 1988).

7 Stathis N. Kalyvas, *The Logic of Violence in Civil War* (Cambridge: Cambridge University Press, 2006).

8 Jacques Perrier, 'Ces femmes d'Algérie', *L'Aurore*, 27 August 1959. The concept of a 'Third Force', which was central to military thinking throughout the war, was the idea that the French could nurture a moderate alternative political movement to the FLN with whom the French could negotiate a favourable end to the war.

9 A succinct, typical elaboration of this position can be found in two influential books by Germaine Tillion, *Algeria. The Realities* (London: Eyre and Spottiswoode, 1958), a translation of *L'Algérie en 1957* (1958), and *France and Algeria. Complementary Enemies* (New York: Alfred A. Knopf, 1961), a translation of *Les Ennemis complémentaires* (1960).

10 Amin Qasim, *'The Liberation of Women' and 'The New Woman'. Two Documents in the History of Egyptian Feminism* [first published in Arabic 1899–1900] (Cairo: The American University in Cairo Press, 2005 edn). On the context and importance of Amin's work see Leila Ahmed, *Women and Gender in Islam* (New Haven, Conn.: Yale University Press, 1992), 144–65; Margot Badran, *Feminists, Islam, and Nation. Gender and the Making of Modern Egypt* (Princeton, N.J.: Princeton University Press, 1995), 18–19, 47–8; Afaf Lufti al-Sayyid Marsot, 'The Revolutionary Gentlewomen in Egypt', and Thomas Philipp, 'Feminism and Nationalist Politics in Egypt', in Lois Beck and Nikki Keddie (eds), *Women in the Muslim World* (Cambridge, Mass.: Harvard University Press, 1980 edn), 261–94.

11 On Kemalist reform as a process of state-building see Touraj Atabaki (ed.), *The State and the Subaltern. Modernization, Society and the State in Turkey and Iran* (London: I. B. Tauris, 2007); Nilüfer Göle, *Musulmanes et modernes. Voile et civilisation en Turquie* (Paris: La Découverte, 2003 edn).

12 On Iran see Atabaki (ed.), *The State*; Stephanie Cronin (ed.), *The Making of Modern Iran. State and Society Under Riza Shah, 1921–1941* (London:

Routledge, 2003), especially the following chapters: Jasamin Rostam-Kolayi, 'Expanding Agendas for the "New" Iranian Woman: Family, Law, Work, and Unveiling', 157–80; Shireen Mahdavi, 'Riza Shah Pahlavi and Women: A Re-evaluation', 181–92; H. E. Chehabi, 'The Banning of the Veil and Its Consequences', 193–210; also Homa Hoodfar, 'Iranian Women at the Intersection of Citizenship and the Family Code. The Perils of "Islamic Criteria"', in Suad Joseph (ed.), *Gender and Citizenship in the Middle East* (Syracuse, N.Y.: Syracuse University Press, 2000), 287–313.

13 Gregory J. Massell, *The Surrogate Proletariat: Moslem Women and Revolutionary Strategies in Soviet Central Asia, 1919–1929* (Princeton, N.J: Princeton University Press, 1974); Douglas Northrop, *Veiled Empire. Gender and Power in Stalinist Central Asia* (Ithaca: Cornell University Press, 2004).

14 On nationalism and 'state feminism' see Ellen L. Fleischmann, 'The Other "Awakening": The Emergence of Women's Movements in the Modern Middle East, 1900–1940' in Margaret L. Meriwether and Judith E. Tucker (eds), *A Social History of Women and Gender in the Modern Middle East* (Boulder, Colo.: Westview Press, 1999), 107–20; Nikki R. Keddie, '1914–45: Nationalism and Women's Movements', in *Women in the Middle East. Past and Present* (Princeton, N.J.: Princeton University Press, 2007), 75–101.

15 Mehrzad Boroujerdi, 'Triumph and Travails of Authoritarian Modernisation in Iran', in Cronin (ed.), *Making*, 152.

16 Mustapha Kemal stated during a speech to a provincial audience on 10 October 1926, 'The civilized world is far ahead of us. We have no choice but to catch up. It is time to stop nonsense, such as "should we or should we not wear hats?" We shall adopt hats along with all other works of Western civilization. Uncivilized people are doomed to be trodden under the feet of civilized people'. Quoted in Andrew Mango, *Atatürk* (London: John Murray, 2004 edn), 438.

17 Stephanie Cronin, 'Reform from Above, Resistance from Below: The New Order and Its Opponents in Iran, 1927–29', in Atabaki (ed.), *The State*, 81–8.

18 Badran, *Feminists*, 92; Northrop, *Veiled Empire*, chapter 2; Elizabeth Thompson, *Colonial Citizens. Republican Rights, Paternal Privilege, and Gender in French Syria and Lebanon* (New York: Columbia University Press, 2000), 242, 257, 259.

19 There exists an enormous literature on this process: see, for example, Charles Tilly (ed.), *The Formation of National States in Western Europe* (Princeton, N.J: Princeton University Press, 1975).

20 Cronin, 'Reform from Above', 73, notes that Riza Shah and his key personnel 'developed a commandist approach, seeking to impose their will across vast geographical areas and intricate social contexts by diktat, backed up by the threat of military intervention'. On the official visit to Turkey see Afshin Marashi, 'Performing the Nation: The Shah's Official State Visit to Kemalist Turkey, June to July 1934', in Cronin (ed.), *Making*, 99–119.

21 Zehra F. Arat, 'Turkish Women and the Republican Reconstruction of Tradition', in Fatma Müge Göçek and Shiva Balaghi (eds), *Reconstructing Gender in the Middle East. Tradition, Identity, and Power* (New York: Columbia University Press, 1994), 58–9.

22 On the processes by which the modern European state 'invaded' and appropriated the functions of the family see for example, Jacques Donzelot, *The Policing of Families* (Baltimore: John Hopkins University Press, 1997).

23 Deniz Kandiyoti (ed.), 'Introduction' to *Women, Islam and the State* (Basingstoke: Macmillan, 1991), 9, notes that women represent the focal point of kinship-based solidarities, but the dilemma of the modern state is that it must eradicate these particularisms to create universalistic loyalties; Mounira M. Charrad, *States and Women's Rights. The Making of Postcolonial Tunisia, Algeria and Morocco* (Berkeley: University of California Press, 2001); Suad Joseph, 'Theoretical Introduction. Gendering Citizenship in the Middle East', in Joseph (ed.), *Gender*, 3–30.

24 Annelies Moors, 'Debating Islamic Family Law: Legal Texts and Social Practices', in Meriwether and Tucker (eds), *Social History*, 141–75.

25 See Thompson, *Colonial Citizens*, 225–46, on General Georges Catroux and his entourage which rotated between leadership roles in Lebanon and Algeria; also Martin Thomas, 'Women and Colonialism and Colonial Education' in *The French Empire Between the Wars. Imperialism, Politics and Society* (Manchester: Manchester University Press, 2005), 151–84.

26 The French Revolution has been described as the 'supreme point of reference' in Mustapha Kemal's life: see Mango, *Atatürk*, 42, 49.

27 Contemporaries saw a fascistic parallel between the generals' Algiers coup, code-named Operation Resurrection, to topple the Paris government, and General Franco's 1939 'reconquest' of Spain from his base in the Army of Africa.

28 Matthew Connelly, *A Diplomatic Revolution. Algeria's Fight for Independence and the Origins of the Post-Cold War Era* (Oxford: Oxford University Press, 2002), 10–12.

29 On this institutional basis of the separation of 'native' from European-dominated zones see Claude Collot, *Les Institutions de l'Algérie durant la période coloniale (1830–1962)* (Paris: Éditions du CNRS, 1987), 81–162.

30 Claudine Chaulet, *La Terre, les frères, et l'argent. Stratégie familiale et production agricole en Algérie depuis 1962* (Algiers: Office des Publications Universitaires, c. 1984), Vol. 1, 247–50; Neil MacMaster, *Colonial Migrants and Racism. Algerians in France, 1900–62* (Basingstoke: Macmillan, 1997), 41.

31 Claude Meillassoux, *Maidens, Meal and Money. Capitalism and the Domestic Community* (Cambridge: Cambridge University Press, 1991).

32 Schafer, *Deadly Paradigms*, 93–4; Irene L. Gendzier, *Managing Political Change: Social Scientists and the Third World* (Boulder, Colo.: Westview Press, 1985), 50–1, 63–9; John J. Johnson, *The Role of the Military in*

Underdeveloped Countries (Princeton, N.J: Princeton University Press, 1962).

33 On the teleology of development theory and the centrality of a modernist and consumerist vision in French metropolitan culture during the Algerian War, see Connelly, *Diplomatic Revolution*, 27–34; Kristin Ross, *Fast Cars, Clean Bodies. Decolonization and the Reordering of French Culture* (Cambridge, Mass.: MIT Press, 1996 edn).

34 Frantz Fanon, *L'An V de la révolution algérienne* [1959] (Paris: La Découverte, 2001 edn).

35 Particularly influential was Mohammed Harbi's, *Le FLN, mirage et réalité: des origines à la prise du pouvoir (1945–1962)* (Paris: Les Éditions J. A, 1980).

36 Particularly illuminating is Omar Carlier, *Entre nation et jihad. Histoire sociale des radicalismes algériens* (Paris: Presse de la fondation nationale des sciences politiques, 1995).

37 Djamila Amrane, *Les Femmes algériennes dans la guerre* (Paris: Plon, 1991) is a version of her 1988 doctoral thesis. Née Danièle Minne, Amrane is the daughter by a first marriage of Jacqueline Minne, who later married the FLN militant Abdelkader Guerroudj. Danièle joined the maquis in about March 1957 where she married a young FLN dentist, Si Ali Amrane, before she was captured on 26 November 1957 and tried for her role in the Algiers bomb network: see Patrick Kessel and Giovanni Pirelli (eds), *Le Peuple algérien et la guerre. Lettres et témoignages 1954–1962* [1962] (Paris: L'Harmattan, 2003 edn), 177. Currently a professor at Toulouse University, she published a later book of oral testimony by women under the name Danièle Djamila Amrane-Minne, *Des femmes dans la guerre d'Algérie* (Paris: Éditions Karthala, 1994). For an overview of French, Algerian and other state archives see Abdelkrim Badjadja, 'Panorama des archives de l'Algérie moderne et contemporaine', in Mohammed Harbi and Benjamin Stora (eds), *La Guerre d'Algérie, 1954–2004. La fin de l'amnésie* (Paris: Robert Laffont, 2004), 631–82.

38 The military archive known before 1 January 2005 as the *Service historique de l'armée de terre* (SHAT) at the Château de Vincennes, has now been reorganised as the *Service historique de la Défense, Département de l'armé de terre* (SHD-DAT), but throughout this is referred to by using the well-known abbreviation SHAT; the civilian or joint civilian/military administrative archives are held in the *Centre des archives d'outre-mer* (CAOM) at Aix-en-Provence. For an overview of these archives, the problems surrounding their use, and the fields of research being generated by their access, see Raphaëlle Branche, *La Guerre d'Algérie: une histoire apaisée?* (Paris: Seuil, 2005), Part 2.

39 Gilbert Meynier, *Histoire intérieure du FLN, 1954–1962* (Paris: Fayard, 2002); and the 'companion volume' of Mohammed Harbi and Gilbert Meynier (eds), *Le FLN: documents et histoire, 1954–1962* (Paris: Fayard, 2004).

40 See in particular the theses and publications of Diane Sambron and Ryme Seferdjeli referred to later.

41 Marnia Lazreg has warned of the potential pitfalls of such a project in 'Feminism and Difference: The Perils of Writing as a Woman on Women in Algeria', *Feminist Studies*, 14: 1 (Spring 1988), 81–107, although she attempted such a study in, *The Eloquence of Silence. Algerian Women in Question* (New York: Routledge, 1994); on the problems of an Algerian history 'from below' see also Fanny Colonna, 'The Nation's "Unknowing Other". Three Intellectuals and the Culture(s) of Being Algerian, or On the Impossibility of Subaltern Studies in Algeria', *Journal of North African Studies*, 8: 1 (Spring 2003), 155–70.

42 Most studies to date have centred on the experience of urban women, among whom can be found a more educated and vocal minority of FLN militants: very little remains known about the great mass of impoverished and illiterate peasantry or shantytown refugees.

43 Many tens of thousands of photographs can be consulted in the archives of the *Établissement de communication et de production audiovisuelle de la défense* (ECPAD) at Fort-Ivry, Paris; on the historical importance and analysis of the images see Claire Mauss-Copeaux, *A Travers le viseur. Images d'appelés en Algérie, 1955–1962* (Lyon: Aedelsa, 2003).

44 On this myth in Algeria see Baya Jurquet-Bouhoune and Jacques Jurquet, *Femmes algériennes. De la Kahina au code de la famille* (Pantin: Le Temps des Cerises, 2007), 21–59.

45 In Syria Nazik 'Abid, who led a battalion of nurses during the Battle of Maysalun against the French (24 July 24 1920), was dubbed the Joan of Arc of the Arabs and compared to an ancient female warrior, Khawla bint al-Azwar. The majority of male nationalists accepted women's exceptional war service in a time of emergency, but insisted they should then demobilise back to the home on return of peace: see Thompson, *Colonial Citizens*, 120, 124, 188. On 'manly' women in Iran coming to the rescue of the nation, only to be side-lined with the arrival of peace, see Afsaneh Najmabadi, *Women with Mustaches and Men without Beards. Gender and Sexual Anxieties of Iranian Modernity* (Berkeley: University of California Press, 2005), 221–3.

46 Kumari Jayawardena, *Feminism and Nationalism in the Third World* (London: Zed Books, 1986). Egyptian women played a key role the 1919–22 independence struggle, only to be excluded from political rights by the male Wafd government of 1924: see Badran, *Feminists*, 74–88.

47 For an analysis of similar internal divisions in the history of the women's movement in Iran, see Afsaneh Najmabadi, 'Authority and Agency: Revisiting Women's Activism During Reza Shah's Period', in Atabaki (ed.), *The State*, 159–62, 170. Islam was not viewed as inherently anti-women by feminists.

48 *Ibid.*, 174.

49 Leila Ahmed notes the extraordinary plight of 'the Middle East feminist caught between two opposing loyalties, forced almost to choose between

betrayal and betrayal', quoted by Kandiyoti (ed.), *Women*, 7. On the gendering of the nation as female linked to a masculine nationalism as a defence of the purity and honour of the homeland, see Najmabadi, *Women with Mustaches*, 1–7; Nira Yuval-Davis, 'Cultural Reproduction and Gender Relations', in *Gender and Nation* (London: Sage, 1997), 39–67.

50 Thompson, *Colonial Citizens*, 130, 289.

51 Northrop, *Veiled Empire*, 23–4, 59.

52 Helen Callaway, *Gender, Culture and Empire. European Women in Colonial Nigeria* (Basingstoke: Macmillan, 1987), 240, 243–4, notes how the imperial model of conquest and power gave way post-1945 to welfare and educational programmes that were projected as part of a 'transition of power' and 'partnership' with Nigerians.

53 The Lebanese feminist Nazira Zayn al-Din openly addressed her remarkable book, *Unveiling and Veiling* (1928), which strongly attacked the conservative religious establishment, to the French High Commission, 'Representative of France, Mother of all civilization, of liberty and all light'. For this Syrian women nationalists viewed her as a traitor. Thompson, *Colonial Citizens*, 127–36, 146.

54 On the concept of the 'gender pact' see Thompson, *Colonial Citizens*, 7, 146, 150, 268–9, 289; Najmabadi, *Women with Mustaches*, 154–5, comments on the westernised woman demonised in Iran as, 'the enemy within, *fitna*, and the enemy without, the West, thereby making it possible for the previously distinct voices of secular radical modernism and the newly rearticulated Islamism to condemn in unison the "superwesternized" woman'.

55 Deniz Kandiyoti, 'Islam and Patriarchy: A Comparative Perspective', in Nikki R. Keddie and Beth Baron (eds), *Women in Middle Eastern History. Shifting Boundaries in Sex and Gender* (New Haven: Yale University Press, 1991), 23–42. Najmabadi, *Women with Mustaches*, 154–5.

56 Kandiyoti, 'Islam and Patriarchy', 37–8; Joseph, *Gender*, 11–15; Charrad, *States*, chapter 2, 28–50.

57 Joseph, *Gender*, 3–4, 17–18, 22–5; and 'Comment on Majid's "The Politics of Feminism in Islam"', *Signs: Journal of Women in Culture and Society*, 23: 1 (1998), 364–5.

1

From the Sétif Massacre to the November insurrection: the origins of the Algerian women's movement, 1945–54

The centre of gravity of this study lies in the French emancipation campaign from 1956 to 1962, but to understand the extent to which this was innovative or marked a break with the past requires some idea of that which preceded it. This chapter explores a number of issues: first, it provides a brief background sketch of the overall social, economic and political situation of Algerian women during the post-war decade. The triple colonial oppression of women by ethnic or racial discrimination, class and gender goes far to explain why it was so difficult for them to become politically conscious or to engage in any kind of emancipation movement. Secondly, despite these impediments various factors contributed to the emergence of the first significant women's organisations in the main urban centres. Despite the marginalisation of women, the modernisation of large colonial cities like Algiers, Oran and Constantine inevitably led to the appearance of a small, but highly significant strata of young, educated women, mainly students, teachers, secretaries and health workers, who were drawn into the nationalist struggle and provided the backbone of the new women's organisations.

During the decade activism was inspired by the close collaboration between European women, many of them left-wing, communist or Christian militants from metropolitan France, and Algerian women. The former, who had made significant political and social gains after the Liberation, including the vote, now campaigned to extend these rights to Algerian women. Thirdly, the colonial General Government[1] responded to this challenge by close police surveillance of the new women's organisations, and by careful structuring of the Algerian electoral system and 'representative' institutions so as to totally exclude Muslim women. This containment, which was symptomatic of the overall blockage of reform by settler interests intent on preserving their domination, helped drive the nationalists from a reformist towards a revolutionary solution. The failure of reform through the decade 1944–54 enables us to see how the military-led programme of emancipation after 1954, examined in

chapter 2, represented a significant reversal in colonial policy, and why
the long accumulation of under-development and neglect of the rural
and urban poor presented almost insuperable problems of investment.
Lastly, a close examination of the three key women's organisations
reveals various tensions, in particular an incipient division between those
currents that were drawn to a more secular or socialist agenda and those
influenced by an Islamo-nationalist vision of cultural resistance. These
tensions show that the divisions on the issue of women that internally
fractured the FLN during the war and on into the post-independence era
were already emerging well before the insurrection.

Following the invasion of Algeria in 1830, the basic policy of the
French was to establish a settler colony through which European immigrants from the Mediterranean basin would settle on land appropriated
from the indigenous nomadic and peasant population by conquest and
'legal' destruction of communal rights.[2] By 1920 the *colons* had largely
completed the process of taking over the richest and best irrigated
arable land in the valleys, a process achieved by breaking up tribal
society and its forced relocation into poor, rocky and arid marginal
zones. Unable to survive, even at subsistence level, the Algerian rural
population was compelled to seek external resources either by working
as day-labourers for local *colons*, or by temporary labour migration to
northern cities and France. By the 1930s and 1940s the rural population was trapped in a desperate situation: per capita production of grain
and livestock was falling; traditional handicraft industries collapsed as
cheaper, factory-made goods were imported; the majority of men faced
massive under-employment, finding waged labour for one hundred days
a year or less; and cyclical famine, like that of 1942–45, ensued. The
demographic historian Louis Chevalier, in a report of 1947, described
a classic Malthusian crisis:[3] the population growth rate had doubled
between 1921 and 1930, and this demographic transition was to carry
enormous negative consequences for women.[4] Large numbers migrated
from the inhospitable rural interior towards the urban centres, but the
colonial economy was unable to provide enough employment since
metropolitan capitalists had protected their own interests and prevented
Algerian industrialisation.[5] The Algerian urban population expanded
dramatically, but most of this growth consisted of impoverished, illiterate migrants who swelled the rapidly expanding shantytowns (*bidonvilles*).[6] However, despite accelerating urbanisation, by 1948 Algeria
was still a predominantly rural society in which 84 per cent of the
indigenous population lived outside the forty-seven urban centres,[7] and
provided the centre of gravity for a War of Independence that was predominantly a peasant-based phenomenon. Table 1 provides a summary

Table 1: Geographical distribution of European and Muslim populations
c. 1954

Area	European population	Muslim population
Zone 1		
47 major towns	800,000	1,430,000
Zone 2		
Evolved small towns and communes 30,000km²	180,000	1,830,000
Zone 3		
Under-developed rural areas 200,000km²	36,000	5,450,000

Source: *L'Effort algérien*, 1,167 (20–26 February 1959)

of the geographical division of Algeria by 1954 into three zones, with a massive concentration of Muslims in the impoverished interior where very few Europeans chose to live:

While the situation of Algerian women can be understood against this wider background, in general, as the 'prolétaires des prolétaires', they experienced an even more deprived and oppressed way of life than their husbands and brothers.[8] On the eve of war in 1954, while virtually all European children aged six to fourteen years received primary schooling, this was true for only one in five Algerian boys, and one in sixteen girls.[9] In 1948 some 90 per cent of males aged over ten years were illiterate in French and Arabic, and 96 per cent of women.[10] Of the two million women of working age in 1954, some 1.1 million or about 95 per cent of the active female population were engaged in agricultural work,[11] undertaking a range of heavy manual tasks within the peasant economy that were in addition to their domestic role as mothers of large families (fetching wood and water, weeding, harvesting, tending vegetable gardens and livestock, weaving). Outside the domestic economy, particularly within the towns, remarkably few women worked outside the home since any form of labour was regarded as dishonourable: in general, with the exception of a tiny strata of educated women who were entering the service sector (secretaries, nurses, teachers), most female workers came from the pool of desperately poor women who were forced to do so from necessity, repudiated, abandoned or widowed women who had no extended family group to protect them.[12] As will be seen throughout the study, the backward position of women did not derive only from the negative effects of an exploitative colonial order, such as the failure to invest in schooling for Muslim girls, but also from

a patriarchal system that secluded women within the household, isolated them from external political and cultural forces, and removed the
minority of girls who did receive education from school at puberty.

The first organised Algerian women's movement that appeared in
the decade 1944–54 was confined to the towns and made little impact
in rural society because of extreme poverty, isolation and illiteracy.
However, this first urban-based movement appeared historically very
late compared to most other countries in the Middle East. During the
1920s and 1930s dynamic women's organisations were already active
in Egypt, Iran, Turkey, Lebanon, Syria, Iraq, Palestine and India and
a series of international conferences held in Damascus (1930), Tehran
(1932), Istanbul (1935), Cairo (1938) and elsewhere was leading to the
global sharing of ideas on everything from veiling to the franchise.[13]
Algerian women delegates appear to have been totally absent from these
international meetings, a fact that may in part have reflected the wider
intellectual isolation of the Maghreb, and especially of Algeria, from the
more advanced political and religious ferment of the Middle East. Recent
scholarship has shown that Algeria was far less sealed-off from currents
in the Middle East than previously thought,[14] but the repressive French
regime, ever paranoid about any revolutionary or pan-Islamic or pan-
Arab threat to the most prized of the colonies, exercised a formidable
policing of ideas and persons circulating across the borders.[15]

Equally significant was the fact that between c. 1900 and 1944 the
debate on the issues facing Algerian women was monopolised by metropolitan and colonial Frenchwomen.[16] French feminists like Hubertine
Auclert had, since 1900, engaged in a campaign for the emancipation
of Muslim women who were perceived through Orientalist and racist
stereotypes as degraded victims of child-marriage, veiling, seclusion,
polygamy, repudiation and 'feudal' patriarchy.[17] French feminists, such
as the lawyers Maria Vérone and Suzanne Grinberg, were active within
the *Union française pour le suffrage des femmes* (UFSF) and campaigned
for the extension of republican rights, including the vote and secular law,
to Algerian women, as well as for 'modernisation' through education,
employment opportunities and welfare or maternity benefits.[18]

European feminists shared the predominant position of French male
politicians in the more reformist liberal, socialist, communist and left-
republican parties that fundamentally upheld a colonial paternalist
model of the 'civilising mission' and assimilation as in the best interests
of the 'natives'. However, French feminists found it almost impossible to
develop links with, or gain support from, Muslim women, and the UFSF
delegates to the conference of the *Alliance internationals des femmes* in
Istanbul in 1935 bemoaned the absence of grass-roots activity compared

to other Middle Eastern states that were represented: 'In Algeria we live side by side with millions of Muslim women, who are the most backwards of any land'.[19] Compared to most other colonies in the Middle East, Algeria had a large and deeply embedded settler society, and since Europeans dominated most of the spheres of intellectual life, from lycée and university teachers to newspaper editors and writers, French thought and culture exerted a hegemonic power over the small and relatively weak class of educated Algerian women (évoluées). Down to c. 1945 any potential for an independent Algerian women's movement to develop was smothered by, or incorporated into, European-led organisations, from charitable networks to ladies associations and circles.

How and why did this situation change after 1944? While there exists almost no information about the political activity or attitudes of Algerian women prior to 1944, a fairly rich body of oral and archival evidence points to the growth of a dynamic movement in the post-war decade, one that succeeded in reaching for the first time down into the ranks of the urban proletariat.[20] At its peak in 1948–50 this represented a level of autonomous women's mobilisation that was not to be seen again until after 1980. The emergence of a women's movement was an integral part of the wider and almost continuous political ferment in Algeria between 1936 and 1954 as pro-independence nationalism penetrated deep into society, and aroused a bitter and often violent response from colonial interests. After the Allied landings in Algeria in November 1943 and the fall of the Pétainist regime, the nationalists increased in self-confidence, buoyed up by the Atlantic Charter of August 1941 which pronounced the rights of people to self-determination. The end of the Second World War led in the Maghreb, as it did globally across the declining European empires, to a massive acceleration in the pressures for decolonisation. Algerians were highly optimistic that the new political order that emerged from the long war to defeat fascism would finally lead to radical change. The immediate response of the colonial regime to this challenge was to unleash the extremely violent repression at Sétif in May 1945, and to imprison thousands of nationalists, but far from bringing the independence movement to a halt this simply deepened the political crisis and drove the nationalists towards the preparation of an armed insurrection.

The women's movement that appeared after 1943, far from being unified, was divided by deep and often bitter internal divisions that reflected the more global tensions between different political strands of the anti-colonial struggle. The three main umbrella parties under which the women's organisations grouped were the *Parti communiste algérien* (PCA), the reformist *Union démocratique du manifeste algérien*

(UDMA) headed by Ferhat Abbas, and the nationalist, pro-independence *Mouvement pour le triomphe des libertés démocratique* (MTLD) and the associated *Parti du peuple algérien* (PPA) of Messali Hadj.[21] Eventually, after the outbreak of the War of Independence, the communists and the reformists disbanded their organisations and dissolved their membership into the FLN. This assertion of FLN hegemony from 1956 onwards was to carry important consequences for the future women's movement since it marked the marginalisation of a more secular and 'western' brand of feminism, and the dominance of a more conservative and religious current. The following sections look at these three movements in turn to show in more detail the new forms of activism and organisation that emerged after 1944, and the differing ideological currents at work.

The Communist Party and the *Union des femmes d'Algérie*

Throughout the history of the Algerian nationalist movement, between the foundation of the ENA in 1926 through to the outbreak of the War of Independence in 1954, the relationship between the French and Algerian communists and the Messalist movement was one of bitter antagonism. The *Parti communiste français* (PCF), and the PCA which fell very much under its control, was opposed to the idea of Algerian nationalism and the struggle for independence, a movement which it derided as backward and manipulated by conservative, fascist and fanatical interests, a 'xenophobic nationalism of primitives'.[22] True liberation would only come about under the aegis of France, through the prior revolutionary and class struggle of the French proletariat. This 'Marxist' analysis tended to go hand in hand with an 'assimilationist' and colonialist agenda: Algerians were far too backward to manage their own affairs in an independent state,[23] and they would best find the road to full citizenship and civilisation by full integration into metropolitan France. The deep, almost visceral hostility of the rank-and-file European militants in the PCA towards the PPA reflected the general fear of the 'poor white' settlers towards being outnumbered by a growing Algerian population that was facing endemic poverty, and which threatened at any moment to boil over into a bloody insurrection.

However, as the PCF came to recognise the growing strength of the nationalist movement after 1934, so it came to see the need to establish a more autonomous Algerian Communist Party, which through a programme of 'arabisation' would seek to extend its influence among urban and rural Muslim workers, and to develop policies that would reflect their experience and ambitions. Between 1935 and 1936 the number of Algerian party members increased from 60 to 700.[24] In 1946, after the violent repression of Sétif by a Gaullist government which included communist ministers, the PCA made a significant change in policy by approaching the Messalists, as well as the more moderate nationalists of Ferhat Abbas' UDMA.[25] The PCA tried to re-establish contact with the Algerian masses by organising party cells in both urban and rural zones, and by campaigning on a range of progressive issues, including agrarian reform, extension of equal state welfare provision, health care, education, and an end to discriminatory distribution of rationed food to settlers.[26] It was as part of this wider change in the Algerian Communist Party towards 'arabisation', and a drive to organise among the peasantry and urban proletariat, that the first significant women's movement appeared, the *Union des femmes d'Algérie* (UFA).[27]

The leading figure in the UFA, which was established in 1944, was its general secretary and leading politician Alice Sportisse. After de Gaulle's ordinance of 21 April 1944 which granted the vote to metropolitan and European women in Algeria, she was one of thirty-three women who were elected to the Constituent Assembly. In the Assembly she campaigned for the extension of the franchise to Algerian women, and although the Organic Law of 20 September 1947 in principle granted this, underhand measures were taken to ensure this would not be implemented.[28] In the early years of the UFA the organisation was run largely by and for European women: for example, at a major public meeting in Algiers on 9 April 1946 only two Muslim women were present among the 300 European women and fifty men.[29] However, the movement was able to attract talented and highly dedicated radicals (exiled Spanish republicans, Marxist intellectuals from metropolitan France, left-Catholic militants) who were prepared to organise among the largely illiterate and impoverished mass of Algerian women in the *bled*, or in the shantytowns and 'native quarters' of the urban centres.

These militants were particularly successful in establishing a communist organisation that reached out from the urban centres into the rural hinterland of the Department of Oran: a penetration that may have been more successful than anywhere else in Algeria because of the more 'advanced' proletarian condition of labourers on the *colons* estates.[30] Typical of these new women activists were Lisette Vincent, Myrian Ben and Jacqueline Guerroudj, who were posted as teachers to rural schools where they were shocked by the hardship faced by peasant women and children, the constant malnutrition, their primitive dwellings, and an almost total absence of any modern infrastructure, including roads, electricity, water supply and primary health care.[31] Jacqueline Guerroudj travelled on foot with her husband into the outlying *douars* (villages) of Ouchba, Chouli, Terny and Oum Oulalou, where she held meetings with local women, providing advice on hygiene and child-care, reading from newspapers and debating current events.[32]

The UFA militants became radicalised through their ability to break through the normal segregationist barriers and to gain a direct, personal experience of indigenous society.[33] The UFA provided a framework in which women from the three religious communities (Christian, Muslim, Jewish) were brought into contact and could share elements of their differing cultures. The European militants began to develop a first-hand experience of the cultural and linguistic problems of organising among Muslim women who were largely illiterate, spoke only Arabic or Berber dialects, and were hampered by the strict rules of gender segregation. The extent to which female seclusion served to prevent wider education or involvement in the main-stream associational and political life of the colony should not be under-estimated. Once girls reached puberty or were married extremely powerful forms of family, community and self-regulation came into force, the main object of which was to prevent women having any contact whatsoever with males outside the boundaries of the immediate family and household grouping.[34] In general Algerian males were prepared to tolerate women's social networking outside the domestic space within certain 'traditional' female spheres such as private houses, Turkish baths, weddings, circumcision fêtes, or visits to cemeteries and holy sites, activities from which men were excluded or in which mutual surveillance and kinship links could guarantee that honour was safe. By 1947 the UFA had adapted to this situation by organising strictly female meetings in the major urban centres and this succeeded for the first time in drawing in Muslim women in large numbers. Baya Allaouchiche, perhaps the most influential of Algerian women in the UFA, notes:

> Everywhere was used to hold discussions: cemeteries, Moorish baths, marriages and baptisms. We were always ready to explain the rights and role of women in the world. We thought we could advance the cause of women in this way. On their side they found pretexts to get out of the house saying they were going to the Moorish baths. We organised cinema shows with hired films. One or two women explained the film [in French, Arabic or Berber], the meaning of the theme, and discussion then took off . . . they used extraordinary ingenuity to come and get educated.[35]

Such women-only meetings, which also used Arabic and Berber interpreters, and cinema and theatrical performances to appeal to the illiterate, succeeded by 1948 in attracting, at least by Algerian standards, enormous numbers of Muslim women to UFA public meetings. Police informers reported in October 1948 the presence of 800 Algerian women at a meeting in the Algiers' *Foyer Civique* to mark Aïd-el-kébir, at which the general secretary Alice Sportisse attacked the failure to implement the vote for women, 'who have to struggle in a situation close to poverty'.[36] The UFA, probably through studying the methods of the PPA nationalists, also proved adept at using propaganda techniques and cultural forms that would appeal to illiterate Arab or Berber speaking women, particularly through popular films like the Egyptian *Gawhara*, theatrical sketches, and Arab female orchestras such as 'Aissa', and 'El Nedjema'. Success can also be measured by the spread of UFA women's groups across Algeria into the main urban centres of Algiers, Oran, Constantine, Relizane, Bône, Sétif and Sidi-Bel-Abbès.[37]

The UFA also helped to create for the first time an internationalist dimension to the Algerian women's movement, which before 1945 had been so isolated from external contacts. This was an era during which the Cold War reached its zenith and the UFA, in line with international communism, attacked the danger to the Soviet Union of global imperialism led by the United States and NATO. Equally prominent was the theme of the international solidarity of women engaged in anti-colonial struggles across the globe. At the Third Congress of the UFA held in May 1949 in the Algiers town hall the number of Muslim women outnumbered Europeans by 400 to 250, and among the main speakers was a delegation of women from the *Women's International Democratic Federation* (WIDF), the socialist and anti-colonialist organisation founded in 1945. Archimède Gertie, a lawyer and deputy from Guadaloupe, described how in her country 'natives, as in Algeria, were considered in the same way as "beasts of burden"', and encouraged Algerian women to engage in the struggle of all peoples against colonialism. The delegate Thai-Thi-Lien denounced the ongoing French colonial war in Vietnam and emphasised the key role of women in the 'struggle for total liberation', both through support for combatants and, on the social front, through a mass drive against illiteracy.[38] Algerian women delegates attended, and reported back from, international women's conferences held in Budapest, North Korea, Peking, Cairo and Stockholm. By 1952 the attention of the UFA had turned to the violent military and police repression taking place across the border in Tunisia and on international women's day, 8 March 1952, at a meeting attended by 300 women in the Cinema Suffren Mme Mandouze spoke against, 'The massacres of children, the rape of women, the destruction of crops, carried out by the forces of repression in Tunisia'.[39]

The UFA played a particularly prominent role in organising campaigns that were directed more towards social and 'class' issues, than towards the nationalist struggle. During 1944–45 the Algerian populace was

confronting a situation of widespread famine, and the communists demonstrated against the high cost of living, black-market traders, and the
discriminatory supply of rationed rice to European families.[40] They also
demanded the extension of social security and pension rights to Muslim
women on a par with those available to European women, attacked the
conditions in the *bidonvilles*, and encouraged women to challenge the
exclusion of their children from state primary schools by getting them
enrolled. The movement also attacked the deepening repression of the
Algerian government as it tried to keep a lid on the growing strength of
the nationalists, campaigned for the release of political prisoners, and
exposed the flagrant corruption of electoral procedure by the Governor
Naegelen after 1948, including the refusal to implement the vote for
Muslim women. Quite exceptional, if not unique, was the decision of
the PCA to stand two Muslim women in the municipal elections of
1945, Bendjaoui Kateb at Bône and Mérami Fatma at St-Cloud in the
Oran department, both of whom won council seats.[41]

Through the organisation of petitions, protest meetings, strikes and
street demonstrations the UFA undoubtedly succeeded in raising the
political awareness of large numbers of lower-class women. These
Muslim women were not, as was often claimed, quiescent victims
of Islamic patriarchy or the passive followers of European militants.
Algerian women, records Lucette Laribère, were always at the forefront
of demonstrations, which could be met with extreme levels of police violence, including gunfire. 'I remember how during the dockers' strike in
Beni-Saf an Algerian woman gave birth, and she had absolutely nothing
to clothe her baby, she wrapped it in newspaper'.[42] The UFA had a
particularly strong presence in the Oran region and on one occasion a
column of about a thousand veiled women marched on the Prefecture of
Sidi-Bel-Abbès to hand in a petition demanding the right to vote. During
the agricultural workers strike of 1951–52 women in the same region
lay down on the railway line to stop a train departing with male prisoners for the notorious prison of Berrouaghia.[43] During the 1953 strike to
blockade ships destined for Indochina during the colonial war, women
interposed themselves between the *Compagnie républicaine de sécurité*
(CRS) riot police as they were about to attack the dockers, and removed
and tied their long veils (*haïks*) around their waists so that their hands
could be free to bombard the police with stones.

How successful was the UFA movement during the decade 1944–54?
As a section of the wider communist apparatus, the UFA possessed the
advantages of a sophisticated, well-funded and experienced party, with
its own printing presses, journalists, bureaucracy, communications and
links into both the trade unions and local and national government.

Between January 1945 and April 1946 the membership climbed rapidly from 7,000 to 20,000.[44] Algerian historians have often claimed that this dynamic movement in the long term undermined the PPA and weakened the key battle for national independence. In reality the extremely turbulent politics of the period, the constant tensions and battles *internal* to different currents, the complex and cross-cutting party alliances and splits, makes it difficult to impose a simple grid, a binary opposition, between the pro-independence PPA and the 'assimilationist' PCA. During 1946–47 Alice Sportisse made repeated efforts to approach Messali Hadj to create a united front organisation, the *Front national démocratique*,[45] and the UFA and the nationalist sister organisation, the *Association des femmes musulmanes algériennes* (AFMA), maintained a dialogue through members who attended joint meetings.[46] However, any move to unity was doomed to fail: the Messalists could not overcome their hostility towards the communists who had for decades sought to obliterate their movement, and the PCA retained a deep ambivalence towards nationalism. European communists frequently betrayed an underlying assimilationist stance towards Algerian identity, the assumption that in time and with progress Muslims would caste aside their supposedly inferior religion, culture and society for a secular and modern way of life. At a UFA rally in September 1947 one speaker reported on her attendance at a meeting of the recently formed nationalist AFMA at which the audience had 'declared itself in favour of keeping the veil until independence of the country', but on the contrary, she claimed, the veil should be suppressed.[47] Tensions were exposed within the UFA in the preparation for the 1949 Congress when Muslim delegates, supported by a minority of Europeans, objected to the decoration of the stage with numerous red, white and blue flags.[48] Many of the rank-and-file women supporters of the PCA were unable to overcome the visceral racism and superiority towards Algerians that was endemic in *pieds-noirs* society.[49] As Muslims attending UFA meetings began to outnumber Europeans after 1947 there are signs of the latter withdrawing in increasing numbers and failing to re-new membership,[50] precisely the same pattern of 'white-flight' that, as will be seen later, army Women's Circles began to experience after 1958.

The *Union démocratique du manifeste algérien* and secular feminism

The second strand in the Algerian women's movement was smaller in scale than the UFA, but of interest for the light it throws on an important secularist and westernising tendency. This feminist current grew under the aegis of Ferhat Abbas' party, the *Union démocratique du manifeste algérien*, which was created in early 1946 by a generation of reformist politicians who had originally subscribed to a moderate assimilationist agenda.[51] This movement found its early roots in an elite strata of professionals, mainly doctors, lawyers, politicians and teachers, who had received a high level of education within the French lycée and university system. This francophile group, sometimes referred to as *'évolués'*, was headed by Ferhat Abbas who during the 1930s was unreservedly in favour of full assimilation: 'either the population becomes completely French or it will perish'.[52] With the Manifesto of 12 February 1943 Abbas was forced to recognise the failure of the assimilationist project and accepted that some form of Algerian independence was desirable, but he still favoured close links with France, a kind of Dominion status, and preferred to achieve this goal through peaceful parliamentary and legalistic methods.[53]

On 1 May 1949 the UDMA established a new youth organisation, the *Jeunesse de l'union démocratique du manifeste algérien* (JUDMA), which during 1951 to 1954, in the columns of the party weekly *La République algérienne*, widely debated the issues facing Algerian women. In 1951 the paper carried a number of interviews with leading Egyptian feminists, including Saiza Nabarawi and Mounira Charaoui of the Egyptian Feminist Union, and Fatma Nimet Rashid of the National Feminist Party.[54] Egypt had a far more advanced and mature women's movement than Algeria and during the post-war era served as a beacon for emerging feminist and Arab nationalist struggles.[55] The message conveyed by the Egyptian militants to their Algerian sisters was a highly radical and political one, by the standards of the repressive French colony. They described the enormous role that Egyptian women had played, including in the mass street demonstrations of 1919, in the revolt against British rule: 'For the first time ever one saw veiled women taking the lead of demonstrations'.[56] Most crucial was the Kemalist idea that the Arab nation could only liberate itself through harnessing the full potential of women through education.[57] But if women were to liberate themselves and play a full role through education, training and employment, they would have to battle against traditional customs, seclusion and the veil: 'against the absurd, if not criminal, habits and customs that keep the Arab woman a slave outside the life of the nation . . . The veiled woman cannot assume any meaningful role in society . . . The veil is a rampart that it is absolutely necessary for Arab women to climb over if they wish to definitively emancipate themselves from the tight restrictions of imperialism'. This liberation was entirely legitimate, they claimed, since veiling and seclusion had no basis in the Koran and 'had nothing to do with Islam'.[58] Throughout 1951–54 *La République algérienne* internationalised the issue of Muslim emancipation through articles on the women's anti-colonial struggle in Pakistan, India, Syria and elsewhere. Numerous photographs of strong Muslim women as uniformed soldiers, aviators, telephonists, doctors and engineers provided icons of unveiled, liberated women placed in association with visual symbols of scientific progress and modernity (aeroplanes, cars, electric machines).[59]

The liberationist message made an enormous impact on young, educated Algerian women and through the letter columns of *La République algérienne* during 1953–54 they launched an extraordinary and virulent frontal assault on conservative religious forces in Algerian society, propounding the thesis of a 'double imperialism' that depicted custom as a form of oppression that was equal to colonialism itself. One correspondent, 'Nadia G', attacked the daily suffering of young women forced to work for derisory wages or into prostitution: we are told 'it's the fault of colonialism', but more blameworthy were the prejudices of parents and Muslim opinion, 'who insult us, denigrate us, expel us from their bosom like evil beasts that one wants to crush'. The male leaders of political parties and of Islamic organisations were indifferent to their fate, blind to 'this pain that gnaws young hearts smothered by the "protective" shadow of white veils that conceal so much dark suffering'.[60]

The idea of a double oppression seems to have gained some currency in 1953, and Fadila Ahmed, in an article in the Arab newspaper *Al Manar*, entitled 'The twin jailors of women', wrote: 'we Algeria women have two jailors: colonialism . . . and those listless beings who cling to the customs and traditions inherited, not from Islam, but from their ignorant fathers. The second jailor is worse than the first'.[61] Another young woman from Constantine wrote, 'In the atomic age it is absolutely unacceptable that women be odiously locked up, sequestrated, ridiculed', and also opposed the veil, 'noxious ancestral ideas' and the 'double imperialism' of both colonialism and conservative Muslim society.[62] A woman from Tlemcen attacked the veil and spoke of the humiliation of being photographed in the street by American 'gentlemen' tourists like freaks, 'a spectre looming up from by-gone ages'.[63] These militants were demanding, in particular, to be freed from the constraints of arranged marriage, not to be traded like cattle between families and thrown into 'the bed of a stranger who rapes them' and for the right to chose a partner on the basis of mutual attraction, 'to make a marriage of love'.[64] As will be seen in later chapters, this feminist discourse was identical to that which was solicited and reproduced by the army psychological warfare campaign for emancipation after 1956, and provides an important clue as to how one key current in the pre-war nationalist movement, that of the *évoluées*, resurfaced later in the French camp.

The radical voice of the young feminists was not, however, representative of the wider, male-dominated leadership of the youth movement and
parent UDMA. The anonymous editor (J. A) of *La République algérienne* dissociated himself from the more outspoken letters, chastised one
contributor for talking of 'noxious ancestral ideas', and warned against
abandoning principled behaviour for the superficial licence and decadence of the west.[65] The JUDMA feminists were undoubtedly aware of
the contemporary campaign being orchestrated by populist elements in
the PPA and *Ulema* to attack, often through violent street actions, alcohol
consumption, dance halls, cinemas and cafés in which Algerian women
were thought to flaunt themselves unveiled, in make-up, aping European
fashion and insulting all notions of honour, morality and national integrity.[66] JUDMA feminists who went unveiled reported that they were being
subjected to constant harassment in the street by men who 'follow them
right along the road, wolf whistle, bother them and finally even insult
them', so that they were being driven back into domestic seclusion.[67]

Such male aggression can be seen as a hostile reaction to the threatening 'invasion' of women into the previously banned public spaces
of the city. The UDMA press received numerous letters from men
who deployed a standard discourse of westernised female decadence
to attack an emerging Muslim feminism.[68] The Third Congress of the
JUDMA in 1954 passed a resolution which warned against Algerian
women who were taking, 'only the superficial varnish and licentious
libertinage of western civilisation, deliberately neglecting their role as
women, spouses, mothers and citizens'.[69] Faced with this male backlash
the female militants of the JUDMA went to great pains to argue that
emancipation was perfectly compatible with Islam, and that customary
restraints on women represented a corrupt deviation from the Koran
upheld by archaic patriarchy or conservative Islamic scholars. They
emphasised that the veil was no guarantee of moral behaviour, indeed it
was argued that some women used the anonymity of the *haïk* to engage
in clandestine liaison, and engaged in a form of self-policing to show that
unveiled women could demonstrate an irreproachable modest, respect-
ful and pure bearing: 'Have no fear dear brothers and dear fathers . . .
Above all do not think that we imitate certain European women in their
flashy finery, fancy show and low-cut dresses. On the contrary, we walk
with our head held high, always maintaining for ourselves the modesty
of the young Muslim girl'.[70] Some JUDMA feminists argued that the
dispute about the veil was sustaining a false and divisive debate, and
sisters had the right to veil or not as they chose.[71] Afsaneh Najmabadi
has argued that the simplifying and damaging binary opposition that
contrasted secular modernisation (unveiling) with conservative Islam

(veiling) failed to see that Iranian feminism contained a strand that regarded modernity, the veil and Islam as perfectly compatible, and some elements of this voice can be recognised in Algerian feminism.[72]

Overall the UDMA leadership, despite its modernist pretensions, maintained a quite conservative and cautious position on women's emancipation, and the focus on specific issues like the veil, education and training helped disguise a failure to address the issue of political rights, including the female vote which was not included in the party programme until 1955.[73] The reformist movement was in constant struggle to try and find an equilibrium or juste milieu, what one leader, Oussedik, called 'a harmonious synthesis between the two currents of civilisation: the materialism of the West and the spirituality of the East'.[74] But the UDMA leaders clearly felt ill at ease with the mixing of sexes in party or public meetings, and photographs show rigidly separated audiences with men to one side, and veiled women to the other.[75] While the party press gave space to young women, it sought to distance itself from what it viewed as the intemperate language of inexperienced juveniles. There existed a tension between those young women who were feeling their way, under exceptionally adverse conditions, towards a concept of personal development and individual fulfilment *as* women, and a party which subordinated their interests to those of the nation or 'people'. In general the UDMA discourse, including that of many women, saw the education and progress of women as instrumental or secondary to the needs of national liberation led by men. Ibnou Cherqui emphasised three key roles for women: first as providers of 'the constant comfort of her help' to militant husbands, brothers and fathers; second, of moral support for combatants; and third, as mothers and educators of children 'in the course of nationalism'.[76] Once again nationalism was threatening to lock women into the private family sphere in their 'natural' gender role as reproducers. Soon the small number of young and educated Algerian women who shared a more radical, secularist and personalist agenda were to find themselves politically isolated, particularly as the UDMA was first banned by the French government and then absorbed into the far more integral nationalist movement of the FLN.

Religious reformism and the *Association des Ulema musulmans algériens*

The reformist movement of the *Ulema* (or Islamic scholars) is of considerable importance to this study overall since, although it was not directly involved in any women's organisation, it helped formulate the core ideology of Messali Hadj's PPA-MTLD and of the FLN which became dominant after 1954, including the position on women. Until the 1980s the historiography of Algerian nationalism, most of it written from a left or Marxist perspective, tended to ignore or under-estimate the deep religious continuities within the independence movement and post-colonial state: but this has begun to be revised by historians following the post-1988 resurgence of Islamism.

From the moment of the French conquest of Algeria in 1830 until about 1920 the dominant form of religion was constituted by the holy men or *marabouts* castes, and the Sufi mystical confraternities (*tariqa*) that were located in monastic-type centres of pilgrimage and scholastic teaching (*zaouias*). By the early twentieth century scholastic learning was moribund, and both *marabouts* and official *imams* declined in popular legitimacy since they were closely associated with the colonial regime that funded and nurtured them as an instrument of political control. This sclerosis was challenged by the Islamic reform movement that arrived from the Middle East in the early 1920s and was led by Sheikh Abd al Hamid Ben Badis, member of a patrician Constantine family, who helped to found the AUMA in 1931 which rapidly spread through the urban centres of Algeria.[77] Islamic reformism, not unlike the Protestant Reformation in Europe, represented a rejection of populist forms of superstition, magic and saintly intercession, and a return to pure scriptural sources (*salafiyya*). This austere, disciplined and individualistic faith leant itself well to the rationality and modernising ambitions of the Algerian urban bourgeoisie that expanded with the rapid economic growth of the early twentieth century.

Although Ben Badis attempted to keep the *Ulema* clear of any political entanglements, it provided a powerful vehicle for emerging nationalism.[78] The assertion of Algerian exceptionalism, the deep historical roots of identity, Arabic language, culture and Islamic faith that could never be assimilated into French civilisation, expressed a new found pride, a cultural nationalism that stood firm against the humiliating and depersonalising impacts of colonialism. In April 1936 Ben Badis refuted Ferhat Abbas' famous statement that he could find no evidence for the existence of an Algerian nation, by noting: 'this nation has its history, illustrated by innumerable remarkable deeds; it has its religious and linguistic unity; it has its own culture, traditions, and values . . . it is a nation totally unlike France by its language, its values, ethnic origins and religion. It has no desire for assimilation. It has its very own fatherland, Algeria, with its established and well known frontiers'.[79] Unlike the highly fragmented and segmentary structures of moribund tribalism and *maraboutism*, that were rooted in particular localities and shrines, the puritan individualism of the *Ulema* provided a kind of 'Jacobin Islam',[80] the basis for a new national identity that unified Algerians across space, class and clan.[81] Reformism also separated Islamic spirituality from the sphere of natural science, which meant that Koranic orthodoxy was compatible with material progress, so that its followers could simultaneously defend religion against the inroads of westernisation while embracing the techniques of modernity, economic change and rational organisation.[82] Finally, under a highly repressive colonial regime that constantly harassed and crushed any overt form of Algerian political or party opposition, reformism constituted a 'non-political' religious base of cultural resistance that the government found difficult to proscribe.[83]

During 1930 to 1936 Messali Hadj distanced himself increasingly from secular communism and moved towards reformist Islam. He proposed the teaching of courses in Arabic language and history to migrant workers in France, deployed a political rhetoric infused with Islamic *jihadist* terms, and abandoned European dress for the beard, long gown and head-wear (*chéchia*) of the religious leader and prophet.[84] Much of the basic thinking and attitude of the PPA towards women derived from the *Ulema* which, Ali Merad notes, was 'both defensive and conservative'. The *Ulema* rejected the ideas of the progressive Muslim feminists of Turkey, Egypt, Iran, Syria, Iraq, Palestine and Tunisia, and adopted the ideas of the conservative Egyptian reformist Rashid Rida (1865–1935) as the supreme authority in this field.[85]

Rida was a puritanical moralist who expressed horror at the spectacle offered by the life-style of American women, the nudity in sea-side resorts, the rampant hedonism and individualism of western women who had ready access to divorce, and who destroyed the sacred unity and stability of the family. It was essential to combat what he perceived as a Christian and atheist conspiracy to weaken Islam from within by an insidious subversion of morality and family life, and this could be best achieved by a stout defence of traditional Sunni orthodoxy. Rida, unlike the Egyptian feminists, opposed the abolishment of veiling, and reaffirmed patriarchy, polygamy and unilateral male repudiation. Ben Badis and his followers stood at the opposite spectrum from the Kemalist *evolués*, from Ferhat Abbas and the young radical women of the JUDMA, who by abandoning the veil and women's segregation, represented a kind of dangerous Trojan Horse through which Algerian society might be subverted from within by a creeping westernisation. This form of conservative orthodoxy, as will be seen throughout this study, leant itself to one of the most powerful and enduring myths or ideological constructions of Algerian nationalism, the idea that women constituted a bastion and core defence of traditional religious and cultural identity.

The *Ulema*, in an attempt to halt the corrosive effects of westernisation transmitted through the secular French school system, began to expand the number of 'free schools', the secondary *médersa* schools that could provide both boys and girls with a modern Arabo-Islamic education.[86] The free schools played a crucial role in the formation of a whole generation of youth who became nationalist militants between 1936 and 1954. Although the data are unreliable or contradictory, the number of schools appears to have increased from 70 in 1934–35 to 181 in 1954, and by 1955 to have taught 21,093 boys and 14,097 girls.[87] The *médersa* received no government funding and were organised by a central association and local committees which allowed them a degree of independence that was worrying to the French authorities which subjected them to close police surveillance. Many of the male pupils, including the future FLN military leader and President Houari Boumédienne, went on to complete their education at the universities of Zitouna in Tunisia and El Azhar in Egypt, a connection that facilitated the flow of external Arab and Islamic cultural and nationalist influences into the Algerian lower middle class. Eventually, when the *Ulema* rallied to the FLN during 1956–57, the *médersa* were subjected to severe repression and some 133 schools were closed and many teachers were interned.

Typical of these centres of nationalist culture was the *médersa* 'Chabiba' of Algiers, a school that was funded by an association of parents and supporters, which had been temporarily closed by the government in July 1934 after the arrest of a militant teacher, Chama.[88] Nationalist families that nurtured Arab culture as a form of resistance frequently moved their daughters from French state schools into the *médersa*. The PPA militant Isa Benzekri was withdrawn from the French school when thirteen years old on the insistence of her maternal uncle and placed in the Algiers 'Chabiba', as was another future activist Malika Zerrouki. There they received a modern education in both Arabic and French language, infused with a strong nationalism including Algerian history and the learning and singing of patriotic hymns or songs (*nachid*).[89] Another activist Fatiha Bouhired comments: 'I was in the French school up to CM2 [Cours moyen 2, age group 10–11 years], then I studied Arabic in a "free" school of the Casbah, the "Lalla Chemma". It was a modern school, not like the impoverished Koranic schools [*Sid el Ouhate*]. We studied the Coran, the holy sayings [*hadith*], Koranic commentary [*tefsir*], arithmetic. It was a political school. Although the nationalist hymns were banned, we still learned them. It's there that we learned, still young, that we were colonised and that one day we would have to make a revolution against colonialism'.[90] Among the five members of the first clandestine women's cell of the PPA in 1946 were two future *médersa* teachers,[91] and the key activists of the youth branch, the *Jeunes filles musulmanes algérienne* (JFMA) created in June 1948, were predominantly teachers and students from the free schools. A police report noted that the JFMA, like the parent UDMA, was opposed to '"the occidentalisation" of the indigenous woman'.[92]

The *Ulema* thus supported girls' education as integral to the process of national regeneration, as long as they were segregated from boys in the classroom, their moral behaviour was closely policed, and knowledge, according to Ben Badis, was diffused 'on the basis of our religion and our national character'.[93] The reformist thinkers did not advocate education for girls and women on the basis of equality of opportunity and individual emancipation, but rather as a key to an Arabo-Islamic renaissance. Most of these young *médersa* women, who came to form the backbone of the PPA women's organisation, were drawn from a particular strata in urban society, a class of relatively well-off small shopkeepers, traders and skilled artisans who remained independent from the state patronage system and retained a degree of 'traditional' Arab culture and learning.[94] The petit-bourgeois nature of the *médersa*, influenced by a European disciplinary model, is captured in class photographs of Tayeb El-Okbi's *médersa* in Algiers which, notes James McDougall, 'show girls in neat, knee-length white dresses, their hands folded in their laps, and rows of boys in jackets and fez, flanked by their teachers (all in European dress, sometimes with a *burnūs* over the jacket)'.[95] The reformist-led *médersa* schools played a progressive role in facilitating the expanding education of girls: the *Ulema* leader Ahmed Tawfiq al-Madani, who represented the liberal wing of the movement,[96] in a speech to a meeting of 800 young women in Algiers stated: 'In order to be free, independent, it is necessary that our women be instructed and educated. She must be the equal of man and not his slave'.[97] But the overall position of reformism towards women was conservative and sought to reinforce Sunni regulation of family, marriage and gender segregation. Thus in one *médersa* programme dedicated to Arab language and history Sheikh Belkacem Djebali taught women from behind a curtain,[98] while the president of the AUMA Bachir al-Ibrahimi wrote in the newsletter *El Basaïr* (28 February 1950) opposing the extension of the vote to Algerian women on the grounds that it would provoke discord among Muslims.[99]

Populist nationalism and the *Association des femmes musulmanes algériennes*

The fourth and final strand in the growth of women's organisations between 1944 and 1954 concerns the foundation by the PPA-MTLD in

1946 of a network of clandestine women's cells, followed by the establishment of the AFMA in July 1947.

Throughout the long period from the foundation of the *Étoile nord-
africaine* in 1926 through to the outbreak of the War of Independence
in 1954, the Messalist movement never formulated a detailed or clear
policy in relation to women.[100] Until 1936 the ENA organised a political
base among the community of emigrant workers in mainland France, but
this was a society of single men with which Algerian women, left behind
in the colony, had little direct contact or input.[101] From 1936 onwards
Messali Hadj changed the centre of gravity of PPA activism from France
to Algeria, and during the following phase of rapid penetration of the
nationalist organisation in the colony, women began to be drawn into
the radical political currents. The presence of women, uttering characteristic ululations, was noted in mass demonstrations of 1936 and 1939,
when many were injured, and Messali acknowledged the presence of
'women who had come to hear the voice of the people', during his key
speech in the Algiers municipal stadium on 2 August 1936.[102]

However, Messalism, which has been described as a form of populist
nationalism, was in general characterised by a certain disdain for intellectuals, and appealed to the masses more through fiery rhetoric than
by any detailed elaboration of a programme.[103] For Messali everything
was subsidiary to the immediacy of the struggle for independence. Any
mention of Algerian women emphasised their exploitation, poverty and
victim status solely at the hands of the colonial system. Women were
always under 'the yoke of colonialism', or 'suffocated by the poverty
and ignorance that were carefully nurtured by imperialism'.[104] This
analysis of the purely destructive impacts of colonialism on women and
the family continued to provide the staple of FLN discourse through to
1962, and found its most detailed elaboration in Saadia-et-Lakhdar's
sociological treatise of 1961, *L'Aliénation colonialiste et la résistance
de la famille algérienne*.[105] Since, the PPA argued, Algerian women's
plight could only be resolved through the defeat of colonialism there
was no point in elaborating any interim programme: liberation of
women would come about almost instantaneously and totally, as if by
magic, from the removal of the causes of exploitation. 'The Algerian
woman could never advance as long as Algeria was bent under the yoke
of French colonialism',[106] a position that was reflected in a meeting of
the AFMA at which it was agreed the veil should be maintained, 'until
the independence of our land'.[107] This meant in effect that the PPA, as
well as the FLN later on, could avoid making any policy statements
on the issue of women, and a potentially explosive issue could be both
delayed and marginalised. The issues surrounding women were lacking

in any specificity, and were subordinated to or absorbed into the wider demands of the nationalist struggle.

Not until 1954, probably under the pressure of communist and UDMA campaigning, did Messali openly recognise the need for women to participate in the liberation struggle, although he shied clear of taking the issue further: given 'the delicate and sensitive nature of this problem, it is important to approach it with prudence and care'.[108] The masculine discourse of the MTLD-PPA in effect denied women any meaningful role as autonomous political agents, but reduced them to the function of heroic procreators, educators of the nation, and moral supporters of male warriors. 'And you', proclaimed the Central Committee of the MTLD in December 1953, 'women of our Algeria, mothers, sisters, spouses! . . . Remember that it is on you that falls the noble task of giving life and to forging the future generations! It is on you that the future of Algeria rests'.[109] The PPA was relatively at ease with the mobilisation of women in so far as it fitted into a traditional Middle East and Maghrebian myth of women taking over from effeminate or failing men a combative role in a time of danger to the people: the party journal, El Ouma, declaimed a Kabyle saying, 'Women take up arms, since men refuse to'.[110]

But overall nationalism was deeply ambiguous, Janus-faced, in simultaneously politicising women and making them aware of colonial exploitation, while drawing them into an ideology of domesticity and traditional gender roles that would in the long term act as an iron corset on emancipation. In the former area, the PPA was highly successful in bringing women for the first time into the sphere of political activism, an engagement that, apart from the *médersa* schools, was achieved through new forms of cultural activism and via the family cell or kin networks. The nationalists penetrated into urban civil society through a whole range of activities which were aimed particularly at youth, from sports clubs and scouting, to musical circles and festivals.[111] Fatima Zekkal has described the nationalist plays and theatrical sketches written and performed by militants of the AFMA, including male roles that were played by women. At the Algiers Opera, close to the Casbah, they staged 'tableaux that symbolised Algeria before and after colonisation and as we imagined it after independence. I appeared dressed in the Algerian flag. It was the first time that the Algerian flag was shown on stage. The hall was full, bursting at the seams, the police were there'. Later, when Zekkal moved to Tlemcen she seized the opportunity of her wedding celebration to encourage women who were present to set up an AFMA section. 'There was a male orchestra and at the end the gathering sang the PPA hymn [she sings and translates]:

I sacrifice for Algeria my life and possessions
For Liberty
Long live the Party of the Algerian People dear to my heart
And long live North Africa.

Everybody stood to attention, the men separate down below [in the inner courtyard], the women up above and everyone standing and singing. The women made their youyous'.[112] While the AFMA made ready use of family celebrations to overcome the claustration of women, there was at the same time indications of a significant innovation in the major cities as meetings moved away from private houses towards mass performances organised in spacious public halls and cinemas. For many women who attended these mass meetings this was the first time they had ever been inside a cinema, theatre or hall, and the extent to which they were defying convention is indicated by the fact that the turbulent male followers of the reformist leader in Algiers, Sheikh Tayeb El Okbi, disrupted normal cinema or theatre performances in early 1954 to protest against the presence of women.[113]

The most crucial factor preventing the politicisation of women was their high degree of illiteracy, combined with radical seclusion and isolation from political life beyond the threshold of the house. Muslim women were expected to remain silent in the presence of men, not to speak unless first spoken to, and not to express any ideas regarding the external male sphere of politics. To do so was to run the risk of incurring the wrath, and even physical violence, of fathers, husbands and brothers. Fatima Baichi reports how she was beaten and dragged by her hair when her brother caught her 'doing politics'.[114] Mériem Madani, an FLN agent who was later arrested and tortured in May 1959, notes that she had no idea what the revolution meant when it began in 1954, 'I did not know what it was, because I was not educated, I had never studied, I had never been to school, and in our homes the men never talked in the presence of women'.[115] For the tiny minority of urban Algerian women who did become militants before and during the War of Independence, the best chance of achieving a degree of political consciousness and engagement was if they happened to be located in households or extended family networks in which the men were active nationalists. Fatiha Hermouche notes that she was 'through the family circle in touch with the movement of nationalist ideas. One relative militated actively, he brought friends home, and I overheard their discussions. For girls, the influence of the family milieu is vital'.[116] The father and two brothers of Baya Hocine were PPA activists: 'politics was much discussed among the men. What's wonderful about women is that they do not discuss politics, but they understand everything, and suddenly this silent mass, faced with a particular situation, can assume an active role'.[117] But the fact that women's nationalism emerged largely as a component of the politics of the male-led family group, and from which it was unable to break free, meant that this radical current was subsidiary to or dependent on males who would rapidly reverse or demobilise the new-found momentum at independence.

Equally significant was the fact that patriarchal or kinship solidarities bound together members of the same family, fraction or clan in which individualism had little place, so that if 'conversion' took place to support the PPA, or later the FLN, the *Mouvement national algérien* (MNA), or the French side in the war, it was frequently the whole group that would 'go over' collectively (*ralliement*) in a single instance.[118] Such en bloc political mobilisation included all wives and daughters as an integral part of the collective. Baya Hocine notes that all in her family, which lived in the Algiers Casbah, were PPA militants, and that this was the case for all those who had emigrated to the city from their Kabyle village: 'It's the whole village that agrees on this, that's how it is with us, the Ighil Imoula'.[119] Committed PPA nationalists were more willing to admit women into the previously male-dominated and closed sphere of politics or to attend AFMA meetings, even if this meant some breaching of traditional boundaries of female exclusion and segregation, since this was legitimated by the exceptional circumstances of clandestine nationalist struggle. The FLN militants Malika and Louisette Ighilahriz recall the solemn occasion when their father, instead of eating separately from the women as was usual, called all the family around the table and announced his political engagement and his expectation that they too would suffer and sacrifice themselves for the liberation of their country: 'I want you to be very courageous and that you follow my example'.[120] However, as will be seen, this channelling of women's political energies into the nationalist struggle was to carry portentous implications, since there was no guarantee, no implicit 'contract', that women would be compensated for such a sacrifice by recognition of their political right in the post-independence order.

The response of colonial government to the emergence of the Algerian women's movement, 1944–54

This concluding section examines the response of the Gouvernmente générale (GG) to the challenge offered by the growth of Algerian women's organisations. During the decade after 1944 the government was intensely preoccupied with the rapid extension of the nationalist movement, and how to weaken or contain it through repressive means, including mass arrests of militants, seizure or closure of the press, fixing elections and other well-worn techniques. The women's organisations, especially the AFMA, were undoubtedly weakened by the general climate of repression, and the interest of the Algiers government to keep a close eye on the various associations is shown by the extensive volume of intelligence and informer reports. But, given the relatively small membership of the various organisations, the GG showed no particular concern, and was happy to monitor the situation through surveillance. What the archives reveal is concern in a rather different field, a high-level ambition to block the access of Algerian women to the franchise and to do this in such a way as to fend off international criticism of the colonial regime.

A fundamental political issue that faced the colonial regime throughout the period after 1900 was how to retain settler domination, despite the republican rhetoric of universal rights, and in a situation in which indigenous Algerians greatly outnumbered Europeans. The *sénatus-consulte* law of 1865 codified a radical difference between Europeans (and soon after Jews under the Crémieux decree of 1870) who had full French citizenship and Algerians who were given second-class status as 'subjects' since they fell under Muslim personal status law (*statut personnel*). The dike which was constructed to retain the flood of Algerians that threatened to inundate the settler monopoly of political power was crucially defined in religious terms: as long as Algerians remained Muslims then they fell subject to the separate laws and customs of Islamic courts which regulated marriage, the family and inheritance. The French exclusionary ideology claimed that as long as Algerians remained subject to 'barbaric' Islamic practices such as arranged and child-marriage, polygamy, repudiation, dowry and veiling so it was inconceivable that they could become full citizens since this would be in contradiction with 'universal' French law that, by definition, should apply to all individuals without exception.[121] In principle the 1865 law enabled Algerians to become French citizens through 'naturalisation' by renouncing Muslim personal status: time and again colonial spokesmen cynically offered Algerians this immediate and ready access to citizenship as a warranty of their own 'democratic' principles, while knowing full well that such an act of apostasy was deeply abhorrent to almost all Algerians: as General Reibell remarked in 1928, 'If they [the Algerians] want to become French citizens, then they can naturalise, that's up to them. They can become French citizens any time they choose'.[122] The settler regime thus used personal status, constantly reiterated through an Orientalist discourse of female oppression and male sexual violence, as a key blocking device: in such a system colonials had every interest in sustaining and exaggerating the 'backward' features of Algerian family law rather than emancipation.[123]

From time to time the settler regime conceded, under intense pressure from liberal reformers and Algerian elites, as with the Jonnart law of 1919, tiny additions of carefully selected categories of male Algerians to the European electorate, such as war veterans, property owners and the holders of educational qualifications. However, with the Liberation the political climate in metropolitan France was one of intense expectation of radical change and the institution of a new, democratic constitutional order, an optimism that was symbolised by the extension of the vote to all French women. The challenge facing the colonial regime in Algeria was how to engineer an electoral system that could be defended in the republican language of universal rights and democracy, while in reality built to guarantee the political domination of the European minority. Basically this was achieved in relation to the Algerian male electorate through the device of a dual chamber. After lengthy debate in the First and Second Constituent Assemblies (October 1945 to October 1946), as well as the first National Assembly, the Organic Law of 20 September 1947 continued the classic colonialist system of separate and grossly unequal electorates.[124] The law established a quasi-parliamentary body of limited competence, the *Assemblée algérienne*, divided into a First College of sixty delegates, elected by 469,000 Europeans and 63,000 Muslims from the conservative elites, and a Second College of sixty delegates elected by 1,300,000 Muslim male voters. Since all major decisions had to pass both Colleges and by a two-thirds majority, the European minority could always control the agenda and block any legislation to which they took exception.[125] Even with this institutionally corrupt system, designed to guarantee settler hegemony, the GG was finding it difficult to contain the explosive pressures of nationalism and Naegelen was appointed Governor in February 1948 to keep a lid on the situation by overseeing the first elections to the Algerian Assembly. Under his supervision the regime proceeded to rig the elections on a huge and systematic scale, using a range of corrupt practices from the intimidation and arrest of nationalist candidates to the stuffing of ballot boxes.[126]

However, the colonial regime was faced with a further dilemma in that the enfranchisement extended by De Gaulle to all European women in metropolitan France and Algeria would, in principle, have to be extended to Muslim women. Under Articles 4 of the Organic Law of 20 September 1947, 'Algerian women of Muslim origin possess the right to vote', but a decision on how this would be implemented was left, by a slight of hand, to the future Algerian Assembly which in turn was so rigged as to carry an automatic European majority.[127] During the decade from 1948 to 1958 the Algiers government repeatedly claimed that the women's franchise was *not* blocked by the French powers but by Muslims themselves in the Second College. Deputies of the Algerian Communist Party, most notably Alice Sportisse and René Justrabo,[128] the mayor of Sidi-Bel-Abbès, continued to push for implementation of the franchise in the National Assembly and the Algerian Assembly during 1948 and 1949, and also through the campaigns of the UFA. For example, at a UFA meeting in Algiers during October 1948 attended by some 800 women, nearly all of them Muslims, Sportisse made a speech in which she noted that the Communist Party 'had fought and continues to fight to obtain the right to vote for Muslim women', and indicated that a UFA campaign for the political education of Muslim women would prepare them for the exercise of this duty.[129]

Naegelen, in concertation with the Minister of the Interior, responded in 1949 to such pressure with the trivial proposal that some 300 women from the Muslim educated elite be added to the electoral list of the First College, a measure that the European delegates quickly buried.[130] Given the predominance of highly conservative Algerian delegates in the Assembly, so-called 'Yes-men' or 'Beni-Oui-Oui', supporters of the colonial regime chosen through corrupt electoral procedures, it is not surprising that they clamped down on any meaningful extension of the female vote. Naegelen's cynical and widespread use of electoral fraud represented the final blocking of the way to any peaceful solution to the Algerian crisis and drove the PPA towards the only option left to it: armed rebellion.

The Algiers administration seemed quite relaxed about its cynical fixing of the electoral system and its exposure in the media: this, after all, is what it had been doing for over a century. Nor did it see the communist-led campaign for implementation of the female franchise as a matter of concern. But behind the scenes, largely unknown to the Algerian nationalists, Paris and Algiers appear to have been much more anxious about the potential impacts on international opinion. The source of this preoccupation in the Ministries of Foreign Affairs, Justice and the Interior originated from pressure that was bought to bear by Marie-Hélène Lefaucheux, a politician who played a leading role in the post-war international women's movement. From 1945 Lefaucheux was elected as deputy for the Aisne for the *Mouvement républicaines populaires* (MRP), a Christian Democrat party which in the immediate post-war years, inspired by the experience of the Resistance and progressive Catholicism, adopted with exuberance the mantle of the Gaullist 'liberation' of women.[131] Lefaucheux held a powerful, diplomatic position in the French delegation to the UN, and in 1946 she played a leading role alongside Eleanor Roosevelt in the establishment of the *Commission on the Status of Women* (CSW), as well as in the drafting of the Universal Declaration of Human Rights (1948). During 1946–47 Lefaucheux pressed the Commission to monitor the status of women in protectorate and colonial territories, and in the following years the CSW, which aimed to achieve 'equality with men in all fields of human enterprise', engaged in centralising a huge volume of comparative information on women's political, economic, civil, social and educational rights across the globe.[132] Between 1948 and 1952 Lefaucheux, as chairwoman of the CSW, played a key role in overseeing the monitoring of the legal rights of women in marriage, especially in relation to repressive customary practices, and in advancing full political suffrage for women, a radical agenda at a time when only twenty-five of the fifty-one UN member states allowed women equal voting rights with men. Lefaucheux travelled widely to the French colonies of North and Sub-Saharan Africa and, as will be seen later (chapters 5 and 8), came to play a crucial role in the formulation of Algerian emancipation policy and reforms during 1957–59. Her work as chairwoman of the CSW culminated in the adoption by the UN General Assembly on 20 December 1952 of the Convention on the Political Rights of Women, an instrument that helped highlight the ongoing denial of rights of indigenous women under colonial regimes.[133]

Lefaucheux, as chair of the CSW, was placed in an uncomfortable position by her own government's policy in Algeria. During 1951 and early 1952 she kept the French government informed of the CSW preparation of the Convention which was to include, 'the political rights of women, their situation in common law and their access to education' and in a report she recommended 'it would be advantageous to our country to show evidence of initiative in relation to the advancement of women'.[134] In a letter of 1955 Lefaucheux explained that her concern for women's rights in the French colonies did not arise from her 'feminism', but her deep regret that the government failed to recognise the political interest in favouring 'the progress of women'. In particular she was aware of the bitter discontent among young educated women, the 'elite' of nurses, teachers and students, who 'harbour much bitterness because of the total indifference with which the administration allows unacceptable customs to continue'. France should be offering their best chance of progress, but these women were being drawn into, 'movements with communist or nationalist leanings'.[135]

Lefaucheux had clearly recognised the nature of the frustration building up among the Algerian *évoluées*, and the appeal that she was making to the French government during 1951–52, in order to head off the growth in nationalism, was directly in line with the policy that Algiers would adopt after 1956. The Minister of the Interior, who had authority over the Governor General, relayed Lefaucheux's concerns as UN delegate, as well as those of the French Ministry of Foreign Affairs, to Algiers and recommended in a letter of 16 January 1952, 'vis-à-vis international opinion, that France could show evidence of progressive measures in this area', and requested a report on the voting rights of Muslim women.[136] Although the French government was concerned primarily with diplomatic window dressing, rather than with the substance of reform, its anxiety was justified since in the long term the political battle within the UN over the Algerian colony was to prove almost as decisive in opening the way to independence as the FLN armed struggle.[137] There was evident French government concern over this issue and the Ambassador in Moscow, the former Governor General Yves Chataigneau, sent a dispatch to the Foreign Minister, Robert Schumann, providing evidence of the failure of the Soviets after thirty years to emancipate Muslim women in Central Asia from the veil (parandja) and other repressive practices.[138] These facts, he suggested, could be used against Soviet delegates in the CSW if they should attack French policy in the Maghreb.[139]

Over a two-year period between July 1951 and August 1953 there was an extensive correspondence between the Minister of the Interior and the Governor General Léonard, on the position that France should take in regard to the Convention on the Political Rights of Women. This is of interest for the insight which it provides into the standard arguments and discourse deployed by the colonial regime to deny rights to Algerian women throughout the Fourth Republic between 1944 and May 1958.[140] Léonard advised Paris that the colonial distinction between French citizens and Algerian-Muslim subjects meant that as long as the latter remained wedded to 'the principal institutions of Muslim law, contrary to our Western concept of social equality', such as the abhorrent practices of polygamy, enforced child-marriage, repudiation, segregation and the veil, Muslim women were not able to exercise the vote freely.[141] Léonard, utilising a standard argument of settler society, remarked that the UN and international opinion should be informed that all Algerian women were free to exercise the right to vote by the simple choice of naturalisation.

Léonard went on to construct a smoke-screen: resistance to the franchise, he claimed, did not stem from the French government, which had laudable progressive motives, but rather from Muslims themselves. International opinion should be told that France had already granted voting rights to Muslim women by the Statute of 20 September 1947. But implementation lay with the Algerians themselves and when Naegelen, it was claimed, had proposed in 1949 adding 300 Muslim women to the electoral lists of the First College in the Algerian Assembly, this had sunk without trace under the 'indifference, or even the hostility of Muslims'. Léonard brushed over the concern expressed by Lefaucheux that the fate of Muslim women lay in the hands of an undemocratic quisling Assembly, 'hostile to any advancement of women', one which was so constructed as to prevent any power reaching the Algerian electorate. The government had no power to intervene in the 'private' sphere of religion and, 'It has to take account of the reactions of a society attached to its customs, essentially religious, and extremely touchy and oversensitive to any measure which may appear to violate their conscience'. The UN, he noted, should be informed that the best means of achieving full rights for Muslim women would be through the education of Algerian girls, 'that is when the Muslim milieu does not itself oppose its doubts', a long-term evolution that the administration would need to approach with 'prudence'. The Governor was thus able to relegate political change to some distant and indeterminate future, while concealing the fact that the colonial regime carried prime responsibility for preventing access of Muslim girls to state education.

Lastly, Léonard quickly skimmed over the most crucial political issue in all this, that of settler opposition to enfranchisement of women. Even the tiniest concession, he admitted, 'will be disliked by the European element of the population, hostile to any numerical increase in the first college'. Since the 1930s settlers had been deeply worried by the rapidly growing birth rate of the Muslim population and by the prospect of Algerians virtually swamping the European minority.[142] It had proved difficult enough to gerrymander the electoral system so as to contain the voting power of Algerian men, without engaging in the folly of granting the vote to women which would double the Muslim electorate from 1,900,300 to 3,800,600. By mid-1957 the Algiers administration estimated that a female franchise would reduce the European proportion of the electorate from 25 per cent to 14.5 per cent, and that such a change would radically alter the electoral balance of power, would lead to the European loss of control of all urban municipalities, with the possible exception of Oran and Algiers, and result in 'such an abrupt loss of influence for the Europeans that a sharp reaction is to be feared on their part'.[143] The administration in 1957 was secretly examining various ways to restrict women's access to the vote, through requirements of literacy, age and marital status, or by the argument that Muslim women were unsuited to exercise such a right because they were illiterate, would be forced to vote according to the interests of male family members, or because of the veil, which would prevent identification at polling stations. The idea of registering only those women who requested it might backfire since nationalist women might do so, while 'moderate women would fear a collision with tradition'.[144] It was on similar grounds that Léonard had opposed the UN Convention on the Political Rights of Women,[145] and when Lefaucheux eventually signed the protocol on behalf of France on 31 March 1953, this was not a ratification, and a get-out clause was added: 'The French government, given the customs and religious traditions in existence in its territories, reserves the right to suspend the execution of the present Convention in relation to women residing in these territories'.[146] French diplomats were thus able to present themselves to international opinion as keen supporters of the Convention, but would have to wait on conservative Algerian public opinion and their Assembly to change before progress could be made.

In conclusion to this chapter, it can be noted that the decade from 1944 to 1954 witnessed the first significant political organisation of and by Algerian women. This movement, after a peak in 1948–49, began to lose impetus during the early 1950s. This reflected in part the decline of the post-Liberation women's movement in metropolitan France, to which the Algerian movement was closely linked, particularly with the advent of the Cold War and the exclusion of the PCF from government.[147] The Algerian nationalist movement also entered a phase of deepening crisis after 1949, a process of internal fission that paralysed the PPA until a final split between the Messalists and the new FLN in late 1954. Because of the major electoral advances made by the MTLD in November 1946, as well as the constitution of a clandestine terrorist network, the *Organisation spéciale*, the French government appointed two successive hard-line General Governors, Marcel-Edmond Naegelen and Roger Léonard, who engaged in a ferocious repression of the nationalists. The fledgling women's movement fell victim to this harsh phase of repression and the decline in attendance at meetings of the two principle associations (UFA, AFMA) provides a barometer of the overall crisis in the nationalist movement. By early 1953 attendance at UFA meetings had declined from gatherings of several hundred to meetings of ten to forty,[148] while the PPA militant Isa Benzekri, after returning in 1951 from a year's absence in a French sanatorium, found 'the Association [AFMA] had practically ceased to exist, it had suffered from the repercussions of the divisions in the heart of the PPA/MTLD'.[149]

The women's organisations, even at their peak, only attracted a tiny percentage of Algerian women, mostly educated women in the main towns. Estimates of the communist UFA that it had at its peak between 15,000 and 20,000 female supporters appear to be inflated while the all-Muslim AFMA, lacking the elaborate organisational base of the PCA, was even smaller with a peak membership of several hundred women.[150] However, although the Algiers government had no difficulty in keeping the fragile women's movement under close police surveillance and restricting its activities, this phase of militancy undoubtedly helped to politicise a whole generation of young women who were to form the core of FLN militants during the War of Independence.[151]

But the history of this immediate post-war mobilisation is most interesting for what it tells us about the emergence of deep underlying tensions internal to the women's movement, ideological oppositions that prefigure the profound contradictions that were to bedevil Algerian nationalism throughout the War of Independence, and on into the post-colonial age. While Algerian women showed remarkable resilience in mobilising and finding cultural and political expression within the constraints of a patriarchal society, at the same time we can see the inner tensions emerging between the minority who were drawn to a more secular, 'western' and 'Kemalist' agenda of liberation, and those who accepted the *Ulema*/Messalist formulation of a nationalist struggle that embedded women in the subordinate gender position of mothers and guardians of the home. The FLN essentially inherited the latter position from the PPA, and was able to exert its ideological hegemony over the 'westernising' trend when it forced both the PCA and the liberal reformists (UDMA) to dissolve and join its own organisation during 1956–57. At the same time the colonial regime moved in the opposite direction. While during 1944–54 it had bitterly resisted any form of female franchise or emancipation of women, it now engaged in a 'U-turn' and moved to recuperate precisely the most radical and secularist trend that had been voiced by young women nationalists in their attack on the 'dual imperialism' of retrograde colonialism and reactionary Islamist patriarchy. During 1944–54 women who shared these two positions, which cut across the communist UFA, secularist JUDMA and Messalist AFMA in complex ways, could still engage in open dialogue, but with the coming of war the opposing visions became radically split and fixed by association with either French power (western female liberation) or Algerian national authenticity. In the process the Algerian women's movement was diverted into a suffocating cul-de-sac for the next quarter of a century.

Notes

1 The General Government (*Gouvernement générale*), the central colonial administration, employed some 2,000 civil servants located in a vast building in Algiers. Before the balconies of the façade was situated the ceremonial square, the Forum, on which the unveiling parades of May 1958 took place.

2 Space does not allow a detailed treatment of the complex history of Algerian society. There exists a large literature on the subject: for the English reader the following provide an overview: Mahfoud Bennoune, *The Making of Contemporary Algeria, 1830–1987* (Cambridge: Cambridge University Press, 1988); John Ruedy, *Modern Algeria. The Origins and Development of a Nation* (Bloomington: Indiana University Press, 1992); Charles-Robert Ageron, *Modern Algeria: A History from 1830 to the Present* (London: Hurst, 1991); Pierre Bourdieu, *The Algerians* (Boston: Beacon Press, 1962); Benjamin Stora, 'Introduction' to *Algeria 1830–2000. A Short History* (Ithaca: Cornell University Press, 2001); and MacMaster, *Colonial Migrants*, chapters 1, 10.

3 Louis Chevalier, *Le Problème Démographique Nord-Africain*, Institut National d'Études Démographique, Travaux et Documents, Cahier No. 6 (Paris: Presses Universitaires de France, 1947).

4 J. H. Meulemen, *Le Constantinois entre les deux guerres mondiales. L'évolution économique et sociale de la population rurale* (Assen: Van Gorcum, 1985), 184.

5 Daniel Lefeuvre, *Chère Algérie. La France et sa colonie, 1930–1962* (Paris: Flammarion, 2005).

6 R. Descloitres *et al.*, *L'Algérie des bidonvilles. Le Tiers monde dans la cité* (Paris: Mouton, 1961).

7 Maurice Borrmans, *Statut personnel et famille au Maghreb de 1940 à nos jours* (Paris: Mouton, 1977), 459.

8 Caroline Brac de la Perrière, *Derrière les Héros.. Les Employées de maison musulmanes en service chez les Européens à Alger pendant la guerre d'Algérie, 1954–1962* (Paris: L'Harmattan, 1987), 25–47.

9 Stora, *A Short History*, 24. However, the average statistics conceal considerable geographical variations: some 26.5 per cent of girls were in primary education in Algiers, but in rural areas this could fall to 2 per cent or less; see Borrmans, *Statut personnel*, 460–1. Mahfoud Kaddache, *Histoire du nationalisme Algérien. Question nationale et politique Algérienne, 1919–1951* (Algiers: Société Nationale d'Édition et de Diffusion, 1981), 743, estimates that in 1948 some 6.57 per cent of all Algerian children (aged six to fourteen years) were in primary education.

10 Borrmans, *Statut personnel*, 462; see also Kamel Kateb, *École, population et société en Algérie* (Paris: L'Harmattan, 2005), 26–35: three times more was spent on the education of each European child than on one Algerian.

11 *Ibid.*, 462.

12 Willy Jansen, *Women Without Men: Gender and Marginality in an Algerian Town* (Leiden: E. J. Brill, 1987); Dahbia Abrous, *L'Honneur face au travail des femmes en Algérie* (Paris: L'Harmattan, 1989).

13 The rich proliferation of international conferences in which Muslim women were involved in the inter-war period is under-studied, but some details, including the Congress of Eastern or Oriental Women (*Congrès musulman général des femmes d'Orient*), can be found in Fleischmann, 'The Other "Awakening"', 113, 117; Thompson, *Colonial Citizens*, 138–9, 144, 272–5; Afsaneh Najmabadi, 'Authority and Agency', in Atabaki (ed.), *The State*, 171–3; Charlotte Weber, 'Unveiling Scheherazade: Feminist Orientalism in the International Alliance of Women, 1911–1950', *Feminist Studies*, 27: 1 (Spring 2001), 125–57; Borrmans, *Statut personnel*, 88–92.

14 Odile Moreau, 'Echoes of National Liberation: Turkey Viewed from the Maghrib in the 1920s', *Journal of North African Studies*, 8: 1 (Spring 2003), 59–71; and especially James McDougall, *History and the Culture of Nationalism in Algeria* (Cambridge: Cambridge University Press, 2006).

15 Kaddache, *Histoire du nationalisme*, Vol. 1, 37–42, 286–8.

16 For the background on female European writing or perceptions of Algerian women see, Benjamin Stora, 'Women's Writing Between Two Algerian Wars', *Research in African Literature*, 30: 3 (Fall 1999), 78–94; Lazreg, *Eloquence*, 20–97; Peter R. Knauss, *The Persistence of Patriarchy. Class, Gender, and Ideology in Twentieth Century Algeria* (New York: Praeger, 1987), chapter 4; Jeanne Bowlan, 'Civilizing Gender Relations in Algeria: The Paradoxical Case of Marie Bugéja, 1919–39', in Julia Clancy-Smith and Frances Gouda (eds), *Domesticating the Empire. Race, Gender, and Family Life in French and Dutch Colonialism* (Charlottesville: University Press of Virginia, 1998), 175–92. For inter-war ethnography see Mathéa Gaudry, *La Femme Chaouia de l'Aurés* (Algiers: Librairie Orientaliste Paul Geuthner, 1929: re-edited Algiers, Chihab-AWAL, 1998); Thérèse Rivière, *Aurès-Algérie, 1935–1936. Photographies de Thérèse Rivière, suivie de Fanny Colonna 'Elle à passé tant d'heures. . .'* (Paris: Éditions de la Maison des Sciences de l'Homme,1987); Nancy Wood, *Germaine Tillion, une femme-mémoire. D'une Algérie à l'autre* (Paris: Éditions Autrement, 2003), chapter 1.

17 Hubertine Auclert, who lived in Algeria from 1888 to 1892, published *Les Femmes arabes en Algérie* (Paris: Société d'Éditions Littéraires) in 1900: see Julia Clancy-Smith, 'Islam, Gender, and Identities in the Making of French Algeria, 1830–1962', 167–72, in Clancy-Smith and Gouda (eds), *Domesticating the Empire*, 167–72.

18 Sara L. Kimble, 'Emancipation Through Secularization: French Feminist Views of Muslim Women's Condition in Inter-war Algeria', *French Colonial History*, 7 (2006), 109–28.

19 *Ibid.*, 123–4. At a UFSF conference held in Constantine in 1932, one rare Muslim delegate, Sehir Hacène, condemned the European women present for ascribing the suffering of Algerian women to Islam, rather than to social deprivation.

20 The key oral sources have been recorded by Djamila Amrane/Danièle
    Minne (see bibliography), and by Andrée Dore-Audibert, *Des Françaises
    d'Algérie dans la guerre de libération* (Paris: Karthala, 1995). A particularly
    rich source are the police intelligence reports, based in part on the evidence
    of informers, contained in CAOM 10CAB155.
21 The MTLD represented the electoral machine and facade for the more clan-
    destine PPA.
22 Kaddache, *Histoire du nationalisme*, 142; Danièle Joly, *The French
    Communist Party and the Algerian War* (Basingstoke: Macmillan, 1991).
23 Kaddache, *Histoire du nationalisme*, 139, a Muslim victory would inevita-
    bly, 'reduce women and children to slavery'.
24 On the process of 'arabisation' see Claude Collot and Jean-Robert Henry
    (eds), *Le Mouvement national Algérien. Textes, 1912–1954* (Paris:
    L'Harmattan, 1978), 54–60, 85; Kaddache, *Histoire du nationalisme*,
    321–7, 576.
25 Kaddache, *Histoire du nationalisme*, 746–7.
26 *Ibid.*, 656–9.
27 The PCA had established an earlier women's organisation in April 1937,
    the *Union franco-musulmane des femmes d'Algérie*, with the aim of estab-
    lishing 'a rapprochement between European and Algerian women', but the
    initial membership of well-off women was only thirty-six: see Fatima Zohra
    Saï, *Mouvement national et question féminine. Des origines à la veille de la
    guerre de libération nationale* (Oran: Éditions Dar El Gharb, 2002), 66.
28 Diane Sambron, 'La Politique d'émancipation du gouvernement français
    à l'égard des femmes musulmanes pendant la guerre d'Algérie', Doctoral
    thesis, Paris IV, October 2005, 315: the Communist deputies Sportisse,
    Djemeed, Mokhtari and Fayet placed a bill before the National Assembly
    as early as 13 March 1947 with a clause, 'All Algerian men and women,
    without distinction of origins, race, language or religion enjoy full demo-
    cratic liberties', later amended in August to include specifically the 'right to
    vote'.
29 CAOM 10CAB155: report of police commissioner; this European domi-
    nance is confirmed by its Muslim General Secretary Baya Allaouchiche, in
    her recent book under her married name, Baya Jurquet-Bouhoune, *Femmes
    algériennes*, 94, 97.
30 On the proletarianisation of day-labourers in the wine-producing area
    of Oran see Michel Launay, *Paysans algériens. La Terre, la vigne, et les
    hommes* (Paris: Seuil, 1963).
31 Amrane-Minne, *Des femmes*, 181–4; Dore-Audibert, *Des Françaises
    d'Algérie*, 36–9, 167–70, 179–84., Saï, *Mouvement national*, 71, notes
    among the leading urban militants Gaby Gimenez, Joséphine Carmona,
    Mme Espasa and the Laribère sisters.
32 Amrane-Minne, *Des femmes*, 182–3.
33 For a vivid account of rural activism see Jacqueline Guerroudj, *Des douars
    et des prisons* (Algiers: Bouchène, 1995), 12–15.

34 On the system of female segregation in Algeria, as for the Maghreb and
    Middle East in general, there is an extensive literature, but see in particu-
    lar the ethnographic work of Camille Lacoste-Dujardin, *Des mères contre
    les femmes. Maternité et patriarcat au Maghreb* (Paris: La Découverte,
    1996).
35 Dore-Audibert, *Des Françaises d'Algérie*, 30.
36 CAOM 10CAB155.
37 See Dore-Audibert, *Des Françaises d'Algérie*, 31.
38 CAOM 10CAB155, report of *Renseignements généraux* (RG), 25 May
    1949.
39 CAOM 10CAB155. Mme Mandouze's husband was Professor André
    Mandouze, a leading anti-colonial academic.
40 Kaddache, *Histoire du nationalisme*, 696, lists numerous riots across
    Algeria involving thousands of women, including by 2,000 women in Oran
    who on 6 March 1945 besieged the Governor General shouting 'bread,
    bread'.
41 Saï, *Mouvement national*, 68: both candidates held French citizenship.
42 Dore-Audibert, *Des Françaises d'Algérie*, 33.
43 *Ibid.*, 33–4; Amrane, *Les Femmes algériennes*, 42; Kaddache, *Histoire du
    nationalisme*, 859–60, notes this action concerned the transfer of forty-
    seven prisoners of the clandestine *Organisation spéciale* (OS) after their trial
    in Oran; Baya Jurquet-Bouhoune, *Femmes algériennes*, 105–7 also notes the
    extreme militancy of Muslim women, and gives a figure of 8,000 involved in
    an Oran march on international women's day, 8 March 1952.
44 Saï, *Mouvement national*, 68; Dore-Audibert, *Des Françaises d'Algérie*, 31;
    Amrane, *Les Femmes algériennes*, 41. These figures appear to be inflated
    and are identical to those given by Mohammed Harbi, *L'Algérie et son
    destin. Croyants ou citoyens?* (Paris: Arcantère, 1992), 92, for the entire
    PPA. Jurquet-Bouhoune, *Femmes algériennes*, 105, indicates a member-
    ship of 15–16,000 after 1951. It is of interest to note that of the 480 new
    members who joined during January 1945 alone, 180 (38 per cent) were
    Muslim.
45 Kaddache, *Histoire du nationalisme*, 756.
46 Jurquet-Bouhoune, *Femmes algériennes*, 101–2, notes links between the
    two organisations.
47 10CAB155, RG report, 1 September 1947.
48 Jurquet-Bouhoune, *Femmes algériennes*, 102–3.
49 Tensions between European ex-Communists and Algerian nationalist
    women may have surfaced later when they were forced to share prison
    space: see Meynier, *Histoire intérieure*, 183, note 155.
50 Jurquet-Bouhoune, *Femmes algériennes*, 104.
51 On the 'liberal' current in the nationalist movement see William B. Quandt,
    Revolution and Political Leadership: Algeria, 1954–1968 (Cambridge,
    Mass.: MIT Press, 1969), 25–42.
52 *La Défense*, 3 May 1935; in February 1936 Abbas published his notorious

article claiming that there was no such thing as an Algerian nation: see Kaddache, *Histoire du nationalisme*, 375, 421–2.

53 On the Manifesto see Kaddache, *Histoire du nationalisme*, 641–7.

54 On these Egyptian feminists see Badran, *Feminists*; Lazreg, *Eloquence*, 92–4, is critical of the Egyptian feminist Huda Sha'rawi for giving advice in 1951 that failed to recognise the specific conditions facing Algerian women, but Sha'rawi had died in 1947.

55 See Badran, 'Arab Feminism' in *Feminists*, 223–50.

56 *La République algérienne*, 9 March 1951, Mostafa Bechir, 'The Egyptian Feminist Union and the Role of the Woman in the Nation'. On the demonstrations, during which several women died, see Badran, *Feminists*, 74–8.

57 Such a position had been adopted by the First Congress of the UDMA at Sétif, 25–27 September 1947. 'If our women do not become our equals, informed and educated, our society will remain amputated from half its body and remain backward from modern society', quoted by Saï, *Mouvement national*, 32.

58 *La République algérienne*, 9 March 1951.

59 See, for example, *La République algérienne*, Supplement to No. 18, February 1954, with numerous photographs of Pakistani women; more generally for such modernist images see Sarah Graham-Brown, *Images of Women. The Portrayal of Women in Photography of the Middle East, 1860–1950* (London: Quartet Books, 1988).

60 *La République algérienne*, 23 October 1953.

61 *Al Manar*, 24 July 1953.

62 *La République algérienne*, 30 October 1953.

63 *Ibid.*, 30 October 1953.

64 *Ibid.*, 30 October and 20 November 1953.

65 *Ibid.*, 30 October.

66 On these violent campaigns see Kaddache, *Histoire du nationalisme*, 671, 674–5; CAOM 81F1218, police note dated 24 April 1954.

67 *La République algérienne*, 15 January 1954, 'Young Muslims Respect Our Young Girls in the Street', a letter signed 'B. A of Constantine'; for an identical pattern in Iran, see Najmabadi, *Women with Mustaches*, 154–5.

68 See for example, *La République algérienne*, 12 March 1954, a letter signed 'Omar M. A. of Montpellier', which argued that the veil protects, 'our family better than a whole arsenal of laws. A people is strong through the strength of the family. A civilisation dies most often through an overturning of morality; such disarray is a consequence of the indulgence of women, their ascendancy over men through turning them aside from their religious and political duties'. On the image of the 'westoxicated' woman in Iran, see Najmabadi, *Women with Mustaches*, 8, 138, 154, 239.

69 *La République algérienne*, 1 October 1954.

70 *Ibid.*, 6 November 1953, letter from Tlemcen,

71 *Ibid.*, 15 January 1954, letter from B. A of Constantine.

72 Najmabadi, 'Authority and Agency', 159–61, 175–6; and *Women with Mustaches*, 133, 136.
73 See CAOM 81F1218, report on the UDMA and female franchise, Ministry of the Interior, 18 December 1954.
74 Saï, *Mouvement national*, 33.
75 See for example a photograph of the UDMA section at Tiaret in *La République algérienne*, 16 March 1951.
76 *La République algérienne*, 7 December 1951, 'The Role of the Algerian Muslim Woman in the Anti-colonial Struggle'. M. Z., a JUDMA member, also saw the role of militant women as aiding and supporting 'their brothers, their spouses, their fathers', *ibid.*, 30 March 1951.
77 The classic study is Ali Merad, *Le Réformisme musulman en Algérie de 1925 à 1940* (Paris/La Haye: Mounton et Co., 1967); but see also Kaddache, *Histoire du nationalisme*; and McDougall, *History*.
78 See Fanny Colonna, 'Cultural Resistance and Religious Legitimacy in Colonial Algeria', *Economy and Society*, 3: 3 (August 1974), 233–52; Ernest Gellner, 'The Unknown Apollo of Biskra: The Social Base of Algerian Puritanism', a 1974 article reprinted as chapter 6, in his *Muslim Society* (Cambridge: Cambridge University Press, 1981), 149–73; Jean-Claud Vatin, 'Religious Resistance and State Power in Algeria', in Alexander S. Cudsi and Ali E. Hillal Dessouki (eds), *Islam and Power* (London: Croom Helm, 1981), 119–57.
79 Merad, *Le Réformisme*, 398–9.
80 McDougall, *History*, 110, borrowing a phrase from Jacques Berque.
81 Colonna, 'Cultural Resistance', 241–2.
82 On this strategy of nationalist ideology see the analysis of Partha Chatterjee, which is applicable to Algeria, in 'Colonialism, Nationalism, and Colonialized Women: The Contest in India', *American Ethnologist*, 16: 4 (November 1989), 622–33.
83 Gellner, 'Unknown Apollo', 167.
84 Benjamin Stora, *Messali Haj, Pionnier du Nationalisme Algérien (1898–1974)* (Paris: L'Harmattan, 1986), 108–18, 137–8, 157–8.
85 Merad, *Le Réformisme*, 316–31.
86 John Damis, 'The Free-School Phenomenon: The Cases of Tunisia and Algeria', *International Journal of Middle East Studies* 5: 4 (September 1974), 434–49; Kateb, *École, population*, 43–6.
87 Kateb, *École, population*, 44–5; Kaddache, *Histoire du nationalisme*, 337; Saï, *Mouvement national*, 17–18; Amrane, *Les Femmes algériennes*, 28–30.
88 Kaddache, *Histoire du nationalisme*, 221, 302, 358, 493.
89 Amrane-Minne, *Des femmes*, 26, 88. For the text of typical *nachids* see Kaddache, *Histoire du nationalisme*, 963–4.
90 Amrane-Minne, *Des femmes*, 129.
91 Amrane, *Les Femmes algériennes*, 36.
92 CAOM 10CAB155, RG, 16 June 1948.

93   Merad, *Le Réformisme*, 328–30.
94   Colonna, 'The Nation's "Unknowing Others"', 163–4 defines 'a highly defined stratum, that minuscule, urban petite bourgeoisie, of middling education in Arabic or French but of relatively marked acculturation', that furnished the cadres of PPA nationalism. Kateb, *École, population*, 45, notes that the school-leaving certificates of the *médersa* received no recognition from the French administration, which indicates the way in which this nationalist strata remained apart and un-integrated into the French clientele and 'rewards' system. The social roots of Moroccan nationalism were almost identical, and from the 1920s women of the urban bourgeoisie inspired by reformism organised a 'free school' movement which educated many women who later became nationalist militants in the *Istiqlal*: see Alison Baker, *Voices of Resistance: Oral Histories of Moroccan Women* (New York: State University of New York Press, 1998), 21–2, 47–54, 93–114.
95   McDougall, *History*, 112.
96   Tawfik al-Madani (1899–1983) illustrates clearly the continuities and links between the AUMA and the independence movement: an important nationalist historian and ideologue, he became general secretary to the AUMA in 1952, and later rallied to the FLN in 1955–56, for which he became an external emissary in Cairo and Minister of Cultural Affairs in the provisional government (*Gouvernement provisoire de la République algérienne*, GPRA), September 1958: see McDougall, *History*; Benjamin Stora, *Dictionnaire biographique de militants nationalistes algériens (1926–1954)* (Paris: L'Harmattan, 1985), 348; Meynier, *Histoire intérieure*, 53, 189–91, 248.
97   CAOM 81F1218, note of 24 November 1948.
98   CAOM 81F128, Ministry of Interior, 18 December 1954; report of 19 May 1953.
99   CAOM 81F1218, Ministry of Interior, 18 December 1954.
100 CAOM 81F1218, a report of the Ministry of the Interior, 18 December 1954, notes that the MTLD, 'has never defined its doctrine on the political evolution of Muslim women'.
101 Thousands of inter-war Algerian migrants co-habited with or married European women: see Neil MacMaster, 'Sexual and Racial Boundaries: Colonialism and Franco-Algerian Inter-marriage (1880–1962)', in Maire Cross and Sheila Perry (eds), *France: Population and Peoples* (London: Pinter, 1997), 92–108. It is possible that European partners (including Messali Hadj's wife, Emilie Busquant) had more influence in 'modernising' male attitudes to women than did distant wives in Algeria.
102 Kaddache, *Histoire du nationalisme*, 469, 534; Collot and Henry (eds), *Textes*, 83.
103 See especially Carlier, *Entre nation et jihad*.
104 Saï, *Mouvement national*, 40–1, quoting from the PPA journal *L'Algérie libre*.

105 This book, published in Lausanne in 1961, was probably by Rabah Bouaziz and his wife: communication from Gilbert Meynier.

106 *L'Algérie libre*, 18 August 1949, quoted in Saï, *Mouvement national*, 42; see also Amrane, *Les Femmes algériennes*, 32–3.

107 CAOM 10CAB155.

108 Amrane, *Les Femmes algériennes*, 34.

109 Collot and Henry (eds), *Textes*, 328.

110 *El Ouma*, March 1939, quoted in Kaddache, *Histoire du nationalisme*, 504, 938.

111 Kaddache, *Histoire du nationalisme*, 337, 512–13, 536–7.

112 Amrane-Minne, *Des femmes*, 21–2.

113 CAOM 81F1218., police note, 24 April 1954.

114 Amrane-Minne, *Des femmes*, 112.

115 *Ibid.*, 156.

116 *Ibid.*, 64.

117 *Ibid.*, 144.

118 In the peasant village (*douar*) the regulation of 'political' life, of law and custom, was undertaken by the collective decision of a council of the male elders, the *djemâa*.

119 Amrane-Minne, *Des femmes*, 144.

120 *Ibid.*, 147; Louisette Ighilahriz, *Algérienne* (Paris: Fayard/Calmann-Lévy, 2001), 45–6.

121 In December 1936 parliamentarians for the Department of Oran declared that French and Algerians could not exercise equal electoral rights to the same assemblies, 'when there are on the one hand those completely subject to French civil law and on the other those who can preserve a religious status contrary to those same laws and which notably permits polygamy, the pure and simple repudiation of women, and for the most part denies inheritance to girls': quoted in Kaddache, *Histoire du nationalisme*, 413.

122 Kaddache, *Histoire du nationalisme*, 239: see *ibid.* 887, between 1865 and 1916 only 1,725 Algerians were naturalised (a rate of thirty-five per year); on the *Ulema* view of individual naturalisation as an act of apostasy, see 100, 336, 460, 587–8; Laure Blévis, 'La Citoyenneté française au miroir de la colonisation: étude des demandes de naturalisation des "sujets français" en Algérie coloniale', *Genèses: Sciences sociales et histoire*, 53 (December 2003), 25–47.

123 See Clancy-Smith, 'Islam, Gender', 169–70. The instrumental nature of Islamic marriage law as a political barrier was highlighted by the fact that in other French colonial regimes, notably Senegal, citizenship was granted to natives who retained their personal status.

124 On the debates that concluded in the voting of an inegalitarian dual chamber see Abderrahmane Farès, *La Cruelle Vérité* (Paris: Plon, 1982), 32–43.

125 Collot, *Les Institutions*, 220–2.

126 Ruedy, *Modern Algeria*, 150–3; the crude nature of electoral fraud is reflected in voting figures, at Aïn Témouchent on 25 March 1949, 10,166 Algerians voted for the administrative candidate, nil for the UDMA candidate: see Kaddache, *Histoire du nationalisme*, 847.

127 SHAT 1H246/1*, report of P. Marmey, *Le Droit de vote de la femme musulmane*, Centre de Haute Études d'Administration Musulmane, 16 January 1958.

128 René Justrabo's wife was president of the Sidi-Bel-Abbès section of the UFA.

129 CAOM 10CAB155, RG report, 22 October 1948.

130 CAOM 81F1218; CAOM 10CAB22, letter of R. Léonard to the Minister of the Interior, 12 March 1952; Sambron, 'La Politique' (Doctoral thesis), 320–7.

131 Claire Duchen, *Women's Rights and Women's Lives in France, 1944–1968* (London/New York: Routledge, 1994), 34–47, 55. Lefaucheux was a leading member of the Resistance, and later served as president of the *Conseil national des femmes français* and of the *International Council of Women* (1957–63).

132 *Short History of the Commission on the Status of Women*, www.un.org/womenwatch/daw/csw/CSW/CSW60YRS/cswbriefhistory.pdf(accessed 14 March 2006).

133 Devaki Jain, *Women, Development, and the UN. A Sixty-Year Old Quest for Equality and Justice* (Bloomington, Indiana: Indiana University Press, 2005), 23–4.

134 CAOM 10CAB22. R. Léonard to Minister of the Interior, 12 March 1952.

135 CAOM 81F1218, Lefaucheux to de Lacharrière, 4 January 1955.

136 *Ibid.*

137 See Connelly, *Diplomatic Revolution*.

138 Lefaucheux was a close childhood friend of the Schumann family.

139 CAOM 81F1218, Chataigneau dispatch to Robert Schumann, 26 July 1951. The USSR, unlike France, went on to ratify the Convention.

140 The question of Léonard and the women's vote is discussed briefly by Diane Sambron, 'La Politique d'émancipation du gouvernement français à l'égard des femmes algériennes pendant la guerre d'Algérie', in Jean-Charles Jauffret (ed.), *Des hommes et des femmes en guerre d'Algérie* (Paris: Éditions Autrement, 2003), 231–2; and in more detail by Ryme Seferdjeli, 'French "Reforms" and Muslim Women's Emancipation During the Algerian War', *Journal of North African Studies*, 9: 4 (Winter 2004), 21–5.

141 CAOM 10CAB22, Léonard to Minister of the Interior, 12 March 1952.

142 Lefeuvre, *Chère Algérie*, 73–5, on the 'fear of being submerged'.

143 CAOM 81F1218, 'Note sur le vote des femmes en Algérie' (n.d. 1957).

144 CAOM 81F1218, 'La condition de la femme musulmane en Algérie. Aspect politique', July 1957; SHAT 1H2461/1*, report of P. Marmey, *Le*

Droit de vote de la femme musulmane algérien, Centre de Haute Études d'Administration Musulmane, 16 January 1958.
145 CAOM 81F1218. Léonard to the Minister of the Interior, 31 March 1953: 'In the actual state of her evolution, the Muslim woman has no opportunity to exercise freely and with dignity the right to vote conferred on her'.
146 CAOM 81F1218.
147 Duchen, *Women's Rights*, 57–9.
148 CAOM 10CAB155, RG reports.
149 Amrane-Minne, *Des femmes*, 27.
150 Evidence of the AFMA president, Mamia Chentouf, in Amrane, *Les Femmes algériennes*, 37.
151 Djamila Amrane's astonishing finding, *Les Femmes algériennes*, 11, 43, that only six of the 10,949 women officially registered by the Algerian government as former *moudjahidates* had any political involvement in the pre-war communist or nationalist movements, seems puzzling and may indicate a massive under-registration or refusal of an older generation of female militants to seek any form of recognition from post-independence governments.

The origins of the emancipation campaign, November 1954 to May 1958

The military coup of 13 May 1958[1] was marked by demonstrations of 'fraternisation' when Muslim women unveiled en masse on the Algiers Forum. This has been widely seen as a quasi-revolutionary moment that dramatically initiated the emancipation campaign. However, as will be seen in chapter 3, the illusion of a revolutionary break in May 1958 was successfully created by the propagandists of the psychological warfare bureau. Emancipation, far from springing forth perfectly formed as a triumphant expression of the popular will, represented the moment that a slowly maturing, but largely unseen, movement that had been gathering force over the previous two years suddenly came into the limelight. This process has gone largely unnoticed by historians in part because the government and army moved initially towards an agenda on Muslim women through a series of piecemeal initiatives and tentative experiments that were wrapped in considerable secrecy so that the FLN might be caught unawares, but also to conceal from French and international opinion the underlying military and intelligence logic of measures that it wished to dress in the clothing of liberal and democratic reform. However, an examination of this early stage is of interest, since the timing, and how and why the various initiatives were first undertaken, is informative as to the underlying concerns and objectives of the colonial authorities in moving towards such a strategy.

This chapter, which covers the first half of the Algerian War from 1 November 1954 until the coup of '13 May' 1958, falls into two parts. During a first phase from 1954 until mid-1956, which was dominated by the governorship of Jacques Soustelle, the Algiers government made little attempt to formulate a policy that was directly or explicitly aimed at Muslim women. The main initiative of Soustelle, who surrounded himself with fellow ethnologist advisers, was a classic 'Third World' developmental policy that aimed to improve the economic position of Algerian society as a whole, of which women just happened to constitute one category. However, from this reformist agenda emerged a number of new organisations, in particular the *Section administrative spécialisée* (SAS) and *Centres sociaux*, that were later to play a significant role in an overall strategy that targeted women.

The second and most important phase, which lasted from the summer of 1956 until the spring of 1958, saw the appearance of an intense debate that was focused for the first time specifically on Algerian women. It is difficult to determine whether the FLN or the French army was the first to deploy a 'liberation' strategy for Muslim women that the opposing side then responded to by adopting forms of counter-emancipation. However, two events during July–August 1956 made a big impact on French opinion and created a general climate in which the issue of Muslim women moved onto the agenda. In July the European public was astonished to see in the press photographs of three young nurses in military uniform who had been captured by the army in the maquis, images that shattered the Orientalist stereotype of secluded and powerless Muslim women.[2] A few weeks later, on 13 and 19 August, the newly independent states of Tunisia and Morocco announced major reforms of the marriage and family law. Suddenly the nationalists of the Maghreb seemed to be adopting a progressive position on Muslim women that threatened to harness their energy through modernisation, and to isolate France in international opinion as a reactionary colonial power. The Algiers government of Robert Lacoste responded over the next year, from behind the scenes, with a range of initiatives that included a propaganda campaign on emancipation and un-veiling, a working party on the reform of the marriage law, a debate on the extension of the vote to Muslim women, and a secret pilot operation to create and test new women's organisations.[3] However, throughout 1957 we find evidence of growing tensions within the civil-military apparatus over a reform programme aimed at women: on the one hand Lacoste and an older generation of leaders were concerned that emancipation might trigger a strong religious backlash among conservative Algerians that would play into the hands of the FLN. Lacoste placed both the issue of the women's franchise and the project to reform the marriage code on the back-burner. On the other hand, late 1956 and early 1957 saw the surge to power within the army of a radical new force, the young colonels who detested the sclerosis of the Fourth Republic and supported the ideology of revolutionary warfare. This radical current was far more prepared to engage in unconventional forms of warfare and to develop a highly proactive 'liberation' of Muslim women that aimed to induce a profound psychological shock both in the French establishment and the FLN. While the colonels secretly tested out such new methods during 1957 in Operation Pilot, by May 1958 they were prepared to grab power

in Algiers and to seize the opportunity to expand the experimental phase
into a full-scale and open campaign of emancipation.

Phase 1: November 1954–February 1956. Jacques Soustelle and the political development agenda

As the Cold War rapidly deepened after 1945 US and NATO foreign
policy centred on an over-riding fear that international communism
was seeking to destroy the west via support for Third World insurrection, preying on the poverty and hunger of innocent peoples that were
the victim of colonialism and under-development. The US government
turned increasingly to academic specialists in the social sciences, including anthropologists, economists and social psychologists, to study the
threat and through the 1950s and 1960s they produced an influential
model of intervention often referred to as Political Development Theory
(PDT).[4] The model regarded Third World countries as highly vulnerable
to insurgency, according to the adage 'poverty breeds discontent', and
the role of the US and 'west' should be to provide a degree of economic
aid and support so as to nurse fragile regimes through the transition to
modernisation until they could stand on their own feet and establish
democracy, political stability and nationhood. The PDT paradigm was
one of state-building and the creation of efficient bureaucracies that
could provide the necessary planning and administration to ensure economic well-being and security. Where Third World governments were
coming under attack from communist-inspired insurgents they should,
if necessary, be assisted by military programmes to contain this and
to give them time to make the transition to modernity. Some analysts
viewed modern armies as models of progressive, bureaucratic institutions, which could through direct military intervention or coups provide
the most effective route to development and security: a model that had
obvious implications for the French army control of a joint military-
civilian government in Algeria after January 1957.

While French policy documents on development reform and counter-
insurgency during the Algerian War make very few explicit references
to American theory, French practice overall moved towards an identical model. The Paris government, like the USA, utilised a large pool of
academic social scientists to investigate and recommend policies in relation to the 'Algerian problem', and without doubt these specialists were
aware of US thinking and helped to transmit such concepts into the army
and civil service.[5] The Governor, Jacques Soustelle, as a leading ethnologist was well placed to pick up on contemporary PDT and he, in turn,
had recourse to the appointment of experts like Germaine Tillion and

Vincent Monteil. But France had its own long-established institutions of state-planning led by the technocrats of the *grandes écoles* and it should come as no surprise that they should develop Algerian policy documents in a peculiarly French style which, while they carried few references to US doctrine, arrived at similar conclusions on the developmental answer to insurgency.[6] In December 1954 ex-Governor Naegelen claimed that the loss of North Africa would, in a domino effect, lead to the loss of the whole empire, 'It would push France down to the level of a secondary power and even to vassal status', and for General Calliès, 'North Africa has become the No 1 stake in the Cold War'.[7] The immediate response to the insurrection was to design a dual strategy, one of repression and social and economic development.

Less than three months after the outbreak of the Algerian War, on 25 January 1955, Soustelle, a leading Gaullist, was invited by the socialist Prime Minister Mendès-France, and the Minister of the Interior, Mitterrand, to take on the key post of Governor General. The Mendès-France government had taken a progressive stance on the issue of de-colonisation and moved rapidly to end the catastrophic war in Indo-China (armistice of 21 July 1954) and to disengage from Tunisia (Carthage Declaration 31 July 1954). Although the government was brought down in February by a powerful right-wing colonial lobby that feared Morocco and Algeria were also about to be 'abandoned',[8] Soustelle's appointment remained in force and on his arrival in Algiers the European settlers regarded him with deep suspicion and hostility. However, within a year the Governor had become a hard-line supporter of *Algérie française* and had become the hero of *pieds noirs* ultras who mobbed him on his departure from the Algiers docks on 2 February 1956.[9]

From the moment of his arrival in February through to April 1955 the new Governor studied at first hand the conditions in rural Algeria and was particularly struck during an early tour of the epicentre of rebellion in the Aurès mountains by the profound poverty of the people. He quickly elaborated the 'Soustelle Plan' for the accelerated development of the colony.[10] The crisis and endemic poverty confronting Algeria was not, he argued, the consequence of an exploitative colonial system and France had since 1830 brought enormous benefits to a primitive society wracked by tribal wars, disease and famine. Algeria did face major problems of poverty and unemployment but these were not caused by colonialism but rather reflected a classic problem of 'under-development' rooted in such inherent problems as infertile soils, lack of rainfall, a population explosion and other 'natural' or technical aspects. Since, claimed Soustelle, France invested more in Algeria than it received, and future industrialisation and modernisation could only be achieved through French assistance, it was of crucial interest to all Algerians that they remain part of France. For the Governor the way to defeat the FLN rebels, whom he characterised as a small and unrepresentative minority of 'fanatics' supported by external pan-Arab, and particularly Nasserite, interests, was to isolate them from the mass of the Algerian people. The tap-root of rebellion could be cut through economic and social development that would remove the causes of discontent by an increased investment in agricultural reform, irrigation, transport infrastructures, education, health care, training programmes and combating unemployment.

Soustelle appears to have shown little interest in elaborating policies that targeted Algerian women in particular, apart from passing references to their backward condition, 'Often women do not know how to care for a child or to sew'.[11] He, like his advisers at this time, prepared more global economic and social development programmes that through improvement of agriculture, housing, health and education would *implicitly* improve the lives of women, but there was no conscious effort to address specific women's issues or to formulate a policy. In general Soustelle viewed Algerian society as so tied to conservative tradition that there was little point in confronting the issue of emancipation. On his appointment as Governor Soustelle inherited from Mendès-France a brief 'Reform Plan under consideration by the former government', which recommended the integral implementation of the 1947 Statute, including extension of the vote to Muslim women (see chapter 1).[12] Significantly in this instance Soustelle followed the position of his predecessor Léonard, using the excuse of Muslim conservative opposition to block any initiative. It would have been easy, claimed Soustelle, to organise, 'during a first phase a project in favour of women who were sufficiently advanced (*évoluées*). But the enthusiasm shown by Muslims in this respect has been so lukewarm, to put it mildly, that I think it would be a mistake to move too far ahead of their beliefs'.[13] Soustelle was irritated by the opposition he faced to his plans from Alice Sportisse, champion of the female franchise in the Algerian Assembly, and he regarded the UFA as a communist front organisation, which he finally banned with the PCA on 12 September 1955.[14]

However, while Soustelle seems to have shown little interest in the question of Muslim women, he did make other innovations which from late 1956 onwards were to play a big part in the future evolution of an emancipation agenda: the creation of the SAS and the application of ethnographic field practices to the study of Algerian society, particularly through the creation of the *Centres sociaux*. On his appointment as Governor Soustelle travelled almost immediately into the Aurès mountains, long the preferred location for anthropological fieldwork in Algeria, where he noticed the almost total absence of any French administrative structure and personnel, so that the Muslim population was abandoned to desperate poverty, and 'we have allowed a huge void to be dug'. The way of life of such rural people remained profoundly archaic and any attempt to rebuild contact needed to be 'on the solid base of a scientific knowledge of their social structures and their system of values'.[15] There was a long tradition within the French colonial service, as of so many other European imperial regimes, of 'ethnopolitique',[16] utilising the most advanced academic sociological, anthropological and linguistic knowledge to decode 'primitive' societies, the better to control them: indeed, colonial regimes were themselves highly productive of such specialised knowledge through the work of administrators and military officers who spend many years 'up country' in close contact with native customs.[17]

Soustelle's professional background as an ethnologist meant that he was well-equipped to effect such a juncture: Soustelle, and his Tunisian-born wife Georgette, had worked together as ethnographers in Mexico and Guatamala between 1932 and 1934 and 1939 and 1942, and achieved international acclaim as authorities on pre-Colombian Mexican civilisation. Soustelle was much influenced by Mexican rural development projects, the 'cultural missions', which provided an integrated approach to adult education by linking it to basic issues of health, literacy, welfare and housing.[18] This connected approach to issues of poverty was stated in a key definition of June 1955: 'The foundation education addresses itself to all those men, women and children who could not benefit from conventional schooling. It aims to mount a co-ordinated attack on all the causes of poverty by actively involving the subjects themselves in the struggle'.[19]

This developmental approach can be seen at work in Soustelle's creation of the SAS in September 1955, which was to prove to be one of the most innovative organisations in military 'pacification'. This was based mainly on the experience of the old Algerian *Bureaux arabes* and the Moroccan *Affaires indigènes*, by which enterprising officers were permanently located among the isolated and impoverished peasantry of the *bled* where they engaged in a huge range of tasks: building schools, roads and irrigation projects, tackling unemployment through job-creation projects, improving agricultural production, providing medical assistance, regulating local disputes, and all the other tasks that local government should in principle have provided.[20] Although the SAS, at least during the first year of operation, had no explicit instructions or remit to address the problems faced by women, inevitably contact with the harsh reality of the conditions faced by local populations quickly raised pragmatic issues of how to gain the co-operation of illiterate women in relation to child-care, school attendance, water supply, health and other matters. The army command quickly came to see the SAS as a key instrument in its overall emancipation programme at local level.

Soustelle recruited two outstanding sociologists, Vincent Monteil and Germain Tillion, and attached them to his cabinet as advisers. Monteil (1913–2005), whom the orientalist scholar Louis Massignon regarded as his spiritual heir,[21] was one of France's leading experts on Islam which he studied closely during an adventurous army and academic career that took him first to Morocco (1938–48) as an officer in the *Affaires indigènes*, and then as a high-level military attaché to Tunisia, Palestine, Iran, Indo-China, Algeria and French West Africa.[22] A close friend of Mendès-France, whom he had known as a prisoner in Riom during the Second World War, Monteil, who had a deep empathy for Muslim society and later converted to Islam, favoured a federal and an early negotiated settlement of the Algerian crisis. When Soustelle first flew as Governor to Algeria he was accompanied by Monteil as head of his military cabinet with the task of making 'contact' with Muslim society. Monteil became rapidly disillusioned with Soustelle's marked shift towards the right, his tolerance of torture, and growing support for a *guerre à outrance* against the nationalists, and resigned his post on 24 June 1955.[23]

Although Monteil was attached to the General Government for only six months, it seems likely that during this period he was responsible for introducing into the army and administration his expert comparative knowledge of Soviet policy in Muslim Central Asia. Monteil had studied, among other sources, the reports of an Algerian delegation to Uzbekistan in 1950, which was headed by General Tubert, and included the writer Kateb Yacine.[24] This was informed by its Soviet hosts of the advances made in the emancipation of Muslim women, particularly through the great campaign against veiling of 1926–27 and the Constitution of 1936 that made it illegal to engage in acts of resistance to female liberation including marriage of minors, polygamy, refusal to educate girls, or opposition to their full voting and political rights.[25] The problems that the Soviet Union faced in the inter-war period as a secular colonial power trying to impose its political authority on a deeply resistant Muslim and traditional tribal society provide close historical parallel to the situation faced by France in post-war Algeria.[26] Monteil was fascinated by the lessons that could be learned from the earlier Soviet experience, and was aware that in Algeria, as in Central Asia, no global social, economic and political progress could be made without a radical emancipation of women. However by the 1950s, after forty years of Soviet endeavour, many traditional practices, including veiling, seclusion, pre-pubescent marriage and polygamy remained entrenched, even among members of the Communist Party. Monteil attributed this failure to an external political emancipation imposed on Asian society that had not undergone a real, internal transformation of values, and held up the best and most optimistic sign for progress in the Maghreb in the enormous aspiration of Muslim women for education.[27] Although Monteil left the cabinet in June 1955, his understanding of the Soviet experience would have reinforced Soustelle's belief that the situation of Algerian woman could only be transformed by long-term reform, and that any replication of a Soviet style radical confrontation with Muslim society was doomed to failure: a position that Soustelle seemed to abandon three years later during the events of '13 May' 1958 (see chapter 3).

The second key member of Soustelle's small team of expert advisers was the ethnologist Germaine Tillion. From 1934 to 1940 Tillion had, along with Thérèse Rivière, carried out fieldwork in the isolated mountains of the Aurès region, an experience that had provided her with intimate knowledge of the language, culture and traditions of women in the Chaouia tribes.[28] The main centre of the rebellion of 1 November 1954 was in the Aurès mountains and Louis Massignon, deeply disturbed by the fear that the French air-force would bomb the hill tribes with napalm, was able to arrange a meeting with Mitterrand, the Minister of the Interior, to which he invited Tillion.[29] Tillion, as an expert on the Aurès, was given a three-month mission to study and report on the conditions underlying the revolt.

On her return via Algiers Tillion reported her findings to Soustelle, whom she had known twenty years earlier in the Musée de l'Homme, the pioneer centre of French inter-war ethnography. The Governor invited Tillion to join his cabinet team as a *chargé de mission*, where she worked closely alongside Monteil on a study of the economic and social problems faced by Algeria. Despite the fact that Tillion, who had lived for years sharing the daily lives of Chaouia women, had a closer knowledge of rural women than almost any other European, and several years later was to write one of the most influential studies of Muslim women, *Le Harem et les cousins* (1966),[30] she does not appear to have developed specific proposals in relation to them during 1955–56. This is in part because Tillion's remit was to study the enormously complex and global problems facing colonial Algeria as a whole, as can be seen in a study which she wrote in late 1956, misleadingly published as *L'Algérie en 1957*.[31]

However, this study does contain a powerful, but implicit, policy in relation to Algerian women. When Tillion arrived in the Aurès region in December 1954 after a fourteen-year absence she was profoundly shocked by the massive economic dislocation and 'pauperisation' of the previously stable 'archaic' society.[32] For Tillion the root causes of this deepening poverty did not lie with colonialism, 'that hoary scape-goat', which she characterised as a nineteenth-century phenomenon, but rather with a classic Malthusian crisis in which a galloping growth in population would massively outstrip natural resources. France was not viewed by her as in an exploitative or damaging colonial relation-ship with Algeria: on the contrary the best, and perhaps only, chance for Muslim people to avoid catastrophic Third World poverty was through an ongoing French presence and assistance in the form of investment by Paris, the skills of the European minority, the income generated by labour migration to the metropolis, industrialisation and mass education. A nationalist victory would spell total disaster: an independent Algeria would be unable to 'go it alone', incapable even of developing the enormous potential of the newly discovered Saharan oil fields. Tillion's analysis was not particularly original and reflects the conventional post-war analysis of French demographers and techno-crats like Louis Chevalier who also elaborated a Malthusian agenda that remained blind to the destructive impacts of colonial domination.[33] Tillion's reformist position up to 1957, which can be characterised as an 'ethnographic liberalism' or a diffuse Christian socialism,[34] like that of Monteil, Camus and other humanists, suffered from the illusion that a reformed colonialism could even at this late hour endure within the paradigm of a French-Algeria.[35]

Tillion's answer to the 'woman question' in Algeria, in line with her developmental model, did not address the issue of a political solution, or relate Muslim women to the question of nationalism or independence, but rather provided the answers through an economic and modernis-ing agenda. Algerian women were viewed in global terms, in relation to a Malthusian model, as rapid breeders of babies. The solution to the inevitable process of pauperisation was not birth control, a practice that was seen as a 'cruel joke' within the logic of an 'archaic agricultural civilisation',[36] but rather universal education. Tillion estimated that some 98 per cent of all Muslim women were illiterate, while only one in sixteen girls was receiving primary education. But this did not mean that women were sunk in ignorance as to the possibilities of a better life: 'In the towns, they now go to the cinema, they listen to the radio, either at home or a neighbour's, they gossip among themselves, they get to know things, and even in villages out in the back of beyond I heard remarks of an astonishing bitterness last year', a bitterness that related to repudiation, lack of rights over children, and other features of Islamic law and custom.[37] Tillion had optimistically recognised here a popular thirst and potential for education as the key to modernity, and this perception led her to establish the *Centres sociaux*.

The *Centres sociaux*, created by the decree of 27 October 1955, although financed by the Ministry of National Education, were not part of the conventional school system, but training programmes designed for illiterate adults and youths who had received little if any state education: teams of teachers, social and health workers that according to Soustelle would work, 'without dogmatism or inflexibility, combining basic instruction, post-school education, hygiene, and simple trade skills'.[38] Although Soustelle and Tillion have been widely credited with the invention of the *Centres sociaux*, the prototype for such training centres had existed from about 1951 in the deprived shantytowns of Algiers. In 1953 Father Scotto, in collaboration with professionally trained social workers, Marie-Renée Chéné, Emma Serra and Simone Galice, established, with the support of the municipality of Hussein-Dey, a social centre in the shantytowns of Bel Air.[39] Chéné had arrived in Algeria as a militant of the *Service civil international* (SCI), an NGO that specialised globally in social work in impoverished urban slums.[40] The deepening crisis in traditional rural society had, since the 1930s, driven huge numbers of impoverished peasants from the interior into the mushrooming shantytowns of Algiers and other major cities, a flight from the land that accelerated further after 1955 as the army, through its 'free-fire' zones, created a serious refugee problem (see chapter 6).[41]

The shantytown of Bel Air, in which the Scotto team operated, provided a typical example of a general urban crisis: 6,500 people lived there in appalling unhealthy conditions, with no piped water, sewerage system or surfaced roads, and the nearest medical dispensary was ten kilometres away. By 1962 the rural exodus had inflated the population to 35,000.[42] The social workers established a small dispensary in the *bidonvilles*, delivered water by tanker, and set up courses to help Muslim women with literacy, domestic skills and health care. In early 1955 Germaine Tillion, accompanied by another ethnologist, Georgette Soustelle,[43] visited the centre at Hussein-Dey, while Father Scotto was invited to a meeting with the Governor, Tillion and Monteil, to discuss his work.[44] The Bel Air centre thus served as a practical model and Tillion invited Emma Serra to help set up the new *Centres sociaux*, which grew in number from eleven in late 1957, to 125 at independence. Nelly Forget, who worked in the *Centres sociaux*, notes that they marked a significant breakthrough by attracting large numbers of young women, who until then had been confined to low-skill, exploitative labour as domestics, and trained them as health and domestic skill monitors. This, combined with a mixed-gender work environment, began to create a new, positive image for Algerian women:[45] but one, as will be seen below, which attracted the unwanted attention of both European ultras and of the army intelligence services.

Phase 2: March 1956 to May 1958. Lacoste and radicalisation of the emancipation agenda

Soustelle, after his departure on 2 February 1956, was replaced by Robert Lacoste, after the new Prime Minister Guy Mollet was forced into a humiliating withdrawal by violent Algiers demonstrators to abandon General Catroux, his first choice as Governor. This February crisis marked a major watershed in the war, the abandonment of a possible early negotiated settlement with the nationalists for a deepening military repression that locked France into one of the longest and bloodiest wars of decolonisation.[46] On 16 March 1956 parliament passed a Special Powers Act that enabled Paris and the minister in Algiers[47] exceptional authority to introduce measures to combat the FLN, including the surrender of both civilian and military authority to the generals. At the same time Mollet announced the extension of conscription and the massive increase of the army presence in Algeria to 450,000 men, an expansion that marked an overall militarisation of Algerian government and civil society. The rapid increase in the power of the generals, which was capped by the appointment of General Salan as overall commander in December 1956, led to a radicalisation in the doctrine and practice of colonial warfare.

Robert Lacoste, as *ministre résident* between 9 March 1956 and 10 May 1958, has generally been seen by historians as responsible for overseeing a phase of unprecedented military violence and repression, including the widespread use of torture. Daniel Lefeuvre has criticised this accepted opinion by noting Lacoste's involvement in a major programme of economic and social reform to tackle, 'the problems posed by the poverty of the majority of the population'.[48] But the simultaneous pursuit of both repression and reform, far from being incompatible, was a key feature of French military strategy, and Lacoste's simultaneous acceleration of both aspects deepened the central, and ultimately fatal, contradiction of the war as a whole. At the centre of this dual agenda lay the emergence, particularly from August 1956 onwards, of a new policy that was specifically aimed at the 'conquest' via emancipation of Algerian women.

One indication of a change of direction appeared on 5 February 1957 in the form of an influential and provocative article by the journalist Monique Difrane in *Le Figaro*, under the title 'Liberation for Algeria? Yes! That of Women'.[49] The French right-wing press served, throughout the war, as the unofficial voice of the army, and journalists, as was undoubtedly the case here, frequently served to transmit propaganda on behalf of the armed forces. It is significant that Difrane's article appeared at this particular moment in time, and the argument and style of the piece provides interesting evidence of a propaganda discourse that undoubtedly reflected the new thinking of the army but which it did not, as yet, wish to publicise.

Difrane claimed to have just returned from a journey to the interior of Algeria, a trip that would only have been possible under the protection of the military, where she had visited and conversed with Kabyle and Arab women of all ages and classes who had raged in despair against their oppression by Muslim patriarchy. The author reassured her conservative readership that her agenda was not 'a more or less futile story of "suffragettes" lending itself to laughter and mockery', but a question of representing the authentic and insistent voice of Algerian women who were demanding change. The Muslim woman, 'is a prisoner for life, confined, isolated, cooped up between the four walls of her house or hut', a baby-making machine subject to 'annual pregnancies', who could at any moment be repudiated and expelled penniless into the street. Difrane's emphatic claim to convey the authentic voice of all Algerian women, their precise words and experience, needs to be treated with caution and her text appears to reproduce the discourse of the minority of educated *évoluées* (see chapter 1) rather than the opinions of the great mass of illiterate peasant women.

Difrane presented an argument that fell into two parts. Firstly, she analysed the various social forces at work within the colony that conspired to maintain women in such a state of servitude, in particular the Algerian 'taboo', the fearful conspiracy of silence surrounding the issue. Even those husbands of Muslim women who would like to change things by, for example, going out in public as a couple, were afraid to break with tradition because of the reprobation of Algerian society and 'what the neighbours may say'. The status quo was also reinforced by the religious leaders and *imams*, the *Ulema* heads like Tawfik al-Madani, who defended the sacred right of Islamic law and custom not to be interfered with by secular government. One highly educated woman, described as 'very *évoluée*', had buried her head in her hands, saying: 'If anybody congratulates themselves before me on this respect for our religion, our customs, our personal status, I think: "He's an enemy!". Since he drives us into a different world from his own, and slams shut the ancestral status on us like an iron gate!'.

But, claimed Difrane, the taboo was also sustained by European society: the main culprits here were the French women, the wives of army officers and other 'ladies of good deeds', whose benevolent work with Algerians was limited to charitable hand-outs, 'baby clothes for the fifteenth child . . . the cooking of fritters, embroidery' and who 'preach to Muslim women resignation to an unbelievable fate, as if the latter was without a mind or heart'. The European woman regarded the Muslim woman as so inferior, so abject and 'absolutely vacuous' that she was thought incapable of expressing any opinion, and was treated as a passive object rather than as a human being. European charitable workers had thus failed to pick up on the volcanic pressures building up among Muslim women for radical change, and also served to block reform through a dangerous 'respect for customs'. Difrane was reflecting here the idea of a 'double imperialism' that had been expressed by young Muslim nationalists and *évoluées* of the JUDMA during 1951–54 (chapter 1) according to which women were crushed under the double weight of conservative Muslim and European colonial forces. Soustelle had also expressed this idea: while European ultras persisted in refusing Muslims full citizenship 'on the pretext that the latter would be incompatible with their Islamic "personal status", on the Muslim side the extremists push their fellow believers to reject this same citizenship as incompatible with their salvation'.[50]

Secondly, Difrane argued that, breaking through the 'taboo' on women's condition, she was able to uncover among frustrated Muslim women an enormous pressure for change: 'For long these cloistered and crushed beings have remained silent, rendered stupid by their suffering, but the undeniable fact of the present is the awakening of their consciousness'. France, one Muslim told her, had abolished slavery, but not for women and she then appealed for measures that, probably not a coincidence, were identical to the legal reforms secretly being explored by the Lacoste government at that moment: 'Give us marriages in the town-hall, give us new laws, suppress the Muslim magistrates (*cadis*), suppress the ease with which husbands use repudiation, arrange things so that we can hang the veil in the window since it's only useful as a curtain!' Difrane argued that the key plank of government policy, to retain the colony through integrating the French and Muslim communities and by reform of the electoral system could not work until a revolution like that of Atatürk had been achieved. 'One cannot dissolve two societies into one when one reflects the Middle Age and the other the Twentieth Century'. This was no time for half measures: what was needed was education and modernisation for women and tackling the most urgent problem facing Algerian society, the demographic explosion. The stakes were high and, since four million Algerian women were looking to France, this was an opportunity to be seized: 'Behind the blind walls seethes an inevitable revolution which will be made against us if it is not made with us and by us'. Difrane was giving voice here to an emerging current of thought among the radical advocates of psychological warfare: victory would be dependent on the emancipation of Algerian women and France must move urgently to appropriate this agenda before the FLN. Behind the scenes this U-turn in colonial government and armed forces thinking on Muslim women was dramatically precipitated by the rapid move of Tunisia and Morocco towards radical reform of the marriage and family codes.

The Tunisian challenge: reforming the personal status law

One of the most important steps that Muslim nation-states were able to take during the twentieth century to emancipate women was to introduce a comprehensive and radical legal code on women, marriage and the family (*statut personnel*).[51] On 13 August 1956 Tunisia introduced, only five months after independence, what has been widely regarded as one of the most progressive Codes ever passed by a Muslim country.[52] Six days later, by the order of 19 August, the King of Morocco also established a commission for the reform of the code of personal status.[53] The Tunisian Code established a minimum age for marriage (fifteen for women, eighteen for men); made the consent of both spouses mandatory, preventing the tradition of enforced marriage; required that marriage be a civil matter, with formal registration; banned male repudiation of wives, while requiring divorce to be also a civil matter, enacted in a court; banned polygamy; and set out clear rules in relation to dowry, property rights, inheritance and care of children after separation. Such legislation was not without precedent, and Tunisia was able to draw upon the experience of earlier reforms, including those of Kemal Atatürk in 1926 and the Syrian Code of 1953, as well as international resolutions like that of the Third Congress of the *Union féministe arab*, passed by representatives from Egypt, Lebanon, Syria, Jordan, Palestine and Iraq at Beirut in June 1954.[54]

This innovation was watched very closely from across the border by the Algiers government, and three months after the promulgation of the Bourguiba Code Robert Lacoste secretly consulted Prefects and the super-Prefect (IGAME)[55] of Constantine on proposals to reform the personal status law. Lacoste noted that it was important to keep up

with changes in society, and 'not to ignore the efforts of renewal and
modernisation of Muslim law being pioneered for many years now by
the Muslim countries of the Mediterranean basin'.[56] Bourguiba, in two
speeches of 3 and 10 August 1956 announcing the new Tunisian Code,
noted that change was in the national interest, so that 'Tunisia does not
remain an abomination among the civilised nations of the world', while
social justice could not tolerate half of society being grossly marginalised.[57] France was reacting to an embarrassing situation in which its
Algerian colony might begin to appear highly retrograde on women's
rights by comparison with its newly independent neighbours. Tunisia
and Morocco, as soon as the authority of France was removed or weakened, were able to forge ahead and prove themselves to be more liberal
on women's emancipation, so dangerously exposing French symbolic
claims as the very founder and defender of revolutionary universal
rights.

Further light was thrown on official thinking in a report drawn up
for the government by Henry Le Breton, Emeritus professor of law at
Algiers University. In a close legal critique of the Tunisian legislation,
while arguing that the substance of the Code was not as radical as it
might appear, he praised the suppression of polygamy and repudiation, which helped stabilise the family. The danger was that the Code
threatened to stir up opposition among religious conservatives, but 'let's
be thankful that it has been carried out in Tunisia by a Muslim government. We thus have, in the near future, the demonstration of what
is possible in this field in Algeria'. The Bourguiba reform was an act
of bravery for a Muslim government and, 'for the modernisers of the
Neo-Destour Party, a resounding propaganda success which they have
not been reluctant to use'.[58] Le Breton was pointing to the fact that the
over-cautious Algerian government had for decades simply refused to
consider any significant reform in the sphere of women's rights because
of a real, or imagined, backlash by powerful religious interests. The
Bourguiba Code had the merit of demonstrating that reform of personal
status law was not necessarily an agenda imposed from without by a
western and infidel regime, but was perfectly compatible with orthodox
Islam. It opened the path to France doing likewise, and demonstrated
that this was not only politically possible but also desirable.

In late April 1957 Lacoste sent an order to Champeix, Secretary of
State for Algerian Affairs in the Ministry of the Interior, to prepare as
a matter of urgency draft proposals (*avant-projet*) for a reform of the
legal status of Muslim women.[59] A working party met in four sessions
in the Paris Ministry of the Interior during May–June 1957, and among
its rather changing membership were experts in Muslim family law and

senior members of the Algerian administration, including the chair, Eugène Simoneau, *Directeur des affaires d'Algérie* in the Ministry of the Interior, and Louis Milliot, former dean and professor of law in the University of Algiers. Milliot was given the task with Raymond Charles, *Conseiller* of the Paris Appeal Court, of drawing up the highly technical draft Code.[60] The recommendations of the final report,[61] which was shelved until late 1958, will be considered in a later discussion of the final statute introduced by the Gaullist government in 1959 (chapter 8), but here the concern is with what the working party reveals about the motivation of the government in undertaking an emancipation agenda in mid-1957.

The chairman repeatedly emphasised the great urgency of the project, and that this clearly arose from the need to respond to the enormous public interest generated by the Bourguiba Code and for France not to be perceived as more backward than Tunisia. The group had been instructed by government, noted the chairman, 'to go as far as possible in the direction of a real emancipation of the Muslim woman, and to go at least as far as the new Tunisian Code'.[62] It is noticeable that the working party contained no Algerians, although it was intended that the proposals be later referred to some Muslim religious 'notables'. Nor were there any women members until the penultimate meeting agreed that Marie-Hélène Lefaucheux, president of the *Union des femmes françaises et musulmanes d'Algérie*, should be briefed and invited to the final session.[63] As we have seen, Lefaucheux, as chair of the UN Commission on the Status of Women, had already placed pressure on the government for reform during 1951–53. After the UN General Assembly on 1 October 1955 voted to place the Algerian problem on the agenda, a shocked French government became intensely concerned to fend off international criticism of its colonial regime.[64] After the UN adoption of the Convention on the Political Rights of Women (20 December 1952) the attention of the CSW turned to the global reform of discrimination in marriage (consent to marriage, minimum age, civil registration) as well as traditional or customary practices that were harmful to women, such as claustration and genital mutilation.[65] This international UN agenda brought further pressure to bear on the French government, and Lefaucheux, with her intimate knowledge of the CSW, may have been brought on board to help formulate a reform that would counter the critics of French colonialism.[66]

Lacoste, in parallel with the establishment of the working party, sent instructions on 9 May 1957 to the Algerian Prefects and IGAME to seek their opinion on seven specific themes: the general desirability of reform, the act of marriage (consent, age, etc.), repudiation, polygamy, veiling, seclusion, inheritance and political rights. The replies provide an insight into official thinking on emancipation across the different regions of Algeria at an early stage in the debate.[67]

Most Prefects were in favour of ending repudiation and ensuring that divorce was legalised by a court decision, a measure that was seen to help stabilise the family unit. Likewise polygamy could be readily banned since it was in decline and survived only among a small number of rural traditionalists. But the general tone of the reports was one of caution and a reluctant acceptance that some change was needed to catch up with inevitable social change and to contain growing pressures for reform. Change, however, could not be too advanced since it was likely to stir up opposition of older men who, as the Prefect of Orléansville noted, feared 'an overturning of religious principles'. Such caution was particularly advisable in a situation of war: as the Prefect of Tlemcen remarked, reform was desired by young *évoluées* women, 'But in the present conjuncture of events such an initiative is inopportune and carries the danger of playing into the hands of the FLN'. The Prefect of Sétif expressed the opposite concern, 'We must avoid allowing ourselves to be overtaken in this field by the nationalists'.

The tension between those who argued against reform on the grounds that it would alienate an intensely religious society and reinforce support for the FLN, and those who defended the urgency of reform, or risk seeing the FLN seizing the initiative, was to plague the French government over the next three years. The majority of Prefects avoided this dilemma by favouring a gradualist and long-term preparation of Algerian society, particularly through the education of women. The Prefect of Bône, who opposed enfranchisement since, 'the FLN will give out orders that will be followed by women', thought reform would be best carried out by Muslims themselves 'in a pacified Algeria'. The IGAME of Constantine, Maurice Papon, agreed the time was not right for reform, and in line with his espousal of the techniques of psychological warfare,[68] he placed more emphasis on propaganda (producing 'a psychological shock') based on prior scientific investigation of Algerian public opinion: 'Opinion polls and preparatory campaigns through the intermediary of the press and radio to study the reactions of the Muslim masses. The development of women's cultural, social, and political organisations as well as the increase in contacts with European women'.

It is difficult to piece together from the archives the line of thinking of Lacoste between mid-1957 and the collapse of the Fourth Republic in May 1958, but it seems likely that he was sufficiently worried by the political repercussions of a religious and nationalist backlash against legal reform, that he decided to shelve the draft Code submitted to him in June 1957, while holding the line with some minor, window-dressing measures. The law on labour relations of 6 August 1954 granted Muslim women the right to take part in elections to industrial tribunals (*prud'hommes*), a fairly limited right that was first exercised on 16 June 1956 and was regarded by the colonial government as a 'success'.[69] The law of 11 July 1957 (*régime des tutelles*) made one significant change to the complex mosaic of personal status or family law by enabling married women to retain care of their children on the death or long-term disappearance of their husbands, whereas previously, under Islamic law, children reverted to the guardianship of male relatives.[70] Significantly, even this minor reform which was hedged about with conservative restrictions, met with strong resistance from Muslim justices and was viewed as a daring innovation by the Algiers government.

The main tactic of Lacoste was to put off both full enfranchisement as well as introduction of a complete code on women's status until implementation of a new local government act (*loi cadre*) passed on 5 February 1958. In several debates in the Senate and National Assembly on the law during November 1957 to January 1958 two centre-right deputies, Marcelle Devaud and Francine Lefébvre, failed to carry amendments to guarantee the extension of the vote to Algerian women. They argued that their exclusion was discriminatory and in breach of the French Constitution. Devaud noted that this exclusion was in contradiction with, 'the dramatic global emancipation of women . . . Do we have to wait to be shown the way by Nasser in Egypt, Bourguiba in Tunisia, and Mohamed V?'[71] Francine Lefébvre in the National Assembly on 28 January 1958, attacked the blatant racial and sexual discrimination: 'as a woman, I am shocked to see that you care so little about the opinion of women. One really gives the impression of believing that Muslim women are absolutely incapable of forming an opinion or expressing themselves'. She also held up the dangers of revolt: 'If today we do not know how to respond to the hopes of these women they will begin to pay attention to the siren voices that sing from Cairo'.[72] It is noticeable that Devaud, Lefébvre and Lefaucheux, who were agitating for the rights of Algerian women between 1951 and 1958, shared a similar background, that of the generation of Resistants who, although members of conservative or centrist parties, came to play a major political role in the organisations of French feminism.[73]

In reply to Lefébvre's attack in the National Assembly Robert Lacoste, the Minister for Algeria, noted that the Organic Law of 20 September 1947 had insisted that Muslims be consulted on such a crucial issue as the vote and that this had been delegated to the Algerian Assembly (see chapter 1). Now that the Assembly had itself been dissolved by decree (12 April 1956), this power should pass on to future regional assemblies, proposed by the *loi cadre*, in which Algerians would be represented. At the same time Lacoste insisted on the need to be cautious and to avoid a backlash from Muslim society.[74] Through this sleight of hand, Lacoste was following closely in the footsteps of his predecessors, Naegelen and Léonard: firstly, any major reform relating to women could be deferred and elected Muslim political leaders could be expected to block any such initiative. Secondly, even if significant changes were introduced this would be seen to be coming from Muslim representatives themselves and thus dampen any potential opposition and unrest to French interference in the religious sphere that might play into the hands of the FLN. This was in keeping with the advice of an official in the General Government, that no matter how hard Muslim feminists were pushing for 'revolutionary' change of their status, 'any initiative coming directly from us carries the risk of being falsely interpreted and giving rise to tendentious reactions'.[75] As in 1948, Lacoste, by deferring action to local assemblies, was able to delay reform safe in the knowledge that conservative Muslims could be relied upon to prevent any 'revolutionary' agenda and that any failure of reform could be blamed on 'backward' Algerians themselves.

The 1957–58 debate on the women's franchise and the personal status law reflected the more overt public and reformist side of Lacoste's dual approach. Investigation of these policy initiatives lay very much in the hands of civil servants or administrators, advised by lawyers and academic specialists in Muslim law, who tended to reflect the cautious and conservative traditions of the General Government in relation to any innovations that affected the religious sphere. However, in tandem with this, but working in a far more secretive way were the psychological warfare officers of the Fifth Bureau who were interested in the counter-insurgency and repressive implications of women's emancipation. This newly emerging force that was gathering strength within the army was far more prepared to engage in bold initiatives that might directly challenge the 'reserved area' of Muslim faith and practice.

Rural counter-insurgency: Jean Servier and the emancipation programme, 1956–58

The single, most distinctive feature of the French army in Algeria between 1954 and 1962 lay in the enormous political influence of the doctrine of 'revolutionary warfare' which permeated all levels of the armed forces and came to constitute a parallel structure within the military hierarchy and government.[76] The theory was developed primarily by army officers, most notably Colonel Charles Lacheroy,[77] who had recently experienced 'unconventional' methods of anti-guerrilla warfare in Indo-China. After the humiliating and crushing defeat of the French army at Dien Bien Phu (7 May 1954), and the subjection of 12,000 prisoners to techniques of brainwashing and communist indoctrination, military theorists began the process of examining the hard lessons to be learned from Indo-China and how these could be applied to colonial warfare in Algeria. Most of the key exponents of psychological warfare were inspired by a virulent anti-communism and an apocalyptic vision of a global communist encirclement of the 'west' through support for anti-colonial and Third World struggles for independence. Faced with this mortal threat military strategists like General Chassin argued that the French army must adapt to the new kinds of totalitarian warfare developed by the enemy: 'The time has come for the free world, unless it wishes to die a violent death, to apply certain of its adversary's methods'.[78]

The key idea, and indirectly the most relevant to the position of Algerian women, was drawn from Mao Tse-tung's work on the strategy of revolutionary warfare (1936) in which guerrilla forces could best survive, like fish in water, when they found logistic and moral support from the people: 'But if you drain the water or a drought should come, then the fish dies or disappears'.[79] From the very first shots of the insurrection in the Aurès mountains on 1 November 1954, the War of Independence, despite its dramatic urban dimensions, was primarily a war of guerrilla fighters in the mountainous interior who could not have survived without the support of the peasantry, and primarily of women, who supplied them with food, accommodation, clothing, medical aid and intelligence. In reality, as we will see, such support was never a simple matter, a question of the spontaneous and automatic resistance of an oppressed people, but had to be gained and constantly sustained by the ALN through its political organisation, the *Organisation politico-administrative* (OPA), and traditional or tribal leaders, propaganda, social work, 'revolutionary justice' and terror. The French specialists of revolutionary warfare proceeded from the idea that it was crucial to 'drain the swamp', to remove the support base of the relatively small number of guerrillas among the peasantry, by winning the mass of the population over to the French side, by protecting them from ALN terrorism, and eventually forming villages into armed auto-defence units that could take on the enemy and guarantee safe-zones in which the 'civilising' mission of schooling and economic reconstruction could continue. Essentially warfare was seen as a 'total' phenomenon, not simply a question of guns and armed conflict, but a matter of fighting for the hearts and

minds of entire populations, a battle that reached far into every aspect
of everyday 'civilian' life. From late 1956 onwards counter-insurgency
officers and specialist advisers began to recognise that such an agenda
could not afford to neglect women, half of the total population.

The key phase in the penetration of the doctrine of psychological
warfare into all levels of the military and civilian government hierarchy came, under the aegis of the Minister of Defence and later Prime
Minister, Maurice Bourgès-Maunory, between July 1956 and August
1957, culminating in the creation of the Fifth Bureaux.[80] A significant
moment was reached with the creation of a body of officiers itinérantes
in July 1956, all of them former prisoners of the Viet Minh camps, who
were attached to commanders in the field so as to lead, 'a vast campaign of disintoxication and re-education of the Muslim population'.[81]
But the key turning point came immediately after the Suez debacle on
5–6 November 1956 with the appointment of the Vietnam veteran,
Raoul Salan as commander in Algeria. Salan brought with him a team
of specialists in counter-insurgency, including Colonels Trinquier and
Goussault, who played a role in elaborating subversive actions aimed at
Algerian women.[82] By August 1957 the Fifth Bureau had established a
structure that reached through all levels of the army command, a 'hiérar-
chie parallèle' that studied, prepared and implemented propaganda and
counter-insurgency actions.[83] This organisation came to exercise, partly
through its officer training centres at Arzew and elsewhere, a powerful ideological hegemony throughout the forces, and began to develop
proto-fascist and far-right Catholic theories that encroached dangerously into the sphere of politics. It was with the arrival of Salan and
Goussault in December 1956 that we see the first clear, although highly
secret, signs of a new programme directed specifically towards women.

A key objective of Lacheroy and other officers of the Fifth Bureau was
how to deploy counter-revolutionary warfare to win the hearts and minds
of the Algerian population. In such forms of non-conventional warfare
intelligence not only about the FLN but also about the attitudes and
morale of the ordinary people was crucial to the design of propaganda and
other measures, from welfare to education. As Stathis Kalyvas has noted,
civil wars in which there are no front lines, and in which insurgents may
be present but 'invisible' in the civilian population, present a particular
'identification problem' to occupying forces. Local populations, fearing
terrorist retribution, may refuse to identify combatants hiding among
them, a situation which leaves the security forces highly vulnerable.[84]

The French army, faced with this problem, resorted to a combination
of methods, from deployment of paid informers to systematic torture,
but the approach that is of most interest here involved a 'strategy of

contact', the creation of organisations that could build bridges between the much feared army and a civilian population that remained stubbornly silent and hostile. The French colonial army had a long experience of such so-called rural 'pacification' methods, the elaboration of welfare and health programmes in tribal or peasant societies, that would *simultaneously* win the trust of the population and enable sound intelligence to be gathered. The outstanding example of such a specialist organisation during the Algerian War was the SAS set up by Soustelle in 1955, but by late 1956, in line with the emergence of a women's emancipation agenda, the army was tentatively exploring how to establish methods that would enable 'contact' with Muslim women. Such an agenda posed formidable problems in the *bled*, the rural interior in which 80 per cent of all Algerian women lived, the zones that served as the base of the FLN maquis. How could a strategy of contact be created for that half of the population that was radically segregated and isolated from the public sphere behind the walls of the home? It was this challenge that was first addressed during 1957 by the ethnologist Jean Servier, in a secret experiment code-named Operation Pilot that proved to be so successful that it came to provide the standard model for counter-insurgency 'pacification' for the whole of rural Algeria until the end of the war. Servier appears to have been the first person during the war to design a military programme that was directed specifically at peasant women.

Jean Servier, a *pied-noir* ethnologist, carried out fieldwork during 1949 and 1954 for a doctorate on the different Berber peoples of Algeria, and his linguistic skills and knowledge of Kabylia, an area of intense growing nationalism and banditry, was of political interest to the Algiers government that funded and commissioned him to prepare reports in 1952–53.[85] It was by chance that Servier was carrying out fieldwork in the Aurès mountains, the epicentre of the insurrection, on 1 November 1954. He achieved considerable publicity and fame because of his rescue of the wounded teacher Mme Monnerot from a bus ambushed by the FLN, and for his defence of the besieged town of Arris through the distribution of fifty rifles to the first improvised *harki* unit of the war.[86] This Beau Geste moment brought the young ethnologist to the attention of Soustelle,[87] and after the presentation of his thesis at the Sorbonne in 1955,[88] Servier was recruited by the army. He received training in Paris during the spring of 1956 from Colonel Goussault, later head of the Fifth Bureau, in revolutionary and psychological warfare, and in turn taught courses to SAS officers at the *Centre militaire d'information et de spécialisation pour l'outre-mer* (CMSIOM).[89]

From March to August 1956 Servier was, as *chargé de mission aux affaires politiques*, closely associated as a specialist adviser during the planning of one of the most secret and controversial operations of the Algerian War. The aim of Operation K or Opération Oiseau Bleu was to create and arm a 'Third force' counter-maquis among the tribes people of the Iflissen, whom Servier had studied in 1952–53.[90] Operation K turned out to be a bloody catastrophe for the French army since the maquis which it armed and supported was pro-FLN and in a counter sting operation inflicted heavy casualties on a French unit during an ambush on 1 October 1956.[91] Despite this débâcle Servier's credit remained sufficiently high with the army command for him to be placed in charge of a second clandestine Operation Pilot in January 1957. Operation Pilot is of particular interest since this experimental counter-insurgency operation was particularly focused on Algerian women and led to the establishment of the single most important war-time initiative to reach out to Muslim women, the EMSI. In late 1956 Servier was in Paris when he read a newspaper account of how the peasants of Bou Maad, located in the Dahra Mountains to the north of Miliana, had revolted against the terrorist grip of the FLN and had handed over money collectors to the gendarmerie.[92] Servier, who knew this area well from his fieldwork in 1949 and 1950, was so excited by this potential for breaking FLN power in the *bled* that he left immediately for Algiers and submitted to the Minister, Lacoste, a proposal that General Salan called, 'an in depth action for the reconquest of the population'.[93]

Servier's timing could not have been more propitious: Salan, newly arrived as commander of the combined forces in Algeria in December 1956, brought with him a circle of ex-Vietnam veterans who were dedicated to the techniques of revolutionary warfare, and who were prepared to experiment with daring and unconventional methods. At the same moment General Massu, on assuming both civilian and military powers on 7 January 1957, unleashed the massive operations known as the 'Battle of Algiers' to root out the FLN terrorist networks in the capital. The same month saw the creation of the Fifth Bureau, headed by Colonel Goussault, and so everything was pointing to a radicalisation of the war. It seems likely that it was Goussault who arranged a meeting between Servier and General Salan on 16 January to agree a plan that was strongly opposed by the conservative 'Grands Services' of the General Government who were shocked by a project that went against the policies they had followed for years.[94] Salan gave the green light and the next day summoned the military and civilian heads of the Orléansville region, General de Brébisson and the Prefect Chevrier, to brief them on 'Pilote 1', which was planned to take place in their area of command between 26 January and 26 March.[95]

The genesis of Servier's thinking on emancipation can be traced back to August 1956 when he had been working as *chargé de mission* under Lucien Paye, *Directeur des affaires politique*,[96] at the very moment that Lacoste's cabinet was turning to the implications of Bourguiba's radical Code of Personal Status. The ethnologist had a close knowledge of the way of life of peasant women in the most isolated mountain zones, and was in a good position to formulate policy.[97] On the 12 August Servier sent Paye two reports from the army HQ in Tizi-Ouzou, where he was involved in the 'Oiseau Bleu' operation, one of them a *Note sur le Statut de la Femme Kabyle*. Bourguiba had first announced the new Tunisian code in two speeches on 3 and 10 August, and it seems likely that Servier was responding to this news when he wrote to his director, Lucien Paye, who several months later was to sit on the working party for the revision of the Algerian law on marriage and the family.

Servier argued in his paper on the personal status of Kabyle women that they were subject to the patriarchal group and 'remain minors in law . . . They cannot participate in the public life of the village. They are neither voters nor electable and are not allowed to give witness before the village assembly (*djemâa*)', and given present conditions, 'it would seem unwise to change radically the status of women'.[98] However, he noted that Kabyle peasants were favourable to the education of their daughters, but were held back by the fear of dishonour and disapproval of conservative society and what neighbours might say. The answer to this was for the government to impose universal schooling on all girls, a step that Kabyles would welcome. In addition, he predicted a coming offensive of the FLN against French schools: 'It is likely that the FLN will undertake the initiative of an obligatory Koranic education of girls from October [1956] as part of its offensive against the French school'. Servier outlined a counter-programme:

> The teaching of girls should be <u>practical</u> and based on domestic skills and child- care that take as their point of departure what one finds in a normal Kabyle house . . . The place of the Kabyle women within the household, her role in overseeing the home and the education of children, means that the day that the 'old Matriarchs' – the elderly mothers of the husbands – are replaced by the pupils of the French school, Kabylia will tip over as a block into western civilisation. This evolution can only occur if France, in a first phase, seeks to form the future mistresses of the house rather than to transform those who stay squatted round the hearth.

This recommended programme was very similar to the approach that was taken a year later by the EMSI teams.[99] Servier announced what was to become a central tenet of military-led emancipation, that since *was Bourdieu ever involved in these policies?*

women constituted the very bastion of Algerian-Muslim identity, culture and tradition, and its point of reproduction, a key aim of psychological warfare must be to intercept and re-shape this habitus.

Early in 1957 Servier set out his ideas for propaganda activity with women in a further document, *Définition d'une idéologie pour les Operations 'Pilote'*.[100] It announced the idea of a 'New Algeria', emerging truly free and modern, struggling against the privileges of the ruling elite of *grandes familles* and *caïds*; against the prejudices imposed by backward customs and religious traditions that had no foundation in the Koran; and against the: 'subjugation of the woman that maintains her in a veritable state of slavery when in every modern country the woman is today free to live as she chooses, to dress as she wishes, to go out, and to work outside the confines of the house'. The concept of an 'Algérie Nouvelle' was developed in a further directive which advocated a 'religious emancipation' from the *cadis* and *Ulemas*, allies of the FLN which forbade the education of children, and deliberately kept the people in ignorance in order the better to oppress them and extort money.[101] This reflected Servier's discovery from his earlier ethnographic fieldwork that the PPA and later the FLN had penetrated secretly into the most isolated mountain areas during the 1950s in the form of a *Ulema* puritanism, which he detested.[102] Servier forecast that FLN 'cultural commissars' would in a first stage make use of *marabout* prestige to gain influence over the masses and to preach a holy war (*jihad*), but since they were former pupils of the reformist *médersas* they would in a later stage break the privileged position of the *marabouts* castes and force attendance at Koranic schools in which Arab language and culture would displace both Berber and French. Servier proposed blocking this pan-Arab hegemony by ensuring that the *zaouias* taught a modern French curriculum that would also be able to prepare the way for female emancipation.[103]

The Pilot directive, under the rubric Emancipation de la femme, 'Insists on the fact that in modern society all beings are equal: women are and must be the equal of men'. It attacked the barbaric practices supported by Muslim law, by which 'the husband can beat his wife, deprive her of food, and repudiate her by pronouncing a simple formula'. The Muslim woman was treated as a slave, 'a beast of burden', and, 'as a victim of archaic prejudices, is kept isolated from society. From the age of puberty she can no longer go out except when accompanied'. As a result girls did not go to school, were closed to any idea of progress, were ignorant of basic principles of hygiene, and used the most traditional methods in the home, preferring the wood-fired stove (*kanoun*) to Butagas or paraffin cookers. Other Islamic states like Turkey and Tunisia had shown that modernisation was perfectly compatible with religion.[104]

So much for Servier's general ideas on emancipation, but how did this strategy of contact translate into practice on the ground? The idea behind Pilot was to target a particular isolated zone, in this case the mountainous area of the Dahra between the Chélif River valley and the coast, an area defined by the quadrilateral between Orléansville, Ténès, Cherchell and Miliana, an 'infested corner' where the FLN had established a solid military and political structure (OPA). The Dahra, without roads, was so cut-off from the European-dominated plains that there was almost no French presence, administration or infrastructure. One area within the Pilot zone, the military operational sector of Ténès, spread over 2,000 square kilometres, in early 1957 had only two civilian and four army doctors for a population of 115,000 people.

The initial problem facing the army was that FLN terrorism, able to wreak rapid and deadly force against 'collaborators', held the inhabitants in a vice-like grip, so that no intelligence was forthcoming nor any degree of co-operation, even in the case of reforms that might be beneficial to the population. The strategy of 'pacification' of the region was to take place in two phases, summarised as 'destroy and build': firstly, the army would engage in a major offensive to locate and destroy the ALN forces, and then move rapidly to assure protection to the population from FLN terrorism, a crucial precondition for the establishment of a new order in which Algerians would eventually begin to take on responsibility for running their own free society that would eliminate all nationalist influence.[105] The second phase of Pilot, described as a 'work of in-depth pacification', represented an ambitious, 'essentially totalitarian' plan, in the sense that every aspect of local Algerian life would be radically transformed using, 'military, political, administrative, cultural, social and medical means'.[106]

The second phase, one of 'building contact', involved a co-ordinated team moving into selected villages in turn and a frequent initial response of the inhabitants was to flee, terrified, into the forests, but with time the reassured population began to appear. The team typically consisted of a protective military escort led by psychological warfare officers (*officiers itinérantes*),[107] a mobile loud-speaker and cinema lorry (CHPT),[108] small medical teams of army doctors and nurses (*Service d'aide médicale gratuite* or AMG), and the proto-type EMSI, small 'mixed' units made up of one European woman and one or two Muslim assistant-interpreters or *Adjointes sanitaires et sociales rurales auxiliaires* (ASSRA), who had the specific task of making contact with Muslim women.[109] A typical example of such initial contact comes from the Douar Drablia on the morning of 10 July 1957, when the inhabitants were summoned to attend a rally at which 150 men were placed in one group, and 170 anxious women and children in another. After being harangued with anti-FLN propaganda, such as the slogan 'Don't let yourself be devoured by the jackals', one medical team treated the men, while a medical-EMSI team cared for the women. The people were invited to choose a spokesman from each fraction of the tribe and in the following discussion one man asked for weapons to defend the village against the FLN. When the EMSI team departed, the local women ran after the Muslim assistants to thank them.[110]

The action directed towards women was one component of a larger range of measures initiated by Servier's team in the Dahra. FLN prison labour and six bulldozers were used to rapidly build a network of dirt roads (*pistes*) that allowed rapid military intervention to protect villagers from FLN incursions.[111] Servier took particular pride, as he had done in the Aurès in 1954, in arming and training *harkis* to form units (*harkas*) that protected villages (*auto-défense*) and tracked down FLN fighters concealed in the surrounding population. Schools that had been destroyed by the FLN were rebuilt and re-opened with great pomp and feasting.[112] One of the most secretive parts of the operation was the plan to send hand-picked local men, including prisoners and those who had 'rallied' from the FLN side, to the counter-insurgency training school at Arzew where they were intensely trained, using methods drawn from Vietnam, as 'political commissars'.[113] They were then discretely reintroduced back into the *douars* where they were to provide intelligence, keep watch on individual loyalties and recruit for the *harkas*.[114] Servier's vision of the future seems to have been linked to Lacoste's 'Third Force' strategy and the important legislation of the *loi cadre* by which Algerians would themselves come to play a major role in the reorganised structures of elected local government, so building up a new participatory democracy from the grass-roots that would eliminate the enemy OPA. The political commissars would play a key part in establishing sufficient security to enable the inhabitants to elect local assemblies that were cleansed of any 'sleeper' FLN terrorists.[115]

During 1957, after the initial contact with village women, Servier took particular care to develop the EMSI teams, paying and equipping them from a special secret fund of 600 million (old francs) allocated to him by the Algiers government.[116] Since few of the European women who were recruited to head each team could speak Arabic or Berber dialect and had little close knowledge of Muslim customs, it was absolutely crucial to attach to them young Algerian women who could serve as interpreters and cultural intermediaries (ASSRA). It proved difficult to recruit '*évoluées* favourable to France', but psychological warfare officers, following on from their Vietnam experience, took an obvious delight in being able to use ex-FLN militants in this task, women who it was thought would know the enemy better than anybody.[117] For example, the army captured a young FLN nurse, a former student and daughter of a *cadi* who, Servier claimed, had fallen into the hands of the ALN band of Si Mourad who used her as a sexual slave. Enraged by her experience, she proved easy to 'turn' and was readily recruited as an assistant, providing a model for the rapid engagement of other young Muslim women.[118] The journalist Jean Piverd described in glowing terms his departure for a two-day tour of villages 'into the outback', with a team of four, a doctor, a driver and Denise B., a twenty-five-year-old woman who had previously been a secretary in the Paris Ministry of Defence, and Touria B., an eighteen- or nineteen-year-old Muslim who, it was claimed, had been forced into an FLN unit where she had served as a nurse for nearly a year.[119] Touria's ambition was now to train for a diploma in a school for ASSRA being built by Servier.[120] As the team arrived in each village Piverd described the enormous crowds of people who queued up with every possible kind of malady, from purulent eye disease to infected cuts, and the EMSI paid particular attention to child-care, cleaning, bathing and weighing babies.

Piverd's report on the EMSI, which emphasised the heroic self-sacrifice of young French women in harsh and dangerous conditions, was to become one of the favourite subjects of army propaganda through the rest of the war, and endless photographs and films recorded smiling, blond and white-coated assistants tending to the needs of grateful peasant women and their babies.[121] The outstanding example of such hagiography was Christiane Fournier's, *Les EMSI: des filles comme ça!*, which includes a photograph of hundreds of women and children seated on the ground waiting their turn, with the caption: 'A crowd that has descended from the four corners of the *djebel*, prisoners of an anachronistic Middle Ages, reach out towards a better life'.[122] Servier claimed that in some villages the women had begun to form their own committees and, with army assistance, to initiate various self-help projects such as weaving carpets for sale in local markets.[123]

How successful was the first Operation Pilot, and the EMSI in particular? Internal army reports are rather contradictory, and reveal major and damaging internal battles over the operation between different branches of the civil and military hierarchy. Relations between General de Brébisson and the local Prefect Chevrier were strained, and the project was plagued by the lack of a coherent and unified command, so that it suffered from disputes between different 'fiefdoms' over personnel, funding and decision-making. Colonel Ameil, commander of the sub-sector of Orléansville was sceptical about the project from the

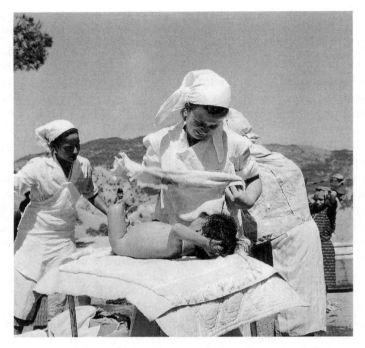

1 One of the early EMSI teams during Operation Pilot at
Bou Maad, 1957

beginning, and later refused to support psychological actions, the EMSI
or Arzew training programme, an opposition which led to his posting
back to France.[124] It seems likely that this opposition was a reflection of
the hostility of some 'conventional' officers to the growing penetration
and influence of Goussault's Fifth Bureau into the army command, and
by early summer Goussault, following a tour of inspection, was livid at
the failure to expand Operation Pilot into zones that were in the original plan, and demanding to know what commanders had done with the
considerable resources in extra manpower and materials allocated to
them under Pilot.

   From early March onwards General de Brébisson and General
Allard, commander of the *Corps d'armée d'Alger* (CAA), marginalised
the Servier operation by developing their own agenda, and rapidly
extending the experiment into the departments of Algiers, Médéa and
Mostaganem,[125] and in particular as Operation NK-3 in the Palestro
area. A series of top-level meetings had to be called in the Government
General to sort out the seething discontents (13 May and 29 May), and
Salan instructed Allard in June that any further extension to Pilot would

need to be based on a detailed plan approved by Lacoste.[126] Goussault wisely, if opportunely, decided to halt his criticism of the powerful army commanders, unlike Servier who, standing outside the conventional military hierarchy and endowed with a sense of his superior mission, had no hesitation in circulating withering criticisms of both Goussault and the generals. Among Servier's criticisms of the army command was the treatment of *harkis* as second rate mercenaries, lacking proper pay and conditions, and the failure to see that revolutionary warfare did not consist of 'pure and simple brutal repression, that is to say, in most instances, blind, collective and unintelligent', a comment that has been marginally annotated in red crayon, 'idiot'.[127] Servier, whose concerns seem well founded,[128] recognised the central contradiction of army 'pacification', that indiscriminate violence and repression fatally undermined any 'good works' achieved by SAS and EMSI to win the hearts and minds initiative. It seems not too surprising that the outspoken Servier was sidelined to a meaningless desk job in the General Government and soon returned in April 1958 to an academic post in the University of Montpellier.[129]

The instability and in-fighting surrounding the Operation Pilot clearly damaged the outcomes of the programme during 1957, and, along with it, the creation of the first EMSI. The teams lived a hand-to-mouth existence, were lacking in adequate and secure funding, and by July the ASSRA under Mme Guilles had still not been paid. The colonel in charge of the army medical service was sabotaging the work of the EMSI, either by attaching them to his own service, or, instead of providing them with decent accommodation, posted them to live under tents in dangerous zones where they could not carry out their welfare mission.[130] Opinion on the success of the EMSI was divided: in May General Huet was lavish in his praise of their 'excellent work' and seeking further sources of funding, but good results depended on the overall degree of security established in their zone of operation. In some areas the FLN made a sustained push to re-enter zones from which they had been driven, and in some instances cut the throats of local women who had provided water to French soldiers.[131] In December one colonel noted, after an initial positive response to the EMSI, a deterioration in the climate owing to FLN pressure: assistants were badly received, and local women said they had no need for medical or other help, which was patently untrue. The loud-speaker lorries (compagnie de haute-parleurs et de tracts, CHPTP) were greeted with a 'hint of scepticism and irony', and the commander concluded that despite six months of psychological campaigning by Pilot, 'the hold of the rebel OPA is still strong in regions considered to have been pacified'.[132]

But overall the EMSI proved sufficiently successful for the experiment to be extended, and the five initial teams,[133] had by August 1957 been expanded to eleven, three based at Orléansville, two at Miliana, three at Cherchell and three at Ténès. Lacoste, by an order of 25 October 1957, then extended the system to the rest of the colony, and a special induction course was set up in Algiers.[134] Among the key factors that inspired the high command to expand and generalise the EMSI, as will be seen (chapters 4 and 7), was the realisation of the propaganda advantages to be won via the international media, the lure of intelligence to be won by penetrating the intimate world of the Algerian family, and the advantages to be gained from seizing the initiative on emancipation that out-manoeuvred the FLN which, for religious and political reasons, was unable to support a progressive agenda for women.[135]

Urban counter-insurgency: emancipation and the 'Battle of Algiers'

The final factor that led the Algerian government and military to advance an emancipation strategy was the growing awareness that it needed to pre-empt the FLN, which was developing a similar agenda. The guerrilla forces of the FLN had from the very beginning of the war received the crucial logistic support of peasant women who cooked, washed clothes, acted as look-outs and concealed the fighters, but such support, the 'natural' domestic role of mothers and sisters, was rarely if ever acknowledged by either side in the war. However, during the course of 1955–57 the FLN began systematically to recruit educated young women from urban society either to serve as nurses in the maquis or as liaison agents in the terrorist networks. The role of Algerian women within the FLN structure will be examined in detail in chapter 9; here the aim is to consider the process by which the French army became aware of this growing involvement and reacted to it.

Army officers, who entertained Orientalist assumptions of Muslim women as veiled and timid beings, lacking in any initiative, subservient and crushed under the boot of male power, were astonished by the growing number of Algerian female militants caught in 1955–56 during military operations. Between June 1955 and the end of 1956 some twenty-eight women were arrested for transporting weapons and ammunition and housing FLN militants, but the biggest shock came after the first arrest in July 1956 of three nurses in the maquis and the realisation that women were now serving with ALN guerrilla forces.[136] Doctor Nefissa Hamoud, an Algiers paediatrician and the first woman to go regularly into the Kabyle maquis to provide medical aid, was arrested in an ambush in October 1956.[137] Documents found on the body of an FLN political cadre killed on 4 October 1957 indicated that Algerian women were serving as armed combatants in the North Constantine area, after receiving medical training in early 1957. At the very moment that the first EMSI experiment was underway in Operation Pilot, the women fighters in the ALN were taking on an identical function as political propagandists and as 'veritable social welfare assistants in the service of Algerian women'.[138] *The moudjahidat* ♀

However, the biggest shock for the French came during the 'Battle of Algiers' of 1956–57 when Massu's parachutists arrested a number of young women who were closely involved in the transmission of messages, guns and bombs for Yacef Saadi's terrorist network.[139] The centre of gravity of the rebellion may have been in the *bled*, but during 1956–57 the world media turned with fascination and horror to the stories of Zohra Drif, Djamila Bouhired, Samia Lakhdari, Djamila Bouazza and others who planted bombs in the milk bars of crowded Algiers from September 1956 onwards. It was the female urban terrorist, later depicted in Gillo Pontecorvo's remarkable 1965 drama-documentary *The Battle of Algiers*, that provided the most powerful and enduring image of Algerian women's new-found capacity to defy convention and assume a new role as nationalist militants and fighters.

The involvement of young women in the FLN networks of Algiers had become clear to the French authorities some time before the bombings, most notably through the lycée and student strike of May 1956.[140] The army was increasingly preoccupied with the problem of how to penetrate into, and gain intelligence on, the FLN networks that found a bastion within the warren of the ancient Casbah. It was precisely at this moment that signs first appear of the army trying to engage in a 'strategy of contact' with Muslim women through the manipulation of the *Centres sociaux*.

The military were fully aware of the extent to which the dedicated and idealistic social workers of the *Centres sociaux*, through their welfare work in the *bidonvilles*, had built up close relationships and trust with the urban poor, a source of contact that could potentially provide a mine of intelligence. A first sign of military attempts to intrude onto the terrain of the social workers came on the night of 26–27 May 1956 when the police and army mounted a huge operation to surround the Casbah, a key fortress of FLN militancy, during which over 4,000 men were arrested. On the 26 May all eighty social workers in Algiers were assembled by order of the head of the public health services, divided into ten teams, and asked to go in police lorries to carry out an unknown task. When they discovered that they were expected

to unveil and frisk Muslim women to make sure they were not FLN
men in disguise or carrying weapons, the team of eight led by Marie
Chéné, and half the team of Emma Serra, refused and were threatened
as 'traitors' and held in lorries or police cells overnight. On the 28 May
Chéné wrote to the *Association nationale des assistants socials* (ANAS)
in Paris, complaining that, 'our mission as social workers will be seriously compromised through participation in this policing operation'.[141]
The national president of the ANAS, Mlle de Laage, managed to gain
a retraction from Lacoste and the Paris government and a recognition
that the action had breached the professional and legal code of social
workers. However, the crisis revealed a serious split within the corps
of assistants and a majority, perhaps mainly *pieds noirs* favourable to
Algérie française, wrote to Lacoste opposing the ANAS, claiming that
the police mission assigned to them was not incompatible with their
professional ethic, particularly under the exceptional conditions in
Algeria, and that it was proper 'to humanise the system of control'.[142]
Mme R. Bley, head of the *Service social familiale nord-africain* in Paris,
who was shocked by this 'regrettable state of mind', was to find herself
during 1961 in the forefront of opposing a similar onslaught on the
social services by Maurice Papon's police before and after the massacre
of 17 October.[143]

Despite the Algerian government's retreat on this issue in May, the
writing was on the wall, and increasingly through 1956–57, especially
with the 'Battle of Algiers', the police and army moved to interfere
with, or control, the work of both the *Centres sociaux* and of the social
work teams established by Scotto. However, despite enormous pressure
and intimidation, the authorities largely failed to harness the centres as
auxiliaries to their repressive agenda. The army then adopted a quite
different tactic and began publicly to denounce them as hot-beds of FLN
sympathisers and arrested, tortured or expelled them back to France.
Annie Steiner was arrested as early as 15 October 1956 and sentenced to
five years in prison; Hélène Gautron was arrested on 21 February 1957
and tortured; Nelly Forget, a SCI militant, was arrested on 5 March
1957 and tortured; and eventually thirty-five liberals appeared in a kind
of 'show trial' on 23 July 1957. A virulent campaign in the Algerian
press made the *Centres sociaux* a target of *pieds-noir* hostility and led
eventually to the murder by the *Organisation armée secrète* (OAS) of six
leading members, including the writer Mouloud Feraoun, on 15 March
1962.[144]

The history of the *Centres sociaux* during 1956–57 indicates how the
security services were becoming increasingly interested in the processes
by which a 'strategy of contact' could be constructed and developed,

especially in order to penetrate the segregated universe of Algerian women. When they found the professional social workers, who were supported by their national association, resistant to such manipulation, the army went ahead and began to develop its own parallel institutional base for such an initiative, particularly through the creation of women's local associations or circles that expanded dramatically after '13 May 1958'.

The single event, however, that galvanised the army to accelerate an emancipation agenda arose from the final capture on 26 August and interrogation of Zohra Drif, the outstanding woman member of Yacef Saadi's underground. The intelligence service was able to capture documents that revealed Drif's advanced plan to set up a totally new clandestine organisation for women based on the classic secure form of cells of three arranged in a hierarchical pyramid. During her interrogation on 2 October Zohra Drif, who remarked, 'I insisted on the importance of the social role of women', revealed how she intended to organise a team of women in each Algiers quarter which would provide medical and social aid for poor families, support the families of FLN prisoners, engage in propaganda through tracts and demonstrations, serve as liaison agents and collect intelligence on French informers.[145] This structure, which seems to have been in part modelled on the cells of the former PPA *Association des femmes musulmanes algériennes*, would have included 357 women in all. Identification and recruitment of 'sisters' was already under-way when Drif was arrested, and since it had been particularly difficult for the army to search or arrest veiled Muslim women liaison agents the proposed network offered a formidable potential for the regeneration of the *Zone autonome d'Alger* (ZAA) that had been decimated by army repression.

The high command, including Generals Salan and Allard, took a keen interest in the discovery of this previously unknown plan, and intelligence analysts reported, 'Such an organisation constitutes in the hands of the rebels a powerful means to control the Muslim popular masses. On these grounds, it merits our fullest attention'. From this moment the army and civil administration began to pay particular attention to, and collect intelligence on, the role of women within the FLN organisation.[146] From the summer of 1957 onwards the Fifth Bureau had organised a series of propaganda radio broadcasts on the theme of unveiling, and the modernisation and liberation of Algerian women (see chapter 3). The army placed letter boxes in the Casbah in which Algerians could discreetly put messages to the authorities: one such anonymous letter dated 8 April 1958 from a woman expressed appreciation of the 'Radio Casbah' broadcasts against veiling, and claimed that for Muslim women to become modern and civilised it was necessary to ban the veil, 'that suffocates her, that hinders her in work or education . . . and which above all deprives her of liberty and imprisons her between four walls'. General Massu forwarded this letter to Allard, noting this sign of, 'the aspiration of Muslim women for rapid progress'. He argued that the veil should be banned immediately and, 'I have already had occasion to express my fear of seeing us outdistanced in this area by the FLN that could advocate a similar radical transformation of customs, with guaranteed good results'.[147]

By the winter of 1957–58 the military were impressed by the results of their own emancipation strategy achieved during Operation Pilot, but they had become simultaneously aware of, and disconcerted by, the extent to which the FLN was also harnessing the enormous potential of women to the nationalist struggle. Until this moment most aspects of the army's highly secretive emancipation agenda in the Dahra and elsewhere remained unknown to the public. While the Fifth Bureau had covertly utilised propaganda by radio, film and newspapers to try and change, or gauge public opinion on female liberation, as in Difrane's *Figaro* articles, the government was not able to gain any prestige among the Muslim population or international opinion for its still secretive emancipation campaign. The discovery of Zohra Drif's detailed plan for a woman's clandestine organisation made clear the very real danger that the FLN might seize the initiative, and trump the army. On 6 May 1958, General Allard, a key advocate of psychological warfare, forwarded Massu's letter to Salan, noting:-

> The action undertaken in relation to women for over a year by the free medical teams, by the women's circles, and through propaganda, has obtained un-hoped for results.
>
> The time has come to go officially public on the emancipation of Muslim women so as to prevent the rebels from profiting from the current change in the state of mind brought about by us through so much effort.[148]

Exactly one week later, on 13 May 1958, the military coup by the Generals in Algiers provided the ideal conditions for the achievement of this goal, the launching of a co-ordinated and open campaign for emancipation.

Notes

1 Much confusion has been caused by the practice of using the date of 13 May to refer to both that specific day, as well as to the overall three-week crisis: I

have used 13 May (no quotes) to refer to events on that day alone, and '13 May' or the *'journées* of 13 May' (in quotes) to denote the entire phase of the crisis that ended with De Gaulle's inauguration on 1 June.

2 Amrane, *Les Femmes algériennes*, 221–2; Kessel and Pirelli, *Le Peuple Algérien*, 130–4: Safia Bazi, Fadila Mesli and Meriem Belmihoub were not the first women captured in the maquis, but did trigger a huge media interest.

3 The shift towards an emancipation agenda during late 1956 and early 1957 did not come about through a clear policy initiative made centrally by the government and army, and there exists no documentary evidence for this in the archives. Rather, the change can be deduced from a sequence of initiatives or actions 'on the ground' that appeared about the same time and reveal that the issue of emancipation was widely diffused.

4 Shafer, *Deadly Paradigms*; Gendzier, *Managing Political Change*; Christopher Simpson, *Science of Coercion. Communication Research and Psychological Warfare, 1945–1960* (Oxford: Oxford University Press, 1994).

5 Connelly, *Diplomatic Revolution*, 27–38; and 'Taking Off the Cold War Lens: Visions of North–South Conflict during the Algerian War for Independence', *The American Historical Review*, 105 (June 2000), 221–45; Paul and Marie-Catherine Villatoux, *La République et son armée face au 'péril subversif'. Guerre et action psychologiques, 1945–1960* (Paris: Les Indes Savantes, 2005), 437, on the military use of Sorbonne specialists in sociology, propaganda, demography, etc., and on US counter-insurgency theory and the training of French officer at Fort Bragg, USA (1952–56), *ibid.*, 188–95, 263, 363, 432.

6 On the background to planning for the Algerian economy between 1945 and 1958, see Lefeuvre, *Chère Algérie*, 240–348.

7 *Ibid.*, 265, 267.

8 On the background to the fall of Mendès-France see Jean-Pierre Rioux, *The Fourth Republic, 1944–1958* (Cambridge: Cambridge University Press, 1987), 225–40; Alexander Werth, *The Strange History of Pierre Mendès-France and the Great Conflict over French North Africa* (London: Barrie Books, 1957).

9 On Soustelle and Algeria see Stephen Tyre, 'From *Algérie Française* to *France Musulmane*: Jacques Soustelle and the Myths and Realities of 'Integration', 1952–1962', *French History*, 20: 3 (September 2006), 276–96; James D. LeSueur, *Uncivil War. Intellectuals and Identity Politics During the Decolonization of Algeria* (Philadelphia: University of Pennsylvania Press, 2001); Todd Shephard, *The Invention of Decolonisation. The Algerian War and the Remaking of France* (Ithaca: Cornell University Press, 2006).

10 A detailed account is provided in Jacques Soustelle, *Aimée et souffrante Algérie* (Paris: Plon, 1956), 23–94.

11 *Ibid.*, 83.

12 *Ibid.*, 54.

13 *Ibid.*, 88.

14 *Ibid.*, 138–42, 160–1.

15 *Ibid.*, 26–7.

16 This neologism is taken from Mohammed Harbi, *L'Algérie et son destin*, 136.

17 For this in general Philippe Lucas and Jean-Claude Vatin, *L'Algérie des anthropologues* (Paris: Maspero, 1982).

18 Soustelle, *Aimée et souffrante Algérie*, 83; Denis Roland, 'Jacques Soustelle, de l'éthnologie à la politique', *Revue d'Histoire Moderne et Contemporaine*, 43: 1 (January–March 1996), 137–50; Grégor Mathias, *Les Sections administratives spécialisées en Algérie. Entre idéal et réalité (1955–1962)* (Paris: L'Harmattan, 1998), 24.

19 *Comité algérien pour l'éducation de base*, 10 June 1955, quoted in Nelly Forget, 'Le Service des Centres Sociaux en Algérie', *Matériaux pour l'histoire de notre temps*, 26 (1992), 45–6.

20 On the SAS, created by an order of 26 September 1955, see SHAT 1H2556/1; Mathias, *Les Sections administratives*; also Lieutenants Lasconjarias and Jouan, 'Les "Sections Administrative Spécialisées" en Algérie: Un outil pour la stabilisation', Centre de Doctrine d'Emploi des Forces, Ministry of Defense, 2005, located on the site www.cdef.terre.defense.gouv.fr (accessed 14 January 2009); on the Moroccan background see Jim House and Neil MacMaster, *Paris 1961. Algerians, State Terror, and Memory* (Oxford: Oxford University Press, 2006), 45–6.

21 On Louis Massignon see Edward W. Said, *Orientalism* [1978] (London: Penguin Books, 1987 edn), 264–74.

22 Vincent Monteil, *Soldat de fortune* (Paris: Grasset, 1966).

23 *Ibid.*, 189. On Soustelle's conversion to a 'hard' repressive position see Wood, *Germaine Tillion*, 158–74.

24 Vincent Monteil, 'Essai sur l'Islam en URSS' and 'Supplément a l'Essai sur l'Islam en URSS' in *Revue des Études Islamiques*, 20 (1952–1953) (Paris: Paul Geuthner, 1953–4); General Tubert, *L'Ouzbekistan, république soviétique* (Paris: Édition du Pavillon, 1951).

25 Monteil, 'Essai sur l'Islam', 32–42; and 'La Femme libre', in *Les Musulmans soviétiques* (Paris: Seuil, 1957), 105–17.

26 Massell, *Surrogate Proletariat*; Northrop, *Veiled Empire*.

27 Monteil, *Les Musulmans*, 116–17. Soustelle notes, *Aimée et souffrante Algérie*, 87, that his inspiration for Algerian legal reform was in part drawn from Soviet and Yugoslav policy towards Muslim minorities.

28 Wood, *Germaine Tillion*, 'Humanisme éthnographique dans les Aurès: la mission Tillion/Rivière', 14–51; the volume of photographs by Germaine Tillion, with Nancy Wood, *L'Algérie aurésienne* (Paris: Éditions de la Martinière/Perrin, 2001); T. Rivière, *Aurès/Algérie, 1935—1936* (Paris: Éditions de la Maison des Sciences de l'Homme, 1987), which includes an important essay by Fanny Colonna, 'Elle a passé tant d'heures. . .', 125–90; special issue 'Les Vies de Germaine Tillion', *Esprit* (February 2000), 82–169; Jean Lacouture, *Le Témoignage est un combat. Une biographie de Germaine Tillion* (Paris: Seuil, 2000).

29 Tillion, *France and Algeria*, 24–5.
30 Germaine Tillion, *Le Harem et les cousins* (Paris: Seuil, 1966); translated into English as *The Republic of Cousins* (London: Al Saqi Books, 1983).
31 References here are to the English translation, *Algeria, the Realities* (London: Eyre and Spottiswoode, 1958).
32 *Ibid.*, 18–22.
33 Chevalier, *Le Problème démographique Nord-Africain*; see MacMaster, *Colonial Migrants*, 184–6.
34 See Philip Dine's discussion, '*Ni victims ni bourreaux*: The Liberal Dilemma', in *Images of the Algerian War: French Fiction and Film, 1954–1992* (Oxford: Clarendon Press, 1994), 64–88.
35 See in particular Nancy Wood's excellent discussion of Jean Amrouche's critique of *L'Algérie en 1957* in *Germaine Tillion*, 187–95; Wood has however (see *Germaine Tillion*, 44–51) significantly qualified Fanny Colonna's argument in *Aurés/Algérie 1935–1936*, 159–60, in which Colonna claims that Rivière and Tillion radically failed to identify the profound political and religio-nationalist transformations already evident in the Aurès during 1934–40, a failure of French ethnology in general, 'the collective aphasia of a dominant society faced with a reality that radically escaped it'.
36 Tillion, *Algeria. The Realities*, 29.
37 *Ibid.*, 54, 58.
38 CAOM 12CAB192, 12CAB230, dossiers on *Centres sociaux*; Soustelle, *Aimée et souffrante Algérie*, 83–4; LeSueur, *Uncivil War*, 59–62.
39 For an important account of this little known enterprise see Dore-Audibert, 'L'action sociale', in *Des Françaises d'Algérie*, 41–80; Jean Scotto, *Curé Pied-Noir, Évêque Algérien* (Paris: Desclée de Brouwer, 1991); Forget 'Le Service', notes action also centred on the shantytown of Boubsila-Bérardi.
40 Forget, 'Le Service', 40, notes the role of other SCI workers, including Rachel Jacquet and Simone Chaumel-Tanner. The history and archival resources of the SCI, founded in 1920, can be located at www.sciint.org (accessed 14 January 2009). On the similar operations of the SCI in the shantytowns of Nanterre during the Algerian War, see Monique Hervo and Marie-Ange Charras, *Bidonvilles* (Paris: Maspero, 1971), and Monique Hervo's extraordinary memoirs in *Chroniques du bidonville: Nanterre en guerre d'Algérie* (Paris: Seuil, 2001).
41 On the growth of the Algiers shantytowns see Descloitres, et al., *L'Algérie des bidonvilles*.
42 Dore-Audibert, *Des Françaises d'Algérie*, 46.
43 Georgette Soustelle (1909–1999), like her husband, was a specialist on Mexico: her fieldwork in Lacandon in 1940–42 for a Sorbonne doctorate was published as, *Taquila: un village nahuatl du Mexique oriental* (Paris: Institut d'Ethnologie, 1958). In 1956 she provided the preface to, *Boubsila, bidonvilles algérois. Étude sociale du bidonville de Boubsila dit Bérardi à Hussein-Dey*, which suggests a close or 'patron' association with the *Centres sociaux*.

44 Dore-Audibert, *Des Françaises d'Algérie*, 60, 72.
45 Forget, 'Le Service', 44–5.
46 On the February crisis and its significance see Alistair Horne, *A Savage War of Peace: Algeria 1954–1962* [1977] (London: Macmillan, 1987 edn), 147–57; Sylvie Thénault, *Histoire de la guerre d'indépendance Algérienne* (Paris: Flammarion, 2005), 118–32.
47 By the decrees of 15–16 February 1956 the functions of the governor general were transferred to a *délégué générale* who was no longer under the authority of the Minister of the Interior, but of the Prime Minister assisted by a *sécrétaire d'État aux Affaires algériennes*.
48 Lefeuvre, *Chère Algérie*, quoting from Lacoste's speech to the Algerian Assembly, 21 February 1956.
49 *Le Figaro* 5 February 1957. SHAT 1H1147/1 file of press cuttings, shows that Difrane wrote several articles on emancipation for *Le Figaro* between 1957 and 1959, and later claimed (13 June 1959) that she was proud to be the first in the national press to break the 'taboo' on the subjection of Muslim women and to show that 'France has the right, the duty and the power to finally remove the barriers erected by a facile conformism'.
50 Soustelle, *Aimée et Souffrante Algérie*, 70.
51 J. N. D. Anderson, 'The Role of Personal Statutes in Social Development of Islamic Countries', *Comparative Studies in Society and History*, 13 (January 1971), 16–31, and *Family Law in Asia and Africa* (London: Allen and Unwin, 1968); Moors, 'Debating Islamic Family Law'; John L. Esposito with Natana J. Delong-Bas, *Women in Muslim Family Law* (Syracuse, NY: Syracuse University Press, 2nd edn 2001).
52 On the 'Bourguiba Code' see Mark A. Tessler, Janet Rogers and Daniel Schneider, 'Women's Emancipation in Tunisia', in Beck and Keddie (eds), *Women in the Muslim World*, 141–58; Susan E. Marshall and Randall G. Stokes, 'Tradition and the Veil: Female Status in Tunisia and Algeria', *Journal of Modern African Studies*, 19: 4 (December 1981), 625–46; Norma Salem, 'Islam and the Status of Women in Tunisia', in Freda Hussain (ed.), *Muslim Women* (London/Sydney: Croom Helm, 1984), 141–68; Charrad, *States and Women's Rights*; the most specialised and informed treatment is Borrmans, *Statut personnel*, Part 2, 275–421.
53 Borrmans, *Statut personnel*, 153–274.
54 *La Condition de la Femme dans le Moyen-Orient Arabe* (Paris: La Documentation Française, October 1955): copy consulted at CAOM 81F1219.
55 An *Inspecteur général de l'administration en mission extraordinaire* (IGAME), was a kind of super-prefect who held special civil and military powers during periods of national emergency.
56 CAOM 13CAB7, Lacoste letter (secret), 5 November 1956; various documents and legal opinions on the Tunisian Code are in CAOM 12CAB207 and 81F1218.
57 Salem, 'Islam and the Status of Women in Tunisia', 156.

58 CAOM 12CAB207 Henry Le Breton, 'Note sur le Code Tunisian du Statut Personnel', undated, but probably just after September 1956.

59 CAOM 81F1219, Lacoste telegramme to Champeix, 25 April 1957; Champeix telegramme to Lacoste, 27 April 1957, informing him of the decision to consult a panel of legal experts.

60 CAOM 81F1219, minutes of the *Groupe de Travail*, 14, 20 and 27 May, 3 June 1957. Other members were Michel Rosier, Fusil, Ferrandi, Bauer, Casanova, Lucien Paye, Colombe, Colonel Pierre Rondot and Lefaucheux; further documentation from the Ministry of Justice can be located at the Centre des archives contemporaines (CAC) at Fontainbleau, see CAC 19950236, including Raymond Charles, *Rapport préliminaire à l'avant-projet de code portant statut de la femme musulmane en Algérie*, 7, which placed the need for reform within a broader context of codification in Morocco, Tunisia and elsewhere.

61 Copies of the *Projet de réforme du statut personnel de la femme musulmane et de la femme Kabyle en Algérie*, Ministry of the Interior, Direction des Affaires d'Algérie, June 1957, 142, are located in SHAT 1H112/3 and CAOM 14CAB165–6.

62 CAOM 81F1219, minutes, 14 May 1957.

63 CAOM 81F1219, minutes, 27 May, and 3 June 1957. Lefaucheux was in correspondence with the *Figaro* journalist Monique Difrane, who seized the opportunity to send a copy of her article, 'Indépendance en Algérie! Oui! Celle de la femme' to Simoneau, chairman of the working party.

64 See Connelly, *Diplomatic Revolution*, 92–3, on this major blow to French diplomacy.

65 *Short History of the Commission on the Status of Women*, 5–6.

66 CAOM 81F1219 contains much documentation on this issue, including UN resolution 547 H (XVIII) of 12 July 1954, requesting all member states to assure women entire freedom of choice as to marriage partner, suppression of bride price, of marriage of pre-pubescent girls, etc. Forget, 'Le Service', 40, notes that the General Government was in June 1955 collecting data on the early *Centres sociaux* in preparation for a UN session.

67 CAOM 12CAB207. *Opinion des IGAMES et préfets sur le problème de l'évolution de la femmes musulmane*, Algiers, 3 July 1957.

68 On Papon and psychological warfare see House and MacMaster, *Paris 1961*.

69 Seferdjeli, 'French "Reforms"', 25.

70 CAOM 81F1224, Note on Projet de Loi, 1 July 1957; National Assembly, session 27 April 1956, and 16 June 1957; D. Sambron, 'Évolution du statut juridique de la femme musulmane à l'époque coloniale', in *La Justice en Algérie. 1830-1962* (Paris : La Documentation française, 2005), 135–8.

71 CAOM 81F1218, Conseil de la République [Senate], 16 January 1958. Devaud, born in Constantine in 1908, married Stanislaus Devaud, elected deputy for Constantine in 1936. Active in the Paris Resistance, she was later Senator for the Seine from 1946 to 1958, and played a high-level national

and international role in the women's movement, acting as French representative on the UN Commission on the Status of Women (1975–83): see http://annuaire-au-feminin.net/bioDEVAUD.html (accessed 11 June 2007).

72 CAOM 81F1218, National Assembly debate, 28 January 1958. Francine Lefébvre (1908–1979), was deputy for the Seine from 1946 to 1958.

73 On the formation of this progressive strata of bourgeois activists see Sylvie Chaperon, 'Feminism Is Dead. Long Live Feminism!', in Claire Duchen and Irene Bandhauer-Schoffman (eds), *When the War Was Over: Women and Peace in Europe, 1940–56* (n.p.: Continuum International Publishing, 2000), 146–60; on Francine Lefebvre and the MRP see Patricia E. Prestwich, 'Modernizing Politics in the Fourth Republic. Women in the Mouvement républicain populaire, 1944–1958', in Kenneth Mouré and Martin S. Alexander (eds), *Crisis and Renewal in France, 1918–1962* (Oxford: Berghahn Books, 2002), 199–220; Hilary Footit, 'The First Women *Députés*, "les 33 Glorieuses"?', in Harry Roderick Kedward and Nancy Wood (eds), *The Liberation of France: Image and Event* (Oxford: Berg, 1995), 129–41.

74 CAOM 12CAB207, National Assembly, 28 January 1958. An undated note, 'L'Intégration et le statut personnel', stated in relation to the draft personal status law of June 1957: 'The Ministerial Cabinet has finally decided that this project will be left to the consideration of the local assemblies competent in the matter of "personal status"'.

75 SHAT 1H246/1*, note, 'Action sur la femme algérienne', by Laperronieux [?], 18 May 1957, based on discussion with two officers of the *Service des liaisons Nord-Africains*.

76 There is a considerable literature on Algeria and 'revolutionary warfare', also referred to as 'psychological warfare': the fullest study is the joint doctorate of Paul Villatoux and Marie-Catherine Villatoux (University of Paris I, 2002), that has been published as *La République et son armée face au 'peril subversive'. Guerre et action psychologique en France (1945–1960)* (Paris: Les Indes Savantes, 2005). For an excellent short account see Peter Paret, *French Revolutionary Warfare from Indochina to Algeria. The Analysis of a Political and Military Doctrine* (London: Pall Mall Press, 1964); see also Paul Villatoux and Marie-Catherine Villatoux, 'Le 5e Bureau en Algérie', in Jean-Charles Jauffret and Maurice Vaïsse (eds), *Militaires et guerrilla dans la guerre d'Algérie* (Brussels: Éditions Complexe, 2001), 399–419; Mathieu Rigouste, *L'Ennemi interieur postcolonial. De la lutte contre subversive au contrôle de l'immigration dans la pensée militaire française (1954–2007)*, doctoral thesis, Paris VIII, 2007.

77 Paul Villatoux, 'Le Colonel Lacheroy, théoricien de l'action psychologique', in Jauffret (ed.), *Des hommes*, 494–508.

78 General Chassin, 10 October 1954, quoted in George Armstrong Kelly, *The French Army and the Empire in Crisis, 1947–1962* (Cambridge, Mass.: Massachusetts Institute of Technology, 1965), 24.

79 Villatoux and Villatoux, *La République*, 294, 312.

80 *Ibid.*, 369–71, 422–3, on Bourgès-Maunory's conversion to the doctrine espoused by Colonel Lacheroy.

81 *Ibid.*, 228, 388–9: letter of R. Lacoste to commander 10th Military Region (Algeria), 5 July 1956.

82 *Ibid.*, 422.

83 *Ibid.*, 422–35, on the structure of the Fifth Bureau.

84 Kalyvas, *Logic of Violence*, 89–91.

85 CAOM 12CAB221: the GG provided Servier with official letters (3 April 1952, 9 January 1953) requesting sub-prefects, mayors and administrators to give him full assistance in the *bled*. The GG funded two payments of 150,000 AF each in September 1953 and June 1954, and commissioned research on the spread of Berber language.

86 On these events see Horne, *Savage War*, 88–93; and Jean Servier's account, *Dans l'Aurès sur les pas des rebelles* (Paris: Éditions France Empire, 1955), 7–29; for biographical details of his career see Maurice Faivre, 'Un Ethnologue de terrain face à la rébellion algérienne', Institut de Stratégie Comparée, www.stratisc.org/Faivre_7.htm (accessed 22 November 2005).

87 On Servier's background as an ethnologist see Jacques Cantier, 'L'Ethnologue et les savoirs autochtones: Jean Servier et les Berbères d'Algérie, étude de cas', *Outre-Mers. Revue d'histoire*, 352–3 (December 2006), 47–56.

88 Servier's original thesis has been lost (personal communication of Fanny Colonna), but was published as *Les Portes de l'année, rites et symboles: l'Algérie dans la tradition méditerranéenne* (Paris: Robert Laffont, 1962); and later without change, rather confusingly, under the different title of *Tradition et civilisation Berbères: les portes de l'année* (Monaco: Éditions du Rocher, 1985).

89 SHAT 1H2563/2*, note on Servier, État-major, Bureau Psychologique, 28 June 1957; CAOM 13CAB7, Jean Servier to Directeur Général de la Fonction Publique et des Affaires Politiques (GG), 12 August 1956.

90 This operation, and Servier's role in it as adviser, has been studied by the leading ethnologist of Kabylia, Camille Lacoste-Dujardin in *Opération 'Oiseau Bleu': des Kabyles, des ethnologues et la guerre d'Algérie* (Paris: La Découverte, 1997), see especially 47–9, 254–72; also by General Maurice Faivre, 'L'Affaire K, comme Kabyle (1956)', *Revue d'histoire, guerre mondiale et conflits contemporains*, 191 (1998), 37–67; see also Yves Courrière, *La Guerre d'Algérie*, Vol. 2, *Le Temps des léopards* (Paris: Fayard, 1969), 244–63; for Servier's own rather opaque account see *Adieu Djebels* (Paris: Éditions France Empire, 1958), 13–118, a book that was banned by the government.

91 Camille Lacoste-Dujardin has replied to an attack by General Faivre on her critique of Servier in 'Une auto-intoxication de services secrets. Histoire et ethnologie dans la guerre d'Algérie', in Pierre Brocheux et al. (eds), *La Guerre d'Algérie au miroir des décolonisations françaises* (Paris: SFHOM, 2000), 573–91.

92 Servier's accounts of his adventurous exploits need to be treated with some caution: a document in SHAT 1H2536/2* of the Bureau Psychologique, 28 June 1957, probably by Goussault, notes that the essentials of Operation Pilot had already been presented to the Paris *École Supérieure de Guerre* as early as May 1956.

93 Servier, *Adieu Djebels*, 144–56; SHAT 1H2536/2*, note of Salan 29 January 1957. The term 'reconquête' bears an interesting resemblance to the Spanish 'reconquista', the centuries-long process of Christian warfare that eventually led to the expulsion of the Muslim population.

94 SHAT 1H2536/2*, Bureau Psychologique, Algiers 16 January 1957, 'Fiche au sujet de l'opération de Monsieur Servier'.

95 SHAT 1H2536/2*, Colonel Goussault to Général Dulac, 17 January 1957.

96 Courrière, *La Guerre d'Algérie*, Vol. 2, 23. Lucien Paye (1907–72) was another of the academic specialists on the Maghreb that advised Soustelle: he was later Minister of Education (February 1961–April 1962) and ambassador to Senegal and China (1964–69).

97 Part of Servier's doctoral thesis of 1955 was on, 'Chants rituals et chants de circonstances des femmes de l'Aurès'.

98 CAOM 13CAB7. Servier to Paye, 12 August 1956: the second report was on the *marabouts* and the Koranic schools (*zaouias*).

99 CAOM 13CAB7, note for Monsieur Villeneuve, 20 August 1956 [from Paye?], instructing him to plan with Le Tourneau, the Rector, a project for 'a school of domestic science for young Kabyle girls'.

100 SHAT 1H2536/1*, undated; no author is given, but the document, on internal evidence, can be attributed to Servier.

101 SHAT 1H2536/1*, *L'Algérie française pivot de l'Eurafrique*, undated.

102 Servier, *Dans l'Aurès*, recounts how during fieldwork during 1949–54 he found much evidence of *Ulema* penetration into the Berber tribes and its violent opposition to traditional festivals, singing, dancing, cafés, alcohol, coffee, tobacco and cinemas: see 8–9, 149–54, 248. Fanny Colonna, *Les Versets de l'invincibilité. Permanence et changements religieux dans l'Algérie contemporaine* (Paris: FNSP, 1995), confirms this early *Ulema* penetration into rural Algeria.

103 CAOM 13CAB7, Servier, 'Note sur les Écoles Koraniques de Kabylie Maritime', 12 August 1956.

104 SHAT 1H2536/1*, *L'Algérie française pivot de l'Eurafrique*. This undated document, probably by Servier, was later reused verbatim to form the core of a standard guide for army officers engaged in propaganda on emancipation: see SHAT 1H2582, Fifth Bureau, État-Major, 21 November 1958.

105 SHAT 1H2556/1, Lacoste circular, 'Action civique par les SAS', 4 February 1958, outlines this two stage model of pacification.

106 SHAT 1H2536/2*. A detailed eye-witness account of the operations was provided by Jean Piverd in five articles in *L'Aurore*, 26 June to 1 July

1957, the first titled 'J'ai vu les hommes de bonne volonté travailler à l'édification de l'Algérie Nouvelle'. General Dulac was furious that Servier had broken orders by escorting Piverd, who revealed the location and nature of the operation: see SHAT 1H2536/2*, note of General Dulac, Chef État-Major, Algiers 28 June 1957.

107 There were initially ten of these allocated to Pilot, all of them ex-prisoners of the Viet Minh who had experienced 'brain washing' techniques: SHAT 1H2409: Salan report August 1957.

108 On the CHPT units see chapter 4.

109 During Operation Pilot the term *Assistance médicale sociale rurale itinérante* was used, which then became the official ASSRA (*Adjointes sanitaires et sociales rurales auxiliaires*) in October 1957. The term *Équipes medico-sociales itinérantes* (EMSI), which referred to each team of two or three ASSRA, does not seem to have come into use until late 1957, but I have used it here to refer to the earlier experimental organisation. A fuller account of the EMSI is given in chapter 7.

110 SHAT 1H2536/1*.

111 *L'Aurore*, 27 June, 1 July 1957.

112 Piverd's fifth report in *L'Aurore*, 1 July 1957, centred on the festivities of opening a new school, titled, 'Une école détruite, c'était la disparation de la France . . . Alors, j'en ai construit une autre'.

113 SHAT H2536/2*, Salan to commander Division Militaire d'Alger [n.d], provides orders for the careful selection and training of nineteen officers, 'to provide supervision for the Centre for Training of Political Commissioners'.

114 Villatoux and Villatoux, *La République*, 464–6. On Arzew see Frédéric Guelton, 'The French Army "Centre for Training and Preparation in Counter-Guerrilla Warfare" (CIPCG) at Arzew', in Martin S. Alexander and J. F. V. Keiger (eds), *France and the Algerian War, 1954–62: Strategy, Operations and Diplomacy* (London: Frank Kass, 2002), 35–53.

115 SHAT 1H2536/2*, a report (probably by Goussault), Algiers Bureau Psychologique to Salan, 17 July 1957, notes three of five *douars* north of the Chélif valley were now entirely 'pacified' and, 'Local councils have been elected by the population and our former trainees from Arzew are in place and are undertaking excellent work both in relation to politics and intelligence gathering'.

116 SHAT 1H2536/1*, Bureau Psychologique, 28 June 1957; Courrière, *La Guerre d'Algérie*, Vol. 2, 27.

117 SHAT 1H2536/1*, a note (probably by Servier), sees the ASSRA as typically coming from an educated, urban background, 'usually belonging to wealthy families', who could initiate peasant women to 'modern life': the FLN *moudjahidates* nurses came from a similar background (see chapter 9).

118 Servier, *Adieu Djebels*, 188–94; Courrière, *La Guerre d'Algérie*, Vol. 2, 26; confirmed by SHAT 1H246/1, Fiche 18 May 1957, on Louisa Fadli.

119 *L'Aurore*, 29–30 June, 1957, titled, 'With Denise, the Parisian welfare
     assistant, and Touria, the Algerian, who was, against her wishes, a nurse
     with the bandit gangs'.
120 Servier, *Adieu Djebels*, 204–5. This school does not seem to have ever
     started operation, probably because of Servier's later removal by the mili-
     tary command.
121 ECPAD – ALG 57/392 contains some of the earliest photographs of the
     EMSI taken by an army photo-journalist, 16 August 1957, who visited the
     team headed by Mme Guille that operated in the Bou Maad area.
122 Christiane Fournier, *Les EMSI: des filles comme ça!* (Paris: Arthème
     Fayard, 1959).
123 Servier, *Adieu Djebels*, 196; Courrière, *La Guerre d'Algérie*, Vol. 3, 32.
124 SHAT 1H2536/2*, Goussault report, 17 July 1957.
125 Villatoux and Villatoux, *La République*, 475–8, provides a detailed recon-
     struction of the extension of Pilot to Casseigne [now Sidi Ali], north-east
     of Mostaganem.
126 SHAT 1H2536/2*, Salan to General CAA, 30 June 1957.
127 SHAT 1H2536/1*, *Note sur l'emploi des musulmans dans l'armée*,
     3 September 1957 [n.d. or author, but almost certainly by Servier];
     Servier told Courrière, *La Guerre*, Vol. 3, 27, that Fifth Bureau officers
     allowed 'their nostalgic memories of Indochina to influence the Algerian
     situation'.
128 SHAT 1H2536/2*, Goussault to Salan, 17 July 1957, noted in the
     Ouarsensis (where 'Pilot 2' was originally planned): 'The artillery and
     aviation are deployed frequently without much concern for the damage
     inflicted on the population'.
129 SHAT 1H2536/1*, in a note of 28 June 1957 Goussault made a detailed
     critique of Servier's failings.
130 SHAT 1H2536/2*, Bureau psychologique, fiche on Operation NK-3, 3
     June 1957.
131 SHAT 1H2536/2*, note of Lt-Colonel Besson, Fifth Bureau, CAA, 24
     May 1957.
132 SHAT 1H2569, report by Lt.-Colonel Beaudu, Chargé Action
     Psychologique, Secteur Saint-Charles, 4 December 1957.
133 Courrière, *La Guerre d'Algérie*, Vol. 3, 26, initially five army nurses,
     Personnel féminine de l'armée de terre (PFAT), released by General
     Allard.
134 SHAT 1H4395/7, Lacoste, order of 25 October 1957. A detailed assess-
     ment of the EMSI is provided in chapter 7.
135 SHAT 1H2536/2*, General de Brébisson note to Algiers Command, 24
     February 1957: 'The key idea of Servier must be the liberation of the
     masses from poverty and ignorance, and the emancipation of women,
     aims that the FLN, by its very nature, is unable to pursue'.
136 Amrane, *Les Femmes algériennes*, 220–3; Kessel and Pirelli (eds), *Le
     Peuple algérien*, 130–4. Of the total number of 10,949 women militants

officially registered after the war with the Ministry of Veterans (Ministère des Moudjahidine), 0.29 per cent joined the FLN in 1954, 7.9 per cent in 1955, and 23.5 per cent in 1956, see Djamila Amrane, 'Approche statistique de la participation de la femme algérienne à la guerre de liberation nationale (1954–1962)', in *Majallat et-Tarikh*, No. 10, 1981, Algiers, 90, quoted in Diane Sambron, *Femmes musulmanes. Guerre d'Algérie 1954–1962* (Paris: Éditions Autrement, 2007), 30.

137 Courrière, *La Guerre d'Algérie*, Vol. 1, 98–9.

138 SHAT 1H2582, FLN Circular No. 9, 2 May 1957.

139 There is an extensive literature on the 'Battle of Algiers', but see in particular: Yacef Saadi, *La Bataille d'Alger*, 2 Vols (Paris: Publisud, 2002 edn); General Jacques Massu, *La Vraie bataille d'Alger* (Paris: Plon, 1971); Pierre Pallissier, *La Bataille d'Alger* (Paris: Perrin, 1995).

140 For a detailed account of a typical itinerary of engagement see Commandant Azzedine's account of his niece Zehor Zerari in, *On nous appelait fellaghas*, reprinted in Jean-Claude Carrière and Commandant Azzedine, *C'était la guerre. Algérie 1954–1962* (Paris: Plon, 1992), 338–58.

141 *Ibid.*, 49.

142 *Ibid.*, 53–4; thirty-six assistants signed the letter.

143 House and MacMaster, *Paris 1961*, 144–6.

144 On the campaign against the *Centres sociaux*, in which Colonel Gardes, head of the Fifth Bureau, played a key role, see LeSueur, *Uncivil War*, 62–86; Forget, 'Le Service'.

145 SHAT 1H2461/1, Fifth Bureau, Action Psychologique sur l'organisation féminine de la Zone Autonome d'Alger (ZAA), 11 October 1957; 1H2582, Second Bureau État-Major, 10e Région, 14 October 1957, Organisation féminine de la ZAA.

146 CAOM 81F1218, Directeur Générale des Affaires Politiques, 19 December 1957.

147 CAOM 14CAB162, Massu to IGAME, Algiers, 26 April 1958.

148 CAOM 14CAB162, Allard to Salan, 6 May 1958.

3

Unveiling: the 'revolutionary *journées*' of 13 May 1958

Throughout the period from early 1956 to early 1958 putschist forces had been gathering strength both within the army and among right-wing settler organisations and these eventually coalesced on 13 May 1958 when crowds gathered in the Forum and stormed the General Government buildings. The military rapidly used the crisis to effect a bloodless coup and to install a temporary 'revolutionary' authority headed by a Committee of Public Safety (*Comité de salut public* or CSP) under Generals Massu and Salan. There then followed a tense stand-off between the army in Algeria and the new Paris government headed by Pierre Pflimlin, a three-week period during which civil war was a real possibility, until de Gaulle agreed to assume, once again, the role of 'saviour of the nation', and was voted into power by the National Assembly on 1 June.[1] '13 May' was one of the great turning points in modern French history, not only because it marked a key stage in the Algerian War, but more significantly the collapse of the Fourth Republic, de Gaulle's return to power, and the beginnings of the new constitutional regime of the Fifth Republic.

The planning of the coup and its implementation was extraordinarily complex – the Bromberger brothers in *Les 13 Complots du 13 mai* counted thirteen strands[2] – but basically two antagonistic political formations reached agreement to rally to the call for de Gaulle's return to power. On the one hand there was a secret plot by Gaullists, most notably Michel Debré (soon to become Prime Minister), Jacques Soustelle, Léon Delbecque and Jacques Chaban-Delmas (acting Minister of Defence), to engineer the return of the General so as to resolve the political crisis of the 'system', the dead hand of the party system of the Fourth Republic, which they viewed as destroying the *grandeur* of France. The second trend was composed of various extreme-right-wing plotters, mainly from the *pieds-noirs* community, neo-fascists, poujad-ists, die-hard colonialists and army officers who shared the Gaullist fear of national degeneration, but who were even more concerned about a 'sell-out' in Algeria and were determined to fight to the bitter end for the political supremacy of the million European settlers. On 11 May the far-right Pétainist editor, Alain de Sérigny, published an overt appeal to de Gaulle to seize the helm, and this set the stage for the various clandestine trends to converge in the coup d'état of 13 May when extreme-right settler activists stormed the General Government while the parachute regiments looked on.[3] The plotters, in a move reminiscent of General Franco's rebellion of 1936 when the army of North Africa flew from Morocco to attack the Spanish Republic, were laying plans to topple the government by an airborn invasion of Paris.

On the evening of 13 May General Massu, commander of the armed forces in the Algiers region, took control of the situation by announcing from the balcony of the General Government to the huge and excited crowds of Europeans packed into the Forum below, the intention to form immediately a CSP.[4] During the twenty-three days between 13 May and 4 June, when de Gaulle made his triumphal appearance before delirious crowds of *pieds-noirs*, the large open space of the Forum, which was separated from the white bulk of the General Government by high iron railings, was the scene of daily parades, of huge popular gatherings that often continued late into the night. In keeping with the symbolism of the Jacobin committee of public safety of 1793–94, the massed and euphoric crowd in the Forum was represented in the endless speeches and media discourse as an expression of the spontaneous 'revolutionary' will of the people, an assertion of a noble and colossal force that carried its own inherent message of populist legitimacy. The most dramatic and memorable part of the 'revolutionary' and highly theatrical crowd scenes that were played out here over three weeks was the extraordinary 'fraternisation' from 16 to 18 May between Europeans and Muslims.[5] On Friday 16 May contingents of Algerian men, elderly war veterans wearing decorations, *harki* and other pro-French elements, marched into the Forum where they were encouraged to join hands with, or embrace, their 'brother' Europeans in a symbol of reconciliation and friendship that was photographed and filmed by the international media. This was deemed such a spectacular propaganda success that Psychological Action officers of the Fifth Bureau decided to extend 'fraternisation' to include Muslim women, a far more novel and controversial action.

On the evening of the following day, Saturday 17 May, the dramatic arrival of the hero of the *Algérie française* crowds, Jacques Soustelle, after his escape from virtual house-arrest in Paris, was marked by unprecedented scenes as a group of young Algerian women removed and burned their *haïks* before the General Government. The next day this

action was accelerated when hundreds of women from the Algiers slums
marched into the Forum carrying banners and placards, removed their
haïks or had them taken off by their European 'sisters', and applauded
speeches by Muslim women expressing their desire for emancipation
and modernity as full French citizens. From the 19 May to early June
these elaborate ceremonies of unveiling were extended to urban centres
throughout Algeria.

Before examining in closer detail the orchestration of 'fraternisation'
ceremonies, it is necessary to examine their underlying political meaning
and purpose. The aim of the military and Gaullist organisers of the '13
May' coup was to force Pierre Pflimlin, who had been invested as Prime
Minister by the National Assembly early in the morning of 14 May, to
stand down in favour of General de Gaulle. However, there was no rapid
resolution of a crisis that appeared to be slipping dangerously towards
civil war: the Pflimlin government began to take military steps to protect
Paris, while de Gaulle remained evasive, refusing to respond to the call
of the Algiers plotters by openly agreeing to take on the role of national
saviour. In a Paris press-conference on 19 May de Gaulle stated that he
had no interest in heading a military dictatorship, but indicated his willingness to come forward if so delegated by the 'Republic': 'Now I shall
return home to my village and there I shall hold myself at the disposi-
tion of the country'.[6] For the next ten days, during which the military
plotters invaded Corsica, there existed a dangerous vacuum of power
and de Gaulle seemed to hang back while desperate haggling took place
for a constitutional resolution. In a situation of chaos the outcome of
the three-week crisis remained unpredictable and at times the situation
of the plotters in Algiers, who faced an economic embargo, appeared
desperate, especially as their key player remained elusive and failed to
respond to their appeals.

The officers of the Fifth Bureau, specialists in propaganda techniques
and the manipulation of public opinion, knew that it was of crucial
political importance to win over both the national and international
media. It was important in the first few days of '13 May' to dispel the
hostility of the international media which tended to present the Algiers
generals as proto-fascist dictators, on a par with Franco in 1936, who
were intent on guaranteeing a white supremacist regime. A primary
purpose of the propaganda offensive was to negate this image and to
gain legitimacy for their coup by showing that the 'New Order', far from
being a colonial despotism, was based on full equality and 'integration'
of both Europeans and Muslims. When the ad-hoc CSP was established
on the night of 13–14 May, Massu insisted that Algerian representatives
be added (Mahdi, Madani, Berkani, Sheikh Taïeb) and he read from

the balcony Communiqué No. 1: 'The Committee beseeches General de
Gaulle to break his silence by addressing the country . . . We are proud
to be able to prove to the world that the people of Algiers have been able
to give a perfect demonstration of total fraternity between the European
and Muslim populations, united under the folds of the French flag'.[7]
However, in the heady euphoria of 'revolution' few noticed that the four
handpicked Algerians on the CSP had no popular mandate and made
up only 7 per cent of the fifty-five-man body, whereas Muslims made
up 89 per cent of the population. The mass 'fraternisation' of Algerian
men on 16 May was organised to demonstrate the totally 'spontaneous'
and euphoric support for inter-racial unity and *Algérie française*. During
the following two days this message was given a far more dramatic and
newsworthy support by the parade of Algerian women, the 'other half'
of the population, who signalled their wish for emancipation within the
French nation. The function of mass 'fraternisation' was to convince the
world that the coup was a genuine and almost miraculous expression of
the unity of the two warring communities, but in addition it served the
crucial function of bringing de Gaulle on side. The General was wary of
being perceived as the leader of a military and white supremacist coup,
but if the mass of ordinary Europeans and Algerians were spontaneously and genuinely united in calling for his aid, then he might well be
able to cross the Rubicon in answer to such a call of the 'nation'.[8]

A key issue that was debated endlessly by contemporaries, and subsequently by historians, was whether the 'fraternisation' was indeed
a spontaneous expression of the popular will. Journalists and other
eye-witnesses present in the Forum were deeply divided on this issue:
on the one hand, as will be seen, there were those who claimed that
the army had coerced many Algerians who were brought in by lorry to
the parades, or that the women who unveiled were prostitutes and the
dregs of the slums. Opposed to this was the claim that an extraordinary
and electric fervour had swept through the crowd of Europeans and
Algerians, an emotional outpouring of joy and optimism that signalled
an end to the bloody divisions, and the powerful solidarity of the two
peoples as they faced the future together. Typical of this highly charged
impact is the claim of Colonel Jacques Romain-Desfossés that he, like
all his comrades, was swept away: 'This immense flood of the crowd of
Europeans and Muslims fraternally intermingled had something fantas-
tic about it'. He would never forget, 'the deeply moving emotion that
seized hold of me'.[9] Dr Sangline also would always remember with deep
emotion the joy of the crowds in the Forum, 'where the crowd formed
an immense chain of friendship, each person linking arms with his
neighbour, all mixed together: Europeans, Muslims, civilians, soldiers,

men, women, children and adults. A glittering ant-heap, bright colours on the long, unfurled banners, thousands of flags. It was truly a joy to be alive!'[10] The peculiar psychodrama was frequently likened to that of 4 August 1789 when representatives of the National Assembly, in a strange and intoxicated atmosphere, voluntarily renounced the seigneurial rights and privileges of the Ancien Régime. It may be the case that many *pieds-noirs* and a significant number of Algerians who favoured French control, such as the *harkis* and conservative war veterans, were swept by a wave of euphoria or by a willing suspension of disbelief in their wish to grab at the hope of peace after four years of bloodshed. But although historians like Jean Lacouture and Alistair Horne have seen 'fraternisation' as 'authentic' or 'genuine',[11] in itself perhaps a testament to the skill of the Fifth Bureau, the events were indeed closely orchestrated by the military. It was crucial to the whole strategy of the army that its role be kept secret, otherwise the objective of demonstrating popular 'spontaneity' would have imploded, and this is why the events continue to be wrapped in some mystery because the Fifth Bureau was so keen to cover its tracks. The potent myth of 'fraternisation' was far too politically important to be picked apart and discredited.[12]

The Fifth Bureau and the 16 May 'fraternisation'

Although the main interest of this study is in the emancipation of Algerian women, it is useful to examine the all-male 'fraternisation' ceremonies of 16 May, before moving on to the symbolic unveiling on 17–18 May, because of the light that it sheds on the organisation of the psychological warfare offensive. The Forum demonstration of 16 May did not consist, as often claimed, of Algerians spontaneously pouring down into the square from the neighbouring Casbah, but of a highly theatrical and ritualised procession of groups of medalled war veterans, boy scouts and girls carrying tri-coloured bouquets of flowers, delegations from different parts of the city and suburbs carrying banners and flags; and marching bands, which as they arrived were marshalled by loudspeaker instructions.

In a sense there was nothing new about the demonstration: colonial Algeria, even before the war, sustained a rich culture of public ceremonials and parades, often centred on war memorials, which in part reflected a *pieds-noirs* overcompensation, a symbolic assertion, of an insecure French national identity. But as an examination of the Algerian press reveals, with the arrival of a huge army presence that almost equalled the total European population, and the militarisation of civilian life, there was an endless round of parading, official presentations of prizes, speech making and martial music in every town and outpost, presided over by generals, colonels, their wives and Algerian *bachagas*. The army was constantly organising such events with military precision, but where '13 May' differed was in the scale and complexity of the events and, given their crucial political importance, the intervention of the Fifth Bureau to ensure the right media and propaganda impacts.

The key personnel involved in planning the Forum events were Colonel Charles Lacheroy, the leading theorist of psychological warfare who was placed in charge of press/media affairs by the CSP on 13–14 May; Colonel Michel Goussault, head of the Fifth Bureau for the 10th Military Region (Algeria) and patron of Jean Servier; Colonel Jean Gardes, soon to succeed Goussault as head of the Fifth Bureau; Colonel Roger Trinquier, parachute commander and specialist in urban counter-insurgency; Captain Paul-Alain Léger, expert in 'dirty tricks' operations; and Captain Sirvent.[13]

The propaganda techniques of the Fifth Bureau will be examined later (chapter 4), but here it can be noted that the training programmes of the schools or centres of psychological warfare in Paris and Algeria, such as Arzew which formed over 7,000 officers, included methods for the indoctrination of crowds. The army was particularly interested in contemporary theories of 'brain-washing', crowd psychology and behaviourism by which conditioned reflexes could be implanted into the popular masses. One of the 'bibles' or key references here was Chakotin's *The Rape of the Masses* (1939), by a leading Russian microbiologist and pupil of Pavlov, who had studied and witnessed at first hand the crowd propaganda techniques of the Russian Revolution and Nazi Germany. Chakotin believed that there was a true scientific technique of crowd conditioning based on four instincts (of struggle, nutrition, sexuality and maternity) and that 90 per cent of the population could be influenced, not by rational data or argument, but by 'senso-propaganda' that played on the emotions through *repetition*. Central to Chakotin's experience of Russia and Nazi Germany was the extent to which such manipulation of the masses was achieved by vast rallies or spectacles, like those at Nuremberg, in which a key role was played by marching uniformed men, flags, bands, symbols (the Swastika), slogans and 'the formidable technical equipment afforded by the modern state'.[14] The Fifth Bureau had no hesitation in adapting 'totalitarian' techniques, and at Arzew and Paris instructors taught officers scientific methods for organising mass rallies, including 'son et lumière', the diffusion of psychologically tested slogans on banners and placards, the types and duration of music (Arabic and military), mobile public address systems, 'by appealing not to our intelligence, but to our instincts and common sense'.[15] Such methods were deployed by the army not only in urban centres, but also in the isolated interior during mass ceremonies (*ralliement*) when dissident populations or sections of tribes passed over to the French side in elaborate ceremonials of surrender. As the Villatoux's note, by 1957 the Fifth Bureau saw such psychological actions, 'as the miraculous solution capable of finally achieving the real and lasting pacification of the country',[16] and this explains in part the centrality of the Forum parades during the *journées* of '13 May' which can be considered as a form of *ralliement*.

How did the Fifth Bureau get Algerian men to assemble on 16 May for the displays of 'fraternisation'? In part this was achieved through Algerian ex-servicemen's associations, highly conservative and pro-French organisations that were patronised by the army and provided with various rewards in the shape of club buildings (Dar el Askri), employment, pensions and handouts (medals, blankets, food).[17] It was Auguste Arnould, head of the *Comité d'entente des Anciens Combattants*, who made a loudspeaker appeal on 16 May to link arms and 'to create the chain of friendship' between Europeans and Algerians.[18] A second element in the mobilisation was provided by a highly sophisticated system, created by Trinquier during the 'Battle of Algiers', for the total control of the Algiers population: the city was divided up into arrondissements, blocks (*îlots*) and individual buildings and at each level the army appointed European 'ultras' and pro-French Algerian informers to spy on the population and report on FLN suspects.[19] The *Dispositive de protection urbaine* (DPU), which derived from Nazi and Soviet models of urban control,[20] constituted an armed and parallel police of about 7,500 men, and it was they who coerced unwilling Algerians to swell the ranks of the 'fraternisation' parades. Trinquier had already proved his ability to mobilise, via the DUP, both Algerians and Europeans in an impressive joint Forum demonstration on 11 November 1957, and this well-oiled and tested machine was put into action on 14–15 May.

Trinquier, and his close aid Léger, depended primarily on Captain Sirvent of the 9th Zouave Company, which was stationed at the Palais Klein to control the FLN fortress of the Casbah, to orchestrate the first 'fraternisation' demonstration. Sirvent, a *pied-noir* born in Algiers, became a teacher at a school in the Casbah at the end of the Second World War, and gained an intimate knowledge of 'his' people and Arab dialect.[21] On 14 May General Petit, a key Gaullist conspirator who liaised between Paris and Algiers, called Sirvent to the General Government, emphasised the crucial political importance of gaining Algerian support for the coup and to bring de Gaulle to power, and asked if he could organise this through, 'the Muslim elites, the leaders who were able to pull the mass of the population into the movement' under the banner of full equality and Soustelle's old mantra of 'integration'.[22]

The following day Trinquier, concerned that the 'revolution' was losing impetus[23] and, meeting opposition in the Oran, Kabyle and Constantine regions, relayed a similar order to Léger and Sirvent to organise a demonstration through the DUP and specified the precise slogans to be used on the banners.[24] On the night of 15 May Sirvent called all the Algerian Casbah heads of street units (*chefs d'îlot*) to a meeting, some 280 men, whom he addressed in Arabic: 'This is the big revolution. We are all equal, all French . . . we will provide you with flags and placards. So you will be demonstrating like and alongside the Europeans!'. The Algerians, hesitant and frightened that they would be exposed to attack by 'ultra' Europeans, were promised protection by armed Muslim militias (the *bleu de chauffe*) and they then elected to form their own Casbah *Comité de Salut Public* headed by Fahrès, an ex-FLN militant and technician of Radio-Alger, who next day was to make a speech at the Forum of fealty to France on behalf of the Casbah CSP.[25] Throughout the night of 15–16 May Sirvant's HQ was a hive of activity as Zouave soldiers and the wives of the *îlots* bosses sewed and painted banners and placards with the chosen slogans, 'The Casbah replies: all present' and 'We are French, and we wish to stay French'.

As the march set off on the afternoon of 16 July, Sirvent ordered that not a single uniformed French soldier be present so as to sustain the necessary illusion of an authentic and spontaneous Algerian movement. However, not all Algerians on the demonstration were the euphoric and joyful participants that the army claimed and at least three observers, the protestant Pasteur André Trocmé, active within the international pacifist movement the International Fellowship of Reconciliation, Albert-Paul Lentin, and Léon-Etienne Duval, Archbishop of Algiers, reported incidents of coercion by the armed DUP which rounded up Algerian men and forced them into lorries using various forms of intimidation, including confiscation of their identity cards that would only be returned after the parade. Only a few hundred men gave way to such pressure and most of the prefabricated banners remained unused.[26]

Unveiling ceremonies of 17–18 May

The 16 May demonstration was undoubtedly a huge success for the Fifth Bureau, and made a major impact on the national and world media, but this 'fraternisation' was significantly an all-male affair, as was illustrated by one of the army leaflets showing a turbaned Algerian carrying a

un même cœur

un   seul
Drapeau
tous français!
Dans L'algérie française

2 'Fraternisation' propaganda leaflet, *journées* of '13 May' 1958

tri-colour flag and holding hands with a European under the slogan, 'A single heart, a single flag: all French! In an *Algérie française*'.[27]

How exactly the Fifth Bureau then passed on to the far more novel and daring plan to up the stakes by extending the movement to include women remains unclear, but the initiative did not originate here but had an earlier history. The most likely candidate as initiator is Colonel Goussault, head of the Fifth Bureau in Algiers, who had already played a key role in the elaboration of female emancipation strategies, including Servier's Operation Pilot during 1957.[28] Army propagandists had undoubtedly initiated a media campaign on this theme, and in particular against the veil, as early as the summer of 1957. In July 1957 Radio-Alger broadcast in both Arabic and Kabyle editions of the programme *Magazine de la femme* the thoughts of a Muslim presenter called 'Nadira' in which she excoriated the veil and called for the emancipation of Algerian women. It seems highly likely that the broadcast by 'Nadira' to her Muslim sisters, as well as the letters of listeners that were read out, were scripted by psychological warfare officers, as were similar broadcasts to Algerian women after 13 May 1958 (see chapter 4).[29]

The Fifth Bureau was already engaged in a clandestine propaganda campaign against the veil in mid-1957, concurrent with Servier's Operation Pilot and the first working party on the revision of the Code of Personal Status (May–June). The campaign for unveiling began to peak in the weeks immediately before the 13 May coup. On 8 April a group of seventy-five women from the Casbah sent a petition to the head of Radio Casbah expressing satisfaction at the broadcasts on emancipation within the context of an 'Algérie Nouvelle et Française'. In order, they claimed, 'that the Muslim woman becomes a modern, civilised woman, it is necessary that she builds a plan for the future like the French woman and in order to achieve this each Muslim woman must remove the veil or the *cachabia* that smothers her, that impedes her in her work, or during her education, . . . and which above all else deprives her of her liberty and imprisons her between four walls'. The veil was not prescribed, they claimed, by the Koran, only by reactionary parents. The road to modernity and a better future was now open and, 'alongside the Muslim woman Algeria will live and remain French without the veil in Peace and Liberty'.[30] This petition, which may have been circulated by one of the officers of the *Section administrative urbaine* (SAU) who had set up women's circles, asked that the veil be banned. General Massu, in forwarding this letter to General Allard and Salan's cabinet, noted that surveys of public opinion had shown that young Muslim women 'wish to enjoy greater liberty' and would follow the side in the war that first led them towards, 'a modern concept of existence. The suppression of the veil will mark an important step in this direction . . . It seems to me absolutely necessary that the order for "unveiling" should be given now firmly and unambiguously'.[31] The same Casbah letter was used by a Muslim councillor, the *cadi* Mohammed Benhoura, during a speech he made to the Administrative Commission of the Department of Algiers on 7 May, as a sign of the urgent need for Algeria to follow the revolutionary movement for the liberation of women sweeping through the Maghreb, notably in Tunisia and Morocco.[32]

Before looking more closely at the unveiling ceremonies it is necessary to place these elaborate and propagandistic performances within the context of the 'sociological' meaning and uses of the veil in Algerian society, as opposed to stereotypical and Orientalist constructions. Historico-anthropological studies of veiling throughout the Muslim world demonstrates, in contrast to western Orientalist stereotypes of a uniform or homogeneous dress-code, a huge range of constantly evolving designs and practices that vary from country to country, and within states from one region to another, from urban to rural contexts, according to ethnic, cultural and class background. In general, peasant or nomadic women in rural societies, particularly among the Berber mountain peoples, tended not to wear the *haïk* and face veil (*hadjar*) of urban society (on the latter see illustration 4, p. 130).

Part of the reason for this is that peasant women engaged in very heavy manual labour (collecting wood, transporting water) and such an encumbering garment was not practical. But more importantly, villages like those of Kabylia, constituted quasi-fortified communities which 'foreigners' would not enter, or only rarely under close supervision and surveillance by male inhabitants, and so women could move about in public spaces relatively freely without running the dangers of contacts that might bring dishonour. The physical layout of the village, of groups of houses, shared courtyards and lanes, was a reflection of extended family and lineage structures,[33] and the only males that women would meet, within the confines of the spaces they habitually moved within, were close relatives. All inhabitants of the village, male and female, as part of a community based on blood ties, understood almost intuitively the unwritten rules that regulated gender roles, segregation and honour: so for example, males would make sure that they were not near the path that women took each day, at certain fixed times, to carry water from the fountain or spring.

Veiling, as throughout the Mediterranean world, was historically a feature of urban society.[34] A number of factors came into play: firstly, veiling was in the town a mark of social status, a symbol of the relative wealth of the trader, shopkeeper or official and the fact that his wife did not work. In contrast to the rural peasantry, very few urban women would engage in any kind of labour outside the fortress of the household, and if they did this was generally seen as an indication of extremely low and even immoral status. Secondly, urban public spaces almost inevitably presented far greater danger from contact with every type of stranger, males who were not restrained by the powerful lineage codes of the village and for whom, in the classic double-standard of societies of honour, seduction of women belonging to exogamous 'other males' was fair play. In general any woman of the lower classes who did not veil would be regarded as a prostitute, or run the risk of being treated as such.

The distinction between unveiled-rural and veiled-urban societies represents a useful, but overly simple, model, and tends to obscure the way in which each individual would alter or adapt her dress code according to the context in which she found herself. In the bigger cities of the northern littoral like Algiers, Oran and Bône there was significant spatial segregation between predominantly European zones, and the poorer 'ghettoised' sectors, the old Casbah, the tenement slums and shantytowns or *villages nègres* of the Muslim population. A minority of older working women and younger *évoluées* women who might travel daily on foot or bus between the Muslim quarter, where they lived with their families, and the European commercial centre, where they might work as cleaners and secretaries or attend lycée classes, would often wear the *haïk* within the home streets in which they were known to neighbours, and then remove it in the more anonymous space of the European city.[35] Since the *haïk* was a very light and simple wrap around piece of cloth, women could wear under it western style clothing. However, for a far larger number of urban Algerian women who lived in extreme poverty the simple and cheap but elegant *haïk* had the advantage of enabling them to go into public spaces or into the centre of Algiers with some self-respect, and despite the fact that the clothing they wore underneath was often ragged and patched. Captain L. P. Fauque, an army expert on Muslim society, wrote:

> The veil is a mark of respectability and to leave the house without it is for some equivalent to going out undressed and to be exposed to the wounding jeers of men. Every girl who goes unveiled is considered in popular and traditionalist milieu as a girl of light reputation who risks not being able to find a husband . . . This urban custom comes into play, when populations are brought together, in relation to strangers from outside the homogeneous group. Thus in the resettlement camp of Aïn-Mimoun (Kenchela) the women stay hidden away and only appear outside when veiled whereas before, in the *douar*, they moved about freely inside the hamlet (*mechta*) with their faces uncovered. The veil is also sometimes the only decent piece of attire that can conceal their thread-bare clothing'.[36]

In general terms the process of modernisation and urbanisation during the twentieth century, fuelled by the crisis in rural society which accelerated internal migration to the towns, increased the numbers of women who changed to wearing the veil. An increase in veiling was also a response to the conquest and penetration of Europeans into Algerian society, a way in which indigenous peoples could express their separation and cultural resistance from an invasive infidel (*roumi*) presence. Radical female segregation and seclusion remained a paramount value in post-Second World War Algeria, and even the minority of better educated or more progressive nationalist families found it extremely difficult to defy such conventions (see chapter 1). Any attempt by the military government to conduct a campaign against the veil was likely to arouse a hornet's nest of opposition, not only among pro-independence nationalists, but also among the conservative religious authorities and Algerian elites that the French needed to keep on side.

Part of the answer to this apparently high-risk strategy can be found in the considerable historical precedents available to the Fifth Bureau of unveiling campaigns. As the history of Orientalism shows, the image of the veil has for centuries served Christian Europe or the west as the crucial symbol of the 'otherness', the perceived archaic and barbaric nature, of Islamic society.[37] The great advantage of the veil to European propagandists is that it offered such a highly visible and even dramatic symbol of the totality of a 'barbaric' and anti-modern Islamic social, political and cultural order, a potent signifier or convenient short-hand for a wider field of gendered practices, from seclusion and arranged marriage, to polygamy and sexual violence. In contemporary European society the veil has continued to serve this function, as can be seen for example in the case of the French headscarves controversy that has raged in fits and starts since 1989.[38] The archives of both the civilian and military administrations in Algiers during 1957–58 show that the experts on Muslim affairs were fully aware of the precedents for organised or ritualised unveiling as a keystone of authoritarian modernisation campaigns in Turkey, Iran, Soviet Central Asia, Morocco and elsewhere from the 1920s onwards. Mass unveiling demonstrations had taken place in Egypt (1923), Uzbekistan (1927), Syria (1942), Lebanon (1944) and elsewhere.

Closer to home was a major debate on women and the veil in Tunisia during 1929–30. On 8 January 1929 the Socialist Club organised a meeting to discuss the status of Tunisian women during which Mrs Menchari dramatically removed her veil at the podium. Bourguiba, the future president, opposed this stance and argued that reform of Tunisian society was impossible as long as colonial domination remained, and that in the meantime the veil should continue as a defensive expression of national identity.[39] Bourguiba's position here was similar to that of the future FLN which saw the true emancipation of Algerian women less as an integral component of the liberation struggle than as a something that would be achieved by post-colonial liberation. The following year Al-Tahir Al-Haddad published *Our Woman in the Law and in Society* (1930), which caused outrage in conservative circles for its argument that emancipation was compatible with a correct reading of the Koran and Islamic tradition. Al-Haddad made a violent attack on the veil which was, he argued, not imposed by the Koran and which he likened to 'the muzzle used to prevent dogs from biting', and 'the concrete proof of man's basic belief that women are essentially immoral'.[40]

Psychological warfare officers in 1957–58 also referred frequently to the highly mediatised unveiling of Lalla Aïcha, the daughter of the King of Morocco. On 11 April 1947 the young princess made a famous speech from a balcony in Tangiers city square to thousands of women in which she aligned herself with the nationalist movement and spoke of the need for women to become educated and to assume a role as full participants in Moroccan society as a condition of a national 'renaissance'. According to one eye-witness, this was 'the first time, in the history of Islam, either in the East or the West, that a great woman from a great imperial family *dared* to tear off her veil in public'.[41] This format of young women from aristocratic families unveiling and addressing crowds from public balconies was to be reproduced by the army in the major towns of Algeria during May 1958. What drew the Fifth Bureau towards such precedents was that it showed how Muslim societies had themselves attempted to engage in internal reform and to ban the veil, a development that was frequently used by army propagandists to show that emancipation was perfectly compatible with Islam and was not merely a dangerous 'western' agenda imposed by secular or Christian powers.

By far the closest parallel to the French reforming agenda in Algeria was that of the Soviet Union in Central Asia between 1919 and 1929, when a highly secular and revolutionary power attempted, within a colonial context, to use a drive for the emancipation of Muslim women as a means to penetrate and control Islamic-tribal societies that were extremely resistant to any 'civilising mission'.[42] Experts in the Fifth Bureau did not refer explicitly to Central Asia but, bitter anti-communists and anti-Marxists to a man, they were unlikely to have publicised any affiliation to a Soviet model. However, Islamic experts in the Algerian administration were very interested in the Soviet experience and, as has been seen (chapter 2) Soustelle's adviser Vincent Monteil had made a close study of Central Asia. The most well-known aspect of the Soviet emancipation drive, reported widely in the international press, was the great processions of thousands of Muslim women in Uzbekistan that began in March 1927. The columns, organised by party officials and guarded by militiamen, surged through the urban centres and, fired up by female orators, revolutionary songs and music, proceeded to the *en masse* burning of the veil or to the forced unveiling of richer, conservative women.[43] It seems likely that Fifth Bureau specialists, who were so intrigued by totalitarian methods of crowd control, drew their inspiration for the highly theatrical 'fraternisation' parades of 17–18 May from the Soviet Union. As Borrmans notes, the iconoclastic image of the burning veil was also diffused in popular culture through *The Fall of the Veil* of the celebrated singer al-Zahâwî:

> Tear off your veil, O daughter of Iraq
> Unveil yourself, since life demands a profound change
> Tear it up; thrown it without delay into the fire
> Since for you it provides a misleading protection.[44]

3 Young women at the Forum prepare to burn their veils, 17 May 1958

Elaborate unveiling rituals were organised by the army in separate events on the 17 and 18 of May. On the evening of the 17 May Jacques Soustelle, after his dramatic clandestine escape from France, appeared on the balcony of the General Government before the ecstatic crowds of the Forum. As a leading Resistance member and Gaullist, as well as an ex-Governor who had come to embrace the cause of *Algérie française*, he symbolised the temporary, but crucial, alliance between the extreme-right-wing settler movements and the Gaullist plotters. The atmosphere of the crowd was one of huge elation at the prospect of Algeria remaining French, and it was in this context that the Fifth Bureau organised, at short notice, a daring *mise en scène* of veil burning.

As darkness descended, a group of about twelve young Algerian women, guarded by *harkis*, burned their veils inside the protective iron gates of the General Government. The army photographer Daudu took nine pictures of the scene, which he called a 'symbolic auto-da-fé', which show a group of apprehensive girls aged about fourteen to sixteen being encouraged by two older Algerian women dressed in a European style and an elegant European woman, probably the wife of General Salan.[45]

Their identity remains unknown, but it seems likely that these young women had been recruited from a lycée or typing pool, and Trocmé identified them as 'a bit more *évoluées*'. The little evidence that does exist on the identity of young women who played a prominent role in unveiling rituals supports the idea that they were from well-educated, relatively well-off and Francophile family backgrounds, as in the case of Monique Améziane at Constantine, Malika Massu at Blida (see below), or the lycée-educated Kebtani, later a deputy, who with other Algerian women removed her veil on 16 May 1958 at the behest of General Gandoet in the theatre of Sétif.[46] Immediately after the veil burning a delegation from the group went to join Soustelle and Generals Salan and Massu on the balcony of the General Government.

Salan made use of this first 'fraternisation' of women to persuade Paris that a vast movement of support for continuing French power was sweeping spontaneously through the Algerian population: in a telegram to the Minister of Defence he claimed, 'I stress the exceptional patriotic fervour of the crowds that reveals an extraordinary revolution in attitude in the sense of a total spiritual fusion of the two communities . . . Yesterday evening groups of Muslim women burned their veils of their own accord, saying, "Today we are French!"'. Salan went on to describe as 'absolutely deceitful' the claims of some Prefects who were hostile to the coup that demonstrations were being orchestrated by the army when they were evidently spontaneous.[47] It was of crucial political importance to the Gaullist plotters that metropolitan and international opinion be convinced of the authenticity of the popular Algerian support for *Algérie française*.

However, the veil burning incident of 17 May quickly became viewed by the army leaders and their advisers as a far too radical and provocative act which threatened to alienate Muslim opinion. General Massu in particular was much influenced by his wife who, deeply engaged in social work with Algerian women, had a much more informed and sensitive understanding of their culture. 'Several *passionarias*', noted General Massu later, concealing his own involvement in the ritual, 'several inflamed women burned in the Forum this symbol of their "servitude" . . . but they were not the most representative or thoughtful of women [. . .] Always this taste for the theatrical, for the scandalous, but for Algerian women obsessed with tradition, this gesture was shocking'.[48]

However, the burning incident was quickly overlaid by a massive and far more widely reported unveiling demonstration on Sunday 18 May. In a highly elaborate and theatrical event large groups of women representing and carrying banners from all the main Muslim shantytowns and quarters of the Algiers region, including towns as far away as Chiffalo, Ménerville and Castiglione (modern day Khemisti Port, Thenia and Bou Ismail), some thirty miles distant.[49] The groups marched through

4 Arrival of women demonstrators at the Forum, 18 May 1958

the dense crowds of applauding Europeans into the open space inside
the railings of the General Government where they were welcomed by a
military band, lined up and exhorted to remove their veils.

Outside the railings some European women, under the amazed eye
of *pieds-noirs* onlookers, unveiled some of their Algerian 'sisters'[50] who
said in Arabic, 'It's good, it's good, you are right my sister, you are right,
thank-you, thank-you'.[51] Who were these women, and how were they
organised? From the 15 May onwards the army moved rapidly to establish local CSP in every commune in the Algiers area, and the most active
role in this creation of a 'parallel' revolutionary government was taken
by the officers of the SAU who, in most instances, had been operating
from the Spring of 1957 to built up contacts with the local population.[52]
The SAU/CSP were in an excellent position to mobilise local women for
the demonstration of 18 May, as can be shown by two of the most active
groups from Ménerville and the Cité Mahiéddine. Women organised by
ex-servicemen of the Ménerville CSP, quite possibly the wives of political activists, had spent the morning dying three *haïks* red, white and
blue, so as to form a huge tri-colour flag that was presented to Soustelle
and hung from the balcony of the General Government.[53]

5 Banners of the women demonstrators at the Forum, 18 May 1958

Even more prominent was the role of women from the Cité Mahiéddine, a dense central *bidonville* of 10,000 people, many of them dockers' families,[54] where Captain de Germiny had headed the SAU since March 1957. De Germiny, in a report on the 'psycho-political methods' employed to rebuild contact with the population after the violent Battle of Algiers, noted the establishment of what was an early example of a women's circle or 'club', in a 'a pleasant location where young girls and young women from the Cité Mahiéddine can meet to look at encyclopaedias or journals. Also here, radio, television, and twice a week cinema shows, attract an ever increasing public'.[55] Such an early phase of social work with Muslim women prepared the way for their mobilisation during the unveiling ceremonies of 18 May,[56] and one of their number, who had rather unusually been selected onto the local CSP, was delegated to make a speech from the balcony of the General Government, a moment that received enormous coverage in the international press. Algerian women, she said through the microphones, were aware of the aid that they had been receiving from the army over recent months: 'We are aware of how far our traditional dress, our reclusive existence, are factors that separate us from our French sisters of a different religion to ours. We wish to engage fully in the route to modernity and to profit from the exciting epoch which Algeria is currently traversing to accelerate our progress'.[57] Switching from French into Arabic she then called on her 'sisters' to remove their veils, 'the barrier between two communities', and then led the vast crowd of 100,000 people into singing the *Marseillaise*.[58] Some women followed this appeal with trepidation and lowered their face veils, although trying to cover their face with their hands, and were encouraged and applauded by the European crowds.[59]

The Algiers 'fraternisation' of 17–18 May was seen as such a huge success by the Fifth Bureau that it rapidly co-ordinated plans for similar 'revolutionary' parades to be organised throughout towns and villages across Algeria, an attempt to consolidate the military coup that had met strong resistance from Prefects and some generals in Kabylia, Oran and Constantine. On 20 May the Fifth Bureau sent out an urgent telex to commanders of the three army corps (Algiers, Oran, Constantine):

BEFORE SUCCESS ALREADY RECORDED PARTICIPATION MUSLIM WOMEN IN DEMONSTRATIONS OF NATIONAL REGENERATION – PRIMO – SUPPORT TO MAXIMUM PARTICIPATION FEMALE POPULATION FROM ALL BACKGROUNDS IN ALL MASS DEMONSTRATIONS – STOP SECUNDO – ENCOURAGE PARTICIPATION OF UNVEILED MUSLIM WOMEN THROUGH APPLAUSE AND SIGNS OF SUPPORT – STOP. TERTIO – PREPARE ALL MOBILE MEDICO-SOCIAL TEAMS TO CREATE IMMEDIATELY WOMEN'S CIRCLES BRINGING TOGETHER EUROPEANS AND MUSLIMS – STOP AND END.[60]

The order was for the 'spontaneous' wave of emancipation to be extended throughout Algeria through organisations working at the local level, including the SAS, the EMSI, the newly created Committees of Public Safety and a secretly planned *Organisation de l'action civique* (OAC) which was to establish a 'total' control of population through an extension of Trinquier's DUP system to all towns and villages.[61]

In the interior the army coercion or manipulation of crowds was even more evident than in Algiers, and the military placed pressure on each SAS during what became known as Operation Lorry to organise trucks that would carry a minimum of twenty people from each village to a local rally. This contributed to a little known crisis in the ranks of the SAS, who saw this use of force as counterproductive and ruining several months' work, and seventy-five to eighty recalcitrant officers were removed and some of them sent back to France.[62] How these orders filtered down to isolated villages in the South-Oranais was recounted by a journalist for *Elle* magazine: two Muslim soldiers went in a jeep round all the scattered *douars* with an order from the local army Captain for a mass meeting next day. Several hundred silent men and a thousand women, highly excited by rumours of the Algiers 'fraternisation', were addressed by a widow who 'spontaneously' seized the microphone: 'In an instant, this woman electrified the audience. Without a veil, she faced up to the crowd, and with a stentorian voice spoke of peace'. All Muslim women, she said, were to become like their French sisters, and some women then unveiled themselves accompanied by shrill ululations.[63] An EMSI assistant, Ginette Thévenin-Copin, recounts how her company located in the Soummam valley received orders by radio on the eve of 18 May to organise a convoy of villagers to a rally in Sidi-Aïch. Thévenin-Copin and her colleagues spent the night making impromptu banners with white cloth and paints. Next day, 'Muslims arrive spontaneously from all the surrounding *douars*', and Thévenin-Copin was pleased to see large numbers of women of all ages present: 'it was a revelation, the first time since my arrival there that I saw the smiling, open faces of women: a moment worth waiting for that opened the door to hope, their optimism to see a better life one day'.[64]

However, the most elaborate ceremonials of unveiling, which made the biggest impact through the media, took place in a series of massive demonstrations organised by the army in the major towns from 18 May onwards. In particular the leaders of the military coup (Soustelle, Salan, Massu, Allard) and other generals and dignitaries, transported by helicopter, engaged in a lighting tour of Orléansville, Mostaganem, Blida, Boufarik, Oran, Philippeville, Bône, Sétif, Constantine, Tizi-Ouzou and Biskra between the 18 and 28 May. On each occasion an almost identical and theatrical *mise en scène* took place: groups of veiled women marched in mass parades through the streets alongside medalled Algerian ex-servicemen associations and *harkis* to the traditional locations of official ceremonial (central squares, town halls, war memorials). On arrival young female delegates, dressed either in a modern European style or with *haïks*, shared the rostrum or balconies with the generals and dignitaries and presented them with bouquets, before making speeches in favour of emancipation and casting their veils to the crowds.

Two of these parades, at Constantine (26 May) and Blida (28 May), are particularly revealing of the military structuring of these events. On Monday 26 May Soustelle, Dr Sid Cara and Generals Noguez, Gilles and Dulac made a rapid tour of 'fraternisation' demonstrations in Biskra, Bône and Constantine. In Constantine a young woman, Monique Améziane, read a prepared speech from the imposing balcony of the theatre, the headquarters of the CSP: 'I stand before you in a veil. But the definitive emancipation of Muslim women is on its way. Also, in

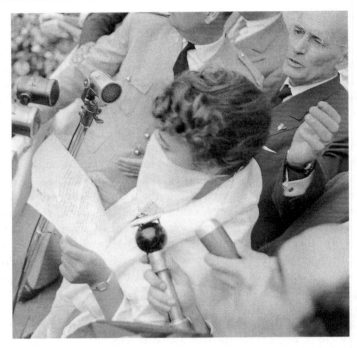

6 Monique Améziane reading the 'emancipation' text from the balcony of the
Constantine theatre, 26 May 1958

a symbolic gesture, I wish to open the way to our new existence so that
finally we can stand equal with our sisters of every confession'.

She then 'spontaneously' tore off her face veil and *haïk* and threw it to
the crowd below, where several women followed suit and ululated.[65]

Monique Améziane was an eighteen-year-old lycée student, the
daughter of a wealthy and pro-French *bachaga* who in April 1955 had
fled to Paris since he feared assassination by the FLN.[66] In his absence the
farm, managed by his son Mouloud, was used by the FLN as a support
base until it was seized by parachutists on about 20 April 1958 and
turned into what was to become the most infamous torture centre of the
Algerian War.[67] On 8 May Mouloud was arrested and tortured by the
army at the farm. Two weeks later army officers, who had been unable
to find any Muslim women to lead the unveiling ceremony, came to
find Monique Améziane at her lycée: her co-operation, they said, would
save the life of her brother and guarantee her ability to take the baccalaureate exams. For the demonstration on 26 May a seamstress fitted
Monique Améziane in Marianne style, with a blue dress and a tri-colour
rosette, over which she wore a veil and *haïk* for the first time in her life.

Key case
(la Ferme
Améziane)

Immediately after the demonstration she was taken to the farm to see her imprisoned brother who was released the following day.[68] The grim contradictions of the emancipation policy is shown by the fact that this was symbolised by Monique Améziane bedecked in classic republican and French revolutionary style while other women of Constantine, like Djamila Guellal and Zéléïkha Boukadoum, were subjected to torture and sexual degradation on the family farm that carried her name.[69]

The biggest propaganda coup of the army during the Constantine demonstration of 26 May was, however, a speech that Sheikh Lakhdari made alongside Monique Améziane just before her unveiling. Abdelali ben Ahmed Lakhdari, a religious leader of national and international importance, had been educated at the Zitouna university in Tunis before becoming in 1949 *imam* of the Sidi Kittani mosque and director of the *médersa* al-Kittania of Constantine, a centre that rivalled the famous neighbouring *Ulema* institute of Ben Badis.[70] French intelligence reports noted his 'certain loyalty' and he was cultivated by the government, like so many conservative religious leaders, through honorific rewards like the *Légion d'honneur* and material benefits, including inscription on the official list which provided him with free funding for the pilgrimage to Mecca. Documents seized on an FLN militant killed in Constantine on 20 August 1955 showed that Lakhdari was condemned to death for, 'collaboration with the enemy, opposition to the revolution, a first class traitor and renegade to his country and religion'. Twice during 1956–57 Lakhdari sought refuge over the border in Cairo and Libya.[71] A 1959 government telegram noted: 'his very considerable influence in Muslim milieu at national level and has incessantly shown favourable feelings for our cause'.[72]

In his speech Lakhdari praised France and the freedom of religious practice under its governance. In the drive for renovation in Algeria Muslim women had a special role: 'Know well, O woman, that the time has come for you to play your role in the history of the New Algeria! [. . .] God has said, "Women have the same rights and obligations as men"'. You are not 'a being who can be bought and sold . . . This imaginary and over-blown veil has nothing in common with the Muslim faith'.[73] This speech provided a considerable boost to the army propagandists: it was important to be able convince Algerians that women's emancipation was not part of a political agenda imposed by an atheistic colonial power, but was supported by Algerian religious leaders and compatible with the Koran. The journalist André Seguin recognised the importance of the speech by, 'one of the highest placed religious authorities in North Africa and the Muslim world',[74] and in following years Lakhdari's speech was to be constantly quoted in emancipation propaganda, on the radio and in government tracts.[75] In late 1958 the *imam* was also consulted by the government, along with other influential religious leaders, on the crucial reform of women's legal status (*statut personnel*) (chapter 8).

The second provincial 'fraternisation' rally of particular interest was that at Blida, to the south of Algiers, on 28 May when Generals Massu and Desjours took the podium before 30,000 demonstrators. During the usual orchestrated events, which included a fly-past of jets in a cross of Lorraine formation, a tiny fifteen-year-old girl called Malika 'spontaneously' forced an entry onto the stage and read to the microphone: 'I, I love the French . . . We are all united behind the Army and have sworn to fight to the end for Algeria and France to live together'.[76] Malika came from a relatively privileged and deeply pro-French family: she had received an education up to the school leaving certificate (CEP), her father was a foreman on a colon farm, and four of her brothers were serving in the French army, including two in parachute regiments. The Massus adopted Malika, an act that established a trend among other senior officers, and served as a symbol, the General claimed, for the principle of integration declared in the Forum during '13 May'.[77] Malika also played a part in the emancipation movement as a speaker for the *Mouvement de solidarité féminine* (MSF).[78] By 'integration' it would appear, however, that General and Madame Massu meant assimilation since they raised Malika as a Catholic rather than as a Muslim,[79] and as will be seen later emancipation did indeed involve the attempted social and cultural transformation of Algerians into Europeans.

How the FLN and the Algerian population, and in particular women, responded to the overall army emancipation campaign will be treated in chapters 9 and 10, but here I look at the more specific reactions to the '13 May' unveiling parades. There is some evidence from intelligence reports that the FLN leadership was disconcerted by the 'fraternisation' demonstrations,[80] which threatened to win over many Algerians, to impact on international opinion, and to bring de Gaulle, a formidable opponent, onto the side of the conspirators. The FLN newspaper *El Moudjahid*, in an article 'Operation "Fraternisation"' of 29 May, noted that although de Gaulle claimed to be impressed, the parades constituted a pure 'mise en scène' 'orchestrated with science and cynicism by a leading specialist in psychological action', Colonel Lacheroy. On the 18 May it was the SAU that had forced women to come to the Forum: not the hundreds announced by the press, but 'in fact twenty veiled women who were forced to attend by the military or their stupid war veteran husbands who obey orders. And there they timidly half-opened their veils, while here and there one could see several cleaning ladies firmly flanked by their European employers or by "patriotic" social assistants'.[81] *El Moudjahid* had a limited, clandestine circulation, so more important to FLN counter-propaganda were broadcasts from Morocco (*La Voix de l'Algérie libre*) and from Tunisia (*La Voix de l'Algérie soeur*) that detailed how demonstrators in Constantine, Bône, Algiers, Oran and elsewhere had been coerced and rounded up into army vehicles.[82]

What was the social, political and class background of the women on the unveiling demonstrations and how numerous were they? In general two categories of women can be distinguished: firstly relatively poor and illiterate women from the *bidonvilles* and slum enclaves of the city, who were most readily manipulated by the SAU and women's circles and who provided the main mass of the contingents that marched in procession into the Forum and other town centres. Secondly, the much smaller contingent of more educated, younger *evoluées* who can be categorised as radical modernisers or militants who provided the leadership for the first group and made the key speeches. *El Moudjahid* pointed mainly to the presence of the first group, domestic servants (*fatmas*), or cleaning ladies of the General Government and prostitutes.[83] The widespread claim of a deliberate recruitment of prostitutes probably reflects more a propaganda bias than any reality,[84] but some undoubtedly were domestic servants, of whom there were from 12 to 20,000 in the city, by far the largest category of employment for Algerian women in Algiers (70 to 80 per cent).[85] The dominant Algerian ideology was that women should not enter the labour market, but remain within the home raising children, a keen point of male honour since employment threatened to breach domestic seclusion, and those women who did have to work from necessity because they were single, repudiated or widows, what Willy Jansen calls aptly 'women without men', constituted a 'dangerous' or liminal category since they threatened to escape from male control of their sexuality.[86]

The most interesting and richest source of information on the mental universe of these poor, single women is provided by Caroline Brac de la Perrière's oral history project based on interviews with domestic servants. Firstly, it is interesting to note that five of the twenty women in the case study did not normally wear the veil at all, mainly because as single women they enjoyed a degree of independence and escaped the pressure of husbands or the wider kin group to conform. For example, Mme F., who was separated from her husband at this time and described herself laughingly in an interview as 'free' did not wear the veil, including when she went with friends to see the events in the Forum, although she did wear it later when she returned to live with her husband, 'to avoid trouble'.[87] The most common practice, as for the great majority of Algerian women in the city, was for the domestics to wear the veil in public spaces as they travelled from their homes in the *bidonvilles* to their place of work, where once indoors it was immediately removed.[88] Many Algerians, once they had crossed from 'Arab' zones into the highly segregated streets of the European quarters of the city, either the commercial centre or the bourgeois residential areas of the 'heights', would remove the *haïk* and stow it away in their handbag.[89]

What was perceived by Fanon and the film-maker Gillo Pontecorvo as a revolutionary innovation of women in the Battle of Algiers, the 'cross-dressing' into a European style so as to pass weapons through the parachutist check-points, was the extension of a current practice of Muslim women in the urban environment. Malika Ighilhariz, a courier, describes how the FLN provided her with a big American car:

> I was to be seen getting out of the car, dressed like a French woman; I went into a building where I put on my veil and small face veil, then came out veiled and went down to the Casbah. I deposited what I had to hand over and picked up whatever had to be taken out from the Casbah, messages, weapons. And played the same game in reverse. In the corridor of a building I removed the veil, retouched my lipstick, put on my glasses, I came out and got back into my fine car.[90]

In the European areas the women were protected by a certain anonymity, and could escape the attention of neighbours and kin or were protected from the verbal condemnation and physical violence of other Algerians and might even 'pass' as Europeans: as A. N., who lived in as a servant, noted, 'I did not wear the veil, no problem. Besides, I did not live in an Arab quarter so I had no problem at all'. In only one instance, that of Mme K. Z., is there evidence of a domestic coming under pressure from her employer to attend the Forum events, notably during de Gaulle's visit on 4 June, but she detested the General for killing 40,000 Algerians at Sétif and only pretended that she had been to the rally. Some Algerian women who participated in the unveiling campaign, noted K. Z., were said to have been bribed with semolina.[91] On one occasion she had passed weapons for the FLN hidden under her veil and on another occasion she was in a house raided by the army when she exacted a mocking revenge: a female agent was brought in to search all the women, 'I said: "Yes". I removed the veil, the scarf, I was going to take everything off. "Stop, stop". I said, "no, no, I'm getting undressed". "Stop, stop". Everyone laughed'. K. Z. illustrates an awareness of the complex, instrumental and ludic uses of the veil and expressed her resistance to the army unveiling campaign by pushing the act to an absurd level of total nudity.[92]

Such evidence provides a small but valuable window into the complex universe and dress codes of Algerian women for whom the veil could assume a whole range of styles, of meanings, of bodily expression and symbolism. As David Macey notes, the *haïk* is subject to modification: it can be made of cotton, silk or artificial fibre; be held around the body or face in different ways; and 'her sisters recognize an individual by the way she holds herself and wears her *haïk*; Algerian men learn to do the same'.[93] All the French press, radio and official accounts refer to 'unveiling' as if it involved a single and uniform act, the discarding of one, often indeterminate, item of clothing. However, Algerian women wore both a small, triangular face-covering (*hadjar*) held in place by elastic, and the lose *haïk* wrapped round the body and over the head, and the many hundreds of press photographs taken during the 'fraternisation' ceremonies show those who paraded into the Forum and squares engaged in a variety of highly expressive acts: some slipped the *haïk* round their shoulders, but retained the face veil, some removed the veil, but clutched the *haïk* or put their hands in front so as to conceal their face, others lowered both veil and *haïk* to shoulder level, while a very small number removed the *haïk* entirely. But the great majority of the veiled women who paraded into the Forum and elsewhere did not engage in any uncovering whatsoever, including most of the women delegates from Mahiéddine that appeared on the balcony of the General Government alongside Soustelle on 18 May.[94] Frequently the Algerian press was so keen to record the success of the campaign that some photographs of massed ranks of marching or assembled women, all of them entirely covered up, carried captions in total contradiction with the visual evidence: 'they were all unveiled' or the reader was reassured, 'note that later these demonstrators all unveiled themselves'.[95] Observers also noted that of the women who did, under the pressure of the moment, lower their veil or *haïk*, many were seen to replace them as soon after the event as possible. In general, the unveiling ceremonials, contrary to the impression given by the media, did not initiate a dramatic and lasting transformation of veiling practices.

If Algerian women were reluctant to unveil, this has been usually ascribed to religio-cultural factors and the psychological shock of exposure that was subjectively experienced as a form of gross nudity. As the psychiatrist Fanon noted, 'The veil protects, reassures, isolates . . . The unveiled body seems to escape control, to fall to pieces. The feeling of being badly dressed, even of being naked . . . A horrifying sensation of disintegration'.[96] But for many women this was more than a state of mind since they really were 'badly dressed'. The *haïk*, a kind of cheap uniform, enabled destitute women to move in public with some degree of self-confidence when their undergarments were worn, patched and, by European standards, even indecent. At the mass unveiling of 18 May in the Forum women shouted, 'Give us clothes so that we can dress like our European sisters!' and the next day the radio appealed to European women to take their second-hand clothing to local police stations for Muslim women who wanted to abandon their traditional costume.[97]

A far more immediate and dangerous political reality also underlay this reticence. Low-status women who moved about unveiled in public spaces were morally suspect and generally equated with prostitutes, but such condemnation was massively reinforced during the course of the war since wearing European dress was associated with anti-national religious apostasy and, even more dangerously, as a sign of working directly with Europeans.[98] The policy of the FLN nationalists was to drive a wedge between the European and Algerian communities through strike actions, boycotts (alcohol, tobacco), destruction of schools and creation of a parallel 'state' structure or OPA (FLN law courts and justice, social services) so as to block any attempt by French reformist programmes to build links, and retain influence over, the population. For any Muslim woman to be seen anywhere near to, or associated with, Europeans, the army or government institutions, was to run the risk of being regarded as a potential collaborator and spy. Mme F., a domestic, was forced to travel to work in an army lorry, 'I did not like this since I was afraid that the others on seeing me with them would think that I was passing on information', and when her son was rushed to a military hospital this was 'annoying because they could think I was an informer'.[99] Mme B., a Europeanised Kabyle Protestant who did not wear the veil, was treated at work by others with derision as an apostate ('m'tournia'), 'They criticized me a lot because I went out without a veil'. This became particularly threatening when she travelled from the European into the Algerian urban zones: 'I went down with a neighbour into the Arab quarter, we went together because of my European looks [for protection]. I suffered because they thought I was Spanish; they spoke in Arabic, I replied in French. There were some who asked why then did I speak Kabyle'.[100] In the street passers by said to Mme F., who did not wear the haïk, 'Why have you removed your veil? Are you becoming French?'.[101] This could potentially become very dangerous and as the spiral of violence deepened after 1954 Algerian women were frequently accosted and badly assaulted on their way to or from their European workplace. The FLN ordered women to stop working for Europeans, although the ALN commander Azzedine stated that officially they were tolerant of the poor who were reliant on this income and even recruited some domestics as informers on European activities.[102]

In general very poor and needy women who worked for Europeans were left undisturbed by the FLN, but it was quite a different matter for such a strata to join the mass of the *haïk*-clad ranks that paraded through town centres. A report of the French secret service (SDECE) noted that the heads of Wilaya V (Oran region) had sent out an order banning any participation in 'fraternisation' parades and to oppose the '"pseudo evolution of the Muslim women" and to forbid in the name of religion participation in all demonstrations . . . According to the FLN the Muslim women who had participated in demonstrations with their faces uncovered, had been forcibly unveiled by French soldiers'. Three hundred grenades were to be sent into the urban centres to increase commando attacks.[103] Captain Bernhardt, the head of the SAU of Belcourt and a keen advocate of psychological action, in a detailed report on the events of May, noted that eighty lorries and seven cars had been used by the SAU to transport ex-servicemen and 300 women to the Forum on 18 May, while another 500 women had attended the demonstration to greet de Gaulle on 4 June. He was enthusiastic about the joyful atmosphere and dancing among the women at these events, 'despite the threats and insults that several young trouble-makers showered on the women', mainly unemployed and turbulent youths aged eighteen to twenty-five. Attempts had been made to combat this through the formation of two auto-defence groups who were currently helping the SAU to 'purge the quarter'. Most women, claimed Bernhardt with the usual exaggerated optimism of army reports, wished for 'progress but the male reaction is violent and paralyses their desire for change by threats of divorce, some instances of which have already been put into effect'.[104] The sense of this is ambiguous, but would seem to point to husbands who were angry because the protesting women had drawn down the ire of the nationalist community and threatened their own honour and position as males that were expected to keep 'their females in order'. Overall, it can be seen that for lower-class women to participate in army demonstrations was a quite risky thing to do and, although the FLN would not seek to assassinate them (it recognised that these illiterate women were victims of coercion), most women would seek to avoid involvement or, in the last resort, to cling to their veils and to conceal their identity.

Finally, turning to the second but much smaller category of more proactive and radical modernisers, it can be seen that they were in a far more vulnerable position because of their higher level of visibility, more prominent leadership and unambiguous political embrace of the French cause. The so-called *évoluées* constituted an elite strata, characteristically young women aged from about sixteen to thirty, well-educated by Algerian standards and from relatively well-off families, who could fall into two opposing camps according to differing circumstances: militant idealists who supported *either* the struggle for national independence

or its radical opposite, assimilation into western culture. Teenage girls
who ended up on opposite sides often began by sharing a similar French
culture and wish for progress towards a future modern society in which
women would enjoy equality and cast aside the most conservative features of Muslim patriarchal oppression (see chapter 1 on young UDMA
militants). The origins of this divide can be found in differing family
backgrounds: on the one hand were young women from well-off families whose interests were wedded to those of the French because they
benefited in various ways from rewards or employment by the colonial
state (functionaries in the central and local government, secondary and
higher level teachers, employees of large companies, etc.), and on the
other, the families of small shop keepers and businessmen who sustained
a 'traditional' Arab cultural nationalism and had little economic stake
in the colonial regime. For the pro-French radical liberation of women
would be achieved through integration, a total embrace of republican
secularism and western civilisation, while for the nationalists this goal
would be achieved through revolutionary liberation from colonialism
and a newly independent order.

This division manifested itself during the unveiling campaign of
May 1958. As has been seen, Monique Améziane, the daughter of a
wealthy pro-French *bachaga*, got caught in the cross-fire: on returning
to her lycée after her notable unveiling and speech from the balcony
of the Constantine Theatre, she was praised by French pupils, 'but the
young Muslim girls tore her Gaffiot dictionary'. Her father wrote in a
panic to criticise his wife for allowing this to happen: 'You have signed
the death warrant of my daughter', but she was saved from possible
assassination because local people knew that she had been coerced.[105]
Monique Améziane was more of an exception, since the army found
many other young *évoluées*, mostly coming from wealthy families that
were protected by their location within the bourgeois European areas
of the city, or the largely European-dominated sectors of local government and business, who were prepared to engage with a flamboyant and
'revolutionary' zeal in attacking the perceived medieval symbols of religious oppression. A journalist described a characteristic manifestation
of the radical modernisers during the 'fraternisation' parade at Boufarik
on 19 May, 'Young girls dressed in European style took the tribunal
by assault and came to shake Soustelle's hand!'.[106] These *évoluées*,
noted Fanon, along with the ex-servicemen, 'are the shock troops
instructed to destroy the cultural resistance of a colonised land'.[107] The
photographs taken during the burning of veils on the night of 17 May,
perhaps the most provocative iconoclastic act, show the leadership role
of two slightly older Algerian women, distinguished by their more chic

European dress, encouraging the girls to throw *haïks* onto the flames (see illustration 3, p. 128). Behind the group in the shadows is a heavily armed *harki* guard.

An older and less headstrong group of *évoluées* was symbolised by the three Algerian women who were elected as deputies to the national assembly in November 1958, Nafissa Sid Cara, Rebiha Kebtani and Khedira Bouabsa: a proclamation issued by Wilaya II in 1959 warned against these unveiled women, 'and similar traitors to religion and the father-land', depraved beings who haunted dance halls and cabarets, and asked that names of such collaborators be handed to FLN militants.[108] The radical supporters of France were potentially far more at risk from the FLN than the illiterate women who took part anonymously in the parades: the wish for revenge ran high, and when the ALN army finally occupied Algiers at independence in July–August 1962 the soldiers, in a climate redolent of the 1944 Liberation when women accused of collab-orationism or sleeping with Germans were subjected to public humilia-tion, engaged in a hunt for unveiled women, the 'girls of 13 May', and 'girls of the paras'.[109]

In an opposite camp to the pro-French activists were the young nationalist *évoluées* who responded to the unveiling campaign by leaping to the defence of Muslim dress codes and cultural-religious identity that needed to be saved from the depredations of western secu-larism. During the baccalaureate exams in June 1958 female students wore the veil, something never seen before and in defiance of an official ban.[110] The FLN claimed that more Algerian women were now wearing the veil in the street as a symbol of patriotism,[111] but such an instru-mentalisation of the veil could, in this instance, only have applied to the very small number of urban women who had previously *not* worn the *haïk*. The inverse relationship is provided by Monique Améziane, forced by the army to wear a *haïk* for the first time, so that she could participate in an orchestrated unveiling. Fanon pointed to such forms of symbolic resistance in relation to the Moroccan nationalist move-ment in which women began to wear black instead of traditional white veils, but he seems to have had an inkling that such a defensive cultural agenda in Algeria might reinforce conservative social and cultural practices[112] and impede the revolutionary transformation of gender roles that he hoped to see develop under the impact of the struggle for independence, a foreboding that proved tragically correct (see chapters 10 and 11).

In conclusion, how far were the army-led unveiling parades of May 1958 a success? Despite the evident orchestration, there appear to have been many high-level officers and politicians who were bowled over by the events and referred to them in an emotionally charged and even quasi-religious language as a 'miracle' or 'resurrection'. Fanon refers to Europeans who were 'overexcited' and evoked a psychology of 'conversion' to explain the climate of euphoria.[113] This derived in part from the feeling of relief that four years of war would end in both reconciliation and preservation of *Algérie française*, as well as from the neo-fascist and fundamentalist (*intégriste*) Catholic convictions of the plotters that the French nation had been rescued from the moral and political decadence of the Fourth Republic. Commander Cogniet, an expert on psychological warfare, wrote, 'it is Christ who is coming and who demands this liberty, demands this equality, who calls to the Roman citizens that . . . men are brothers, and it is this that the revolutionaries call Fraternity'.[114]

But the most crucial political impact of all was that 'fraternisation' should serve to persuade de Gaulle to 'offer his services' as saviour at the moment when the plotters were very much at risk of failure and being arrested by the Pflimlin government. De Gaulle did not wish to be associated with a military coup that would damage his democratic credentials, whereas a huge, populist appeal by both settlers and Algerians could provide the needed legitimacy for an extra-parliamentary seizure of power. The General had little time for the theory of psychological warfare or 'integration',[115] and he frequently asked trusted army officers whether 'fraternisation' was indeed spontaneous and genuine. They assured him that it was, and this was enough to persuade the General to come on board: during his famous speech in the Algiers Forum on 4 June he said, 'I know what has happened here . . . I can see that the route you have opened in Algeria is that of renewal and fraternity'.[116] De Gaulle, desperate to end his years in the political wilderness, was opportunely affected by a willing suspension of disbelief, but once ensconced in power he wished to break away from the hold of the army and so reopened the question in his entourage on 28 June: 'It is advisable to verify if these demonstrations, moving as they were, really correspond with the deeper feelings of the Muslim masses'.[117] But for the army command in Algeria and for Colonels Lacheroy, Goussault and Trinquier, the ideologues of the Fifth Bureau, there was no stepping back and the *journées* of 13 May immediately gave a massive impetus to a 'reconquest' of the Muslim population as signalled by a directive sent by Salan to all civil and military authorities throughout Algeria on 2 June.[118] Central to this was the emancipation of Algerian women and the next chapters investigate three aspects of this 'strategy of contact', the role of propaganda and the mass media, of the urban-based MSF, and of the EMSI teams in the rural outback (*bled*).

Notes

1 For an account of the events see Horne, *Savage War*, 273–98.
2 Merry and Serge Bromberger, *Les 13 Complots du 13 mai* (Paris: A. Fayard, 1959).
3 There is a huge literature on '13 May', but recommended for the background to the plot is Christophe Nick, *Résurrection: naissance de la Ve République, un coup d'état démocratique* (Paris: Fayard, 1998); and Odile Rudelle, *Mai 58: De Gaulle et la République* (Paris: Plon, 1988).
4 Jacques Massu, *Le Torrent et la Digue: Alger du 13 mai aux barricades* [1972] (Paris: Éditions du Rocher, 1997 edn), 37–54.
5 Many contemporary, press and historical accounts of the complex series of 'fraternisations' reflect a high degree of confusion and error as to the sequence of events and the dates on which they occurred: journalists, for example, who were absent from Algiers frequently drew up reports from press or army agencies as if they were present, so repeating a cascade of mistakes as to the chronology. David Macey, *Franz Fanon. A Life* (London: Granta Books, 2000), 402, notes that Fanon in *L'An V de la révolution algérienne* made the 'extraordinary slip' of placing the unveiling events of 16 May on the 13 May, but Macey in turn makes the error of situating this demonstration, as do many other historians, on 16 May when in reality it took place on 18 May. The following account reconstructs the framework from two key sources: the many hundreds of pictures and typed reports of army photographers deposited in the ECPAD archives, and 10,662 pages of fifteen Paris-based and ten Algerian newspapers for the period 10 April–2 June 1958 reproduced by the *Service internationale de microfilms*, which was consulted at the British Library (Colindale), M. misc. 39–53.
6 Horne, *Savage War*, 293.
7 Massu, *Le Torrent*, 52–3.
8 *Ibid.*, 89, 'de Gaulle could only commit himself if he knew that the Muslims were also calling for him'.
9 Jacques Romain-Desfossés, 'A la conquête des coeurs', *Historia Magazine, la guerre d'Algérie*, 347 (October 1973), 2869–75.
10 Henry d'Humières, *L'Armée française et la jeunesse musulmane: Algérie 1956–1961* (Paris: Godfroy de Bouillon, 2002), 155.
11 Jean Lacouture, *De Gaulle: The Ruler, 1945–1970* (London: Harper Collins, 1991), 169; Horne, *Savage War*, 291.
12 See the tortured contradictions in Massu, *Le Torrent*, 86–90 where he denies that the action was 'concerted and teleguided', and then indicates in detail how it was orchestrated by the army.
13 The role of this group during '13 May' can be reconstructed, in addition to the archives, from various sources, including: Villetoux and Villetoux, *La République*; Courrière, *La Guerre d'Algérie*, Vol. 2; Roger Trinquier, *Le Coup d'état du 13 mai* (Paris: Esprit nouveau, 1962) and *Le Temps perdu*

(Paris: Albin Michel, 1978); Paul-Alain Léger, *Aux carrefours de la guerre* (Paris: Albin Michel, 1983).

14 Serge Chakotin, *The Rape of the Masses. The Psychology of Totalitarian Political Propaganda* (London: George Routledge, 1940), first published in Paris as *Le Viol des foules* in 1939. The application of Chakotin's theory by the Fifth Bureau can be found in SHAT 1H2460/1, *Étude sur une campagne de fraternisation en Algérie* (undated).

15 Villatoux and Villatoux, *La République*, 82–3, 426–9, 442–6, 487–9, 494–6.

16 *Ibid.*, 421.

17 *Ibid.*, 465, 468–9, on veterans (along with women, youth and village notables) as one of the four key social categories targeted by the Fifth Bureau.

18 Massu, *Le Torrent*, 93.

19 Roger Trinquier, *La Guerre moderne* (Paris: Éditions de la table ronde, 1961), 53–5. Each habitation was painted with the equivalent of a modern postal code to enable easy and rapid identification by the intelligence services: a photograph in Courrière, *La Guerre d'Algérie*, Vol. 2, shows a building in the Casbah with such a code, '10A8'.

20 Jean-Charles Jauffret, *Soldats en Algérie, 1954–1962. Expériences contrastées des hommes du contingent* (Paris: Éditions Autrement, 2000), 180; the Minister of Defence, Chaban-Delmas, was so concerned by the growth of this fascistic militia that on 14 November 1957 he removed Trinquier to France.

21 Massu, *Le Torrent*, 86–7.

22 Claude Paillat, *Deuxième dossier secret de l'Algérie, 1954–1958* (Paris: Presses de la Cité, 1962), 532.

23 The political importance of 'fraternisation' on 16–18 May was accentuated by the fact that it was organised, and helped turn the tide in favour of the coup, at the very moment that the Gaullist plotters in Algiers seemed most vulnerable and even risked arrest by Salan who was threatening to support the Paris government: see Rudelle, *Mai 58*, 184–9.

24 Trinquier, *Le Coup d'état*, 140–2; Léger, *Aux carrefours*, 320–1.

25 Paillat, *Deuxième dossier*, 533–5; Massu, *Le Torrent*, 88–9, 93.

26 *Le Monde*, 24 May 1958; *L'Humanité*, 24 May 1958; *Manchester Guardian*, 24 May 1958; Henri Alleg (ed.), *La Guerre d'Algérie* (Paris: Temps actuels, 1981), Vol. 3, 51; André Debatty, *Le 13 Mai et la presse* (Paris: Armand Colin, 1960), 308–9; Marc Ferro (ed.), *Le 13 Mai 1958. Les Médias et l'événement* (Paris: La Documentation Française, 1985), 54. Forcing participation on demonstrations by confiscating identity cards was a technique used by inter-war authoritarian or fascist regimes in Spain and elsewhere.

27 The best source as to the demonstration, its all-male nature, slogans, etc., are sixty-three photographs taken by two official army photographers Vandy and Michalowki, see ECPAD ALG/58/235 to 237.

28 Goussault was also credited with the creation of the *Mouvement de solidarité feminine*, CAOM 13CAB61.

29 SHAT 1H2461/1*, Letters received by *Magazine de la femme*. One of the letters to 'Nadira' sent by a listener Mademoiselle C. Z. of M'Sila was undoubtedly bogus since it was identical to that from a young women of Tlemcen published in the UDMA journal *La République algérienne* on 30 October 1953 (see chapter 1).

30 CAOM 14CAB162, petition 8 April 1958.

31 CAOM 14CAB162, General Massu, Fifth Bureau, 26 April 1958.

32 CAOM 14CAB233, minutes of Commission administrative du Département d'Alger, 7 May 1958.

33 See the map and analysis of social structure for the Kabyle village of Aït Hichem in Bourdieu, *The Algerians*, 14–15.

34 Tillion, *Le Harem et les cousins*.

35 See especially Abrous, *L'Honneur face au travail des femmes*, 119–20. For the astonishing range of western and traditional clothing worn in the Maghreb by individual women in different locations and contexts see the interviews and photographs, especially of Saadia Bouhaddou and Rabia Taibi, in Baker, *Voices of Resistance*, 183–201, 252–66. It can be noted that Algerian males too could alter dress code according to changing context; thus early labour migrants to France slipped from the village at night to put on European clothing before taking the ferry, and reversed this on their return home, see MacMaster, *Colonial Migrants*, 73.

36 Captain L. P. Fauque, *Stades d'évolution de la cellule familiale musulmane d'Algérie*, 19, a printed pamphlet (restricted) of the General Government, 20 May 1959: copies can be located at SHAT 1H112/3 or CAOM 2SAS7.

37 There is a considerable literature on the symbolism and politics of the veil: in addition to the seminal work of Edward Said, *Orientalism*, see for example, Rana Kabbani, *Imperial Fictions. Europe's Myths of Orient* (London: Pandora, 1988); Reina Lewis, *Gendering Orientalism. Race, Femininity and Representation* (London: Routledge, 1995); Ahmed, *Women and Gender in Islam*; Fatima Mernissi, *Beyond the Veil: Male-Female Dynamics in Muslim Society* [1975] (London: Al Saqi Books, 1985 edn); Fadwa El Guindi, *Veil. Modesty, Privacy and Resistance* (Oxford: Berg, 1999); Unni Wikan, *Behind the Veil in Arabia, Women in Oman* [1982] (Chicago: University of Chicago Press, 1991 edn). On the erotic and pornographic postcards and images of unveiled women see, Malek Alloula, *The Colonial Harem* (Manchester: Manchester University Press, 1987); Leïla Sebbar and Jean-Michel Belorgey, *Femmes d'Afrique du Nord. Cartes postales (1885–1930)* (Saint-Pouçain-sur-Sioule: Bleu autour, 2002); Carole Naggar, 'The Unveiled: Algerian Women', *Aperture*, 119 (Summer 1990), reprinted in Liz Heron and Val Williams (eds), *Illuminations. Women Writing on Photography from the 1850s to the Present* (London: I. B. Tauris, 1996), 422–6.

38 Françoise Gaspard and Farhad Khosrokhavar, *Le Foulard et la République* (Paris: La Découverte1995); Sharif Gemie, 'Stasi's Republic: The School

and the "Veil", December 2003–March 2004', *Modern and Contemporary France*, 12: 3 (2004), 387–97; Neil MacMaster and Toni Lewis 'Orientalism: From Unveiling to Hyperveiling', *Journal of European Studies*, 28: 109–10 (March–June 1998), 121–35.

39 Salem, 'Islam and the Status of Women in Tunisia', 149–50.

40 *Ibid.*, 141–7; Borrmans, *Statut personnel*, 123–46.

41 On this event, including a photograph of Lalla Aïcha unveiled at the microphone, see Baker, *Voices of Resistance*, 50–4; there are also photographs of her with other Moroccan delegates, all in western dress, at the 1957 Congress of Arab Women in Damascus, pp. 29, 81.

42 Massell, *Surrogate Proletariat*; Northrop, *Veiled Empire*.

43 Massell, *Surrogate Proletariat*, 226–46, 262–3; see Northrop, *Veiled Empire*, 85–6, 180, 316, 340–1 for photographs of mass rallies and burning or removal of veils.

44 Borrmans, *Statut personnel*, 93.

45 ECPAD, ALG 58/241, two of the nine photographs can be found in Massu, *Le Torrent*, 128. The likely identification with Lucienne Salan has been made through comparison with other known photographs of her.

46 Report of Jacques Perrier in *L'Aurore*, 3 September 1959.

47 Raoul Salan, Vol. 3, *Mémoires. Fin d'un empire* (Paris: Presses de la Cité, 1972), 321.

48 Massu, *Le Torrent*, 102.

49 Army photographers Michalowsky, Vandy, Daudu and Boissay took 102 pictures in all, which enable a close reconstruction of the events, see ECPAD ALG58 251. From these and other press photographs and reports it is possible to identify other groups from Mahiéddine (CSP), Clos-Salembier (SAU), Hussein-Dey (SAU), Maison-Carrée (SAU), Kouba, Belcourt (SAU), Haut-Casbah (SAU), Basse-Casbah (SAU), Public-Fontaine (CSP), Tagarine, Champ-de-Manoeuvre, El-Biar, Birmandreis. The location and urban structure of these places can be found from maps and data in Descloitres et al., *L'Algérie des bidonvilles*, 41, 43, 63, 72–3.

50 *Paris Match*, 477 (31 May 1958), shows pictures of such unveiling by Europeans, one of which is reproduced in Todd Shepard, *The Invention of Decolonization. The Algerian War and the Remaking of France* (Ithaca: Cornell University Press, 2006), 188 (but incorrectly dated 16 May).

51 *La Dépêche quotidienne d'Algérie*, 19 May 1958.

52 The SAU was an extension of the system of rural-located SAS officers into urban centres, with the task of establishing close contact with the Algerian inhabitants of the most deprived slum zones.

53 *Le Figaro*, 19 May 1958, report of René Janon; *La Dépêche quotidienne d'Algérie*, 19 May 1958.

54 See Descloitres et al., *L'Algérie des bidonvilles*, 67–71.

55 SHAT 1H1215/3, report on Cité Mahiéddine, 1 February 1958.

56 See the photograph of the arrival of women from the Cité Mahiéddine in the Forum, Debatty, *Le 13 Mai*, 155.

57 *L'Écho d'Alger*, 19 May 1958.
58 *La Dépêche quotidien d'Algérie*, 19 May 1958.
59 *La Dépêche de Constantine*, 19 May 1958.
60 SHAT 1H2461/1.
61 SHAT 1H2460/1, Salan directive 2 June 1958 to civil and military authorities; on the OAC see SHAT 1H2467/2, dossier 'Organisation voulant developer l'esprit du 13 mai 1958'; FNSP, fonds Beuve-Méry 139, Directive No. 38 du Cabinet Civil, 9 June 1958, Annexe No. 3 relative à l'organisation et au contrôle des populations; and Villatoux and Villatoux, *La République*, 472.
62 FSNP – Fonds Beuve-Méry, BM 139, intelligence from an officer in Algeria, note dated 30 June 1958.
63 Report by 'S.F.' in *Elle* magazine, October 1958 (SHAT 1H1147/1).
64 Ginette Thévenin-Copin, *Plaidoyer pour la paix* (Montpellier: Mémoire de Notre Temps, 2001), 77–8.
65 *La Dépêche quotidienne d'Algérie*, *L'Écho d'Alger* and *La Dépêche de Constantine*, 27 May 1958. The speech was also broadcast by radio.
66 Jean-Luc Einaudi, *La Ferme Améziane. Enquête sur un centre de torture pendant la guerre d'Algérie* (Paris: L'Harmattan, 1991), 87–90. The Prefect, Maurice Papon, visited the Améziane estate frequently during 1949–51 and in 1954 the *bachaga* was decorated with the *Légion d'Honneur* by François Mitterrand, Minister of the Interior.
67 Pierre Vidal-Naquet, 'Rapport sur la Ferme Améziane' (February 1961) in *La Raison d'État* (Paris: Éditions de Minuit, 1962), 284–7; Raphaëlle Branche, *La Torture et l'armée pendant la guerre d'Algérie, 1954–1962* (Paris: Gallimard, 2001), 268–77. Mauss-Copeaux, *A Travers le Viseur*, 100, has a photograph of a naked, skeletal prisoner at Améziane in 1959 being jeered at by guards.
68 Einaudi, *Ferme Améziane*, 100, 105–6: accounts based on interviews with Mouloud and Monique Améziane, September–October 1987.
69 Einaudi, *Ferme Améziane*, 11–23.
70 On this *médersa*, at which the future president Houari Boumédienne was a student, see McDougall, *History*, 69, note 23.
71 CAOM 13CAB7, notice individuelle, 1958.
72 CAOM 14CAB9*, (secret) telegram 6 May 1959.
73 *La Dépêche quotidienne d'Algérie*, 27 May 1958.
74 André Seguin, 'Vers l'émancipation de la femme musulmane', *La Dépêche quotidienne d'Algérie*, 27 May 1958.
75 For example, CAOM 13CAB61, transcript of a women's programme broadcast in French and Arabic, 13 November 1958 and 7 December 1958; CAOM 81F74, a resolution to de Gaulle from forty-seven Algerian women of the Hussein-Dey Cercle féminine 29 September 1958 which requested, after their first ever vote in the referendum of 28 September, full equal rights with men and quoted from the Lakhdari speech.
76 Massu, *Le Torrent*, 107.

77 *Ibid.*, 114, 117; the book is dedicated in the name of 'integration' to his natural daughter Véronique, and his two adopted Algerian children Malika and Rodolphe.

78 *Ibid.*, 247.

79 See the photograph of Malika wearing a cross at the confirmation of Véronique, *ibid.*, 264.

80 CAOM 81F888: SDECE report 31 May 1958 indicates confusion and perplexity among the 'internal' FLN in Algeria at the 'fraternisation' campaign.

81 *El Moudjahid*, 24 (29 May 1958).

82 CAOM 81F367 and 81F888, transcripts of radio intercepts, 6 June and 11 July 1958.

83 *El Moudjahid*, 26 (4 July 1958).

84 General Bollardière, the only high-ranking officer to resign over the issue of torture, claimed 'pimps and prostitutes of the Casbah were brought in by lorry', *Nouvel Observateur*, 368 (29 November 1971), quoted by Massu *Le Torrent*, 94; although Léger, *Aux carrefours*, 322, hints that prostitutes from the main 'red light' area of the Casbah offered their support.

85 Brac de la Perrière, *Derrière les Héros*, 40.

86 Jansen, *Women Without Men*; and 'The Economy of Religious Merit: Women and *Ajr* in Algeria', *The Journal of North African Studies*, 9: 4 (Winter 2004), 1–17.

87 Brac de la Perrière, *Derrière les Héros*, 274–5.

88 *Ibid.*, 296.

89 *Ibid.*, 259; Léger, *Aux carrefours*, 231.

90 Amrane-Minne, *Des femmes*, 149.

91 See Fanon, *L'An V*, 20: 'It was primarily poor and starving women who were laid siege to. Every kilo of semolina handed out corresponded to a dose of indignation against the veil and confinement'.

92 *Ibid.*, 233–41.

93 Macey, *Frantz Fanon*, 406–7; he makes reference to Rachida Tita, *La Galerie des absents. La Femme algérienne dans l'imaginaire masculine* (La Tour d'Aigue: Éditions de l'Aube, 1996).

94 Photograph in *L'Écho d'Alger*, 19 May, showing only about one in ten of the delegation with their head uncovered.

95 *La Dépêche de Constantine* 23 and 24 May 1958.

96 Fanon, *L'An V*, 42.

97 *La Dépêche quotidienne d'Algérie* 12 August 1959; Debatty, *Le 13 Mai*, 154.

98 The *Ulema* had as early as 1944 preached against young women who worked as domestics for Europeans since this led to cultural assimilation and undermined Arab-Islamic identity: see Kaddache, *Histoire du nationalisme*, 672.

99 Brac de la Perrière, *Derrière les Héros*, 250, 252.

100 *Ibid.*, 265–7.
101 *Ibid.*, 275.
102 *Ibid.*, 145–7, 308–9.
103 CAOM 81F888, SDECE report, 6 June 1958.
104 CAOM 2SAS53, Bernhardt, *Bulletin de Renseignements. Mai 1958*, 7 June 1958.
105 Einaudi, *La Ferme Améziane*, 106–7.
106 *La Dépêche quotidien d'Algérie*, 20 May 1958.
107 Fanon, *L'An V*, 21.
108 Meynier, *Histoire intérieure*, 227; on the three deputies see Seferdjeli, 'French "Reforms"', 47–54.
109 *Ibid.*, 643. On the Liberation see Fabrice Virgili, *Shorn Women: Gender and Punishment in Liberation France* (Oxford: Berg, 2002). There exists little information on the number of Algerian women who were assaulted or killed during the violent lynching of *harkis* and other 'traitors' during 1962.
110 *Vie Catholique Illustrée*, 30 November 1958.
111 *El Moudjahid*, 26 (4 July 1958).
112 Fanon, *L'An V*, 30–2.
113 *Ibid.*, 24.
114 Villatoux and Villatoux, *La République*, 540; and for an overall assessment of the 'fraternisation' strategy in May 1958, see 471–5, 488–91, 550–2.
115 Rudelle, *Mai 58*, 59.
116 Michèle Cointet, *De Gaulle et l'Algérie française, 1958–1962* (Paris: Perrin, 1996), 46–7.
117 *Ibid.*, 47.
118 SHAT 1H2460/1, Salan directive 2 June 1958 for an acceleration of action at all levels in order to achieve 'integration' and to profit from 'the present psychological climate'.

4

The propaganda offensive and the strategy of contact

The French army faced a major problem in its campaign of emancipation, how to reach out to the mass of over four million women, 98 per cent of whom were illiterate and scattered over the surface of a huge territory in villages or secluded settlements that were hours away by foot or donkey from the nearest roads. As we have seen (chapter 2) during 1957 Operation Pilot tested integrated methods of psychological action in the *bled* under the direction of itinerant propaganda officers, utilising tracts, slogans, loud-speaker lorries, mobile cinemas and other means of communication. This, and two further chapters, examine in more detail three key dimensions of the accelerating attempts at bridge-building, a 'strategy of contact': firstly, this chapter looks at the role of mass media communication (print, film and radio) which was developed centrally by the government and military to reach women across the entire geographical space of Algeria. This is followed by chapter 5 on the role of the MSF, local associations that operated mainly in the big cities and the smaller, European-dominated provincial towns; and chapter 7 on the mobile welfare teams (EMSI), which provided the main form of contact in the rural interior. This does not exhaust all of the multifarious ways in which the French attempted to transmit their ideas to the female population, but provides a fairly comprehensive picture of the overall strategies deployed by the colonial power.[1] Three questions can be asked of this propaganda offensive: what *techniques* or methods were deployed to maximise communication? What does the content tell us about the ideological message and the underlying model of emancipation that was diffused? And, lastly, did the propaganda have any lasting effect on Algerian women?

By the outbreak of the Algerian War in 1954 the French military had a long established theory and practice of propaganda as a necessary component of modern warfare. The First World War (1914–18) and the Russian Revolution of 1917 had ushered in the age of 'total war' and the standard military perception that the outcome of international conflict rested as much on the civilian populations that sustained war economies (now subject to direct attack, bombing and demoralising propaganda), as on the strength of regular armies. The growth of new forms of mass media, particularly film and radio, greatly increased the ability of states to develop powerful forms of propaganda that aimed covertly to alter or manipulate mass attitudes, frequently through non-rational processes (use of symbols, manipulation of emotions and prejudice).[2] The French state, like most western powers, had since the First World War established its own specialised organisations, mainly within the Ministry of Defence, to study, research and test methods of psychological warfare.[3] The French army, in its bid to counter the FLN and to win the battle for the 'hearts and minds' of the indigenous population, was thus able to draw upon a well-established 'science' of communication theory. The adaptation of psychological warfare to the specific conditions of the Algerian theatre, in which the Fifth Bureau (1957–60) played a dominant role, drew upon or merged two major contemporary currents of thinking. On the one hand there existed a sophisticated body of academic communication research, pioneered and financed by the US military after 1945, a field of psychological warfare that was linked to a multitude of social science programmes in social psychology, psephology, advertising, journalism, market research, behaviourism, radio and television studies and other related disciplines.[4] Such research was of considerable interest to the Fifth Bureau since it held out the promise of refining techniques that would shape the attitudes of target groups (in this instance women) by identifying their social characteristics, and testing and refining various propaganda techniques through effects research, opinion surveys, questionnaires and statistical analysis.

The second influence sprang from the context of the Cold War. During the early 1950s the Korean War had given rise to a 'brain-washing' panic in the west that 'Oriental' communism had found the means to assert a total control over the human mind using Pavlovian techniques.[5] Many French officers of the Fifth Bureau in Algeria had passed through the Vietcong retraining camps in 1954 and were impressed by such methods of psychological indoctrination.[6] The 1950s was an era in which behaviourist theories, which would today be viewed as crude or overly simplistic, held wide currency, and this translated into an acceptance among many propaganda specialists that it was certainly possible, using correct scientific techniques, to imprint upon, or transform, the mind-set of Algerian people so as to achieve a compliant psychology.[7]

The organisation of psychological warfare went through various complex changes in the course of the conflict, but the most important phase (with which this study is mainly concerned) corresponded with the period of domination by the powerful Fifth Bureau between its inception in early 1957 and its disbandment in February 1960. The Bureau consisted of a central body in the État-Major (HQ) of the 10th Army (10th Région Militaire) in Algiers, under the dual guidance of Colonel Lacheroy and Goussault, and later of Colonel Gardes, and which had three operational sections: *Études*, which studied doctrine and the key themes, aims and objectives, to be transmitted via action plans to the various army units; *Action*, which was concerned with media production, information and the methods of transmission (press, radio, film); and *Relations nationales*, which liaised with the national and international media.[8] In August 1957 the Minister of the Interior, Bourgès-Maunory, a keen advocate of psychological warfare, ordered that Fifth Bureau officers be attached to each of the three Army corps (Oran, Algiers, Constantine), and within the corps down as far as the battalion or sector level.[9] The tentacular Fifth Bureau came to constitute an extremely influential and quasi-autonomous 'parallel hierarchy' manned by the equivalent of Soviet political commissars, doctrinaire exponents of revolutionary warfare who infiltrated into every level of the armed forces.

While the governments in Paris and Algiers made the key decisions as to which propaganda campaigns were to be launched, in line with major political initiatives, the Fifth Bureau HQ undertook to research, develop and produce films, photographs, radio broadcasts, press releases and other media material, or to issue directives to the officers attached to the different levels of command on the style and manner of propaganda to be implemented at local level. To give just one example, the Fifth Bureau, influenced by behaviourist theory on conditioned reflexes and psychological imprinting, ascribed a particular importance to repetitive slogans which it tested on Algerians, since, it was claimed, 'the Muslim has different reactions from that of the European', according to age, background and other criteria. The key slogans were then relayed throughout the Fifth Bureau network to be used in leaflets, posters, banners and painted on road-side walls.[10] Such psychological testing of propaganda even extended to culture-specific theories of colour symbolism: for example, it was believed that Islamic tradition associated green with positive attributes (peace, happiness), while yellow was rather disliked, and the voting ballots for the referendum of September 1958 were printed white for a 'Yes' to de Gaulle, and violet, 'the colour of death', for a 'No'.[11]

However, it would be a mistake to accept the claims to 'scientific' methodology and professionalism at face value. There is much evidence to show that the senior 'experts' of the Fifth Bureau, all males and with long careers as army officers, held extremely doctrinaire opinions about revolutionary warfare, 'Orientalist' and male Eurocentric views of Algerian women, and had, in many instances, a shallow and quite amateurish knowledge of propaganda theory and research. For example, the major school of psychological warfare at Arzew, which between October 1957 and September 1959 trained 7,172 officers, was directed by Lieutenant-Colonel Bruges, and later by Colonel de Maison Rouge, neither of whom had any expertise in psychological warfare and had to undertake a crash-course reading of Jung, Mao Tse-tung, Marx, Lenin, Chakotin and other 'classics'.[12] Servier was highly scathing of the work of Bureau officers in the field which he likened to 'a mediocre publicity campaign mounted by amateurs full of good intentions', and few of the specialists that ran the Fifth Bureau could even speak Arabic or Berber and had to depend on interpreters.[13]

The task of developing forms of communication that could reach all Algerian women presented a formidable challenge. The 1954 census counted a total of 4,880,800 females, of which 83.65 per cent lived in rural areas, in most instances scattered over a huge landmass and located in isolated *douars* that were without electricity and road links. Yet it was particularly important to the army propaganda offensive that it reach into the *bled* since this contained not only the majority of women, but also the terrain in which the guerrilla forces of the ALN had their major support base. The overall level of female illiteracy was 98 per cent, and while attempts were made in the 1950s to rapidly expand basic education for girls, in 1954 only 10.7 per cent received any form of primary schooling. This meant that the army was faced with the problem of how to influence or persuade a female population that had an extremely low level of political education, no understanding of abstract western concepts (such as the meaning of 'democracy'), and were unable to read newspapers, posters and leaflets. Algerian women lived in an intensely oral and visual culture in which the main sources of daily information about the outside world derived primarily from the spoken word and rumour.

During 1960–61 the French government carried out a sophisticated survey, based on statistical analysis of a questionnaire, in an attempt to gauge the different channels through which Algerian women received political information, so that the army could more effectively use those methods of communication likely to reach the 'target' audience. The study, which was carried out by the *Laboratoire des sciences humaines appliquées* (LSHA) based in Algiers, although completed late in the war, provides an insight into mass media communication and Muslim women. The LSHA was established under the control of the *Comité d'action scientifique de défense nationale* (CASD) in Paris following an exploratory meeting of leading academics at the General Government in March 1960 under the chairmanship of General Guérin.[14] Guérin noted that a key objective of the initiative was to 'better inform the population of the *bled*', and the LSHA that undertook this task, which was created in October 1960, employed a small staff of trained academic psychologists. Among various projects carried out into the 'penetration and effectiveness of information in the Muslim milieu' was a survey of Algerian women that was to be based on 1,500 questionnaires carried out by fifty EMSI interviewers across Algeria and which were synthesised in August 1961 in a report, *Étude sur l'information en milieu musulmane féminine*.[15]

The report indicated a number of methodological weaknesses in the collection of the data and its analysis that was indicative of the problems of 'psychological profiling' of the female population. Firstly, the LSHA was dependent on the assistance of fifty EMSI teams to provide thirty questionnaire returns each, but the welfare assistants were not necessarily very well equipped to carry out this task and only 1,016 forms, rather than the 1,500 questionnaires planned, were actually returned. Of these 198 could not be utilised, leaving 818 forms. But the statistical analysis for these 818 women aged fifteen to eighty-five years revealed a very high percentage of blanks or 'non-returns' (NR) in relation to specific questions: for example in reply to the question, 'Do you read the newspaper or have it read to you?', about a half (46.3 per cent) made no reply. The director, Lacavalerie, was much exercised by this problem, since the statistics could be greatly falsified, and initially he tried to separate out, but without success, those women who did not reply since they were ignorant, from those who refused because they were suspicious or hostile towards the French. The EMSI were asked to make a note as to whether they thought each woman was favourable towards France, indifferent, distrustful or hostile, and some 30 per cent were placed in the last two categories of 'distrustful' or 'hostile'.[16] That about a third of women were negative or hostile towards the exercise is high, if we keep in mind that those questioned would have almost certainly been those in the 'pacified' zones who were best known to the EMSI and had volunteered to attend the women's circles regularly.

As will be seen later (chapter 6) there is a mass of evidence, from army reports and autobiographical accounts, of the extent to which enquiries by the French were met by an almost impenetrable wall of silence that became known as *attentisme*. For the Algerian population in general, the best form of self-defence when threatened from both sides, by the army and the FLN, was not to disclose one's personal

position. But in addition, the silence of women was reinforced by deeply
entrenched cultural values: it was held reprehensible for them to speak
at all in the presence of strangers or males, and certainly not on 'political' issues that were a male preserve. Reticence was not necessarily only
an expression of a colonial power relationship, of women who were terrified by the questions posed by an occupying force that often deployed
extreme force or repressive violence: Hélène Vandevelde-Daillière, in
a very similar opinion poll carried out in post-independence Algeria a
decade later, found it very difficult to gain access to women, and when
she did so was met with a high level of non-replies and of resistance.[17]
A third of rural women (30 per cent), Vandevelde-Daillière found,
thought politics was not the business of women, and another 26 per
cent that politics 'served no purpose'; only 11 per cent ever discussed
politics with somebody they knew, 39 per cent never did so, while 50
per cent refused or failed to answer the question.[18] The extraordinary
difficulty faced by the French army in trying to assess the opinions of
Algerian women thus arose from a complex of factors, including seclusion in the domestic space, male honour and sensitivity to any attempt
to approach their wives and daughters, fear of the occupying forces,
refusal to answer questions relating to the public sphere controlled by
males, and a high level of ignorance arising from illiteracy and isolation
from the outside universe of information, political events and current
affairs.

Despite these difficulties, the 1961 investigators concluded that the
data returned still provided useful information as to the *general* trends in
media communication. Firstly, the survey confirmed that print sources,
including newspapers, whether read directly by the literate or read by
them to the illiterate, constituted a minor channel of information. Under
10 per cent of rural women in the sample received news in this way, as
opposed to the two outstanding means by which information was diffused, the radio and oral communication through social networks. Some
42.4 per cent of rural women listened to the radio one or more times
a week, while about a half preferred to exchange information through
social converse. The intensely oral and aural nature of Algerian culture
reflected both the high level of illiteracy, as well as the traditional forms
of female associational life, based on women's networks, gatherings in
the Turkish baths (*hamam*) or at various family-based social functions
(weddings, circumcision, Aïd, local pilgrimages) in which local news,
story telling and the exchange of information played a key role.

The report showed that reading of newspapers and listening to radio
was frequently not an individual and private act, but a group activity. Newspapers, for example, which were relatively expensive, were

Table 2: Social practices of listening to radio broadcasts (%)

Where do you listen to the radio?

	Men	All women	Rural women
At home	38.2	38.0	28.2
At a neighbours or friends	14.2	25.7	28.1
Public or collective radio	8.2	4.5	6.7
No reply	39.4	37.8	38.0

Source: SHAT 1H2463, *Étude sur l'information en milieu musulmane féminine* (1961), Appendix K.

frequently read out aloud by those who were literate to a wider kin or social circle. This was also true of the radio as is shown in table 2.

Since information was transmitted within a group setting, this meant that it was not simply received by each individual in an unmediated way, but was subjected to intense debate and evaluation by kin, neighbours and local leaders. As Daniel Lerner found in a not dissimilar situation in the Turkish village of Balgati in 1950, a wealthy and conservative headman who owned the only radio ceremoniously played the news to a select group and afterwards subjected it to a commentary.[19] Since access to the media occurred within the ambit of the extended family or kin group, it would seem highly likely that information was both selected and shared upon the basis of pre-existing group loyalties. Michel Launay, as an anti-war conscript, went every Saturday evening to listen to the nationalist *Voix de l'Algérie libre* in the family of his friend Mazouzi.[20] Fanon emphasised the collective nature and group mediation of listening to the radio, 'The old resistance to intra-familial contact disintegrated and one can see in a *douar* family groups of fathers, mothers and daughters elbow-to-elbow gazing at the face of the radio in the expectation of *Voix de l'Algérie*'.[21] As the 1961 study concluded, what was more important than the 'raw data' of news items received by radio or newspapers, was the 'transformation' or interpretation of the information within the social circle. However, the majority of women showed little understanding of politics, of abstract concepts like 'democracy' or the significance of expressing their voice through the ballot box. The report found that in its present form information tended to be adapted to the needs of the minority of educated women, while its penetration among the mass of illiterate women was feeble, and among rural women preference was shown for radio transmissions of popular music and songs (55.2 per cent) than for news items (14.6 per cent). A decade later members of Vandevelde-Daillière's team found a similar situation, particularly in rural areas and shantytowns, where many women had absolutely no access to radio, newspapers or other sources, and responses in reply to questions ranged from, 'do not understand what is being said to them' to showed 'inertia and total indifference': 'For these women there is a total ignorance of the world outside the family, the world of public affairs'.[22]

However, the French army, as well as Franz Fanon and the FLN, were quite right to see radio as the most powerful instrument for reaching out to an illiterate audience that was isolated and scattered over a huge and difficult terrain. But before examining the content of the radio programmes that were specifically designed for women, we take a look at the propaganda use of film which provided another powerful, visual means for reaching an uneducated audience: as General Jacquier noted in November1960, 'The film is, along with the radio, the most effective means of communication that we have in our action upon the Muslim population'.[23]

Film and photographic propaganda

In the half-century before the outbreak of the Algerian War there had been a significant production of commercial, long métrages films shot on location in the Maghreb. Most popular were exotic Orientalist genre films located in the desert or Arab souks in which typically a European beauty, captured by a lascivious sheikh, was rescued by the French hero from a harem: cinema goers to *Yasmina* (1926), for example, were promised 'all the magic of the Orient, all the sensuous display of the harem, all the voluptuous lyricism of its captives, the precious flowers of an enchanted hot-house'.[24] However, while this production is of interest for what it may tell us about the stereotypical perceptions of Algerian women that many French soldiers brought with them to North Africa, what I am concerned with here are the short documentary or news items filmed by the army for, or about, Muslim women during 1954–62.

The *Service cinématographiques des armées* (SCA), founded in August 1946, centralised both photographic and film production and diffusion for the Algerian armed forces from its HQ in the Martimprey barracks in central Algiers.[25] The SCA included a team of professional army photographers and cameramen who were sent out daily to cover key events, such as the Forum demonstrations, or to cover particular propaganda themes, of which a favourite was the heroic medical work of EMSI teams in the *bled* and the 'modernisation' of Muslim women. Photographic film was rushed daily from the 'field' by plane, helicopter, van or train to the SCA laboratory for development and rapid diffusion to the various press agencies of the Ministry of Defence and the Fifth Bureau, and by daily plane to Paris for distribution to the national and international press agencies like Keystone and International.[26] Documentary films, printed in multiple copies, were likewise distributed to French television and to commercial cinema companies or, internally within the army, in both French and Arab-language versions, via the Fifth Bureaux hierarchy to army units and mobile propaganda teams (CHPT).

The Fifth Bureau exercised a close control over the themes or subjects that were to be emphasised, including various aspects of women's emancipation, but also those topics to be avoided, such as 'the systematic destruction of *douars* or villages', heavy artillery and tank shelling, 'shantytowns, poverty-stricken quarters, houses in ruin', and 'slovenly, hirsute soldiers'.[27] A censorship committee exercised a control, not always with success, over the commercial films shown in Algerian cinemas, and among examples of those which raised concern was the Resistance film *La Bataille du Rail* (1945) in which railway workers sabotaged a Nazi troop train and which, after its projection in Bouira in November 1956, was thought to have triggered FLN attacks on the Algiers–Constantine line.[28] Also banned was *Hiroshima Mon Amour* (1959), perhaps seen as creating opposition to the nuclear test programme in the Sahara, and the cowboy film *L'Homme de San Carlos* (USA: *Walk the Proud Land*, 1956) in which an Apache reservation moved away from submission to the US army towards peace and autonomy.[29] Egyptian Arab-language films were of particular concern to the French since they conveyed the spirit of Arab nationalism and depicted a 'modern and prosperous country' to the disadvantage of colonial Algeria.[30] Psychological warfare officers were concerned that Egypt might offer an image of modernity, particularly in the female sphere of domesticity, that demonstrated how the Arab state could reach levels of consumer prosperity well in advance of colonial France. One report noted how a film broadcast on television, 'gives an extremely flattering idea of the standard of living of Egyptians that one sees living "à l'américaine". Ultra-modern interiors, luxurious cars, etc. . . . giving an impression obviously in contradiction with the real way of life of the Egyptian people'.[31] By 1956 over 250 Egyptian films had been granted import licences for screening in the thousand cinemas across Algeria but, despite a blanket ban imposed in 1958, the army was unable to stop them reaching a wide popular audience. Egypt retaliated by producing *Djamila Bouhired*, an account of the FLN terrorist bomber and heroine who was captured by the French, tortured and sentenced to execution. A further blow for anti-colonial film-making was struck when fifteen Algerian trainees at a French film school defected to Tunisia to work with the FLN.[32]

Once a week the head of the SCA, Captain Rouy, met in a briefing meeting with the head of the Fifth Bureau to agree on the appropriate themes to be covered by the SCA film unit, and during the course of 1957 attention turned increasingly to the making of documentaries that illustrated the emerging emancipation strategy and which could be shown to audiences of Algerian women to convince them of the benefits of 'modernisation'. For example, a SCA unit was sent in August 1957 to the heart of the Operation Pilot pacification programme in the Bou Maad area to photograph the new EMSI teams at work (see illustration 1, p. 96). The journalists described the primary purpose of the teams as 'the penetration of the Muslim feminine cell and child-care training', disclosing the primary intelligence function of the operation as much as its social welfare purpose.[33]

In July 1957 the SCA also produced a three-minute documentary, *Nurses of the Bled*, which showed the new mixed EMSI teams of young European and Algerian women at work, symbols of 'fraternisation', heroic self-sacrifice and medical progress. The opening scene of the film showed villagers living in squalor and hunger, and the narrator emphasised that these were the conditions faced by people living under the control of the FLN before the French army arrived to liberate them from terrorism and poverty: 'The young women of Algeria and the Metropolis have agreed to be "harnessed" to this tremendous task with courage and faith'. The EMSI was then shown departing every day on foot, by horse or army helicopter to the most isolated villages that could not be reached by road, and where the care for children and the sick established a new trust with the population. During subsequent visits to the same villages men, women and children were shown pressing round in greeting: 'Here, a warm and sympathetic friendship is created . . . here the smiles of all the little children of Algeria who will keep for ever the memory of these young women from the Metropolis and Algeria, a symbol of French solidarity'.[34] The months after the events of '13 May' 1958 was especially productive in documentaries about the process of unveiling, the general emancipation of Algerian women, and the campaign to persuade them to exercise their new right to vote in the September referendum and National Assembly elections of November. The SCA produced 500 prints of 'A Full French Citizen', 600 of 'Vote Yes', and a range of other titles that included 'How to Vote', 'The Arab Woman of the *Bled*', 'The Falling Veil', and 'Woman, Blessing of God'.[35]

The Algerian government was fully aware of the crucial importance of this photographic and film propaganda in the battle for international public opinion. The SCA was highly successful in its distribution of free images that were passed via major agencies in such a way

(referend 9 Sept. 1958)

that they carried credits such as Keystone or Agence France-Presse, so that their military source was concealed, 'to avoid giving the impression that information had been orchestrated'.[36] The SCA was proud to claim that between 50 and 75 per cent of global press, TV and cinema images during the Algerian War, unknown to the public, originated with army journalists. A particularly prominent part of this propaganda was devoted to the EMSI, since images of blond young nurses bathing or inoculating Algerian babies while smiling and grateful peasant mothers looked on neatly encapsulated a multitude of messages: the peaceful nature of colonial rule, the enthusiastic acceptance of the Algerian populace, the love and self-sacrifice of the French, the warm inter-communal relations of both sides, liberation from backwardness and squalor, and the building of a new society (see illustration 1, p. 96).

The head of the SCA, Captain Rouy, pressed for the 1957 documentary *Nurses of the Bled* to be completed as quickly as possible so that it could reach commercial cinemas in metropolitan France and be dispatched to New York in time for a coming session of the UN which was about to debate the Algerian War.[37] An important production and distribution role was played by the private company Tangent Films in ensuring that French propaganda films of the Algerian War, most of them illustrating the civilising process of 'pacification', reached a wide American audience.[38] One of these productions, *The Falling Veil* (c. 1960), showed de Gaulle arousing Muslim women from their mental torpor, so that they were 'electrified' into liberating themselves from patriarchal oppression, and able to achieve progress towards modern civilisation that was illustrated, notes Matthew Connelly, by French women taking 'their Algerian counterparts in hand to hat shops and post offices, enacting practices of modernity for their protégés to mimic'.[39] This propaganda battle for American public opinion was to prove of crucial long-term importance since the eventual termination of the war, and the withdrawal of the French, came about as much through pressures exerted by international diplomacy, and in particular by the USA and the UN, as it did from FLN guerrilla warfare.[40]

How did films reach the domestic audience of Algerian women, and what kind of influence, if any, did they have? The colonial government had used the Ciné-bus from 1943 onwards to show official films in the more isolated regions of the colony,[41] but such methods were greatly expanded during the course of the war. Films were distributed by the SCA to army units and the SAS/SAU, which had some 400 projectors, to show to local audiences in village halls, women's circles and other venues. In addition specialised propaganda units, the CHPT, copied in 1956 from American *Loudspeaker and Leaflet Companies*, began to deploy mobile cinemas, including a type of screen (*cinéma jour*) that could be viewed in the open air during daylight.[42]

SCA reports during 1957 show an increasing ambition to reach audiences of Algerian women, in line with the centrally directed campaign of emancipation. In December 1957 it noted that during the previous year Algerian attendance at army-mounted film shows had doubled and, 'among these spectators we can now count numerous Muslim women, a happy portent for the evolution of these women and for the whole of Algeria'.[43] A tour by a Ciné-bus unit in the Department of Mostaganem in October 1957 had in ten shows attracted an audience of 19,150, of which 8,600 were Muslim women, and it was thought that women were being drawn in increasing numbers by films.[44]

There is little evidence as to the impact of such documentary films but relatively high attendances may have reflected the novelty and entertainment value for women who had, in many instances, never seen a film in their life. Certainly the army liked to use film-shows, frequently including Hollywood cartoons, as a means of drawing in a female audience that could then be subjected to speeches by EMSI and other women propagandists. Jean Servier and his commando associates cried with laughter at the seriousness of a captain seeking their advice on the advisability of showing an English-language version of *Donald Duck* to the villagers of Tifra in Kabylia: implying that the psychological warfare units revealed an absurd lack of understanding of the potential audience.[45] But in general women, who watched films in segregated sessions with their children, seem to have been enthusiastic, even if, as the wife of an SAS officer noted, they understood nothing and reacted with nervous laughter to occasional romantic scenes and kissing.[46] The soldiers who manned the CHPT rarely had any knowledge of Arab or Berber dialect, and were in little position to judge whether the messages were suited to the culture of the audience. Music that was played over loudspeakers from disks was sometimes more suited to a brothel, and Monique Eoche-Duval notes that, 'the words of the songs and the music was a little bit too suggestive in this land where the men would not listen to such things in the presence of their wives'.[47] General Crépin, in a directive which ordered the projection of a new SCA film, *Femmes*, throughout Algeria, remarked that it was difficult for such short documentaries to suit the tastes and the complexity of different types of audience that varied from one region to another, and in this instance, where 'the female rural milieu has only a very vague idea of the way of life in the town'.[48]

Such evidence would seem to indicate that cinema propaganda was not so professionally produced to match the needs of respective female audiences as the Fifth Bureau often liked to claim. The overall impact

See also [film]
FLN use of film (add to my chapt 2)

on attitudes or political opinion may have been quite superficial, but in addition the FLN political cells (OPA) certainly encouraged people not to attend film shows or, in some instances, to actively disrupt proceedings. In 1957 one projection by a Ciné-bus was disrupted by youths, some of whom were arrested, and by the audience whistling, while in 1959 another screening was sabotaged by the cutting of electricity cables. It was reported from pro-FLN villages that no women would attend screenings,[49] while Captain Montaner of the SAU of Clos-Salembier (Algiers) recorded during July 1958 that the cinema hall he had organised was stoned by turbulent youths.[50] As always the effectiveness of propaganda has to be gauged against the local political background, and in most instances the allegiances of women were determined not by individual choice but by the political colouring and solidarity of the extended family, kin or village group to which they belonged.

Radio: the 'battle of the airways'

From the First World War down to the age of satellite TV, radio broad-casting represented the single most powerful instrument in the armoury of state propaganda. During war-time it had the advantage of diffus-ing messages very rapidly across a national space, penetrating across borders or globally to reach into the privacy of the home of an 'enemy' population. It was a source of information that governments found particularly difficult to control or police. During the inter-war period most advanced states established powerful, short-wave transmitters that could broadcast to global audiences: France, for example, estab-lished the *Poste Colonial* in 1931 which by 1938 was broadcasting in thirty languages. The full propaganda potential of radio was not lost on General de Gaulle whose political career as national leader of the French Resistance was founded on his famous appeal from London on 18 June 1940.

In 1959 Frantz Fanon published his famous essay, 'Here is the Voice of Algeria', in which he argued that radio, particularly in the form of the new, portable transistor, represented a revolutionary tool for the nationalist movement.[51] Fanon argued that until the War of Independence *Radio-Alger* was a 'transmission belt for the colonial power' and was produced for a predominantly European settler audi-ence, who owned some 95 per cent of all radio sets.[52] This colonialist hegemony was, however, challenged increasingly by neighbouring Arab nationalist stations and in particular by the *Voix des Arabes*, transmit-ted from Nasser's Egypt, which supported the Algerian struggle from its very inception.[53] But, for Fanon, the most dramatic and revolutionary potential of radio was realised during 1956 when the FLN was given a voice by Moroccan and Tunisian stations, notably the Tunis-based *La Voix de l'Algérie arabe soeur*, and finally in December with its own transmission, *Radio de l'Algérie libre et combattante*. For Fanon, the Algerian masses which had previously shunned *Radio-Algers* and radio-listening in general as a form of penetration of alien European cultural-imperialism into the very heart of the Muslim family, now flocked to gain access to the radio as a source of information that shattered French propaganda and blanket control over the media, and also became in its own right an act of resistance. Immediately Algerians rushed to buy-up every new and second-hand radio they could lay their hands on and Algerians apprenticed to European radio-electricians began to open their own workshops.[54]

The French government was confronted with the difficult problem of responding to this threat to its previous tight censorship and control of news media. Historically, the growth of radio war propaganda had confronted modern states with a dilemma: attempts to capture or reach 'home' audiences was very much dependent on the mass ownership or availability of radio sets, but such a proliferation might also enable the public to tune-in to 'dangerous' overseas or clandestine air-waves. Despite the drawbacks, the Nazis had been so convinced of the enormous propaganda potential of radio that they encouraged the manufacture of millions of cheap, mass-produced sets, the *Volksempfänger* ('people's receiver') so that by late 1939 over 70 per cent of households owned one.[55] The French army had experimented with radio propaganda in 1951 during the war in Vietnam but had abandoned the idea because of the paucity of receivers among the population, even among the Viet Minh elite.[56] In Algeria the total number of officially registered sets increased by 41 per cent from 418,325 in May 1958 to 590,782 in late 1960, in part due to the rapid spread of the new transistor radios, and between a sixth and a third of Algerians may have owned a set by 1960.[57]

The French government was well-informed of the pro-FLN propaganda being transmitted across the borders, mainly through the *Groupement des contrôles radioélectriques* (GCR) located at Fort du Mont-Valérien in the Paris suburb of Suresnes and its Algerian listening posts. The GCR produced a daily *Bulletin d'écoutes générales* with transcriptions of key intercepts.[58] One response to the growing volume of pro-FLN broadcasts was to engage in the technically difficult and expensive process of jamming, which seems to have only succeeded in part,[59] and the FLN *Voix de l'Algérie libre* responded by constantly changing wave-length.[60] The government also tried to restrict the sale of

7 Women knitting and listening to the radio in the MSF circle of Palestro,
January 1959

radios and batteries to Algerians by the decrees of 16 and 20 December
1957, particularly the light and portable transistor which was ideal for
the isolated areas without electricity, while the army during its operations tried to seize or destroy as many sets as possible.[61] But this only
succeeded in creating a black market in radio equipment, including a
cross-border trade organised by the maquis.[62] The government seems
to have recognised that it was impossible to prevent Algerian access to
the radio, and moreover such a policy was counterproductive since it
stopped people listening to official propaganda broadcasts. As the 1961
LSHA survey showed (see above), half of all women listened to the
radio once or more a week, and this was regarded as by far the single
most important source of information, particularly for the great mass of
illiterate women in the *bled*. An alternative strategy considered by the
Fifth Bureau, reminiscent of the German practice, was to mass produce
a cheap standard radio that could then be widely installed in SAS, SAU,
village halls, women's circles, youth clubs and other locations where
group listening would be under the control of local officials, settlers and
army officers.[63]

But the FLN OPA appears to have organised its own listening circles or group reception of nationalist transmissions and Zohra Drif, in her 1957 plan for a clandestine network of FLN women's cells in Algiers, included group discussion of the political situation based on listening to *Radio-Tunis*, *Rabat* or *Radio Algérie Libre*.[64]

The ethnologist Jean Servier appears to have been among the first to have commented on the considerable interest shown by Algerian women in listening to the radio, in particular the Kabyle-language broadcasts of *Radio-Alger*.[65] In May 1957 General Noiret, commander of the Constantine region, undoubtedly aware of the newly emerging agenda on women, forwarded a report of the local *Renseignements généraux* (RG) which commented on the great popularity of Paris Arab-language broadcasts, particularly 'the latest songs', 'listener's letters', cultural programmes and 'those that relate to the life of Muslim women, the emancipation of the Arab woman and the evolution of customs'. A radio 'referendum' on the wearing of the face veil (*hadjar*) had aroused much interest among young women, 'among whom the desire for emancipation is very great and who begin to speak of equality of attitudes'. The RG's view was that much attention should be given to the organisation of radio transmissions to women: 'Besides the fact that these broadcasts could turn young Arabs away from listening to xenophobic and racist Arab radio, they are of a nature to accelerate the evolution of the Muslim woman and via her of Arab society as a whole towards previously unknown forms of liberalism'.[66] This current of thinking was followed up during the summer of 1957 by *Radio-Alger* in its Arab and Kabyle versions of the *Magazine de la femme*, which welcomed a listener's debate on the veil and emancipation through its popular speaker, called 'Nadira'. But it was above all the events of '13 May' that was to give an enormous boost to radio propaganda, a key component of the wider campaign of emancipation that was accelerated throughout Algeria.

The remaining section of this chapter looks at the content of a particularly important weekly programme, the *Magazine social de la femme*,[67] which was broadcast by *Radio-Alger* from early August to December 1958 in league with the newly formed MSF led by Lucienne Salan and Suzanne Massu.[68] One of the first acts of the army conspirators on 13 May was to seize the building of *Radio-Alger*, an almost standard move in any modern coup. On the 17 May, the day on which veils were burned in the Forum, Massu, inspired by the heady atmosphere of 'fraternisation', claims to have gone on the spur of the moment into the radio station where she used her rank to demand of the parachutist guard an immediate access to the studios to make a spontaneous radio appeal. In the transmission she called on all women to come to her aid to ensure that the joyful flame of love and reconciliation demonstrated in the Forum should be nurtured by a nation-wide women's movement, 'This, my sisters, is our affair. Help me, come to me: this is Suzanne Massu in Algiers and I appeal to your assistance'.[69]

This appeal gave rise to the creation of the MSF, which will be examined in the following chapter, but what can be noted here is the considerable potential of radio to the emancipation movement, and this was soon to be translated into the regular broadcasts of the *Magazine social de la femme*. The *Magazine*, a fifteen-minute programme broadcast every Thursday and Sunday morning at 7.15 am in French, and repeated the same day at 6.60 pm in demotic Arabic, ran for eighteen weeks until its closure on the recall of General Salan and his wife to France in December 1958. After several weeks the programme began to assume a regular format which consisted of five elements, a four minute editorial presented by leading members of the MSF, medical advice (*billet de docteur*), brief news items mainly relating to charitable activities of the MSF, letters from listeners, and, most interesting of all, a popular address to Algerian women by 'Lalla Safiya'.

Mme Salan, as a highly active president of the MSF, exercised a tight control over the programme and it was she and her advisers in the General Government who decided on the theme of each week's editorial and approached the wives of leading generals, officers or functionaries to speak to these topics. Among those who participated in the editorials were, in addition to Salan herself, the wives of Generals Massu, Réthoré, Saint-Hillier and Jouhaud, Mme Goussault (wife of the head of the Fifth Bureau), and Mme de Marie, wife of the head of Salan's cabinet. Suzanne Massu, for example, on 11 August under the title '*Croisade de l'amitié*' spoke of the inter-faith solidarity of Christian, Muslim and Jewish women who were able to meet now in the women's circles of the MSF, 'activities include meetings of friendship, country picnics, group walks, seaside excursions, infant nurseries', where in spite of language differences they could speak 'the eternal language of women'. In contrast to the world of men, of politics and conflict, 'our weapon is the sewing machine'.

Other editorials addressed social issues, such as high unemployment, poor housing, the cess-pit anarchy of the *bidonvilles*, and solutions that promised to improve the quality of life for Algerian women, such as vocational training, the work of the *Centres sociaux*, schooling for girls, and new building programmes, solutions that were 'revolutionary and effective'. However, the key issues that were repeatedly addressed throughout 1958 related to the government campaign on the two most important planks in the emancipation movement: firstly, to persuade Muslim women to exercise their right to vote for the very first time in the referendum of 28 September and the legislative elections of November 1958, and secondly, to persuade women of the fundamental importance of a reform of the personal status law. These issues are examined more closely in chapter 8, but briefly it can be noted how the dominant radio discourse was one that emphasised the necessary struggle by Algerian women to escape from a medieval and oppressive past. Mme Goussault, in her editorial on 'Algeria in 1830', re-iterated a standard discourse used by colonial ideologues to legitimate both the conquest of Algeria, and the need for an enduring French presence. Goussault dwelt on the misery and backwardness of Algeria before the arrival of the French, the bloody tribal conflicts, cruel Turkish despotism, crushing taxes, piracy, general filth, lack of any hospitals and other 'odious abuses' that only France was able to abolish. Under the beneficent hand of France Algerian women could now emerge into the full light of modernity, an era marked by a high standard of living, good housing, clothing, food and health care for themselves and their children, self-fulfilment through education and leisure, and full economic and political equality with European women. Such a bountiful future could only be achieved under the governance of France and the almost superhuman and all-loving father figure, de Gaulle. As Mme Salan claimed in another editorial, only by voting 'Yes' for de Gaulle could a 'pacific revolution' be achieved: 'What a radiant future is promised for an Algeria that finds itself integrated and united with the Motherland, benefiting from the economic riches, the cultural treasures and techniques that are the fruit and inheritance preciously accumulated by France through the centuries'. To abstain from voting was to 'betray the Fatherland that has cherished you, it is to prepare the victory of the separatists and of international Communism'.

Other programmes approached the well-worn theme of unveiling, which was then linked by speakers to other issues of personal rights, polygamy, forced marriage and repudiation. Particular importance was attached to re-assuring Muslim women that reform of the personal status law, or exercising the vote, was not against their religion, but had already been addressed by other Islamic states, including Turkey under Mustapha Kemal, Egypt, Syria, Lebanon, and more recently Tunisia and Morocco. Frequent mention was made of the speech of the eminent religious leader Sheikh Lakhdari in Constantine on 26 May 1958 (see chapter 3). Princess Lalla Aïcha of Morocco and the 'beautiful Soraya', wife of the Shah of Persia, were held up as examples of royal women who had adopted reform, and Algerian women were encouraged to demonstrate that they too could be proud to embrace modernity. It was

frequently suggested, in a discourse that must have sounded surreal to
Algerian women living in shantytown slums, army resettlement camps
and isolated *douars* without roads, running water or electricity, that
they too could aspire to become the equal of their French sisters who
historically had also to fight to achieve their rights and now enjoyed
equality with men, able to, 'to go out, to engage in sport, to follow
university courses, to become doctors, pharmacists, lawyers, or directors of industrial or commercial enterprises'. The radio, as did the MSF
women's weekly magazine *Femmes nouvelles*, held up powerful role
models of modernity, from champion rock-climbers and swimmers, to
atomic scientists, film stars and princesses.[70] A series of Arab-language
broadcasts, *Voter Oui, c'est assurer l'emancipation de la femme musulmane*, informed Algerian women that their vote placed them on the
same level as, 'a great scholar, a great writer or a great engineer. Such as
Jacqueline Auriol, the fastest woman pilot in the world'.[71] The French
propagandists, unwittingly or not, were here following very much in
the footsteps of an earlier tradition of middle-class Arab feminism and
nationalism, particularly in Egypt, which centred on the life narratives
of exemplary 'famous women', including non-Muslim subjects like Joan
of Arc, Catherine the Great of Russia, Queen Victoria, George Sand and
the American astronomer Maria Mitchell.[72]

Possibly the most effective part of the *Magazine* was the regular
broadcast by 'Lalla Safiya', who presented herself as a simple and
uneducated woman of the people who shared the tribulations and
concerns of her 'sister' Algerians: 'I', she claimed, 'I am only a poor,
ignorant woman'. In contrast to the more formal style of the editorials
by elite European women, which were intended as much for a settler
as an Algerian audience, this supposed mother of six addressed herself
to illiterate Muslim women in a close personal and even affectionate
way and larded her talks with popular aphorisms or religious epithets
(*Inch' Allah*!). However, 'Lalla Safiya' was certainly a fiction and radio
actresses played her role reading from scripts that were prepared by psychological warfare specialists.[73] Such concealment was a standard tool
of propagandists since revelation of the true identity of the organisation
lying behind the message would create an immediate disbelief or doubt
in the audience.

'Lalla Safiya' developed themes identical to those of the editorials
(the role of education, the importance of the vote, reform of the personal status law, unveiling), but her message was packaged in a simple,
but more subtle and user-friendly format. The style of the populist
broadcast can be illustrated by that of 14 September 1958 on the theme
of 'progress' in which Lalla argued against religious conservatism.

Addressing herself to her 'dear sisters', she remarked that some of you will ask what is the point, 'All is in the hand of God!': to such religious fatalism she replied that we also are religious, respect our ancestors and visit their tombs, 'We also, we obey *Islam* . . . But Islam is a religion that is worth the effort: – The Proverb says: "Fasten your camel, and have trust in God"'. How can we possibly turn the clock back and live like our ancestors, she asked: 'In order to do that would we, the women, not have to destroy the mechanical mills and bring the hand mill back into every house? – Do we have to smash the water pipes and the fountains to go, as we did in the past, to fetch water at the spring? Do we have to burn down the hospitals and schools?'.

Lalla claimed to be won over to change by the example of her young and progressive (but fictitious) daughter. At one time Lalla had been backward and tried to stop her going to school, but she was now happy and enthusiastic to encourage her daughter: so listeners should do likewise with their sons and daughters and they would be richly rewarded, 'Inch' Allah!'. In a broadcast on the veil (21 September) Lalla again used her daughter as a foil, a symbol of progress, and noted that she herself has not worn a veil for two years since, 'When I saw my daughter so happy to go out without a veil, I wanted to do like her'. Much of her advice was couched in a sensible, pragmatic and non-doctrinaire way: thus it was impossible to lead an active life dressed in the *haïk*: 'To come and go in the town, to cross the road in the middle of the automobiles, to see well, to hear, to carry a parcel, you must, I can assure you, be dressed like a French woman. The habit is quickly learned!'. Women of the Aurès or Sahara had never worn the veil, but did that make them any the less Muslims? And how were they to manage veiled, 'to go and fetch water at the spring or well?'. In other programmes 'Lalla Safiya' reported her arguments with her fictitious grandmother, who initially refused to vote, or her conservative friend Malika who claimed that according to the Koran men were superior to women whose role it was to obey and remain within the home. Lalla, through kindly argument, won both of them over to her side: women should not 'remain like an animal that men can sell or buy . . . like an old, blind horse that has to work the water-wheel', and the Prophet had declared, 'All the faithful are brothers'. In a programme on 30 November, a few weeks before the *Magazine de la femme* was closed down, Lalla announced that she was off to join an SAS in the interior as a social worker dedicated to the welfare of mothers and children. So 'dear friends of the *bled*' might in the future be able to recognise Lalla by her 'sympathetic voice' as she moved anonymously among them, no fiction but a living reality.

The 'Lalla Safiya' broadcast, with its use of simple characterisation, its direct appeal to ordinary Algerian women through the voice of a warm and personable 'sister', shows how the army was able to invent more plausible and possibly successful propaganda. As the LSHA survey of 1961 indicated, at least half of all Muslim women listened to the radio one or more times a week, so a considerable number were likely to have listened to the *Magazine* or similar French propaganda transmissions. Today, even under the most sophisticated laboratory conditions, it is notoriously difficult to measure the impact of the mass media in changing basic attitudes or opinions, and the effectiveness of French propaganda cannot be conclusively assessed. Frantz Fanon, through what David Macey has called his 'revolutionary romanticism', entertained an exaggerated radical optimism as to the potential of pro-independence radio to forge a new Algerian national and political consciousness: but the overall impact of French army propaganda was probably even less than that of the FLN. It should be kept in mind that listening to the radio was frequently a group or quasi-public process that was mediated by other women, kin and villagers and where there existed support for the FLN, or deep hostility to the occupying armed forces, French propaganda would have been either subjected to withering criticism, switched off or re-tuned to nationalist wavelengths. Algerian women listening at home were also highly selective as to what they chose to hear, and French research showed that the majority of women (59.3 per cent) preferred to listen to music and songs, rather than to news or current affairs (18.6 per cent).[74] It seems unlikely that French radio broadcasts had any *transformative* effect on the emancipation of Algerian women, although the spread of the transistor radio into the isolated villages of the interior, in the absence of other means of mass communication, undoubtedly provided them with an important window on the rapidly changing events of the War of Independence.

Notes

1 In particular this study does not examine in detail the French policy of expanding educational opportunities for Algerian girls, especially at primary level, a long-term strategy that would only begin to change or affect women's attitudes well after the War of Independence was over.

2 For an overview see Garth S. Jowett and Victoria O'Donnell (eds), *Propaganda and Persuasion* [1986] (London: Sage Publications, 3rd edn 1999).

3 For a detailed history see Villatoux and Villatoux, *La République*, Parts 1 and 2.

4 Simpson, *Science of Coercion*.
5 Susan L. Carruther, '"Not Just Washed, But Dry-Cleaned": Korea and the "Brainwashing" Scare of the 1950s', in Gary D. Rawnsley (ed.) *Cold-War Propaganda in the 1950s* (Basingstoke: Macmillan, 1999), 47–66; see also above, chapter 3, the influence of the Soviet Serge Chakotin.
6 Sylvie Thénault, 'D'Indochine en Algérie: la rééducation des prisonniers dans les camps de détention', in Brocheux et al. (eds), *La Guerre d'Algérie au miroir*, 235–49.
7 An overview of theory can be found in two seminars by M. Bonnemaison, a specialist in social psychology, *Fondement de la guerre psychologique* (7 November 1957) organised by the Fifth Bureau in Algiers in which he distinguished the 'American school' of 'mass-man' characterised by Carl Jung (the unconscious, archetypes, the image), and the 'Soviet school' based on Pavlov (instincts, conditioned reflexes): SHAT 1H2409.
8 Villatoux and Villatoux, 'Le 5e Bureau en Algérie', 409.
9 SHAT 1H2409, Instruction of Bourgès-Maunory [probably August 1957]. The French army in Algeria, which constituted the 10th Military Region, was subdivided under the central command in Algiers into three army corps (Algiers, Oran and Constantine), and each corps into zones corresponding to the twelve departments (fifteen after March 1958) and held by a division. The zone was further subdivided into sectors corresponding to an arrondissement and held by a regiment, and each sector was further sub-divided into quartiers: see Guy Pervillé, *Atlas de la guerre d'Algérie* (Paris: Éditions Autrement, 2003), 31.
10 SHAT 1H2409, *L'Arme psychologique en 10e Région Militaire*, August 1957.
11 SHAT 1H2409, *Contrôle et sondage des resultants de la propagande à destination des musulmanes et rebelles*, 23 February 1957; Monique Eoche-Duval, *Madame SAS, femme d'officier. Algérie 1957–1962* (Paris: F.-X. de Guibert, 2007), 89.
12 Villetoux and Villetoux, *La République*, 445–6.
13 *Ibid.*, 489, 486.
14 SHAT 1H2463, minutes of foundation meetings of LSHA, Algiers 23–24 March 1960. Among those present were Professors Marçais, Yacono and Malméjac, and Hadj Sadock of the Lycée of El-Biar.
15 SHAT 1H2463, *Étude sur l'information en milieu musulmane féminine*, 4 August 1961, 33, by Chef de Bataillon Lacavalerie, director of the LSHA.
16 The returns also showed a bias towards the European-dominated Oran region, where the EMSI were most present; also towards urban rather than rural women, and those who were better educated. The percentage of returns for illiterate (76.8 per cent) was well below the expected norm of 96–8 per cent.
17 Hélène Vandevelde-Daillière, *Femmes algériennes à travers la condition feminine dans le Constantinois depuis l'indépendance* (Algiers: Office des

Publications Universitaires, 1980), 94–8, 228–65. The survey was carried out between February 1969 and February 1970, using a team of female students.

18 *Ibid.*, 241, 263.
19 Daniel Lerner, *The Passing of Traditional Society. Modernizing the Middle East* [1958] (New York: Free Press of Glencoe, 1964 edn), 27.
20 Launay, *Paysans algériens*, 255.
21 Fanon, *L'An V*, 67.
22 Vandevelde-Daillière, *Femmes algériennes*, 229.
23 SHAT 1H2515.
24 Cited in Pierre Boulanger, *Le Cinema colonial* (Paris: Éditions Seghors, 1975), 62. On Orientalism and colonial film production in Algeria and the Maghreb see, in addition to Boulanger, Abdelghani Megherbi, *Les Algériens au miroir du cinéma colonial: contribution à une sociologie de la décolonisation* (Algiers: SNED, 1982); Richard Abel, *French Cinema. The First Wave, 1915–1929* (Princeton: Princeton University Press, 1984), 151–60; Matthew Bernstein and Gaylin Studler (eds), *Visions of the East. Orientalism in Film* (London: I. B. Tauris, 1997); Ella Shohat and Robert Stam, *Unthinking Eurocentrism. Multiculturalism and the Media* (London: Routledge, 1994); David H. Slavin, *Colonial Cinema and Imperial France, 1919–1939: White Blind Spots, Male Fantasies, Settler Myths* (Baltimore: John Hopkins University Press, 2001).
25 Benjamin Stora and Marie Chominot, 'Photographes sous l'uniforme: regard croisés sur la guerre d'Algérie', in Laurent Gervereau and Benjamin Stora (eds), *Photographier la guerre d'Algérie* (Paris: Éditions Marval, 2004), 39–41. The SCA succeeded from the older *Section photographique et cinématographie des armées* founded during the First World War. The rich deposit of films and photographs can be consulted in the *Établissement de communication et de production audiovisuelle de la Défense* (ECPAD) at Fort d'Ivry, Paris. I have been unable to consult the recent thesis of Marie Chominot, *Guerre d'indépendance de l'Algérie, l'image, source et objet de recherche historique*, May 2008, Paris VIII: see also her unpublished research paper, 'Armée et photographie en guerre d'Algérie', Institut d'Histoire du Temps Présent (IHTP), Paris, 2 March 2004.
26 SHAT 1H2515 contains a wealth of information on the operations of the SCA.
27 SHAT 1H2515, directive 10 RM, 15 April 1957. A useful comparison with French film censorship and cinema in colonial Syria and Lebanon can be found in Thompson, *Colonial Citizens*, 197–210.
28 SHAT 1H2409.
29 SHAT 1H2515.
30 On French control and censorship of cinema and films in Algeria, especially Egyptian productions, see Sébastien Denis, 'Cinéma et panarabisme en Algérie entre 1945 et 1962', *Guerres Mondiales et Conflits Contemporains*, 226 (2007), 37–51.

31 *Ibid.*, 49, intelligence note 20 February 1957. The 6,000 TV sets in the Algiers area reached an audience of about 25,000.
32 SHAT 1H2515, General Challe note, 15 March 1960; Boulanger, *Cinéma colonial*, 8, 272; Connelly, *Diplomatic Revolution*, 28–9.
33 ECPAD – ALG 57/392, twenty-eight photographs taken 16 August 1957.
34 SHAT 1H2515, note of Captain Rouy, head of SCA, 6 July 1957, with analysis of film sequence and script. ECPAD was unable to locate for viewing any of the films relating to emancipation and Algerian women. Diane Sambron, *Femmes musulmanes*, 104, note 120, remarks that many of these films have been deposited at Aix with CAOM, archives du ministère de la Culture/films cinématographiques, but they cannot be viewed because of their poor condition. Connelly, *Diplomatic Revolution*, 216–17, was able to view some of these films and makes interesting comment on their content.
35 SHAT 1H2515, SCA, *Réalisation de films de propaganda pour le référendum*, 15 September 1958; Sambron 'La Politique', in Jauffret (ed.), *Des hommes*, 238.
36 SHAT 1H2515, SCA fiche, 15 September 1958. *Paris Match*, 476 (24 May 1958), showed several photographs of the unveiling ceremonies at the Forum on 17–18 May taken by its own photo-journalists Joël Le Tac and Daniel Camus under the rubric, 'The events of Algiers in photo, as seen by our special correspondents'. But two of the photographs of veil burning credited to Le Tac and Camus were taken by SCA photographers.
37 SHAT 1H2515, note of Captain Rouy, 6 July 1957.
38 Pacal Pinoteau, 'Propagande cinématographique et décolonisation. L'Exemple française (1949–1958)', *Vingtième Siècle. Revue d'Histoire*, 80 (2003/4), 55–69.
39 Connelly, *Diplomatic Revolution*, 216. *The Falling Veil*, Tangent films, London, c. 1960, was directed by Robert W. Schofield. Schofield had links with the French producer J. K. Raymond-Millet, who specialised in making propaganda films in colonial North Africa between 1929 and 1955.
40 The FLN was clearly aware of the importance of emancipation to French international propaganda: one captured internal document commented on the 'publicity aims: the newspapers, the films, and declarations enable the world to be informed of the so-called "humane task" undertaken by France for the Algerian people', SHAT 1H2461/1, report captured 26 November 1958 on the corpse of Si Boumédienne.
41 Boulanger, *Cinéma colonial*, 271; Villatoux and Villatoux, *La République*, 382.
42 SHAT 1H2515, SCA note on *cinéma jour* project, 17 October 1957. A photograph (ECPAD ALG57 83 R06) shows such a cinema in operation.
43 SHAT 1H2515, *Le Role du Service de Diffusion Cinématographique depuis la naissance d'une Arme Nouvelle. L'Arme psychologique*, by Plassard, Chef Adjoint, 5 December 1957. Underlined as in the original text.
44 SHAT 1H2516, report of Murati, head of the Service de Diffusion Cinématographique (SDC), 9 November 1957.

45 Servier, *Adieu Djebels*, 49–51.
46 Eoche-Duval, *Madame SAS*, 57–8.
47 *Ibid.*, 190.
48 SHAT 1H2515, Crépin directive, 3 May 1960.
49 SHAT 1H2516, reports of SDC.
50 CAOM 2SAS59, monthly report for SAU Clos-Salembier, July 1958.
51 Fanon, *L'An V*, 51–82.
52 *Ibid.*, 51, 77; see also Macey, *Frantz Fanon*, 328–30.
53 Charles-Robert Ageron, 'Un aspect de la guerre d'Algérie: la propaganda radiophonique du FLN et des États arabes', in C.-R. Ageron (ed.), *La Guerre d'Algérie et les Algériens, 1954–1962* (Paris: Armand Colin, 1997), 245–6.
54 Fanon, *L'An V*, 66–7.
55 David Welch, *The Third Reich: Politics and Propaganda* (London: Routledge, 1993), 30–4.
56 Villatoux and Villatoux, *La République*, 253.
57 Ferro (ed.), *Le 13 Mai 1958*, 16; Ageron, 'Un aspect', 249.
58 CAOM 15CAB118, 'La Propagande radiophonique de la rebellion', 10 March 1961; copies of the daily bulletins are in CAOM 81F367 and 81F888.
59 SHAT 1H2516, reports on jamming (*brouillages*), include a note of 8 June 1961 that jamming of medium waves was failing to 'counter effectively an aggressive propaganda'; CAOM 15CAB118, 'La Propagande radiophonique', reports that jamming of medium waves was more effective than short wave transmissions, and for towns than for rural or frontier areas.
60 Fanon, *L'An V*, 69, 72.
61 Launay, *Paysans algériens*, 315, notes that by 1960 the transistor radio had become almost a necessity of the peasant household. The main impediment to their regular use was the cost of batteries.
62 Fanon, *L'An V*, 68–9.
63 SHAT 1H2409, Réunion du Comité Mixte d'Action Psychologique, 4 October 1957; Welch, *Third Reich*, 30–4, notes that the mass produced 'people's receivers' had a limited range so foreign broadcasts could not be listened too; community listening, or broadcasts by loudspeakers in public spaces and factories, also ensured a sense of national belonging and conformity.
64 SHAT 1H2582, 2e Bureau, *Organisation féminine de la Z. A. Alger*, 14 October 1957.
65 CAOM 13CAB7, report from Tizi-Ouzou, 12 August 1956.
66 SHAT 1H2461/1, note of R. G. Constantine, 7 May 1957.
67 While unclear from the archive sources it is likely that *Magazine social de la femme* was a re-named version of the older women's programme *Magazine de la femme*.
68 The full script for most of these broadcasts, in CAOM 13CAB61, provide an invaluable source for the propaganda content of radio programmes directed towards Algerian women.

69 Massu, *Le Torrent*, 99–101; CAOM 13CAB61, Mme Massu, *Message aux amies de toutes confessions* [n.d].
70 *Femmes nouvelles*, 20 February 1959, special issue on 'The Empress and Simple Citizen: SORAYA', and 6 March 1959, with numerous photographs of female mountaineers and swimmers.
71 SHAT 1H11471/1, Operation Referendum, transcripts of twenty-eight RTF programmes, August–September 1958.
72 Marilyn Booth, 'The Egyptian Lives of Jeanne d'Arc', in Lila Abu-Lughod (ed.), *Remaking Women. Feminism and Modernity in the Middle East* (Princeton, N.J.: Princeton University Press, 1998), 172; and '"May Her Likes Be Multiplied": "Famous Women" Biography and Gendered Prescription in Egypt, 1892–1935', *Signs*, 22: 4 (1997), 827–90.
73 The internal evidence of a fictional character can be found in the bizarre contradictions in 'Lalla's' biography, detailed technical annotations to the scripts and other features.
74 SHAT 1H2463, *Étude sur l'information en milieu musulman féminine*, 4 August 1961.

5

The *Mouvement de solidarité féminine*: army wives and domesticating the 'native'

The campaign by the French army for the emancipation of Algerian women offered to displace the 'traditional' Muslim family and gender roles by a particular western model of the couple and companionate marriage. It is particularly significant that this model was rarely reflected upon or recognised by the French as a specific cultural and social form, but accepted in an automatic and unquestioning way, as 'natural' and proper. It was precisely this unreflective agenda that provided Europeans with the overpowering sense of self-confidence about the inherent superiority of European life-styles that constituted the *mission civilisatrice*. While many of the hard-working and dedicated European women who tended to Algerian babies and women in the *bled* saw their role as bringing humanitarian relief and medicine to a neglected population (treatment of trachoma, inoculation, sterilisation of wounds), such aid was not just about scientific intervention, but was generally an integral part of a wider set of complex values, beliefs and actions that involved an attempt to form Muslim women in a particular mould.

During the last two decades there has been much research on the process of 'domesticating the empire', the methods by which British, Dutch, Portuguese and French imperial regimes attempted to intervene in, regulate or remake indigenous family life in its own image.[1] This chapter aims, in part, to investigate the overt and implicit meanings of the model of family life, companionate marriage and gender roles that underpinned the emancipation campaign. The paternalistic origins of domesticity are complex and varied from one colony to another, but one key source of interventionism can be traced back to late nineteenth and early twentieth centuries in western Europe when social imperialists, eugenicists and welfare reformers, concerned by the 'racial degeneration' of the proletariat in urban slums, were concerned to educate working-class women into scientific methods of hygiene, diet, child-care and household management that would guarantee the fitness of infants and husbands.

Intrinsic to social imperialism and Christian welfare was a petit-bourgeois class model of family life that emphasised particular moral and disciplinary virtues, such as cleanliness, teetotalism, saving of money, rational use of limited resources, punctuality and self-help.[2] The metropolitan model of charitable and state intervention in the sphere of the family could be readily exported and adapted to the colonial context, particularly as the categories of class and 'race' were interchangeable, the European inhabitants of slums being viewed by the middle-class as African savages in urban jungles that required missionary and police intervention. Omnia Shakry has shown how metropolitan national-ist discourses on mothering and child rearing influenced the forms of Egyptian middle-class feminism that emerged in the early twentieth century. Just as with European social imperialism, Egyptian feminists viewed the education of girls and women, the ending of superstitious practices and the inculcation of a science of home-management, hygiene and child-care as a national duty, the key to future progress and eventual independence.[3] A similar evolution appeared among Iranian women nationalists: the opening of two girls schools in Tehran was celebrated in 1909 in the following terms: 'in the future, every household is headed by a learned lady who knows household management, child rearing, sewing, cooking and cleaning and from whose breast the milk of love of the homeland will be fed to infants so that they shall be deserving of [national] service and sacrifice'.[4]

By the early 1900s it was a truism throughout the educated classes of the Middle East that the roots of national regeneration lay with the education and modernisation of women, but Algeria followed a very different path until the Second World War. Firstly, Algeria lacked a suf-ficiently large and dynamic Muslim urban middle class to support an elite women's movement of the kind to be found in Turkey, Egypt and Iran.[5] The discourse that presented the educated mother as the national saviour was not taken up by Algerian women and made their own, but was captured after the 1920s by the male-dominated *Ulema* which, while acknowledging the importance of the education of girls, gener-ally harnessed this to a conservative defence of Islamic family values. In addition between 1900 and 1945 women in settler society, unlike their metropolitan counterparts, showed very little interest in reaching out a hand to help 'regenerate' or modernise the Algerian family: on the con-trary most believed that Muslim women should be left in an uneducated and 'primitive' condition where they offered less of a competitive threat. After 1900 the main drive towards a progressive welfare agenda on Algerian women and the family came not from inside the colony, from settlers or Muslim women, but from metropolitan writers like Georges

Vabran of the *Musée Social* who argued that European women were best suited to take on the difficult task of gaining access to native homes, since 'Only the hand of a woman can lift the veil which protects Muslim women', and to organise lessons in hygiene and home economics.[6] The French feminist, Hubertine Auclert, who lived in Algeria between 1888 and 1892, also believed that assimilation should be achieved through European women penetrating into the secluded space of the Muslim home so as to offer a progressive cultural model.

However, such reformist ideas appear to have made almost no impact in the first half of the twentieth century, and it was only after the outbreak of the rebellion in 1954 and the arrival of many hundreds of wives of army officers and administrators that this model of female interventionism became dramatically activated. Army wives brought with them a range of experience that encouraged their intervention in an emancipation agenda. Firstly, only the wives of senior officers and certain types of female army personnel (mainly nurses) were allowed to serve with active forces overseas, and it was precisely this category of women who played the key role in forming the MSF. The leaders, Lucienne Salan and Suzanne Massu, had both served as professional nurses in the Resistance,[7] and belonged to the cohort of young women who before and during the Second World War had participated in the 'home front' training programmes of the *Union des femmes de France*, which included stretcher bearing, automobile driving and mechanics, and defence against gas attack.[8]

After 1945 this experience was carried into the French colonies, most notably during the war in Indochina, where both Massu and Salan had served as military nurses. The French forces in Vietnam developed a programme of welfare work with indigenous women, and after 1954 this experience was brought into Algeria. It was French policy in Africa, Indochina and elsewhere to encourage wives of the military and colonial service to volunteer for welfare work with native women since they had unique access and, surrounded by servants, had the free time to do so.[9] In Lebanon and Syria during the French mandate the colonial civic order was highly paternalist and the wives of high commissioners, such as Madam Catroux, played a prominent role as the patrons of women's associations and glamorous charity balls, or by visiting hospitals, soup kitchens and clinics.[10] In a strongly hierarchical organisation like that of the French army women, in marrying officers, were as 'incorporated wives', expected to share closely in their husband's occupational identity and culture and in many instances to represent the human face of the military to the outside world through official functions, welfare work and ceremonials.[11] The wives of generals and colonels in Algeria, through charitable work with poor Muslim women and children, were thus fulfilling a traditional function,[12] and the wife of the Algerian governor, as part of her quasi-official functions, would also invite selected wives of the Algerian elite to receptions or undertake various benevolent functions that were well-publicised in the colonial press.[13] It was this long practice of involvement by colonial and military elites in charitable work, and which typically deployed a discourse of universal sisterhood as wives and mothers, that prepared the ground for the MSF initiative. Although the leaders of the MSF held quite conservative values they were mostly newly arrived in Algeria, did not share the racist attitudes towards Muslim women to be found among the *pieds-noirs*, and tended to support the bourgeois ideals of the post-Liberation Gaullist women's movement: Lucienne Salan, for example, had close links with Hélène Lefaucheux, the most influential representative of this reformist current.

As we have seen (chapter 3), the events of '13 May' and the successful 'fraternisation' movement in the Forum led within days to a major drive by the joint military-civilian government headed by General Salan to accelerate the emancipation of Muslim women. On the 17 May Suzanne Massu made a radio-appeal to all her European and Algerian 'sisters' that led to the creation of the MSF.[14] The basic idea behind the MSF was that European women should take the initiative in forming hundreds of local clubs or associations which would attract women from the Muslim, Jewish and Christian communities into shared social and cultural activities, reach over religious and political divisions, and unite all women in a common purpose as wives, mothers and agents of progress. Through direct personal contact in local clubs 'backward' native women, it was thought, would emulate or absorb through a kind of osmosis the superior moral and domestic behaviour of Europeans. The hierarchical structure of the new organisation closely matched the system of army ranks so that the position of each member matched the status of their husbands. Both Lucienne Salan and Suzanne Massu, as wives of the top commanders, were addressed directly, and in the media, as 'madame la général' or 'mon commandant', and army wives were keen to assert a 'correct' hierarchy in their own relations, following the dictum 'they carry the stripes of their husbands'.

Although both Salan and Massu claimed that the MSF was a purely voluntary and charitable organisation established through the spontaneous enthusiasm of European women, in reality it was another tool of military operations and mainly funded by the army. The MSF was founded on the secret initiative of the Fifth Bureau as part of its psychological warfare strategy, and a number of army initiatives during

1957 prepared the way for the new organisation. In 1957 the Bureau had already begun to establish local women's circles like one reported in early July: 'a women's circle has been opened in Algiers where Muslims and Christians can freely exchange their points of view so as to know and understand one another better. From these contacts can be drawn precious lessons on the methods to be used to hasten, as smoothly as possible, the emancipation of Algerian women'.[15] Some of the newly founded SAU in Algiers, such as those in the Cité Mahiéddine and Belcourt under Captains de Germiny and Bernhardt, began to establish women's clubs during 1957.[16] During this time Suzanne Massu assumed a particularly proactive role in this sphere and, after visiting and studying the work of the *Centres sociaux*, she established welfare assistance for orphaned street boys (*yaouleds*) many of whom were refugees from the war zones in the interior. The first *Centre jeunesse* was established at Bab-el-Oued in March 1957, funded by 20 million francs 'given' by General Massu to his wife, and located in a building and with full-time male personnel supplied by his *État-major*.[17] Suzanne Massu's daily presence, along with the wife of General Navarro, soon attracted a flood of Algerian women who were desperate to obtain information about their husbands, sons or brothers who had 'disappeared' or been arrested by the army during the violent Battle of Algiers. Through this contact the *Centre* quickly developed a role of welfare assistance to women, including the project 'Home knitting' (*tricot à domicile*) through which poor Muslim women earned income through a domestic knitting industry that supplied clothing to various outlets, including department stores. The ambiguity of the altruistic role of Mme Massu was highlighted by the fact that she provided welfare assistance to women and children who were the immediate victims of the massive repression, torture and murder inflicted by the parachutist regiments under the command of her husband.[18]

Although General Massu claimed disingenuously, 'No political move lay behind the beginning of this organisation [MSF] which rose in response to a simple human need',[19] there is evidence as to the way in which the Fifth Bureau began to manipulate women's circles to its own ends. In August 1957 Madame Tournemine, the wife of an officer, began to pioneer a women's circle in the small settler township of Héliopolis near Guelma (examined below) and this appeared so successful to the commander of the sector, Colonel Bravelet, that he gave army backing to an experimental action during which Algerian women were summoned by army loudspeaker vehicles and coerced to attend a foundation meeting in the local school-yard. Cinema shows were used to attract them to the weekly meetings and women, he claimed, seemed to be growing in confidence as shown by rising attendance and a quarter of them unveiled spontaneously during sessions.[20]

In October 1957 the head of the Fifth Bureau in Constantine reported to Algiers on the activities of Thérèse Godet who, under the aegis of the metropolitan based *Union nationale des associations familiales* (UNAF),[21] had organised numerous women's groups in *douars* in which European instructors, mainly the daughters of settlers, and Muslim women were trained by Godet as teachers of domestic skills. This project proved so successful that Godet was planning to extend it to the departments of Oran and Algiers. This private initiative, which claimed to be apolitical and non-confessional, was funded by the French UNAF and by small grants from the Prefecture of Constantine, but had no links to the army. The army report went on to recommend that the Constantine organisation be secretly lured into co-operating with the military through the inducement of 20 million francs to finance the cash-strapped programme and to achieve a process of 'convergence': 'We know from a reliable source that the UNAF would agree to discretely link its actions to those of *pacification* and to allow us to exercise an effective control over the political and psychological activities of its Training Centres, if the Civil and Military authorities provide the aid which it needs'.[22] That the Fifth Bureau was seeking to manipulate such a prestigious institution as the UNAF indicates the extent to which covert operations was penetrating into the civil sphere of the state.

Thus by the time of the events of '13 May' the army was already well on the way to exploring the potential of women's circles as part of its strategy of contact and intelligence gathering. The radio appeal of Suzanne Massu on 17 May evoked a large response from European women who wished to participate in the exciting 'revolutionary' movement that was unfolding and, with the assistance of Jacqueline de La Hoog, the wife of an oil executive, a foundation meeting was held on 20 May at which 200 welfare assistants were present.[23] The very same day Colonel Goussault sent an urgent telex to the regional army commanders, 'to create immediately women's circles that bring together Europeans and Muslims', which confirms the close links between the Fifth Bureau and the creation of the MSF.[24]

Within days the nascent MSF was almost wrecked by a power struggle between Suzanne Massu and Lucienne Salan for control of the organisation. Overtly this clash was about military hierarchy and protocol: the imperious Salan, as wife of the head of both the armed forces and government of Algeria, was not prepared to accept a position within the MSF below Massu, the wife of a mere *Général de brigade*.[25] Superficially this problem was resolved by the creation of a structure that placed Salan as president and head of the Central Committee, while Massu was president of one of the three regional committees (Algiers), along with the wives of Generals Réthoré (Oran) and Olié (Constantine). Under the surface the conflict rumbled on until in October 1958 Massu tried to block Salan's attempts to control or interfere with the Algiers regional committee by establishing her own legal statute, for which she was accused by Salan of threatening to split the MSF and creating 'a disastrous malaise among all the women'.[26]

The dispute between Salan and Massu reflected in part a clash of two strong personalities, but at the same time is revealing of a number of tensions and contradictions within the MSF organisation. Elizabeth Thompson has analysed the way in which a paternalist form of charitable welfare in the Lebanese and Syrian mandates during the 1920s gradually gave way to a 'colonial welfare state' in which Arab citizens no longer received benefits as a 'gift' but as a basic right, providing a powerful impetus to the eventual recognition of full political rights.[27] But in Algeria a peculiar hybrid situation continued, a mixing of charitable and state welfare functions, of which the MSF was symptomatic. One of the peculiarities of the situation in Algeria, as General Salan and the army assumed increasing control over civil government, was that the demarcation between military command and budgets and civil rule became increasingly confused and inextricably intertwined. This situation is illustrated most clearly by the mobile welfare teams (EMSI) which were pay-rolled by the civil authority (Prefectures), but being desperately short of funds, of vehicles, buildings and materials were almost totally dependent on the good will of local commanders to make these available. One of the most extraordinary, and under-researched, features of the Algerian War is the way in which all the organisations which worked on the ground to bring welfare to women and children, from the SAS/SAU to the EMSI and MSF, were literally reduced to forms of scavenging and make-shift fixing, to get hold of or commandeer scarce resources from doors and cement, to second-hand clothing, soap, bed linen, tents and food supplies.[28] Since, particularly in the *bled*, the army frequently constituted the only meaningful governmental structure on the ground and, with its huge budget allocations, monopolised most resources, the ability of women's welfare organisations to function effectively depended on the skill with which they could gain the patronage of local or centrally placed army commanders.

The wives of the senior generals, and in particular Salan and Massu, were ideally placed to influence their husbands, each of whom directly controlled massive resources on the ground, from army vehicles and drivers to stocks of materials. The ambitious Lucienne Salan had no hesitation in playing a forward political role in the Algerian crisis and intervened directly to act alongside her husband and to advise him, as head of government, during the events of '13 May'.[29] Through this intervention she gained immediate and privileged access to the civil and military apparatus in the General Government which was carefully managed by Jacques de Mari, a senior administrator (*chargée de mission*) in General Salan's cabinet, while de Mari's wife served as the general secretary to Salan as head of the MSF Central Committee. However, Suzanne Massu, who claimed to be 'totally apolitical', was incensed by Lucienne Salan's imperious style of control of the MSF and her diktat as to how all funds were to be spent, including those of the regional Algiers committee that Massu presided over.

This tension led Lucienne Salan, in a rather extraordinary move, to set up a quite separate private bank account for her personal 'social welfare fund' into which she got General Salan's cabinet to divert half of government relief funding. The single biggest government grant to the MSF in November 1958 of 60 million francs came from funds that were allocated in the budget for emergency relief to the poor (Chapters 203–42 of Section D of the Budget), but diverting this from its proper use caused considerable anxiety to the head of the Civil Cabinet, General Hubert, who noted that he was already short of funds to alleviate the desperate situation of the population in *regroupement* camps and the victims of recent catastrophic floods.[30] Thirty million francs diverted from the emergency relief fund was thus paid into Lucienne Salan's private account and then disbursed by her, often to needy Europeans as much as to Algerians, according to her own whim and in a way that always presented it to the public as a personal gift (*à titre personnel*) from her private resources.[31]

Salan was thus able to bring to her position as 'first lady' in Algeria a highly paternalistic and traditional style as an aristocratic dispenser of charity. From June to December 1958 she undertook an exhausting itinerary, constantly visiting with a team of assistants and army personnel, schools, hospitals, crèches, SAU centres and women's groups in Algiers or going out on tour into the provinces. Always welcomed in formal ceremonies by local commanders, dignitaries, mayors, their wives and little girls offering bouquets of flowers, Salan confirmed her personal status and power as a benefactor through handing out to poor Algerians an endless stream of blankets, clothing, sweets and foodstuffs.[32] But Suzanne Massu, who was described by journalists as the antithesis of the elegant and elitist Salan, always down-to-earth, dressed in a Prisunic dress and sandals, had little interest in fashion and was inspired by a more populist approach and a social conscience that was rooted in her

strong Catholic faith.[33] Massu, in a barely disguised and barbed attack
on Salan's style of dispensing charity, told the press, 'You know, I am
not a "pretty lady", wife of a prefect or colonel, who is going to bring
sweets to the ordinary soldiers in the army hospitals. CHARITY, PITY,
GIVES ME THE HORRORS!'[34]

Behind the scenes the differing approaches of Salan and Massu to the
work and role of the MSF was fought out over the crucial issue of membership. In the early weeks of the MSF Suzanne Massu had set membership fees of 'adherents' at a nominal 100 Francs, probably to be inclusive
of the poorest Algerian women, but Lucienne Salan and her military
advisers tried to raise this in July 1958 since, 'we risk being infiltrated by
undesirable elements',[35] a not ungrounded fear since the FLN had given
instructions for its female supporters to infiltrate the women's organisations.[36] Despite these differences, however, Suzanne Massu was equally
dependent on military aid. She, along with members of the Algiers
regional committee, represented a 'counter team' to that of Lucienne
Salan, and through the attaché Captain Pasquelin gained access to the
resources of General Massu's regional *État-major*. As the latter noted, in
spite of the enthusiasm of the MSF women, 'only the army can provide
the framework and the "means" to set up such an organisation'.[37] Why
did the MSF organisers cling on to a style of welfare work that presented a public image of entirely voluntary or charitable assistance to
Algerian women, when in reality this was only made possible through
army resources and as an extension of the military apparatus? Firstly,
most army wives, along with many other women on the colonial side
of the conflict, created a protective false consciousness in relation to the
violent nature of the war being fought by the French forces. The destructive and inhuman aspects of French intervention, which were there for
all to see, were dealt with by a whole complex of psychological tricks, of
self-denial and wilful blindness. Here there was a fundamental refusal to
acknowledge the possibility of illegal or morally unacceptable forms of
army violence and, most crucially, to enter into any debate of the issue:
for Suzanne Massu this blocking out was sustained through the myth of
a water-tight division between the political sphere, controlled by males,
a zone in which she refused to 'intervene', and the autonomous sphere
of women's voluntary work inspired by spiritual and Christian values:
as such there existed a radical dissociation between the grim reality of
the war being waged by the army (and her husband), and her own social
work: 'the weapon of us women is the sewing machine'.[38] The feminisa-
tion of welfare relief, which was expressed by a discourse that emphasised the maternal instincts and self-sacrificing role of European women,
a kind of 'Florence Nightingale' symbolism, served a very powerful

propaganda and media role in humanising what was a bloody colonial war. But in order to sustain this image the army was happy to conceal the fact that it funded this welfare work and, through the Fifth Bureau, determined the key propaganda campaigns in which it engaged.

What kind of support did the MSF find among European women as it tried to expand its organisation across Algeria? At the top levels we find that the list of key women involved in the MSF reflected a roll-call of the names of generals and colonels and undoubtedly for any senior army wife *not* to have participated would have been regarded within elite army circles with opprobrium. In late 1958 Lucienne Salan decided to built up her private charitable fund through a standard letter sent to the directors and presidents of all major private companies in Algiers: in this she noted that the movement of '13 May' and 'fraternisation' imposed on them an, 'imperious duty', and 'it is essential that your spouse devotes part of her spare time to a circle of the Action Sociale et de Solidarité Féminine'.[39] Non-participation could perhaps be interpreted as a signal of political disaffection from the 'revolutionary' movement and even have had negative implications for their husband's career. But, sometimes we gain a glimpse of women who seem to have got involved with the MSF because of a genuine concern for the plight of Algerian women: for example, Mme Delignette, wife of a doctor in the small township of Rabelais, decided to set up a circle in October 1958 since she had accompanied her husband in his tours of duty in the rural zones and witnessed the terrible poverty and suffering of the Algerian women.[40] It seems likely that many 'incorporated wives' in Algeria, like those in the British colonies, were glad to throw themselves with energy into welfare work with the 'natives' because of the *ennui* that many of them faced in their daily lives when a supply of low-paid servants alleviated even the need for domestic work, or because they were located in the small townships and army posts of the *bled*.[41]

However, given that far more European women in Algeria were of settler rather than metropolitan French origin it was noticeable how far the former were under-represented in the overall MSF organisation. As Captain Bernhardt of the Belcourt SAU noted, after the 'fraternisation' parades, 'the impetus of Muslims towards France has not been matched by the impetus of Europeans towards Muslims. The young women who have responded to the appeal of Madame Massu are the wives of officers and engineers, foreigners to the country. The locals have not responded'.[42] The EMSI reported frequently on the lack of support for MSF circles: thus from Palestro, '*European women*: one word sums them up – indifference. The emancipation of Muslim women is of absolutely no interest to them'.[43] This, as will be seen, was in part because a significant percentage of colonial-born women came from a 'poor white' or lower-middle class background and had little inspiration to get involved in such an elitist movement as the MLF and, more significantly, because they shared the racial values of a highly segregationist colonial society.[44] By contrast the 'incorporated wives' of army commanders, colonial officials and businessmen were largely metropolitan French in origin and so, as recent arrivals in Algeria, brought with them into the colony more liberal perceptions of both women's and 'native' rights. The MSF leaders, along with army officers in general, shared a jaundiced view of settlers as racist, egocentric beings who, through their defence of entrenched privileges and a failure to recognise and accept the need for economic and social reform for Algerians, threatened to undermine a progressive agenda that held the only chance of maintaining *Algérie française*.

This is significant since, if we are to understand the values that underlay the model of female Algerian emancipation promulgated by the MSF, it is necessary to look for the origins of this more in the social and political experience of women in mainland France than in the conservative colonial milieu.[45] There is not space here to give a full analysis of the post-war women's movement in France, but suffice it to say that in general the majority of women active in the MSF were moulded or influenced by a conservative and predominantly Catholic culture that emphasised the 'natural' role of women as mothers, wives and guardians of the home.[46] The 'familial feminism' sustained by the MSF was one of domesticity (child rearing, cuisine, hygiene) that reflected the contemporary bourgeois ideology in mainland France.[47]

This linkage to the metropolitan context is also shown by the close links that the MSF leadership established with the main women's organisations in France, particularly with the *Conseil national des femmes françaises* (CNFF) and its president, Marie-Hélène Lefaucheux. The CNFF, founded in 1901, federated numerous associations of women's organisations, and represented the opinion of a largely privileged, middle-class constituency which campaigned for a moderate reformist agenda which, after the final winning of the vote in 1944–45, included the advancement of women in numerous domains of education, civic rights, health, family life, employment and political education.[48] As has been seen (chapter 1), Lefaucheux, in her position as French delegate to the UN's Commission on the Status of Women, had a key role in the international movement for political and legal rights, and as president of the CNFF (1954–64) and of the *Conseil international des femmes* from 1957 to 1963, supported the post-'13 May' campaign for the emancipation of Algerian women. Lucienne Salan corresponded regularly with Lefaucheux, and the latter welcomed a delegation of twenty Algerian and European girls sent by the MSF to participate in the 14 July parade in Paris, before heading an exchange visit of twenty French girls to Algeria.[49] The MSF affiliated to the CNFF, and Salan and Lefaucheux liaised on a number of issues, most significantly on the campaign to extend the vote to Algerian Muslim women in the referendum of 28 September 1958. They also, behind the scenes, planned the move to stand three Algerian women in the parliamentary elections of November.[50] One of those duly elected deputy was Nafissa Sid-Cara, later president of the MSF, who was soon promoted to Secretary of State in the Gaullist government and for whom Lefaucheux acted as *Chef de cabinet* and close collaborator during the meetings of the 1959 commission to revise the personal status law.[51]

The role of the MSF in the campaign to extend the vote to Muslim women and to reform the law on personnel status will be explored later (chapter 8): the concluding part of this chapter examines in more detail the local function of the circles and the problems of contact which they faced. By May 1959 the MSF claimed to have organised 438 circles,[52] but many of those in the *bled*, in the absence of European settlers, had a brief and rudimentary existence or were organised primarily by the EMSI teams (chapter 7). So the effective MSF circles were largely an urban phenomenon, located in the large cities of the northern literal or in the scatter of smaller provincial centres like Aumale, Bouira and Relizane in which their were enough women, the wives of officers, administrators and professional cadres, to support and sustain the organisation. Three circles, Héliopolis, Rio-Salado and Palissy, for which there exists a rich body of material, have been selected as case-studies to illustrate the inner workings of the local MSF.

An early experiment: the women's circle of Héliopolis, 1957–58

Colonel Bravelet, commander of the Guelma sector and a keen advocate of emancipation, was impressed by the work of Mme Tournemine, the wife of an officer, in creating two circles in the small townships of Héliopolis and Guelaa Bou Sba.[53] Just before Tournemine returned to France, Bravelet persuaded her to write down the detail of the methods she had developed between August 1957 and June 1958 to make contact with Muslim women, so that this could serve as a model for future grass-roots action. The document she produced, *Action psychologique féminine*, is interesting for the inside detail it provides of how European women set about the task of establishing contact with Muslim women in the interior, and is revealing of the highly paternalistic and manipulative attitudes towards those seen as child-like and suggestible creatures who required authoritarian direction.[54]

Tournemine, rather in the way of an amateur ethnologist or missionary, outlined a series of progressive steps by which European women could enter into contact with Algerian women and manipulate and pressurise them to attend regular meetings. Firstly, working either with medical teams or alone, the European was to win the initial trust of native women through providing health care for them and their children, and to gain entry to the jealously guarded private world of the home and family:

> Use the occasion of this health care to go to their home, without ever forcing your way into their huts, which they will usually not refuse.
>
> Don't be surprised by anything (the place, smell, filth, darkness, smoke, primitive tools or utensils). Nothing should put you out; copy right away their way of doing things; sit on the ground or on a bench, drink coffee just as it is offered.
>
> Respect their customs and modesty; gently but firmly brush aside their superstitions and their false sense of shame (the dirty amulets of the babies, poultices of rotten leaves on wounds, women refusing to undress for an injection or medical examination, etc.).

During the initial contact in the home the European should consolidate her influence through praise of the women's children, clothes and utensils and by gifts of sugar, coffee, medicines or sweets for the children. *'Before satisfying their heart and soul with kind words and good advice, you must first fill the stomach and flatter the coquetry of the women* . . . They really understand nothing except when it concerns their affections, their children, their coquetry or vanity'. After an initial contact the European should begin to assert a series of escalating demands, the first of which was to insist that women were properly clean and washed before any care was provided. If they should resist they were to be ostracised, 'walk past their hut without stopping, stay deaf to their appeals . . . "I prefer to go to see the neighbour"', and if they tried to cheat, 'get very angry'.

When trust had been established the next step was to gather the women into the first meeting, which needed to be segregated in a closed space if husbands were to allow their wives to attend. The women should be put at their ease by inviting them to breast feed their babies, then speak for ten minutes to express your sincere friendship, explain that meetings were for French women of all faiths to unite, and that we all have much to learn from each other. What particularly intrigued the Algerian women, she noted, was if you talked of your own family and showed personal photographs. The initial meetings would be attended mainly by older, often widowed women who were able to do so since they presented little threat to deeply held values of honour, and these influential matriarchs should be cultivated so that in time they would permit the young women (a particular goal of action), such as daughters and daughters-in-law to attend, 'while still acting as strict chaperon'.

Particular attention was given by Tournemine to veiling and the tactics for its gradual abandonment. At a first meeting the veil should be allowed to pass, but at the second, 'invite the women to lower their "*haïk*" on the pretext that you cannot recognise them, that you cannot speak to "eyes" but only to "friendly faces". To remain "veiled" is a sign of distrust'. If by the third meeting some continued to wear the *haïk* they were to be ridiculed by the European holding a veil to her own face, or bluntly told that only the very old and sick could do so: 'If one or another persists, pretend not to know her, do not speak to her. She will not resist for long'. Then gradually the women should be persuaded to go as a group unveiled in public and, 'two months later they will find it completely normal to go out into the street unveiled, even on their own'.

Tournemine showed a particular concern, common to the traditions of colonial administration, that the European must always retain psychological mastery and infallibility over the 'native', since any sign of weakness could open a dangerous chink in the armour-plating of French hegemony. Thus the discussions in the circle should appear a free and open dialogue but, in reality, 'you must always dominate, direct the discussion, while seeming not to do so, with much sympathy and understanding'. If the Algerians asked a question she was unable to answer it was imperative not to appear to lie or deceive while remaining in the driving seat, 'say that you are going to look into this question in depth . . . The best means to never find yourself inferior to them is to never lie . . . Appear in their eyes very strong and sure of yourself. Never give the impression of being afraid and, from time to time, set out to prove it . . . do not hesitate to appear very strict on occasions'. For example, it was often difficult to retain order when women pressed around during the distribution of food and clothing, 'call on the soldiers, which is nearly always necessary, and whom they are frightened of'. Until this point in the text the relationship between Tournemine and the Algerians of Héliopolis, for all its patronising force, appears to be an intimate face-to-face encounter between women alone in a courtyard or cactus enclosure, but suddenly we become aware of the wider power relationship and context of this encounter. The authority of Mme Tournemine rested less perhaps, as she claimed, on her strong personality and moral force as an inherently superior European woman and more on the reality of military presence and coercion.

Most of the accounts by European women of their work in the MSF circles or EMSI teams presents a discourse in which their relationship to Algerian 'sisters' is an immediate friendly and moral bonding based on a shared universal identity as women and mothers, while the ever-present retinue of army bodyguards and interpreters is not mentioned at all and rendered invisible. Now and again the façade drops to reveal the under-lying power relationship, as in an account by the EMSI worker Ginette Thévenin-Copin of passing in the countryside a man riding on a donkey, followed by his exhausted wife on foot carrying a huge load of sticks. 'I ordered the husband to get off the donkey, freed the women of her heavy load, and advised the husband, who did not seem to appreciate my inter-vention, to put the pile of wood on the back of the animal'. It seems that the courageous young woman had single-handedly confronted what she called obnoxious 'ancestral customs', but then we become aware almost coincidentally of another presence: 'it was then that the young soldier who was given the order to escort me said, "Pitchounette, perhaps you should not have done that, you have made yourself an enemy"'.[55] The 'writing out' of the military underpinning of MSF actions was neces-sary to retain the illusion of a humanistic and progressive agenda in which the conversion of Muslim women must appear to be carried out with their full and voluntary assent since coercion would betray the fundamental values to which the civilising mission laid claim.

Evidence of this ambiguity, one that underlay all social welfare during the war, can be found in the confidential reports of Captain Schlumberger who organised a tour by Lucienne Salan through western Algeria in September 1958 to address rallies of both European and Muslim women to found or participate in MSF circles. At each location visited the Fifth Bureau would try and gather as many local Muslim women as possible, and then using loud-speaker lorries attempt to 'heat up' (*chauffées*) the enthusiasm of audiences, before they were addressed by Lucienne Salan, followed by distributions of clothing, condensed milk and blankets. Many thousands of these women were located in army resettlement camps and were living in tents. At Marbot Schlumberger noted, 'A timid welcome. Appearance of poverty and mediocre health conditions – lack of milk and water'; at Pont de Caïd, 'A hundred women giving a rather strained applause appear anxious: many of these families have been recently subject to *regroupement* and are without milk or food'; at Nedromah, 'The women appear to be intimidated and frightened'.[56] The question of the harsh conditions faced by rural women will be explored in more detail in the next chapter, but in relation to the everyday opera-tions of the women's circles it can be noted that even where European volunteers (or EMSI) were highly dedicated and inspired by genuine and altruistic concern for the plight of Algerian women the relationship was always embedded in, or underscored by, the more or less visible presence of the colonial power and its armed might.

The MSF circles of Rio-Salado and Palissy

The local circles which have left the most detailed record were located in the Oran region, where the dense settler population in the prosperous, wine-growing areas created optimum conditions for volunteer work by European women in small towns that bore a striking resemblance to the traditional agro-villages of Provence or Languedoc. The following account is based on the circle of Rio-Salado (today El Malah), situated sixty kilometres to the west of Oran, which prided itself on the being the finest in Algeria, and Palissy (Sidi-Khaled), a few miles to the south-west of the garrison town of Sidi-Bel-Abbès, HQ of the Foreign Legion.[57]

Of the two the MSF circle of Rio-Salado operated on the largest and most elaborate scale. At a foundation meeting held in the town hall on 10 June 1958, attended by fifty European women under Mme Rethoré, wife of the General in command of the Oran region and president of the MSF region, a multi-faith CAS was established headed by Odette Bour and three vice-presidents representing the Muslim, Christian and Jewish communities. Over the next year, this dynamic and well-endowed group found accommodation first in a temporary building, the children's nursery, and later in a permanent centre that it was able to buy with the assistance of local wine producers.

The CAS quickly set about investigating the social conditions and needs of local Muslim women by sending out teams of volunteers to visit them in their homes. This appears to have been the first time that the women settlers of Rio-Salado, who lived in a highly segregated society, gained direct experience of the mass poverty that existed on their doorstep. Many of the townships that developed from the mid-nineteenth century onwards in the Oran region had a bi-polar structure, with the settlers inhabiting the European administrative and commercial centre, and the Muslim population segregated in peripheral ghettoes or shantytowns commonly known as *villages nègres*. From the 1930s onwards, with the deepening crisis of Algerian rural society under the impact of colonialism, many thousands began to migrate to the *villages nègres* to scratch a living as day-labourers, a process that accelerated dramatically during the war.[58]

Although the archives of the Rio-Salado circle make no mention of it, the 'village' of Sidi-Saïd disguised the existence of a *centre de regroupement* (see chapter 6), into which thousands of peasants from outlying farms had been forced by the army which destroyed their homes.[59] Michel Launay, who studied the area directly, discovered that within the prosperous wine-growing arrondissement of Ain-Témouchent in which Rio-Salado was located, the *colons* faced a problem of labour recruitment or demands for higher wages, which arose from FLN and trade union pressures, including total withdrawal of labour and strikes. The *colons* supported the mass resettlement of outlying peasantry into camps in order to undermine the FLN, and to create huge reserves of cheap labour, 'disciplined' by the army, on the door-step of each European township.[60] By the later stages of the war, women and children within the camps constituted a particularly large pool of low-waged seasonal labour. Between 1956 and 1960 the French army decimated the population of younger males of working age in the arrondissement of Témouchent, some 5,000 men in a total population of 116,000, and this had left an estimated 2,000 to 2,500 widows and many more orphans.[61] The desperately poor women in the camps and 'new villages' like Sidi-Saïd, particularly since their husbands were dead or absent in the FLN, were forced to work, especially during the intense phase of seasonal grape-picking (*vendange*). The *colons* were glad to be able to tap into the pool of female and child labour, especially since they constituted a more docile work force that could be paid below the legal minimum wage for men.[62]

In October 1958 the Rio-Salado MSF organised one of the numerous petitions sent to de Gaulle for a reform of the law on female personal status (see chapter 8), and among the 837 women who 'signed' it (816 of them by finger-print indicating 97.6 per cent illiteracy), were many from Sidi-Saïd who were categorised as widows and agricultural labourers.[63] Launay's study suggests that the desperately poor inhabitants of the 'village' shared a culture of poverty that was marked by the ecstatic rituals, dancing, feasting (*Ouahda*) and hashish smoking of the Sufi and marabout sect of the Aïssaoua: forms of populist hysteria and release that tended to oppose the more austere puritanism of the neighbouring *douar* of Messaada, a centre of *Ulema* culture and FLN activism.[64] The European women of the Rio-Salado Committee, on first 'discovering' the quarter of Sidi-Saïd, inhabited by over 4,000 Muslims located a kilometre from the colonial centre, seem to have been shocked by the conditions which they found: 'During our daily visits to the *douar*, and in the Muslim quartier of the town, we discovered a frightening number of widows or abandoned women each with four or five children in their care'.[65] The MSF Committee soon began to recognise the crucial need for single Muslim women with children to work, most of them as agricultural labourers, and to facilitate this established a crèche for 150 children, an initiative which proved especially timely for the grape-picking season. The local *viticulteurs* were generous towards a crèche project that supported their interests as employers by facilitating access to a large pool of cheap female labour, and they provided the funds to buy a permanent building to house it.[66] But once the intense seasonal need for *vendange* labour was over many women were once again unemployed and, to help alleviate this, the MSF opened a carpet-weaving and ceramics atelier that provided some income for twenty women.[67] The MSF committee of Palissy was exercised by similar social concerns and its president, Mme Husson, reported the need to:

> Get employers to recognise that a minimal basic wage exists (domestic staff) . . . To accept the dignity of each family by guaranteed work for the men, and for widows and abandoned mothers. Improvement of housing conditions, water supply, electricity, and heating. Guarantee of daily work (harvesting, the *vendange*, and pruning vines provide insufficient income).

Overall the MSFs of Rio-Salado and Palissy could do little to ameliorate the fundamental problems of mass underemployment and endemic poverty. The level of job-creation barely scratched the surface: the carpet atelier of Rio-Salado could only employ a tiny fraction, below 2.3 per cent of the 837 women with which they had most contact, while at Palissy the local Foreign Legion battalion provided only intermittent relief work for men on various public works schemes. In addition there is evidence that the call for intervention and reform in the job market, such as respect for a minimum wage, was coming largely from women like Husson who as recent arrivals from France were regarded as outsiders, while the local *pieds-noirs* community was deeply opposed to any move to challenge its entrenched social, economic and political domination.[68] Settler identity was created and sustained by the founding myth of a heroic ancestry that as pioneers had cleared the 'uninhabited' malarial scrublands and swamps of northern Algeria single-handed and transformed it into an agrarian paradise: nothing was owed to the primitive and nomadic Algerian tribes that were incapable of unlocking such wealth.[69]

In Pallisy, after an initial surge in interest, European women quickly dropped away and Husson virtually ended up running the circle single-handed: she noted 'the lack of European ladies that can serve as instructors is a major deficiency', while the idea for a crèche had to be abandoned. A collection for second-hand clothing in August so that Muslim children could return to school raised nothing at all, while a further appeal by the Mayor (president of the *délégation spéciale*)

Champtassint, as well as an army loud-speaker lorry, for funds or materials led to 'nothing'. The Europeans of Pallisy appear to have turned their back on the MSF, or treated it with open hostility, and Champtassint, who supported the organisation, advised Husson not to make any further appeals for money or gifts in kind.[70] The Pallisy MSF would clearly have collapsed without the support of the civilian authorities and the army, which supplied some funds, materials, interpreters, cinema films, EMSI/ASSRA assistants and other back-up.

At Rio-Salado, where the Committee enjoyed greater local backing, a second line of attack on the poverty of women was achieved through a classic, but well-policed, system of charitable relief. European members visited the homes of the indigent on a daily basis and established a dossier (fiches) that recorded family information, social and economic position, and cross-checked or verified this with identity cards and their employers: a system that must have caused much apprehension for most Algerians, and certainly for the FLN which, correctly, sensed an extension of army intelligence. The bigger colon employers in the Oran region, like the Spanish caciques and latifundia lords of Sicily, held almost feudal powers of granting or withholding employment that created a climate of fear among the 'deferential' workers of the region. In some instances the MSF gave advice to women and directed them towards the social security, doctors or pharmacies, but material aid (wheat, semolina, clothing, milk) was only provided to 'non-indigent' women facing a temporary need. This would suggest that the Committee operated a screening policy through which, as in Victorian England, only the 'deserving poor' were to be helped, those Algerians that had the moral qualities to achieve self-improvement.[71] Most astonishing of all was a report of the MSF that the main beneficiaries of welfare were not Muslim women at all, but Europeans who received 80 per cent of all aid.

The standard activity which most of the circles across Algeria organised consisted of ouvroirs, sewing and knitting groups, in which women of the three communities could converse and break down the barriers of segregation, while at the same time engaging in useful employment (see illustration 7, p. 166). At Rio-Salado the women, 'while knitting', exchanged cooking recipes, while building trust between 'women of different races and customs'. As has been seen for Héliopolis, a central idea was that Algerian women would absorb a progressive model of behaviour from their western 'sisters': the opening of the Pallisy ouvroir in the village hall was attended by 130 Muslim women with their babies where, 'A dozen European ladies made good use of their experience and generously dispensed useful advice to their Muslim sisters'. The organisers tried to increase attendance at such meetings through various forms of light entertainment, including cinema shows provided by the army, singing of popular songs, or listening to the radio or carefully selected gramophone records (at Pallisy carefully selected 'records of children's songs'). A key objective was to reach out to the generation of girls or young women who were seen as more receptive to western influences. But as reported in Héliopolis and other locations, the MSF encountered initial problems with sessions being monopolised by more conservative and older women in order to protect the seclusion and honour of the young. At Pallisy it was reported that matriarchs, 'come along for the pleasure of getting out, but refuse to learn to sew. It seems they wish to represent the family so that the girls, young women or daughters-in-law remain at home'.

At Rio-Salado a basic schooling was established for 150 young women who were taught some French and arithmetic, but most significantly the essential European values of domesticity, hygiene and morality (politeness, correct behaviour). 'The less evolved benefit from advice relating to domestic life (lessons in cookery, cutting, dress-making, knitting)', and making clothing, 'a skirt, a baby vest, a brassiere'[72] or 'dress', was itself a means to draw girls away from indigenous towards western styles of dress. The national woman's magazine of the MSF, *Femmes nouvelles*, contained endless images of the latest Paris fashions, such as 'the Winter 58 collection',[73] but instead of such styles being beyond the reach of its Muslim readers, they were encouraged to make their own dresses using the cut-out patterns provided in the magazine.[74] At Rio-Salado the success of this process of modernisation was quickly seen in a transformation of everyday comportment, in 'the good dress-sense of the young girls', 'their correct welcome, the care taken with their cleanliness, even their coquetry', and their personal hygiene (cleaning teeth daily) and table manners. The *Femmes nouvelles* conveyed a similar message on how young women should learn 'the secrets of elegance' by knowing not only how to choose a dress or hat and appear chic, but also to learn an appropriate body language, how to stand properly or sit elegantly not with legs apart: 'an art in itself'. At Pallisy the MSF entertained identical objectives through, 'lessons in hygiene, cleanliness, baby-care, morality, solidarity, the sense of duty, family life, and life in society'. Trivial as much of this may seem, as Norbert Elias and others have shown, the historical development of manners has been the very hallmark of the European concept of *civilité* or 'civilisation' (eating with knives and forks, use of the handkerchief) as opposed to the uncouth world of the barbarian or savage.[75] The MSF circles were thus engaged not only in attempts to remove the veil, but also in the far more complex processes of inculcating a total *savoir faire*, a set of manners and cultural bearings that revealed an assimilationist rather than integrationist agenda.

A second type of MSF activity, sometimes referred to as *causeries*, consisted of much larger weekly public meetings of women (and men separately), in which the presidents of the local circles, usually assisted by a team of interpreters, EMSI or local dignitaries such as the Mayor or army commander, addressed wider and more political issues, such as anti-veiling, the campaign for women to register and vote in the 28 September referendum, and for reform of the law of personal status. An unusually detailed and revealing insight into the political operations of the Pallisy MSF is provided by a meticulous daily log, significantly given the military title of a *Journal de marche*, kept by its President Madame J. Husson who, like Massu and Salan, had served in 1944 as an army nurse or PFAT. Husson constantly liaised with the commanding officers of the Foreign Legion based a few miles away in Sidi-Bel-Abbès. Much of this routine exchange concerned quite pragmatic issues of material or organisational aid for the cash-strapped MSF, such as the provision of a radio set or gramophone, old army shirts to be reused in the *ouvroir*, cinema projections, supply of army interpreters and small cash grants.

Husson's journal provides evidence of the way in which the local Fifth Bureau exercised a direct control over the political activities and themes of the MSF. On 1 September Husson contacted Commander Hallo to gain clarification of how the MSF Committee was to receive its instructions under the new post-coup 'revolutionary' framework of the CSP. Hallo replied that the local CSP, which should operate in parallel with the MSF Committee and support the same aims, normally received its orders from the Fifth Bureau, and a female member of the CSP should be delegated to regularly attend meetings of the Pallisy committee and serve as liaison. In reality most of the liaison seems to have been undertaken by Sous-Lieutenant Collin of the Fifth Bureau who was delegated to this role, and one archival photograph shows Collin deep in conversation with Husson, the Mayor Champtassint and his wife.[76] For the most important political gatherings a senior officer, usually Commandant Grandidier, would share the MSF platform at public meetings and address the Algerian women. Husson, who could only address the Algerian women in French, was always accompanied by an official translator, and in most instances this was again a service provided by the Fifth Bureau (Lieutenant Roche).

In the *Journal de marche* Husson reports on an important foundation meeting on 6 August to persuade the Algerians of Pallisy to support the infant MSF. This appeal, which was organised by the Fifth Bureau, took place in separate sessions for men and women. Because adult males exercised close control over the behaviour and honour of women, and whether they would be allowed to attend MSF meetings, it was of crucial importance to win them over first.[77] At 11 am on the 6 August the men, first drawn in by a short film, were then addressed by Husson: 'My friends, I thank you all for agreeing to help me in the difficult task that has been entrusted to me', and afterwards, she claimed, they applauded and pressed round to 'show their joy at having been understood'. A Fifth Bureau officer then replied in Arabic to questions the men might have about wages, social security payments and other issues. Husson then welcomed the Algerian women in a separate session at 5 pm:

I love you all.
I wish to help you progress.
I wish to turn you into complete women, truly happy and new women.
I am your sister, accept me! And love me like I love you already.

She was able to reassure them, following the meeting of that morning, that husbands and brothers would be supportive ('they all understood me'), and then tea was served for everyone to get to know each other.

In a *causerie* on 4 September Husson spoke at length on the topic of the veil. By then, she claimed, twenty young local girls had shown a deep desire for 'evolution' and demonstrated this by permanently discarding their veils and handing them to Husson for safe keeping in the town hall, possibly a tactic encouraged to prevent families forcing them to retain the *haïk*. Husson praised this act of courage and asked all the girls and mothers present to do likewise in a collective unveiling. The president then supported this by arguing that neither the Koran nor Islamic religious leaders insisted on the wearing of the veil, and that Algeria, compared to Egypt, Morocco, Tunisia and other Muslim states, was the last bastion of this practice. There was no shame in showing one's face,[78] and in moving into the public sphere to assert their rights as Frenchwomen, just as did the wife of President Coty who despite her public functions remained in high esteem.

It is difficult to penetrate through the glowing and self-congratulatory discourse of Husson, as of all leading figures in the MSF movement, to gauge how Algerian women participants viewed the circles or whether their ideas and behaviour were modified.[79] But at an important indoor meeting of the MSF at Palissy on 25 September to organise the imminent referendum vote a photo-journalist on the stage clearly caught the segregated audience of unveiled women by surprise and the instinctive reaction shown to the camera flash by the rows of startled and anxious women, apart from the normally unveiled and smiling young girls, was to swing in unison away from the camera and to clutch their *haïks* to their face. This would suggest that the MSF in Pallisy made little, if any, impact on the wearing of the veil. But in addition there is evidence of political resistance by Muslim women to MSF action in the townships of Rio-Salado and Pallisy.

In May 1959 General Gambiez, commander of the Oran region, after a visit to the MSF of Rio-Salado, supported the request of Mme Bour for an increase in the government grant from half to twenty million francs: 'a rich work of fraternity has been pursued in depth . . . and in this radiant commune there is no longer any place for the OPA'.[80] While it was the case that 'pacification' was most successful in Oranie and provided the best conditions in Algeria for European women to organise the circles, even in these areas of massive settler presence the Algerian population showed signs of deep, if *attentiste* resistance. Bour reported that due to the 'events' her group was not able to extend its activities beyond the town suburbs, suggesting a degree of insecurity in the surrounding countryside. FLN resistance simmered in the area and undoubtedly influenced local Muslim women, most of whom never attended any form of meeting, or, even when they did, could be secretly opposed to its objectives (as with the older women who attended to impede or control its effects), or drawn by a variety of motives from an interest in film shows, to the handouts of semolina and clothing. The FLN had a real, if clandestine, presence inside the township: for example, Husson reported in August 1958 that the local mosque had been closed down by the army for several months as a 'disciplinary sanction'. Two soldiers were usually placed to guard MSF Committee meetings, and on the eve of the important referendum vote on 28 September the FLN carried out an attack in which one sentry was severely wounded. At a big meeting of the MSF on 9 October the commander asked the Algerian women if they had any requests, and one had the courage to ask that General de Gaulle should liberate their men who had been arrested two days earlier in relation to the attack. The commander, clearly angered by this, and responding in 'severe terms', remarked that three or four terrorists had penetrated into Pallisy, 'guided by the inhabitants of the village', and several suspects had been arrested and 'confessed'. The women had voted in the referendum to stay French, but this was, he said, in contradiction with the attack: 'If you ask to stay French, you do not become accomplices of the bandits (*fellaghas*); you do not engage in a double game'. In the referendum the 234 Algerian women of Pallisy who had voted returned a 100 per cent 'Yes' for de Gaulle, but concealed beneath this apparently total and unanimous support for the French government one has the sense of a deep, if usually un-stated, hostility to the MSF which, as will be seen later, only began to surface openly from the end of 1959.

In conclusion it can be noted that the comparative study of empire tends to show that there was nothing particularly unusual about the French approach to carrying out welfare work with indigenous Algerian women during the period from 1957 to 1962. To date historians have examined most closely the situation in the British African colonies, and this work shows a range of welfare interventions by European women from the 1920s onwards that included, for example, training in mother-craft, hygiene, diet and domestic sciences that bore a striking resemblance to the MSF and EMSI initiatives.[81] In the case of the British colonies like Nigeria and Ghana, in which there was a relatively peaceful transition to independence, feminist historians have, in spite of their strictures about Eurocentric interventions in 'native' domestic culture, provided a sympathetic and positive picture of the considerable contribution that European women made towards achieving progress for women and preparation for a post-independence society. The role of metropolitan French women in the running of the colonial empire has received little attention from historians,[82] but as has been seen the tragedy in Algeria arose from the fact that similar forms of welfare intervention that in a 'normal' peacetime context might have been welcomed by all sides as part of a progressive agenda, was radically distorted and 'corrupted' by the military who hitched it to the purposes of 'pacification'. A few professional women social workers, as in the *Centres sociaux*, resisted this perversion of the welfare function, but more generally European women seem to have leant themselves to this process. As we will see in chapters 6 and 7, the irresolvable contradictions between emancipation and military violence became most evident in the work of the women's welfare teams, the EMSI, in the peasant and nomadic societies located in the vast and sparsely inhabited interior.

Notes

1 There is a considerable and growing literature on imperialism and domesticity: for an introduction to this field and bibliography see Karen Tranberg Hansen (ed.), *African Encounters with Domesticity* (New Brunswick, N.J.: Rutgers University Press, 1992); Nupur Chaudhuri and Margaret Strobel (eds), *Western Women and Imperialism. Complicity and Resistance* (Bloomington and Indianapolis: Indiana University Press, 1992); Frederick Cooper and Laura Stoler (eds), *Tensions of Empire. Colonial Cultures in a Bourgeois World* (Berkeley: University of California Press, 1997); Clancy-Smith and Gouda (eds), *Domesticating the Empire*; Margaret Strobel, 'Gender, Sex and Empire', in Michael Adas (ed.), *Islamic and European Expansion* (Philadelphia: Temple University Press, 1993), 345–75.

2 There is a large literature on this subject, but for Britain see especially Gareth Stedman Jones, *Oucast London. A Study in the Relationship Between Classes in Victorian Society* (Harmondsworth: Peregrine, 1976 edn), chapter 18; Anna Davin, 'Imperialism and Motherhood', *History Workshop*, 5 (1978), 9–65; for France, Janet R. Horne, 'In Pursuit of Greater France: Visions of Empire Among Musée Social Reformers, 1894–1931', in Clancy-Smith and Gouda (eds), *Domesticating the Empire*, 21–42.

3 Omnia Shakry, 'Schooled Mothers and Structured Play: Child Rearing in Turn-of-the-Century Egypt', in Abu-Lughod (ed.), *Remaking Women*, 128–69.

4 Najmabadi, *Women with Mustaches*, 195; also 'Crafting an Educated Housewife in Iran', in Abu-Lughod (ed.), *Remaking Women*, 91–125.

5 It has often been claimed that between the late nineteenth century and the Second World War an indigenous tradition of Arab intellectual life was moribund in Algeria, a view that has been challenged by McDougall, *History*, and Mostefa Lacheraf, *Des noms et des lieux. Mémoires d'une Algérie oubliée* (Algiers: Casbah Éditions, 1998). While the field has been under-researched, it would appear that Algerian women played little part in an Arab-language culture that was monopolised by men, and that those few women who were able to gain a secondary or further education were drawn more entirely into a francophone culture.

6 Georges Vabran, *La Femme française et la femme musulmane en Tunisie*, Musée Social, 1913, cited in Horne, 'In Pursuit', 38.

7 CAOM 13CAB61, in an undated manifesto to promote her claim to head the MSF, Lucienne Salan referred to her Resistance record as, 'Senior nurse (wounded at Montbéliard)'; Massu in a similar manifesto claimed, 'Having had the honour of leading many women in wartime, both in the Leclerc Division during the campaign in France, as well as later in INDOCHINA, I know what they are capable of'. Donald Reid, 'The Worlds of Frantz Fanon's "L'Algérie se dévoile"', *French Studies*, 61: 4 (2007), 471, notes that in 1944–45 Massu led the Rochambeau ambulance division during the Second World War.

8 Fiona Reid, 'The Croix Rouge Française: Femininity and Female Patriotism in Inter-war France', unpublished paper, conference 'Refugees, Outcasts and Migrants, 1930–50', University of Glamorgan, 23 February 2008.

9 Conklin, Alice. L., 'Redefining "Frenchness": Citizenship, Race Regeneration, and Imperial Motherhood in France and West Africa, 1914–40', in Clancy-Smith and Gouda (eds), *Domesticating the Empire*, 65–82.

10 Thompson, *Colonial Citizens*, 85, 240.

11 On the concept of the 'incorporated wife' see Hilary Callan, 'The Premise of Dedication: Notes Towards an Ethnography of Diplomat's Wives', in Shirly Ardener (ed.), *Perceiving Women* (London: Malaby Press, 1975), 87–104; Hilary Callan and Shirley Ardener (eds), *The Incorporated Wife* (London: Croom Helm, 1984).

12 Philanthropic work with Indian women (hygiene, education, domestic training) was also an expected role of colonels' wives in the British army in India: see Mary A. Procida, *Married to the Empire. Politics and Imperialism in India, 1883–1947* (Manchester: Manchester University Press, 2002), 43–7, 165–89. In the British and French armies it was also traditional for colonels' wives to adopt a welfare function in relation to the wives of lower-ranking soldiers or to assume a 'motherly' role towards men in the regiment, for example visiting and comforting the sick or wounded in hospital: see Mona Macmillan, 'Camp Followers: A Note on Wives of the Armed Services', in Callan and Ardener (eds), *Incorporated Wife*, 100–2; Rosemary McKechnie, 'Living with Images of a Fighting Elite: Women and the Foreign Legion', in Sharon Macdonald, Pat Holden and Shirley Ardener (eds), *Images of Women in Peace and War. Cross-Cultural and Historical Perspectives* (London: Macmillan, 1987), 131–2.

13 CAOM 9CAB100, *Oeuvres de bienfaisance*, by Mme Naegelen 1951; 10CAB20, *Thé dames musulmanes* and receptions by Mme Léonard, 1951–54.

14 A fuller official title was *Mouvement d'Action Sociale et de Solidarité Féminine* and the local organising committees were named *Comité d'Action Sociale* (CAS).

15 SHAT 1H2409, report, *L'Arme psychologique en 10 R.M*, August 1957; Ryme Seferdjeli, 'The French Army and Muslim Women During the Algerian War (1954–62)', *Hawwa*, 31 (2005), 43–4.

16 SHAT 1H1215/3, SAU Cité Mahiéddine; CAOM 2SAS53, SAU Belcourt.

17 Dore-Audibert, *Des Françaises d'Algérie*, 74; d'Humière, *L'Armée française*, 149–66; Massu, *Vraie Bataille*, 189–96.

18 Reid, 'The Worlds', 472, note 53, remarks, 'some said General Massu made orphans and his wife took care of them'. Reid, 460–1, 472, also comments on the acerbic analysis of Roland Barthes, 'Tricots à domicile', *Les Lettres Nouvelles*, No. 7 (April 1959), reprinted in *Oeuvres complètes*, Vol. 1, 1942–1965 (Paris: Seuil, 1993), 805–7.

19 Massu, *Vraie Bataille*, 196.

20 SHAT 1H2461/1, report of Colonel Bravelet, 151e RIM, Guelma Sector to Fifth Bureau, 26 October 1957.

21 The UNAF was established by the Ordinance of 3 March 1945 to co-ordinate all associations relating to women and family policy.

22 SHAT 1H2569, Chef Bureau Psychologique Constantinois to Cabinet Militaire, Algers, 23 October 1957.

23 Massu, *Le Torrent*, 100–1.

24 SHAT 1H2461/1, telex from Fifth Bureau, 20 May 1958; Goussault's secret role in creating the MSF is noted in an unsigned Aide-mémoire, 17 October 1959, CAOM 13CAB61.

25 Massu, *Le Torrent*, 103, dismissed this as silly women's business (*'rififi' féminins*), but admitted that the row threatened to cause problems for their husbands as senior commanders.

26 CAOM 13CAB37*, letter of Mme Salan to Massu, 17 October 1958.
27 Thompson, *Colonial Citizens*, 66–70, 76.
28 The memoirs of EMSI, MSF and SAS/SAU personnel reveal the constant search for resources, see for example, Thévenin-Copin, *Plaidoyer*.
29 See Salan, *Mémoires*. Vol. 3., 293, 296, 312.
30 CAOM 14CAB88, General Hubert to Madame Salan, 20 November 1958.
31 After General Salan was recalled to France in December 1958 his replacement as *délégué générale*, Paul Delouvrier, as part of the Gaullist strategy to reassert civil political control over the army, severely pruned the MSF budget and subjected it to careful audit: see CAOM 14CAB88, note of Mafart, director of cabinet, 22 May 1959; Delouvrier letter to General Secretary MSF, 4 June 1959.
32 See for example SHAT 1H2461/1, report of Captain Schlumberger on Salan's tour through the Orléansville region in September 1958.
33 Simone Galice, a dedicated member of the *Centres sociaux* movement, described Mme Massu as 'honest, intelligent and humane', see Dore-Audibert, *Des Françaises d'Algérie*, 74.
34 SHAT 1H2483, press cutting: interview with Jacques Perrier, *L'Aurore*, 31 August 1959. See also Massu's personal undated MSF 'manifesto', CAOM 13CAB61.
35 CAOM 13CAB61, unauthored *Aide-Mémoire*, 17 October 1958, probably by Jacques de Mari. The legal Statutes established four kinds of annual membership, adherents (100 Fr.), active members (1,000 Fr.), sympathisers (2,000 Fr.) and benefactors (5,000 Fr.).
36 CAOM 81F888, a SDECE report, 6 June 1958, noted that the FLN 'has passed orders to flood all the organisations newly created by the French authorities with militants'.
37 Massu, *Le Torrent*, 103.
38 CAOM 13CAB61, transcript of Mme Massu radio broadcast, in series *Magazine social de la femme*, 11 August 1958. The radical silence regarding the negative aspects of military action can be found in the accounts of most *Algérie française* participants in the EMSI, SAS and MSF, such as Thévenin-Copin, *Plaidoyer*: a singular exception is Monique Eoche-Duval, *Madame SAS*, who shared with her SAS husband a difficult and dangerous opposition to senior officers who engaged in torture and mindless brutality. Sambron, *Femmes musulmanes*, 78–84, argues that the EMSI failed to implement the propaganda side of the military agenda and engaged in disinterested welfare activities: but this is to accept at face value the ideological 'humanism' of Thévenin-Copin and others which created a smokescreen for the reality of the EMSI deeply embedded within a repressive military apparatus.
39 CAOM 14CAB88, draft of standard letter by Madame Salan.
40 CAOM 13CAB37*, letter of Mme Delignette, 23 November 1958.
41 See, for example, on the role of colonial service wives in Uganda, Beverley Gartrell, 'Colonial Wives: Villains or Victims?', in Callan and Ardener (eds), *Incorporated Wife*, 176–80.

42 CAOM 2SAS53, Bernhardt, *Bulletin de Renseignements* for May 1958.

43 SHAT 1H2569, EMSI report, July 1958. Another report from Tablat in November 1958 said that the only way to get Europeans and Muslim wives of local notables to assist was through pressure from the authorities who should make them see they were not, 'the only ones to gain from the benefits of European civilisation'.

44 Launay, *Paysans algériens*, 94, who was present in the rich Oran region during 1960–61, notes, 'The wives of the small *colons* cordially detested the wives of the big *colons*, these arrogant people who claimed to undertake charity while ruling over the Comités de Solidarité Féminine created after the "13th of May"'.

45 There is a remarkable precedent for the MSF in the *Union des femmes coloniales* which was constituted by the wives of civil servants and colonial agents in the Belgian Congo, whose main remit was to 'civilise' Black native women through infant care, hygiene, and sewing and knitting circles (*ouvroirs*): see Catherine Jacques and Valérie Piette, 'L'Union des femmes coloniales (1923–1940). Une association au service de la colonisation', in Anne Hugon (ed.), *Histoire des femmes en situation coloniale. Afrique et Asie, XXe siècle* (Paris: Karthala, 2004), 95–117. The fact that in the Congo such an intervention by women from metropolitan Europe could occur some thirty years before Algeria seems to be linked to the fact that the former was not a colony of settlement, so that no white society was entrenched (as in Algeria, South Africa, Rhodesia, etc.) with racist and segregationist interests that tended to block social welfare and interventionist programmes for indigenous women.

46 For the general background see Duchen, *Women's Rights*, on the conservative implications of natalist policy, Jean-Noel Biraben and J. Dupâquier, *Les Berceaux vides de Marianne: l'avenir de la population française* (Paris: Seuil, 1981).

47 Ross, *Fast Cars, Clean Bodies*.

48 On the history of the CNFF and Lefaucheux see the on-line introduction and catalogue to the *Fonds du CNFF (2AF)* held at the *Centre des Archives du Féminisme* (CAF), University of Angers: www.bu.univ-angers.fr/index.

49 CAOM 13CAB37*, report of Central Committee of MSF, 20 August 1958.

50 On the three candidates see Seferdjeli, 'French "Reforms"', 19–61.

51 *Christian Science Monitor*, 2 March 1959, interview with Lefaucheux; CAOM 81F1219: Sid Cara and Lefaucheux presented a joint draft decree to the commission.

52 CAOM 14CAB88, R. Martinet to Mafart, 22 May 1959.

53 Just a decade earlier Héliopolis had been at the epicentre of the Sétif massacre and settler militias had burned Algerian corpses in the lime kilns of the town.

54 SHAT 1H2461/1, report by Mme Tournemine, 8 pages typed, forwarded by Bravelet to General Vanuxem, commander of ZEC, 9 June 1958.

55 Thévenin-Copin, *Plaidoyer*, 108–9. The Muslim husband on a donkey before his heavily laden wife on foot, or of the husband driving a plough team of mule and wife was a standard colonial caricature in Algeria: see the image titled 'Bonheur conjugal' in Mauss-Copeaux, *A Travers le Viseur*. 66–7,

56 SHAT 1H2461/1, reports of Captain Schlumberger to Colonel Goussault, 5 and 20 September 1958.

57 The key sources are CAOM 14CAB88 and CAOM 81F74 and, unless otherwise specified, provide the basis for the subsequent analysis. Rio-Salado was famous throughout Algeria for the wealth of its European wine producers, and later as a major centre of recruitment for the OAS: interview with Michel Launay, Paris, 25 June 2008.

58 On rural–urban migration and the *villages nègres* in Oranie see Xavier Yacono, *La Colonisation des plaines du Chélif* (Algiers: E. Imbert, 1955–56), 2 Vols; and more generally Descloitres et al., *L'Algérie des bidonvilles*; and André Prenant, 'Facteurs du peuplement d'une ville de l'Algérie intérieure: Sétif', *Annales de Géographie*, Vol. 72, Nov.–Dec. 1953, 434–51.

59 Launay, *Paysans algériens*, has detailed information on Sidi-Saïd, Rio-Salado, and the region by an academic and SAS conscript who carried out field research in 1960–62. Sidi-Saïd was also the location of a prison camp (*Centre de tri et de transit*) for male and female FLN detainees: Michel Launay, interview, Paris, 25 June 2008.

60 *Ibid.*, 58–9, 82.

61 *Ibid.*, 173–4, 282–3.

62 *Ibid.*, 282–5, 303–4: the minimum wage for men was 6.91 Fr. per day; 5 Fr. for women, 4 Fr. for children, whose productivity frequently matched that of men.

63 CAOM 81F74, petition from Rio-Salado. Launay, *Paysans algériens*, 283, estimates the number of widows in Sidi-Saïd at 250–300.

64 Launay, *Paysans algériens*, 144–51, 362. The local tension between Reformist, pro-FLN supporters, and a more a-political populism reflected a class division between relatively better-off Algerian landowners and self-employed (shopkeepers, traders), and the mass of poor day-labourers.

65 The French army and administration disguised the fact that Sidi-Saïd was a resettlement camp, and it shared in the extreme poverty of such forced locations: see Michel Cornaton, *Les Regroupements de la décolonisation en Algérie* (Paris: Éditions ouvrières, 1967), 156–8; Launay, *Paysans algériens*, 184.

66 Cornaton, *Les Regroupements*, 160, notes for this region bitter complaints by men that low-paid female labour was being used by *colons* to displace them.

67 Launay, *Paysans algériens*, 330, describes this as a form of charity rather than a meaningful economic project.

68 *Ibid.*, 279–340, has a detailed analysis of the methods used by both Algerian and European landowners to avoid implementation of welfare legislation

relating to minimum wages, paid holidays, family benefits, limits on daily hours of work, and other social rights.

69 On the racial founding myths of *colons* identity see Peter Dunwoodie, *Writing French Algeria* (Oxford: Clarendon Press, 1998); Pierre Nora, *Les Français d'Algérie* (Paris: Julliard, 1961). A contemporary *pieds-noirs* web-site for Rio-Salado fully sustains the myth of how courageous settlers transformed 'these wild and deserted places', and established in this, 'ungrateful and infertile soil . . . these fine properties, these magnificent vineyards' and a village with numerous squares and gardens, 'spacious, perfectly tendered, prettily laid out, pleasantly adorned with flowers and perfectly fragrant'. Algerians were air-brushed from this paradise. http://coundris.chez-alice.fr/f_repertoire4.htm (accessed 22 September 2006).

70 Mme Tournemine, from her experience in Héliopolis, advised that women organising circles needed to be courageous and meet 'the hostility of her entourage and most of the Europeans in the area': SHAT 1H2461/1.

71 See Stedman-Jones, *Outcast London*, Part 3, on the austere Victorian idea that indiscriminate charity could only encourage the indolence, vice and 'demoralisation' of the under-class.

72 The brassiere, not worn by rural women, was an evident sign of western propriety: when one ASSRA team distributed bras and explained their use, they later found them made into hats for children, see Mathias, *Les Sections administratives*, 86.

73 *Femmes nouvelles*, 6 (November 1958): this can be consulted at the Paris Bibliothèque nationale, FOL-JO-10185.

74 *Ibid.*, 13 (6 March 1959).

75 Norbert Elias, *The Civilizing Process. Vol. 1. The History of Manners* [first published in German, 1939] (Oxford: Basil Blackwell, 1978 edn).

76 CAOM 81F74.

77 Separate meetings with Algerian men was a standard Fifth Bureau procedure during the MSF campaign; the British in Ghana also recognised the need in a patriarchal society to 'bring men on-side', see Anne Hugon, 'La Redéfinition de la maternité en Gold Coast, des années 1920 aux années 1950: projet colonial et réalités locales', in Hugon (ed.), *Histoire des femmes*, 154–5.

78 See a reproduction in Sambron, *Femmes musulmanes*, 53, of an army poster of an unveiled Muslim woman with the caption, 'Are you not pretty? Unveil yourself': SHAT 1H2504/1.

79 Such oral history information is available for Ghana: Jean Allman, 'Making Mothers: Missionaries, Medical Officers and Women's Work in Colonial Asante', *History Workshop Journal*, 38 (1994), 23–48, argues that Asante women were profoundly disinterested in the agenda of 'maternal imperialists', learned nothing new from mother-craft lessons, but were active agents who pragmatically negotiated or shaped the process to gain access to medicines, soap and clothing.

80 CAOM 14CAB88, Gambiez to DGG, 24 May 1959.

81 See Callaway, *Gender, Culture and Empire*; Hugon, 'La Redéfinition', 145–71; Allman, 'Making Mothers'.
82 Hugon (ed.), *Histoire des femmes*, represents a move in this direction; John Iliffe, *The African Poor. A History* (Cambridge: Cambridge University Press, 1987), 206–8 has information on French post-war social services in colonial Africa, but this was relatively under-funded and fragile compared to the British colonies.

6

Military 'pacification' and the women of Bordj Okhriss

So far the study of the MSF has centred mainly on grass-roots emancipation processes in *urban* society, but in many ways the French attempt to elaborate a strategy of contact was even more important in the isolated high plains and mountains of the interior since this is where 80 per cent of the population lived and in which the ALN maquis found its local support. This terrain provided an excellent base for the insurgents, zones that were almost impenetrable to modern armed forces, and in which the guerrilla fighters, knowledgeable of every sheep-track, cave and gully, could move with ease and quickly melt away to avoid any pursuing commandos. A fundamental problem for the army in the zones of pacification was how to engage in actions that would destroy guerrilla bands, their bases and logistical support within the local peasant community, with all its attendant violence, and simultaneously win the population over to supporting the French political order through providing them with security, schools, medical centres, roads and a 'higher order' of progress and civilisation than the 'bandits' could ever offer. Algerian peasant women found themselves, as have women universally in so many theatres of war from Palestine to Vietnam, caught in the eye of the storm and in order to understand the difficulties facing the EMSI teams, their success or failure in winning over the inhabitants (see chapter 7), it is necessary first to take into account the context of insecurity, the accompanying and contradictory violence of the armed forces, with which they were inevitably associated.

The historian faces little shortage of evidence, from participant memoirs of combatants to extensive archive sources, to establish the general features of military operations and their impact on local Algerian civil populations. What is singularly lacking, and difficult to research, are first-hand accounts by Algerian peasant women of their experiences of the war and how they related, if at all, to the attempts by the French to extend an emancipation agenda to them.[1] Did Muslim women welcome or oppose the French initiative and how did this vary across class, between for example those from an educated bourgeoisie and illiterate peasantry; across the complex map of Algerian space by urban and rural or regional affiliation; and through time, as the fortunes of each side ebbed and flowed?[2] Amrane, using the official data of registered women militants, has been able to provide important statistical insights, but what is needed here is more in-depth, qualitative information on the mental universe of female combatants and 'sympathisers'. Of the few interviews that have been carried out with Algerian women about their experience of the war, the majority have been with educated women of urban origin, and very few indeed have been with rural women, most of whom were illiterate and have left little if any record.[3] In the absence of a detailed ethnography or oral history of the war,[4] one of the most potent, alternative sources of information lies in the evidence of the many thousands of photographs that were taken of peasant women in the *bled* that recorded their contact with, and reactions to, the French army and administration and the various agencies, like the EMSI, that were designed to assist in their emancipation.

The most famous war photographs that relate specifically to Algerian women in the *bled* were taken by the young conscript Marc Garanger in 1960–61. Garanger, an unofficial regimental photographer, based with his army unit in the isolated village of Bordj Okhriss 120 kilometres to the south-east of Algiers, was ordered by his commander to take identity-card photographs of some 2,000 men and women located in the villages and resettlement camps of Aïn Terzine, Bordj Okhriss, le Mesdour, le Meghnine, S'Bara and Souk el Khrémis.[5] While on home-leave in 1961 Garanger, with the aid of FLN sympathiser Robert Barrat, was able to go clandestinely into Switzerland with his photographs and six portraits of women appeared in the *Illustré Suisse* with a text by Charles-Henri Favrod with the basic message, 'here is what France is doing in Algeria'.[6] From the very beginning the photographs, like several other iconic images of Garanger such as that of the captured FLN commander Ahmed Bencherif, were associated with a pro-FLN and anti-war position. In 1966 the images of women, reformatted from cropped 'passport' size to more aesthetic waist-length portraits, gained the prestigious Niepce Prize, and in the following years were exhibited world-wide and finally published in 1982 as *Femmes Algériennes 1960*.[7]

The women of Bordj Okhriss were coerced by the army to remove their veils in order to have their photographs taken and the images have been widely interpreted, including by Garanger himself, as a symbol of the inherent violence of colonial domination and war, and capturing the moment when the women expressed their angry defiance and proud dignity before the eye of the invasive camera.

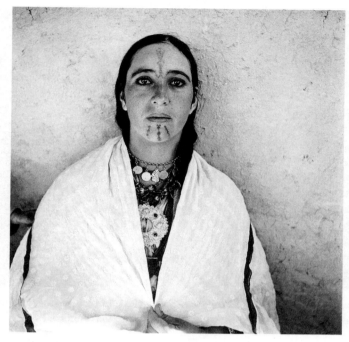

8 Woman unveiled for identity photograph, Bordj Okhriss 1960. The tattoos
indicate that the local Arabophone people still carried the trace of their
original Berber culture

[handwritten note: "Berber?"]

In each village the population was summoned by the officer of the army
post. It was the faces of the women which impressed me so much. They
had no choice in the matter. They were under the obligation to unveil and
to let themselves be photographed. They had to sit outside on a stool in
front of the white wall of a *mechta*. I was on the receiving end of their
point-blank stares, first witness to their silent and smouldering protest. I
wish [in these photographs] to bear witness to them.[8]

Some of the women resisted having their photograph taken and one of
them, Yamina Boukaf, told Garanger in 2004, 'I remember very well the
day the photos were taken. If I am not among them, it's because I didn't
want to do it. When we had to go, I pretended to be ill'.[9] In later years
Garanger elaborated further on the conditions under which the photographs were taken: 'I was circled by armed soldiers to take the shots. The
response of the women to the act of aggression against them is visible in
each of their expressions'.[10] In the light of such comment, the dynamics
of the situation begins to shift: as with numerous French accounts of
contact with Algerian women, as with the EMSI and MSF in general in

9 Zohra Gacem, Bordj Okhriss, holding the identity photograph taken
forty-four years earlier by Marc Garanger

which the presence of the military is occluded, we are suddenly made
aware of the fact that each Algerian women is seated facing not only a
lens, but also a line of armed soldiers. Similarly, no matter how peaceful and caring may seem the myriad depictions of EMSI nurses tending
to Algerian babies and their mothers, French welfare intervention was
always under the immediate or imminent sign of the gun, and no matter
how much the Europeans protested it, the relationship could never be
one of equality.

In 2004 Garanger was able to return to Bordj Okhriss for the first
time in over forty years and to locate and meet several of the surviving
women, including Cherid Barkaoun, one of the two wives of the silversmith of Bordj Okhriss. Here another detail emerges: the women of
Bordj Okhriss, like most of those in rural Algeria, did not wear a face-veil
but, if they wished to protect themselves from the gaze of a stranger, they
could draw the loose *haïk* together with their hand. The conditions under
which the *haïk* was removed were not determined by Garanger with the
soldiers as a silent guard, but by the direct intervention of an officer:

> In the beginning the women lowered their veil [*haïk*] which they draped
> over their shoulders, but kept their head-scarf. Immediately the officer
> demanded that they take this off too. This was a terrible humiliation
> for these women, to appear with uncovered hair in front of the French

10 Cherid Barkaoun, one of the two wives of the silversmith of Bordj Okhriss, expressing her distress

soldiers. Some literally looked at me to kill. Above all most of them expressed an incredible distress. This is the case here, as with Cherid Barkaoun. Her look tells us all about the drama she was experiencing at this moment.[11]

The identity photographs were ordered by the army command in a climate that was suffused with sneering contempt and racism for Algerian women: when Garanger placed the prints on the desk of a captain in the Aumale HQ, he called out to other officers, 'Come and see, come and see how ugly they are! Come and see these baboons, just like monkeys!'[12]

The *Femmes algériennes* sequence provides powerful visual evidence of the nature of the interrelationship between the occupying French forces and peasant women. Here, what may appear to be a relatively low-key and mundane event encapsulates the climate of coercion and fear under which Algerian women lived constantly. Disempowered and voiceless, they were still able to express an inner resistance, or to use Marnia Lazreg's phrase, 'the eloquence of silence', a defiance and sense of integrity and honour that no humiliations could breach.

The images of *Femmes algériennes* have been widely discussed and analysed, but mainly from a literary and deconstructionist angle that deploys critical theory to interpret the structure and meaning of the 'gaze'.[13] However, there exists a danger in failing to provide a careful reading of these images that places them in a historical, sociological or anthropological context. The failure to examine the background encourages a largely subjective approach in which the author is able, in some magical way, to tell us what the silent women looking at the camera are thinking and feeling.[14] Subjectivity is here often grounded in the assumption that Algerian women and French forces were locked into a self-evident conflictual opposition, a Manichean relationship between two homogeneous blocks, the oppressor and the oppressed. Algerian women universally hate and resist all things French, while all Europeans are part of the same, undifferentiated block of colonial oppressors. The problem with this, apart from the tendency to caricature, is to engage in an over-simplifying and reductionist approach that fails to note what is most interesting about the situation, the extraordinary complexity and internal divisions of the local society in which these women lived, and the often ambiguous relationship of Algerian peasants to the occupier. For example, Garanger took a number of photographs of the local *harkis* who fought with the French army, including intimate domestic scenes with their wives and children, and these women would also have been among those who had their identity photographs taken.[15] They also may have objected to having their photographs taken, in breach of the code of female honour, but their attitude to the armed forces is likely to have been quite different since their safety from FLN assassination depended on the protection of the French. That the relationship between peasant women and the French was not always one of unmitigated hostility is captured in another sequence of photographs that Garanger was able to take of women inside their homes, usually a forbidden (*haram*) space, since he was able to accompany a team of female welfare assistants who had already established a basis of trust.[16] Among these domestic scenes are intimate portraits of women, smiling and relaxed as they breast-fed their babies, wove or prepared food.[17]

A further level of complication in the taking of these identity photographs is that, although described vaguely as intended for policing purposes, and therefore as part of the apparatus of control and repression, they had also a more benign function. As will be seen in chapter 8, the French administration faced considerable difficulty in implementing its emancipation agenda because of the failure, especially in isolated rural areas, to register births, marriages and deaths, and to constitute a civil register (*état civil*). The difficulty in identifying women then carried a

11 Smiling woman breast-feeding her baby, Bordj Okhriss 1960

number of negative consequences when it came to the implementation of various rights, including from September 1958 onwards the right to vote, the granting of family allowances, and the application of the 1959 marriage law which included checks by officials to ensure brides were above the new minimum age of fifteen years. The senior civil servant André Jacomet in December 1959 ordered a crash programme of registration, especially of women, and in September 1960 the Sub-Prefect of Aumale was co-ordinating major census operations in Bordj Okhriss and the surrounding resettlement camps.[18] While identity cards were used to control movements of people they were also, and this is a typical contradiction of the war, a necessary part of trying to extend reforms and to create a functioning civil society.

The remaining part of this chapter sets out to move beyond the identity-card sequence, which has often been treated in isolation from the context in which the photographs were taken, by looking at the larger oeuvre of Marc Garanger, which consists of over 10,000 photographs that provide an outstanding and sympathetic record of both the daily life of the conscripts, as well as of the local Algerian community.[19] This record is unusual since not only was Garanger a professional

photographer who was left free to wander through the villages, but
unlike most army photographers who were dispatched daily to cover
specific military operations and events right across Algeria, the corpus
provides an in-depth view into the life of *one* locale, a rural war zone
that experienced the full brunt of conflict as well as welfare reformism
and emancipation. A second source of information about Bordj Okhriss
can be found in the extensive army and civil archives for this area.[20] The
overall aim here is not so much to engage in a close critical examination
of Garanger's oeuvre but to use the region in which he was located as
a case-study, a starting point, from which to illustrate the difficult and
often violent conditions faced by Algerian rural populations during
the so-called 'pacification'. It is with these conditions in mind that we
then move on in chapter 7 to look more closely at the difficulties faced
by the strategy of contact, and in particular the EMSI teams that were
operating in zones of continuous violence, destruction and uprooting.

The military sector of Aumale[21] to which Garanger was posted in
early March 1960 covered a huge area of high and impenetrable mountainous terrain, which towards Aumale sloped into the grain-farming
region of the High Plains, and further south, the arid and treeless wastes
of the Saharan fringe. Away from the main highways, much of the
settled or semi-nomadic peasantry lived in dispersed farms (*mechtas*) or
douars that could only be reached by mule along small dirt tracks, until
the army, using bulldozers and *corvée* labour, began to blast strategic
routes to supply military posts and control the interior.[22] This huge
zone, larger than the county of Norfolk, was, apart from the small
towns of Aumale and Aïn Bessem, almost completely devoid of settlers,
and in the quartier of Aïn Terzine in which Garanger was located, there
were only ten civilian Europeans for an Algerian population of 14,000.
Historically, through the early twentieth century, the *pieds-noirs* farmers
had deserted the *bled* for the towns and, after 1954, because of FLN
raids on isolated farms,[23] this evacuation had accelerated further, so that
by 1961 the tiny colonial population of the Aumale sector (2,328) was
cooped up in the townships, outnumbered by a largely hostile Algerian
population of 210,978. In this situation, redolent of a fragile American
frontier society constantly endangered by turbulent Indian tribes, by far
the biggest European presence (4,400 men) was that of the army.[24]

In this zone of low and unreliable rainfall and poor soils the great
mass of the peasantry scratched a bare living from cereal and livestock,
using primitive farming techniques, and the army reported that 'eighty-
five per cent of the population live in poverty on an average annual
income of 200 new francs'.[25] The men at Aïn Terzine faced seasonal
unemployment for most of the year and, after the intensive labour of

the harvest, in which many worked as day-labourers or share-croppers (*khammès*) for bigger Algerian landowners, many were either hired by the SAS for relief work on road and housing construction or migrated towards Algiers and France.[26] After a century of neglect by the colonial government the rural population of Aumale was almost devoid of any supportive investment or infrastructure, including basic medical provision and schools. For the whole sector of 200,000 people there were only five civilian doctors in 1960, and before 1954 in the vast arid tracts of the south and mountain zones some inhabitants had never seen a European.[27] One SAS officer reported, 'No health centre, no civilian doctor, no technical assistant, no nurses, no welfare assistants, and isolation because of the insecure roads (Masqueray) or distance (Maginot)', areas in which neither civilian nor military doctors were prepared to go and work.[28]

The endemic poverty and underdevelopment of the peasant and pastoral societies of the Aumale sector was in most respects quite typical of the deep rural crisis to be found across the mountainous zones of northern Algeria.[29] Such colonial exploitation and grinding poverty provided good conditions for the spread of the nationalist movement after 1945,[30] but Aïn Terzine was to play a particularly important strategic role throughout the War of Independence since the impenetrable mountain zone immediately to the north, the Forest of Bordj Okhriss, and to the south, the hilly Bougadouen, provided a refuge for the maquis of both the ALN and the opposing MNA. ALN units, in particular the hundred-man Katiba 611, carried out constant attacks into the plains, cutting telegraph posts, laying siege to army posts, and ambushing patrols and road convoys, but their most important function was to provide secure resting places, food and local guides for long-distance columns bringing weapons and equipment from Tunisia via the Saharan fringes to supply the important Wilaya IV (Algiers) and Wilaya III (Great Kabylia) to the north. An army report noted: 'A cross-roads too for the rebels who profit from the strips of wooded and mountainous terrain to maintain their communications between the Ouarsensis and the Bibans chain, and to supply Wilaya III with livestock from the high plateaux'.[31] During early May 1958 army intelligence tracked a convoy of 160 porters carrying arms supplies (a mortar, machine guns, rifles, ammunition) as it moved from the south through the Bordj Okhriss Forest towards Haizer in the Kabyle mountains to the north: by the 4 June the French army had attacked this unit and killed ninety-eight men.[32]

By late 1957 the ALN maquis, having won a long and bloody civil war to defeat the MNA in this region,[33] was at the height of its military power and it was at this stage that General de Maison Rouge, who had gained a reputation for the successful pacification of the Aïn-Témouchent region in Oranie, was appointed commander of Aumale. The crucial strategic importance of the sector was fully recognised by him as a cross-roads, 'a veritable nerve-centre between the Mitidja, Kabylia and the Constantine region', and General Allard on appointing Maison Rouge in January 1958 instructed him, 'Your mission is to cut Algeria in two between the Blida Atlas and the High Plateaux. If you succeed the rebellion will not be able to survive in the Algiers region'.[34] This explains why Bordj Okhriss, sitting astride the FLN transit corridor and with a powerful maquis in the hills above, was the centre of intense military operations that impacted constantly on the lives of the local people.

Women and the maquis[35]

During 1955–56 the FLN began to recruit both qualified and trainee nurses from the towns to go into the maquis to provide crucial medical care for wounded men in make-shift hospitals concealed in forest huts and caves. This professional core was expanded during 1957 through the arrival of lycée and university students, many of them fleeing the towns to escape arrest by the army after the student strike of May 1956 and the Battle of Algiers. These young women, the *moudjahidates*, led an extremely harsh and dangerous life,[36] and as army operations penetrated deeper into the mountains after 1958 they were, along with their ALN units, forced into interminable marches at night to avoid detection or encirclement. Often hungry, living in caves, lean-to shelters and holes in the ground, infested with lice, facing extremes of hot and freezing or rainy weather, the maquisards showed extraordinary resilience in tending severely wounded soldiers and, often short of medicine and equipment, improvising splints, herbal remedies, treatment of gangrene and amputations without anaesthetics or penicillin.

Equal, if not more important, to the ability of the ALN forces to survive in the *bled* was the day-to-day support provided by local peasant or nomadic women. When ALN units, which were almost constantly on the move, arrived in an isolated mountain village or desert encampment, the local women would volunteer (or be coerced) to improvise and cook for dozens of men in a situation where they and their children faced desperate poverty and food shortages.[37] In addition the peasantry washed clothes, kept guard, provided shelter, carried messages and arms, and transported supplies into the mountains from the markets, shops and FLN depots of the towns in the plains. As one interviewee told Amrane, with typical brevity and self-effacement: 'I was a *moussebila*: I carried weapons, I washed the clothes, did the cooking, collected money, and reported any intelligence'.[38] A maquisarde recalled, 'The women of the hamlets helped us. All the hard work, it was them that did it: they milled the wheat, rolled the couscous, and made the bread. When we arrived exhausted, they had prepared the meal . . . They suffered . . . We, we could escape when the soldiers came and we were armed, we could defend ourselves'.[39]

The 'domestic' and invisible gendered work of the local civilian *moussebilate* and 'sympathisers', which was vital to the ALN maquis, went largely unreported in post-war Algerian histories and autobiographies by men who recorded their own heroic fighting deeds, and yet the peasant women and their children were far more exposed to the punitive violence of the French army, including burning of houses and rape, than the younger, celibate and mobile men and women of the ALN. In areas like Bordj Okhriss in which the conflict between French army and nationalist forces was most intense and long-lasting a high percentage of the able-bodied, married men deserted the villages in order to join the maquis, to escape forced recruitment into MNA bands, to avoid constant army and FLN harassment, or to find work in the cities of Algeria and France. The ALN, cut-off in the mountains by the army, became increasingly dependent on the liaison and support of communities of women: as a Kabyle peasant noted, 'There are only women left in the village . . . The women have stayed behind; if the women had gone there would be no-one left to feed the fighters (*fellaghas*)'.[40]

Small numbers of *moudjahidate* operated in the ALN maquis in the Aumale sector, and in the mountains between Bordj Okhriss and Bouira.[41] For example, army intelligence which constantly monitored the movements of ALN Commando 322–1 through the Forest of Bordj Okhriss during 1960 reported the creation of a new HQ camp for twenty men and one woman nurse, along with various food and clothing caches.[42] The special French Commando units (*Commando de chasse*), like the 'Kimono 11', sometimes found women in ALN fighting units in the area,[43] but far more important was the extensive supply role played by women living within the villages like Aïn Terzine and Bordj Okhriss. The OPA, the FLN clandestine political network, penetrated deep and silently into the social fabric of the townships of Bordj Okhriss and Mesdour[44] and was able to infiltrate militants into the main French civilian and military institutions: for example, three town councillors were reported to be acting as FLN collectors in early 1960 and Gestraoui, a sergeant in the Mesdour *harka*, was arrested for FLN collaboration and was photographed by Garanger along with his family at the moment of their deportation.[45] The battalion at Aïn Terzine deployed exceptional, but standardised, forms of violence to extract information from captured

ALN fighters or arrested militants. When men were intercepted during operations in the mountains or *zones interdites* they were often beaten on the spot,[46] and while key suspects were whisked away for interrogation, other less 'valuable' fighters were killed under the guise of the infamous wood collection fatigues (*corvée de bois*) or 'shot in escape'.[47] Despite constant surveillance, numerous arrests and torture by intelligence officers (OR), army reports reveal deep frustration at the ability of the FLN cells to recover and reorganise no matter how harsh the repression.

As the peasant population was uprooted and moved from the isolated mountain zones into camps, so the maquis became increasingly dependent on food supplies that filtered in from the *douars* and markets in the valleys below. The important weekly market at Bordj Okhriss, attended by up to 2,000 traders who came in from miles around on foot or by mule and horse, was closely policed by the SAS soldiers (*maghzen*) to prevent foodstuffs reaching the ALN. A report noted the need to suppress, 'the small-scale and un-monitored dealing in the *douars*. The population must be brought to make its acquisitions only with the retailers established in the markets and village centres, surveillance allowing us to detect if the purchases exceed the needs of the family'.[48] But an army map showed that Bordj Okhriss continued in late 1959 to be the main supply centre for three maquis bases in the mountains to the north, north-west and south.[49] Much of the provision supply into the mountains was effected by local women, and the sector commander laid down plans in November 1960 to intercept aid reaching the ALN from the re-settlement camps: 'control of the night-time isolation of these New Villages, control over food supplies being taken by inhabitants of the village, especially women', into the interior (*bled*).[50] Commando units in the Aumale sector were constantly intercepting mule trains moving into the mountains, often accompanied by women, some of whom were married or related to ALN fighters, who fled on sight or were arrested.[51] ALN units operated by establishing carefully hidden supply caches of arms and food scattered over several square miles between which they constantly moved, and as French commandos led by Algerian trackers located and destroyed the depots they found evidence of the sophistication of the support network, tons of potatoes, flour, tinned goods (sardines, peas), coffee, oil, condensed milk, type-writers, transistor radios, medicines and clothing, some of which had been made by local women.[52]

Women, 'pacification' and military violence

The women of the Aumale sector, as in so many other parts of Algeria, were closely implicated in the activities of the FLN and as the level of army repression deepened after 1957 many of them, in the absence of males, began to exercise a degree of initiative and independence of action through 'man's work' that had traditionally been denied to them by a conservative, patriarchal society.[53] Algerian peasant women, playing such a key (but often 'invisible') role, became victims of army repression on a vast scale. It is necessary to grasp the nature and scale of such violence in order to begin to understand the difficulties that welfare and medical teams, and particularly the EMSI, faced in trying to elaborate programmes that would reach out to a constituency traumatised by war. The following section examines two kinds of violence, first the direct impact of the French army on civilian populations in the zones of combat, and second the more insidious but destructive process of resettlement (*regroupement*) that uprooted and dismantled peasant society.

Violence impinged deeply on the lives of women in the *bled* in many forms, including through the enormous mortality rate of husbands, sons and brothers. During 1958 some 70 per cent of all major operations in the Aumale sector were concentrated in Bordj Okhriss and the area to the south (Bougaouden) and here, between 1 January 1958 and 1 October 1959, the army killed 1,870 'rebels' and captured or wounded 1,847.[54] Certainly a good number of those killed in the ALN would have originated from outside the area,[55] but the official figures fail to include many of those men, including locals, who were summarily executed in large numbers. Some army commanders in the area regularly displayed dead fighters on the bonnets of army vehicles and forced terrorised villagers to file past the corpses as an 'exemplary lesson'.[56] The Kabyle writer Mouloud Feraoun describes scenes where, after mass killings by the army, distraught women, 'are wandering on the national highway, crying with despair and anger. There is not one single man alive in the village . . . In Azouza, there are no longer enough men for the funerals: the local women have to perform that chore'.[57] The ethnologist Camille Lacoste-Dujardin has recorded through the songs and oral traditions of women in the Iflissen tribe of Kabylia the trace of the long-term trauma following massive destruction and death, the suffering, 'of a depth that was until now unrecognised and which will leave them profoundly marked for ever'.[58] The scale of the military repression in the Iflissen was reflected, a decade later, in a demographic catastrophe: of the young men aged twenty to thirty-five in 1956, 41 per cent had been killed, adult women outnumbered men by over two to one, and traditional patriarchal families were radically dislocated, many households being now headed by single widows.

From 1956 onwards, as the army became increasingly aware of the direct involvement of Algerian women in the guerrilla, so attitudes changed from 'gentlemanly' respect for the 'weaker sex' towards treating women with the same brutal violence as men, including summary execution, systematic torture and rape. The most frequent occasion for brutal treatment of entire civilian populations arose during major army operations in the more isolated mountainous areas, the *zones interdites*, in which the maquis forces were based. In May 1955 General Parlange, the commander of the Aurès region, issued a directive by which any rebel act of sabotage or attack would have, 'as a consequence the collective responsibility of the nearest *douar*', a policy that was extended to all Algeria in July.[59] During operations that involved major clashes with the ALN the army regularly destroyed mountain villages by fire, explosives and bulldozer, both as a reprisal and to force inhabitants, suspected of supporting ALN forces, to flee into the plains. There are endless accounts, like the following, which is typical of reprisal operation:

> On the hillside I saw the advance of army sections into eleven villages indicated by columns of smoke rising from the farm-houses, mills and shacks as they caught fire. The next day the villages were positively plundered: not only did the units live off the land, but the shops were systematically raided, money stolen, the goods smashed, etc. The women were all herded together in order to place pressure on the men; they could not even go out to relieve themselves. While this was going on the men from whom one wished to extract denunciations were put to the 'question' [tortured].[60]

The reference here to using women as an instrument to place pressure on Algerian males leads to the issue of rape, a widespread practice by the French army that was long concealed on both sides, by ex-soldiers, the army authorities, women victims and the FLN. The occultation in French society of sexual violence during the war, a practice that most radically contradicted the self-proclaimed 'civilising mission' of the army, changed dramatically after 2000 following the revelations by Louisette Ighilahriz of the implication of senior commanders, including General Massu, in her rape,[61] the extraordinary Mohamed Garne affair,[62] and the publication of Raphaëlle Branche's *La Torture et l'armée* (2001).[63] Branche has established the widespread nature of rape, usually a collective act, used as an expression of power, humiliation and revenge against Muslim Algerian society in its most essential values based on female honour and purity of descent: 'through the woman, assaulted, sexually abused, raped, the soldiers got to her family, her village, and all the circles to which she belonged, right down to the last of them, the Algerian people'.[64] Algerian men, often forced to look on, were humiliated in their most sacred role as protectors of women.[65] On occasions French soldiers took trophy photographs of

12 An old woman protests to Commander de Mollans at the rape of her daughter by French soldiers

their exploits in a standard pose that consisted of two mates 'sharing' a naked woman who stands like a prisoner between the two men.[66] While the extent of rape varied from one locale to another (some officers would not tolerate such criminal abuse, while others were permissive or turned a blind eye), it was generalised and certainly existed at Bordj Okhriss as elsewhere. Jean-Louis Gérard, who was attached to the intelligence unit at Aïn Terzine notes that in January 1960 the OR organised a 'routine patrol . . . so that the lads could unwind', and although he was opposed to what was going on, admitted that on one occasion, 'I mounted guard outside while the others carried on their dirty work!'[67] Jean-Paul Meurisse, a friend of Garanger's at Bordj Okhriss, recounts how he arrived one day at Meghnine, 'The boss was waiting . . . with a dozen women next to him. "My lieutenant, you choose", he said. I was staggered. My predecessor had assumed a droit de seigneur'.[68] A photograph of Marc Garanger shows an old woman wiping tears from her face at the door of the army post of Le Taguedine where she had come to complain to the commander de Mollans about the rape of her daughter.[69]

'Bernard X' who operated with the *Commando de chasse* K11 just to the south of Bordj Okhriss notes that although their captain strictly banned such violence, on occasions a gendarme and SAS officer accompanied the unit because of complaints of 'exactions', and during an operation the commandos were astonished to see a terrified woman and her two daughters appear, 'their faces were covered with mud and blood, which gave them the appearance of spectres . . . it was to protect her daughters from eventual violence by the soldiers'.[70] This was undoubtedly a form of magical protection and mothers' traditionally left their new-born babies dirty in order to ward off the evil eye.[71]

Rape, although not constituting a system of ethnic 'pollution' and genocide as during the Balkan war, led to many unwanted pregnancies. Feraoun reported how during major operations the army behaved as if they were in a 'free brothel': at Aït Idir, 'only twelve women are willing to admit that they were raped', while people have 'counted fifty-six bastards in a village of the Béni-Ouacifs'.[72] In some instances abortions were carried out, but some women were able to stand strong against the enormous weight of male values of lineage and honour and insisted on keeping and raising the children. Mimi Ben Mohamed, a senior nurse who worked in a maquis near Palestro, to the north-west of Aïn Terzine, remarks that when they raised the issue of rape and pregnancies with the Commander Si Lakhdar, his suggestion was to kill the babies. '"No, that's impossible", objected the nurses, "we cannot kill the innocent. The kids have nothing to do with it, neither do the women since they were taken by force" . . . and in effect the women did not do it, but kept all these children. The fathers did not want to have these children, but eventually they kept them'.[73]

While army brutality against women assumed direct and overt forms, such as bombing of villages with napalm, rape and killings, a less direct but more generalised form of violence arose from the policy of population *regroupement*. This highly destructive uprooting of the peasantry needs to be understood within the wider context of the process of 'pacification'. As was seen in chapter 2 the Operation Pilot experiment in the Dahra tested the pacification of isolated rural zones controlled by the ALN in a series of stages and proved so successful that from late 1957 it was extended into other areas of Algeria. Under the impulse of General Challe, army strategists further refined the Pilot model into a standard four-stage process for the 'reconquest' of 'rotten' zones.[74] This involved a first phase of intense military action against the ALN maquis using huge sweep operations and newly formed *Commandos de chasses*, mobile units that included *harki* trackers that pursued the enemy night-and-day inside the *zone interdite* or free-fire areas. In a second phase, the inhabitants of the mountainous interior were to be evacuated by force, their

villages destroyed, and resettled in militarised camps protected by army
posts. Third, once removed from FLN pressure and terror, the population in the camps would find the confidence to establish their own armed
auto-defence units and to provide an increasing flow of intelligence about
ALN networks and collaborators. When security had reached a safe level
in a particular area, now designated a 'quartier de pacification', the army
could reduce its presence and move on to repeat the process in an adjacent
rebel zone. Finally, the ALN would have been virtually destroyed and the
army could hand over security to the SAS and their *maghzen* guards,
and simultaneously engage in economic and social welfare programmes,
including the EMSI, women's circles and female emancipation.[75] At the
core of the pacification programme was the mass resettlement of the rural
population into camps, a process aimed to achieve, according to the
Maoist dictum, the 'draining of the swamp' so that the guerrillas would
no longer move around like fish in water, but be left stranded from their
support base. By the end of the war three million people, up to half of the
rural Algerian population, had been uprooted and had either fled to
urban shantytowns or been confined in vast, soulless camps surrounded
by barbed-wire and look-out towers, where many starved.[76]

This standard strategy was implemented by General de Maison
Rouge in the Aumale sector after January 1958. In a key briefing to the
Prime Minister during his official tour to Aumale in February 1959,
Maison Rouge noted that the rich agricultural valley near Bouira had
been chosen as a 'pilot priority zone', and this was now well advanced
through resettlement. Having procured this area, pacification was now
being extended southwards into the Aumale sector, first to the quartier
of La Baraque, and then on towards Aïn Terzine where 'the forest of
the Oued Okhriss to the East [of Aumale], classified as a *zone interdite*,
and the termination of the mountain chain of the Bibans and Monts du
Hodna, constitutes a zone of communication with Tunisia that is crucial
to the rebels . . . Search and destroy operations are necessary here in
1959, but also the total *regroupement* of the population which is the
only means to deny the rebels' food supply and shelter'.[77]

The 'rolling' programme of the Challe juggernaut that marched
through Algeria from west to east through 1959 to 1961 came to focus
its attention specifically on the quartier of Aïn Terzine during 1959: a
new *Commando de chasse* 'Kimono 13' was formed and based here
in March to destroy the last remnants of the ALN in the hills above[78]
and a programme of resettlement was accelerated. During the year
between June 1959 and June 1960 a sequence of camps was planned
by the Algiers architect Bouvet in the Aïn Terzine quartier at Mesdour,
Guetrini, Souk el Khémis, de Mettane, Tagdid, Bordj Okhriss, Tarfa,

S'Bara and Meghnine.[79] The number of camps in the Aumale sector, or what were now called 'New Villages', increased rapidly from twenty-five centres in March 1959, housing 931 families, to sixty-seven centres in November 1960, and the objective was to finally house 60 per cent of the population in this way.[80]

As early as May 1957 the SAS of Bordj Okhriss had reported that the inhabitants, living in dispersed settlements, were so exhausted by the constant raiding by opposed nationalist forces (MNA, ALN) seizing men, livestock, money and food supplies, that they were demanding return of their confiscated guns to mount an auto-defence against men from the north, the 'Kabyles'. The SAS expressed the ambiguity of the position in June 1957, 'the peasants wish to be protected by the army, but do not seem to want to openly take sides against the HLL [hors-la-lois or bandits]'.[81] By 1959 senior officers in Aumale were reading in a far more doctrinaire way the confusion and desperation of the peasantry as a sign of their moving to the French side and actively supporting *regroupement*: thus in November 1959, the Aumale commander noted, 'the population hopes more and more for peace and is very favourable to the *regroupements* in the New Villages. They are working hard and courageously to build them and one can assert that where a good preparation has been undertaken on the material and psychological plane, a real social transformation is under way'.[82] The thinking of the military was that camps would not only isolate the FLN from its support base in the local population, but also by concentrating the peasantry in quasi-urban centres with shops, schools, dispensaries and electricity would have a transformative function in modernising the culture and mentality of Algerian women and their families, a pre-requisite of emancipation.

Nowhere in the extensive army documentation for Aumale and Bordj Okhriss is there any mention of local Algerian opposition to *regroupements*. For one significant incident on 20 May 1960 the battalion log states laconically, 'CCAS: removal work ROUABAS',[83] and if it was not for Garanger's photographs this moment of resistance would have remained meaningless or passed into oblivion. The inhabitants of the *douar* of Rouabas at Aïn Terzine had just been informed of a decision to resettle them in the camp of Meghnine or Bordj Okhriss, and all the men, including village elders, marched in a file to complain to the Commander de Mollans, who ordered a 'half-track' machine-gun (CCAS) to halt their advance.[84]

The photographs show that the protest was an all-male affair, entirely in keeping with this patriarchal society in which men were the sole political actors, yet for the 'invisible' women of Aïn Terzine *regroupement*

13 A machine-gun 'half-track' blocking the advance of a column of men come to protest against the imminent resettlement of the *douar* of Rouabas

would have carried particularly tragic consequences, not only in the direct form of deepening hunger and illness, infant mortality and material poverty, but through the destruction of the home, a deeply religious and magical space that in Algerian tradition 'belonged' to women, and its replacement by a sterile western form that disrupted customary practices and symbols.[85] The elders negotiated with de Mollans: 'What you are doing is inhuman. You are deporting us. We cannot cultivate our land. What are we going to live on?', who replied, 'I understand your situation and I am sorry. But I can't do anything: it's an order from the colonel'. But Garanger knew this was completely untrue, de Mollans personally made this decision because he felt insulted by the night-time movement of the FLN among the Rouabas fraction, 'under his very windows'.[86] From the beginning forces in the maquis had recognised the danger of such *regroupments* to its own support base, and in September 1957 the MNA was trying to force families that had fled to Bordj Okhriss for safety to return to their farms.[87]

There is a considerable body of evidence which shows that the uprooting of the peasantry and the 'fixing' down of pastoral nomads carried particularly devastating implications for women and children throughout Algeria. The inhabitants of entire *douars* were forcibly

14 Aerial view of peasant houses destroyed by the French army during resettlement in the region of Bordj Okhriss

removed from their ancestral lands by the army and their houses were burned down or demolished.[88]

Often this was carried out by the military without any prior planning and construction of reception centres, so that the refugees were dumped in virtual prison camps. Commander Florentin of the *Inspection générale des regroupements*, in a devastating critique of resettlement, noted: 'The population flees empty-handed and a human avalanche streams towards the valleys that are under the control of the army but where nothing has been prepared to receive them . . . The people are penned behind barbed-wire around a small, neo-burgrave style fortress'.[89]

In the 'temporary centres' the inhabitants, often parked behind barbed-wire entanglements, lived in tents or bivouacs until the army could find the materials and deploy refugee labour to build more permanent houses.[90] The new locations, often far removed from the village of origin now in *zones interdites*, meant that the peasants were unable to work their fields or herd livestock, and the population began to suffer from serious malnutrition, disease and catastrophic infant mortality. On average in camps with over 1,000 people one infant died every two days,

15 Aerial view of the military resettlement camp of Mesdour, north-east of Bordj Okhriss

mainly from malnutrition, and on a visit to one centre Michel Rocard, the future Prime Minister, remarked to an officer that he seemed not too upset when a baby died in his arms, 'He replied, "Monsieur, this is the fourth in three days"'.[91] The SAS officer of Bordj Okhriss reported on 'the deplorable health conditions in the *regroupement* of Mesdour' and other centres, and the high incidence of typhoid, tuberculosis and other diseases.[92] The standard houses designed for the settlements were too small and lacked in insulation, boiling in summer and freezing at night or in winter, and they were placed in geometrical grids that reproduced the soulless layout of military barracks.[93]

> Deprived of their traditional economic base as farmers and herders the inhabitants of the camps were reduced to desperate poverty, and a demoralising dependency on army handouts of food, clothing and blankets. General Parlange, who headed the camp inspectorate, spoke of a veritable 'burned-earth' policy, and of a radical dislocation of traditional family structures and a process of turning people into tramps (*clochardisation*):the traditional social hierarchies are over-turned, and the taste for work, when it existed, disappears since it is easy to become a client of the Public Assistance. In brief, moral degradation, encouraged by over-crowding, accelerates and threatens to become generalised . . . the means to engage in farming are abandoned, with fields too distant,

pack animals lost or sold; it's total ruin and the uprooted settle down with
fatalism into a life of poverty.[94]

Garanger's identity photographs were taken in the newly founded
settlement camps, and the subjects constituted a virtual refugee
population that had been dramatically uprooted. The attitude of each
individual can only be guessed at, but the overall context was one of
ambiguity towards an occupying force that offered on the one hand
some degree of protection, medical aid and food, and on the other
was destroying their homes and an existing way of life, and complicit
in extreme brutality, rape and murder. On rare occasions even the
command acknowledged the impossible contradictions of such a war:
as General de Maison Rouge told the Prime Minister in February
1959, to crush the FLN networks (OPA) would require a long process,
'and requires a hardening of methods towards the population which is
in contradiction with the policy of détente undertaken since the month
of May [1958]'.[95]

Civil war, insecurity and *attentisme*

This final section aims to show that peasant women were not faced with
a simple choice of allegiance to one of two sides, the ALN or the French
army, but by the extraordinary ambiguities and contradictory pressures
of civil war. The apparent 'silence' of women was not only an expression
of ignorance, illiteracy and seclusion, but also of a family or clan-based
omerta. The French attempts to emancipate women, to extend a strategy
of contact to the *bled*, was faced not only with problems of language
and communication, but also with impenetrable forms of defensive
silence behind which lay concealed the 'hidden transcript' of peasants
skilled in the arts of verbal resistance.[96]

   That the conflict in Algeria was as much a civil war as a war of decolonisation is highlighted by the fact that the 200,000 Algerian soldiers and
auxiliaries (*supplétifs*) fighting on the French side greatly outnumbered
the 50,000 men in the ALN.[97] As Mohand Hamoumou notes, the reason
why some Algerians joined the French forces and others the FLN cannot
in many instances be understood through the ideological decisions of
these individuals, by 'a "political" grid', but rather by 'local contingencies', such as blood-feuds between local families, tribal allegiances and
disputes over property.[98] Stathis Kalyvas has analysed the *intimacy* of
civil war violence, how in small-scale, face-to-face social settings the
tensions and conflicts of peacetime (disputes over land, livestock, marriage alliances, insults and honour) that were normally mediated and

settled, now became the basis of denunciation that unleashed deadly force, and pitted neighbour against neighbour.[99]

At the outbreak of the Algerian War on 1 November 1954, the major nationalist movement was the MNA led by Messali Hadj. It took the FLN until late 1957, after a long and bloody internecine battle for power, to assert its dominance. However, the situation was unusually complex in the region of Bordj Okhriss since, until the end of the war in 1962 this continued to lie on the frontier between the MNA, a predominantly 'Arab' movement that continued to survive as a powerful force entrenched within Wilaya VI to the south of Aumale, and the ALN that filtered southwards from its Kabyle stronghold to the north. The French secret services provided funding, arms and equipment to a number of MNA groups in the south led by Bellounis,[100] Si Cherif and Rabah Benaissi who, acting more like freebooting war lords than regular soldiers, engaged in cattle raiding, forced recruitment and other depredations. For example, a Bellounis force of fifty to sixty men surrounded the *mechta* of Sidi-Abdelkader on 25 January 1958 and seized ten men as recruits, along with a large stock of cows, goats, sheep and mules; 'They then rounded on the women whom they thrashed, in the absence of their husbands'.[101] The Bellounist force, secretly funded by the French from May 1957 until July 1958, placed constant pressure on the population of the Bordj Okhriss area for money, supplies and recruits.[102] Although Bellounis, who proved recalcitrant to French control, was finally tracked down and killed by the army on 14 July 1958, the bands of Si Cherif and the ex-Bellounist Benaissi continued to operate until at least 1961. General de Maison Rouge, who had turned against Bellounis in May 1958,[103] was by early 1959 facing the same problems with Si Cherif: as he informed Michel Debré during his tour of inspection, 'But with 800 men in arms, living like rebel bands whose exactions are very difficult and never entirely preventable, he is the cause of incessant problems. In fact he operates more often for himself than for France and often acts outside the bounds of legality'.[104] Ex-MNA guerrillas were constantly disbanding or rallying to join the French army as *harkis*, or crossing over to the ALN side. So anarchic and confused was the situation in the Aumale sector, with an incessant ebb-and-flow of MNA and ALN units, that it became increasingly difficult for both the French and local populations to distinguish one side from the other. By the summer and autumn of 1959 the SAS of Maginot reported that the French-backed forces of Si Cherif was running amok, engaging in rape, kidnapping and drunken violence: 'it is certain that the FLN benefits from the support of the population which has suffered too much from the violence of the *Djich* without the latter ever being brought to account'.[105]

The peasants of Bordj Okhriss were caught in a complex and paralysing web of conflicting interests: they faced not simply a split between the French occupier and Algerian nationalists, but a triangle of MNA, ALN and French-*harki* forces. Both the MNA and the FLN demanded, on pain of death, monthly payments, food supplies and male fighters, a burden that impoverished peasants could barely sustain, while the French threatened to arrest, torture and even liquidate anybody who did so. The state of confusion and paralysis affecting the peasants was described by the SAS officer for Bordj Okhriss when on 11 May 1957 1,200 people crowded onto the market place to express their predicament to the French authorities: 'The population, without protection, abandoned to the violence of the rebels, no longer know what to think and the differences of opinion and action that daily are becoming more intense inside the ranks of the nationalist movements leaves them facing a situation that they no longer understand'.[106] The officer saw the opportunity here for the villagers to move over to the French side and to set up an auto-defence force that would enable them to stand up against both MNA and ALN, but this hope was constantly frustrated by a deep 'mutual mistrust' and what was generally referred to as a psychology of *attentisme*. By 1960 the situation had barely improved, and the SAS reported that the FLN was locked into major conflict with the MNA infiltrating into Bordj Okhriss from the south, 'but the different organisations are so closely intermingled that it is often difficult to identify them. Overall the population of these regions is disconcerted and pulls back further into itself'.[107]

The term *attentisme* is not easily translated: for the French authorities this was often used in a conventional sense of a 'wait and see policy', that during a long war in which it was unclear which side would be the ultimate victor, it was wise to hedge one's bets by retaining a certain neutrality and by not becoming too closely associated with one side or the other.[108] But *attentisme*, a refusal to declare one's hand, had a far more potent logic: in small and isolated communities like Aïn Terzine and Bordj Okhriss in which everybody knew everyone else, the total networks of family, fraction and other kin alliances, and in which it was impossible to move or carry out the smallest transaction without being observed, the best chances of survival from MNA or FLN gunmen or *harkis* violence was to remain silent. The climate of distrust and fear was accentuated by the fact that each side cultivated informers, among them the grocer of Rouabah, Saadi Riah, who tried to survive ALN and French pressures by supplying both with information. Garanger describes him less as a collaborator than a poor victim: 'He was quite simply trapped by this war. His behaviour was typical of local notables, carried away on a storm that was beyond them, on which they had no grip, and who desperately tried to protect their interests, those of their relatives and of their village or hamlet'.[109]

The journal of Mouloud Feraoun provides a rare insight into the mechanisms of *attentisme* in Kabyle village society: the writer, able only to confide to his diary, expresses a Kafkaesque climate of paranoia in which neighbours were unsure of who might be acting as informer for FLN or army, and who may be falsely denouncing another to settle scores for old quarrels over land and honour. In April 1957 Feraoun was told by an old man how he was travelling on a bus which was stopped by the army: everyone was ordered out and a local informer pointed men out. 'My God, I was afraid. He could have pointed his finger towards me. He had reasons to. Last year, his father sold me a mortgaged field. I sued him and won. And last year I beat up their shepherd when he let his herd damage my young fig trees. Yes, I beat him up. And I won my suit. That young recruit could have avenged himself using the army, and I was afraid'.[110] The people, noted Feraoun, 'have nothing to say to one another' but pass by and 'hastily exchange a weary and meaningless greeting . . . It is as if each person feels trapped and sealed in an airtight bell jar'. The streets are empty, but 'there are shadows moving about . . . Given this situation, you must trust no one, because words misunderstood are often misinterpreted', like the old woman fined for a hasty comment, or Hocine's sister-in-law executed because she spoke 'ill of them'.[111]

In the Aïn Terzine quartier the same forces were at work: the SAS and intelligence officers continually expressed their frustration with the *attentisme* of the population, estimated at 70 per cent in 1959,[112] and their inability to uncover what was going on under the surface of local society. The better-off avoid talking, 'they sit on the fence and continue to give promises to both sides', or the people are 'thrown off balance and fall back even more on themselves', and Algerians told SAS officers what they want to hear so they produced radically different versions of 'the deepest thoughts of the population'.[113] In places the archive provides a hint of the internal splintering at work. In November 1956 three men of the Ouadi family of Bordj Okhriss were assassinated by either the MNA or FLN, and the following year another member was threatened by a money collector in the market who said, 'You are crazy. I saw the rebels yesterday evening and I spoke to them about you (the Ouadi) – You can be allowed to go back home by paying 100 or 150,000 Frs. This is nothing compared to what you own (your farm is worth nearly two millions). – Anyway France is the loser and will abandon you – You will then see what position you find yourself in'. Not surprisingly the

Ouadi appear to have sought safety by joining the SAS *maghzen* and in July 1960 this included two soldiers from the family.[114] It was not uncommon for extended families to have men fighting on both sides, and in some instances having a foot in both camps was a deliberate group insurance policy against the unpredictable outcome of the war.[115]

To conclude, with the background knowledge of the situation in Bordj Okhriss, it can be seen why the response of Muslim women to the French presence was so complex and difficult to decode. Some of the women who faced Garanger's lens had husbands, brothers or sons who were in the maquis, or who had been arrested, imprisoned or killed by the army. Others, like the young woman from Mesdour on the cover of *Femmes algériennes*, had had their villages destroyed and been moved behind the barbed wire entanglements of the resettlement camps. Others again were members of families or clan groups that had tried to find protection with the army, and the men had joined the *harkis* or formed self-defence groups.[116] At least one woman physically resisted being photographed and some are glaring defiantly at the camera, while other young women have dressed up elaborately in their most precious possessions, huge silver broaches and gold-coin necklaces. But for all the nuances of position, for the women of Bordj Okhriss, as throughout Algeria, the French army represented a dangerous and powerful force associated with mass destruction, brutality and rape. As will be seen in the next chapter, the central contradiction facing the EMSI teams was how to gain the trust of Algerian women and to bring them social progress and emancipation when they themselves were part of an army that had destroyed their villages and driven them into refugee camps. In a situation in which being seen to converse or associate with the armed forces risked attracting the counter-violence of the FLN, most women sought to maintain a safe distance from the welfare teams. Also since the outcome of the war remained uncertain or, from early 1960 onwards, a French retreat became more likely, then it was rational to remain disengaged from either side or to maintain an *attentiste* position so as to be able to opt eventually as the winning side became evident.

Notes

1 This is a wider theoretical issue addressed constantly by historians of colonialism, ethnographers and 'subaltern studies': on Algerian women specifically see 'Decolonizing Feminism' in Lazreg, *Eloquence*, 6–19.
2 The only attempt to analyse the geographical variations in female militancy is Djamila Amrane, 'Répartition géographique des militantes de la guerre de libération nationale (Algérie, 1954–1962)', *AWAL*, 8 (1991), 1–19.

3 There is a strong bias in oral history research towards the representation
   of more educated militants of urban origin; as with the eighty-eight women
   interviewed by Amrane, *Les Femmes algériennes*; of the twenty-six interviews in Amrane-Minne, *Des femmes*, only four (15 per cent) were with
   women from a rural or peasant background. There are valuable interviews
   with working women by Brac de la Perrière, *Derrière les Héros*, but these
   were confined to urban Algiers. Research has yet to be carried out among
   the hundreds of thousands of 'ordinary' women in the *bled* and urban
   shantytowns as to their experience of the war and attitude towards the
   French presence and emancipation agenda. The best insight we have into
   the condition and experience of peasant women during the war is provided
   by the oral history research of the ethnographer Camille Lacoste-Dujardin,
   particularly 'La Guerre vécue par les Iflissen', in *Opération 'Oiseau Bleu'*.
4 In spite of the immense volume of research and publication on the Algerian
   War, there still exists a noticeable absence of an adequate social history: a
   lack that reflects a complex of factors, from the past refusal of the Algerian
   government to allow fieldwork, extreme insecurity during the recent civil
   war, and the refusal of many to talk about a conflict that left deep scars.
5 The army unit of Garanger was based at Aïn Terzine a few miles outside the
   main township and market centre of Bordj Okhriss: I have used the latter
   to refer in general to the area. Garanger was appointed by the commander
   at Aïn Terzine, de Mollans, as his personal but unofficial photographer and
   was frequently taken by helicopter during operations into the *zone interdite*,
   with the aim of increasing the colonels standing with army superiors. De
   Mollans, who strutted about with a riding crop, was proud of action photographs of ALN captives, which he referred to as, 'my hunting scenes': Marc
   Garanger, *Marc Garanger: Retour en Algérie* (Paris: Atlantica, 2007), 6.
6 Marc Garanger, *Femmes algériennes 1960* [c. 1989] (Anglet: Atlantica,
   2002), 122.
7 *Femmes algériennes 1960*, first published by Éditions Contrejour in 1982,
   used a selection of fifty-five portraits of women from the many hundreds
   that were taken.
8 Garanger, *Femmes algériennes*, 1. Marc Garanger, sensitive to the charge
   of complicity in military force, insists that he was never in the position of
   the official army photographers like Marc Flamand whose heroic images
   of Bigeard's parachutists placed him firmly on the side of the occupying
   forces. Most of the 10,000 to 20,000 images were taken by Garanger in his
   spare-time in Bordj Okhriss and are a testament to, and an expression of,
   his personal opposition to the war: 'I had only one idea in mind: to shoot
   the maximum of pictures to show the reality of life for Algerians and what a
   colonial war was like', Garanger, *Retour*, 6. Even when photographs had a
   more 'official' status they expressed a subversive intent, as with his famous
   image of the captured ALN commander Ahmed Bencherif taken under
   order of the commander to be printed on an anti-FLN leaflet, but which
   was rejected because 'he perceived a message that was opposed to the one he

wanted to make', a striking portrait of a proud and defiant leader, *Retour*, 7; *La Guerre d'Algérie vue par un appelé du contingent* (Paris: Seuil, 1984), 16–17.

9 Garanger, *Retour*, 53.

10 Marc Garanger, with text by Leïla Sebbar, *Femmes des Hauts-Plateaux. Algérie 1960* (Paris: La Boîte à Documents, 1990), 7.

11 Garanger, *Retour*, 13. The 2004 images were first published in a special edition of *Le Monde*, 28 October 2004, to commemorate the fortieth anniversary of the end of the Algerian War. For Garanger the warm reception that he found in 2004 among the people of Bordj Okhriss, including some of the women he had portrayed in 1960, was an emotional and personal affirmation: one of them, Zohra Gacem, was excited to see her photograph, burst out laughing, and said to Garanger, '"you are in my heart". Tears sprang to my eyes . . . she was offering me what was worth more than anything: her gratitude', see *Retour*, 8–9. But in the case of two other subjects pictured in 1960, a woman from the Saou family and Zohra Laamouri, long negotiations to take photographs had to take place in 2004 with their husband and an elder son, hostile to this 'brutal intrusion into their privacy', *Retour*, 54–7.

12 Garanger, *Femmes algériennes*, 121.

13 This is particularly true for Karina Eileraas, 'Reframing the Colonial Gaze: Photography, Ownership, and Feminist Resistance', *MLN*, 118: 4 (September 2003), 807–40. Ranjana Khanna, *Algeria Cuts. Women and Representation, 1830 to the Present* (Stanford: Stanford University Press, 2007), 21–2, analyses the 'extraordinary photographs' not through a reading of Garanger's books, but by an unnamed secondary source that must be David A. Bailey and Gilane Tawadros (eds), *Veil. Veiling, Representation and Contemporary Art* (London: Institute of International Visual Arts, 2003), 86–7, since she reproduces the dreadful mistranslation of Garanger's account of inhabitants being called together by the army officer in charge (*chef de poste*) as the 'postmaster': 'Interestingly', notes Khanna, 'it was the postmaster who assisted Garanger in his task, calling up the women to lift their veils and be photographed'. Instead of making any attempt to examine the context in which Garanger took the photographs, Khanna races off to impose a reading elaborated through a mass of references to Lacan, Deleuze, Simmel and others. For other comment see, Kaja Silverman, *The Threshold of the Visible World* (New York: Routledge, 1996), 146–61, 'How to Face a Camera', which explores the act of violation and 'the horror of being photographed for the first time'; Winifred Woodhull, *Transfigurations of the Maghreb. Feminism, Decolonization, and Literatures* (Minneapolis: University of Minnesota Press, 1993), 42–5, and 'Unveiling Algeria', *Genders*, 10 (Spring 1991), 112–31; Naggar, 'The Unveiled: Algerian Women'. The literary approach to Garanger has been reinforced by interest in the major Algerian writer Leïla Sebbar: in *Shérazade: 17 ans, brune, frisée, les yeux verts* (Paris: Stock, 1993), 219–21,

the central character, a young Parisian *beur*, discovers as a revelation a copy of *Femmes algériennes 1960*, 'these faces had the hardness and violence of those who suffered the arbitrary knowing that they will find inside themselves the strength to resist'. But Sebbar in her commentary to Garanger's photographs in *Femmes des Hauts-Plateaux* runs the danger of a subjective 'poetic' text that obscures rather than enhances our understanding: thus on page 51, she describes a group of veiled women sitting in a circle in an arid landscape as if in a cemetery, missing the point that they were waiting to be photographed by Garanger, and are more likely to be sharing their opinions about how to confront the camera.

14 Eileraas, 'Reframing', 814–15, notes that the 'women's looks [cannot] be interpreted without reference to the social and historical context of Garanger's images', but then manages to avoid making a single reference to the context.

15 For the *harki* at home, see *La Guerre d'Algérie*, 60–1, *Hauts-Plateaux*, 68–71; for men in the auto-defence group, *La Guerre d'Algérie*, 31. SHAT 1H1895/2, fiche 12–15 March 1959, notes in the Aumale sector there were 1,787 Algerians fighting with the French army (*supplétifs*); SHAT 1H4334, État-Major Aumale, 22 January 1958, indicates fifty *harkis* at Bordj Okhriss, and seven at Aïn Terzine.

16 Garanger interview, Paris, 18 October 2005.

17 Garanger, *Hauts-Plateaux*, 13–27.

18 CAOM 2SAS29*, SAS Bordj Okhriss, Journal de Marche, 14 September 1960.

19 Garanger's photographs of Bordj Okhriss, apart from the identity-card portraits, can be found in three books, *La Guerre d'Algérie*, *Hauts-Plateaux* and *Retour*.

20 The highly bureaucratic system of the French civil and military apparatus has left a considerable body of evidence for the sector of Aumale, now located in the archives of Aix-en-Provence (CAOM) and Vincennes (SHAT) (see the bibliography and notes below); in addition I have used soldiers' diary records, and interviewed Marc Garanger (Paris, 18 October 2006) and Jean-Louis Gérard (Paris, 10 June 2007).

21 The sector of Aumale, covering 6,640 square kilometres, was in 1959 under the command of General de Maison Rouge from his HQ in Aumale town, while under him the sector was sub-divided into seven quartiers, of which one was Aïn Terzine, the terrain of action of the 1st Batallion of the 2nd Infantry Regiment, under Colonel Henri Amador de Mollans: SHAT 1H1895/2 and SHAT 1H4334/2.

22 See Garanger, *La Guerre d'Algérie*, 25, photograph of an army ceremony to open the piste at Oued Tarfa; see SHAT 7U21*, JMO, 2e Régiment d'Infanterie, 1er Bataillon, 16 May 1960 on this opening.

23 SHAT 1H1895/2, Fiche, 12–15 March 1959, notes that for security reasons local councillors (*délégués spéciaux*) had deserted the *douars* which they were appointed to administer for the safety of towns; CAOM 3SAS18, ELA

Aumale, in the report for February 1959 noted the assassination of two *colons*, and 'the ditch between the two communities gets deeper'.

24 SHAT 1H4334/2, table of population, 2 September 1961; SHAT 1H1895/2 shows in March 1959 the total French armed force in the Aumale sector was 7,245, including various kinds of Algerian auxiliary soldiers. The USA frontier comparison was ever-present among French soldiers, and Garanger, *Femmes algériennes*, 121–2, was inspired in his own work by Edward S. Curtis's photographs of North American Indians.

25 SHAT 1H1895/2, report, May 1960. Grain production was only 5 quintals per hectare. 200 NF was equivalent to about £20 in 2007 prices.

26 CAOM 3SAS29*, reports of SAS at Bordj Okhriss: in 1957 the SAS issued 280 permissions to go to France.

27 Thus for Aumale there was only one doctor for 36,000 people, compared to one for 5,137 in Algeria as a whole, and one for 1,091 in metropolitan France: see M. Michel Rocard, *Rapport sur les camps de regroupement* (Paris: Fayard, 2003), 126.

28 CAOM 3SAS18, ELA Aumale, report for 15 June to 15 July 1960.

29 There is a large literature on the long-term crisis of the Algerian peasantry under the impact of colonialism: see, for example, D. Sari, *La Dépossession des fellahs (1830–1962)* (Algiers: SNED, 1975) and the classic work of Pierre Bourdieu and Abdelmalek Sayad, *Le Déracinement: la crise de l'agriculture traditionnelle en Algérie* (Paris: Éditions de Minuit, 1964).

30 M. Bennoune, 'The Introduction of Nationalism into Rural Algeria: 1919–54', *The Maghreb Review*, 2: 3 (May–June 1977), 1–12.

31 SHAT 1H1895/2, Étude sur la Pacification, Aumale sector, May 1960. From the earliest days of the insurrection Abdelkader Amrane and the student leader Mohammed Rachid Amara organised the clandestine links between the FLN leaders in Algiers and the maquis via Aumale and Bordj Okhriss: see obituary on Amrane in *El Watan*, 24 December 2006.

32 SHAT 1H4706/2*, fiche de renseignements, 5 May and 4 June 1958. An idea of the arduous and dangerous conditions faced by ALN convoys, especially as electrified fences were built along the Tunisian and Moroccan borders, is given by the group of fifty-six men led by Commander Ahmed Bencherif that crossed into Algeria on 2–4 April 1960 and finally reached the Aumale sector in August. Tracked by commandos and decimated, the final surviving group of nine men was surrounded on 23 October, among them Bencherif who was photographed by Garanger: see the maps in Maurice Faivre, *Les Archives inédites de la politique algérienne, 1958–1962* (Paris: L'Harmattan, 2000), 409, and Pervillé, *Atlas*, 38; Garanger photograph, *La Guerre d'Algérie*, 16–17.

33 A band of 180 MNA fighters surrendered to the French army at Bordj Okhriss on 24 July 1957: CAOM 3SAS29*.

34 CAOM 81F107, report by General de Maison Rouge to PM, Michel Debré, Aumale, 11 February 1959.

35 The most detailed data on women combatants has been taken from the

moudjahidat stats:

official registers of the Ministry of the Moudjahidine, a significant procedure since 'veteran' certificates bring major honours, as well as material
rewards (pensions, early retirement benefits, access to 'reserved' jobs, right
to import a car tax free, etc.). Amrane, *Les Femmes algériennes*, 219–32,
273–4, had access to the files for the 1974 census, which listed 10,949
women. Ryme Seferdjeli, in her thesis, '"Fight With Us, and We Will
Emancipate You": France, the FLN and the Struggle over Women during
the Algerian War of National Liberation 1954–1962', PhD, University of
London, 2004, 86–7, 145–51, has subjected these data to a close scrutiny,
noting a puzzling increase to 26,078 registrations in the 1995 census. The
inflation in numbers is almost certainly due to fraud, and casts serious
doubts on the statistical reliability of the data. The Soummam congress of
August 1956 defined three categories of male combatants: the *fidaï* (commando), the *moudjihad* (ALN soldier) and the *moussebel* (partisan), see
Harbi and Meynier (eds), *FLN: Documents*, 243–4. The post-independence
register adapted these categories to women and, although not always con-
sistent or easy to apply, the following terms are used: the *fidayate*, or urban-
based fighters, who were very few in number (sixty-nine); the *moudjahidate*
who made up under 10 per cent of combatants, were the nurses attached
to the mobile ALN units; the *moussebilate* were the local, civilian women
who provided logistic support. Outside these categories were the hundreds
of thousands of women '*adhérents*' or 'sympathisers', largely unregistered
and unrecognised, who paid FLN dues or provided occasional assistance.

36 Amrane, *Les Femmes algériennes*, 231–2, of the 10,949 registered militants,
948 (8.6 per cent) were killed and 14.4 per cent imprisoned.
37 CAOM 3SAS29* includes numerous reports of women in the Bordj Okhriss
area harbouring guerrilla forces; for example Dahmane Bellili housed a
group of seven men under the command of Si Yahia during the night of
26–27 January 1957.
38 Amrane, *Les Femmes algériennes*, 119.
39 *Ibid.*, 121.
40 *Ibid.*, 123.
41 Amrane, 'Répartition', in mapping the geographical distribution of registered militants, notes large numbers to the north and north-east of Bordj
Okhriss: 113 for Palestro (now Lakhdaria), thirty-seven for Bouira, and
eight for Aïn Bessem, but dropping away to the south, with eight for
Aumale (Sour El Ghozlane).
42 SHAT 7U21*, JMO 1st Batallion, 2–3 December 1960.
43 See the on-line journals of Jean-Marie Buquet who served in a commando unit in the Aumale area, www.megabaze.com/page_html/142a-
Algeria-1956-1959 (accessed 4 December 2007).
44 Jean-Louis Gérard, a member of the intelligence gathering team at Aïn
Terzine led by the *Officier de renseignement* (OR) from early 1958 to 1959,
confirms the solid implantation of the OPA: interview in Paris, 10 June
2007.

45 CAOM 3SAS18, monthly report of Aumale ELA (SAS), 15 February to 15 March 1960; SHAT 7U21*, JMO 1st Batallion, arrest of *harki* Sergent-chef Mohamed Ben Labiad (Gasraoui) 15 March 1960; Garanger, *La Guerre d'Algérie*, 26–7.

46 Garanger, who was frequently taken by de Mollans in his helicopter to record operations, captured such moments of violence: see the violent battering of a shepherd and combatant, *La Guerre d'Algérie*, 105, 121.

47 Of the eight men captured with FLN commander Bencherif on 23 October 1958 (see note 32 above), seven were shot on the spot; Garanger photographed the corpse of Ouaïl Mohammed, the body-guard of Saïd Bouakli (*La Guerre d'Algérie*, 129), as well as that of the political commissar wounded on his arrest in March 1960 by a bullet wound in his leg, but subsequently killed by several shots by the OR of Bordj Okhriss, *La Guerre d'Algérie*, 122–9, *Retour*, 46–9; Jean-Louis Gérard of the OR has confirmed the case of a suspect forced to dig his grave and then killed by machine-gun fire, interview Paris, 10 June 2007; as well as the fact of torture at Aïn Terzine, often in the shower to make it easier to clean away the blood and excrement, see Branche, *La Torture*, 322–4, 327–8, 333.

48 SHAT 1H1895/2, inspection report, 12–15 March 1959.

49 SHAT 1H1895/2, report of tour of inspection by Lt.-Colonel Rafa, 13 October 1959, with a map 'Markets supplying the rebels'.

50 SHAT 1H4334, Note d'Orientation, commander Aumale sector, November 1960 (underlined as in document).

51 Jean-Marie Buquet on-line journal (see note 43); also Jean-Louis Gérard, interview Paris, 10 June 2007.

52 SHAT 1H1895/2, the report of Lt.-Colonel Rafa, 13 October 1959, notes that the ALN diet was 'plentiful and varied'.

53 See Mouloud Feraoun, *Journal, 1955–1962* [first published in French, 1962] edited and with an introduction by James D. LeSueur (Lincoln, Nebraska University Press, 2000), 242, 257, on how women were beginning to 'wear the trousers' and gain emancipation. A comparable transformation of gender roles in the Moroccan independence struggle is explored in detail by Baker, *Voices of Resistance*.

54 CAOM 81F107 and SHAT 1H1895/2.

55 SHAT 1H1895/2, report, 13 October 1959, estimates 30 per cent of the ALN in Aumale were local men.

56 See the anonymous on-line journals of a soldier who served in the 'Kimono 11' commando in the Aumale area: www.algeriademes20ans.net (accessed 5 December 2007). He reports at Masqueray, 25 March 1958, how the body of an important ALN officer was carried on a donkey and 'was exposed on the bonnet of an army lorry (GMC)'; see Branche, *La Torture*, 283–9 on the symbolism of such degrading 'mises en scène' that were pioneered by Colonel Argoud during 1957 in an area to the east of Aumale; see Antoine Argoud, *La Décadence, l'imposture et la tragédie* (Paris: Fayard, 1974), 138–49 for his justification of such methods, including torture and public 'executions'.

57 Feraoun, *Journal*, 208.

58 Lacoste-Dujardin, 'La Guerre vécue par les Iflissen', in *Opération 'Oiseau Bleu'*, 127–71.

59 Jean-Charles Jauffret, *Les Officiers qui ont dit non à la torture: Algérie 1954–1962* (Paris: Éditions Autrement, 2005), 27; Courrière, *La Guerre d'Algérie*, Vol. 2, 126–7.

60 *Ibid.*, 84–5, account of François Durteste, private archive. See Feraoun, *Journal*, 150–1, on bombing of three Kabyle villages, the women and children wandering aimless, 'The soldiers have spread death, terror and destruction. Here are three villages that have been emptied, destroyed, and erased from all maps, oh Oradour!'.

61 *Le Monde*, 20 June 2000; Ighilahriz, *Algérienne*; Neil MacMaster, 'The Torture Controversy (1998–2002): Towards a 'New History' of the Algerian War ?', *Modern and Contemporary France*, 10: 4 (2002), 449–59.

62 Khéïra Garne, arrested and gang raped by soldiers in the barracks of Theniet al-Had in August 1959, gave birth to Mohamed Garne, who was then adopted. He searched out his unknown mother, then living half-crazed in an Algiers cemetery, in 1988 and eventually won a long court action in November 2001 by which the French state recognised him as a war victim and French: see Florence Beaugé, *Algérie, une guerre sans gloire* (Paris: Calmann/Lévy, 2005), chapter 8; and Mohamed Garne, *Lettre à ce père qui pourrait être vous* (Paris: J. C. Lattès, 2005) and his website at www.garnemohamed.org (accessed 23 October 2006).

63 See also Raphaëlle Branche, 'Des viols pendant la guerre d'Algérie', *Vingtième siècle. Revue d'histoire*, 75 (July–September, 2002), 123–32; and 'Etre soldat en Algérie face à un ennemi de l'autre sexe', *Annales de Bretagne et des Pays de l'Ouest*, 109: 2 (2002), 143–50.

64 Branche, 'Des viols', 128.

65 Feraoun, *Journal*, 166–7, 189, 262–3, comments on rape as an attack on the key values of honour, 'the living flesh of the Kabyle soul', and how one man committed suicide after being tied up 'and forced to watch some soldiers who were sexually humiliating his wife or his daughter'. On the testimony of rape see also Beaugé, 'Violées', in *Algérie*, 169–83.

66 For obvious reasons few such photographs have survived, but see Gervereau and Stora (eds), *Photographier la guerre d'Algérie*, 84; the MNA found an almost identical image on captured French soldiers that was reproduced on a Paris wall poster titled 'Pacification' in June 1956: APP HA31, 'Propagande nord-africaine'.

67 Branche, *La Torture*, 292–3.

68 Garanger, *Retour*, 79.

69 Garanger, *La Guerre d'Algérie*, 130–1, and AL469843: this complaint does not appear to have led to any investigation or disciplinary action; in an interview in Paris, 18 October 2005, Garanger noted that rape was not considered a serious crime by the privates (*bidasses*), and was the subject of 'jokes'.

70 This practice is also reported in Branche, *La Torture*, 291; Lacoste-Dujardin, *Opération 'Oiseau Bleu'*, 159; Garne, *Lettre*, 133.
71 Nefissa Zerdoumi, *Enfants d'hier: l'éducation de l'infant en milieu traditionnel algérien* (Paris: Maspero, 1982), 151.
72 Feraoun, *Journal*, 29 February 1959, 262.
73 Amrane, Les *Femmes algériennes*, 84; Commandant Azzedine, *On nous appelait fellaghas*, 294–8, recounts the extraordinary courage of this nurse.
74 For the Challe Plan operations between February 1959 and April 1961, see Pervillé, *Atlas*, 36–9.
75 See Maurice Challe, *Notre Révolte* (Paris: Presses de la Cité, 1968), 140–1 for a detailed mapping of the pacification model; Keith Sutton, 'Army Administration Tensions over Algeria's Centre de Regroupement, 1954–1962', *British Journal of Middle Eastern Studies*, 26: 2 (November 1999), 248–51, examines the four-stage model.
76 The major study is Cornaton, *Les Regroupements*; Rocard, *Rapport*, which includes Rocard's original inspection report of 17 February 1959 on the camps, along with essays by Gilles Morin, Sylvie Thénault and Claire Andrieu; Bourdieu and Sayad, *Le Déracinement*; Charles-Robert Ageron, 'Une dimension de la guerre d'Algérie: les "regroupements" de la population', in Jauffret and Vaïsse (eds) *Militaires et guérilla*, 327–62; Keith Sutton, 'The *Centres de Regroupement*: the French Army's Final Legacy to Algeria's Settlement Geography', in Alec G. Hargreaves and Michael J. Heffernan (eds), *French and Algerian Identities from Colonial Times to the Present* (Lampeter: Edwin Mellen Press, 1993), 163–88.
77 CAOM 81F107, presentation of de Maison Rouge, 11 February 1959.
78 Garanger, *La Guerre d'Algérie*, 94–5, 102–5, 108–21, for photographs of Commando 13 and various operations.
79 CAOM 3SAS18, ELA, Aumale, monthly reports, August 1959–60; CAOM 3SAS29*, JMO Bordj Okhriss; SHAT 7U21*, JMO, 1st Batallion of 2nd Infantry Regiment.
80 SHAT 1H1895/2, Fiche de liaison, 12–15 March 1959; SHA1H4334, Note d'Orientation, November 1960. The map in Cornaton, *Les Regroupements*, 125, shows in December 1960 that the arrondissement of Aumale had 29.3 per cent of its population in centres, compared to the average for Algeria of 24 per cent.
81 CAOM 3SAS29*, SAS Bordj Okhriss, report for June 1957.
82 SHAT 1H4334, General Briand, Note d'Orientation, November 1960.
83 SHAT 7U21*, JMO 1st Batallion, 2nd Infantry Regiment.
84 Garanger, *La Guerre d'Algérie*, 42–5. Although the army frequently claimed that movement into camps was voluntary, in many instances populations had to be starved into surrender, see Lacoste-Dujardin, *Opération 'Oiseau Bleu'*, 151; SHAT 1H2460/1, directive Corps d'Arméé Constantine, 8 June 1957, ordered that villages refusing to resettle should be 'punished . . . by making life unbearable'; Cornaton, *Les Regroupements*, 196, reports women, 'furious and indomitable', who returned four or five times to their homes after being evacuated.

85 On the symbolic form of female space embodied in the traditional Algerian house see Mohand Khellil, *L'Exil Kabyle* (Paris: L'Harmattan, 1979), 42–55.

86 Garanger, *Retour*, 30–1.

87 CAOM 3SAS29*, Bordj Okhriss SAS report, 5 September 1957.

88 See Garanger, *La Guerre d'Algérie*, 49, aerial photograph of a destroyed *douar*.

89 SHAT 1H2574, J. Florentin, report, 11 December 1960. The inspection service was created in November 1959 in response to the mounting scandal of the *regroupements*.

90 Garanger, *La Guerre d'Algérie*, 56–7, shows the inhabitants at the S'Bara tent camp building houses in June 1960.

91 Rocard, *Rapport*, 126, 197; on starvation in the camps see C.-R. Ageron, 'Une dimension', 345–6.

92 CAOM 3SAS18, ELA Aumale, November 1959; de Mollans objected to such SAS reports, 'nothing supports this manifestly exaggerated assessment'. As with so many officers, he seemed keen to report to higher command the faultless management of his own quartier.

93 Garanger, *La Guerre d'Algérie*, 50–5, aerial photographs of three camps, including Mesdour; also *Retour*, 28–9. Garanger in a television programme on the ARTE channel, 12 February 2003, described Mesdour as a, 'concentration camp for the civilian population, surrounded by barbed-wire, and built by their own hands'. His former commanding officer de Mollans was so enraged by this he asked the Ministry of Defence to take legal action, which it refused to do since it would be against press freedom: see www.lecri.net/les_pages/rocard.htm (accessed 5 December 2007).

94 SHAT 1H2574, report of General Parlange, 15 February 1960. However, for a far more positive picture of a *regroupement* see Eoche-Duval, *Madame SAS*, on the careful planning of Sidi Naamane to the west of Médéa.

95 CAOM 81F107, briefing of General de Maison Rouge to Michel Debré, Aumale, 11 February 1959.

96 James C. Scott, *Domination and the Arts of Resistance: Hidden Transcripts* (New Haven: Yale University Press, 1990).

97 Pervillé, *Atlas*, 50.

98 Mohand Hamoumou, *Et ils sont devenus harkis* (Paris: Fayard, 1993), 29.

99 Kalyvas, *Logic of Violence*.

100 For a detailed investigation of the Bellounis force see Jacques Valette, *La Guerre d'Algérie des Messalistes, 1954–1962* (Paris: L'Harmattan, 2001), 133–290. The private army became so troublesome to the French that they eventually tracked down and killed Bellounis in July 1958.

101 CAOM 3SAS29*, report, 26 January 1958.

102 CAOM 3SAS29*, report, 2 July 1957 on Bellounis incursions into the *douars* of Meghnine, Taguedide and Intacen.

103 Valette, *La Guerre d'Algérie des Messalistes*, 247.
104 CAOM 81F107, presentation of de Maison Rouge, Aumale 11 February 1959.
105 SHAT 1H4334/3*, reports SAS Maginot, July–September 1959. Si Cherif was widely known as 'le Djich', meaning in this context 'war lord'.
106 CAOM 3SAS29*, SAS Bordj Okhriss, report, 11 May 1957.
107 CAOM 3SAS18, ELA Aumale, report for 15 February–15 March 1960.
108 I have examined this more closely in a paper to the conference, 'The French Colonial Mind', Exeter University, 12–14 April 2007, 'The "Silent Native": *Attentisme*, Being Compromised, and Banal Terror during the Algerian War of Independence, 1954–62', forthcoming in a volume edited by Martin Thomas.
109 Garanger, *Retour*, 82–3.
110 Feraoun, *Journal*, 204; also p. 139, the maquis is made up of malcontents and 'old scores are quickly settled in the name of the resistance', and p. 200, the rich 'who made people sweat under their hats for a living are now sweating with fear'.
111 *Ibid.*, 11, 140–1, 242.
112 SHAT 1H1895/2, report, 13 October 1959.
113 CAOM 3SAS18, ELA (SAS) Aumale reports, 1959–60.
114 CAOM 3SAS29*.
115 See Garanger's photograph of two brothers at S'Bara, one a *harki* and the other a reputed FLN sympathiser: *La Guerre d'Algérie*, 59.
116 Garanger, *La Guerre d'Algérie*, 60–1, a young *harkis* soldier at home with his family; on his return in 2004, nobody knew the fate of this man, who may well have been killed at independence.

7

The mobile socio-medical teams (EMSI): making contact with peasant society

The army faced a particularly daunting task in its ambition to create a strategy of contact, which would enable it to penetrate into the lives of the great mass of Algerian women that inhabited the interior. Here, as chapter 6 has shown, conditions were particularly adverse to such a project due to a combination of poverty, illiteracy and isolation, combined with forms of military action that alienated rural communities. The key instrument of contact that was developed during Operation Pilot and then extended to the rest of Algeria from late 1957 onwards was the mobile socio-medical teams (EMSI).[1] It was widely recognised that any strategy of contact, in order to breach the traditional protective carapace of gender segregation, would have to be carried out by women agents and an examination of the organisation of these teams, their methods and experience in the *bled*, is revealing of the relative success and failure of the army in achieving one of its key goals.

The new organisation was established in late 1957 under the direction of Mme Maugé, a formidable character, who had had a long experience as a military nurse during the campaign to repress the revolt in Madagascar (1947), and was then promoted major for her leadership skills in the crash-training of some 900 young women for service with the army in Indochina.[2] The initial backbone of the EMSI was constituted by some forty-five volunteers from the army ranks (PFAT), many of whom had considerable experience during operations in Indochina and elsewhere and were habituated to military life. But the majority were young civilian women recruited by a radio and press campaign in France and Algeria, and who came from a diversity of backgrounds. While some women brought to the task a prior experience of nursing, first-aid or welfare work, this was not a requirement, and the regulations for the new ASSRA, as each individual in the teams was known, simply required applicants to be aged eighteen to thirty-five years, physically fit, educated up to school leaving certificate level (CEP) and of good morals.[3] Many of these women appear to have been highly idealistic, inspired by an ambition to undertake some form of humanitarian work, or by the opportunity to exchange the tedium of secretarial life for one of adventure. But most were ill-prepared for the Spartan existence, hardship, danger and daunting medical and welfare work which they faced in the *bled*.[4]

The new recruits, on arrival in Algiers, were passed at breakneck speed through a month-long training programme which included elements of basic nursing and midwifery, child-care, Arab language, the history and sociology of Muslim society, the role of the EMSI in relation to the 'evolution of the Muslim woman', the rudiments of Muslim law and how to settle local disputes (*chicayas*).[5] This first course, like others that followed later, was not simply pragmatic but included a heavily ideological component: for example, the introduction to psychological warfare was taught by Commander Cogniet, an officer who held the most extreme far-right Catholic and ultra-nationalist vision of a global crusade against communism.[6] The European trainees were then allocated to an army sector that had achieved a degree of 'pacification' and relative security against FLN attacks. Often after a long journey by train and jeep they were abruptly pitched into the intensely all-male universe of the military post where they came under the orders of the commander and the officer of the Fifth Bureau.

The general function of the ASSRA was to support the mobile army doctors (AMG) as they travelled through outlying villages to provide emergency aid to the isolated peasant population, particularly during mass campaigns against trachoma. But in particular, each newly arriving ASSRA was allocated – usually on the advice of the Fifth Bureau – three or four outlying villages or *douars* on which the assistant was expected to concentrate her effort over a period of several months, building a relationship of trust with the local women through the provision of baby-care, lessons in hygiene, medical aid (baby milk, antibiotics, bandages), and women's circles (*ouvroirs*) that through knitting, sewing and entertainment, such as radio and cinema, aided weekly contact and social relations. The key idea underlying the intervention was that each European ASSRA would be expected to win over the local women, and be able to locate and recruit one or two young Muslim women of sufficient skill and potential to train 'on the job' as ASSRA. Each EMSI, generally a mixed team of one European and one or two Algerians, was thus formed over a period of time in each locality, and once it had achieved a solid basis of support through 'in depth work', the EMSI leader was supposed to move on and restart the process in another group of *douars* so that the process of emancipation could spread gradually throughout a sector.

Thérèse Vieillefon, posted to a resettlement camp, almost certainly Mesdour or Bordj Okhriss, described in a letter the typical conditions faced by a young ASSRA on first arrival:

> I am quite alone, but I think that soon I will find an assistant from among the population. The inhabitants are very poor and hungry. Since the departure of the rebels they can move about freely and come to the weekly market every Tuesday. The women are very fearful as well as the children that I find difficult to get near. But one has to proceed cautiously and I am certain that when they understand why I want to see them, I will win their trust.[7]

Marie-Clothilde Robilliard, in a similar vein, reported:

> I started to work as of yesterday. And I am quite disconcerted. It's so different from working in a hospital where you have to run about all day long, that I don't know how to adapt to the work of making relations, chatting with the women, laughing and dawdling. And I think I need some time to adapt to this way of life. However, I already have a lot of sympathy and friendship towards these women in their lost and dusty villages. But I am truly very concerned not to be able to speak their language yet.

But she was thankful not to be housed, like some ASSRA, in a tent.[8]

How successful the new ASSRA was in establishing links to the local population and in creating an EMSI team depended partly on her personal qualities and organisational skills in overcoming numerous problems, including shortage of buildings, basic materials and money, and partly on the degree of active support received from the sector commander who controlled the key resources, including allocation of transport, accommodation and support personnel. Although sector commanders received orders from Algiers to provide full assistance to the EMSI, clearly some senior officers regarded the presence of young women as a tiresome diversion from their role of combating the FLN,[9] although others were enthusiastic and called for an increase in their numbers.[10]

The formation of the EMSI was relatively slow at first, but then accelerated rapidly after the events of 13 May 1958 when Salan gave the teams a key role in orchestrating 'fraternisation' campaigns in the *bled*.[11] By August 1960 there were 171 EMSI units, sixty-three in Oranie, sixty in the Algerois, and forty-eight in the Constantinois regions. These were made up from 315 ASSRA, of whom eighty were Europeans from metropolitan France, ninety-four *pieds-noirs*, and 141 Muslim women, reinforced by forty army personnel (PFAT).[12] Ryme Seferdjeli notes a further increase in the number of teams to a peak of 223 in February 1961,[13] but the number of qualified ASSRA remained static at 315, and any growth was achieved through the accelerated recruitment of some 230 *harkettes*, young assistants lacking in even the rudimentary training of the ASSRA and who received lower levels of pay.[14] This 'watering down' of the composition of the EMSI reflected, as will be seen, a deepening crisis of recruitment in the final stages of the war.

In the assessment of the work of the EMSI it is necessary to make a distinction between the glowing image presented by the French media and official army propaganda, and the underlying reality. Dealing with the first of these, the presentation of the ASSRA as 'blue-eyed' and flaxen-haired angels, self-sacrificing Florence Nightingale figures who brought succour to the oppressed Algerian people, is in itself of more than passing interest: the publicity surrounding the EMSI was of almost as much importance to the Fifth Bureau as their welfare achievements. As has been seen (chapter 4), the SCA played a key role in the promotion of the EMSI, and had already produced the documentary film, *Nurses of the Bled* as early as July 1957 during Operation Pilot. The Fifth Bureau also orchestrated the collective visits of the national and international press in minute detail and among the favoured scenes that journalists were whisked away by car and helicopter into the *bled* to witness were teams of white-coated EMSI weighing and bathing infants (see illustration 1, p. 96).

Typical of the numerous reports in women's and Catholic journals, was one in *Elle* magazine of a visit in October 1958 to a commune in the Sud-Oranais where Thérèse Durand, with her assistant Guermina, were photographed bathing thirty Algerian babies; a report followed by an appeal for readers to send in baby clothes and toys.[15] But the doyenne of the propagandists was the popular Catholic journalist and writer, Christiane Fournier, who had already written on the heroic exploits of the French army in Indo-China. Mme Maugé, who knew Fournier, encouraged her to write a book on the EMSI and also persuaded her superior Colonel Gardes, head of the Fifth Bureau, to organise her visit to Algeria and to provide eight photographs for the publication.[16] *Les EMSI, des filles commes çà!*, with a Preface by General Challe who was currently directing the brutal Operation Jumelles, is suffused in a religious bathos, in which the EMSI were likened to the twelve disciples who, 'regenerated the world because they believed that love is stronger than hatred'. The self-sacrificing EMSI were presented as the finest flower of idealistic French youth, by contrast with the decadent beat generation of Paris, 'the cheats, always on the pull, all those stars of the dissolute life'.[17] Maugé, no doubt with the full backing of Colonel Gardes, was tireless in her attempts to promote the book during trips to Paris in September 1959, as well as through book fairs, press conferences, and radio and television interviews with Fournier. The media impacts were taken sufficiently seriously by the FLN to inspire it to attack Fournier on the *Voix des Arabes* of Radio Cairo in December 1959: 'your dirty book on the EMSI can only contain lies, racist talk, nasty quarrels, propaganda and services on behalf of French psychological actions in Algeria'.[18]

Political and propaganda functions

How correct was the FLN in its assertion that the EMSI constituted a key part of the psychological warfare strategy? Firstly, the EMSI were directly controlled by the Fifth Bureau, and its successor from early 1960 the Third Bureau, and Mme Maugé, from her office within the General Government, liaised constantly with her superior Colonel Gardes who was located in the same building. The EMSI teams in the *bled* were also answerable to the parallel hierarchy of the Fifth Bureau and its officers who were attached to commanders at the local sector level. In general it is possible to recognise a division of labour between Maugé and her assistants, who were given some independence of action in the day-to-day running of the organisation, and the Fifth Bureau, which occasionally interceded via classified directives to define key lines of action and political objectives. At the local level the Fifth Bureau officer kept an eye on the EMSI in relation to the political impacts of their work, required that EMSI action plans be submitted to him,[19] and guided strategic decisions, such as which particular *douars* offered the best political and social conditions to be selected as a target for 'in-depth work'.[20]

The single most important directive which defined the purpose of the EMSI, *Action sur les milieux féminins en Algérie*, was issued by the État-major, signed by the Commander in Chief General Challe, on 27 March 1960.[21] Directive 257, offered a detailed reflection on the work of the EMSI, 'the fruit of three years experience throughout Algeria'. The key role of the teams was to make contact with 'the feminine milieu', and to demonstrate 'in a concrete way the modern future that France holds out to them . . . Our mission is to transform Algeria to enable her population, in particular the population of Muslim women, to make the easy transition to the formation of a modern civilisation'. The fundamental, long-term objective of the EMSI was seen as essentially transformative, and in the widest sense educative, a process by which Algerian women could be gradually liberated from the constraints of conservative religious and customary practices that gave 'to Muslim society its immobility and sclerotic character'. But the directive was at pains to note that women, far from being the powerless, oppressed creatures as was widely believed, in reality were not submissive within the privacy of the household circle but held very real power and respect, and it was by building on this base that women needed to expand their influence into the public social and political sphere as full citizens and voters. It was recognised that such a transformation of deeply engrained attitudes would require a long time-scale, even several generations, and this acknowledgement confirmed a deeper shift in the army command away from the naive 'revolutionary' agenda of 1958 that had believed in a dramatic utopian conversion of Muslim women to modernity.

Directive 257 showed an unmistakable prioritisation of intelligence and repressive goals over those of welfare reform; reflecting on three years of EMSI activity, it warned: 'The principal pit-fall to be avoided is to allow the EMSI to become absorbed by its medico-social work without moving on to its true task'. The welfare and medical support provided by the teams was primarily a *means* not an end. It was through this initial aid, such as baby-care, that the EMSI could persuade Muslim women to emerge from the seclusion of the home and make contact, and which enabled the EMSI to identify potential political 'leaders' who could gradually be trained to run the women's organisation enabling the European team leaders to eventually move on to other villages. To this end it was recommended that the EMSI begin to withdraw from 'the direct practice of medical and social matters', which could be handed over to army doctors, the SAS or other agencies, to concentrate on the formation of the women's circle, in which a transformative model of modernisation and the 'new woman' could be offered. 'It is the circle that provides the education which in the end is the true mission of the EMSI'.

The instrumental and subsidiary purposes of welfare and social work to a political agenda was made quite clear by the army command. Colonel Gardes, head of the Fifth Bureau, in a general letter to the EMSI in October 1959, beseeched them not to get too emotionally bound up with their humanitarian work: 'I ask you to understand the importance of this and not to be dictated to only by your heart, to be drawn there where a child cries, or where a woman calls on your help; do not forget that your action goes beyond the question of medicine or hygiene and that you must win the support of the total body of women entrusted to you for the cause that we are fighting for, that of a France united across the two shores of the Mediterranean'.[22] Directive 257 implied that the over-emphasis on good works would simply encourage a supine dependency on hand-outs without any transformative élan, 'her natural tendency to passivity without encouraging a sense of effort or social dynamism'.

The more overtly political agenda of the EMSI operations can be recognised in a number of areas and in the following analysis this has been divided into four aspects: the promotion of a model of western femininity and domesticity, the use of standardised propaganda directives (*fiches*) in the local circles, the provision of intelligence, and the campaign for the first ever vote by Algerian women in September 1958.

One of the key roles of the EMSI was to offer, both through example and lesson, a model of western modernity that Muslim women could be led to admire and emulate. As Commander Cogniet remarked in a message to the EMSI, 'Do not forget that for "your women" you are France!'.[23] Each individual ASSRA was expected to offer, through her everyday behaviour, comportment, language, style of dress, moral tenor, generosity of spirit, diligence and fortitude, a role model to all young Muslim women. When women were recruited as ASSRA, one of the key factors that was taken into account was the moral behaviour of the candidates and, in the Muslim case, their degree of receptivity to western styles of dress and behaviour. Mme Maugé, and the EMSI departmental leaders, exercised a constant and often draconian surveillance over the behaviour of the ASSRA, including directives that they were to act in a seemly way and, for example, not to smoke in public or wear shorts which were both seen as objectionable to Muslims.[24]

A particularly thorny issue was presented by the fact that the ASSRA were often the only young and single European women with whom male soldiers, starved of female company, had any daily contact. Almost inevitably many relationships developed and, although these often ended in marriage, there existed numerous 'immoral' liaisons, including one instance of a colonel who retained an ASSRA as his mistress. Commanders were concerned that the local population might mistake the *harkettes* for the prostitutes of the mobile army brothels, the *Bordel mobile de campagne* (BCM), so that, noted one memorandum, 'it is unthinkable that a father will open his doors or allow any contact with his daughters, or a husband with his wife. We cannot think of a worse caricature of the emancipation of the Algerian woman'.[25] A significant number of ASSRA were regularly dismissed from the teams on the grounds of 'indiscipline'.[26]

The young Muslim women who were cultivated by the EMSI for potential recruitment as ASSRA were keenly watched and assessed for the extent to which they conformed to a western model of femininity. Afsaneh Najmabadi has shown, in the case of Iran at the beginning of the twentieth century, how complex was the transition from marriage as a procreative contract, in which the wife was selected neither for love nor sexual passion but for the begetting of offspring, to a romantic contract in which women were now required to invest affection in the husband.[27] However, far from representing an unambiguous emancipation from segregation and oppression, the change towards unveiling, and the life of the companionate couple, required a re-education and disciplining of the body, including how to comport oneself so as to remain chaste in public spaces. If women were now to take on the duty of educating the future nation, then they in turn had to undergo an education that would make them the rational managers of the household, adept in the science of cooking, sewing and child-care, as well as acquiring a moral behaviour that was linked to a healthy body and sport.[28] Although in the case of Algeria we are looking at changes some sixty years later and in a rather different context, the modernisation of peasant women rather than of educated elites, Najmabadi's insights help to understand the enormity of the transformational process underlying the EMSI emancipation programme.

An EMSI circular noted that young Muslim trainees should for several months undergo a 'kind of "detribalisation"' by which they would be enabled to sever their ties to the bed-rock of local custom and family tradition through the milieu of the EMSI acting as a surrogate 'family':[29] at Kerrata, for example, five women groomed for the EMSI were expected to abandon the veil and to live 'totally as Europeans'.[30] Among a series of evaluation reports on whether trainees should be accepted as ASSRA or not, was one for Fatima Be.*,[31] who had worked for several years with a doctor in Oran and spoke French: 'Has learned excellent habits of cleanliness and hygiene. A convinced partisan of the evolution of the Muslim woman: takes particular care of her appearance and dresses with taste . . . serves as an example for the women and young girls of the village'. Likewise Fatima H.* and Zohra K.* both spoke French, were 'convinced partisans of the evolution of women', understood 'the modern principles of cleanliness and hygiene' and showed no hesitation in abandoning the *haïk* for a track suit when teaching physical education to Muslim girls. By contrast Fatma Bo.* was to be rejected, since she 'provided a bad example through her undisciplined character, her frivolous conduct, and morality which leaves much to be desired'.[32]

Although, as has been seen, the 'revolution' of May 1958 espoused a political model of 'integration', of full equality between Europeans and Algerians while claiming to respect the religious and cultural identity of the latter, underlying EMSI practice was a powerful Eurocentric and assimilationist agenda. The EMSI habitus operated through a disciplining process, involving for example advice on the modest use of make-up, a 'correct' dress sense, and a certain bodily comportment and language, as well as of deference and politeness to superiors, a model that essentially derived from the conservative and largely catholic petit-bourgeois values of the EMSI hierarchy.[33] The esprit de corps cultivated by the organisation, especially evident during training programmes, was like that of an English girls' boarding school, bound together by a chaste self-discipline and healthy sporting enthusiasm.

The EMSI ranks, perhaps hardly surprising for so many young and single European women, was also suffused with a highly romantic atmosphere, in which the aspiration was to find a prince charming, most often in the ranks of the army, to marry, quit work and settle down to raise children. Implicit in this aspiration was a model of the couple and nuclear family based on sentiment that was placed in sharp contrast to the supposed loveless world of the Muslim arranged marriage. Ginette Thévenot, like many ASSRA, encouraged her women's circle to create panels of selected photographs on particular themes of modernity: one of these panels titled '*La Femme dans le monde*', consisted of various pictures of famous women which Thévenot carefully selected and cut from magazines, making sure they were suitably modest, 'worthy of example', and not from among 'the proliferation of little stars who give rise to scandal'. Held up here as the ideal model was the recent marriage of the Shah of Persia with Farah Diba, everyone being aware of 'this marvellous fairy story . . . that races the imagination into a world of dreams'.[34] Sometimes the young Muslim ASSRA missed the nuance: Ourida Rahmani wrote to the EMSI magazine *Toubiba*, 'I will continue with my efforts to turn my women into "B.B's"' [Brigitte Bardot's], which received the acid comment from Maugé, 'NO! Let B.B. take care of being an international French star: as for you be – and make of your women – an ordinary little French lady'.[35] The women's magazine *Femmes nouvelles*, which was circulated through the MSF-EMSI network, carried serialised romances adapted to a Muslim readership: thus in one typical story the heroine, Zina, after much inner turmoil rejects an arranged marriage and finally falls into the arms of her true love, Mahmoud.[36] Following on from the reform of the personal status law in February 1959 (see chapter 8), local EMSI correspondence constantly referred with great enthusiasm to the instances of Muslim couples now getting married by free choice, in civil ceremonies before French officials, and in a European dress style.

The second political aspect of EMSI work to be considered related to the use of what today would be termed 'teaching packs', standardised recommended programmes (*fiches*) that were produced by the Fifth Bureau on the basis of the experience of ASSRA during Operation Pilot.[37] These were identical in many ways to the step-by-step procedures recommended by the MSF in making initial contact and stabilising

FEMMES d'ALGÉRIE

**LA RÉBELLION BARBARE
C'EST POUR VOUS:
LA MAISON SANS HOMME
LA PEUR-LA MISÈRE
LES ENFANTS QUI ONT FAIM**

16 Army propaganda leaflet to 'Algerian Women', distributed at Bordj
Okhriss 1957: 'The barbaric rebellion means for you: a home without a man,
fear, poverty, and hungry children'

relations with Algerian women in the *douar*, primarily through lessons
on hygiene and child-care, but were far more overtly political in context.
Each separate lesson, following the practical introduction (*prise de
contact*) to groups of Muslim women, had a section on 'Propaganda'
which related specifically to the FLN as an enemy that harmed the interests of women and their children.

The 'rebels' were presented in the *fiche* as a blood-thirsty and destructive force that abducted their men-folk or savagely cut their throats,
leaving women to carry the burden of supporting the household on their
own. The FLN seized their money, depriving their children of food,
to buy arms that were turned against the people. They also destroyed
schools, leaving their children un-educated, whereas France was the
builder of schools, lycées, houses, dams and factories.

In short, 'We know, like you, that the bandits have brought nothing
but suffering. Such demons, beings who are against God, against religion,
can bring no good ... it is in the end you who suffer most from the rebellion'. The underlying objective of the *fiches* was to encourage women to

'rally' to France, by encouraging them to denounce any FLN activists in their midst, or by bringing their influence to bear on men in the village; 'If among you there are wives, mothers or sisters whose husbands, sons or brothers have gone into the maquis, you can tell them to return home. France is generous and knows how to pardon those who have not spilt blood or committed crimes, but have simply been led astray by false shepherds. Here are the authorisations: get these to them'.

It is not clear to what extent EMSI teams utilised such *fiches* or assumed an *overtly* political function in practice. Accounts by ASSRA, predominantly European women, of their activities reveals a quite extraordinary ability to blank out, or a failure to recognise, any form of involvement in counter-insurgency or repressive operations that carried negative implications for the Algerian people and for women in particular. For example, Reine Bellin provided an account of her direct observer participation, along with other ASSRA volunteers, in Operation Jumelles in the Kabyles mountains, one of the most brutal and massive 'steam-roller' army operations of the entire war. For Bellin, this adventure assumed the proportions of an exhilarating camping trip, 'the tins of rations shared with the soldiers; the evening, chatting in the dark on our air-beds . . . bursts of laughter . . . We astonished the Legionnaires by climbing at mid-day at the same speed as them'.[38] Typical is the almost total absence of any self-reflection on the ultimate purposes of such action, apart from the throwaway line of arriving by goat tracks in villages, 'to find a happy and trusting population since freed from terror'.[39] The EMSI maintained a highly gendered self-image in which their own function was purely one of humanitarian aid and nurturing (hence the predominance of images of Algerian babies and small children being washed, clothed and fed) while 'politics' belonged to the male sphere of military superiors and was accepted without question or was not 'our concern'.

However, the Fifth Bureau and army commanders frequently expressed high hopes that the EMSI, through their ability to reach over to peasant women and penetrate the previously impermeable fortress of the Muslim family, would provide important intelligence. But undoubtedly many ASSRA were plunged into a daily round of welfare in which they could readily neglect the more 'political' aspects of their role, to the annoyance of the Fifth Bureau.[40] Colonel Gardes noted that commanders needed to be reminded that the EMSI was created, 'solely within the framework of the riposte to revolutionary warfare with the mission of taking in hand the population of Muslim women', and to detect, and keep the army authorities informed, of 'the currents of opinion among women'.[41] Undoubtedly some EMSI were able to provide commanders and intelligence officers with a check on the degree of collaboration or resistance which they faced in the *douars* that they visited regularly, and in some instances where hostility was particularly entrenched this information could lead to the forced removal of particular families or entire villages into resettlement camps.[42] However, overall the key political function of the EMSI was achieved indirectly, through the attempted conversion of Algerian women to a model of westernised emancipation that would lead them to aspire to enter the portals of modernity that, it was claimed, could only be guaranteed by their support for de Gaulle and *Algérie française*.

Finally, the more overtly political function of the EMSI can be illustrated in their central role in preparing Algerian women to exercise the vote for the first time during the referendum of 28 September 1958. This subject, along with the reform of the personal status law, will be examined in the following chapter, but the particular role of the EMSI is considered here in what was one of their most significant political interventions during their first year of existence. The referendum was a major test for the Gaullist government to demonstrate to international opinion that it carried the support of Algerian women, but in order to achieve this ambition it needed to persuade the mass of illiterate women, who were lacking in any form of political education or experience of voting, first to enrol on the electoral register, then to turn out en masse on the day, and finally to exercise their vote 'correctly'. In the interior of Algeria the EMSI teams, with their Arab and Berber speaking ASSRA and assistant *harkettes*, provided a crucial instrument in this task. Many men, bound by traditional codes of honour and strict female segregation, were deeply hostile to their wives and daughters voting since they feared, often as a result of FLN counter-propaganda, that they would be forced to unveil or be exposed to the prying eye of strangers. In July 1958 Salan's cabinet sent out orders for the preparation of 'special bureaux staffed by female personnel' so that women could be registered 'without any reluctance' and likewise for segregated polling stations on the day, 'protected from public gaze'.[43]

The MSF, through its circles in the urban centres and an intense radio campaign,[44] as well as the EMSI set out to engage in a crash civic education of Algerian women.[45] An example of this is provided by the MSF of Palissy when its president, Mme Husson, addressed a special meeting of 150 Algerian women. To illustrate the choice between a 'Yes' and 'No' vote she held up, 'a magnificent piece of nylon lace and said, "you can see it's very beautiful and you would love to have some on a skirt"' (the audience replies 'Yes'). She then compared it to a 'torn and ragged cloth', asking which would they prefer? 'Yes, the pretty lace, that is FRANCE, in all its richness and opulence'. But to choose the rag was to stay in poverty, renounce emancipation, reject the opportunity to become like European women and, 'was to agree with the bandits and with foreign powers'. A week later the Pallisy MSF, three days before the referendum, held a further mass meeting of 200 Algerian women at which an EMSI team demonstrated voting procedure, the use of voting slips (white for 'Yes' and purple for 'No'), and an Algerian ASSRA harangued the crowd in Arabic as to why they should vote 'Yes': 'God created men and women, without any distinction of race or religion'.[46] What is striking about this is not only the condescending and infantile treatment of Algerian women, but also the extent to which the military authorities interfered directly in the electoral procedure to ensure a 'Yes' vote.[47] On the day of the election MSF and EMSI personnel not only assisted Algerian women at the voting stations, but helped them in selecting the 'Yes' voting slips.

The EMSI and Algerian resistance

From the external official and media accounts of the EMSI, highly publicised in films, photographs, radio broadcasts and newspapers, one would gain the impression of an efficient, trouble-free organisation, impressive in its humanity and scope. But the reality was somewhat different, and this concluding section examines first the inherent weakness and incapacity of the organisation, and secondly the extent to which the propaganda drive met resistance from the Algerian peasantry.

Firstly the EMSI organisation was severely hampered by a lack of funding and access to adequate material resources (vehicles, accommodation, medical supplies). A series of quarterly reports from the Army Corps in Oran complained constantly about the fundamental lack of budgetary and material allocations to enable commanders to assist the EMSI within their sectors, complaints that appear to have gone largely unheeded.[48] On occasions the work of EMSI teams threatened to grind to a halt. A regional organiser, Mme Fourcade, reported that they were expected to 'do everything with nothing', while the ASSRA were demanding payment of the danger bonus they had been promised.[49] The EMSI of the Constantine region, who were on the payroll of the civil administration and not the army, were so frustrated by the long delays in back pay that they invaded the cabinet of the Prefect to confront him in person.[50] The EMSI, along with the SAS, spent much of their time begging or trying to lay their hands on materials controlled by various military organisations, from bricks and cement to clothing, milk and paper. It is difficult to know if this penury represented a basic strain in the overall military budget, which by 1959 was absorbing 20 per cent of the total state budget,[51] and/or the reflection of a fundamental lack of commitment within the echelons of the military-governmental apparatus to treating *action sociale* as a priority. Certainly there were many reports that commented on the failure of sector commanders to provide adequate support to the small EMSI teams that found themselves abandoned and left to their own devices without proper hierarchical supervision.

A second, pragmatic weakness of the EMSI was that their overall number was far too low to make a significant impact on the huge number of Algerian peasantry. The main target of EMSI action was young women in the age group fifteen to thirty-five, because they were viewed as most susceptible to modernisation, while older women (*adjouzat*) were much disliked by the Fifth Bureau since they were stout defenders of religious custom, carried much power within the household, and were less open to French influence. The authorities calculated that two million women aged fifteen to thirty-five were served by some 300 ASSRA, an average of 6,000–7,000 women per assistant.[52] But in reality when EMSI teams arrived to give medical aid in isolated villages, in which the population was normally devoid of access to any kind of modern medical help, they were swamped by huge crowds, not only of women, but also babies, children and elderly men.[53] In the Oranie, where the number of EMSI was 'insufficient for the area and size of population', the command was seeking in 1960 to double the 110 ASSRA.[54]

The army, concerned that the EMSI would spread themselves too thinly and try to cover too large a population, recommended that no team should take on more than three centres (*douars* or resettlement camps) and 1,500 to 3,000 women at any one time and visit them regularly. Moreover, within each centre the women's circle was to contain no more than thirty to fifty young women, the optimum number for getting to know, identify and train the core of volunteers to take over the future running of the group when the EMSI moved on.[55] In reality it often proved difficult for the EMSI to make regular contact with isolated villages spread over an enormous area of difficult and dangerous terrain: Thévenin-Copin, for example, could only reach one *douar* at a time by travelling out with the weekly military convoy, so that it took one month to make a complete round of the sector.[56] In general the EMSI appear to have been unable to achieve the 'in-depth work' expected of them and the Oran army corps reported as late as April 1961 that most ASSRA still stuck to pragmatic tasks such as knitting and, 'neglected the question of information and moral and civic education'.[57] Most worrying perhaps for the army was the failure of the EMSI to set in motion a multiplier effect, to train autonomous and self-governing Algerian women's circles: it was 'very difficult to locate in the mass of women the leaders and organisers capable of continuing and extending the work set into motion by the teams'.[58]

Thirdly, the army faced considerable difficulty not only in recruiting able ASSRA but also in retaining them. ASSRA were required to have a minimum educational qualification at the standard of the primary school leaving certificate (CEP), and of the 306 enrolled in November 1961, 78 per cent (238 women) had the CEP or equivalent, 17 percent (fifty-three) the higher *brevet*, and 5 per cent (fifteen), of which none were Algerians, the baccalaureate.[59] Particularly important to the entire EMSI project, but rarely acknowledged, was the crucial need for each team to contain at least one Algerian ASSRA who could communicate with Arab or Berber-speaking women, act as interpreters to the European team leaders, and who were sensitive to the complex religious and cultural values of the population. The problem was that very few young Algerian women had the desired level of French and education to CEP level, and those who did came from a petit-bourgeois, urban class of shop-keepers, teachers, white collar workers and professionals that provided a natural constituency for the nationalist movement.

This may explain in part why such an extraordinarily large number of Muslim ASSRA were recruited from FLN militants who were captured and then 'turned'. Quite typical of this process was the recommendation of Captain Ricart to employ as ASSRA two captured FLN women being held by the *Détachement opérationnel de protection*: one Bahia L.*, twenty-three years old, was a former secretary to the Sub-Prefect of Sebdou, and the second, Tedjania Y.*, eighteen years, was former secretary to Bouazza, political commissar of Douar Sidi-Boumédienne. Ricart said these two intelligent women, who had been educated at the college for girls in Tlemcen, were 'full of goodwill' and had only worked for the FLN under threat. If handed over to the courts they would be definitively lost to the army, while they could provide valuable aid as ASSRA.[60]

There are numerous accounts of this kind in the press: an almost standard practice of the army was to introduce journalists visiting the interior to the ASSRA who, it was claimed, provided a living witness of young Muslim women who had been cruelly or treacherously recruited by the FLN through force, often used as sex objects, or who had joined the maquis in desperation to escape forced marriage. These ASSRA provided proof of the abhorrent oppression of women by the nationalists, while within the EMSI ranks they found both freedom and a fulfilment of their deepest desire to gain access to an enlightened modernity. Christiane Fournier told the story of Aziza who, after escaping to the maquis to avoid forced marriage with an old man, was captured by the

French army and offered a place with the EMSI: whisked away from the *djebel* to the capital she was entranced by visions of a future that could be hers, 'Aziza opened her eyes full of wonder on the shop-windows of Algiers . . . The young girls, their blond hair falling on their shoulders, resting on the arms of the boys they had chosen to love'.[61]

Despite the highly propagandist construction of these accounts, they were not entirely fictitious, and many dozens of ex-FLN women were recruited into the EMSI. As has been seen (chapter 2) such a policy of conversion had been started by Jean Servier during Operation Pilot, and by August 1959 Colonel Gardes was planning to establish a permanent centre run by PFAT that would retrain up to thirty ex-FLN militants at a time.[62] The danger of such a policy is that the army risked integrating into the EMSI women who were hostile to the logic of 'pacification' or were even covert agents that had penetrated into the ranks of the ASSRA under FLN orders. Many of the Muslim ASSRA, far from showing the deep bonds of 'fraternisation' with their European sisters depicted by Thévenin-Copin and Fournier, often revealed signs of fractious resistance: at Saint-Charles several ASSRA were asked, or forced, to resign since they objected to sharing quarters with their European comrades, and had fallen under the influence of one, Samira, 'who by her anti-French intrigues creates much damage wherever she goes'.[63] That ASSRA often felt themselves discriminated against was not surprising: one general recommended that recruitment of Jewish women as ASSRA was to be avoided, while General Bertron favoured Christian ASSRA and when EMSI teams arrived 'he had acquired decent rooms for the Europeans while the Muslim women had to put up with makeshift accommodation'.[64]

By September 1958 there were already signs of disquiet that recruitment of ex-FLN women was enabling suspect elements to enter the EMSI ranks and a senior organiser, Mlle Desfretiere recommended that it was important to prevent, 'the women who were taken during military operations, or who themselves sought safety with the soldiers, from automatically joining the EMSI'. She attached to her report an intelligence file on an ex-rebel (Aziza B.*) who had joined the EMSI at Bordj-Menaïel in March and qualified as an ASSRA in June 1958 and asked for an urgent investigation of her weekly visits to a male contact in Algiers.[65] The fear that the FLN was deliberately planting its militants, or trying to win over ASSRA, was well founded. In September 1961, for example, it was reported from the Oranais that the FLN was openly soliciting ASSRA and two of them were arrested for collusion.[66]

Former EMSI note that the local FLN tried to make contact with Muslim ASSRA to win them over, and teams had to be vigilant that women did not pass medicines to the maquis. One response to FLN pressure threatening to compromise individual ASSRA was to move them quickly to an entirely different sector.[67]

Evidence of the infiltration of an active FLN militant can be found in a report of the SAU officer for the Bas Casbah in 1959 relating to Zoubida Belkebir, aged twenty-two years, currently seeking qualification as an ASSRA or *attaché feminine* with the SAS. Belkebir, who had 'strong nationalist or pro-FLN sentiments', came from a family of dedicated militants. Four brothers and a brother-in-law were currently in the maquis, while another brother-in-law, Si Ali or Sid Ali, a landowner at Boufarik, had been a high-level FLN organiser in the Sahel, before his escape via France to Spain, Morocco and Tunisia. Zoubida had been arrested during the early stages of the Battle of Algiers in 1957 and 'interrogated quite energetically' (i.e. tortured) before departing for Morocco, where she worked as a nurse with the nationalist Dr Bendouali and resided with her brother-in-law, Sid Ali. During 1959 Zoubida went to the French consulate to apply for a visa, dressed for the occasion with veil and *cachabia*, although she normally wore European clothing, and then returned to Algiers where she presented herself as an aspirant ASSRA.[68]

In general it can be concluded that the 140- to 200-odd young Algerian women who, at any one moment, served as ASSRA during 1958–62, were not uniformly dedicated supporters of *Algérie française*, as official propaganda suggested. Some appear to have become disillusioned with the racism they faced in the ranks of the army, others became uncertain and worried about their position as French withdrawal became a possibility from late 1959 onwards, shifted from a pro-French to pro-FLN position, or were actively recruited or infiltrated into the EMSI by the FLN. These signs of disillusionment with, or hostility to, French operations is significant, since the Muslim ASSRA with their knowledge of French, Arabic and Berber dialect, of local social and cultural mores, and sensitivity to the universe of Algerian women and of family relations, offered the greatest potential to implement a strategy of contact. The type of young women from which the ASSRA were recruited, aged eighteen to about thirty, literate in French, educated to at least CEP standard, constituted a tiny urban class and a potentially invaluable but scarce political resource that both FLN and the French government competed for as potential cadres. This pivotal group, an elite of Francophone women from the urban lower middle-class or old urban families that had traditionally served the French state (*cadis, bachagas,* army officers), were deeply attracted to a vision of modernity that could, according to their families' political culture, be realised *either* through the promise of emancipation and integration into French civilisation (a universe portrayed by the glamour of Parisian teenage life and romantic love) *or* through dedication to a nationalist struggle that would liberate women, although in some often undefined way, through independence.

Undoubtedly many ASSRA, as portrayed by propaganda and the media, in nailing their colours to the French mast, became extremely enthusiastic and militant missionaries in the task of converting their Algerian 'sisters' and winning them away from the stifling traditions of female oppression and segregation. But the environment of French modernity was one in which pro-nationalist women also found themselves completely at ease. The entire class of French speaking and educated young women occupied an ambiguous and even volatile position, and this explains in part the ease with which they could pass from FLN ranks to the EMSI, and back again. For the Fifth Bureau and the leaders of the EMSI this began to cast an atmosphere of doubt and insecurity over the reliability of Muslim ASSRA in their crucial task of bridging over to local Algerian women. The European ASSRA, with a few exceptions, had little if any linguistic competence in Arabic or Berber, and were hugely dependent not only on Algerian ASSRA as interpreters and intermediaries, but also on the accuracy of translation and whether nuances of meaning and tonal inflection might conceal or not messages of disapproval or resistance. Even the formidable Mme Maugé, director of the EMSI, could find herself frustrated and on uncertain ground: during a tour of inspection of two resettlement camps she was met by many poorly clothed women and dirty children, 'The army Muslim interpreter used by me did not seem to translate faithfully the words of the population, nor my own for that matter'.[69] But of course she was unable to be certain, and therein lay the deep insecurity of the whole 'pacification' endeavour.

This leads in to the question of the kind of reception that the EMSI teams met when they began to make contact with isolated rural populations. Thévenin-Copin claims that, after an initial timidity, she invariably received a warm and generous welcome from peasant women wherever she went.[70] The archives reveal a rather different picture, and in general two separate, but often interrelated, forms of village hostility and resistance can be identified: firstly, a socio-religious and cultural opposition, and secondly, a nationalist inspired political resistance. Looking at these in turn, it can be noted that for many, if not the great majority of, women attachment to customary family and gender roles, including arranged marriage and seclusion, was a sacrosanct tradition legitimated by religion and custom, an internalised system of values rather than forms of practice simply imposed by external male authority and force. Indeed, married women, as the educators of children (in the widest sense) and guardians of the sacred space of the household, were widely regarded as the transmitters of core identity. This is why the EMSI were keen to try and marginalise or exclude the older *adjouzat* from the women's circles.

However, in most areas the core of socio-religious opposition to the EMSI came from the men who were deeply anxious about any agenda for emancipation and continued to hold the whip hand as to whether wives and daughters could leave the house to attend EMSI or MSF activities. EMSI teams working in the Kabyle mountains to the north of Bouira described their reception in some villages as warm and positive, and in others quite cold, particularly on the part of men like those of Guendoue who remained distant and were 'somewhat fierce, spoke very little, and did not say what they thought of the situation'. Elsewhere they made some progress and after a difficult first contact, 'the population approaches us readily', except for Tassala, inhabited by a traditional, conservative religious elite, 'a *marabout* village, where the men are all very religious and do not like their wives to leave the house, even to go to the *ouvroir*'.[71] Directive 257 in a section 'Action on men' noted that past attempts to change the status of women through a radical agenda rather than by a gradual evolution had produced a justifiable and 'perfectly understandable' opposition among men. It recommended a sensitive management of local male feelings since it was crucial to bring on-side men who provided a 'lever' for change.[72] But in many areas, as in Eastern Oranie in April 1960, it was reported that EMSI teams were making little impact despite frequent visits because of the sheer grinding poverty and illiteracy of the inhabitants: 'The mentality of Muslim women remains on the whole very primitive', and despite much work, 'poverty, the passivity inherent in the milieu, and male dominance, impedes and even blocks this timid evolution'.[73]

The depth of socio-cultural resistance to the EMSI agenda was not necessarily political and was shared right across the populace, often regardless of whether they were pro-French or nationalists. This embedded nature of popular attachment to traditional familial and gender structures is illustrated by the fact that the EMSI frequently faced difficulty in persuading the wives and daughters of police or army auxiliaries, an almost natural constituency under the direct wing of the army, to attend meetings or circles. One inspector of the EMSI reported the difficulty of penetrating, 'the female milieu of the local Muslim (FSNA) authorities, the *Moghaznis* and *Harkis*, which instead of giving an example of such evolution, are a hindrance to this action'.[74] However, the FLN undoubtedly made its presence felt in organising resistance to the EMSI at village level through its clandestine political network (OPA).

The FLN at the higher level, as has been seen, organised opposition to the emancipation strategy of the army through its radio broadcasts and by orders to threaten or attack the MSF and EMSI. In some instances the FLN mounted direct attacks on ASSRA on leave,[75] and killed them: Thévenin-Copin records the death of at least nine women by assassination.[76] After the death of four ASSRA in an ambush in the Ghribs in January 1961 the army reported an undeniable demoralisation in the EMSI ranks.[77] But the widest impact of FLN opposition, which varied enormously in intensity from one region or village to another, was to create a generalised boycott of the circles. In general the FLN did not discipline or threaten women who received material aid from the EMSI or SAS, a procedure which would have been highly counterproductive given the wretched conditions faced by the peasantry (lack of medical aid, food and clothing) and the fact that such French supplies were also channelled to the FLN maquis, but it did challenge those who showed too keen an attachment and association with the French. Typical of many army reports were those from Baraki, where the EMSI team faced great difficulty in establishing contact with women, 'it seems that a clandestine OPA is the cause of this reluctance', or in Oranie where an OPA operated at village level, 'in which women often played an active role'. At La Baraque near Aumale, 'where one day the women of the Circle refused care and tea on the order of the rebels – There is certainly an OPA operating here'.[78] Quite typical here was both the uncertainty of the EMSI, as well as of the intelligence officers, to know whether the FLN was active or not in particular villages, and their powerlessness to do anything about it. As the army reported from the western Oranais, a clear stagnation or regression in the work of the EMSI in rural areas, 'seems due to the pressure or orders of the milieu under the influence of the rebels, thus to causes that the ASSRA have a mission to neutralise but which, it has to be said, escapes their control'.[79]

The final point to note is that the work of the EMSI, as of the MSF, became increasingly difficult as the end of the war drew in sight. Although by 1959 the FLN had significantly lost the military battle (but not the war itself), there were growing indications of a deep shift in Algerian popular opinion, a new-found self-confidence that took the form of an increasing willingness openly to defy or challenge the army and French authorities. One SAS reported in June 1961 a sudden increase in hostility towards welfare assistants who had previously been well received: 'during the course of their visits to the *douars* our social teams have noticed a very clear deterioration in the ambiance and hostile comments have been made to us in certain *bidonvilles*, especially at Staouéli and Zéralda that have always given us an excellent reception'.[80]

Following de Gaulle's speech of September 1959 the Algerian nationalists were aware of the growing signs of a possible French retreat, and
began to sense that the settler population was nervous and running
scared. The real turning point in nationalist self-confidence (see chapter
10) was marked by the *journées* of December 1960 in Algiers, when the
populace was prepared openly to chant nationalist slogans during street
demonstrations.[81]

This deeper shift carried serious implications for the EMSI. Firstly,
it became increasingly difficult for the organisation to retain or recruit
both able European and Algerian women. Under 'normal' conditions
there was already a high level of turn-over among the ASSRA, and
between November 1957 and September 1960 some 43 per cent, 235
women out of 557 recruits, had left.[82] Many young women failed
to cope with the Spartan and demanding conditions that they faced,
others were removed for various failings, while there was a considerable
'leakage' of those who got married, invariably to French soldiers.[83] This
instability of personnel meant that individual ASSRA were just building up experience of the job on the ground, when they departed to be
replaced by novices who had to begin all over again.

The problem of recruitment deteriorated further as uncertainty about
the outcome of the war deepened. This anxiety became particularly
evident among the Algerian ASSRA, since they had far more to lose: if
the war terminated in an FLN victory they risked becoming the target
of nationalist vengeance. Moreover, as any sign of association with the
French authorities became increasingly risky or worrying, the families
and relatives of ASSRA placed pressure on the young women to cut their
ties to the army since this might tarnish and endanger the family group
as a whole in the eyes of the nationalists. Numerous reports during
1960–61 comment on the growing difficulty of recruiting Algerian
ASSRA and of demoralisation in the EMSI ranks, 'due in particular
to the pressure of comrades and neighbours who reproach them for
working "with the soldiers"'.[84] In Oranie in July 1961 EMSI teams
were met with a hail of stones at Saint-Denis-du-Sig, Bedeau, Oran and
Aïn-Témouchent.[85] In this deteriorating situation the army was forced
to increase dramatically the number of inexperienced *harkette* recruits
and to cut back on the size of EMSI teams.[86]

With the dramatic radicalisation of overt popular nationalism from
the end of 1960, there were growing signs of women's resistance inside
the EMSI circles. Algerian women were passing from an earlier phase
(1957–59) during which they generally remained mute in the immediate presence of SAS, MSF and EMSI personnel, in a situation in which
silence was the best form of defence, of not disclosing one's true opinions

while gaining access to the material resources of the army, to a phase (1960–62) in which resistance could be expressed openly and often with impunity. In the towns, in particular Algiers, Algerian women attending the circles began to talk openly of independence 'as if it was already an accomplished fact', younger women aged sixteen to twenty were particularly fractious, 'oversensitive and quarrelsome', and they made it quite clear that they were unprepared to be subjected to any more propaganda and that their motive in attending circles was purely material and instrumental.[87] 'The Muslim female population, especially in the *douars*, is more interested in the small and immediate material benefits to be gained from contacts, from these meetings, than by the ideas of social emancipation that one tries to teach them'.[88] As the balance of forces tipped remorselessly in favour of the nationalists, so the work of the EMSI became increasingly untenable and inspections by senior army officers reveal their own deepening demoralisation and a growing recognition that the MSF and ASSRA actions had been superficial and never achieved the effective and durable transformation of Muslim women that had been optimistically claimed in earlier years.

Notes

1 A very similar function to the EMSI was played by the SAS, either through the volunteer work of the wives of officers, or by social assistants who were attached permanently to the teams: for a detailed account see the autobiography of Monique Eoche-Duval, *Madame SAS*; Sambron, *Femmes musulmanes*, 84–92. Seferdjeli, 'French Army', 45–6, notes that the *attachées*, who numbered 561 by June 1960, were more numerous than the EMSI. Much less is known about these assistants, in part because they were not the subject of intense media attention, but their functions were very much the same as that of the EMSI.
2 Fournier, *Les EMSI*, 41–7, Maugé appears here under the thin disguise of 'Pat'.
3 SHAT 1H4395/7, the order of 25 October 1957, which established the ASSRA.
4 Ginette Thévenin-Copin, in her autobiography, *Plaidoyer pour la paix*, provides an insight into the daily life of the ASSRA.
5 Fournier, *Les EMSI*, appendix, 183–7; interviews with Ginette Thévenin-Copin and Edmée Barbier, former EMSI, Montpellier, 3–4 November 2006. The foundation order (*arrête*) of 25 October 1957 specified that ASSRA would later attend a four-month training programme leading to a diploma, but this requirement was never implemented and may have been designed to conceal the lack of qualifications and expertise.
6 Edmée Barbier interview, 4 November 2006; on Cogniet's extremism see Villatoux and Villatoux, *La République*, 539–41. ASSRA trainees later

reported on how Cogniet's courses had enlightened them as to the nature of the struggle in which they were involved, 'It was not a question of two opposed armed powers, but of two philosophies. The Marxist philosophy that considers man as a material being who must be enslaved, which is what the FLN wishes to impose: and the Occidental philosophy, which is what we represent, that recognises that man has spiritual qualities which he wishes to develop so that his country can live in liberty and self-fulfilment', *Toubiba*, 12 (25 June 1959). *Toubiba*, an internal EMSI journal edited by Mme Maugé, private archive of Ginette Thévenin-Copin.

7 *Toubiba*, 1 (25 July 1959).
8 *Toubiba*, 16 (25 October 1960).
9 Thévenin-Copin, *Plaidoyer*, 59–60; SHAT 1H2569* records the opposition, for example, of General B. in Oranie, and of a medical officer (captain) at Telagh who was hostile to the EMSI because of 'their incompetence in medicine'. For opposition to the early EMSI experiment during Operation Pilot, see above chapter 2.
10 SHAT 1H2461/1, General Hubert to Algiers HQ, 30 May 1958, complained that only one EMSI existed in his sector and requested three more as crucial to building contact with the population.
11 See chapter 3.
12 SHAT 1H2461/1, EMSI statistics, 29 August 1960.
13 Seferdjeli, 'French Army', 50–1.
14 The *harkettes*, who were trained 'on the job', were paid 20–25,000 old Francs (AFr.) per month, compared to ASSRA pay of 43,000 AFr.: see SHAT 1H2461/1.
15 SHAT 1H1147/1, press cutting from *Elle*, October 1958.
16 SHAT 1H2461/1, Maugé notes to Colonel Gardes, 15 May, 29 August 1959.
17 Fournier, *Les EMSI*, 12, 19.
18 *Toubiba*, 3 (25 September 1959); 6 (25 December 1959); 14 (25 August 1960).
19 SHAT 1H2409, État-Major, Fifth Bureau, 24 October 1958 notes that EMSI role in 'pacification' will be 'controlled by psychological officers working in close liaison with the intelligence officers', including their submission of any modifications to the 'work plan'.
20 Colonel Gardes, in *Toubiba*, 4 (25 October 1959).
21 SHAT 1H2088, Instruction pour la pacification en Algérie No. 4 (257/EMI/3/PH), 27 March 1960, 36 pages, hereafter referred to as Directive 257. This document was issued down to commanders at sector level, but was kept secret from the EMSI for security reasons that almost certainly derived from a justified concern that the FLN had infiltrated agents into the organisation.
22 *Toubiba*, 4 (25 October 1959).
23 *Toubiba*, 13 (25 July 1960).
24 SHAT 1H4395/7.
25 SHAT 1H4494/2, quoted by Seferdjeli, 'French Army', 67–8. Among the FLN and French anti-war militants there was a widespread propagandist

perception of the ASSRA as 'prostitutes'. On the BMC and prostitution in the Maghreb see Christelle Taraud, *La Prostitution coloniale. Algérie, Tunisie, Maroc (1830–1962)* (Paris: Payot, 2003). In the ECPAD archives is a sequence of photographs, FLAM R637 to 6382, by Marc Flamand of Colonel Bigard, a sub-prefect, and senior officers during a visit to the resettlement camp of Sidi Moumoun, seated in 'Oriental' style on cushions while being entertained by ASSRA dancing girls: such events could be readily construed by Algerian society as immoral.

26 SHAT 1H2569*; *Toubiba*, 2 (25 August 1959), records the departure for 'indiscipline' of Noëlle Fernandez and Malika Touabi, and of Louise-Marie de Kerjegu, 'victim of her over-vivid imagination'; *Toubiba*, 7 (25 January 1960), for 'indiscipline', Aïcha Messaoudi, Yamina Toury, Claire Charpentier, Michèle Braquessac.
27 Najmabadi, *Women with Mustaches*, 158–9.
28 *Ibid.*, chapters 6 and 7.
29 SHAT 1H2556/1, directive of P. Hosteing, Directeur général des affaires politiques, 3 December 1957.
30 SHAT 1H2461/1, report, 12 December 1957.
31 In line with the conditions of being given access (*dérogation*) to archives that are normally closed, I have respected the anonymity of some individuals: these are indicated by initials and an asterisk.
32 SHAT 1H2569*, report of Captain Bidaud, 27 August 1958. In another report of 18 September 1958 the EMSI organiser Mlle Desfretiere warned that commanders were accepting young Kabyles women into the EMSI teams, who 'do not possess sufficient qualities to serve as an example for village women . . . women of questionable morals'.
33 This question of proper dress codes, personal hygiene and correct comportment was similar to that promulgated by the MSF circles and its publication *Femmes nouvelles*: see above chapter 5.
34 Thévenin-Copin, *Plaidoyer*, 177; a copy of this panel in Thévenin-Copin's private archive shows a central design of a veiled Muslim woman holding hands with a European woman, and surrounding this couple, various images of dynamic women (athletes, nurses), and the 'fairy-tale' marriage of King Baudouin of Belgium and Fabiola in December 1960.
35 *Toubiba*, 11 (25 May 1960).
36 *Femmes nouvelles*, 19 (20 April 1960).
37 SHAT 1H2461/1, five *fiches* distributed by Fifth Bureau, 30 June 1958.
38 *Toubiba*, 3 (25 September 1959).
39 Thévenin-Copin, *Plaidoyer*, 124, justifies a captain using a human shield of local villages, including women, to walk in front of army convoys along roads that were being mined by the FLN.
40 Sambron, *Femmes musulmanes*, 80–4, notes that propaganda and intelligence was never a main concern of the EMSI; see also Launay, *Paysans algériens*, 316–17, an SAS nurse at Trois-Marabouts (Oranie), 'The Captain had asked her to skilfully interrogate the patients and to provide him with

"intelligence". But she did not like informing and knew that the Muslims quickly saw through such silly games if she engaged in them'.

41 SHAT 1H2661/1, dossier action EMSI, 20 May 1958–March 1962.
42 SHAT 1H4395/7, reports on EMSI for the Bouira sector.
43 CAOM 13CAB64, Salan cabinet note, 24 July 1958.
44 In addition to the MSF *Magazine de la femme* (see chapter 4), SHAT 1H1147/1 has transcripts of Operation Referendum, twenty-eight RTF Arab-language broadcasts on the theme, 'Vote Yes. To Assure the Emancipation of the Muslim Woman'.
45 Seferdjeli, 'French Army', 57–60, for detail of the referendum campaign.
46 CAOM 81F74.
47 Several model directives sent out by the Fifth Bureau insisted on the 'Yes' vote: see SHAT 1H2461/1.
48 SHAT 1H2569: for example General Fouquault, report of 28 June 1960, 'The activities of the teams is more and more limited by the poverty of the material and financial means already noted'.
49 SHAT 1H2569, note, 3 May 1958.
50 Thévenin-Copin, *Plaidoyer*, 194–7.
51 Lefeuvre, *Chère Algérie*, has demonstrated the extent to which the underdeveloped Algerian colony, contrary to popular perception, was dependent on budgetary transfers from metropolitan France.
52 SHAT 1H2088/4, Directive 257, 27 March 1960.
53 Thévenin-Copin, *Plaidoyer*, 139, and photographs of huge waiting crowds.
54 SHAT 1H2569/2*, quarterly report, April 1960.
55 SHAT 1H2088/4, Directive 257, 27 March 1960.
56 Thévenin-Copin, *Plaidoyer*, 66.
57 SHAT 1H2569/2*, quarterly report, CAO, 12 April 1961. On the problems of the EMSI on the ground see also Seferdjeli, 'French Army', 63–5.
58 SHAT 1H2569/2*, quarterly report, CAO, 28 June 1960.
59 Seferdjeli, 'French Army', 52–3.
60 SHAT 1H2569*, note of Captain Ricard, 28 March 1958.
61 Fournier, *Les EMSI*, 49–56, and her account of Aïcha of Oran, kidnapped by the FLN, 73–80; see for example also, Thévenin-Copin, *Plaidoyer*, 104–5, the case of Fatima, captured in the maquis, who had been a brilliant school student, but escaped to the FLN to avoid an arranged marriage; Jacques Perrier in *L'Aurore*, 27 August 1959, on his meeting Zoubida, who had been taken by force at Mascara in 1957 along with seven other women 'to serve as a distraction to the men of Wilaya V'.
62 SHAT 1H2461/1, Gardes to commander in chief, 24 August 1959. It is unclear whether this centre was ever established, but a similar retraining camp at Arzew did exist for captured ex-FLN male cadres.
63 SHAT 1H2569, reports from Saint Charles, March–April 1958.
64 SHAT 1H2569/2*, quarterly report, ZOC, 28 June 1960; report of Mme Maugé on inspection tour, Oranie, 26 February 1958.
65 SHAT 1H2569/2*, report of Desfretiere, 18 September 1958.

66 SHAT 1H2569/2*, quarterly report, ZCO, 26 September 1961.
67 Interview of G. Thévenin-Copin and E. Barbier, 4 November 2006.
68 CAOM 2SAS56, intelligence report of SAU officer, Bas Casbah (Algiers), 22 July 1959.
69 SHAT 1H2569/2*, Maugé report, 26 February 1958.
70 Thévenin-Copin, *Plaidoyer*, 67, 172.
71 SHAT 1H4395/7, EMSI reports for sector of Bouira, January and April 1960.
72 SHAT 1H2088/4, directive 257, 27 March 1960.
73 SHAT 1H2569, quarterly report, ZEO, 21 April 1960.
74 SHAT 1H2569/2*, report, 15 March 1961. FSNA (*Français de souche nord-africaine*), was the term used currently by the government to denote Algerians.
75 SHAT 1H4395/7, report of Third Bureau, 4 March 1960.
76 Thévenin-Copin, *Plaidoyer*, 184–5, 214.
77 SHAT 1H2569/2*, quarterly report, Oranie, 11 May 1961.
78 SHAT 1H2569/2*, reports 1959–60.
79 SHAT 1H2569/2*, quarterly report, ZOO, 26 September 1960.
80 CAOM 2SAS72 Chéragas, monthly report, 20 May–20 June 1961.
81 Mahfoud Kaddache, 'Les Tournants de la guerre de libération au niveau des masses populaires', in Ageron (ed.), *La Guerre d'Algérie et les Algériens*, 51–70; see also Seferdjeli, 'French Army', 61, who notes that former *harkettes* participated in the Oran demonstrations.
82 Seferdjeli, 'French Army', 63.
83 *Toubiba* refers to many dozens of resignation for reasons of marriage: see, for example, 4 (25 October 1959), 'Again another who abandons us to marry a Lieutenant-Colonel'. It appears that some women volunteered for the EMSI because of the attractions of an active marriage market.
84 SHAT 1H2569/2*, quarterly report, ZNE, 12 October 1961.
85 SHAT 1H2569/2*, quarterly report, Oran, 12 July 1961.
86 The word '*harkette*', a diminutive and feminised form of the term '*harki*', may have been related to the fact that cash-strapped commanders funded these women from the budget allocated to military auxiliaries (*harkis*): interview E. Barbier, 4 November 2006; on this widespread form of 'creative funding' see Mathias, Les *Sections administratives*, 95.
87 SHAT 1H2569*, quarterly report, 11 May 1961.
88 SHAT 1H2569*, quarterly report, ZCO, 15 December 1960.

8

The battle over the personal status law of 1959[1]

Of the different measures taken by the French government for the advancement and emancipation of Algerian women none was potentially more important than the 1959 reform of marriage and family law (*statut personnel*). It is no co-incidence that throughout the Muslim world during the last hundred years political battles over reform and modernisation have inevitably been framed in relation to the legal position and rights of women. The structure of the family cell constituted the fundamental bedrock of the total socio-political order that determined everything from socialisation of children, gender relations, property ownership and economic activity, to social networks and political power. While some attempts to transform the position of women involved long-term change, most notably access to education, others, including the personal status law, leant themselves more readily to interventionism and attempts to bring about or impose radical transformation from 'above'. This explains why the French moves to reform family law proved to be such an extremely sensitive issue. Most Algerians, whether supporting the FLN or the French side, were not in principle opposed to women receiving education, training, improved health care or even the vote, since at the end of the day such change could be absorbed without altering the fundamental ground rules and shape of the religio-social order: but interference with the regulation of family life was perceived, across political and class lines, as a dangerous and subversive innovation. Why then did the French choose to undertake such a reform at so inopportune a moment when, embroiled in a seemingly endless colonial war, it threatened to alienate all sectors of public opinion and to strengthen FLN support?

As has been seen (chapter 2) by early 1957 the head of the Algiers government, Robert Lacoste, in the light of the Tunisian and Moroccan reforms of family law, was acutely aware of the extent to which the colony was lagging behind the times and how this threatened to undermine claims of *Algérie française*, before the court of international

opinion, to an enlightened and progressive stance. Lacoste had in early
1957 quietly established a working party under Simoneau to draft a new
code but this, after consultation with the Prefects, was shelved. Lacoste
was surrounded by European specialists on native customs and Islamic
law, advisers from the *affaires indigènes*, judges and professors of law,
who upheld a highly conservative consensus or tacit alliance with the
official-backed religious leaders (*imams*) and lawyers (*cadis*), that no
major changes to Islamic law would be implemented by non-Muslim
French secularists.[2]

The colonial government was traditionally attuned to the danger of
religious inspired revolt and the French security services kept a constant
watch on religious leaders and the confraternities, which still retained
considerable popular support, as potential fomenters of anti-French
discord and 'fanaticism'.[3] The crucial strategic political importance of
the statute was that throughout the twentieth century the government
had been able to deny citizenship and full equality to Algerians as long
as they retained their *statut personnel*, a legal status as Muslims. It was
argued by colonial ideologues that it was precisely because Algerians
clung to un-Christian traditions such as polygamy, child-marriage and
other barbaric customs that they could not enter into the French *cité*.
But, in a kind of perverse collusion, conservative Algerian religious and
political leaders, locked out from full citizenship and equality, erected
the *statut personnel* as *the* true fortress of national identity, a counter-
weight to exclusion. Religious leaders not only fought tooth-and-nail
to defend the statute from secular subversion, but defined core Muslim
identity in terms of the sacrosanct family structure: as the reformist
Ulema Lamine Lamoudi claimed, 'It represents our traditions, our
customs and our beliefs. This regards three principal issues: marriage,
divorce, and inheritance'.[4] Fundamentally European Islamic experts and
advisers, as well as the elite of official religious leaders, both had a career
investment as highly trained conservative exegetes of the most abstruse
details of Muslim law and supported the status quo or a 'gender pact' in
relation to the family code.

The advice given by the Prefects on the proposed 1957 law veered on
the side of caution, and Lacoste was not prepared to stir up a hornets'
nest that would benefit the FLN (chapter 2). But the events of 13 May
1958 brought to the fore the dynamic and radical colonels of the Fifth
Bureau who were fully prepared, in a climate of heady excitement, and
encouraged by the impact of women's 'fraternisation', to implement a
'revolutionary' transformation of the marriage code. The propaganda
drive against the veil during 1957, along with the success of Operation
Pilot, had created a high level of confidence in an emancipation agenda,

and the generals were concerned to seize the initiative before the FLN, which was discovered to be laying its own plans for a new women's organisation. However, even the colonels proceeded with caution on the delicate issue of personal status and the Salan-led government took the decision to prepare the way for such a radical initiative by *first* extending the vote to Algerian women in the referendum of 28 September 1958. The thinking behind this was to test the degree of support among Algerian women for the new Gaullist regime and, once their political 'maturity' and reliability had been demonstrated, the government would then proceed immediately to the next phase, legal reform of the statute. Since the two-phase project for the vote and legal reform were closely interrelated this chapter looks briefly at the first before examining the marriage code in more detail.

Algerian women and the franchise

Algerian women had, in principle, gained the right to vote, along with European women, by the Organic Law of 20 September 1947, but as has been seen (chapter 1) this right was in effect blocked by a carefully constructed fixing of the system of dual assemblies. As late as January 1958 a report on *Le Droit de vote de la femme musulmane algérienne* asked if it was possible any longer to maintain the exclusion of half the population from political life when it was in sharp contradiction with the French policy of integration.[5] But the thought of adding 1,900,300 voters to the electorate further primed the deep fears of Europeans of being politically inundated by a large and rapidly increasing Algerian population. The report fell back on three reasons to justify continuing exclusion: the mass of illiterate women, unable to read a leaflet or voting slip, could not make a rational or informed decision; no vote could be freely exercised because of the control and interference by male relatives; and it would not be possible to verify the identity of veiled women at the voting stations. It concluded with the standard formula of colonial government in resisting the extension of political rights to natives: such enfranchisement should come *after* the long-term education and evolution of women would make them fit to enter the portals of democracy. This typical line of thinking was dramatically swept aside after 13 May 1958.

On 27 June 1958 General Salan, who held full military and civilian power in Algeria, ordered the enrolment of all Algerian women on the electoral registers,[6] and from 8 July onwards the government orchestrated a major propaganda drive so that women would both register in time and turn out in force at the referendum to express support for de Gaulle and *Algérie française*.[7] For Salan the goal was not only to win the 'Yes' vote but also to maximise the number of women on the electoral rolls and of participation so as to demonstrate to the world that Muslim women were fully prepared to integrate and to engage as citizens in the political process.[8] This concerted campaign for registration and the 'Yes' vote was carried out at local level with the aid of the MSF and EMSI, as well as through radio broadcasts and the distribution of specially made films such as 'Vote Yes' and 'How to Vote'.[9] Lucienne Salan, the quasi-official voice of her husband, dedicated a significant part of the weekly broadcasts of her MSF, the *Magazine social de la femme*, to the coming election (chapter 4), and in addition there was a special Operation Referendum which included twenty-eight French and Arabic transmissions over a four-week period. The latter placed particular emphasis on the extent to which the franchise represented both a pathway to progress and material prosperity and a form of empowerment that placed Muslim women on the same plane as men as well as the most outstanding figureheads of French womanhood and modernity, scientists, lawyers, doctors and aeronauts. Every woman was a 'human being just as worthy, as intelligent, and as respectable as men'.[10] The propaganda significantly framed the vote in terms of the full equality of Algerian women in all spheres of education, employment and civic rights, and carried an implicit signal: if they could demonstrate their political maturity via the ballot box, the door would rapidly be opened to the next phase, the reform of the personal status law. One radio broadcast announced, 'To vote is a duty, a duty that gives you rights. No abstentions on Sunday. Tomorrow the life of the emancipated woman begins'.[11]

The referendum of 28 September was regarded as an outstanding triumph by the colonial government since, despite FLN intimidation, an extraordinarily high percentage of Algerian women turned out to the poll to help inflate the overall 80 per cent in favour of the all-important 'Yes' vote.

General Massu in a letter to Salan noted with satisfaction the unexpectedly high women's vote in favour of the referendum: Muslim women had, 'seized hold of their chance with alacrity: the movement for emancipation is well under way, it is advisable to make best use of this'.[12]

Although the high vote gave a green light to the reform of the marriage code, it is important not to interpret it, as did many French, as a mass rejection by women of the FLN and nationalism. The concerted propaganda campaign of the Algiers government and military for a 'Yes' vote undoubtedly constituted systematic electoral gerrymandering on a vast scale: for example, the colour purple was chosen for 'No' voting

17 Algerian women voting for the first time, referendum of 28 September 1958

slips because of its negative associations in Muslim culture and electors brought in by army lorry were forced to show the unused 'No' ballot slip after the vote.[13] The FLN provisional government (GPRA) lodged a complaint with the UN and later, after the legislative elections of 30 November, opposition candidates brought the issue to the *Conseil constitutionnel* which, against all the evidence, validated the elections for the first parliament of the Fifth Republic.[14]

If Algerian women showed enthusiasm on the day, this seems to have related as much to the excitement of a festive opportunity to meet up with other women, or because of the attraction of food, clothing, soap and blankets usually handed out on such army-led mobilisations. In some areas, particularly in Oranie and Mitidja, the big *colons* estate-owners told their workers, especially the women who supplied seasonal labour, how to vote, and in some communes like that of Pallisy this led to a 100 per cent 'Yes' vote.[15] But of most importance, the great majority of women were both illiterate (96 per cent) and lacking in any political education, and appear to have had little political awareness or understanding of why they were voting, apart from being lured by propaganda

of a virtual paradise of riches tomorrow or giving expression to hopes
for a quick resolution of the war and a return to peace.[16] As one EMSI
reported of later cantonal elections in 1959: 'They [Algerian woman]
absolutely don't understand the significance of this vote and ask the men
of their family what they need to say . . . In general, women have little
interest in the vote and mainly wanted advice on hygiene and care . . .
They did what we asked them to do [on the vote]'.[17]

The initial and superficial enthusiasm shown during the referendum
appears to have rapidly evaporated in later elections, and already by
the legislatives of 30 November 1958 Captain Montaner of the SAU
of Clos-Salembier noted a higher level of abstention for women than
men. Female turnout at the La Redoute voting station was down from
82 per cent in the September referendum to 60 per cent, while abstentions were much higher in the areas of conventional housing, where
about 45 per cent of women voted, than in the shantytowns (75 per
cent).[18] This would suggest that the big turn-out for the referendum of
28 September in the shantytowns was largely an expression of the political ignorance and 'culture of poverty' of those who had recently arrived
as refugees from the interior, who Montaner described as 'a mass that
is easy to manage, to organise, to convince and to attach to us', as
opposed to the relatively better-off and politically aware population
of longer urban standing. The inhabitants of the *bidonvilles*, he noted,
showed little interest in politics: their main concern was to find employment and decent housing, 'an obsession with this population that lives
in dire poverty'.[19] This class basis to the voting patterns of Algerian
women is confirmed by the turnout for the referendum in Tlemcen
where the better educated bourgeois women, strong FLN supporters,
abstained, while women from the poor quarters of the city turned out
enthusiastically in force.[20]

However, the acclaimed success of the referendum undoubtedly
opened the way to an immediate campaign to reform the family code.
Behind the scenes the authorities had begun to explore the possibility of
a new reform as early as June 1958. On 14 June General Massu wrote to
Salan suggesting the urgency of sustaining the momentum generated by
the revolutionary events of '13 May' and the integration strategy by the
suppression of the *statut personnel* and its replacement by the French
civil code. Such a 'Spectacular measure' would create 'in the Muslim
masses a deeper psychological shock than even the 13 of May'.[21] Salan
then instructed M. Villeneuve, deputy director of political affairs, to
investigate the issue and provide a written report.[22] Villeneuve, possibly the most influential of the senior administrative advisers on the
reform of family law, had already in July 1957 produced a report in

which he made clear his conservative stance, which reflected that of the Algerian civil service, and warned against tampering with the religious status quo.[23] He warned that the detailed reform project prepared by the working party under Simoneau in 1957 (see chapter 2), was far too radical, and represented an incursion of the French civil code that was, 'a profound assault on the Muslim personal status'. Villeneuve was ringing the warning bells of an Islamic revolt: at the very least it would be necessary to consult Muslim religious leaders and theologians so that the initiative would not appear as an imposition by secularists on Koranic law, but he noted that earlier changes to family law (as with the Kabyle law of 1930–31) had little impact on behaviour because of the backwardness of women. What was required for a code to have any impact was 'an exceptional campaign of female education' and a prior evolution of the family cell towards a conjugal model of modernity. The observation was sound, but it also fell squarely into the traditional mechanisms of the colonial elite in which political advance for Algerians was to be delayed into some distant and nebulous future. In Paris such doubts were received by René Brouillet with some concern, particularly the prospect of a reform of the personal status law generating opposition that could be seized on by the FLN, and he decided to consult de Gaulle on the matter.[24]

The reform of the personal status law

Following the military coup in Algiers of 13 May, de Gaulle became Prime Minister on 1 June and swiftly moved to lay the foundations of the new Fifth Republic. A great deal is known about the way in which the emancipation programme was quickly expanded by the Algiers military government of Salan, and the work of Frantz Fanon has tended to reinforce a general perception of unveiling and reform as the singular work of 'revolutionary' colonels. This view has tended to obscure or neglect the position of de Gaulle in relation to the question of Algerian women, a silence that is all the more puzzling when it is kept in mind that the peak in the expansion of the emancipation process came during the first year of the new Gaullist government.

De Gaulle's views on emancipation need to be understood within the context of his overall policy on Algeria, but the latter continues to divide historians because of the general's penchant for secrecy and Delphic ambiguity. The Minister of Public Works, Robert Buron, for example, was none the clearer about de Gaulle's intentions on Algeria eighteen months after his return to power, asking himself, 'where then is the prince of equivocation leading us?'.[25] Julian Jackson has

identified three schools of thought among historians: first that de
Gaulle, before coming to power in 1958, had already decided to work
towards Algerian autonomy; second that he was intent on keeping
Algeria (hence the accelerated investment of the Constantine Plan and
the Challe offensive); and third, that he preferred some form of 'association' or union with France. Jackson's support for the third position
has its attraction: during a first phase of government that lasted from
June 1958 until early 1960, although de Gaulle was still feeling his way,
his basic impulse was to retain French links to, or control over, Algeria
even if it should eventually gain a degree of self-government, not unlike
that of a British dominion. But ideally France would negotiate such a
union from a position of strength, hence the need to consolidate military
victory and a 'Third Force' strategy that would organise a moderate
Algerian 'nationalist' movement to counter the FLN, with which France
could then negotiate a peace that would guarantee its economic, oil and
strategic interests. This is why de Gaulle essentially continued with the
policies of Lacoste and Salan, with their contradictory mix of repression (the Challe offensive) and reformism (Constantine Plan), and in
the case of Algerian women de Gaulle was inclined to push ahead with
emancipation in so far as it would help to win over the Algerian people
to such 'association' and simultaneously assist the social and political
modernisation of a future state that could provide a dynamic partner in
union with France.

However, de Gaulle held racist views that were incompatible with
Soustelle's 'integration': he told Alain Peyrefitte that Muslims, with their
turbans and *djellabas*, were clearly not French and, like oil and water,
the two could never mix:

> Arabs are Arabs, the French are French. Do you think that the French
> body politic can absorb ten million Muslims, who tomorrow will be
> twenty million and then forty? If we undertake integration, if all the Arabs
> and Berbers of Algeria are considered French, how could we stop them
> coming to live in the metropolis where the standard of living is so much
> higher? My village would no longer be called Colombey-les-Deux-Églises
> but Colombey-les-Deux Mosquées.[26]

De Gaulle, in promoting the emancipation of Algerian women, first
through the franchise and then by reform of the personal status law,
clearly carried none of the illusions of *Algérie française* radicals that
Europeans and Muslims could meld through 'fraternisation' into a new
and egalitarian nation. But, as has been seen (chapter 3), the events of
'13 May' had been so orchestrated by the Fifth Bureau as to persuade
the hesitant General that he did indeed have a popular mandate from

the will of the people, the settlers and Muslims united. De Gaulle had his private doubts about the genuine nature of 'fraternisation', but in public he was quite prepared to exercise a willing suspension of disbelief since this 'revolutionary' pseudo-élan served his own interests in returning to power through a 'democratic coup'.

Perhaps the single most significant but well-concealed component of de Gaulle's overall Algerian policy in his first eighteen months of power was the gradual reassertion of the authority of the Paris government over the generals in Algiers who had assumed virtual autonomy, a process that was symbolised by the eventual removal of Salan, Massu and Challe and the insertion of his own place-men, including Delouvrier. Although by early 1960 de Gaulle had taken a number of steps to undermine the political power-base of the generals in Algeria, including the order for all army officers to be withdrawn from the Committees of Public Safety and the dissolution of the Fifth Bureau in January 1960, this staged 'containment' of army political power did not necessarily involve a U-turn or change of direction in the policies adopted by the militarised Algiers government: the issue at stake was one of the locus of sovereign power, not of specific agendas.

From the moment that de Gaulle became head of government in June 1958 he showed himself willing, on the specific question of emancipation of women, to comply with the pressure of Salan and the '13 of May' Algiers radicals to maintain this 'revolutionary' agenda. Indeed, contrary to expectation, de Gaulle was prepared to accept a major reform of the statute even when this was opposed by some of his own advisers, including Delouvrier. But underlying this apparent agreement between Salan and de Gaulle was the fatal 'misunderstanding' between settlers and the General that was symbolised by his notorious, 'I understand you' ('Je vous ai compris') speech: whereas Salan and Soustelle regarded emancipation as a key to the survival of *Algérie française*, de Gaulle secretly saw it as a means to assist the modernisation of a future 'partner' or semi-autonomous 'associate' state.

On his return to power during his famous speech in Algiers on 4 June de Gaulle announced elections in a single electoral college, and the registration of Algerian women was officially announced a month later. It was rather fitting that the General, who had first pronounced on the future franchise of all French women in Algiers on 24 March 1944,[27] should now, in the same city, provide this as a 'gift' to Muslim women. De Gaulle was probably reassured that this would not open the floodgates to FLN power by the comforting fact that women in France had since 1947 used their new voting rights to reinforce the conservative parties against the communists and socialists. However, the family code was a rather more delicate matter, and while the General's Paris advisers on this issue (Brouillet, Tricot, Lenoir) seem to have hesitated through August and September, the generals in Algeria took a far more proactive role in persuading de Gaulle to take this step.

The Salan campaign to reform the personal status law

Immediately after the resounding success of the women's vote in the referendum of 28 September General Salan sent a telegram to de Gaulle noting that the 'massive participation of Muslim women' had given a green light to the next stage of emancipation. 'Their spontaneous support for the new order proposed to them must inspire the government' to pursue a new ordinance on the personal status law.[28] Simultaneously Lucienne Salan as president of the MSF, undoubtedly with the support of her husband and the Fifth Bureau, orchestrated a propaganda campaign to persuade de Gaulle and public opinion of the urgency of a new family code. On 2 October Lucienne Salan wrote a long and legally sophisticated letter to de Gaulle, insisting that the mass 'Yes' vote by Algerian women had demonstrated their wish to remain French.[29] During her recent tour, she recounted, of the Algerian provinces as president of the MSF, Algerian women had spontaneously and unanimously expressed their wish to modernise.[30] In the name of the MSF she submitted to the General a range of recommendations that should be put into effect as quickly as possible and accompanied by 'a psychological offensive'. The reform should include obligatory education for all girls which would in turn lead them to abandon the veil, 'which constitutes the symbol of isolation, seclusion, and enslavement'. But most central was a reform of the marriage code, which should include a minimum age for marriage, suppression of marriage enforced by the father or guardian (*droit de jebr*), suppression of polygamy, and an end to unilateral repudiation by husbands.

Two days later the central committee of the MSF, under the presidency of Lucienne Salan, sent to women's circles throughout Algeria a model petition requesting de Gaulle to implement reforming measures.[31] The petitions in French and Arabic provide a fascinating insight into the grass-roots campaign of the MSF and the response of many thousands of illiterate Algerian women. Many neatly typed petitions were evidently drawn up by the European leaders of the MSF circles or by ASSRA, and then read out to mass meetings of Algerian women who, in most instances, 'signed' with a fingerprint.[32] These tend to reflect the standardised set of both legal and social welfare demands circulated in the model petition: a request for reform of the marriage code, particularly in relation to repudiation and marriage before the mayor; the extension of full welfare rights, especially family allowances, on a par with those already enjoyed by Europeans; and the provision of decent housing and regular employment for their husbands. But other petitions, often written by Muslim women with biros in school exercise books in broken French, were more individualised and reflected the hopes and aspirations of the more educated young Algerian women in the circles. For example, Dalila Benached of Hammam-bou-Hadjar, noted, 'I am proud to have voted with my Muslim sisters for General de Gaulle', and was also honoured because she was able to read and write and so able to present the petition on behalf of all those who had 'signed' below with a fingerprint:

> Our European sisters want to help us to live like them, but to do that we must help them to pass the laws to make this possible. Marriage must take place before the Mayor [*monsieur le maire*] so that we can have a family registration book (*livret de famille*), and divorce must be less easy so that so many women and children are not left abandoned – our children must go to school and learn a trade. We must be better housed so that there are no longer six or eight in one room: above all fathers, brothers and husbands must understand that we are their equals in life and in the eye of the law.
>
> Also, when there is an inheritance to divide up the boys have the biggest share: all their life girls are badly considered.
>
> We have confidence in de Gaulle and all my Muslim sisters join me in spelling out our gratitude and a full-hearted, thank you.

The petitions, although in part reflecting an agenda imposed by the European leaders of the circles, also give a sense of the injustice Algerian women felt towards a repressive system of patriarchal authority and their deep hope for a better life, but one which would be implemented through the much-admired father figure, de Gaulle. Some of the young women expressed, above all, a wish to be able to form a free and loving relationship with their future husband with whom they could share a western style of conjugal equality. The petition from Aïn Farès noted, 'We now understand that we are not only slaves in the service of the master. Our husbands also understand this. They realise that we are their companions, their companions through all the ups and downs of life: in joy, in hardship, trouble, and success'. Aïcha Chérif wrote from Fornaka to de Gaulle on 12 October in a similar vein:

> I hope that you will give us peace. I do not want to be sold like a beast; I want to get married according to my own taste with the one I love. I do not want my husband to abandon me with the children and to leave me in poverty, without assistance. I do not want to be forced to veil, since the Good Lord gave us a face that we should not be ashamed to show. When I

am big I also want to have trust in my husband and that he lets me do my shopping for myself, because if I feel like having a red dress, I don't want to wear a yellow one! . . . Muslim women admire you General, and give you their full trust.[33]

It is striking how far propaganda after '13 May' for the new order was centred in thousands of posters, tracts and films on the personal appeal and charisma of de Gaulle. Captain Jean Claude Racinet exemplified this position in his 'pacification' propaganda, 'I relied on the archetype of the Father that's much more alive in the collective unconscious of oriental crowds than in ours. I idealised de Gaulle before my audiences . . . We needed a great man'.[34] The de Gaulle fixation was particularly prominent in the emancipation campaign and the Fifth Bureau, through endless portrayal of the General as the father-figure who entered into a direct appeal to, and moral relationship with, each Algerian woman, believed that such a personalisation of male authority would be in rapport with the values of patriarchal society and the Muslim 'mind'. The women's petitions reflect this position: some were decorated with the tri-colour or pasted in pictures of de Gaulle cut from magazines while one from Hammam-bou-Hadjar was drawn up by, 'I, Talbia Kaddour, née Naoum, am a passionate admirer of General de Gaulle. At my employers I listen with strong emotion to the BBC. I want to gain a better life for my Muslim sisters'. Life was tough for this mother of six since her husband was ill, but she looked forward to the improved housing promised by de Gaulle, 'and I know that he always keeps his promises'. The women of Hussein-Dey claimed that after their 'Yes' vote on 28 September, 'We wish to live with the same rights and duties [as men], as the General, so generous and so just, has himself promised us'. During the first year of de Gaulle's presidency, before his relations with the 'ultras' turned sour, there existed a strong concordance between the optimistic faith of the settlers and of some évoluées Muslim women, in his image as a strong, autocratic leader and father-figure.

How did de Gaulle respond to this campaign? On 3 October de Gaulle announced in Constantine an ambitious five-year investment plan for the modernisation of the Algerian economy, and such a project was clearly concordant with parallel moves to educate and emancipate Muslim women. Specialist advisers had been working on various versions of a draft marriage code from June 1958 onwards, but the key message coming through from the Algiers civil administration was a warning of the dangers of legislating in the reserved area of Islamic law and custom. De Gaulle took note of the repeated claim that it would be crucial for the success of any reform that it should be seen by Algerians to have followed consultation with religious authorities and received their assent.[35] At the cabinet meeting on Algerian affairs (*Comité interministériel*) on 15 October, the first one to be held since the triumphant referendum vote, de Gaulle announced his decision to consult a delegation of Muslim religious leaders in Paris.[36]

Having gauged the situation at first hand and received the MSF petitions signed by thousands of Algerian women, on 15 November de Gaulle sent a key directive to Salan: 'Following consultation with several Algerian leaders, and taking account of petitions that have been addressed to me by important Algerian social organisations, I esteem that it is advisable to undertake a reform of the personal status of Muslim women. This programme must be undertaken with all necessary caution'. A distinguishing feature of the order was the speed and urgency with which the reform was to be pursued: a commission of Algerian and European experts in Muslim law, building on earlier drafts, was to submit its proposals within a month. This project was then to be referred to eminent religious authorities for their opinion, and if the response was favourable, the government could issue an outline law or Ordinance, which it did eventually on 4 February 1959.[37] However, the government very quickly ran into opposition to the projected reform.

Division in the government ranks

In the four months following de Gaulle's order to Salan a complex battle ensued, behind closed doors and largely unseen by the public, which deeply divided the French government and administration, and pitched the conservative and the reformist wings of the Algerian elites against each other. In order to understand the extreme sensitivity of the personal status law, a particularly explosive issue in the context of a colonial war in which government could ill-afford to strengthen the FLN by stirring up popular resistance and alienating its own 'natural' constituency among conservative elites, it is useful to look briefly at the fundamental significance of marriage to the basic socio-political and cultural structures of Algerian society.

Ethnologists and sociologists have demonstrated the extraordinary importance of the customary, religious and magical practices, the basic 'ground rules', that regulated the functioning and reproduction of peasant societies in the Mediterranean world.[38] In the Maghreb the kinship group (extended family, fraction or tribe) constituted, long before the emergence of the modern, centralised state, the key social organisation for the *biological* survival of the local society under conditions imposed by a harsh environment in which the durability of the lineage (and the individuals that constituted it) depended on maximising access to land and livestock, water, food reserves and reproductive power.[39] As Germaine Tillion showed in her classic work *Le Harem et les cousins*, a crucial mechanism for preventing the long-term erosion of the kin group's land and property through marriage of women to outsiders (exogamy) was both to restrict their inheritance rights, as well as to uphold marriage between couples from the in-group, preferably with first cousins.

It is salutary for contemporary western societies, shocked at the perceived 'primitive' practices of Muslim familial customs such as arranged marriage, to bear in mind that such traditions had evolved over millennia as sophisticated and 'rational' systems for survival that depended on prioritising the interests of the group over that of the individual. In many advanced west European nations, within living memory, the Christian peasantry had also regarded arranged marriage as necessary, a strategy that could all-too-readily be destroyed by modern individualism and romantic attachment, by rebellious couples carried away by a strong sentiment ('love') that peasant wisdom likened to a form of dangerous madness since it carried the potential to destroy the long-term future survival of the group.[40] Crucial, however, to Algerian reactions to legal reform was the fact that through many centuries Islam had adapted itself to, and sanctified, the underlying 'ground rules' that regulated marriage strategies. The populace did not oppose legal reform in so far as it threatened the rationale of customary regulation that cemented the framework of social and economic practice, rules that might be extrapolated by the anthropologist, since few consciously recognised such a logic: rather they reacted in terms of the religious ideology that sanctioned the rules of marriage strategies. As the Algerian jurist Mohammed Benhoura remarked in June 1958, 'the personal status constitutes for Muslims more than something mystical, it is their religion itself, and no human force can succeed in making them repudiate it'.[41]

In the Maghreb, where the Maliki school of law predominated, family law contained within itself a model of the social order, a blueprint or ideal of the family and social relationships.[42] Within this system marriage did not, as in modern Europe, aim to create a nuclear family unit centred on the close bonds between the couple, but was rather a contract that gave the husband the right to licit sexual relations but in which, even after marriage, his primary allegiance remained to his male line, his father, brothers and uncles (*agnates*). The prime function of married women was to produce male heirs to guarantee the lineage, but this in turn was associated with a deep masculine anxiety about paternity, the obsessive need to guarantee that offspring were really those of the father, hence the constant regulation of honour, gender segregation, bridal virginity and repudiation settlement (*idda*).[43]

This system of patriarchal control, in which all key decisions and power lay with the men of the kin group, inevitably determined the radical subordination of women. The key features of Algerian marriage law and custom on the eve of the 1959 French reform meant that young single women, or even pre-pubescent girls, would have a marriage arranged for them by the father or legal guardian (right of *jebr*).[44] Although in reality the married woman might accrue significant authority and power within the private sphere of the household,[45] husbands tended to remain emotionally distant from their wives and retained legal powers either to contract other, polygamous marriages, or to divorce or repudiate her by a simple unilateral and verbal pronouncement (*talaq*). At separation the divorced woman had few rights: the husband could legally claim control of children or abandon the wife and offspring to their own devices with minimal or no settlement, which meant she would return to the care and protection of her natal kin group, or be forced into degrading employment. The concern of the government to introduce a code, although driven by political considerations to attach Algerian women to the French cause, was also inspired by the social and welfare problems generated by the abandonment of wives and children. While in a recent past the apparent harshness of Islamic law and custom was tempered by the stability of the extended patrilocal kin group that offered a degree of security and protection to repudiated women, the economic crisis in peasant society, the long absence of men as labour migrants or FLN fighters, and the massive uprooting caused by military resettlement, combined to dislocate and erode the traditional support function of the natal extended family. This no longer had the means to provide shelter and protection to its daughters, tens of thousands of which were widowed by the war.

This is a general outline of marriage strategies, but in practice there was an enormously complex variation, for example Kabyle (*qanoun*) and Ibadite customary laws that were traditionally guarded by the meeting of village elders (*djemâa*), were different from the Arab zones and urban societies that followed the majority Maliki and minority Hanafi legal schools. During the complex process of preparing the new marriage code experts in Muslim jurisprudence were appointed to draw up a seemingly endless number of draft projects that were subjected to microscopic examination by various commissions and working-groups. For example, the commission that met on 4–5 December 1958 carried out its debate in relation to three entirely different drafts (*avant-projet*) which it dissected and compared to a myriad of precedents, including the standard legal reference in Algerian courts (Code Morand of 1916), various laws relating mainly to Kabylia (2 April and 2 May 1930, 19 May 1931), the recent Tunisian Code (1956) and Moroccan Code (1957), and the French Civil Code.[46] For our purposes we can move past the dazzling and sometimes esoteric refinements of the debate that took place between the Muslim jurists (*cadis*), European judges and professors of law that drafted the new legislation,[47] and move straight to the very concise and lucid text of the Ordinance of 4 February 1959.[48]

The Ordinance laid down the minimum age at which young women (fifteen years) and men (eighteen years) could contract a marriage, and this had to be by the free consent of both spouses who were to appear in person before a Muslim judge (*cadi*) or before the mayor, or other officer of the *état civil*.[49] The marriage had to be registered and the couple issued with a certificate and a *livret de famille* before they could celebrate the traditional wedding. The marriage could only be dissolved by the decision of a judge at the request of either the husband or the wife, who were to appear in person. The judge was also to attempt a reconciliation between the couple, before a final act that was to be made in the best interest of the children and decided on the level of family support to be provided for them and their mother. This simple text, which was not retroactive or applicable to existing marriages, by implication provided an entirely uniform code for all Muslims in Algeria, including the Kabyles, but with the exception of Ibadite believers of the Sahara. The insistence on the presence of women at both marriage and divorce hearings was to end the Islamic practice of them being represented by a male, and to ensure that they fully agreed to the marriage contract or to the form of its dissolution.

The Ordinance of 4 February, for all its apparent simplicity, undoubtedly offered a radical change in Muslim family law that was fully on a par with the Bourguiba Code on which it was modelled.[50] The provisions of the Tunisian legislation, today widely viewed as one of the most progressive introduced by a modern Islamic state, was almost identical, except for a ban on polygamy. The French legislators excluded polygamy from the act since it was widely recognised that this practice was in long-term decline, was largely confined to elderly traditionalists in the interior, and would gradually disappear of its own accord.[51]

During the accelerated preparation of the Ordinance de Gaulle's agenda had, however, behind the scenes, run into stiff opposition, from both Muslim and European jurists on the commission (5–6 December) and then, more surprisingly, from the newly appointed *délégué générale*, Paul Delouvrier, who arriving in Algiers in mid-December, quickly adopted their cautious or conservative position.

De Gaulle was aware by mid-November that any attempt to tamper with existing marriage and family law carried high risks, and that it was essential to calm Muslim opinion by receiving the backing of religious notables and theologians. Interested more in the propaganda effects of such a consultation process than in any meaningful, open and democratic debate that might have enabled an opposition voice to be heard, the Algiers government drew up a list of suitable clerics or judicial experts who were carefully selected for their influence and leadership role among the populace, as well as for their political loyalty to France. One list of thirteen notables to be consulted from across the three regions of Algeria included five *muphtis*, three *cadis*, two heads of religious confraternities, and the *imam* head of a large *médersa*.[52] The biographies of these eminent religious leaders and jurists shows an elderly elite that had a long track record of close association with the colonial power, including appointment to various official posts, award of honours (*Légion d'Honneur*), and reception of various gratuities, such as pensions or government funding as official delegates on the *hadj*.[53] Among the most influential of these notables, and in many respects quite typical, were Abdelali ben Ahmed Lakhdari, Mohammed ben Bouzar Benhoura and Hamza ben Kaddour Boubakeur.

Lakhdari, born in 1905, and a distinguished Arab scholar trained at the Zitouna university in Tunisia, was appointed in 1948 director of the important *médersa* of Kittania in Constantine, received government funding for the *hadj* in 1948, 1956 and 1958, was awarded the *Légion d'Honneur* in 1948, and attracted the ire of the FLN, which in 1955 condemned him to death for 'collaboration with the enemy'.[54] Lakhdari had made a famous speech in favour of women's emancipation during the 'fraternisation' parade of 26 May 1958 (see chapter 3), a statement that was later extensively quoted by the government in its propaganda campaigns. Benhoura (born in 1890) was much decorated during the First World War, during which he was imprisoned, and had a long career as a Muslim justice from 1911 to 1930. In 1950 he was sent by the Ministry of the Interior on a mission to Jerusalem and Jordan, and was named in 1957 member of the Algiers regional administrative commission and in 1958 to the cabinet of the Minister for Algeria as a technical adviser.[55]

The most influential of those consulted was Hamza Boubakeur (born 1912) who came from a powerful military dynasty (*grande famille*) that had traditionally served France in its conquest of both Algeria and Morocco, and which also headed the powerful *marabout* confederation of the Ouled Sidi Cheikh. On the outbreak of the insurrection in November 1954 he offered to raise an auxiliary force (*goum*) among his tribesmen to fight the 'rebels'. A highly cultured man, who spoke Arabic, German, English and Spanish, he was awarded the *Legion d'Honneur* in 1953, appointed professor of Arabic language in the Lycée Bugeaud, then to the influential post of rector of the Paris mosque in May 1957 and member of the Consultative Committee on the Constitution in 1958.[56]

It might have been expected that if any body of Muslim notables was going to provide the support for the marriage code that the government was so keen to procure, it would have been this group of carefully hand-picked *imams*, *cadis* and functionaries. However, the fact that some of these establishment figures dug in to oppose the project did not bode well for the government and pointed towards the potential for a wider revolt that could only assist the FLN. This opposition became particularly clear during the meeting of the Commission of 5–6 December 1958, which included Boubakeur and three *cadis* (Bouchrit, Turkarli and Benhoura) along with four European legal experts (Raymond Charles, Canac, Roussier and Knoertzer).

The commission agreed that the draft prepared and submitted to them by the administration was hasty and ill-prepared, that the timetable laid down by de Gaulle for completion by 15 December was impossible, and the draft reform far too radical. Boubakeur claimed it was based on the code of President Bourguiba, whom he regarded as a reprehensible, secularised despot, and 'is absolutely revolutionary in relation to marriage, its effects, and inheritance . . . it represents a complete overturning of Muslim law', an opinion shared by the president, Raymond Charles, and by Professor Roussier who was 'a bit surprised by the brutality with which such highly venerated institutions were sabotaged'.[57] The Commission rejected the government's draft and then proceeded to examine alternatives prepared by two of its own members (Roussier and Canac). But by the end of its deliberations the group appears to have been less concerned with the detail of the draft code, for example they were not opposed to giving women a right of consent to marriage, than with a concern that it would lead to a secularisation of marriage through marginalisation of the Muslim justices (*cadis*) and obligatory appearance before an officer of the state. The debate on the Ordinance became inter-twined with a parallel project to reform the judicial system by amalga-mating the *cadis* with the civil French justices, and it was widely felt by the government that the self-interested opposition by Muslim justices to the new law arose from the potential loss of income from the excessive fees extorted during traditional forms of marriage and repudiation.

An insight into the conservative and misogynous mind-set of the religious elite can be found in a long and very detailed critique that

Boubakeur had made, probably in July 1958, of the first attempt
to draft a reform of the personal status law by the 1957 Simoneau
commission (see chapter 2).[58] Firstly, he acknowledged that juridical
reform should match the overall evolution of society, but was dangerous if it was based on abstract principles or forced the pace of
change. By abstract principles Boubakeur appears to have meant an
intellectual importation of a western model of the family, one inspired
by a 'half-Christian, half-secular' sensibility that bore no relationship
to the culture of the Muslim family. What was to be avoided, he said,
was an 'occidental contamination' since the western family was deeply
dysfunctional, especially through the role of the woman who showed
only a superficial religious faith and 'no longer appear to be the ideal
moving spirit of the home, but a woman more preoccupied with her
own independence and amusement, who finds it difficult to support
the sacrifices of motherhood (giving birth, breast feeding, education
of children)'. Liberal legislation was at the root of a general moral
decadence, 'off-handedness, insolence of children, debauchery and an
unsettled way of life. The beaches, amusement halls, parricide, infan-
ticide, battered children, juvenile delinquency recounted in a sensa-
tionalist way by newspapers, reinforces the idea of a decaying family
in Europe and a loosening of morals'. By contrast, he claimed, the
Muslim family showed a remarkable stability, a 'strong vital energy',
that the western model, whether American or Soviet, would endanger.
In addition, the liberal agenda took no account of the true nature of
Algerian women whom, it was implied, required the strict regulatory
framework of Koranic law, since she was 'generally of an impulsive
nature, with a relish for intrigue, machinations, and gossip', and the
traditional religious authorities most favourable to women had noted,
'her fickleness, her acid temperament, her extrovert mood swings, her
tendency to insubordination (nushûz), her hastily formed, absolute
and irrational decisions'. The Algerian woman, unlike the European,
was not bound into a conjugal life, but remained attached to her
family of origin, so that she considered herself to be, 'in the home
of her husband rather as if she were in a family hotel', and presum-
ably lacking in that primordial allegiance to the lineage shared by
all males (agnates). Boubakeur's position on the moral decadence of
western society and the dangers of this working as a Fifth Column to
subvert Islamic values was indicative of the way in which the reformist message of the Ulema had become generalised among the Algerian
elites.

To Hamza Boubakeur it seemed folly to engage in such a major
reform, a 'gift' handed down from above that had *not* been demanded

in any way by Algerian women themselves. Secondly, the reform project
seemed to be offered as a red herring to distract Muslim attention
from the more pressing issue of the war. Finally, and most crucially,
Boubakeur raised the frightening agenda of upsetting the visceral
and blind attachment of the population to its religious practices: a
'milieu ferociously attached to its juridico-customary system, inclined
to an anarchist atavism, subject to the most crazy impulses whenever
its religion is put in question, prompt to indulge a taste for disorder,
to provoke discontent that further aggravates the present troubles'.
Boubakeur clung adamantly to the Malekite tradition of law (*fiqh*) that
he feared was being opportunistically combined with a range of alien
codes and Islamic schools, from Hanefism to Bourguiba and the French
Civil Code, a position that was to be shared a quarter of a century later
by the legislators of the reactionary family code passed by the Algerian
parliament in 1984.[59]

Far more unexpected than Boubakeur's opposition to the reform
was that of Paul Delouvrier, the new head of the Algiers government
appointed by de Gaulle to reassert the authority of Paris over the generals. Delouvrier later, in a significant letter to the Prime Minister on 18
July 1959, made clear the grounds for his opposition to the Ordinance.[60]
Delouvrier recognised that Muslim justices (*cadis*, *bachadels*) were
'relentless adversaries' of the reform, as were the classic elites, both from
traditionalist and modernist (*évolués*) backgrounds, who responded to
the pressure and propaganda of the *Ulema* and the FLN. The elites put
forward the type of argument that had been voiced by Boubakeur: the
legislation represented for them an invasion of the secular state into the
religious field of Islam, there were more important issues to tackle, and
Algerian women needed to undergo a long-term education and evolution before being ready for such changes. Delouvrier acknowledged that
the elite response may have been unrepresentative of the populace since
there was a real problem in gauging the attitudes of the uneducated
masses who had no channel through which to express their opinion.
But in general he viewed the majority of Muslims as mired in a deeply
entrenched conservative attachment to existing socio-religious values
and, 'are prisoners of conformism in the sense that they feel that they
belong to a religious community in which one cannot transgress the
taboos without running the risk of a unanimous reprobation'. In addition the most opportune moment for reform, during the 'revolutionary'
élan of '13 May 1958' when the masses were most receptive, had now
passed by.[61] The one indication of promise arose from the fact that the
younger generation who represented 'the Algeria of tomorrow' were
showing signs of a break, a 'mental rupture', by contrast with adults.

For the colonial government, behind the potential minefield of personal status law lay the ominous shadow of the nationalists. Delouvrier continued in his letter to the Prime Minister: 'The project for the reform of Muslim law is providing a hobby-horse for FLN propaganda. This propaganda is spreading insidiously in Algeria and abroad, especially through a radio campaign: France is accused of "de-islamisation" and of engaging in a "new Crusade against the Crescent"'. The FLN would probably make every possible means to use the issue in the coming session of the UN.

The response of de Gaulle to the resistance of the Algiers Commission (5–6 December), of religious notables, and Delouvrier's administration to a meaningful reform of the personal status law, was to simply by-pass it by establishing a working party in Paris that drafted the final Ordinance without further consultation with Algiers.[62] On 2 February M. J. Mafart, the director of Delouvrier's cabinet, could barely contain his anger at this fait accompli when he read in the press that the *Conseil d'État* was to examine the final text of the Ordinance the next day. In a desperate exchange of telegrams with Paris Delouvrier's cabinet insisted that the new law must not 'cause any offence to the prescriptions and traditions of Muslim religion', while emphasising that any plans to abolish the role of the *cadis* would be a mistake.[63] When Mafart received the text of the revised Ordinance by telegram later that day, it confirmed his worst fears, but it was too late for Delouvrier to do anything about it.[64]

Boubakeur reacted angrily and more publicly to the leaked news that an Ordinance was about to be promulgated without consultation with Muslim jurists and General Renucci, who headed the administrative service for the Muslim deputies in parliament, delivered a letter of complaint to Michel Debré on 31 January.[65] Boubakeur, who held considerable political clout as deputy for the Oasis and president of the Commission for Foreign Affairs, wrote to the Minister of Justice Michelet warning of catastrophic consequences for Franco-Algerian unity: 'As a militant supporter of the union and the collaboration of French and Muslims, I assess with foreboding the grave effects of this measure on Algerian opinion. The discontent of the Muslim masses, the irritation of theologians and ministers of religion, the amazement of the elites, of men and women, in my opinion merits the greatest attention by the government'. He begged Michelet to delay 'to a more favourable date' a measure seen, 'not only as a act of bullying, but even more as an indication of the de-islamisation of the Muslim conjugal union, a theme that runs the danger of fuelling a violent anti-French campaign at a time when prudence and caution is more necessary than ever'.[66] Michelet took the warning seriously and immediately sought the opinion of Nafissa Sid Cara, the Prime Minister, and the Public Prosecutors (*Procureurs Généraux*) of Oran, Algiers and Constantine.

At this point it is of interest to consider the use that Salan and the Paris government made of three Algerian women, whom it promoted as deputies, in order to reinforce the propaganda in favour of legal emancipation. The Ordinance only constituted an outline of the new legislation and it was the task of a *Commission Permanente* that first met on 3 February 1959 to refine the detail of the decree of application that was finally published on 17 September. A prominent role was played in this commission by Nafissa Sid Cara, a newly appointed junior minister, and her close advisor Marie-Hélène Lefaucheux.[67] Exactly how Sid Cara and the other two Algerian women deputies, Rebiha Kebtani and Khedira Bouabsa, were elected to the National Assembly on 30 November 1958, and suddenly propelled onto the political stage remains clouded in mystery, but the evidence points towards another propaganda coup engineered by the Fifth Bureau or other specialists in the Algiers administration, operating through Lucienne Salan as president of the MSF.[68]

Lucienne Salan, during the propaganda drive in preparation for the first ever vote by Algerian women on 28 September 1958, was in close touch with Lefaucheux who, as a UN representative, was particularly well informed on the legal and technical issues involved in the global extension of the franchise to 'Third World' women. Lefaucheux, as president of the CNFF, had publicly intimated to the Gaullist government that the 'wives and mothers' of France would abstain in the crucial elections of the infant Fifth Republic if they were not joined by their Algerian 'sisters'.[69] After the triumphant 'Yes' vote by Algerian women, the MSF leadership began to search among its members for suitable candidates to stand in the legislative elections, and Suzanne Massu participated in numerous electoral meetings to support Sid Cara as a candidate for the Alger-Banlieue constituency.[70] The election of the three Muslim women represented an undoubted propaganda triumph, providing a dramatic symbol of the 'New Algeria' and of the French commitment to emancipation, political integration and equality. The world's press flocked to report on the astonishing phenomenon of women who had been propelled from apparent 'seclusion' into the very public, and male-dominated, arena of parliamentary debate. Much attention centred on the photogenic Rebiha Kebtani, also promoted as the deputy mayor of Sétif, who was widely referred to as the Bardot look-alike, the 'pin up' or 'the blond Kabyle', and who made much of her rapid transformation from veiled recluse to prominent politician.[71]

From the moment that the three women were elected they were immediately used to promote the programme for the reform of the personal status law. It was of particular importance to the government to reassure Algerian opinion that the proposals did not present any kind of secular interference with religious orthodoxy, and this message was far more convincing when directly presented by female Muslims rather than by European spokesmen.[72] But at the same time the government seems to have been nervous at the prospect of the deputies, who had little political experience, making naive or ill-informed statements, and a decision was made to ensure that they were discreetly surrounded by shadowy minders. When the journalist Jacques Perrier interviewed Kebtani in her Sétif office his questions were frequently fielded by a kind of male 'councillor': 'At first I thought he was some kind of professor given the task of guiding Mme Kebtani in her first steps along the often obscure pathways of the administration, but I found out that his role was anonymous and rather peculiar'. The adviser seemed terrified by her naive or inane comments, such as mention of the infantile *La Petite Fadette* as for long her favourite bedtime reading.

However, government advisers were not always able to control the women deputies, and this was to become particularly clear in the case of Nafissa Sid Cara who was appointed, on the departure of Lucienne Salan, as president of the MSF and then appointed by Michel Debré on 8 January 1959 as *Secrétaire d'État aux Affaires Sociales*, the first Algerian woman to serve in a French government. Debré's interest in making this unexpected appointment seems to have been largely for purposes of window-dressing: as her niece informed Ryme Seferdjeli, 'She [Nafissa] had the feeling that she had been chosen because of what she represented and that she was being used'.[73] Sid Cara, for example, was introduced by de Gaulle to President Eisenhower during his official visit of September 1959 to impress the Americans who had a deeply negative view of the colonial war in Algeria, and likewise the glamorous Rebiha Kebtani was sent with a delegation to the UN. However, Sid Cara proved to be far tougher than she appeared, and was keen to pursue a strong and independent line in government.

It is difficult to assess exactly how influential Sid Cara was in the government commission that drafted the new law,[74] but she was able to form a strong alliance with Marie-Hélène Lefaucheux who had a solid technical knowledge of the complex field of Muslim family law and had already participated in June 1957 in the first Simoneau commission to prepare a new code.[75] In 1957 Lefaucheux had taken a quite radical stance on reform, even criticising the Bourguiba Code for not going far enough to prevent repudiation,[76] and as head of Sid Cara's cabinet in early 1959 she worked with the junior minister to present a draft decree to the parliamentary commission that was convened in Sid Cara's bureau. Sid Cara was keen to transfer the power of conservative Muslim justices (*cadis*) to adjudicate on marriage or divorce proceedings to secular officers of the state since it was thought the *cadis* colluded with the worst abuses of arranged marriage, polygamy and repudiation.[77] Sid Cara's career through to 14 April 1962 shows her very real determination to be far more than a mere figure-head and to promote a strong reformist agenda that would make a meaningful difference to the lives of ordinary women in Algeria, but she lacked the overall political weight to make much impact on the Debré government.[78] Sid Cara twice threatened resignation during the drafting of the reform of the personal status law but the final measure still did not come up to her expectations, nor to those of Khedira Bouabsa.[79] The FLN regarded Sid Cara as a traitor, a key symbol of collaboration with French integration, and several attempts were made to assassinate her.[80]

By July 1959, Delouvrier had admitted defeat on the issue of the new personal status law, but the depth and nature of the split in the Gaullist ranks is telling of the extreme difficulty of initiating radical socio-legal and religious change in a time of armed conflict. De Gaulle, in line with the Constantine Plan, was determined to push through a rapid modernisation of the Algerian economy and institutions, and, in his decision to accelerate a radical reform of Muslim law against conservative opposition, shared more with the position of Salan and the 'revolutionary' generals of '13 May' on emancipation than he did the reservations of his placeman, Delouvrier, sent in to exert control over the army.[81] However, as time would tell, Salan and de Gaulle shared a false unity of purpose and were looking to identical means to achieve the opposing goals of *Algérie française* and Algerian 'association' or autonomy. By empowering Algerian women and granting them full citizenship, de Gaulle ensured that they would eventually participate en masse in the referendum of 1 July 1962 that finalised Algerian independence.

The 1959 reform of the personal status law and popular Algerian reactions

What can we know about Algerian responses to legal reform? The archives provide a considerable body of detailed information on this, largely because the army and administration were so nervous about the political impacts on public opinion and support for the FLN that they constantly carried out numerous, detailed investigations of this matter through elaborate questionnaires, surveys and reports. The Prime Minister, for example, sent a telegram to Delouvrier on 15 February to investigate Muslim reactions to the Ordinance, to which the latter replied that an urgent propaganda campaign was required to prepare Algerian opinion before the final decree was published in September 1959.[82] The Algiers government sent out 15,000 questionnaires to the SAS and EMSI teams on 20 February and the responses were synthesised into 432 local reports and then into a global assessment by the Islamic specialist Captain L. P. Fauque in a restricted publication, *Stades d'évolution de la cellule familiale musulmane d'Algérie*.[83]

In July Delouvrier signed a joint circular with General Challe which detailed a massive propaganda offensive by press, radio, film and the MSF, EMSI and SAS networks.[84] This was to include a 'black propaganda' campaign of rumours which targeted the *cadis* as parasites on the people who opposed reform from motives of material self-interest and venality, and who attempted to protect their monopoly of the judicial fees and bribes (*bakchich*) they charged for carrying out marriages and divorce.[85]

During July 1959 the colonial press began to carry numerous articles in favour of the Ordinance, like that in the *Depêche quotidienne* which carried interviews with young men and women who as children had suffered the consequences of repudiation of their own mothers, headed by a large photograph of a sad woman with the caption, 'The obsessive fear of all young women in the suburbs and outskirts: "I do not want to be repudiated"'.[86] After the decree was published, a further campaign was to take place to persuade Algerians to apply the new code in person, particularly through progressive Muslims leading the way by, for example, celebrating western style marriages before the mayor. The EMSI showed particular enthusiasm in encouraging 'their girls', and reporting to higher authorities any instances of marriages 'à la mode de Gaulle'.[87]

In some instances the EMSI reported their success in persuading families to abandon projected marriages, because the spouses were too young, and the man far too old for the bride or even ill and decrepit.[88]

How successful was this campaign in favour of emancipation, or did the French face the imminent revolt predicted by Boubakeur? During 1959 there appears to have been very little reaction to the specific proposals of the new measure among the great mass of the illiterate urban and rural poor who were in no position to know of its existence, let alone to assess its technical implications. The law, as is shown later, only began to impinge on the lower classes in a direct way from the moment that the decree began to be implemented by the courts from late 1959 onwards. As the Procureur of the Constantine Court of Appeal noted in June 1959, 'The example of the past however allows us to predict that

18 An apprehensive couple getting married in the town-hall of Bordj Okhriss
after implementation of the 1959 Personal Status law

if the new arrangements for marriage and repudiation clash too much
with the peoples customs or interests, they will ignore them just as they
have done up to now for all the laws relating to the *état civil*, without
invoking for that matter any argument of a religious nature'.[89] The
reports show a strong consensus that the popular masses that made up
over 90 per cent of Algerian society, 'an extremely conformist society',
clung doggedly to custom. Fauque reported that even labour migrants
to the big cities and to France who had much direct experience of the
European way of life, while convinced of the technical and material
superiority of the west to which they aspired, viewed it as degenerate,
'and they are profoundly convinced of the superiority of Muslim values
over our own'.[90]

Most older men were anxious about losing their traditional powers
and feared that giving their offspring a degree of choice in marriage
would undermine their own long-term security in the family cell, and
also open the way to moral corruption, the 'licentiousness of youth'.[91]
There was evidence of some support for reform among women, particularly for an end to unilateral repudiation, a very widespread practice

described as 'the great fear' of married women since it left them and their children constantly vulnerable to the whim of husbands. But, in general women remained silent in relation to the male sphere of 'politics' and in a society in which 96 per cent of married women were illiterate, most of them remained ignorant of the detail of the family code, and could not understand the terms of the debate, such as the distinction between secularism (*laicité*) and religious authority.

The FLN was, however, able to appeal directly to the general unease relating to the Ordinance on the grounds of both nationalism and religion and played on male insecurities by spreading rumours or exaggerated fears about the nature of the colonial crusade that threatened the very foundations of Algerian society. In November 1959 the commander of the Oran Army Corps reported widespread hostility in his region to the new marriage code because of a failure to consult Muslim representatives, concern that *cadis* were to be abolished, and a perceived 'de-islamisation' and erasure of the Arabic language:

> The sympathisers of the FLN maintain an attitude that derives more from 'tactics' than a deeply held opinion. Fundamentally won over to a renovation of Islam, they none-the-less exploit, systematically, every initiative of France that may seem to clash with the popular conception of Islam and of traditional institutions. Denying us the right to innovate or modify, the moment is favourable to them to accuse us of 'provoking a Holy War'.[92]

An SAU officer Captain Bapst noted a similar opportunist reaction of men to the family code on religious grounds: 'Which seems all the more suspect since these religious arguments often come from the mouth of individuals that have never practised any Koranic prescriptions'.[93] But overall there was no doubt in the mind of the specialist, Captain Fauque, that there existed 'a profound attachment to the Islamic concept of family organisation and this can be interpreted as a defensive reaction against the reforms'.[94]

The reaction of the minority of educated Algerians was more complex and divided. The various surveys indicated a degree of support for reform of the personal status law among the *évolués*, mainly the young men and women who had received a solid French-language education, were deeply influenced by French culture, and who in many instances had a direct stake in the existing political order through state employment as secretaries, junior administrators, doctors, school teachers, interpreters, clerks and technicians. While the young and mainly celibate modernists undoubtedly expressed a strong preference to be able to marry a partner of their choice, to enjoy the life of a conjugal couple 'à la européenne', and to end the destructive impacts of repudiation, when it came to their own marriage most appear to have reverted to custom. Men in particular, while accepting in principle the need for change, were reluctant to abandon their privileged position as males, while family pressures bore heavily on both men and women to follow tradition. But most important in the particular conjuncture of war was the massive influence that the FLN and religious reformists, now united in a common front, came to bring upon the educated, urban middle classes, who during 1959 began to step back from open or strong advocacy of legal emancipation. As Fauque remarked of the *évolués*, 'The crisis of conscience that agitates the young intellectuals holds them back from taking the lead in a movement for the evolution of women'.[95]

As has been seen (chapter 1) during the decade prior to the War of Independence the influence of the *Ulema* reformists had penetrated deep into the nationalist movement of Messali Hadj and among the women of the *Association des femmes musulmanes algériennes*. The *Ulema*, who warned against the dangers of western feminism, secularism and moral decadence subverting the integrity of the Muslim family, after it had rallied to the FLN and moved its key organisers to Tunisia and Morocco in September 1957, came to constitute the official religio-cultural voice of Algerian nationalism.[96] What must have been particularly worrying for the French government were signs that the *Ulema* ideology, as has been seen in the case of Boubakeur, was beginning to make deep inroads into the politically influential class of the Algerian notables and the state funded 'official' *imams* and theologians who had down to 1958 provided a key buttress to French power.[97] Between the heady days of the revolutionary '13 May' of 1958 and the autumn of 1959 there was a deep sea-change in the climate of opinion in Algeria: the optimism of 'fraternisation' and a new dawn for *Algérie française* quickly evaporated, especially after de Gaulle's crucial 'self-determination' speech of 16 September 1959. The emerging possibility of a French withdrawal impelled many of the Algerian bourgeoisie, who had until then publicly backed France, into a prudent silence or *attentisme*.[98] The Procureur of Oran noted that, with the exception of Lakhdari, 'on the part of the ministers of religion there exists the most absolute silence. Agents of the French administration, they abstain from any comment that could make them appear to the rebels as traitors to their cause . . . The well-to-do strata of the bourgeoisie are also refractory'.[99] Delouvrier informed the Prime Minister in July 1959 that the French had lost the initiative on the reform and failed to profit from the élan of '13 May':

> On the other hand it is clear that the 'revolutionary' climate that followed the 13 May 1958 no longer exists today. For a certain time the masses

were carried along by their will-power. They are no longer in the recep-tive state which, at the time, might have welcomed the reforms decided by the government in the sensitive area of the personal status law . . . It is not surprising then to find at present that the classic 'elites' (whether they belong to traditionalist society or a milieu *évolués*) are always very watch-ful of the moment and also influenced by the propaganda and methods of pressure of the FLN.[100]

The French army may have begun to win the military battle against the ALN guerrilla, especially with the Challe offensive, but this came at the very moment that the battle for hearts and minds was tipping in favour of the FLN.

The 'official' religious leaders continued to exercise a significant polit-ical influence inside Algeria, particularly through the Friday sermons in the mosques, and both the French intelligence services and the FLN kept a sharp eye on the 'flavour' of the messages being pronounced.[101] The French were quite prepared to place pressure on *imams* who conveyed a hostile message, including the closure of mosques. In January 1959, for example, General Olié, commander of the army corps in Constantine, sent out a directive noting that Ramadan, which was to begin on 11 March, was a period of religious fervour that the FLN might try to exploit as well as, 'certain religious agents who do not hesitate to exploit the crowds of faithful to engage in an unacceptable propaganda against': in consequence sector commanders were to gather intelligence on the Friday sermons and, if necessary, send police into the mosques and take measures under the Special Powers Act.[102] The FLN in turn threatened to assassinate those religious leaders who were too proactive in support of the authorities. However, in general the ranks of the FLN, far from being hostile to the clerisy or espousing a secular form of socialism, was suffused with a populist Islamic religiosity.[103] For example, in April 1957, the army captured an internal FLN document near Port-Gueydon which ordered that daily prayer should be obligatory for all aged over fifteen, and that Friday prayer (*grande prière*) should be recited in every village.[104]

Both sides in the war recognised the strategic importance of religion in their propaganda campaigns, and this became nowhere more impor-tant than over the reform of the family code since this was almost uni-versally recognised as the touch-stone of the Algerian social order and of cultural identity. In July 1959 the FLN journal *El Moudjahid*, closely reflecting the position of the *Ulema* and Muslim clergy, claimed that the French, 'who moreover are Christian or of the Jewish faith, have dared to deliberately attack the Koran, in its essence immutable, and to impose on Algerian Muslims by the sword the secular laws of France, and this

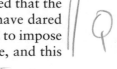

in the most sacred of matters, namely the statut personnel . . . Koranic law is trampled under the feet of French colonialism'.[105] The journal also denounced the erosion of the power of the *cadis*, and although the Algerian government tried to play on popular dislike of the money they engrossed at the expense of the poor, the Muslim justices remained very influential as 'the classic intermediaries of Muslim marriage' and a source of opposition to the reform.[106] Even those traditional religious leaders who were closest to the French expressed a deep repugnance for the family code, an opposition that made itself heard through Friday prayers and other channels. For example, Lieutenant-Colonel Dumas reported on a meeting he had with the religious leaders of Bouira on the reform, Sheikh Abadallah Djermouni, head of the influential Rhamania confraternity, the *imam* of the mosque, and two teachers in the *médersa*. They were totally intransigent in their rejection of the idea that young, inexperienced girls could refuse a choice of spouse imposed by her parents who had the wisdom and maturity to judge what was the best arrangement.[107] Overall the considerable investment made by the 'integrationists' of *Algérie française* and the psychological warfare officers in reform of marriage and family law as a means to win popular support either backfired or, as we shall see next, produced a minimal effect.

Problems of implementing the personal status law

Much of the information from 1959 relates to French surveys of Algerian *opinion* about legal reform, but in many ways the most conclusive evidence about the impact of the Ordinance relates to the way in which in the long term the population reacted to the actual implementation of the new regulations by the local authorities, the judiciary and the court system. Investigation of judicial change relating to family law and Muslim women in general has emphasised the importance of moving beyond the legal texts, which some historians have uncritically assumed to achieve their objectives by the simple fact of promulgation, to explore the way in which legislation, mediated by policing agencies, courts and social practices, translated into outcomes.[108] In the case of Algeria the 1959 Ordinance met strong political resistance from a civil society that quietly avoided or sabotaged the new laws for reasons that often had less to do with ideology than self-protection from the incursion of a hated regime into the intimate affairs of the family, marriage and property. This resistance to modernising French legislation provides crucial evidence as to why the newly independent Algerian state failed to introduce a progressive reform and emancipation of women after 1962 (see chapter 11).

What made resistance possible was the fact that government simply lacked the basic bureaucratic apparatus to enforce its provisions, both in terms of an *état civil* (civil register), local administrators and sufficient courts. While historians have often analysed France as a classic exemplar of the centralised and bureaucratic state, in the case of Algeria there existed an economic and socio-political dualism of space between the European-dominated and more advanced urban societies of the northern literal and the under-developed interior (see Introduction). In the past, through their political domination of the urban centres, the CPE, settlers ensured that state revenue was channelled to the roads, schools, hospitals and other infrastructures of the north, while the 'natives' of the *bled* were abandoned to their own devices. A tacit quid-pro-quo pact seems to have existed between settlers and the local Algerian *caïds* who 'managed' the mass of rural poor on behalf of the French, one by which colonial government in return for failing to invest in rural society would agree not to interfere too much in the traditional way of life of the peasantry, including marriage and family arrangements. The French presence in the *bled* became even more tenuous in the half century after 1900 as settlers abandoned their farms and migrated in growing numbers towards the towns. This 'bureaucratic vacuum' suggests that the 'weak' French state did little to reduce the power of the extended family, clans or tribes as alternative poles of authority and allegiance to central government.[109] During his governorship Soustelle recognised the fact of 'under-administration' as the fundamental problem facing Algeria, but it was beyond the resources of the army to reverse the long-term, accumulated effects of state under-investment in the interior.

One key sign of the absence of a 'strong' state in the *bled* was the failure to establish a comprehensive *état civil*, a civil register of births, marriages, divorce and deaths.[110] The law of 23 March 1882 which regulated registration, including the imposition of a patronymic to identify each person, was not extended to all tribes, especially in the south, and in many areas families failed to register children at birth.[111] In 1913 it was estimated that there were 100,000 lost souls (*omis*), individuals that had no official existence, and despite various attempts to enforce registration, notably by a law of 1925, significantly by 1959 the situation had got worse and the number of *omis* had increased to about 230,000.[112] In 1952 Lucien Fauque reported, 'For long the French administration shrunk back when faced with the practical difficulties to overcome and the inertia of the inhabitants resistant to any census'.[113]

The reasons why Algerians avoided registration were numerous: the key *rites de passage*, birth, marriage and death, had always been viewed as moments of religious and purely private celebration restricted to the family; frequently the officers of the state (mayors, justices) whose role was to register the acts were far distant; while providing such information enabled the state to intrude into the tribe and enforce numerous demands, from taxation to military conscription. While non-compliance with the *état civil* could, in principle, be punished with fines and prison sentences, in practice administrators were reluctant to use such severe methods against ignorant peasants and moratoria on those who had failed to register were still being extended down to 1950. The key factor that worked in the opposite direction after 1945 was the extension of state welfare, particularly family benefits, to some workers and, since claims for child allowance depended on verification of birth certificates, this encouraged registration with the *état civil*.[114]

The problem of under-registration and avoidance of administrative policing deepened dramatically during the Algerian War. Local government at the level of the communes became increasingly disorganised, particularly in the *bled*, as European mayors fled to the coastal cities or France to escape FLN assassination, while Algerians were also reluctant to be installed as officials under Lacoste's *loi-cadre* reform.[115] Over 200 Algerians who served as municipal councillors were assassinated,[116] and the weakening of local government along with its reorganisation after 1956 seems to have been reflected in such dilapidation of the civil registers that the authorities were unable to supply Algerians with copies of the birth, marriage and death certificates required under the new personal status law.[117] Simultaneously there was a massive dislocation of peasant society through *regroupement* and internal refugee movements to the urban shantytowns which made tracking of individuals or families difficult, while adult males who departed in growing number to the cities and France, or into the ranks of the FLN, had every reason to avoid identification.[118] The senior civil servant, André Jacomet, was shocked by the anarchic situation of the *état civil* and, following detailed reports from the senior judges who had to apply the new legislation, realised how this radically undermined implementation of the family code, particularly in relation to the declarations of marriage and divorce.[119] Jacomet immediately ordered the civil and military authorities to engage in a crash programme of registration, particularly of women,[120] what he called 'a veritable "hunt" for the disappeared (*omis*)', and the identity photographs of Marc Garanger taken at Bordj Okhriss in 1960 provide visual evidence of this campaign.

It was against this background that the Algiers government quickly came to realise that it was faced with enormous problems in enforcing the new family code after its publication in September 1959.[121] The large investigation of marriage practices in March 1959, just prior to any attempt at implementation, estimated that about 15 per cent of marriages in the towns escaped registration, 35 per cent in the rural plains, 55 per cent in the mountains, and 80 per cent in the insecure zones, and among these unrecorded marriages were many relating to pre-pubescent girls.[122] In other words the further one moved from urban society into the interior, the more tenuous French authority became, while inversely the local power of the FLN maquis increased along with cultural resistance to the new Ordinance. The problems were particularly pronounced among the conservative populations of the vast southern departments of the Sahara and Saoura. Here it was reported that so few Muslim courts (*mahakma*) and mayor's offices existed that the inhabitants of places like Reggan or Tindouf could be a thousand kilometres distant, and in the absence of any forms of public transport it was almost impossible to register births, marriages and divorce within a matter of days with the *état civil* as required by the law.[123] Religious leaders, noted General Pigeot, were also preaching resistance to the law especially, 'in the zones of influence of the *zaouias* as at Kerzaza and Zaouiet Kounta and in the localities in which the *marabouts* hold a great influence as in Sali and Tamentit'. The inhabitants were so shocked by the requirement for women to appear in person to authenticate their assent to marriage, a dishonouring exposure of women to other males, that villages were asking for marriage ceremonies to take place only at night. General Pigeot warned that the authorities could not afford to be inflexible in its application of the law, 'without risking to see fraud spread with the complicity of the whole population; it will not be the fiancée who appears before the registry officer, but a widow or divorced woman wrapped in veils. The propaganda undertaken for the implementation of the Ordinance will be made a laughing stock'.

Resistance was not, however, restricted to the deep south: the president of the Algiers Court of Appeal reported in the areas of Blida, Orléansville, Bouira and elsewhere opposition that was in part religious and political, and in part pragmatic relating to the greater bureaucratic complexity, higher cost and long procedural delays of marriage and, in particular, of divorce.[124] Considerable problems were faced among the many hundreds of thousands of men who were absent as labour migrants in France or in the northern cities, as conscripts in the army, or in the ALN forces. Ministry of Justice investigation exposed cases like that of Abdelkader Bah who married Habiba Bouklachi in the *mahakma* of Blida on 3 January 1961: but Bah was on this date in Valence, France, and the bridegroom was impersonated by his brother.[125] Abdelkader ben Aberrahmane's *livret de famille* registered his marriage on 26 August 1960 before the *mahakma* of Alger-Sud, but at the time he was in France: he was replaced at the ceremony by his father, and his wife-to-be by another woman. Such abuses suggested that some *cadi* were themselves quietly sabotaging the new law, or lax in the verification of identity.

A particularly difficult problem existed in the case of the clauses on divorce since wives could now initiate proceedings against their husbands, including on the grounds of absence that left families with no means of support. Many male defendants of a petition could not be located or notified of a pending action because they were absent or, even if they were found in time, they could not get permission from the armed forces or their French employers, risking loss of their job if they travelled home.[126] The new law facilitated a 'fast-track' divorce for the disappearance or long-term absence of the husband so that it could be finalised by a judge after one month instead of four years. The aim of this so-called 'colonialist' divorce was to drive a wedge between husband and wife,[127] and to undermine the morale of FLN cadres, a tactic that confirmed the analysis of nationalist theorists that psychological warfare was aimed at penetrating and subverting the family cell.[128] The overall response of the FLN was to dissuade Algerians from having any recourse to French courts or justices and, as will be seen in the following chapter, it set out to establish its own counter-state, *état civil*, and judicial regulation of marriage and divorce.

The weakness of the bureaucracy and *état civil* in the interior meant that many Algerians, as they had always done, simply ignored the law, or utilised numerous and well-worn avoidance techniques. A year after the introduction of the law it was reported that the number of court-registered divorces, which had already been low before the act, had declined even further.[129] This reflected the avoidance of males shocked in their patriarchal sensibilities by the erosion of *talaq*, the empowerment of women, and who were determined to evade the higher costs of settlement enforced by the law. The number of marriages contracted before the communal official by March 1960, despite the enthusiasm of the EMSI for the 'marriage à la mode de Gaulle', had registered zero instances in some locations, even including major towns like Affreville, Relizane, Médéa, Constantine, Bône and Guelma and one Muslim magistrate of Algiers estimated that 60 per cent of all marriages avoided state control.[130]

Although it was widely acknowledged by government officials and jurists that any legislation of this kind relating to family law would inevitably take some while to transform deeply entrenched practices,[131] it was soon apparent that the marriage code was being met by a large-scale resistance, inertia and, the traditional weapon of the peasantry against the colonial power, feigned ignorance, 'stupidity' and silence. As it became increasingly evident from early 1960 onwards that the war would end with a French withdrawal, the judicial and police authorities saw little point in pursuing the strict implementation of such unpopular legislation, while many Algerians sensing this imminent defeat of the colonial power risked little in openly defying its provisions. In late 1961, as OAS violence and anarchy deepened, the Prefect of Oran summarised the situation in what was the most 'pacified' of the three regions: 'The reform of the personal status of women is less-and-less talked about since it has become routine to avoid it. The decree of 17 September 1959 is hardly applied, either in regard to the agreement of the two parties (of the young girl in particular) nor in relation to divorce which has already been replaced by unilateral repudiation'.[132] After independence in mid-1962 the new Algerian state was confronted with a society in which a widespread culture and practice of non-compliance to marriage legislation was deeply entrenched. To understand how the post-colonial state would react to the issue of women's rights requires a closer look at the history of FLN policies on emancipation during the war, the subject of the next chapter.

Notes

1 The French term *'statut personnel'* does not translate readily: the central meaning of the Ordinance and Decree of application introduced in Algeria during 1959 was that of a marriage and family code.

2 The *Ulema* leader, Sheikh al-Uqbi, declared in a *fatwa* of 30 July 1937, 'whoever admits the substitution of a single principle of a non-religious law or regulation for any principle of Islamic law, is an apostate', quoted in McDougall, *History*, 89, note 81.

3 See Julia A. Clancy-Smith, *Rebel and Saint. Muslim Notables, Populist Protest, Colonial Encounters (Algeria and Tunisia, 1800–1904)* (Berkeley: University of California Press, 1997 edn).

4 Lecture of Lamine Lamoudi, 13 March 1936, quoted by McDougall, *History*, 90.

5 SHAT 1H2461/1*, report of P. Marmey, *Le Droit de vote de la femme musulmane Algérienne*, Centre de Haute Études d'Administration Musulmane, 16 January 1958.

6 CAOM 81F1218.

7 CAOM 13CAB20, preparations for referendum.

8 Sambron 'La Politique' (Doctoral thesis), 348–9.

9 SHAT 1H2515, SCA note of 15 September 1958 on propaganda films for the referendum.

10 SHAT 1H1147/1, transcripts Radio-diffusion-télévision française, Operation Referendum.

11 *Ibid.*

12 CAOM 13CAB64, Massu to Salan, 3 October 1958.

13 Sambron, 'La Politique' (Doctoral thesis), 357, 364; Launay, *Paysans algériens*, 83. General Challe and the Fifth Bureau saw electoral pressure as a legitimate counter-weight to FLN terror against voters; Feraoun, *Journal*, 251–2, describes the vote-rigging process.

14 Sambron, 'La Politique' (Doctoral thesis), 356, 362, 364–5.

15 *Ibid.*, 363; on Palissy, chapter 5, p. 16.

16 See Sambron, 'La Politique' (Doctoral thesis), Annexes, 720–2, Document 49, model question and answer directives to be used by the EMSI: these made no attempt to explain to Algerian women the abstruse political implications of the referendum vote, but presented it as a straight choice between peace and prosperity, 'Yes' for schools, hospitals, doctors, nurses, roads, railways, piped water and oil wells, 'No' for their destruction by the FLN.

17 Quoted in Seferdjeli, 'French Army', 60, from SHAT 1H3266/4; Fauque, *Stades d'évolution*, 21, noted, 'At present only a small minority of Muslim citizens have achieved sufficient civic maturity to understand the importance of a ballot paper and its relevance for the issue of public affairs'.

18 CAOM 2SAS59, SAU Clos-Salembier, monthly report, November 1958.

19 CAOM 2SAS60, SAU Clos-Salembier, Montaner, undated report [1960].

20 Sambron, 'La Politique' (Doctoral thesis), 359–60.

21 CAOM 13CAB, Massu to Salan, 14 June 1958.

22 CAOM 13CAB7, Salan to Villeneuve, 16 June 1958.

23 CAOM 13CAB207, Villeneuve, *Projet de réforme du statut personel de la femme musulmane*, 5 July 1957.

24 CAOM 81F1220, minutes of a meeting, chaired by Brouillet, *Secrétaire général pour les affaires algériennes*, Paris, 1 August 1958. In 1959 René Brouillet became the head of de Gaulle's cabinet office.

25 Robert Buron, *Carnets politiques de la guerre d'Algérie (1954–1962)* (Paris : Plon, 1965), 119, quoted in Julian Jackson, 'De Gaulle et l'Algérie: grand dessein ou adaptation empirique ?', 1, conference *Pour une histoire critique et citoyenne. Le cas de l'histoire franco-algérienne*, 20–22 June 2006, Lyon, ENS LSH, http://ens-web3.ens-Ish.fr/colloques/france-algerie/communication.php3?id_article=240 (accessed 14 December 2007); see also House and MacMaster, *Paris 1961*, 3–5.

26 Alain Peyrefitte, *C'était de Gaulle* (Paris: Gallimard, 2002), 65; see also Shephard, *Invention*, 73–7.

27 Susan K. Foley, *Women in France since 1789. The Meanings of Difference* (Basingstoke: Palgrave, 2004), 237.

28 CAOM 14CAB233, Salan secret telegram, 30 September 1958.

29 CAOM 13CAB37*, Mme Salan to de Gaulle, 2 October 1958: this seven-page letter appears to have been drafted with the assistance of specialists in General Salan's cabinet or the Fifth Bureau.

30 This claim is totally contradicted by the reports of the September tour, and

the frightened, impoverished women rounded up to 'welcome' Mme Salan: see this volume, chapter 5, p. 192.

31 CAOM 81F74, contains a mass of petitions forwarded to General de Gaulle, via René Brouillet, on 17 November 1958.

32 Photographs of a typical petition with fingerprint 'signatures' are reproduced in Sambron, *Femmes musulmanes*, 151.

33 Traditionally Algerian men, as throughout the Maghreb and Middle East, undertook the household shopping in order to enforce seclusion and to prevent dishonourable contact with males.

34 Jean Claude Racinet, *Les Capitaines d'Avril* (Paris: Éditions France-Empire, 1976), quoted in Marnia Lazreg, *Torture and the Twilight of Empire. From Algiers to Baghdad* (Princeton: Princeton University Press, 2008), 94.

35 One of the petitions addressed to de Gaulle, that from Perregaux, supported an end to polygamy and repudiation but suggested that since the reform, 'touches on religious law, any changes should be subject to the advice of the "*MEDJLES*" or congress of religious authorities', and without the 'support of this Muslim religious authority', the reform would be compromised: CAOM 81F74.

36 CAOM 81F1219, *Note relative au statut de la femme musulmane et de la femme Kabyle*, 7 January 1959 [anonymous], but certainly an appendix to a letter de Gaulle sent to Delouvrier, 7 January: see CAOM 81F1220. The five-man delegation, which appears to have visited Paris in some secrecy, was composed of a pro-French elite: Sheikh Abdelali Lakhdari of Constantine, Baba Ameur, Muphti of Algiers, Benhoura, a retired *cadi*, and Zerdoumi and Hadj Saddok, respectively professor and head of the Franco-Muslim colleges of Tlemcen and Ben Aknoun. The Algiers intelligence service carried out a prior vetting of the opinion of these religious leaders in relation to their degree of support or opposition to the reform: see 13CAB7, and those who were strongly opposed, like the jurist Mahdi or Boubakeur, were excluded. De Gaulle was thus presented with a biased delegation that would give Paris the mistaken impression that religious notables were united in their support for reform.

37 CAOM 13CAB7, de Gaulle to Salan, 15 November 1958.

38 The French sociologist Pierre Bourdieu (1930–2002) developed much of his classic theory of such peasant structures during his military service in Algeria, see for example, *Outline of a Theory of Practice* (Cambridge: Cambridge University Press, 1977) and his more approachable, *The Algerians*; and John Davis, *People of the Mediterranean: An Essay in Comparative Social Anthropology* (London: Routledge and Kegan Paul, 1977).

39 Meillassoux, *Maidens, Meal and Money*.

40 See Edward Shorter, *The Making of the Modern Family* (London: Collins, 1976); Conrad M. Arensberg and Solon T. Kimball, *Family and Community in Ireland* (Cambridge, Mass.: Harvard University Press, 1968).

41 Mohammed Benhoura, *Le Monde*, 13 June 1958, quoted in Sambron, 'La Politique' (Doctoral thesis), 256.

42 For an excellent analysis of Maghribi family law as the fundamental code of a society built on patriarchal solidarities, see Charrad, *States and Women's Rights*, 4–7, 28–50.

43 Under Muslim law a husband was required, after repudiation and separation, to provide upkeep (*idda*) for three menstrual cycles or months, in part to test whether any ensuing pregnancy and offspring belonged to him or not.

44 Fauque, *Stades d'évolution*, 9–10, 'the family hierarchy is such that in fact the marriage is arranged by a series of negotiations that bring into play the interests and relations between several families. It takes the form of a collective act over which the dominant males retain control'.

45 See Lacoste-Dujardin, *Des mères contre les femmes*.

46 CAOM 14CAB233, minutes of the *Commission d'étude de la situation de la femme musulmane*, 5–6 December 1958.

47 For a detailed analysis of the Algerian jurisprudence see, Jules Roussier, *Le Mariage et sa dissolution dans le Statut Civil Local Algérien* (Algiers: no publisher, 1960); Lucie Pruvost, *Femmes d'Algérie. Société, famille et citoyenneté* (Algiers: Casbah Éditions, 2002); Borrmans, *Statut personnel*; Sambron, 'La Politique' (Doctoral thesis), Part 2, 173–382.

48 The Ordinance of 4 February, an extremely brief bill, provided a summary of the key provisions of the new legislation in thirteen articles: the close detail of how the act was to be implemented was established by the drafting commission that met after 3 February and was published as the decree of 17 September 1959.

49 Ordinance No. 59–274, 4 February, *J.O.R.F*, 11 February 1959, 1,860.

50 There was a considerable difference of opinion among both French and Algerian commentators, some seeing the Ordinance as radical, others as moderate or weak. Part of this confusion arose from the fact that the authorities wished to calm Muslim fears by reassuring public opinion that the law was mild and offered no change to existing Islamic doctrine: for example, SHAT 1H4395/7, *Schéma de causerie*, the standard instructions to be used by the EMSI and SAS in explaining the reform to local populations, describe it as 'limited and measured' and by stripping away the deformations of archaic custom and tradition, 'safeguarding Islam, without undermining through civil marriage the dignity of Muslim marriage'.

51 Charrad, *States and Women's Rights*, 38, gives data on polygamy in Algeria as 3 per cent of all married males in 1948, 2 per cent in 1954 and 1.8 per cent in 1966. According to an extensive survey carried out by the army in March 1959, the official figure of 2 per cent polygamous marriages reflected an under-registration of a practice that was probably closer to 6 per cent: Fauque, *Stades d'évolution*, 10.

52 CAOM 14CAB165-6, report of Jacques-Guy Lenoir, *Directeur des Personnels et des Affaires Administratives*, 10 November 1959.

53 CAOM 14CAB9*, contains much information on the role of the *Affaires Musulmane* in nurturing and rewarding 'loyal' religious leaders: for

example, a telegram from Constantine, 6 May 1959, listed those who were recommended to receive a subsidised pilgrimage to Mecca.

54 CAOM 13CAB7, intelligence report on Lakhdari, October 1958; on the *médersa* see McDougall, *History*, 69, note 23.

55 CAOM 13CAB7, intelligence report on Benhoura, 20 October 1958.

56 CAOM 13CAB7, intelligence report on Boubakeur, 20 October 1958. Boubakeur, who passed seamlessly into the ranks of the post-independence order, remained director of the Mosque (an outpost of the Algerian government) until 1982, and in 1984 his son, Dalil Boubakeur in turn became rector and continues a highly pro-French tradition appreciated by the conservative political establishment: see Alain Boyer, *L'Institut Musulman de la Mosquée de Paris* (Paris: CHEAM, 1992).

57 CAOM 14CAB233, minutes of the *Commission d'étude de la situation de la femme musulmane*, 5–6 December 1958. Jules Roussier subjected the new legislation to a close, legal scrutiny in *Le Mariage et sa dissolution* and concluded (p. 115) that it had been published 'quite brutally' and had 'surprised and sometimes disturbed some excellent souls'.

58 CAOM 14CAB233, Hamza Boubakeur, 'Projet de réforme du statut personnel de la femme musulmane et de la femme Kabyle en Algérie', 27-page typescript, n.d.: the first thirteen pages of this text can be found in Sambron, 'La Politique' (Doctoral thesis), Annexes, 646–59.

59 On the background to the 1984 code see Lucie Pruvost, 'Le Code algérien de la famille: à la recherché d'un projet de société', in *AWAL*, 20 (1999), 7–21.

60 CAOM 14CAB9*, Delouvrier to Prime Minister, 18 July 1959, 7 pages.

61 A mass of evidence confirms Delouvrier's analysis here: for example press reports of the attempt by the army and settlers to relive the heady days of 'fraternisation' during the anniversary parades of 13 May 1959, point to a widespread climate of European demoralisation.

62 CAOM 81F1220, de Gaulle in a note to Delouvrier, 7 January 1959, made clear his unhappiness with the Algiers draft and intimated his intention to revise it once again.

63 CAOM 14CAB165-6, telegram from Mafart to Prime Minister, 2 February 1959.

64 CAOM 14CAB165-6, telegram from Mafart to Prime Minister, 3 February 1959. Further elements of this exchange can be found in CAOM 81F1220.

65 This was published in the *Dépêche quotidienne* on 2 February 1959: see Sambron, 'La Politique' (Doctoral thesis), 262. Boubakeur followed this up with a further public attack in *Le Monde* on 19 February. The deputy for Sétif Ben Djelida also publicly denounced the Ordinance as 'heretical'.

66 CAC 19950236, art. 8, Boubakeur to Michelet, 23 March 1959.

67 CAOM 81F1219, the Commission Permanente was composed of Brasard (president), Julliot de la Morandière (*rapporteur*), Simoneau, Fusil and Sid Cara. The session of 17 April was held in Sid Cara's office, and examined a draft decree prepared by herself and Lefaucheux.

68 That the election of three women deputies did not represent a significant breakthrough for Algerian women into grass-roots politics is indicated by the fact that in the council elections of 15 April 1959 only nine women were elected (0.06 per cent) among the total of 13,995 councillors, 11,558 of which were Muslim men: Sambron, 'La Politique' (Doctoral thesis), 366–7.

69 CAOM 13CAB61, transcript of radio broadcast, *Magazine de la femme*, 31 August 1958.

70 CAOM 13CAB61, Lucienne Salan wrote to M. H. Lefaucheux as president of the CNFF (undated) on the intention to stand at least one Algerian, 'a Muslim female candidate able to collect all the votes (you can see of whom I speak)': probably an allusion to Sid Cara. Khedira Bouabsa in an interview with Ryme Seferdjeli, 'French "Reforms"', 49, 53, says she was approached by French contacts, but refused to give further details. On Massu's role see Sambron, 'La Politique' (Doctoral thesis), 354.

71 *L'Aurore*, 3 September 1959, interview by Jacques Perrier in Sétif. It suited French propaganda to present Kebtani as 'veiled' until the events of '13 May' but in reality she came from a relatively well-off, pro-French elite family, that lived in a large house in Bougie, and was educated at the lycée until at fifteen she married a road haulage contractor.

72 This was the key message conveyed, for example, by an interview by Christiane Lille with the three deputies in *Femmes nouvelles*, 1 January 1959.

73 Seferdjeli, 'French "Reforms"', 50. Michel Debré, in *Gouverner. Mémoires*, Vol. 3 (Paris: Albin Michel, 1988), 14, recommended her appointment to de Gaulle as 'the symbol of a transformation and progress that we wish for Algerian society'. A report in CAOM 13CAB64, shows Sid Cara was subject to the usual intelligence assessment as a suitable parliamentary candidate and found to be conscientious and honest, 'a bit lacking in personality and dynamism, sometimes oversensitive': what the government was looking for in its three women protégés was presentable and compliant pro-French *évoluées*.

74 The key papers from Nafissa Sid Cara's cabinet are held in the Centre des archives contemporaines at Fontainebleau, see CAC 19830229 art. 1 to 9, including her private correspondence, but are not open to consultation because they are held in a store-room that has yet to be decontaminated of asbestos.

75 See above chapter 2, and CAOM 81F1219, minutes of Simoneau Commission, 27 May and 3 June 1957.

76 CAOM 81f1219, minutes of Simoneau Commission, 3 June 1957.

77 CAOM 81F1219, minutes of commission presided by M. Brasard, 3 February 1959. Sid Cara was involved with another project of 1959 to reform the Algerian judicial system so that the *cadis* would be abolished or absorbed into the system of French courts: see CAC 19950236 file 7: Projet de loi relative à la justice musulmane, 4 June 1959.

78 For a later example of Sid Cara's progressive stance, see House and

MacMaster, *Paris 1961*, 145, for her outrage at the police violence during the repression of the Algerian demonstration of 17 October 1961.

79 Shephard, *Invention*, 191–2; *Femmes nouvelles*, 20 (20 June 1959), reported that Bouabsa regarded the Ordinance of 4 February as too timid and less audacious than the Tunisian and Moroccan reforms of the personal status law.

80 Seferdjeli, 'French "Reforms"', 52; among FLN documents seized by the Paris police in November 1961 was a detailed report on the movements and security of 'the traitor Sid Cara': APP H1B21.

81 The continuity between the men of '13 May' and de Gaulle on the question of emancipation was perhaps indicated by the presence of the 'ultra' Soustelle as a cabinet minister in Paris, who signed the Ordinance of 4 February, along with de Gaulle, Debré and Edmond Michelet.

82 CAC 19950236, art. 8, Delouvrier to Debré, 31 March 1959.

83 Fauque, *Stades d'évolution*. A copy of the questionnaire is reprinted in Borrmans, *Statut personnel*, 482, note 55. The local reports are scattered through the archives, for example, SHAT 1H4395/7, return from an EMSI team in the Bouira sector; CAOM 2SAS56, return from SAU Bas Casbah, 3 April 1959; CAOM 2SAS69, SAS Baraki, by Captain Brassens (undated) which was sociologically sophisticated.

84 SHAT 1H4395, circular from Delouvrier and Challe, 21 July 1959.

85 This anti-*cadi* campaign had been already launched by the Fifth Bureau, see SHAT 1H4395, directive from Colonel Lanceron, 11 March 1959. The influential corps of muslim justices was in mid-1959 composed of eighty-one *cadis* and fifty-nine *bachadels*, see CAOM 14CAB9*, report of 10 June 1959.

86 SHAT 1H2476, press cutting, *Depêche quotidienne*, 1 July 1959. Michel Launay, *Paysans algériens*, 354–5, shows from data of SAS officers' adjudication (*chicayas*) that unilateral repudiation was indeed the central concern of married women.

87 See, for example, SHAT 1H2569, quarterly EMSI report, ZOO, 26 September 1960.

88 SHAT 1H4395/7, report of EMSI course at Dellys, 7 March 1960. But Husson of the Pallisy MSF had reported in October 1958 her bitter sense of defeat in not being able to block the arranged marriage of a fifteen-year-old girl who attended her circle or to get it celebrated before the civil authorities, CAOM 81F74.

89 CAC 19950236, art. 8, Procureur of Constantine Court of Appeal to Minister of Justice, 13 June 1959.

90 Fauque, *Stades d'évolution*, 24.

91 SHAT 1H2460/1, Colonel Crozafon, Alger-Sahel sector, report of 3 March 1959 on the Ordinance 4 February.

92 CAOM 14CAB9*, General Corps Armée Oran to Delouvrier, 16 November 1959.

93 CAOM 2SAS56, SAU Bas Casbah, monthly report, 20 August 1959.

94 Fauque, *Stades d'évolution*, 4.

95   *Ibid.*, 28.

96   McDougall, *History*, 140–3.

97   CAC 19950236, art. 8, Procureur of Constantine Court of Appeal to Minister of Justice, 13 June 1959.

98   On the concept of *attentisme* see MacMaster, 'The "Silent Native"'.

99   Procureur général, Algiers Court of Appeal to Minister of Justice, 11 March 1960, quoted in Sambron, 'La Politique' (Doctoral thesis), 273.

100 CAOM 14CAB9*, Delouvrier to M. Debré, 18 July 1959.

101 There exists numerous intelligence reports in the CAOM and SHAT archives on the pro-nationalist messages of *imams* during the Friday prayers: e.g. 2SAS56 Bas Casbah, monthly report, 23 October 1960, gives the outcome of surveillance of two central mosques of Algiers during which the *imams* made 'a clever justification of the rebellion', using such expressions as 'That God help the Islamic fighters for liberty', or 'That God help the *moudjahidines* to replace the tri-colour flag by the Arab flag'.

102 CAOM 14CAB9*, General Olié order, 28 January 1959; CAOM 2SAS56, monthly report of Captain Bapst, SAU Bas Casbah, October 1959, noted that the new *imam* (and ex-*cadi*) of the Mosque of Sidi Abdallah 'does not conceal his hostility to the reform of the statute of women'.

103 On the populist religiosity of the FLN maquisards see Feraoun, *Journal*, 40, on the harangue of an FLN militant during the visit of a commando to Tizi-Hibel: 'you deserve to be burned alive. You are non-believers. You have neither faith nor law. You are all drunkards'.

104 SHAT 1H2582, intelligence report, 2e Bureau, 13 May 1957; another report, 29 November 1957, disclosed an FLN document from the Aurès: 'it is obligatory for each soldier to respect the precepts of the Islamic faith and to follow the teachings. All offenders will be judged by a military tribunal . . . An *imam* must be designated for each Company'.

105 *El Moudjahid*, 45 (6 July 1959), quoted in Borrmans, *Statut personnel*, 494.

106 15 CAB118, Captain Alain de Germiny, SAU Cité Mahiéddine, June 1960; CAOM 2SAS, SAU Bas Casbah, monthly report, 3 February 1959, noted the *cadi*, 'is generally feared and respected, since so many things depend on him. He is even much hated by the majority since his working methods are similar to those of the defunct *corps caïdal* [traditional leaders]'.

107 SHAT 1H4395/7, note of enquiry by Lieutenant-Colonel Dumas, 3 August 1959.

108 Moors, 'Debating Islamic Family Law', 142–3; Ziba Mir-Hosseini, *Marriage on Trial. A Study of Islamic Family Law* (London: I. B. Tauris, 2000), has shown through observation of Iranian and Moroccan court practice how women could manipulate legal process to gain advantage over patriarchal domination. For an early attempt at a sociology of law in relation to Algeria see Jean-Paul Charnay, *La Vie musulmane en Algérie d'après la jurisprudence de la première moitié du xxe siècle* (Paris: Presses Universitaires de France, 1965).

109 This analysis fits in with the work of Mounira Charrad, *States and Women's Rights*, on the failure to legislate on a family code in Algeria compared to Tunisia and Morocco.

110 For an analysis of civil registration to the formation of the modern nation state see James C. Scott, *Seeing Like a State: How Certain Schemes to Improve the Human Condition Have Failed* (New Haven: Yale University Press, 1998); John Torpey, *The Invention of the Passport. Surveillance, Citizenship and the State* (Cambridge: Cambridge University Press, 2000).

111 CAOM 81F1223, a report of president of Tribunal of Batna, sent by the Minister of Justice to the Prime Minister, 20 February 1960, notes the failure to create a civil register for some tribes or to create individual patronymics. The military, police and civil archives of the Algerian War frequently register Algerians as 'SNP' (sans nom patronymique), although this had been required since the law of 1882.

112 CAOM 81F1223, circular from A. Jacomet, General Secretary of Administration, 21 December 1959; A. Jacomet to Prime Minister, 11 April 1960.

113 CAOM 81F1223, L. P. Fauque, note on *état civil*, April–May 1952.

114 CAOM 81F1223, L. P. Fauque, note on *état civil*, April–May 1952: 'In the case of a mass of those refractory to any census, whether from bad motivation, fear of conscription, the pointlessness of declaring daughters, or simply from negligence, the desire to prove the right to receive social benefits has provided a major boost'; see also Borrmans, *Statut personnel*, 463. However, colonial officials frequently used unnecessary bureaucratic procedures to block Algerian access to welfare rights.

115 CAOM 81F1223, A. Jacomet to Prime Minister, 11 April 1960, noted failure of the *état civil* due to the 'profound changes in the administrative structures of Algeria and the installation of inexperienced municipalities'.

116 Hamoumou, *Et ils sont devenus harkis*, 91–2.

117 L. P. Fauque, 'Le Mariage des musulmans algériens', *Revue algérienne, tunisienne et marocain de législation et de jurisprudence*, 1961, Part 1, 66, noted that with the local government reform (*loi cadre*) that abolished the *commune mixte*, attempts had been made to create new centralised registry offices that reorganised the old registers for 1904 to 1956, but this had disclosed, 'the poor condition of certain archives worn to the point of being unusable'. CAOM 81F1223, Jacomet in a note to the Prime Minister, 11 April 1960, elaborated on the problems of upkeep of the *état civil* in the chaotic context of war.

118 The FLN became expert in the falsification of identity, using pseudonyms, the identity of the dead, forged cards, etc., so that its cadres could readily move about and avoid arrest.

119 CAOM 81F1223, in his circular of 21 December 1959, A. Jacomet stated: 'It is profoundly shocking that in a policed society individuals can live without any regularly established juridical connections to their fellows and without the means to prove their identity'. Jacomet was later sacked

as *Sécretaire générale de l'administration* in November 1960 for opposition to the Gaullist policy of self-determination: his removal, while a member of the *Conseil d'État*, has been interpreted as a classic incident in de Gaulle's interference with the independence of the judiciary: Andrew Knall and Vincent Wright, *The Government and Politics of France* [1978] (London: Routledge, 5th edn 2006), 384.

120 The extension of the vote to women had also revealed the problem of verification of their identity during the ballots.

121 Detailed information on the implementation of the law can be found in the numerous reports sent by the Algerian administration and courts to the Ministry of Justice during 1960–61 held at CAC 19950236, art. 8, and at CAOM 81F1223.

122 Fauque, *Stades d'évolution*, 8–9.

123 CAC 19950236, art. 8, General A. Pigeot, deputy of the Saoura, report to Minister of Justice, 24 September 1960. The Minister of the Sahara, Robert Lecourt, in a reply of 26 November 1960, promised the establishment of more tribunals and itinerant Muslim officials.

124 CAC 19950236, art. 8, Algiers president Court of Appeal, 24 May 1960, to Minister of Justice.

125 CAC 19950236, art. 8, dossier on problems of application of the Ordinance.

126 CAOM 81F1223, A. Jacomet to Prime Minister, 23 September 1960.

127 Sambron, 'La Politique' (Doctoral thesis), 268, 297–8.

128 The French tactic appears to have had some effect: see CAOM 2SAS56, the SAU of the Bas Casbah reported in June 1960 the case of the wife of an imprisoned FLN cadre who divorced him, but was now fearful since the FLN lawyer Ould Aoudia had said to her, 'You know, your husband may perhaps become an important leader tomorrow'.

129 CAOM 81F1223, A. Jacomet to Prime Minister, 23 September 1960.

130 Fauque, 'Le Mariage des musulmans', 65–6, statistics of marriages contracted between 19 November 1959 (date of application) and 1 March 1960.

131 Fauque, *Stades d'évolution*, 15–16, Algerians in Bordj-Bou-Arréridj had told investigators that it normally took two to three years for a new law to be understood and progressively applied.

132 CAOM 81F1223, report for third quartier 1961.

9

The FLN and the role of women during the war

The universally held image of women during the Algerian War is that, made famous by Frantz Fanon and Pontecorvo's classic film *The Battle of Algiers*, of Muslim women as heroic resistance fighters. However, this enduring symbol of 'Third World' women confronting the might of colonial armies reflects more the propaganda success of the FLN in manipulating the representation of Algerian women than any real or enduring transformation of their position or rights. For the majority of FLN leaders the 'woman question' did not constitute a significant issue: the immediate life-and-death business of waging war and of national survival was thought to be far too urgent a matter to allow energies to be diverted in this direction and women's equality it was thought would be almost automatically achieved through independence and liberation from colonialism.[1] However, the FLN was forced during the course of the war to take a position on women for two reasons: firstly, women gradually assumed a de facto role in the conflict, playing a major part in urban networks and the maquis as gun and bomb carriers, messengers, fund collectors, nurses, look-outs, cooks and doctors. Inevitably, as often in time of war, such activities presented a challenge to traditional concepts of segregation of the sexes, gender and male dominance. Secondly, the FLN was perfectly aware that a key intention of the French military in undertaking an emancipation agenda was to place the nationalists on the spot, since it was calculated that they would be unwilling or unable to respond by adopting their own progressive reform, while direct opposition to French liberation from custom and patriarchy would expose them in the UN and among international opinion as reactionaries. How the FLN responded to this dual challenge during the war was to set the scene, as will be shown in chapter 11, for the post-independence political marginalisation of women and the long-term failure of a reform agenda.

The ad hoc mobilisation of women

The most interesting and dynamic phase of women's direct engagement in the war came during 1955–57, a more open and experimental period that carried the promise or potential for a real transformation in gender roles, but which was suddenly 'closed down' by the FLN leadership from late 1957 onwards. During this initial phase many thousands of women first became engaged in various levels of direct action as fighters, nurses, ancillaries and providers of logistic support to the ALN. This mobilisation did not occur as the result of a central policy decision but emerged in a piecemeal or ad hoc way in response to the situation that urban and rural male combatants found themselves in, for example facing a shortage of trained nurses to tend to wounded fighters in make-shift field hospitals.[2] In general terms the FLN attitude towards women was *reactive*, a pragmatic and localised response to the direct presence of women who challenged entrenched male misogyny or patriarchy. The ALN commanders of the regions (Wilaya), with weak lines of communication to the external provisional government, often showed considerable autonomy of action and this was reflected in quite different localised attitudes to a female presence in the maquis, from a relatively progressive and more secular or socialist position, to highly traditionalist, religious inspired, patriarchal authoritarianism. But the overall climate within the ALN was conservative, a reflection of the values of the male peasantry, and truly radical officers were very few in number and remained isolated. What glimmering there was of more innovative policies or practices on the ground, as in Wilayas II (Constantinois) and IV (Algiers),[3] was brought to a halt by the central decision in late 1957 to withdraw women from the maquis to Tunisia and Morocco, and there to reassert a harsh discipline over those who had gained a taste of greater freedom and individual autonomy.

In order to understand the reactions of Algerian males to direct contact with women militants on the ground, it is helpful to divide the latter into two quite different categories, the minority of urban-based and usually better-educated commandos (the *fidayate*), many of whom later escaped to the maquis, and the tens of thousands of anonymous peasant women 'civilians' in the rural areas (*moussebilate*) who provided vital support to the *moudjahidines* (fighters in ALN units).[4] These two groups will be examined in turn.

The *fidayate*: the symbol of the urban warrior

The single most enduring and iconic image associated with the Algerian War is of Muslim women in the terrorist networks who transported documents, guns and bombs through the parachutist check-points. Today, in a world in which suicide bombings have become almost commonplace, it is easy to lose sight of the extent to which the detection and arrest of female terrorists from late 1956 onwards caused a shocked or astonished response among both French and international public opinion.[5] Here were veiled women engaging, according to one's point of view, in horrific acts of indiscriminate and bloody violence or in deeds of heroic bravery that seemed to defy all the stereotypes of Muslim women as cloistered and supine creatures totally lacking in willpower or autonomy. Did the activities of young female bombers in the streets of Algiers mark a turning-point in the assertion of women's power or position in Algerian society?

Firstly, the young women who were carefully selected by Yacef Saadi to assist with his terrorist network in the ZAA were recruited in the main from known and trusted petit-bourgeois or modest nationalist families.[6] Many had been educated to lycée level, at a time when only one in ten Muslim girls received even primary schooling, and Samia Lakhdari and Zohra Drif were university law students and daughters of Muslim lawyers (cadis).[7] During the first post-Second World War decade of an organised women's movement most individuals were drawn into militant activity since they had access to the male-dominated universe of political activism by the 'accident' of being located within nationalist family and kin networks (chapter 2) and this pattern continued into the War of Independence. Thus Djamila Bouhired was recruited by her uncle Mustapha Bouhired, an FLN militant, and Louisette and Malika Ighilahriz by their father.[8] The young fidayate certainly were required to carry out tasks that broke the conventions of 'respectability' and honourable behaviour: dressing in a chic western mode of short skirts and make-up so as to pass easily through parachutist check-points, moving about unescorted in urban space, and making contact alone with unknown males.[9] However, most of this breaching of strict gender roles was largely on terms decided by males: the fidayate never assumed positions of command, but always obeyed male orders and even in their most perilous exploits were still their adjuncts (Bouhired was initially appointed to Saadi's top-secret cell as a cook). FLN militants, including even fathers, were prepared to tolerate fidayate breaking the rules of segregation under the exceptional conditions of nationalist struggle, a situation that demanded every sacrifice, but there was an assumption that things would return to 'normal' with the end of the war.

It was undoubtedly the case that some fidayate like Zohra Drif were strong-willed women and Yacef Saadi, for example, through constant daily and close work with Drif in restricted safe-houses and dangerous missions established a degree of closeness and trust that was unusual compared to the normal relations between unrelated men and women in Algerian society.[10] But it should be kept in mind that the urban *fidayate* were very few in number and that most of their actions in breaking through the constraints of conservative gender roles were restricted to a clandestine world that went unobserved by the majority of women. During Saadi's famous secret meetings in Algiers with the ethnologist Germain Tillion, Zohra Drif reverted to the habitual role of the silent and subservient female, serving tea and cakes, taking a back seat and keeping her personal hostile opinion of the ethnologist to herself.[11]

However, the *fidayate* did come to play an enormously important role in FLN propaganda as heroic fighters and martyrs to the nationalist cause. The trial of the leading women bombers and, in particular, of Djamila Bouhired in July 1957, was an international media sensation and the leading FLN defence lawyer Jacques Vergès was skilled in developing a strategy that used the courtroom as a political space for the indictment of French military violence, torture and abuse of human rights, a monstrous violence that he was able to highlight by the inhumane treatment and rape of FLN women.[12] Vergès, who later married Bouhired, collaborated with the novelist Georges Arnaud, author of *The Wages of Fear*, in writing a small booklet, *Pour Djamila Bouhired*, and the heroic exploits of the young terrorist were soon celebrated through an Egyptian film, *Djamila l'Algérienne* (1958) of Youcef Chacine, and by popular singers across North Africa, such as Ouardia El Djezaïria and Sou'ad Mohamed in Egypt, and Hadja Hamdaouïa in Morocco.[13]

In all six *fidayate* received the death sentence during the war, and the campaigns by the French left and intellectuals to save them from the guillotine provided further global publicity. In the later stages of the war (1959–62) came the arrest and trial of the photogenic Djamila Boupacha, whose defence was taken up by the feminist lawyer Gisèle Halimi and by Simone de Beauvoir who set up the *Comité pour Djamila Boupacha* and jointly published *Djamila Boupacha*, illustrated with photographs and a Picasso portrait.[14] The young women militants came to symbolise the Algerian cause, particularly for communists, socialists and liberals throughout the world, as well as for many 'Third World' women then engaged in revolutionary or anti-colonial struggle.[15] The FLN propaganda organisation also distributed to the international media photographs of women soldiers in the maquis, dressed in uniform and displaying the ultimate symbol of manhood, automatic rifles, although in reality the ALN avoided training women as combatants.[16] The images of female combatants were reinforced by the martyrology of women maquisards who, when outnumbered or captured, had fought to the death, like Malika Gaïd and Messika Benziza.[17] The ALN also made use of the image of the martyr to appeal to Algerian women to support the national struggle, as in one tract from mid-1958, 'Algerian women! Listen! Do you not hear the boots of the French occupier clicking on the road? Do you not hear the screams of massacred or tortured Algerian women and men? Do you not hear the proud call of Djamila Bouhired? . . . Heroic and martyrised Algeria has its gaze fixed on you'.[18]

The FLN was quite happy to make use of such propaganda since, while to the outside world it carried a strong revolutionary message, the icon of the female soldier and heroine did not necessarily offer a significant challenge to established gender norms. Throughout the Muslim societies of the Middle East and Maghreb there existed a historical and religious tradition that presented famous real or mythical warriors, like the Algerian Kahina, who in times of exceptional danger to the people had assumed the role of men in resisting invaders and tyrants. A key point of reference here was the role model of Zainab, sister of Imam Hussain, who played a supporting role at the Battle of Karbala. A common structure to this topos was that in a world turned upside down by chaos and defeat, in which men themselves had failed to protect the nation and become 'like women', then it was up to women to assume the masculine role of the warrior and saviour.[19] Afsaneh Najmabadi has noted that the rhetoric of Iranian male nationalists, in 'calling patriotic women manly implied a reassuring restoration of gender order: only men performed such great acts'.[20] This way of thinking surfaced constantly during the Algerian War, as in the case of a young boy, angry and frustrated by his father's unmanly silence towards an oppressive French authority, who dared berate the very symbol of masculine honour: 'Women are in prison, why not the men?'.[21] Many *moudjahidate* internalised the masculine logic of the female warrior: theirs was only a temporary status, not proof of a lasting transformation of gender roles, and with the coming of independence in 1962 they quietly 'demobilised' by withdrawing from public life back into the private, domestic sphere of the home.

The urban *moudjahidate* in the maquis

The proactive role of women militants ruffled few feathers among their male comrades in the major towns, since most of the latter were city born and educated and quite used to a degree of mixing or contact with young 'modern' women who went unveiled and followed a European life-style. The situation was very different in the rural hinterland and it was here that the arrival of hundreds of young and educated women in the maquis during 1956–57 led to widespread disquiet and hostility in the ALN ranks.[22] During 1956 the ALN began to recruit qualified nurses or women with medical experience into the maquis, and this flow was increased after May 1956 by lycée and university students who followed the FLN appeal for a boycott of the educational system, and during 1957 by militants who fled Algiers to escape imminent arrest. Many of these educated women were profoundly shocked by the conditions of extreme hardship and backwardness they found in the interior, but in turn many of the army officers and rank-and-file treated them as unwelcome guests, especially as they presented a threat to the traditional gender roles and rigid sexual segregation that reigned in peasant society and in the universe of the male warrior. A high percentage of the ALN force was constituted of illiterate men, simple but tough combatants who were immersed in the misogynist, patriarchal values of traditional rural society, and in whose eyes single, un-chaperoned women presented a kind of scandal and a disturbing sexual temptation to all men. The success of the French army 'complot bleu', by which they led the paranoid ALN leader Amirouche to believe in a plot to send students and urban intellectuals as agents into the maquis, created widespread suspicious towards the self-assertive, educated and often middle-class young women who were now in their midst.[23] To this was added the distrust of the rough maquisards, the peasantry and clerics towards the city, a place which they associated with the soft living, decadence and sexual dangers of the west. Even Baya Laribi, toughened after a year in the maquis, came to share these perceptions and was hostile to the wave of young women who arrived in the *bled* in 1957: 'They were well dressed, with red varnished nails, pretty shoes, nicely cut trousers, and wore brassieres'.[24]

ALN officers, faced with this unwanted intrusion, frequently felt that it was the duty of the army to act as a surrogate guardian and to impose draconian regulations on the *moudjahidate*, particularly their segregated sleeping arrangements. In Wilaya I it was ordered, 'it is forbidden to nurses to introduce themselves and to sleep among the combatants. They must only keep company with civilians and only with women. Brother Mekki Hihi is in charge of the nurses'.[25] In some regions, notably Wilaya III, women were subjected on arrival to a degrading virginity test, although some strongly resisted this.[26] A circular sent out by a zone council in Wilaya II in late 1958 noted, 'it is formally forbidden for any women to join our ranks; if they should join us, they must be forced back to their place of origin, even if they are captured by the enemy. Those who accompany these women must be punished with the death sentence'.[27]

However, some *moudjahidine* noted that, after an initial shock or surprise, many of those who were hostile or disturbed by the presence of young women gradually came round to accept the valuable role that they played. Yamina Cherrad's experience was quite typical:

> The main problem was the refusal by many of the maquisards to accept our presence. There were some who took us for girls who had come to get married; they could not understand that we also wanted to be militants and to work. Some intellectuals took this in a good way. Others were astonished or intrigued. But certain soldiers were scornful, they tried to assert their superiority, their strength in relation to us. Later, with the passing of months, they came to recognise our worth, especially during a skirmish or on operations.[28]

During 1956–57 in areas controlled by more liberal commanders there were signs of a proto-feminist discourse as in *Renaissance Algérienne*, a publication of Wilaya III. If the 1 November 1954, noted the journal, rang 'the toll bell of colonialism in Algeria, it also marked a new era in the Liberation of women . . . It is no exaggeration to say that nothing could be achieved without their aid'. Women, the 'key-stone of all human societies', had achieved a new level of political consciousness and self-confidence, and recognised, 'that to fight for the Liberation of her country was to fight for her own Liberation . . . The hub on which we will build the Algeria of tomorrow'.[29] As another document of 1957 proclaimed, 'A people among whom women live on the margins of national life is only a half of itself. It is atrophied. Much more serious still, it slides slowly and surely towards a certain death'.[30] However, the *moudjahidate* were invariably required to fulfil traditional gendered support roles as nurses and aids to male fighters, and they were never granted a position within the military gradation of ranks or placed in authority over men. For example the first woman doctor to reach the maquis was Nafissa Hamoud, but when the less experienced Mustapha Laliam arrived he was immediately promoted over her as chief doctor of Wilaya III.[31]

In contrast to the uncomfortable relationship between ALN soldiers and the urban *évoluées*, there is little, if any, evidence that the presence of peasant women (*moussebilate*) was found disturbing or problematic. These illiterate and anonymous women, who at great personal risk provided a global support function that was even more vital for the maquis than the *moudjahidate*, conformed quite 'naturally' to the everyday role that they had always fulfilled in peasant society, carrying wood and water on their backs, preparing food, washing and drying clothes and showing the customary forms of deference to men (reserve, avoidance of eye contact, not speaking unless spoken to, eating apart).[32] The women from the city, educated and more vocal, presented a different challenge to men who were in many instances illiterate, shared a highly patriarchal mind-set, and, imbued with the teaching of religious leaders, viewed the distant city as a place of moral and sexual corruption.

The relationship of ALN fighting units to women in local society was in some instances violent and abusive. ALN units were constantly on the move within the rural-mountain zones, or deployed to carry out missions in distant locations, and the sometimes predatory attitude to women arose in part from the fact that soldiers, far from their home territory, were prepared to act like an army of occupation in their treatment of local populations. For example, Kabyles fighters often carried out raids against the MNA to the south of the Kabylia massive during which the Arab population, suspected of supporting the enemy, was treated with a brutality that was accentuated by regional, cultural and linguistic difference. One ALN report denounced its forces in the Nemenchas as 'a kind of tribal band rather than units of the national army', while elsewhere two cadres were denounced for calling the inhabitants of a village to a meeting where they insulted the women in front of the men, inciting one woman to protest, 'Colonialism comes and tortures us during the day. When you come we are pleased, but you also torture us'.[33] Some maquisard seem to have operated like war lords exercising a *droit de seigneur* over women,[34] but the oft-repeated stories found in the French media of commanders using young women as sex-slaves, until their happy escape to the French side, need to be treated with caution. However, the ALN practiced a classic double-standard in punishing sexual misdemeanours, one order in Wilaya V indicating that those men found guilty of rape should not be beaten or executed, but be given 'a lesson in morality'.[35]

Women and political organisation

Despite the highly subordinate position of women within the FLN, there is some evidence of their beginning to move towards a more structured women's organisation, although their political and social activity was largely restricted to propaganda and educational work aimed at other women. The pro-communist UFA and the Messalist AFMA (chapter 1) had been dissolved in the early stages of the war, and the president of the AFMA, Mamia Chentouf, was expelled from Algeria.[36] There is little evidence of the AFMA 'going underground' and providing a degree of continuity with the generation of militants (*moudjahidate*) that became prominent within the FLN during 1956–57.[37] Djamila Bouhired,

Hassiba Ben Bouali and Zohra Drif organised meetings of women during the general strike of January 1957 on the terraces of the Algiers Casbah to persuade them of the need to continue the struggle.[38] This group was moving towards the idea of a more elaborate clandestine women's network when they were arrested. When Zohra Drif was finally tracked down by the parachutists in the Casbah, they were able to capture documents relating to this new structure, and Colonel Godard, through close interrogation, was able to build up a detailed picture of the proposed organisation which was to consist of 356 militants arranged in a classic network of clandestine cells.

According to Drif a number of cells were to be grouped together, each unit specialising in particular tasks: one group to counter the SAS by undertaking various forms of welfare work (aid to poor families and the sick); another to carry out propaganda and detect informers; one to locate and register individuals or families related to killed, tortured or disappeared militants and to provide assistance; others to act as messengers for the FLN network. The groups were to meet regularly once a week in each quarter for political discussion, or to listen to and debate FLN radio broadcasts from Morocco and Tunisia. The first direct action planned was to be a silent demonstration by women on a Friday at the traditional places of female association, the central mosque and the cemetery, as well as outside the General Government building, to protest against 'the death sentence passed on the two DJAMILA' (Bouhired, Bouazza), and also the imprisonment, execution or disappearance of husbands, brothers and sons.[39] Drif's plan showed clear continuity with the forms of action undertaken by the UFA and AFMA between 1945 and 1954 which centred on social welfare support and demonstrations against the arrest and imprisonment of male nationalists (chapter 1). In the later stages of the war the perimeter of prisons in both Algeria and France continued to provide a focus where the relatives of prisoners could meet in solidarity to protest, sometimes synchronised with hunger strikes by inmates.[40] Djamila Briki recounted how demonstrations developed outside the Algiers prison of Berrouaghia, and on one occasion a refusal to allow visitors triggered off a riot: 'From the barracks next door to the prison the soldiers unleashed their dogs on us and tried to disperse us. Our veils were torn by the dogs, but we did not budge. We threw stones at the prison gates'.[41] The enormously strong emotional bonds between mother and son in Algerian culture,[42] provided a powerful resonance to FLN propaganda and martyrology that depicted the heroic mother as a person who was transported by a superhuman courage in confronting, in the search for a lost son, the brutal parachutists and torturers of the French army. However, it is noticeable that even the most militant of women continued to see their own role primarily in terms of their nurturing and maternal function, a duty to support heroic sons and husbands.

In the rural areas the educated militants played a rather different function as political propagandists (*morchida*) who, when free from nursing *fidayines*, went into the surrounding villages to make contact with local peasant women and to raise their political consciousness. An ALN circular from May 1957 reflected a new stage in the planned organisation of 'women combatants'. The women, who were first to receive medical training at Wilaya level before serving in field hospitals or infirmaries, were also to assist local civilian women: 'the female combatant plays a social and political role in relation to her sisters', acting under the guidance of political commissars. In the first task, which had an unmistakable similarity to the ASSRA, she was 'a veritable social assistant working in the service of the Algerian woman. She must give useful advice to the latter, assisting her to manage the household, to raise the children, and to respect the rules of hygiene'. In the second, political role the task was to educate women on the current situation, explain the nature of the ALN and FLN and the aims of the 'Algerian Revolution', be prepared to answer all questions and act as a role model.[43] French intelligence officers in the Nord Constantinois, in an analysis of this captured document, noted that a drive was already underway to recruit women in Wilaya II where Messaoud Bouali had plans to incorporate fifty women into Mintaqa I. These women were not merely nurses, but 'veritable political agents' and, 'we are seeing, in this domain, a development that it is advisable to watch very closely'.[44] The FLN was concerned at the appearance of the ASSRA that were first tested during the experimental Operation Pilot from 26 January 1957 onwards, and the ALN creation of similar female cadres two months later may well have been a response to this challenge.

Oral evidence by participants in the new organisation is plentiful: Khadra Belami, for example, an eighteen-year-old *médersa* student who joined the maquis of Wilaya II in January 1957, recounts:

> We held numerous discussions with the population. We explained to the women what the revolution was since they had no links with the town and knew nothing about it. We explained to them that the revolution was being made to liberate the country, so that we could live free and so children could go to school. In addition we gave them educational lessons and in the health-care of their children. For example, they did not wash their infants until they were two years old, for fear that they would die.[45]

Malika Zerrouki, who was only fifteen when she joined the maquis in April 1956 to escape arrest, was taught nursing skills by Dr Si Ali: 'I would go out one or two hours walking distance to care for the women and children and to give vaccinations when we had received some. I tried to teach them the elementary ideas of hygiene, I spoke to them about the emancipation of women, about the Algeria of tomorrow'.[46] The young assistants from the city were shocked by the heavy burden of work of the peasant women, not only in raising numerous children but also labouring in the fields or tending livestock, while waiting hand-and-mouth on their husbands. In some instances they were prepared to challenge traditional gender roles. Yamina Cherrad recounted: 'When I tried to give the men some advice about this, they told me to look after my own affairs. But the women adored us'.[47] Fatiha Hermouche gained the trust of women in one hamlet, even learning Kabyle, and discussed the problems which they faced as women. The inhabitants agreed to swap roles for one week, the men undertaking the heavy tasks of carrying water and wood, while the women took care of the house, but after only three days, 'the women missed going down to the spring and the discussions and, finally, everyone resumed their usual occupation'.[48]

Finally, a quite exceptional use was made by the head of Wilaya V, Abdelhafid Boussouf, of a small group of highly trained women agents who were sent in eight mixed teams consisting of one man and one woman, to carry out clandestine investigations of the ALN organisation in each zone. Six of the eight agents (*contrôleuses*) were lycée students and activists in the Oudja section of the *Union générale des étudiants musulmans algériens* (UGEMA) and two were lycée students from Tlemcen.[49] After an individual interview by Boussouf, who was to gain a sinister reputation as the organiser of a powerful police and intelligence apparatus,[50] the recruits received a two-month training in the history and organisation of the FLN, guerrilla tactics, report writing, the use of small arms and other agent skills. Malik Hadjaj was given the task of reporting on MNA activity in Tlemcen, but the general mission of the teams was to report on the structure of the FLN organisation, the morale and combative state of militants, relations with the people and their morale, the state of welfare provision, and receptivity to French propaganda.[51]

The women controllers were also given the special task of investigating 'the feminine world in general', and to engage in political work among the local women. Rachida Miri noted:

> Above all we had to motivate the women. We listened to what they had to say and, among other things, gave them lessons in hygiene. In fact to some extent we carried out the same work as the French. It was necessary to thwart the French agenda and especially of the SAS. During our training

programme Boussouf repeated that the FLN was entrenched in the people, 'like fish in water: if the water was drained, the fish die'.[52]

The agents under Boussouf's direction carried out social and propaganda work that was in many respects like that of the *morchidate* in other Wilaya, but in their training and mission there is a sense of the way in which women controllers were being deployed as part of a highly efficient and centralised apparatus to police the ALN internally, rather than to forward a progressive emancipation agenda.

Marriage and the FLN couple

As has been seen in the previous chapter, the personal status law provided the fundamental touchstone in relation to women's rights and social position, the core site in the contest over modernity, national identity, cultural resistance and patriarchy. This section explores the extent to which the FLN, particularly in the internal maquis, made any impact during the course of the war on the deeply embedded sociocultural, economic and political practices relating to gender, the relative functions and power of men and women, and the overall emancipation of women. FLN regulation of marriage, divorce and relations between couples provides the best evidence of how it translated policy into concrete practice.

Despite the fierce puritanical and authoritarian opposition by many commanders to relationships between soldiers and women in the maquis, in some regions, most notably Wilaya II and IV, more secular and liberal leaders created a climate that was sympathetic and open to the presence of women and, almost inevitably, strong attachments grew between them and the soldiers. The unusual conditions of the maquis, in which young men and women were removed from the influence of the family, which usually controlled liaison, meant that companionate relationships could develop based on mutual love.[53] Local commanders, who acted virtually as guardians, were constantly having to decide how to respond to requests from rank-and-file soldiers (*djounoud*) for permission to marry. A very detailed 1959 directive on marriage in Wilaya IV shows how some of these issues were regulated: the soldier should ideally marry a woman from a family of '*moudjahidines* and Martyrs', must have at least one year of service in the maquis, be of exemplary morals, and make his request via the military hierarchy.[54] There are some indications in the order of a liberalisation of marriage arrangements, perhaps in response to the French reforms of 1959. While the 'act of marriage will be, taking account of the conditions of war, in conformity with the principles of Islam', the traditional bride-price should be kept to a minimum and symbolic sum. The minimum age of marriage for women was set at sixteen years, one more than under the French law, and the maximum age gap between spouses was set at fifteen years. While it was acknowledged that the woman's decision to marry was still under the control of the parents or guardian, who would be consulted where possible, it was also necessary for women to give their free consent. Although the couple was allowed, where possible, a honeymoon of one week, after that the wife was not allowed to accompany her husband in the maquis.[55] Each zone was allowed to grant permission for a maximum of ten marriages per month, but this might be reviewed or stopped in the future if the arrangement caused problems.

How did such orders work out in practice? Yamina Cherrad faced no opposition: 'I was married in November 1960 with Doctor Benaceur. Permission was given to us quite readily',[56] although she went on to indicate the difficulty of sustaining a marriage relationship under the conditions of guerrilla warfare. A month after the marriage her husband was posted elsewhere and was killed in 1961. Yamina was pregnant and for the birth she was sent from the maquis to stay with people in Djijel, 'I did not know them, they welcomed me into their home, I gave birth and rejoined the maquis with the infant two months later. I worked in the infirmary as before. I was well regarded'. Up until late 1957, when the ALN was able to maintain control over large areas of the interior and to establish relatively secure bases, commanders seem to have been more prepared to accept the presence of married couples. After this, as the Challe offensive made for permanent insecurity and the *moudjahidate* were ordered to retreat across the border into Morocco or Tunisia, regulation appears to have become more draconian, as in an order of July 1960 in Wilaya III, 'the maquisard who gets married without authorisation from the ALN and without the knowledge of the people will be executed. If the marriage was not authorised but was concluded according to Muslim law, the person concerned will be condemned to one month prison and then moved elsewhere. Non-commissioned officers and officers will face the same penalties'.[57]

The conditions for relationships to develop between couples within the ALN maquis were exceptional compared to those found in peacetime society. The controlling hand of family males was absent and the ALN commanders acted in *loco parentis* to assume the role of guardian in deciding who could marry and to ensure that the normal interests of patriarchal regulation were respected. The FLN, in its attempt to create a counter-state, also established its own juridical and bureaucratic system to regulate marriage, family law and a civil register for the entire

Algerian population. The Soummam Congress of August 1956, the first opportunity since the start of the war for the FLN to create a coherent organisational structure, showed a clear intent to regulate family life through welfare provision, especially monthly allowances for the families of ALN soldiers, or the dead and imprisoned, as well as by a system of local courts.[58] The judicial system in the rural areas operated at two levels, that of elected *Assemblées du people* in the villages or committee of five (referred to by the French as the OPA) which settled minor issues, and through peripatetic military tribunals for more serious offences.

As the ALN gradually expanded and established its control over new areas of the *bled* it frequently asserted its authority over the local population by integrating existing political leaders, such as the council of village elders (*djemâa*) or tribal heads.[59] This tactic extended to the integration of traditional religious leaders (*imams, talebs, cadis*, educated *Ulemas*) into the OPA structure precisely to oversee and direct areas of local life to do with family law, justice, religious practice and education. A report from the SAU of Clos-Salembier in April 1960 found that the *Ulema*, although constituting only 2 per cent of the OPA, were to be found at all levels of the organisation administering justice: 'In relation to religion they are opposed to any evolution. The fines imposed by the *Ulemas* on those who infringe Koranic regulations are always very heavy'.[60] This conservative application of customary Islamic law is confirmed by other FLN orders, like one sent out in Wilaya III in late 1956 or 1957: 'The heads of the religious foundations (*biens habous*) will watch over the rigorous application of the laws and regulations contained in Muslim jurisprudence when they have to resolve affairs relating to marriage, repudiation, etc.'.[61] This suggests that the FLN, instead of sweeping away the older generation of religious leaders in order to install a new revolutionary order of progressive and more secular justice, integrated them and in doing so maintained at the grass-root level a seamless continuity with pre-war custom and practice.

This conservative ethos was also evident at the higher levels of the FLN judicial system. The minutes of a meeting (*majlis*) of justices (*cadi*) in Wilaya I in October 1960 reaffirmed the practice of the dowry, widely condemned by modernisers, setting this at 6,000 to 30,000 francs. In went on to support early marriage at puberty as an Islamic check on illicit sex: 'Marriage of young girls without a spouse (virgins and older girls). To put a stop to the debauchery that is tending to become generalised, the *majlis* has decided that every effort and honest means should be employed to marry young girls who are still without a husband, especially those who fear marriage or who give themselves over to debauchery'. It was agreed not to accept any accusation of rape brought by a women unless this could, according to the Koran, be confirmed by four witnesses, in the absence of which the accuser would receive eighty lashes of the whip.[62] The fierce puritanical justice of the FLN was reflected in the harsh treatment of moral, and in particular, sexual delinquents. One ALN directive ordered to 'kill all women and men who lead an evil life',[63] and adultery was on occasions punished by execution, including the case of one man who, 'slept with the wives of soldiers and civilians. He would wink at every woman he passed by. And he was a major informer. He was executed by judgement of the ALN'.[64]

The FLN decision to surrender religious affairs and justice during the war to the clerics was to have long-term consequences for women's rights, and set the scene for the conservative policy adopted after independence (chapter 11). However, as Gilbert Meynier has shown, FLN policy and practice at the Wilaya or local level was far from monolithic and a more modern idea of marriage can be found in some areas. Yamina Cherrad remarks how the female propagandists in the ALN spread a more enlightened model of marriage: 'The dowry was limited and it was forbidden to force a girl to marry somebody who was much older than her'.[65] Perhaps nowhere was the potential shift towards a modern concept of the couple more marked than in France. Algerian labour immigrants had been arriving in France since the first decade of the twentieth century and, through their close contact with the French proletariat and urban life, had some experience of European life-styles and culture. In Paris by the 1930s some 10 per cent of all immigrants were married to, or cohabiting with, European women.[66] During the War of Independence the number of Algerian women in France increased dramatically as they fled the violence and resettlement of the French army, and this meant that young immigrant men and women could escape the conservative restraints of family and society in Algeria. However, the FLN *Fédération de France* sought to impose its political and moral authority over the immigrant community, to create a disciplined and autonomous 'counter-state' that would segregate Algerians from attempts by the French police and authorities to control them and to gain intelligence.[67] This included a system of *Comités* or *Commissions de Justice* that regulated all matters of disputes between Algerians, and supervised marriage and divorce. Internal FLN documents, for example, record the celebration of marriages, the payment of fines for unauthorised marriages, and attempts by the Paris *Commissions de Justice* to reconcile couples before they had recourse to divorce: 'Rue Polenceau: Dissension between spouses. Settlement not being possible, divorce was pronounced', and 'Rue des Partants: Divorce pronounced between spouses: a 5,000 Fr. fine'. The Lyons *Comité de Justice* in March 1960

even recorded a 1,000 Fr. fine on a polygamous Algerian who had failed
the Koranic duty to treat wives equitably, and intervened in the case of a
man, 'whose wife has left him and we gave her a warning and made her
return to the conjugal home'.[68]

FLN emigrants struggled, in the absence of religious authorities and
their guidance, to regulate themselves and apply a legitimate interpretation of Islamic law by reference to the Koran. In the autumn of 1959
the anti-terrorist police seized in outer Paris (Seine-et-Oise) a copy of
a detailed FLN instruction to the *Comités de Justice* on how to adjudicate on matters of marriage and divorce, the *Règlement concernant
les marriages et le divorce suivant le droit musulman*.[69] These liberal
regulations appear to have been influenced by the debate surrounding
the new marriage and family code passed by the colonial government on
17 September 1959 (see chapter 8). In particular the *Règlement* insisted
on the ideal of companionate marriage, the happiness of the domestic
circle depending on, 'the good will of the two spouses and their good
relations'. Both women and men, it stated, must give their free consent
to the alliance: 'Above all marriage must be a union based on affection, and agreed together and with complete accord between the two
fiancée and with their reciprocal consent'. The *Règlement*, as in the
case of the Ordinance of 4 February 1959 which required the couple to
attend in person before the officer of the *état civil*, required bride and
groom to appear before the president of the *Comités de Justice* who
would interview both to ensure that neither had, 'undergone any pressure or threats on the part of their parents or guardians . . . All unions
carried out against the will of the young man or the young girl is strictly
forbidden'. The dowry should be quite nominal, not more than 5,000
Fr., and gifts limited. Husbands who used blows or violence towards
their partners would be severely punished by the Committee. Husbands
should not resort to repudiation or divorce without careful consideration and should refrain from appropriating the dowry that was the legal
entitlement of the wife.

Although the *Règlement* contained some quite conservative or conventional formulations, for example that the spouse must 'keep the
honour of her husband intact', there are clear indications of a grass-
roots evolution of emigrant society towards a new model of marriage
and the family.[70] But at the same time this process was being neutralised
by a growing debate within the FLN, inspired by religious conservatives, who attacked the widespread existence of mixed marriages with
European women as a threat to the integrity of Algerian culture and
identity.[71] The debate on mixed marriage, which began to assume
a racist and defensive tone, was to fuel a highly negative current of

opinion within post-independence society that supported the status quo on Muslim women by extolling them as the pure guardians of Algerian identity.[72] In the *Règlement* there are signs of this male agenda to guard the moral purity of the nations women and mothers: 'It is formally forbidden for our compatriots to live in debauchery with our Algerian sisters or to keep them as mistresses'. This puritanical ethic sat rather uncomfortably with the fact that the *Fédération de France* raised huge sums of money through the *spéciaux*, the taxing of petty criminals, pimps and prostitutes. One wife of a bar-owner was recruited by the FLN to organise and lead twenty women, all prostitutes, divided into four cells whose job it was to carry out the monthly collection in the red-light districts of Barbès, Pigalle, Clichy and the Champs-Élysées. The women also acquired guns and bullets from clients, notably American service-men from a base in Orleans.[73]

Demobilisation of the *moudjahidate* from the maquis

In late 1957 and early 1958 the ALN began to remove most of the *moudjahidate* from the maquis, a decision that was to mark a shift away from a more open or innovative policy towards women towards a reassertion of male authority. But, as will be seen in the following section, this left the FLN in a weakened position to counter the EMSI and women's circles at the very moment they were being rapidly expanded after May 1958. From October 1957 onwards the Wilaya commanders took the decision to remove, apart from some exceptional individual cases like Mimi Ben Mohamed,[74] all the nurses and to integrate them back into civilian life in the towns or across the frontier in Tunisia and Morocco. Courrière reports that in Wilaya III this decision was made by Colonel Amirouche at a meeting on 22 October 1957, in an attempt to prevent the tensions created by the fact that some soldiers were allowed to marry nurses, while the rank-and-file had to suffer sexual abstinence or faced execution for sleeping with peasant women.[75] While this was certainly a problem, for example Omar Oussedik was criticised for keeping his wife, Nassera, in the maquis,[76] the primary reason for this change in policy was a significant shift in the nature of the war.

Until 1957 the ALN was able to create quite stable bases or safe zones, including infirmaries, in the mountain villages, so that the *moudjahidate* had a reasonably comfortable, if austere life which they shared with local peasant women. This phase appears to have been one in which it was easier to segregate the nurses, especially in their sleeping arrangements, from the ALN soldiers. However, after Operation Pilot the French army began to pursue a much more aggressive policy of using commando units to harass the ALN in its redoubts and this forced the ALN to abandon static positions close to villages for a constant movement between concealed caves and hide-outs.[77] The constant forced marches, often over long distances at night, were physically exhausting for the fittest of men, and it became clear to the FLN command that few women could cope with the desperate conditions faced by ALN units. Although no central FLN order has been found, it seems likely that such a decision to withdraw women was made since several Wilaya moved in the same direction: Wilaya V at a meeting of 2–7 October,[78] Wilaya III on 22 October, and Wilaya IV in 'late 1957'. Azzedine notes in his memoirs that the nurses were withdrawn by Wilaya IV because of the exhausting physical conditions and growing danger that units faced,[79] and Kheira Bousafi agrees, 'Towards the end of 1957 the brothers called us to a meeting and told us that there had been too many skirmishes, that things were too tough, and that we were going to depart for Tunisia. We cried saying that we wanted to stay with them. But they refused'.[80] By early 1958 most women had been withdrawn, apart from a few, mainly in Wilaya II, IV and V, who showed exceptional resilience and fulfilled particularly valuable work.[81] Baya Laribi was one of the very few who could have stayed, but she admits the conditions were too tough, 'I was too tired, I couldn't carry on'.[82]

However, as ALN units retreated into the mountains away from their provisioning base in the villages, there appeared a rather contradictory practice of recruiting young and extremely tough mountain women (*amilate*) to move constantly with the soldiers to cook bread and wash clothes.[83] Perhaps peasant women were regarded as physically tough unlike the effete women from the towns, but as has been seen, the rural women presented little challenge to customary gender relations, and conservative commanders were eager to seize on any opportunity to marginalise the troublesome *évoluées*. Wilaya II issued an order in December 1958 that any women joining the ranks would be sent back, even if they risked arrest by the enemy, and any males accompanying them were to be executed.[84]

That the door had been firmly shut on any open or progressive agenda was made clear by the subsequent fate of the nurses and auxiliaries who were evacuated across the border to Tunisia and Morocco, and immediately disciplined to conform to traditional gender roles. Malika Zerrouki recounts how she crossed into Tunisia in a group of about fifteen women from Wilaya IV who were then abandoned in a villa: 'there was nothing for us to do, which was really annoying. We could not go out, no kind of life, and this went on for a long while, for some seven to eight months'. The young women, who had gained a strong sense of independence in the maquis, complained bitterly and were locked up in a cellar until rescued by Colonel Ouamrane.[85] That this was no accident can be confirmed by identical events in Morocco: when Michel Launay visited the refugee camps in Oudja in the summer of 1961 he found that the *moudjahidate* had been virtually claustrated in a kind of boarding house, 'The ALN considered itself to be like a father and conducted itself in their case like a head of a traditional family anxious about the reputation of his daughters'. They found it difficult to readjust from the freedom of the maquis to reveiling.[86] The feminist activist Hélène Vandevelde-Daillière was told by her child-minder Sabah how she had joined the ALN in 1957 aged fifteen, only to be evacuated to Oudja where she was one of 108 ex-maquisards, 'locked up like prisoners. We did not even have enough to eat and three of us started a hunger strike to protest. Colonel [Boumédienne] came to see what was going on, and it was me who explained all our demands. He slapped me in the face. That was his reply. I tried to commit suicide'.[87]

Eventually the FLN began to organise structured training programmes for women in both Tunisia and Morocco in nursing, secretarial skills, weapons assembly and radio transmission.[88] In early 1961 the FLN was carrying out a census of all young Algerian women aged fourteen to eighteen years in Fez to progressively enrol them into paramilitary organisations, but this plan does not appear to have come to anything. In general terms Algerian *moudjahidate* found themselves restricted and confined by the powerful hierarchical and severely disciplinary bureaucratic apparatus of the external army (EMG). Even the most well educated and experienced of women were excluded from assuming any significant political role in the FLN. Boumédienne's suggestion that a woman should be appointed to the top executive *Conseil national de la Révolution algérienne* (CNRA) was rejected,[89] and the most prominent women, like Mamia Chentouf, former militant of the AFMA (chapter 1), and Djamila Rahal, were largely restricted to symbolic acts of international solidarity that served the purposes of FLN propaganda such as attending various international women's conferences in Vienna, Copenhagen, Cairo and elsewhere.[90]

There are signs that Djamila Rahal in Rabat attempted to establish an organisation of Algerian women and sent a delegation to discuss the matter with Chawki Mostefaï, a senior FLN diplomat, but this seems to have had no outcome.[91] As Gilbert Meynier notes, the wives of leading army or FLN personnel remained largely invisible in line with the Algerian social norms of excluding married women from the public sphere and preserve of males,[92] an invisibly that contrasted with the political role of the wives of French army officers. From 1958 until the

end of the war the small elite of educated Algerian women was significantly marginalised by the FLN, re-absorbed from the 'heroic' and more
experimental phase of *moudjahidate* engagement of 1956–57, which
most of the male hierarchy came to regard as a threatening subversion
of traditional gender roles, and once again safely constrained within a
subordinate position.

FLN reactions to French emancipation

During the year from May 1958 to May 1959 the FLN found itself
suddenly and dramatically confronted with an aggressive and multifaceted French campaign for emancipation, a propaganda offensive that
included an expansion of the EMSI, the orchestrated unveiling events of
'13 May', the creation of the MSF circles, the extension of the vote to
women in September, and the promulgation of the Ordinance on personal status on 4 February 1959. The French strategy was designed by
the Fifth Bureau to maximise disarray in the FLN by seizing on a latent
contradiction between the growing prominence and liberty of women
militants in urban and rural networks and the weight of conservative
and patriarchal values.[93] The journalist Hansjoerg Kock was fully aware
of the dangers created for the FLN by the French reforms: for the, '
"évoluées women" . . . soldiers, nurses, informers, they take part in the
military struggle hoping that the national Revolution will also grant
them a social Revolution and the benefits of personal liberation. But,
in the heart of the FLN certain strictly conservative forces are opposed
to any kind of emancipation of women'. But, he added, 'it is going to
be difficult for the Algerian rebels to oppose this reform [of personal
status]', since women in the towns have long called for such an emancipation, while young women no longer wore the veil in which they saw
'the detested symbol of a tyranny which is not based on the Koran'.[94]

The ALN inside Algeria was quick to recognise the very real propaganda dangers presented to its own position among both the rural and
urban inhabitants by the French emancipation campaign that could
offer not only rhetoric, but very real material rewards such as medicines,
food supplies and clothing to a desperately poor population. FLN anxieties were revealed in detail in an internal directive, *Propagande et con-
tre-propagande à mener vis-à-vis de la femme musulmane*, which was
found by the French army on the body of an assistant political officer, Si
Boumédienne, killed in the south Oranais on 26 November 1958.[95] The
circular noted that, 'the enemy is proposing to free our Algerian sisters
from archaic traditions that keep her under their yoke. They show a
keen interest in her evolution and do not hesitate to use all means to

hasten her "emancipation" copied on that of the Frenchwoman'. The directive, which instructed ALN cadres how to engage in a planned counter-propaganda campaign, noted that the enemy had two goals: by winning the trust of Algerian women it could get at husbands, brothers and sons, 'the instigators of the Algerian revolution', and secondly achieve important propaganda goals by informing the world of its so-called 'humanitarian task'.

The ALN analysis went on to recognise the sophisticated nature of the French emancipation offensive, how propaganda was tuned to the varying conditions of Algerian women in urban or rural societies. By deploying Muslim women as social assistants who had a close knowledge of local languages or dialects and way of life the army had a better chance of psychological actions that would pierce the vulnerable spots, 'which had the best chance of being effective and gradually succeeding; it exploits maternal and paternal love, the pride of the happy mother that one takes interest in her son'. There was a real possibility that the emancipation agenda would win over women, since they were by their nature susceptible to praise and self-promotion: 'In seeing certain powers granted to her that she did not have before, women, sensitive to this attention, to this interest that is shown in them, will be appreciative and try to impose their opinions inside the household, and will be invited, should this happen, to leave the maquis, to move to *regroupement* camps, to provide intelligence'. The directive provides evidence of the way in which a central theme of nationalist discourse, the idea that the private domestic world of women represented the ultimate bastion of Algerian identity and security, was diffused into the lower levels of the ALN maquis.

The directive then concluded by outlining various forms of counter-propaganda which, in a mirror image of the French campaign, should be carefully adapted to regional or local variations in the condition of women, especially differentiating the more religious societies of the *bled* from the secular urban context. In approaching 'our Bedouin sister', the highly religious and nomadic peoples of the Sahara, the aim should be to remind women of the atrocities, massacres and humiliations imposed by the French, and on the dangers presented to Muslim faith and identity. By agreeing to vote, 'you, Algerian women, you agree to become French, thus to renounce your RELIGION, your COUNTRY . . . you commit yourself to make ALGERIA a French land'. The directive played on the profound populist fear of secularisation, and on one of the great anxieties of rural women that emigration would lead sons and husbands to become 'corrupted' in France, to enter common-law relations with European women, and to break ties with the kin solidarities of

*LANG
(Q?)*
*(1958 FLN
directive)*

home. Equally threatening was the army's educational programme for children through which, 'The enemy teaches them its language so as to de-Islamise them . . . When grown up they will repudiate their parents, marry French women, and will become soldiers to fight for France'.

However, for 'our urban sisters', the better educated and modern women of the towns, the message should be somewhat different and lay less emphasis on the protection of religion and custom, than on the fact that a progressive emancipatory agenda did not have to come from France but was perfectly compatible with the Muslim state once liberated from colonial domination: 'They lure us with the idea of the emancipation of other Muslim sisters in independent countries, like Egypt, Syria, Turkey . . . One does not have to be French to become emancipated'. Finally, it was recommended that the ALN should counter the EMSI and MSF by increasing the vitality of the OPA: political commissars needed to increase their tours of villages to speak to the people, while the material and seductive aid of the French should be countered by parallel operations, the distribution of clothing and money to the needy, and increased activity of ALN nurses.

The Fifth Bureau, in its analysis of this captured document, were ecstatic at this proof of the success of their emancipation strategy and increased its determination to widen the activity of the EMSI.[96] The Bureau in March 1959 circulated extracts from the directive to encourage all the EMSI teams through this evidence of their success.[97] Some of this optimism was warranted since by late 1958 the FLN faced very real difficulty in implementing its own counter-propaganda strategy. The huge, 'steam-roller' offensive of the Challe Plan, combined with the impact of the high-voltage defences along the Tunisian and Moroccan borders in cutting off supplies of manpower and military equipment to the ALN in the interior, meant that the maquis was desperately short of weapons and supplies and was reduced to desperate and continuous long-distance forced marches to survive. This made political and welfare work with local village populations ever more difficult. To make matters worse the ALN decided to demobilise the *moudjahidate* to Morocco and Tunisia, so removing the educated militants who were engaged in political propaganda and welfare work, at the very moment that EMSI and MSF groups were rapidly expanding their activities. Faced with this crisis the FLN appears to have instructed its ex-*moudjahidate* to try and infiltrate the EMSI so as to subvert the French operations from within and to provide intelligence (see chapter 7). But the most direct response of the ALN on the ground to the French emancipation strategy was to engage in compliance terrorism that warned Algerian women to abstain from voting or to boycott EMSI activities, while ASSRA and other social workers were targeted for assassination. However, the ALN in general refrained from using physical violence against ordinary Algerian women for making use of SAS or EMSI welfare: it was too aware of the desperate conditions facing peasant women and their children to try and deny them access to army supplies of medical aid, medicines, food and clothing, and in addition this provided a source of materials that was filtered through to the local maquis.

Finally we need to consider how the FLN decided to respond centrally to the French emancipation agenda through its own public declarations of policy. The most obvious counter, one that was best represented by the work of Frantz Fanon, was to reveal the way in which the French programme was primarily driven by counter-insurgency objectives. However, there was a real danger that a global and all-embracing assault on the French agenda, in denouncing reformism as part of an insidious colonial plot, could end up denigrating the very principle of progressive emancipation and women's rights as alien and anti-national. The remaining part of this chapter examines two key strands in FLN discourse that were used to camouflage its conservative position but which were to carry negative, long-term implications for the post-independence women's movement: firstly, the argument that a programme of women's rights should be put on hold until independence had been achieved, and secondly, the construction of the myth of women as the bastion of Algerian social and religio-cultural identity.

A recurrent feature of wars of national liberation during the twentieth century was the idea that women, who frequently made a huge sacrifice in the struggle, would be compensated with some form of political 'reward' when victory was finally achieved in the form of progressive legislation or socio-political emancipation.[98] The emergency suspension, however, of a clear policy on women appeared to be justified during revolutionary or resistance wars when indigenous forces needed to prioritise the armed struggle in order merely to survive and when the maquis was lacking in any semblance of a state apparatus. FLN propaganda during the war embodied this discursive strategy: liberation from the yoke of colonialism and capitalism would, of itself, create automatically the conditions for female emancipation by restoring the integrity of a non-colonial religio-utopian order. This position carried some obvious dangers in that it proved a useful instrument or cover for *not* having to develop any specific programme, even during the later stages of the war when a fully operational FLN bureaucratic apparatus existed to engage in planning for a post-independence society. However, despite the general refusal to elaborate a blue-print of the position of women in the future socio-political order, FLN documents frequently revealed the mind-set of the leadership, as in a *Notes aux militants du FLN* circulated in early 1957:

> Algerian women living for decades under Medieval material, moral and intellectual conditions constitutes a half of the body of the nation that is almost unconscious.
>
> In consequence, particularly urgent help must be lavished on them, in conformity with the spirit of our National Revolution and the new and numerous demands we face, to prepare them for the tasks of liberation and the construction of the future Algeria within the framework of their natural privileges as wives, mothers, housewives and citizens.[99]

The idea that women in post-independence Algeria would essentially stay confined within their maternal and domestic functions was occasionally affirmed quite bluntly, as by Captain Si Allal in Wilaya V: 'I remind you for the last time that it is forbidden to recruit in the zone, without authorisation, female soldiers and nurses. In an independent Algeria the freedom of the Muslim woman will stop at her threshold. Women will never be the equal of men'.[100]

The claim that the FLN was in no position to develop a cogent policy on women during the course of the war because of the priority and immediacy of armed struggle was flawed since from 1956 onwards it was laying the basis for a state apparatus that by 1958 assumed the form of a Provisional government (GPRA) with a fully-fledged administrative structure. By far the most important foundation was laid at the Soummam Conference held secretly in the interior in August 1956, and this was to provide the only major statement on women until the 'left' Charter of Tripoli on the eve of independence (28 May–7 June 1962).

In the Soummam platform the section *Le movement des femmes* was relegated to the sixth and last place under the heading 'Methods of action and propaganda' after the movement of peasants, workers, youth, intellectuals and liberal professions, and small businessmen and artisans, as if women occupied a separate enclave.[101] Women received the usual accolade as heroic fighters, but their brave sacrifice for the national cause was framed mainly as a form of moral support or succour for the male warrior, 'the moral support for combatants and resistance fighters'.[102] The shining example of female heroism held up, in a display of what Meynier has called an 'everyday Masculine narcissism',[103] was 'the recent example of the young Kabyle girl who rejected an offer of marriage because it did not come from a maquisard'. Overall the Soummam platform represented a step backwards on the position that women had come to occupy in the ALN and it was symptomatic that Ramdane Abbane, the leading ideologue of the FLN, on arriving at Soummam was astonished at the presence of young women who he felt to be 'out of place' in the maquis.[104] As Amrane notes of both Soummam and Tripoli, 'The political texts are clear, the militant woman is courageous and admirable, but she must stay confined within the tasks that are in harmony with her female nature'.[105]

The failure of the FLN to go much beyond grandiloquent, but ultimately vacuous, statements on women's heroic role was reflected in the difficulty that rank-and-file militants had in imagining or conceptualising the post-independence order. Mimi Ben Mohamed, a well-educated militant who achieved the highest position of any nurse in the maquis, recounts the conversations she had with her colleagues about their dreams for the future:

> They each had their little ideas about the future . . . Right, there is the problem of women. In the case of women how was it going to be . . . For example, the beaches . . . some saw private beaches for women . . . On the independent women they were generally not in agreement. Some were against the veil, others were for it . . . We didn't know at all how independence was going to be since we couldn't form a picture.[106]

The absence of a clear political project, the blurred vision restricted to questions of unveiling or a vague utopia based on the segregation of beach swimming, is indicative of the extent to which the FLN had failed to engage in a basic political education of the rank-and-file as to the future position of women. The failure to outline a programme also left the hands of the post-independence regime untied and free to pursue what turned out to be a deeply conservative policy.

Women: the myth of the national bastion

The second and potentially most negative, but insidious strand underlying the FLN failure to conceptualise a coherent policy for women arose from the topos or ideological construction of a 'fortress identity'. The roots of this topos, which were shared equally by Muslim and European intellectuals from at least the 1930s, if not earlier, derived from the recognition of two spheres in Algerian culture and society, the private domestic space of the home which belonged to women and children, and the public sphere of the adult male who represented the family in all external matters. This model derived in part from the classic bourgeois doctrine of separate spheres that became universalised in European culture between the Enlightenment, Rousseau's *Emile* providing a foundation text, and the 1950s. The model crucially essentialised the inherent, and therefore unchangeable, nature of women as nurturing,

(see also Bourdieu)

maternal and sentimental, as opposed to males who were geared to the external universe of physical force, conflict, politics and rational decision making.

From the 1930s onwards the Algerian intelligentsia, particularly the *Ulema*, re-interpreted the western model by idealising the private sphere of the family as a religious space in which women were the guardians of tradition, the transmitters of the essence of Muslim values and identity, through the education or socialisation of children and the future generation. As we have seen (chapter 1) the colonial rulers and the Muslim conservative elites entered into a tacit alliance by which the former would respect the sanctity and autonomy of the religious sphere, defined most crucially as the law of personal status (marriage, divorce), in exchange for the latter quietly accepting the status of subjects without full political rights who would not challenge the colonial order. As the nationalist movement gained strength from the 1930s it, like nationalism in many other 'Third World' struggles of decolonisation, increasingly represented women as the bearers of tradition.[107]

The myth of women as the fortress of religious, cultural and national identity has been widely treated by contemporary historians not as an ideological construct but as an objective, sociological phenomenon that has been used by them as the basis for the understanding of resistance to colonialism. Such interpretations are legion in the analysis of Algerian culture and society, but typical is the comment of Nefissa Zerdoumi that, 'the space of women shrunk to the dimensions of a refuge which was of primary importance to keeping and preserving. Thus women became the guardian of the Algerian-House instituted as a bastion of traditional values against foreign influences'.[108] Frantz Fanon played a key role in the generalisation of this topos among Algerian and European intellectuals, the idea that French military occupation and colonialism since 1830 had profoundly destroyed the structures of Algerian society (tribal associations, landownership, customs) but had failed to penetrate and subvert the last bastion of Algerian identity, the sacred and private sphere of the family. The wisdom of the colonial administrator was phrased by Fanon as follows: ' "If we wish to strike at Algerian society in its structure, in its capacity for resistance, we must first of all conquer the women; we must go and seek them out hidden behind the veil and in the houses where the men conceal them" . . . To convert women, to win them over to foreign values and to tear them away from their personal status, is to gain a real power over the men and, at the same time, to possess the practical and effective means to dismantle Algerian culture'.[109] For Ferhat Abbas also, 'The Muslim woman loves children. As the guardian of moral values, she raises them in the ancestral traditions, the legends and myths. She constitutes the bedrock of the family cell, the dynamic element of tribal life . . . And as she was particularly hostile to European penetration, she concentrated in herself the patriotism and unity of the people'.[110]

Rarely have historians or sociologists attempted to penetrate beyond the myth, to question or challenge this ideological construct. The colonial and nationalist idea of the 'family-as-fortress', rather than being subjected to critical examination, has survived in contemporary political science and sociology as a key interpretative tool with which to understand modern Algerian history. As such, what might be labelled 'Fanonist feminism' has served to reproduce a key element of this discourse: that the essential being of women in a liberated society is to fulfil her domesticated destiny as wife and mother, a destiny made sacred through its core function of guarding the holy nation. Few commentators have stopped to ask what it might mean for any progressive picture of contemporary Algeria if Muslim women should be idealised as the defenders of *algérianité* precisely to the extent that they were isolated from the mainstream of public and political life. It was not necessarily advantageous to the development of a modern society that a key model of basic socialisation and education of the future generation should ideally be placed in the hands of the most secluded, ignorant and un-educated section of society.

The popularity of the formulation of women as the fortress of identity was linked to the sentimental and patriotic theme of wives and mothers as heroic combatants, but at the same time it locked women into the status quo as guardians of the segregated and private sphere of the home, as reproducers and subordinate servants of males. By implication if women should try and encroach on the sphere of men, the public domain of politics, they would risk weakening the walls built around the domestic space which was a guarantee of the purity, integrity and continuity of tradition: emancipation could only be the work of the devil and subversive western design.

Notes

1 The most detailed FLN interpretation of the degradation of Algerian women as almost uniquely due to the impact of the exploitative colonial system is Saadia-et-Lakhdar, *L'Aliénation colonialiste et la résistance de la famille algérienne* (Lausanne: La Cité, 1961).

2 Amrane, *Les Femmes algériennes*, 247, notes the lack of any discussion or document relating to the initial recruitment of women, a process that occurred 'without any prior theoretical reflection'.

3 Meynier, *Histoire intérieure*, 223–37.
4 On the different categories of FLN women combatants see above chapter 6, note 35.
5 Amrane, *Les Femmes algériennes*, 221–5 on press reports during 1956–57.
6 *Ibid.*, 91.
7 Horne, *Savage War*, 184–5; Reid, 'The World's of Frantz Fanon', 465–6, on Hassiba Ben Bouali and Zohra Drif's background as educated women from an upper-class background.
8 Georges Arnaud and Jacques Vergès, *Pour Djamila Bouhired* (Paris: Minuit, 1957), 61; Ighilahriz, *Algérienne*, 45–55.
9 Although less well known, an identical situation existed for women militants in the Moroccan insurrection: see Baker, *Voices of Resistance*.
10 Yacef Saadi, *La Bataille d'Alger*, Vol. 2, 484, refers to Drif as his 'companion in arms'.
11 Amrane, *Les Femmes algériennes*, 112–13. On the Tillion–Saadi meeting see Donald Reid, 'Re-viewing *The Battle of Algiers* with Germaine Tillion', *History Workshop Journal*, 60 (Autumn 2005), 93–115.
12 Sylvie Thénault, *Une Drôle de justice*, 84–8. Jacques Vergès recounted this political and propaganda strategy of the courtroom in *Le Salaud lumineux, conversations avec Jean-Louis Remillieux* (Paris: Michel Lafon, 1990), 178–83.
13 Amrane, *Les Femmes algériennes*, 13, note 1. David Macey, *Franz Fanon*, 431, notes that a film on Djamila Bouhired, *Héroine algérienne* was shown at the Afro-Asiatic Solidarity Conference in Conakry, attended by Fanon and Sekou Touré in April 1960.
14 Simone de Beauvoir and Gisèle Halimi, *Djamila Boupacha* (Paris: Gallimard, 1962), which also includes de Beauvoir's influential article 'Pour Djamila Boupacha' published in *Le Monde*, 3 June 1960. See also de Beauvoir, *Force of Circumstance* (London: André Deutsch/Weidenfeld & Nicolson, 1965), 500–5; Gisèle Halimi, *Le Lait de l'oranger* (Paris: Gallimard, 1988), 352–3; Lee Whitfield, 'The French Military Under Female Fire: The Public Opinion Campaign and Justice in the Case of Djamila Boupacha, 1960–62', *Contemporary French Civilization*, 20: 1 (1996), 76–90.
15 On the abundant literature on the Algiers heroines, see Borrmans, *Statut personnel*, 507, note 126.
16 On the FLN propaganda use of photographs of armed women, see Amrane, *Les Femmes algériennes*, 243–4. Although there are 'official' ALN photographs of uniformed and armed all-women units, there is little evidence that they ever operated. However, many women in the maquis or underground accepted or liked to be photographed by their comrades posed with weapons. In many instances the women are smiling and playful, fully aware of the humorous element in transgressing an ultimate male preserve: see Gervereau and Stora (eds), *Photographier la guerre d'Algérie*, 166; Amrane-Minne, *Des femmes*, 50–1, has a photograph of Kheira Bousafi, rifle in hand, on which she comments, 'I was not armed: in the photo it is a brother

who has leant me his gun. The girls were not really armed, sometimes a little revolver: there were not enough weapons to go round'.

17 Meynier, *Histoire intérieure*, 226; Harbi and Meynier (eds), *FLN: Documents*, 604, 608: among the heroines was a woman 'T', who the day after the execution of her husband by the French, killed a soldier with an axe and seized his machine-gun.

18 Harbi and Meynier (eds), *FLN: Documents*, 612–13, tract of Wilaya IV, 'Appel de l'ALN aux femmes Algériennes'.

19 On these traditions see above Introduction, note 44 and 45; on Morocco see Baker, *Voices of Resistance*, 17–20, 167–8.

20 Najmabadi, *Women with Mustaches*, 221.

21 Launay, *Paysans algériens*, 376.

22 Amrane-Minne, *Des femmes*, 32, gives a figure of 2,000 women joining the maquis.

23 Harbi and Meynier (eds), *FLN: Documents*, 548.

24 Amrane-Minne, *Des femmes*, 78.

25 Meynier, *Histoire intérieure*, 226, minutes of committee for Wilaya I, 22 January 1957.

26 *Ibid.*, 227–30.

27 *Ibid.*, 230.

28 Amrane-Minne, *Des femmes*, 55, interview with Yamina Cherrad.

29 SHAT 1H2461/1, *Renaissance algérienne*, 2 [no date, 1957].

30 Harbi and Meynier (eds), *FLN: Documents*, 648. Wilaya V, 1957.

31 Amrame, *Les Femmes algériennes*, 254; Meynier, *Histoire intérieure*, 227.

32 SHAT 1H2461, the ALN journal *Renaissance algérienne*, 1, published by Wilaya III (seized by the army on 12 December 1957), in an unusual tribute to the peasant women as the unsung heroes of the Revolution, remarked on a change in the strict codes of gender segregation. The women on seeing the *moudjahidines* warmly acknowledged them: 'The most remarkable thing is the break with the old and rigorous custom that forbade women to speak to any stranger to the family circle. Now they do not hesitate to call to the *Moudjahid*, whether it be to offer him a drink or fruit'.

33 Harbi and Meynier (eds), *FLN: Documents*, 204, 245, note 23, 487–91.

34 Meynier, *Histoire intérieure*, 228.

35 Harbi and Meynier (eds), *FLN: Documents*, 448.

36 *Ibid.*, 605.

37 Amrane, *Les Femmes algériennes*, 43, note 2, found that of the 10,949 registered after 1962 as FLN militants, only six were listed as having pre-war political affiliations (two PCA, four PPA-MTLD). This remarkably small number may point to a significant fissure between pre- and war generations of militants, and also a high level of political alienation between ex-communist and Messalist militants and the post-Independence FLN regime. A report of the Ministry of the Interior, 15 December 1955, in CAOM 81F1218, notes that the MNA may have been organising women's cells.

38 Amrane-Minne, *Des femmes*, 139, interview with Zohra Drif.
39 SHAT 1H2583, Organisation féminine de la ZAA, Second Bureau État-Major, 14 October 1957; see also Amrane-Minne, *Des femmes*, 140, for Zohra Drif's comments on the silent demonstrations.
40 On women's demonstrations outside prisons in France see House and MacMaster, *Paris 1961*, 112, 127–9, 233, 240.
41 Amrane-Minne, *Des femmes*, 213.
42 See Lacoste-Dujardin, *Des mères contre les femmes*.
43 SHAT 1H2582, FLN circular of Wilaya II, No. 9, 2 May 1957, found on the body of Said Harane, political officer of the Jemappes *nahia*, killed on 4 October 1957.
44 SHAT 1H2582, Note de Renseignements, 2e Bureau, 7 November 1957. This document is attached to, and provides an analysis of, the FLN circular of Wilaya II, No. 9, 2 May 1957.
45 Amrane-Minne, *Des femmes*, 34.
46 *Ibid.*, 89–90; see also the interviews with Yamina Cherrad and Baya Outata, pp. 58, 82.
47 *Ibid.*, 55.
48 *Ibid.*, 65.
49 Amrane, *Les Femmes algériennes*, 87–9; Ryme Seferdjeli, 'Des femmes dans les missions de contrôle de la wilaya 5 pendant la guerre de libération', in *Aâmal Al-Moultaka Adaouli hawla Nachaat wa tatawor jaïch Al-tahrir Al watani, 2–4 juillet 2005* (Algiers: Publication Ministère des Moudjahidine, 2005), based on interviews with four of the agents, Malika Hadjaj, Aouali Ouici, Rachida Miri and Yamina Chellali. The other four were Samira, Tarik, Khedidja Chellali and Aouicha Hadj Slimane, the last two killed in the maquis. SHAT 1H2582, captured FLN document from the head of Wilaya V to the Captain of Zone Three, 26 February 1957, with instructions on the mission of Yamina [Chellali] and 'Said'.
50 Meynier, *Histoire intérieure*, 336.
51 Amrane, *Les Femmes algériennes*, 87.
52 Seferdjeli, 'Des femmes'.
53 On the evidence of such close relationships, including love letters and photographs of couples, see Meynier, *Histoire intérieure*, 236–7; Harbi and Meynier (eds), *FLN: Documents*, 612.
54 SHAT 1H2582, Directive No. QA-20, Wilaya IV, seized 3 January 1959. CAOM 81F1222, a SDECE note, 18 August 1958, has an identical directive sent from Wilaya V command to the zones.
55 Harbi and Meynier (eds), *FLN: Documents*, 617, letter of Commander Si Mohammed, 17 May 1961, ordering Captain Si Tarik to remove his wife since this, 'appears to us to be damaging to your prestige, to your standing as a conscientious combatant, and to the example you give to all the *moudjahidines*'.
56 Amrane-Minne, *Des femmes*, 61.
57 SHAT 1H1619/1, quoted in Meynier, *Histoire intérieure*, 227–8.

58 Minutes of the Congress of Soummam, 20 August 1956, in Courrière, *La Guerre d'Algérie*, Vol. 2, Appendix, 653–85.

59 Harbi and Meynier (eds), *FLN: Documents*, 619, Instructions on justice, Mintaqa LVIII (South West Oranie), 1956 or 1957 note, 'one must habituate the Tribal Council to render justice, if possible, in the presence of the political emissaries'.

60 CAOM 2SAS60, SAU note, 5 April 1960.

61 Harbi and Meynier (eds), *FLN: Documents*, 586, directive Wilaya III.

62 *Ibid.*, 628–30, minutes of *majlis*, Wilaya I, 10 October 1960.

63 SHAT 1H2582, directive captured 17 April 1957 near Port-Gueydon.

64 Harbi and Meynier (eds), *FLN: Documents*, 628, 631.

65 Amrane-Minne, *Des femmes*, 60.

66 MacMaster, 'Sexual and Racial Boundaries', 95.

67 On the FLN Fédération de France as a 'Counter-state' or society, see House and MacMaster, *Paris 1961*, 61–6; Benjamin Stora, *Ils Venaient d'Algérie. L'Immigration algérienne en France, 1912–1992* (Paris: Fayard, 1992), chapter 19.

68 FLN documents from the private archive of Mohammed Harbi, published in *Sou'al*, 7 (September 1987), 30, 36, 40, 45.

69 The Paris police archives, APP HA/53, SCINA Synthèses quotidiennes, 31 October to 2 November 1959, has the complete text of the *Règlement*; a further copy was sent to the Algiers government, located CAOM 18F122. Borrmans, *Statut personnel*, 499–501, note 106, reproduces the text, but gives no provenance for the document.

70 For a more detailed investigation of the changing position of Algerian women and the family in metropolitan France see Amelia H. Lyons, 'Invisible Immigrants: Algerian Families and the French Welfare State in the Era of Decolonization (1947–1974)', PhD thesis, University of California, Irvine, 2004; and for a later period, Caitlin Killian, *North African Women in France. Gender, Culture, and Identity* (Stanford, California: Stanford University Press, 2006).

71 APP HA/53, SCINA report, 31 October to 2 November, includes other FLN documents found with the *Règlement* which indicated ongoing surveys of the number of mixed marriages. Part of the concern about FLN militants having relationships with young European women was that the latter might be agents of French intelligence (DST).

72 The fullest treatment of the issue was given by the FLN militants 'Saadia-et-Lakhdar', *L'Aliénation colonialiste*, Part 4, 'Émigration et mariage mixte', 145–95, which presented the mixed marriage as a deliberate 'assimilationist' strategy of the colonial power to infiltrate and subvert the integrity of the Algerian family. The increase in the number of Algerian women in France was, they claimed, rectifying this situation and, in line with Fanon's thesis, enabling women to achieve a new revolutionary consciousness and role in the FLN French Federation. But once again this evolution was seen in terms of domestic support, for example undertaking shopping, usually done

by men, so the latter had more time to devote to militant activities. For a later feminist opinion on mixed marriage see Fadéla M'Rabet, '*La Femme algérienne', suivi de 'Les Algériennes'* (Paris: Maspero, 1983 edn), 42–6, 77–80.

73 Amrane-Minne, *Des femmes*, 171–7, interview with 'X'.
74 Commandant Azzedine, *On nous appelait fellaghas*, 297.
75 Courrière, *La Guerre d'Algérie*, Vol. 3, 103–4.
76 Commandant Azzedine, *On nous appelait fellaghas*, 252–3, the problem was resolved by the policy of placing husbands and wives in different units or areas.
77 *Ibid.*, 282–3, 295.
78 SHAT 1H2582, minutes of Wilaya V, 2–7 October 1957, seized by the French army 19 November 1957.
79 Commandant Azzedine, *On nous appelait fellaghas*, 297.
80 Amrane-Minne, *Des femmes*, 52.
81 Amrane, *Les Femmes algériennes*, 250–1.
82 Amrane-Minne, *Des femmes*, 78.; see also Amrane, *Les Femmes algériennes*, 244–5.
83 Amrane, *Les Femmes algériennes*, 85–6.
84 Harbi and Meynier (eds), *FLN: Documents*, 614–5, directive Wilaya II, 15 December 1958.
85 Amrane-Minne, *Des femmes*, 91.
86 Launay, *Paysans algériens*, 351–2.
87 Hélène Vandevelde-Daillière, *Malgré la tourmente. Récit - témoignage* (La Ravoire: Éditions GAP, 1994), 249.
88 SHAT 1585/3*, Second Bureau intelligence fiche on *Organisation féminine à l'extérieur*, 1960–61. Nurses were trained, for example, in several locations in Morocco (Oudja, Larache, the hospitals of Kef and Souk-El-Arba, and by the youth Istqlal at Tetouan), and in Egypt at Alexandria.
89 Meynier, *Histoire intérieure*, 230.
90 SHAT 1585/3*; Borrmans, *Statut personnel*, 508. International solidarity was shown, for example, by the *Ligue de la femme irakienne* that sought permission from the Algerian provisional government (GPRA) for Iraqi women to engage in the ranks of the ALN; see also Seferdjeli, 'Fight With Us', 184–6 on conferences in Vietnam, Albania, Conakry, Bamako and elsewhere.
91 SHAT 1585/3*, SEDECE report, 31 May 1961. Rahal was secretary to the *Bureau fédéral de l'Organisation Scouts Musulmane* in Rabat.
92 Meynier, *Histoire intérieure*, 231.
93 See chapter 2 where the commander of the Operation Pilot had remarked as early as 24 February 1957, that 'The central idea [of Servier] must be the freeing of the masses from poverty and ignorance, and the liberation of women, aims that the FLN by its very nature cannot entertain', SHAT 1H2536/2*.

94 SHAT 1H1147/1, press cutting, *Suddeutsche Zeitung* (Munich), 21 February 1959; for a similar analysis see Serge Bromberger, *Figaro* 18 September 1958, 'Les Femmes musulmanes d'Algérie devant leur destin'.
95 SHAT 1H2461/1. Harbi and Meynier (eds), *FLN: Documents*, 609–12, which reprints this important document, identifies the location as in the region of Béchar, deep in the Sahara, close to the Moroccan border.
96 SHAT 1H2461/1, Fifth Bureau, Étude des 'Directives FLN', 12 February 1959.
97 SHAT 1H2461/1, Fifth Bureau to EMSI, 5 March 1959.
98 On the question of women's rights during nationalist struggle see Jayawardena, *Feminism and Nationalism*.
99 SHAT 1H2582.
100 SHAT 1H1669/1*, quoted by Meynier, *Histoire intérieure*, 230.
101 Minutes of the Soummam Conference, Courrière, *La Guerre d'Algérie*, Vol. 2, Appendix, 676.
102 Amrane, *Les Femmes algériennes*, 251–3.
103 Meynier, *Histoire intérieure*, 229.
104 *Ibid.*, 229.
105 Amrane, *Les Femmes algériennes*, 253.
106 *Ibid.*, 46.
107 See Shirin M. Rai, 'Gender, Nationalism and Nation-Building', in *Gender and the Political Economy of Development* (Cambridge: Polity, 2002); Chatterjee, 'Colonialism, Nationalism, and Colonized Women'.
108 Zerdoumi, *Enfants d'hier*, 38.
109 Fanon, *L'An V*, 19–20; see also Saadia-et-Lakhdar, *L'Aliénation colonialiste*, 151.
110 Ferhat Abbas, *Autopsie d'une guerre* (Paris: Garnier, 1980), 13–14.

10

From women's radical nationalism to the restoration of patriarchy (1959–62)

The final stages of the war from late 1959 until early 1962 saw the most overt and radical phase of women's nationalist activism and evident signs of the failure of the emancipation agenda to make any significant or durable impact on Muslim women. However, this apparent sign of female radicalisation proved to be illusory since at a more hidden, but potent level, it was paralleled during the final years of the war by two developments that in the long term were to carry enormous negative consequences for women in post-independence society. The first of these was the underlying strength and continuity of conservative Islamic religion and culture that was to shape the post-war political order, and secondly, the massive disruption and challenge to patriarchy caused by war-time conditions that determined males at independence to reassert their domination over women and youth with a vengeance.

The failure of the EMSI and the emancipation apparatus

As has been seen throughout this study, the emancipation strategy consisted of a package of different forms of intervention, from unveiling and propaganda campaigns, to mobile socio-medical teams, improved access to schooling for girls, youth training programmes, the joint European–Muslim women's circles, to the granting of voting rights and promulgation of the 1959 personal status law. This emancipation, for a variety of reasons, made very little durable impact on the bed-rock of Algerian society: as Omar Carlier notes, 'If the weight of colonial history is enormous, if the responsibility of the former coloniser for the post-1962 order is not insignificant . . . the internal dynamic of the country is far more decisive'.[1]

The scale of SAS, EMSI and MSF operations was so thin on the ground, under-funded and fragile that they barely scratched the surface of the enormous weight of social and economic problems faced by a desperately poor and traumatised population. The key ideological and transformative intention of the army, to win Algerian women over to a French model of *civilisation*, had little impact since it was associated with the occupying power, and the FLN, which in general terms had mass popular support, directly opposed and countered the enterprise. Statistically the number of women who became associated with the activities of the local women's circles on a regular basis remained infinitely small. For example, most women scattered through the huge territory of the Aumale sector had no circle which they could attend, and those who did, mainly in the small town of Aumale, represented only one or two women in every thousand. Moreover, as it became slowly more evident from late 1959 that an eventual French retreat was likely, so it became more dangerous for young women, as well as for the extended family group to which they belonged, to be seen to become too closely associated with the French. Since women were always regarded as virtual minors, being under the control of males, such association threatened to jeopardise the entire kin group, both in relation to immediate FLN violence and its survival and status in the eventual post-independence order.

It is undoubtedly the case that many hundreds of thousands of women, especially in the *bled*, the camps and urban slums, did have recourse to the welfare operations of the army, especially where the health and well-being of their own children was concerned (treatment of trachoma, inoculation programmes, supply of medicines, food and clothing). The French army misinterpreted the huge queues of women that often came from miles around to attend the sessions of the mobile medical teams as concrete evidence of turning the tide against the FLN 'terrorists' who, it was thought, looked on helplessly. But after the over-optimistic 'revolutionary' phase of emancipation (1958–59), army intelligence reports began to show a much more sober or pessimistic assessment of French influence on Muslim women, and in particular an underlying consensus that Algerians held a highly instrumental attitude to the strategies of 'contact'. Women, it was noted, turned out en masse to gain material goods or services, but increasingly did not even attempt to disguise their lack of interest or open hostility towards ideological propaganda and the broader political goals of the French project. The EMSI of the Oran region reported in December 1960, 'the female Muslim population, especially in the *douars*, is more interested in the small and immediate material benefits they can gain from these contacts and meetings than by the idea of social emancipation that we try to teach them'.[2] The French army, after the radical phase of emancipation, moved towards a more sober assessment that any meaningful transformation of women's lives would require not years, but decades of reform, particularly via the

long-term impacts of universal education. General Challe, in his important directive *Action sur les milieux féminins en Algérie* of March 1960,
noted, 'The evolution of the female milieu is a long-term project since it
involves a transformation of deeply rooted customs. It will be the fruit
of the work of several generations'.[3] However, the time-scale of the
emancipation campaign was at most a mere six years (1957–62), during
the final two years of which the French were merely treading water and
preparing for withdrawal.[4]

The one exception to this pattern of minimal or superficial impacts
of French ideology concerns the numerically very small number of
girls or young women who came from relatively well-off families and
had received a sound education to secondary level. The urban middle-
class elites were deeply divided politically, culturally and linguistically
between a francophone and francophile strata that had been educated
within the French lycée system and were closely tied to the colonial
state as junior civil servants, teachers, lawyers and technicians, and a
class of Arab speakers who, educated in the reformist *médersa* and in
the universities of Tunisia (Zitouna) and Egypt (El Azhar), remained
deeply resistant to French secularism and were often excluded from the
rewards of government employment.[5] One of the tragic consequences
of the Algerian war of decolonisation, which also shared the features
of a civil war, was that the numerically small, educated elite, which was
potentially so valuable to the future independent society, was split down
the middle. The political decisions of young women tended to reflect
their location in families that stood on one side or another of this divide.
The *évoluées* who had received an education within the French system
to secondary or university level, and who had absorbed the intellectual
and cultural traditions of the French humanities and science, and the
universal values that underpinned them, embraced emancipation with
fervour: on the other side stood the 'Arabo-Muslim' nationalists who
fought for an integral Algerian identity. In many respects the two opposing groups shared identical visions of women in the good society, a
modernist future of universal education, access to employment, and full
political participation: but such a potential for unity was over-ridden by
the all-consuming immediacy of the battle for independence or a French
alliance.

Historians, as Ryme Seferdjeli notes, have neglected the study of the
Francophile *évoluées*, not only because they were on the losing side and
therefore of little interest to Algerian and left-wing historiography, but
also because they could be type-caste as traitors to the nationalist cause
and lackeys of the repressive occupying forces.[6] However, this group –
like that of the pre-war JUDMA (see chapter 1) – supported the reformist

side of French emancipation and aspired to a liberal, progressive agenda on women's rights that was not dissimilar to that which was to be later held by many Algerian feminists from the 1980s onwards. The *évoluées*, symbolised by the *Secrétaire d'Etat* Nafissa Sid Cara, did not hold to a militant secularising tendency as the FLN claimed, as puppets of French cultural imperialism, but sought to support a body of reform that was compatible with the Koran and a modern Muslim society through the tradition of *ijtihad* (independent reasoning). However, the *évoluées*, who were viewed by the FLN as 'collaborators', became increasingly nervous as a French retreat approached and which, noted an officer, 'probably means for them a brutal return to an ancestral way of life that they do not want at any price'.[7]

Very little is known about the political fate of this educated pro-French elite at independence: many of those whose families were closely linked to the French army and administration would have departed for France; some may even have been killed by mobs; but the majority probably survived, along with the pro-French families to which they belonged, by either a last minute conversion to independence (sometimes named the *martiens*) or by keeping their heads down. But overall it can be assumed that they were excluded from the official post-independence women's organisations since these tended to promote those who carried the symbolic prestige of FLN war-time militants and who were vetted and registered by the *Ministère des Moudjahidine*.[8] The women's movement post-1962 was considerably weakened by the loss of a significant portion of the tiny class of secondary educated and more politicised women who might otherwise have been expected to play a key activist role.

The radicalisation of nationalist women, 1959–62

The adverse conditions under which the French emancipation campaign began to labour from 1959 onwards can be in part related to a deep shift in the political balance of power away from the French army to the FLN. Relatively little is known about the role of Algerian women during the final stages of the war, in part because the oral evidence gathered by Danièle Amrane and others has been largely based on the testament of the educated *moudjahidate*, most of whom had been killed or arrested by 1958[9] or were removed abroad by order of the FLN in late 1957 and early 1958. As the tide began to turn against *Algérie française*, a process that was marked most clearly by de Gaulle's speech of 16 September 1959 on 'self-determination', and signs increased that the FLN, even if it had lost the military battle, would win an eventual political victory, so the self-confidence of the settler population ebbed away.

Algerian women, especially in the bigger towns, sensing this demoralisation, began to assert an open defiance of the French authorities. For example, on the anniversary of the events of '13 May' the army and government attempted to re-enact the hugely successful Forum mass demonstrations. The conservative newspaper *L'Echo d'Alger* published numerous photographs of columns of veiled Algerian women under the rubric, 'Muslim women come out from the dark. For the first time, their faces revealed, they enter into public life'.[10] But most of the colonial press admitted that the attempt to recapture the heady spirit of May 1958 had failed and Europeans seemed dispirited or lacking in enthusiasm. Most telling of all was the presence of Algerian women counter-demonstrators who had the extraordinary courage, since they ran the very real risk of being lynched, to mount a protest in the midst of tens of thousands of Europeans. One woman waved 'a *fellagha* flag', until it was torn from her hands, while a group shouted 'give us back our prisoners'.[11] In a situation in which Algerian men were absent, often in underground FLN networks or in detention, or in which their open protest would usually lead to arrest or physical violence, women began to replace men in the sphere of public militancy and street demonstrations. The army commander at Tizi-Ouzou reported, 'Very often . . . the male population is happy to maintain a glum passivity while the women show a violent hostility, even attempting to engage in aggression against the forces of order'.[12]

From late 1959 onwards such public signs of protest or disaffection began to multiply. As we have seen (chapter 7), the EMSI and MSF circles were faced with signs of growing and overt political opposition, especially among young women who made clear that their sole reason for attending activities was to profit from material benefits and to gain access to such advantages as sewing machines, clothing and semolina. The army recorded a growing volume of small, but significant acts of resistance: for example, it was not unusual to overhear Algerian women saying to European women, 'We will chuck you out and we will have fine dresses and beautiful houses'.[13] An intelligence report commented, 'the EMSI have noted a deterioration in the climate, much difficulty in getting women to meetings, and think that it is most urgent to deal with the young girls who are more affected by the enemy propaganda. During the organised visits to the beaches (an army chore) they insist on singing in Arabic and when they do, start singing rebel songs'.[14]

Evidence of the extent to which young women, especially of Algiers, were increasingly drawn into militant nationalist activism was provided during the violent street clashes of 10–12 December 1960 which marked, in the words of Ben Khedda, the 'decisive turning-point of the war'.[15] On 9 December de Gaulle arrived in Algeria for a tour of the major cities, but this triggered massive street violence by extreme right-wing settler organisations against both the security forces and the Algerian population. The SAU attempted to orchestrate pro-Gaullist demonstrations by Algerian inhabitants of the Casbah and popular quarters, but this went badly wrong when thousands poured out from the slums waving green-and-white nationalist flags and chanting 'Abbas au pouvoir', 'Libérez Ben Bella' and 'Algérie musulmane'. In the ensuing repression, during which both the *pieds-noirs* and the army fired at the crowds, an estimated 120 Algerians died.[16] The crucial political importance of these four days of rioting lay in the fact that de Gaulle became convinced that *Algérie française* and the integration of the two communities was an impossible dream, and recognised that the FLN constituted a legitimate expression of the popular will of the Algerian people with whom he would need to negotiate sooner or later.

In a society in which women were normally excluded from public spaces and the political sphere arrogated by men, women now came to play an unusually prominent role during these spontaneous mass demonstrations, helping to make dozens of FLN flags, or taking the lead in the advancing columns, dressed in the national colours and galvanising the crowds by singing the Algerian anthem. The SAU officer for the Bas Casbah reported on the 12 December: 'Demonstration Rue de la Lyre, headed by a woman carrying an infant and a rebel flag, dispersed by a charge of the Zouaves (Fifth Company)'.[17] Many of these young women were killed or injured, including a twelve-year-old girl struck by the police while shouting 'Vive l'Algérie algérienne' who later died in hospital.[18] The funeral of this girl was, against the Muslim custom of interment as an all-male affair, organised almost solely by women who turned it into a mass nationalist protest, to which the army responded by further gunfire.[19] Djamila Briki, who took part in these events, explained how the political mobilisation of women in Algiers first developed among the hundreds who gathered daily outside the prisons to bring food and clothing to arrested husbands, brothers and sons, or who attended trials and provided mutual support in the face of execution orders. From this solidarity of women, most of whom were veiled, illiterate and had previously rarely left the confines of the home, emerged a movement that demanded improved prison conditions and visiting rights, and that on occasion resulted in full-scale riots outside the prison gates.[20]

The mobilisation of women during the final stages of the war was in particular a revolt of teenage girls and young married women. Historically, independence or liberation movements, from the Kenyan 'Mau Mau' revolt of the 1950s to the Soweto rising of 1976, have

frequently found a strong support base among the disaffected youth of
sprawling shantytowns, often rooted in youth sub-cultures, street gangs
and anti-authoritarian 'delinquency'.[21] In the case of Algeria, there has
been little research on the links between the nationalist movement and
the rapid increase in alienated urban youth, a consequence of the combination of extraordinary demographic expansion, military deracination
of rural populations, migration of refugees into the northern towns, and
lack of educational and employment opportunities.[22] The reports of
the Algiers SAU provide a detailed picture of growing official concern
at the tidal wave of refugees pouring into the shantytowns and which
was overwhelming attempts to provide welfare, health care, housing
and employment.[23] The FLN-led boycott of schools and subsequent
pupil strikes left thousands of disaffected youths free to congregate in
the street, where they, rather like the Palestinian *Intifada*, harassed the
forces of order or collaborationist demonstrations through stone-throw-
ing.[24] There are indications that teenage girls or young women shared
in this radicalisation of youth and there existed a growing political and
generation gap between them and older, more conservative women. A
Fifth Bureau report noted instances of growing hostility by boys and
girls, influenced by the FLN, towards their mothers for listening to
French propaganda and, 'threaten their mother when she comes into
the house by saying she has been "to listen to propaganda" and they are
happy to think she will be beaten'.[25] When Lieutenant Morel chased and
arrested a girl for carrying a nationalist flag, older women disapproved
of her actions, saying to him, 'Well done, we've had enough', suggesting
a tension between the younger radicals and older women.

    What the older, more conservative women resented was the extent to
which young women, in the absence of males and their authoritarian
control, seized the opportunity to invade public spaces and to engage in
highly expressive acts of militancy. Djamila Briki comments on the demonstrations of 11 December, 'It was a battle by women: there were some
men, especially the young and elderly, but compared to the women one
could count them on one hand. Women were in the majority at Climat
de France . . . it was an explosion: there was shouting, the *you-yous*,
the veils torn up to make flags'.[26] The SAU officer for the Bas Casbah,
Captain Bapst, also remarked on the role of women in his sector,
'Women appeared at the windows and on the terraces. They uttered
violent *"you-yous"* which spread throughout the quarter . . . The demonstrations were made up largely of youths and women: adult male
workers were in a minority'.[27] This spontaneous street action significantly escaped the control of the FLN, which began to fear a dynamic
rank-and-file movement that threatened to challenge its authoritarian

leadership,[28] a challenge that was all the more disquieting since it simultaneously subverted patriarchal authority.

To many journalists and outside observers in the summer of 1962
it looked as if the rising tide of female militancy, the shear energy and
revolutionary élan of the populace, would inevitably result in a radical
transformation of the position of Muslim women in the new society. The
elation of the crowds on independence day, 3 July 1962, that seemed to
promise the dawn of a new age, was captured by a number of contemporary photographers, as in Marc Riboud's picture of a young, unveiled
woman leaning through the open window of a passing car waving the
national flag. She looks straight at the camera, delighted, dark glasses
clutched in her left hand and the caption below reads, 'In the centre
of Algiers women bursting with joy at the prospect of the liberation
of women'.[29] However, as the future was soon to reveal, the nationalist euphoria and energy of mid-1962 did not translate into a vibrant
post-independence women's movement that was able to play a major
political role in the construction of the new Algerian society. Indeed,
Algeria stands today as one of the most remarkable instances of a huge
gap between the often-claimed credentials of a 'revolutionary', 'socialist' and emancipation movement, and the negative, long-term repressive
nature of a post-colonial state that imposed a conservative agenda on
women and imprisoned them as the virtual minors of men. This anti-
feminist politics stood out in even starker relief because Algerian women
combatants had achieved international acclaim as *the* symbol of a fierce
and engaged militancy, the archetypal heroines of anti-imperialism and
anti-colonial liberation. So dramatic was the hiatus between the glory of
the war-time *moudjahidate* and post-independence exclusion of women
from political life that Palestinian women involved in the later *Intifada*
treated Algeria as an exemplary warning of what they should themselves
avoid in their own national struggle.[30]

Why Algeria, which during the 1960s shone on the international
stage as a beacon for anti-colonial, socialist and 'Third World' liberation movements, should have so singularly failed in the area
of women's rights presents a key problematic that has long exercised historians, political scientists and contemporary feminists. To
provide a complete answer would require a further volume on post-
independence Algeria which is beyond the scope of this study. Here
the focus is specifically on the impact of the War of Independence in
shaping the post-colonial order and the long-term failure of a progressive women's movement. The remaining part of this chapter examines
two key elements of the war period that were to carry negative implications for the post-independence order: firstly, the deep continuity

in conservative religious tradition and secondly, linked to this, the disruption of patriarchal family structures which weakened male control over women and which they were determined to reverse once independence was achieved.

K̄s̄v̄ .

The roots of populist Islamic nationalism during the War of Independence

Although many commentators have dated the penetration of radical Islamist currents into the FLN regime from the 1970s onwards, this happened in *some* areas of policy-making from at least 1957–58. Socialist or Marxist interpretations of the Algerian War of Independence as a 'revolutionary' struggle tended during the 1960s and 1970s to underplay the centrality of religion in populist nationalism. FLN documents show that the organisation, wherever it could establish a presence at the local level both in the maquis as well as in the big cities, including Paris, asserted a strict respect for religious practice and a puritanical form of justice based on Islamic principles (*sharia*). Although the FLN assumed a hostile stance towards traditional religious leaders (*imams, sheikhs, marabouts*) who supported the French, and was prepared to assassinate them, it was willing to integrate such men into its own apparatus where possible, especially as they might retain wide influence and prestige among local people. In Wilaya I (south Constantinois), for example, each of the six sub-divisions (Mintaqa) had its own Muslim justice and the minutes of a Wilaya level council of the *cadis* in October 1960 show them making agreement on regulations relating to everything from property disputes, regulation of inheritance and contracts, to issues of marriage, divorce and dowry payments. The FLN *cadis* in Wilaya I exercised a general surveillance over the moral life of the community, 'they lead the people in the path of goodness, stop that which is evil', ensured provision of mosque buildings for Koranic schools and prayer, and recruited *imams* and teachers.[31]

Such a minute regulation of religious life and Islamic justice was not restricted to the illiterate peasant and nomadic populations of the interior, but extended into the shantytowns of the major cities in both Algeria and France. For example, the Paris police captured in October 1959 in Seine-et-Oise an extremely detailed instruction, 'based on the commands of the Holy Koran', to the FLN *Comités de Justice* on how they were to adjudicate on matters of marriage and divorce.[32] In the *maquis* the ALN commanders, many of whom had received a religious education in Koranic schools and *médersas*, often imposed strict religious observance and a rigid control of moral behaviour among both the soldiers and the local population, backed up by draconian punishment.[33]

A number of factors contributed to such a powerful religious culture. Firstly, the origins and long-term evolution of Algerian nationalism, particularly under the leadership of Messali Hadj between 1926 and 1954, was built around a populist discourse and symbolism that was deeply religious. When ALN commanders, who were in many instances of urban origin and education, first arrived in the maquis they came into close daily contact with rural societies that were barely touched by secularism and regulated by age-old customary practices and beliefs. Even the minority of ALN leaders who were personally attached to a more socialist or secular vision recognised that any revolutionary assault on peasant beliefs would be counterproductive. The FLN was far more inclined to adapt its message to the deeply embedded traditional *mentalités* of the peasantry, and the social structures that underpinned it, than to engage in the kind of Bolshevik onslaught on Islam that the Soviet Union unleashed in Central Asia during the 1920s. Indeed, given the enormous difficulties that Algerian nationalism faced in developing a single, binding ideology that could over-ride spatial and cultural fragmentation, the competing loyalties based on region, language and clan endemic in society, religion and the shared community of faith (*umma*) offered the strongest cement.

What this meant in practice was that as the FLN began to infiltrate in the early stages of the war into rural communities where its own position was tenuous it tended to follow a quite pragmatic, rather than overly ideological line in relation to the existing political elites, the assembly of village elders (*djemâa*), and the 'big-men' of the *grandes familles* who carried considerable influence within local clientele and clan networks. Since in the initial stages of FLN penetration into new rural areas the number of ALN militants was frequently very small and fragile in relation to the tens of thousands of inhabitants they were seeking to control, it was more advantageous to co-opt local power-brokers, even when they came from conservative elites (wealthy landowners, *caïds*), than to alienate or assassinate them.

A good example of this process relates to the Ourabah family, the most prestigious and influential *grande famille* in the lower Soummam valley, headed by the ex-deputy Abdelmadjid Ourabah who held quasi-feudal protective powers (*'aiyanaiyya*) over several Kabyles villages. The ALN commander Amirouche tried on several occasions to win the Ourabah clan over to the FLN side, and it was only when this failed that this opened the way to the tragic massacre of Melouza, of villages that were thought to have rallied to the French army or the MNA.[34]

While the ALN was quite prepared to use terrorism against its opponents, in general it preferred where possible to work with pre-existing
political or clan networks: Mintaqa commanders were instructed to use
methods, when making contact with civilian populations, 'stamped with
a total courtesy', including towards any 'member of the *djemâa* or tribal
council'.[35] The model commander of the Wilaya was a leader who should
ensure that his soldiers 'must always respect the people', particularly as
'an abject colonialism' had kept them in ignorance and, '*maraboutisme*,
for example, must be fought intelligently. It is stupid, even criminal, to
treat people roughly'.[36] An ALN report noted that the local five-man
committees which it set up to run village life, the 'People's Assemblies',
tended to be based on the old *djemâa* and, as such, 'are still composed of
wealthy and elderly individuals', or even of individuals 'who in the past
served a colonialism of which the people still carry the scars'.[37] There
are signs of a 're-Islamisation' of Algerian society at grass-roots level as
the poor, faced with an apocalyptic slaughter and destruction, turned
towards a millenarial faith or ecstatic escapism. Mouloud Feraoun
reports, with some irony, how the peasants in his home village of Tizi-
Hibel were impressed by the first mass meetings addressed by an FLN
leader: 'their leader was wonderful. He began reciting from the Koran.
A *fatiha* entirely done in Arabic. You should have heard his pronuncia-
tion, his tone, and his zeal . . . And so, the people of Tizi-Hibel, once the
most villainous on the surface of the earth, have found their faith again;
they are now paying the salary of a muezzin and frequent the mosque
assiduously. God is great!'[38]

It would be a mistake to fall into the trap of assuming a simple
equation between poverty and radicalism, that the more oppressed the
peasantry, the stronger would be their determination to fight against
the colonial system. Although there has been very little investigation
of the class basis of the FLN and nationalist mobilisation in the rural
interior where 80 per cent of the population lived, the evidence suggests
that the core militants came not from the great mass of the landless
poor, but from a strata of slightly better-off independent landowners
and shopkeepers, craftsmen, teachers and petty entrepreneurs who lived
in the small towns and commercial centres of the *bled*. Michel Launay,
in his study of a wine-producing region of Oran, noted hostility between
the category of petit-bourgeoisie that had access to education and the
egalitarian religious ideology of the *Ulema* and provided the cadres of
the FLN, and the mass of impoverished day-labourers who resented
this elite.[39] Eric Wolf noted that poor peasants or landless labourers
have often lacked the tactical power to challenge oppression and were
'often merely passive spectators of political struggles or long[ed] for the

sudden advent of a millennium'. By contrast a more independent strata of middle, 'free' or 'tactically mobile' peasants led the path to revolution. But by a curious paradox this class was also the bearer of tradition and 'it is precisely this culturally conservative stratum which is the most instrumental in dynamiting the peasant social order'.[40]

While at the higher levels of the ALN and FLN a younger generation of militants tended to displace pre-war Algerian political elites,[41] this leadership recognised the shear weight of the conservative religious, cultural and social values that permeated the grass-roots nationalist movement. The Algerian War did not constitute a classic revolutionary movement like that in France in 1789 and Russia in 1917 that sought to sweep away the fabric of the old society. This continuity in the deeper level of culture and the matrix of family and clan life in which it was embedded was to carry fundamental consequences for the position of women.

The war-time challenge to male domination and patriarchy

The post-independence Algerian state prevaricated over emancipation and reform of family law because it recognised the enormous and almost immovable weight of patriarchy, of an embedded system of family structures, sentiment and power that would be difficult to transform without creating dangerous political opposition. Mounira Charrad has, to date, provided the most cogent explanation for the post-independence failure of Algeria to elaborate a family code that would match the needs of a rapidly changing society and bring Muslim women fully into the *cité*. In a comparative study of state formation in the three Maghrebi nations, she argues that the very different outcomes in family legislation between the progressive Tunisian code of 1956, the conservative Moroccan code of 1958, and the peculiar 'stalled' situation in Algeria that lasted until 1984, can be explained by the relative ability of central governments to exert political domination over traditional kin or clan-like bases of power that defended the most conservative readings of Maliki law. Charrad provides a useful macro-level hypothesis for an understanding of post-independence Algeria: the newly formed state showed deep contradictions in its drive to assert national integration over and against localised or regionalist interests, while simultaneously allowing space for kin or clan-based associations which paralysed moves to legislate on family law and to assert control over the private domestic sphere.[42]

Charrad's analysis, while providing a very useful model as a point of departure, remains at a quite general level and does not identify how or why 'tribal' structures were able to remain so powerful over and against the encroachment of the centralising state. What made it possible for socio-cultural patterns of male domination over women, particularly within the family group, to survive through two decades of enormous political and economic crisis and change between 1954 and the late 1970s? Part of the answer to this question can be found in two interlinked phases: first, the massive social disruption of the war dislocated the family group and created a deep crisis for Algerian male virility by temporarily marginalising adults and subverting their 'traditional' role and honour as protectors of women and children. In a second phase that followed independence men, many of whom returned to family life from the maquis, prison camps and French factories, sought immediately to reassert their authority with a vengeance and to restructure patriarchal arrangements.

In the first phase we examine the enormous scale of the war-time dislocation of the family group and its internal structures. The French army programme of 'pacification' involved a massive uprooting of the peasantry from the mountainous interior, the destruction of thousands of hamlets, and relocation into militarised encampments. Between two and three million people, half of the rural population, were definitively torn away from the land and dumped in camps that, in many instances, formed the nucleus of post-war urban settlements (see chapter 6). The General Inspectorate for Resettlement reported how, in response to forced displacement by the army, the population descended like a torrent into the valleys where they were herded into barbed-wire compounds, without even basic housing. 'The people then re-house themselves with relatives or strangers (who hire their filthy huts out at exorbitant prices), are squashed ten to a room, living in a state of promiscuity and disgusting filth . . . such a dislocation of rural society was not foreseen'.[43] In addition a quarter of a million refugees sought safety across the borders in Morocco and Tunisia,[44] or fled the insecurity and hunger of the interior for the shantytowns of the northern literal. The population of some towns doubled in size between 1954 and 1966, including that of Constantine which went from 111,000 to 240,000.[45] Most of this refugee population did not regain their villages of origin on independence since the ties to the land had been definitively fractured, indeed the departure of close to a million *pieds-noirs* during 1962–63 further accelerated rural–urban migration as Algerians moved quickly to occupy empty European properties in the towns.[46] The process of *déracinement* meant that family units were in many instances torn away from the extended kin networks of the village which had in the past structured local, endogamous marriage alliances, and forced into urban zones in which they had to share housing and communal space with strangers.

At the same time displaced family units were stripped of their 'natural' protectors in a time of danger: fathers, brothers and sons. The war was marked by the massive departure of younger, active males from rural society who joined the FLN in the maquis or abroad in Tunisia, Morocco, France and elsewhere, or migrated to the northern cities and to metropolitan France to find employment and to escape violence and forced recruitment by the French army or war-bands (MNA, ALN, Bellounists) that competed for manpower. An approximate estimate indicates that up to a half of all able-bodied men of working age (fifteen to fifty years) would have been either killed or absent from their families for years on end.[47] This meant that in many villages, especially in Kabylia, populations were reduced to women, children and the elderly, a society of 'women without men'. By this term the anthropologist Willy Jansen refers to a key element of Algerian socio-religious culture which regarded celibacy of all adults, but in particular of women, as reprehensible and a threat to good order. Women who lived on their own, or headed households in which adult men were absent, were regarded with suspicion and hostility as a grave danger to the sexual order, and opprobrium extended to the growing number of poor widows and repudiated women who were forced to work as domestic servants, seasonal agricultural labourers, or on the margins of society as prostitutes, bath-house attendants, musicians and washers of the dead.[48]

Although some contemporary observers argued that Algerian women, in the absence of husbands, remained firmly under the power of older males (grandfathers, uncles), most agreed that women had to cope without men and gained experience of a new-found autonomy.[49] Quite typical is a report of the French commander of Azazga in 1959: 'on a large part of the territory villages are practically empty of the active male population, the men being either in France or in the ranks of the rebels'.[50] By 1958 Mouloud Feraoun was noting in his diary how Kabyles women were taking over the kinds of work previously strictly allocated to men, carrying the wounded on their backs, burying the dead, collecting money, standing guard, working the fields. He speculated on signs of a radical transformation of gender roles:

> Perhaps a new world is being constructed out of ruins, a world where women will be wearing the trousers, literally and figuratively, a world where what remains of the old traditions that adhere to the inviolability of women, both literally and figuratively, will be viewed as a nuisance and swept away. This constitutes a form of brilliant revenge for all those peaceful attempts at emancipation that were generally resisted as not at all helpful for the unfortunate woman on the road to liberty. Tomorrow, the

women of Algeria will no longer have any reason to envy other women, except, perhaps, education.[51]

In the second phase that commenced with the coming of independence in mid-1962, Algerian men immediately sought to reassert their lost authority over women, to return to the status quo ante bellum. Part of this was fuelled by a deep psychological *ressentiment* and even revanchism against women that arose from the feeling of humiliation, anxiety and lost honour experienced by many men in their inability to fulfil their protective role towards their wives, daughters and female relatives during the chaos of war.[52] There are close parallels between Algeria and the situation in metropolitan France during the Liberation when men, humiliated and 'feminised' by the defeat of 1940, the *exode*, and mass internment, and challenged by the war-time role of women in the work force and the Resistance, sought to assert their masculinity through the ritual shaving of collaborators (*femmes tondues*).[53] Indeed, since hundreds of thousands of Algerian men had lived through and witnessed the Liberation in France at first hand, it seems likely that the hunting down and violence against Algerian women 'collaborators' in 1962 was a symbolic replay of August 1944.[54] While French men had sought to assert themselves against the super-virility of German soldiers, and then of American GI 'liberators' embraced by young women on tanks,[55] so Algerian men in July 1962 could finally act to erase the experience and memory of Bigeard's crack paratroopers parading machine-like through the streets of Algiers. But in the case of Algerian males the psychological scars of sexual humiliation were far deeper than anything experienced in France because of the way in which a colonial army engaged in actions that represented a deliberate, frontal assault on the fundamental values, the sacrosanct respect of female seclusion and male honour. While the psychological damage of such a subversion could be, to some extent, mitigated by the thought that this was an inescapable fact of war that could be heroically born by the national community, male insecurity was further deepened by the inability of men, in a situation of massive deracination and endemic poverty, to fulfil their classic roles as providers whose duty it was to ensure the well-being of the household (decent housing, clothing and subsistence), the seclusion of women, and obedience to the rules of honour, including avoidance of women's employment.[56]

When the war ended in mid-1962 the desire of most Algerian men was to return to their families, but for hundreds of thousands 'home' was not the peasant house or village that they had last seen but an entirely different location (resettlement camps, shantytowns, urban slums), and the very structure of the family and its kin or village networks was radically dislocated. Hoping to pick up life where they had left it, returning soldiers, prisoners and migrant workers found the domestic circle geographically displaced and dispersed, reduced to smaller, nuclear units cut adrift from the framework of village clan networks, and run by women who had learned to cope without men. The highly educated and Francophile teacher Mouloud Feraoun betrayed a sense of the general male resentment at new-found female independence: 'In the village, the women openly took the places left vacant by the men. This is something that gives them a lot of confidence and even insolence'.[57] Or again, in another passage, 'The men have taken on a haggard look . . . They have lost, my sister told me, all their arrogance as well as their superiority complex regarding women'.[58] Feraoun reveals a prudish anxiety about the deregulation of women's sexuality: the young daughter of Salem, a relative, found refuge in his house after she had run away from her village to avoid rape: 'But I think that she already has been, just looking at her easy manner, the audacious and slightly covert expression on her face, and her fully developed body'.[59]

Returning men felt deeply anxious and insecure in relation to such change, and set about asserting their domination over women with a new energy.[60] As Mohammed Harbi notes, at independence the lower classes surged back into the public spaces from which they had been excluded with a messianic puritanism that sought revenge on all collaborators, the *harkis* and pro-French bourgeoisie and in particular those immoral women who symbolised the subversion of Islamic society:

> Invitations were forced on the bourgeoisie and notables to matrimonial alliances that went against their deepest wish. Things went as far as humiliating them publicly. At Nedromah they were made to sweep the street. The moral order reappeared in full strength, in the name of Islam. At Mila a woman was stoned for adultery. In Algiers they hunted down the 'girls of 13 May' and demanded that men accompanied by a woman show their *livret de famille*. In Adrar a hashish smoker was publicly whipped. In Guelma the population went with the *imam* to the Roman theatre to destroy the statues to shouts of 'no more idols'.[61]

This populist integrism has strong resonances with the moralism of the Taliban and their destruction of the great Buddha statue at Bamiyam. Attacks on women 'collaborators' mirrored the public rituals of humiliation carried out at the French Liberation and by the army and police during the War of Independence :[62] 'The "suspects" are crushed into cells full of human excrement. Women, after being shorn, are locked up separately under the same conditions'.[63]

The attack on the women of '13 May' was directly linked to the emancipation campaign that men had had to endure in silence. Numerous French reports on the emancipation campaign carried out by the EMSI, the MSF and the mobile propaganda units at village level, report the morose silence of the men as they watched 'their' women lined up and harangued by interpreters. Colonel Crozafon ascribed this in an Orientalist way to the primitive jealousy of the Arab, noting the fear, 'of the dispossessed male and it is important to recognise the part played by sexuality in the life of the Oriental, and also the important role played by Muslim women in his household', such that any reform would undermine his privileged position as, 'an unchanging and arbitrary power in the conjugal domain'.[64] The silence of the peasantry was not a sign of disinterest but rather of the fact that the French army practised a ruthless violence and any man showing the least sign of overt criticism or resistance to the military intervention with women ran the risk of immediate arrest, interrogation and incarceration. At independence Algerian men were suddenly released from this restraint and sought to eradicate any indications of the hated emancipation campaign that they had had to bear so long in silence.

What made it possible for men to reassert their authority over women post-independence was, as we see in the final chapter, the flexibility and durability of patriarchal norms and the family structures that underpinned them, and the extent to which the one-party state, recognising the enormous weight of such religiously sanctioned practices, for reasons of political opportunism quietly shelved any meaningful attempt to promote a progressive reform or agenda on women's rights.

Notes

1 Carlier, *Entre nation et jihad*, 28.
2 SHAT 1H2569, quarterly report, ZCO, 15 December 1960.
3 SHAT 1H2088/4, *Action sur les milieux féminins en Algérie*, 27 March 1960.
4 The volume of army reports on the issue of Algerian women and emancipation decreased rapidly from about mid-1959 onwards and this appears to reflect the fact that the civil and military administration no longer regarded the issue as a priority.
5 On this 'cultural and linguistic dualism', see Kateb, *École, population*, 47–9.
6 Seferdjeli, 'French "Reforms"', 20–1, 47–54.
7 SHAT 1H2569, quarterly report, ZEO, 7 October 1961, on the growing anxiety of ASSRA assistants.
8 Amrane, *Les Femmes algériennes*, 273–5.

9 Significantly, the most extensive testament by Djamila Amrane, Louisette Ighilahriz, Jacqueline Guerroudj and others after 1958 relates to narratives of prison life in Algeria and France

10 *L'Echo d'Alger*, 13 May 1959.

11 *Depéche quotidienne*, 14 May 1959.

12 CAOM 13CAB64, commander ZEA Grande Kabylie to General Salan, 13 October 1958.

13 CAOM 2SAS68, monthly report of the SAU of Sainte-Eugène, Algiers, 20 May 1961.

14 SHAT 1H2462/1, intelligence report for Hussein-Dey, Algiers, 22 August 1960.

15 Horne, *Savage War*, 434.

16 For these events see Horne, *Savage War*, 428–34; Kaddache 'Les Tournants', 51–70; Alleg (ed.). *La Guerre d'Algérie*, Vol. 3, 265–74.

17 CAOM 2SAS56, report SAU officer Bas Casbah on events of 9–16 December 1960.

18 Kaddache, 'Les Tournants', 63; CAOM 2SAS60, SAU officer Clos-Salembier, report on events of 8–16 December 1960.

19 Oral account of Djamila Briki in Amrane-Minne, *Des femmes*, 215.

20 *Ibid.*, 208–15.

21 On the colonial authorities anxiety about the 'detribalisation' of African youth pouring into the slums of Nairobi where they came to fuel the 'Mau Mau' revolt, see Paul Ocobock, ' "Joy Rides for juveniles": Vagrant Youth and Colonial Control in Nairobi, Kenya, 1901–52', *Social History*, 31: 1 (February 2006), 39–59; on the culture and violence of youth 'gangs' and emergent nationalism in Bulawayo see Terence Ranger, 'The Meaning of Urban Violence in Africa: Bulawayo, Southern Rhodesia, 1890–1960', *Cultural and Social History*, 3 (2006), 193–228.

22 On the radicalism of youth see Launay, *Paysans algériens*, 374–7; Mark Tessler, 'Alienation of Urban Youth', in I. William Zartman and William Mark Habeeb (eds), *Polity and Society in Contemporary North Africa* (Boulder, Colo.: Westview Press, 1993), 71–101.

23 SHAT 1H2556/1, Pierre Chaussade, Sécrétaire Général du Gouvernement, Instruction aux Chefs de Section Administrative Urbaines, 17 January 1957, spoke of an 'uprooted, "detribalised", and mixed mass'; CAOM 2SAS69, SAU of Baraki, report for 30 November–31 December 1958, noted 2,000 additional refugees had arrived in the previous six months, 'a mobile mass that is difficult to control', that was leading to further expansion of the *bidonvilles*.

24 CAOM 2SAS69, the SAS officer for the Algiers suburb of Baraki, Captain Brassens, *Enquête sur la cellule familiale musulmane* (May, 1959), remarked on the tendency of boys to escape all parental control for the turbulent life of the street, while girls however, 'except for the rare exception, remain under the control of the mother', and a strict surveillance by the father.

25 SHAT 1H2461/1, Fifth Bureau report, 23 August 1958.

26 Amrane-Minne, *Des femmes*, 214–15.

27 CAOM 2SAS56, SAU Bas Casbah, report of Captain Bapst, 14 and 15 December 1959.

28 House and MacMaster, *Paris 1961*, 154; Meynier, *Histoire intérieure*, 207. Launay, *Paysans algériens*, 376–7, notes that at independence military and political leaders regarded the youth elite as deeply suspect because of their independence of mind and anti-authoritarianism: the first words of an ALN sergeant to a local post-war meeting of young people was, 'We are going to bring you to heel'.

29 Gervereaux and Stora (eds), *Photographier la guerre d'Algérie*, 30.

30 Fleischmann, 'The Other "Awakening"', 126, note 35.

31 Harbi and Meynier (eds), *FLN: Documents*, 628–30: minutes of an assembly (*majlis*) of *cadis* in Wilaya I, 10 October 1960.

32 Archives de la Prefecture de Police (APP), HA49, SCINA sythèses quotidiennes, 31 October–2 November 1959 (see above chapter 9).

33 Harbi and Meynier (eds), *FLN: Documents*, 625, provides a list of punishments imposed in Mintaqa I, Wilaya I, 17 November 1957, including, 'Whoever forgets the principles of religion will be condemned and have Muslim law applied to them'.

34 Harbi and Meynier (eds), *FLN: Documents*, 193–4, 444–6.

35 *Ibid.*, 289–90.

36 *Ibid.*, 425–6.

37 *Ibid.*, 424–5.

38 Feraoun, *Journal*, 67–8.

39 Launay, *Paysans algériens*, 176, 371, 396–9.

40 Eric R. Wolf, *Peasant Wars of the Twentieth Century* [1971] (London: Faber and Faber, 1973 edn), 290–2.

41 See Quandt, *Revolution and Political Leadership*.

42 Charrad, *States and Women's Rights*, 179–82; for a similar analysis in relation to legal reform in Iraq and South Yemen, see Mervat F. Hatem, 'Modernization, the State and the Family in Middle East Women's Studies', in Meriwether and Tucker (eds), *Social History*, 73–6.

43 SHAT 1H2574, Chef de Bataillon J. Florentin, *Les Regroupements de population en Algérie*, 11 December 1960.

44 UNHRC, *The State of the World's Refugees 2000* (Oxford: Oxford University Press, 2000), 41, in December 1959 there were 110,245 refugees in Morocco and 151,903 in Tunisia.

45 Vandevelde-Daillière, *Femmes algériennes*, 63–4.

46 On post-1962 changes in urbanism and housing see Marc Côte, *L'Algérie ou l'espace retourné* (Paris: Flammarion, 1988), 181–272.

47 Some 50,000 men were engaged in the ALN and by 1961 263,000 with the French forces, while 330,000 were absent as labour migrants in France and perhaps an equal number in the major cities of northern Algeria. The number of men killed, disappeared or imprisoned in camps was over 250,000. So in round terms over a million men aged fifteen to fifty out of

two million in this age-group were permanently or definitively absent from their families. This figure varied greatly by region and in some zones of Kabylia almost 100 per cent of able-bodied adult males would have been absent.

48 Jansen, *Women Without Men*, and 'The Economy of Religious Merit'; Abrous, *L'Honneur face au travail des femmes*.

49 Vandevelde-Daillière, *Femmes algériennes*, 286; *Temoignage chrétien*, 'Combien de Djemila Bouhired?', 3 January 1958, noted a 'profound transformation' of the role of women: 'All of a sudden they had to go out from the house, to go from prison to prison searching for a disappeared husband, then to bring his regular food basket, to replace him when he has gone into the maquis, to feed her children, to find work, to organise legal proceedings, to appoint a lawyer, confront the police, the administration, the army' .

50 SHAT 1H2461/1, note of Commandant Bouraix, 23 January 1959.

51 Feraoun, *Journal*, 242–3, 257.

52 The reassertion of male authority and gender roles on the termination of conflict can be found in many historical situations: see for example in relation to the Spanish Civil War, Mary Nash, *Defying Male Civilization: Women in the Spanish Civil War* (Denver, Colo.: Areden Press, 1995), and Shirley Mangini, *Memories of Resistance: Women's Voices from the Spanish Civil War* (New Haven: Yale University Press, 1995). Susan Faludi, *The Terror Dream: What 9/11 Revealed About America* (London: Atlantic Books, 2008) analyses the surge in media representations of virility after the perceived humiliation of the terrorist attack on the 'homeland'.

53 Virgili, *Shorn Women*; Michael Kelly, 'The Reconstruction of Masculinity at the Liberation' and Corran Laurens, ' "La Femme au turban": les femmes tondues', in Kedward and Wood (eds), *Liberation of France*, 117–28, 155–79; Luc Capdevila, 'The Quest for Masculinity in a Defeated France, 1940–1945', *Contemporary European History*, 10: 3 (November 2001), 423–45.

54 The Algerian conflict was constantly interpreted on both sides in terms of a narrative and language of 'Liberation' and 'Resistance': see Philip Dine, 'The Inescapable Allusion: The Occupation and the Resistance in French Fiction and Film of the Algerian War', in Kedward and Wood (eds), *Liberation of France*, 269–82.

55 Mary Louis Roberts, 'La Photo du GI viril: genre et photojournalisme en France à la Libération', *Le Mouvement Social*, 219–20 (April–September 2007), 35–56.

56 Under *sharia* law marriage was a contract in which it was the duty of the husband to maintain his wife and to control her outside activities, including the right to engage in employment: see Mir-Hosseini, *Marriage on Trial*, 33–5.

57 Feraoun, *Journal*, 257.

58 *Ibid.*, 241.

59 *Ibid.*, 265.

60 Miriam Cooke, has noted the appearance at this time of anxiety and hostility towards 'monstrous' women in the works of male Algerian writers: see 'Arab Women Arab Wars', in Fatma Müge Göçek and Shiva Balaghi (eds), *Reconstructing Gender in the Middle East. Tradition, Identity, and Power* (New York: Columbia University Press, 1994), 154–5.
61 Harbi, *Le FLN, mirage et réalité*, 364.
62 In Paris the police and the *harki* brigades under Captain Montaner engaged in their own shearing of Algerian women or 'collaborators' with the FLN: see House and MacMaster, *Paris 1961*, 79, 128 and Rémy Valat, *Les Calots bleus et la bataille de Paris. Une force de police auxiliaire pendant la guerre d'Algérie* (Paris: Michalon, 2007), 91–2.
63 SHAT 1H1793/2, note of 18 August 1962, quoted in Harbi and Meynier (eds), *FLN: Documents*, 538.
64 SHAT 1H2460/1, report of Colonel Crozafon, commander of sector Algers-Sahel to commander Zone Nord Algérois, 3 March 1959.

11

The post-independence state and the conservative marginalisation of women

This chapter examines first how it was that the structure of the 'traditional' extended family and its values, often referred to as 'neo-patriarchy', was able to adapt in a dynamic way to the challenge of rapid social and economic change. This survival helps to explain why patterns of male domination remained so all-powerful and generalised within Algerian society, so that politically vulnerable post-independence governments preferred not to challenge the status quo on the position and rights of women. This failure to engage in any significant programme of progressive reform is illustrated by reference, firstly, to the inability to transform the conservative laws of personal status, indeed the government went backwards on this issue compared to the French reform of 1959, and secondly, by reference to a one-party state control and stifling of an organised women's movement.

Neo-patriarchy:[1] family structure and a blocked society

Between 1954 and the 1970s Algeria experienced an extraordinary degree of change: the disruption of war was followed after independence by chaos and economic dislocation as a million settlers, who held the key technical, administrative and professional functions, departed. After 1962 the new government, confronted with economic and social disintegration, mass rural–urban flight, high unemployment and a quite staggering population explosion, attempted to resolve the crisis of rural under-development through an agrarian revolution, while oil revenues were invested in a Soviet style industrialisation programme.[2] One classic modernisation theory maintains that the global, long-term progress in the position of women is a result of economic change, leading to education, entry into the work force, change in the balance of 'traditional' gender roles within the family, and access to health care and family planning.[3] However, a distinctive feature of Algerian socio-economic development after 1962 is that for at least two decades rapid modernisation, including an enormous expansion in female education and literacy, had a quite minimal impact on gender roles, equality and overall rights. Kamel Kateb has measured an explosive growth in girls' education: the percentage of those receiving primary education (age six to fourteen years) increased from 9.5 per cent in 1954 to 71.56 per cent in 1987.[4] However, this dramatic change had, for at least two decades, minimal impact on the position of women and, for example, their level of employment increased from 2 per cent in 1954 to only 2.6 per cent in 1977, one of the lowest in the Muslim world.[5] This apparent contradiction between improved access to education and ongoing exclusion from the labour market can be explained in part by a post-independence model of labour-saving industrialisation that excluded women, and by agricultural reforms that weakened their traditional role in the peasant economy, reducing them to the position of homemakers.[6]

As Kateb and others have pointed out, patriarchy trumped the forces that might have led to social and political emancipation: the Algerian family, faced with the challenge of modernisation, proved to be highly inventive in adapting the 'traditional' male-dominated, extended family so that it served as a basis of economic and political strength, rather than as a conservative corset that led towards inevitable social decline. The anthropologist Camille Lacoste-Dujardin and sociologists like Claudine Chaulet and Lahouari Addi have shown how this dynamic restructuring took place, so that kin networks and marriage strategies could adapt to modernisation and facilitate access to new forms of political and economic power.[7] The typical post-1962 household was constituted of three generations in which, because of the desperate crisis in housing, parents shared the same space with married sons, their wives and children, or, if more wealthy, acquired adjacent flats. This extended family group, instead of fissuring into autonomous, nuclear units, continued to function as a collective and adult brothers and elders were able to insure and protect it best by avoiding putting all their eggs in one basket and diversifying the economic base. Typically one son might emigrate and send remittances from France, another to work in the big cities of northern Algeria, while others remained on the family farm cultivating the land, or used it as a base from which to set up small local businesses (as traders, taxi drivers, hauliers) or travelling daily to jobs in local towns or industry (day-labourers, postmen, masons).

This adaptive, dynamic capacity of the 'traditional' family provided it with considerable strength in times of massive economic and political dislocation and change but went hand-in-hand with a vigorous reinforcement of the patrilineal ideology that maintained women in their 'natural' role of mothers and daughters claustrated within the home. Lacoste-Dujardin says of this family as 'refuge': 'These new families, fragments of lineage groups dispossessed of so many of their privileges, still jealously guarded, according to the length of time passed since its disruption and the degree of links retained with the parental clan, a consciousness of family honour and still adhered to a patrilineal ideology'.[8] Claudine Chaulet rejects the Eurocentric idea that there exists a necessary link between processes of economic modernisation and the evolution of the nuclear family, and points to a flexible, extended family network in which women as individuals were still subordinated to the masculine-controlled interests of the group, 'which aimed to prevent any divisions that could be provoked by the spouse', through arranged, endogamous marriage of young brides who could be easily controlled, and subjected to the strict regulations of gender segregation and seclusion.[9] Kin networks also operated like clientele systems to gain access to political power, for example through relatives in local government who could fix access to jobs, land and favourable planning decisions.[10]

This patriarchal model held true not only for rural and provincial small-town society, but also for large numbers in the big cities, many of whom were refugees or recent migrants from the interior. The traditional Maghrebi house, with its sealed in private spaces (absence of ground-floor windows, inner courtyards) was designed to protect women from the eyes of strangers, a condition of male and familial honour.[11] But the huge population movement into the towns during and after the war created an enormous housing crisis and overcrowding, conditions which made it extremely difficult to maintain the seclusion and privacy of women. The anthropologist Willy Jansen shows how, despite the most adverse conditions, attempts were made to maintain the appearance of segregation. In multi-occupation housing shared by families who were strangers to each other men would follow the rule of giving a warning, such as a cough or calling 'tarîq' (way) whenever they wished to pass through a communal courtyard in which unrelated women might be present, so that they could hide or cover themselves.[12] What can be seen from this is how the family, despite enormous pressures of uprooting, rural–urban migration, overcrowding and promiscuity clung on to the core values of honour and patriarchy. In a situation in which male immigrants to the city faced deep anxiety about the spatial regulation of segregation, in which women of the household were exposed to the dangers of contact with strangers, men frequently resorted to more draconian female seclusion than was normal in the village, including imposition of the veil, strict surveillance and refusal to allow women to go unaccompanied by a male into public spaces.[13]

Some commentators have tended to draw a picture in which the oppression of Algerian women has been ascribed to a 'battle of the sexes', an aggressive male subjugation of women. Certainly Hélène Vandevelde-Daillière produced a considerable body of evidence from her survey in 1969–70, to show that many women felt so isolated within the home that they had no means to escape from a life of resignation and ignorance, and were passive and de-politicised. Typical of the statements recorded is the following by a middle-aged woman, 'No women take part in social life because of customs. Women are made for the house, which basically means they have no life. They rarely go out . . . Put in another way, Arab women are buried alive'.[14] So radical was female seclusion that a third of rural women had no contact even with neighbours, while their husbands avoided conversation with them and some wives were even ignorant of the nature of their husband's employment.[15]

However, as Lacoste-Dujardin has shown, older women as mothers and mothers-in-law could achieve a considerable degree of domestic power and status in so far as they brokered marriages and exercised a strict disciplinary control over their daughters and co-habiting daughters-in-law, thus reproducing the ideology of female submission and serving as 'agents of masculine domination'.[16] Numerous reports by French army itinerant social and welfare teams during the war noted that resistance to emancipation of Algerian women came mainly from the dominant older women or *adjouzat* who blocked any reforming intent and prevented contact between the French and the young women in their households. Patriarchy, far from being solely imposed by force on women by males, was a powerful system of belief and practice that was sustained by both men and women and this explains in part the ability of the ideology to survive post-war changes.[17] It was also in the rational self-interest of Algerian women to aspire to membership of cohesive and extended family networks since this provided them with the best guarantees of a degree of economic security and respect: for example, the usual escape route for wives who suffered abuse at the hands of husbands or were repudiated was to return to the protection of their family of origin. Willy Jansen shows how the situation of 'women without men' was not enviable: they faced extreme poverty and hardship as virtual social outcasts, and the ambition of most widowed or divorced women, as of their male kin or guardians, would be to try and ensure that they remarried as quickly as possible so as to return to the protection and security of the patriarchal collective.

Women and the conservative function of post-independence government

The newly independent state made resounding and high-principled general statements on women's rights. A sequence of 'foundation' declarations such as the Tripoli Programme of 1962, the Constitution of 28 August 1963, and the Algiers Charter of April 1964, as well as Ben Bella and Boumédienne in key speeches, made bold statements on the full equality of women. For example, Article 12 of the 1963 constitution stated, 'All citizens of both sexes share the same rights and duties'.[18] In later years, as an emerging women's movement struggled to assert itself against a conservative, male-dominated political regime, these basic constitutional rights would be constantly referred to, but as many commentators have noted, there continued to exist a fatal and contradictory gap between such general statements of high principle and the failure of the FLN one-party state to develop a coherent programme of reform that would translate basic rights into reality.[19]

One of the reasons for this failure lay in the political turmoil and instability that accompanied the transition to independence, as a range of 'clans', clientele systems and ideological blocks competed for power. Between early July and early September 1962 Algeria came close to a full-scale civil war as the 'external' armed forces headed by Ben Bella moved to crush the 'internal' Wilaya commanders during an advance on Algiers that led to several thousand deaths.[20] Ben Bella, during his brief period as president (13 September 1962 to 19 June 1965) was plagued by political insecurity and this absence of stable authority led him to make a number of compromises with religious conservatives that was to have particularly negative consequences for women whose interests were seen as expendable when weighed against the retention of personal power by FLN apparatchiks. In recent years, especially with the surge of radical Islamist movements after 1988, commentators have begun to revise an earlier historiography that exaggerated the more secular, socialist and progressive side of the Algerian regime, by placing a stronger emphasis on the popular Islamist and archaic features of nationalism.[21] The educated intellectuals who, influenced by French *laïcité* and the Enlightenment, provided a materialist or Marxist analysis of Algerian history and political development, constituted a tiny minority,[22] compared to the masses and the FLN leadership that followed the Messalist tradition which sought to weld the disparate regional, religious and linguistic forces into a cohesive unity and nationalism based on the idealisation of a mythical order that was to be resurrected over and against the hated 'Christian West'. As Harbi notes: 'Algeria advances with its eyes fixed on the past, riveted to its sacred archaisms because they belong to the body of the community. The nationalist ideology combines a nostalgia for the past and the revolutionary hope of a new world'.[23] As has been seen, the defence of an Arabo-Islamic identity was formulated most crucially in terms of women, as mothers and educators, and of the private sphere of the family viewed as a bastion in which core values were transmitted from one generation to the next. In particular FLN propaganda had helped to reinforce the association between French emancipation and counter-insurgency, so that any moves to reform the position of women after 1962 could be aggressively denounced as a dangerous instrument of western neo-colonialist penetration and subversion.

The new political elite that came to power at independence under the leadership of Ben Bella (1962–65) and then Boumédienne (1965–78) recognised perfectly well, in a situation of deep political instability, the profoundly entrenched and unyielding nature of popular Algerian social, cultural and religious tradition.[24] At the core of this lay the patriarchal family, the fundamental building block of the entire social and political order. The political elites quietly turned their backs on the issue of women: there was no reason to meddle in or stir up opposition, in relation to reforms for which there existed little significant pressure or demand. Thus while the FLN elites felt comfortable in utilising the language of 'socialism' and secular law in the technocratic and economic sphere (of oil production, planning, industrialisation, land reform), the cultural-religious agenda was basically drawn from the Ulema tradition. The PPA of Messali Hadj (1937–54), and its successor the FLN, both shared a populist and messianic religious nationalism that was shaped by the Ulema,[25] and its leading ideologue, Tawfiq al-Madani, became Minister of Culture and Religious Affairs in the first FLN provisional government and later under Ben Bella. In the post-1962 political struggle between the minority current of socialism and Arabo-Islamic traditionalism, both Ben Bella and Boumédienne discreetly sided with the latter on the question of women, particularly as in a search for political legitimacy they had most to gain from appealing to populist Islam and the austere salafiyya movement which sought a return to the purity of tradition and sharia. An authentic womanhood was to be located more in the restoration of an essence that was defined in relation to an immutable past than through any process of modernisation. As Mohammed Harbi, a leading oppositional figure within the FLN has argued, the post-1962 governments showed an essential weakness of Algerian nationalism from its very beginning in the 1920s, a form of populism that based unity on a religious and mythical idealisation of a past community that obscured elaboration of a clear ideology or political project, so acting to the detriment of universal and individual rights, a process in which women were the greatest losers.[26]

The dynamics of this failure can be most clearly traced through the post-independence blockage of reform of the marriage and family laws.

The failure to carry out reform of the personal status law

Some feminists have argued that to centre on legal reform and individual rights is to impose a western model that may obscure, as 'declension narratives' claim, the forms of traditional status and community-based power held by Algerian women.[27] However, the modernisation of family codes has been one of the key instruments by which independent Muslim nations, since Kemalist Turkey in the 1920s onwards, have through 'top-down', and often authoritarian, intervention attempted to end the subjugation of women, and liberate the potential of half the population to play a full role in economic, social and political development. Algeria is no exception and reform of the family code has been the single most crucial issue around which both the Algerian women's movement and international feminist organisations have, and continue, to campaign.[28]

As has been shown in chapter 9, the colonial regime faced considerable difficulty in enforcing the new personal status law of 1959, and was confronted by a society in which a widespread culture of non-compliance with the *état civil* and marriage legislation was deeply entrenched. Unlike Tunisia and Morocco, which seized the opportune moment of independence to introduce new family codes while the newly independent state could benefit from high levels of support, the Algerian government simply passed an act (31 December 1962) to leave French legislation on the statute books. This meant that the French Ordinance on marriage of 1959 was to remain in force until the law of 5 July 1975. But it was to take yet another decade before the family code of 1984 came to fill the vacuum. The Algerian government was prepared to quietly leave the 1959 law in place, although preferring not to speak too much about this tacit tolerance of what had been slated as an 'anti-Islamic' measure. Such tolerance was possible precisely to the extent that the law was in practice ignored or flexibly marginalised, both by society and by the courts, and so did not arouse troublesome political opposition from conservative religious forces in society.

The paralysis of government became particularly evident in the long-drawn-out, twenty-two-year failure to legislate a family code to meet the needs of a rapidly changing, post-colonial society. During this period

(1962–84) there were no less than five failed attempts, mainly by secretive committees on which there was no female representation, to draw up draft legislation (1963–64, 1966, 1972, 1979, 1981). Those drafts, which were leaked to the press, showed a general trend through time towards a radical erosion of the 1959 law and the assertion of the core values of traditional Maliki law. The secrecy surrounding the various commissions was in itself an indication of the deep anxiety of the one-party state in relation to the potentially explosive and politically destabilising nature of the issue. Space does not allow a close examination of the detail of the various drafts, but the overall direction of the conservative shift is indicated by the fact that the final 1984 law, in the words of Lucie Pruvost, codified 'a family of a patriarchal type based on respect for agnatic solidarities and hierarchies under which women were treated as permanent minors'.[29] For example, wives owed strict obedience to their husbands as sovereign head of the family, as well as respect for his lineage (parents and kin); women no matter what their age could only marry through the authority of a male guardian (*walî*), which in the case of a widow might be her son; polygamy was retained, and repudiation was restored as a unilateral male prerogative.[30]

The twenty-two-year-long vacuum created by the state and the failure to provide a clear legislative lead on a family code meant that judges and the court system which adjudicated on the reality of marriage, divorce and family life were left adrift to follow their own devices.[31] From 1962 until the abrogation of the code in July 1975, many judges, following their personal religious or ideological bias, simply ignored the 1959 Ordinance which was still in force, and based judgements on classic Islamic law.[32] The way the wind was blowing was clearly reflected during a 1968 conference of jurists on the instability of the Algerian family, during which Mohand Issad of the Algiers faculty of law noted that the supreme court had shown preference for the position that 'the husband held sovereign power to repudiate his wife at will', even if this was an abusive practice and in breach of the statutes. Issad justified this on the casuistical grounds that the law of 31 December 1962 retained French legislation, including the Ordinance of 1959, only on condition that it was not 'of colonial inspiration and discriminatory' or 'contrary to national sovereignty'.[33] The right of husbands to unilaterally end a marriage, even without cause, was thus argued to be in the national interest, and Issad swept aside the progressive law of 1959 that served to give greater protection to women as both a colonial evil and discriminatory.

However, Issad was expressing his individual opinion as a jurist rather than a strict reading of statute law, and this was typical of a situation in

which judges were relatively free to follow their own agendas, a situation that created a mass of confusion and contradictory practices in the
legal process. In many ways this juridical anarchy facilitated and, at the
same time, legitimated the deep conservative currents in Algerian society
that had frustrated or ignored the 1959 law from its inception. In 1968
even the official FLN newspaper *El Moudjahid* was able to offer a *fatwa*
that condoned a strictly illegal disregard for the law. In reply to a question posed by a women who had been married by a *fatiha* ceremony to
a man who later turned out to be already married with two children, it
suggested that she could contest this before a judge, but the *fatiha* marriage was, 'from the point of view of Muslim law pure', and if she was
to contest this in the courts, 'if you are pious you will always have something on your conscience . . . also in Muslim law polygamy is licit'.[34]
Lahouari Addi has gone so far as to suggest that Algeria in failing to
establish a culture of individual rights was not a *Rechtsstaat* and was
prepared to surrender the monopoly of justice in relation to domestic
space and women to the religious-moral order of the community and the
man in the street. For example, the authorities appear to have tolerated
or turned a blind eye to the widespread use of male violence towards
women who they felt had, by appearing alone or 'improperly' dressed in
the street, impugned the moral order.[35]

The conservative turn in marriage and family law after 1962 did
not mean that Algerian women were lacking in agency and that they
were the passive objects of repressive male agendas. Just as civil society
had been able to escape the implementation of the 1959 law, so that
there was a large gap between the statute book and the social reality
of marriage arrangements, so court documents of legal procedure also
reveal the kinds of strategies that women deployed to defend their own
interests in court.[36] Although historians have explored this issue for
the colonial period, little if any work has been carried out for the post-
Independence era.[37] However, some of the published court adjudications
provide a tantalising glimpse of how women attempted to utilise the law
to their own benefit and, rather significantly, did so by appealing to the
colonial Ordinance of 1959. For example, Khedidja Ait Idir brought
a court action against her husband Tahar Nabti in July 1965 because
he had repudiated her, but acted illegally by failing to get the marriage
registered by the *état civil*. However, the great majority of women were
illiterate and too poor to be able to make use of legal process, and if they
did so it was in most instances where, having returned to their parents
home after repudiation, court action was brought by male relatives on
their behalf.[38] But ultimately, the overall conservative direction which
marriage law took after independence in 1962 severely narrowed the

already restricted room for manoeuvre that women had to defend their interests before a judge.

Women's organisations such as the official *Union nationale des femmes algériennes* (UNFA), as well as individual feminists such as Fadéla M'Rabet, voiced with growing concern the failure of the courts to implement current laws inherited from the French. This became particularly clear in the two key areas of enforced marriage and unilateral repudiation. A growing number of religious leaders and *cadis* openly expressed the right of *jebr* by which a marriage partner was chosen by the father or male guardian (*walî*), since, it was argued, women lacked the experience, information or inherent intelligence of men to make such an important decision. The consent of the woman, who they argued must be absent from the marriage ceremony, should always be given by the *walî*. It was precisely this system that the 1959 law had tried to end by insisting that women must be present at the registration before a state official who would verify her assent, as well as her legal age.

From 1962 onwards, however, a mass of evidence points to forced marriage, often of under-age minors, in spite of the Khemisti law of 1963 which extended the age of marriage for girls from fifteen to sixteen years.[39] In the Constantinois region even the official census of 1966 recorded 5 per cent of all girls aged twelve to fifteen years as married (2,774 individuals), undoubtedly the tip of the iceberg since most illegal marriages would have escaped the *état civil* altogether. Vandevelde-Daillière's extensive survey of 1968–72 found that 42 per cent of husbands were imposed on women in urban society, and 65 per cent in rural zones.[40] M'Rabet, after publicising evidence of widespread and increasing psychiatric problems, including 175 attempted suicides in Algiers in 1964 among young women forced into marriage, had her weekly radio programme for women closed down.[41] In addition there was a growing wave of repudiation or divorce in which women and children were abandoned, frequently without any form of support, and in 1963 there was an estimated 10,000 repudiations and abandoned families in greater Algiers alone.[42]

The conservative attack on the colonial legislation of 1959, as on the heritage of French emancipation in general, was powerfully legitimated by the FLN nationalist ideology. Internal documents dating from the war itself show that the FLN was perfectly aware of the extent to which the package of emancipation measures was driven by a counter-insurgency strategy to penetrate, gather intelligence and subvert the FLN base in domestic society.[43] However, in its attack on the 1959 law the FLN fell back on, and reinforced, the conservative topos of the immutable family as a bastion of identity, a form of religious nationalism that bound women into the status quo. The official FLN newspaper *El Moudjahid* noted of the 1959 law:

> Thus the French, who moreover are Christians or of the Jewish confession, as is, it seems, Mr Michel Debré, have dared to deliberately violate the Koran, immutable in its essence, and to impose by the sword on Algerian Muslims the secular laws of France, and this, in the most sacred of things, notably the *statut personnel* . . . a domain that belongs exclusively to the community of believers.[44]

Frantz Fanon sensed the dangers of such a reactive FLN agenda reinforcing traditional practices that might carry negative consequences for women.[45] But while he viewed this as only a temporary sacrifice of the war period this proved not to be the case and the FLN helped to create a long-term, post-independence mental association between almost any form of progressive agenda on women or emancipation, and the idea of an alien, western invasion and subversion of Algerian culture and society. As the conservative ideologue Malek Bennabi remarked in 1968, feminism represented a foreign import: 'Our feminism must not be "made in somewhere". It must be of our own brand'; while for the Minister of Justice, Benhamouda, the goal of any new Algerian code, 'is above all to purify the structure of the family of all its un-Islamic elements'.[46] The close links between the nationalist myth of Arabo-Islamic identity and the emphasis on a necessary reinforcement of classic Islamic law was promoted by Saïd Benabdallah, a leading ideologue and jurist, in his book *La Justice du FLN pendant la guerre de libération*. The nature of Algerian justice, he argued, could only be understood in relation to 'the religious function of the revolutionary myth' and a War of Independence that had been fought by the *moudjahid* (warrior of the faith) as a *jihad* (holy war) which was essentially, 'a dynamic manifestation of auto-defence for the preservation and recovery of a patrimony of the highest value . . . It so happens that it was precisely in Algeria that Islam was the final refuge of these values that were hounded and profaned by an outrageous colonialism'.[47] Nationalist discourse invariably presented women and the domestic habitus as the ultimate redoubt of Algerian identity, and this construct meant that the Islamic code of law which regulated the family would need to be cleansed of all French or western accretions that had polluted the pure tradition. Benabdallah wrote: 'The strength of Algerian Islam resides in effect in the extent to which its spirit is in harmony with that of Algerian civilisation. It contains prescriptions that conform to the traditionalist way of life, and the system of juridical norms that it proposes are in agreement with the deeper structures of Algerian society'.[48] This recourse to tradition appears to have ruled out any attempt to engage in a progressive or liberal interpretation of Islam, but meant in effect a defence of the status quo and the most conservative features of marriage and family law.

In summary, the Algerian government delayed legislation on a post-independence family code since its hold on power was precarious and it preferred to avoid politically destabilising battles over such a sensitive issue between opposing camps that viewed themselves as socialist/secular modernisers or as Arabo-Islamist defenders of 'tradition'.[49] Certainly Borrmans, a close contemporary observer, detected signs of such a split in the secretive workings of the drafting commissions of 1963–64 and 1966, and gave this as a reason why government shelved these projects.[50] It is now evident, especially from the work of Gilbert Meynier, that such a split over the position of women had existed already among the higher echelons of the FLN during the war itself,[51] but the weaker socialist or secularising current eventually lost out to the colonels (Ben Bella, Boumédienne) who seized political power at independence.

Although there were some initial signs of promise on the women's question from the Ben Bella government, particularly in the passing of the Khemisti law of 1963, which increased the minimum age of marriage for girls from fifteen to sixteen years, this quickly evaporated. On International Women's Day, 8 March 1965, a dramatic demonstration passed through central Algiers, during which many women threw their veils into the sea, blocked traffic and shouted slogans demanding an end to discrimination: 'go and do the cooking, we'll take care of the politics'. Ben Bella, during a deeply ambiguous speech in the Majestic cinema, stated there could never be socialism without the participation of women 'within the framework of our Arabo-Islamic values'.[52] On the same occasion one year later, Boumédienne, having seized power through an army coup, made an almost identical speech: progress, he said, 'does not mean in any way imitation of western feminism. We say no to this kind of evolution since our society is an Islamic and social-ist society . . . this evolution must not be the cause of the corruption of our society'.[53] Lazreg, an eye-witness to the event, reports that women who tried to leave in protest were forced back to their seats by armed guards.[54]

Politics and the failure of an organised women's movement

Quite at odds with FLN populist nationalism, was the optimism of many commentators on the international socialist left in 1961–62 that the new republic would mark an extraordinary phase in the simultaneous liberation of Algerian women from the fetters of colonialism and 'feudal' patriarchy. Frantz Fanon, for example, in *L'An V de la révolution algérienne*, optimistically forecast a 'radical mutation' in the role of women, gender relations and traditional family structures and the birth of a 'new society'.[55] Algerian women, it would seem, had through both their heroic sacrifice and the demonstration of an ability to act on a par with men, earned recognition of their moral right to full post-independence equality.

However, this was not to be, and the very group of women who might have been expected to form an avant-garde for a post-independence movement, the *moudjahidate* who had experienced an unusual degree of independence during the war and also enjoyed a high level of symbolic power, returned to a domestic role and withdrew from political activism.[56] The atmosphere of political demobilisation and dejection at the reassertion of male domination and seclusion was typically expressed by Fatma Baichi: 'After independence I no longer worked and I could not militate. My husband prevented me from going out: I could not even go and see my sisters in combat . . . And then even my brothers, even the youngest with whom I militated during the war, encouraged my husband to stop me from going out: "It's all over now, she must not be allowed out, things are different now"'. For Baya Hocine too, 'we [Algerian women] broke through the barriers and it was very difficult for us to go back to how things were. In 1962 the barriers were rebuilt in a way that was terrible for us'.[57] Symbolic of this dramatic shift in the fortunes of women militants at independence was the fate of Djamila Boupacha, the most mediatised heroine, on her release from a French prison on 26 April 1962. Reluctant to return to Algeria where 'the *brothers* [FLN] are going to return me to my life as a woman down there', she was forced by the FLN to leave the protection of her feminist lawyer Gisèle Halimi, and was bundled under guard onto a flight to Algeria.[58]

Why was it that so many of the *moudjahidate*, a highly militant and formidable group of women, should have so readily retreated from public life into domesticity? Many of the women interviewed by Amrane gave personal reasons: they were deeply scarred and exhausted by the war, and by 1962 were yearning for a return to 'normality' and, in particular, to get married and to have the children and family life that had been in many instances put on hold during the long eight-year war. However, such reasons do not explain the widespread disengagement from politics. Typical was the statement of one woman militant: 'Independence, it's the liberation of the country: our goal was achieved, we stopped there', and, 'I fought for independence, I had no other idea in mind. Me, I'm a woman: I thought after it's them, the men, who are going to take over, they know what has to be done for the independent country'.[59] Saleha Boudefa has shown how this position was reinforced by a post-independence official discourse that, by claiming full emancipation of women had been gained at the moment of liberation, rejected any demands for further reform or change as illegitimate since full 'liberation' had already been achieved.[60] Any agitation by women not under the umbrella of the FLN or the UNFA was treated as potentially subversive and anti-national. But in general there was a lack of political education and experience among the *moudjahidate* who were unable to develop a consciousness of the problems faced by women and the kinds of programme or demands that might begin to break the mould of patriarchy. Rather, the war-time élan of militant women was almost entirely captured by a simple, nationalist vision: as Zehor, a student, remarked, 'Independence . . . it was not something clear . . . it was a paradise, a paradisiacal universe where everything would be easy'.[61]

The outbreak of the War of Independence in 1954 had also led to the dissolution of the significant women's organisations that had emerged between 1944 and 1954 (UFA, AFMA, JUDMA) (see chapter 1). By 1962 the majority of militant women who wished to continue political activism could only find an outlet for this within the hegemonic, 'state feminism' of the FLN.[62] As women militants disbanded in 1962 from the ranks of the FLN so they found themselves isolated, cut off from other militant women, without any alternative means of organising outside the conservative and stifling embrace of the one-party state apparatus. Finally, comparative evidence from many other twentieth-century wars in which women were called upon to make a huge sacrifice – both in taking on board roles or forms of work previously reserved for men, as well as extremely dangerous and vital forms of resistance that often went unacknowledged by men (organising clandestine supply routes, safe-houses, look-outs, medical aid) – have shown how extremely powerful the processes of demobilisation and domestic 'normalisation' have been, even in societies that had a much longer and more developed history of feminism. This was particularly true for women in metropolitan France who after the Liberation, despite enfranchisement by de Gaulle in 1944, did not witness any dramatic break with the past.[63] As one woman remarked, 'For me, the Liberation brought no changes. We took our lives up as we had left them before and I was very happy to do so'.[64]

This was also the experience shared by 'Muslim sisters' after radical phases of nationalist resurgence in the Maghreb and Middle East, and there was nothing particularly 'remiss' or unusual in this respect about Algerian women.[65] The most remarkable similarity existed between the experience of Algerian and Moroccan women militants: at the moment of independence in 1956 the majority of Moroccan *moudjahidate* withdrew from post-independence political activity into the role of housewives and mothers. The husband of the resistance fighter Saadia Bouhaddou, for example, insisted that she wear the *djellaba*, 'After independence, my husband told me, "You've proved yourself capable of doing all that. Now it's time for you to stay at home"'.[66] Alison Baker, in her study of Moroccan veterans, found that only one of them, Fatna Mansar, had stayed involved in politics after independence or had any 'concrete ideas of political, economic, and social programs that might have come out of the national liberation movement'.[67] Baker concludes that the majority of the resistance veterans did not emerge from the War of Independence, having radically breached traditional boundaries of gender seclusion, with the developed political consciousness that western observers might have expected: on the contrary they remained conservative on most social issues and shared the views of the men in their milieu.[68]

Some of the best evidence on the enormous difficulties faced by Algerian women trying to mobilise and gain any kind of voice in relation to women's issues and rights in the immediate post-war period comes from the research of Hélene Vandevelde-Daillière. While teaching at the University of Constantine she carried out, with the aid of students, between February 1969 and February 1970 an extensive survey of opinion among 1,059 women and 233 men in both urban and rural zones.[69] Vandevelde-Daillière shows in detail how women were almost totally excluded from the male-dominated political system, both from the FLN one-party apparatus, the trade union movement, as well as from elected representation at local and national level. For example, in the first local elections for the *Assemblées Populaires Communales* (APC) on 5 February 1967, only ninety-nine women were elected to the 10,852 seats (0.9 per cent), and by 1971 this had declined even further to forty-six (0.5 per cent).[70] The sole official organisation for women, the UNFA, which did not even hold its first Congress until November 1966, was an integral part of the FLN machine, followed the party line, and lacked any significant base among the female population. This organisation fits closely Ellen Fleischmann's category of 'state feminism', a form that served to channel and contain any potential movement, stifling and discouraging any initiatives that might challenge male-led conservative policies. When the first provisional Executive Committee of the UNFA organised a street demonstration on 8 March 1964, International Women's Day, the government ordered a change in the membership, leading the entire committee to resign in protest.[71] Most of the more

politicised militants who were involved in the early days of the UNFA
began to drop out from its activities, like the peasant and ex-maquisard
Jemaa: 'At independence I tried to get involved in the UNFA, but I was
of no use to them, they preferred women who make applause and who
do not talk too much like me'.[72]

The majority of women interviewed by Vandevelde-Daillière demonstrated a crushing demoralisation and resignation, and an apparent
inability to conceptualise the political universe beyond the doorstep or
to answer the most basic questions on the outside world, which was
viewed as the domain of men. One sign of the political marginalisation of
women was the tolerance by government in 1967–70 of husbands going
to the ballot station on behalf of their wives, a practice eventually legalised between 1975 and 1991.[73] However, Vandevelde-Daillière's survey
did detect signs of a real, but latent, discontent among both urban and
rural women; a wish to see a major change in values, and a more open
access to social life and the realm of politics. Because such aspirations
were massively blocked by men, who were more content to support the
status quo in relation to gender roles, there was every indication of a profound malaise. The degree of alienation and unhappiness among women
tended to remain buried away and largely invisible, in part because there
was no organisational basis through which women could express their
individual and collective voice: 'It is a matter of concern that the behaviour of women who, for the great majority, appear submissive to social
convention, is in fact constrained by social pressure and that women
submit to social norms because they have no other choice . . . Women
remain submissive in appearance but are internally victimised'.[74]

The role of women during the War of Independence played a significant part in this incipient *prise de conscience*, as well as their ability to
vote, first gained from the colonial regime in 1958. In the opinion poll a
majority of women mentioned the struggle for national liberation as the
prime cause of their interest in politics.[75] But the evidence suggests that
the majority of the *moudjahidate*, and of women in general who had
experienced the radicalising impact of involvement in the war, became
rapidly disillusioned with the post-independence regime and retreated
into the private domestic sphere or, for the better educated, threw their
energy into professional occupations as teachers, doctors and social
workers.[76] But, as Amrane shows, of the eighty-eight militants in her
study, only three profited from any upward social mobility, and in two
of these instances this was primarily due to the elite position of their
marriage partners.[77] More typical perhaps was Kheira, who went into
the maquis as a nursing assistant, but by the 1970s was divorced with
four children and living in a dark, cellar-like room.[78] About a third of

urban and two-thirds of rural women studied by Vandevelde-Daillière believed that their position in relation to men had remained the same or had become 'more submissive' since the end of the war.[79]

This is not to say that there was no active women's movement that challenged the regime during the 1960s and 1970s, but this was largely confined to a few hundred educated and professional women and even they, as the feminist Marie-Aimée Helie-Lucas notes personally, found it difficult to acknowledge the strength of the chains of nationalist ideology and to begin to oppose it.[80] However, the war as a memory and symbol of women's potential did have an eventual, longer-term impact on the emergence of an independent women's movement when it resurfaced after 1980.[81]

Finally, particularly revealing is the overwhelming hegemonic power of the official discourse on women that was internalised by members of the UNFA and other potential activists.[82] This discourse defined women's essential role as that of mother and wife, 'submissive in her function of reproduction and the satisfaction of the needs of men'.[83] But in this domestic function women, far from being separated from the life of the nation, fulfilled their fundamental vocation by giving birth to, and nurturing, male heroes of the past (the soldiers and *chouhada* of the war) and the generations of the future Algeria. To celebrate the Year of the Child in 1979, *El Moudjahid* commented: 'the infant reassures the mother as to her fertility, strengthens her position within the family and social group, attests to the virility of the male, throws light on his capacity . . . Grant us as husband the male who will increase our economic power'.[84] Here the vision of women joined up with the long-established ideology that presented them as the moral and cultural guardians of the core values of national identity. The maternal-nationalist discourse was charged with a sentimental affectivity which valued women through their silent suffering and their willing sacrifice of martyr sons and husbands in the liberation struggle.[85] Implicit in this ideology was that women could only lay claim to heroism *through* Algerian males: and this construction served to conceal and to block investigation of the kinds of economic, social and legal issues that specifically affected women in their own right.

The official discourse further marginalised or isolated the voice of independent women by categorising them as 'feminists', a term that carried particularly negative connotations of a dangerous and foreign movement that threatened the national interest. The conservative discourse of Ben Badis and the *Ulemas* had, since the 1930s, engaged in a strong moralising and puritanical stereotyping of western women as decadent and effete beings, self-centred creatures dedicated to the pursuit of leisure, who had lost touch with the true maternal destiny of women and dedication to child-care and the home. This discourse created a dualistic model in which the authentic Algerian woman, as guardian of the Arabo-Islamic society, was the radical opposite of the western woman.

This discourse was clearly reflected in a series of letters published by the ex-communist newspaper *Alger républicain* in early 1963 in which men engaged in a debate on the emancipation of women. Significantly, men opposed to feminism portrayed it through a stereotyped image that was drawn from the urban west, French cinema, advertising and magazines, the universe of Brigitte Bardot and Roger Vadim's *And God Created Woman* (1956). 'K. I. A' of Climat-de-France in Algiers wrote to say that, with the notable exception of women maquisards and a few highly educated professionals, he did not want to see an emancipation that meant women going to milk bars and dancing the twist or the 'cha cha cha'.[86] Ahmed Agrane of Medea also rejected feminism 'à la "Sophia Loren" or the woman who puts on make-up to go out 'for a walk' while leaving her children to hang about in the street'. Youth was being seduced by western values and losing touch with Algerian customs that remained best preserved in rural society, 'that which our ancestors handed down to us (the wife of the prophet, etc.)'. The solution was to close the doors to Occidentalism and to place emancipation in the hands of men: 'Give work to every man, educate them, teach them the rights of women in Muslim society'.[87] 'K. H.' wrote to *Jeune Afrique*, 'I want to bring the attention of our leaders to the perversion of morals . . . Young ladies have abandoned the veil and, with it, all decency. Obscene, their bodies half naked, with a provocative walk, they infest the streets. They seek to compete with men and, to do this, they smoke and give themselves over to drink'.[88] This conservative moralism, which was in a straight line of descent from the preaching of the puritanical *Ulema*, far from being an expression of uneducated prejudice, could be found at the highest levels of the government.[89]

A minority of men, who shared a socialist perspective and belonged to the FLN French Federation, supported a more progressive agenda on women. For example, Areskiou Lamari wrote from the thirteenth arrondissement in Paris on behalf of several 'brothers' in favour of abolishing seclusion, polygamy, arranged marriage and repudiation and upheld the shining example of the Soviets in Central Asia. 'No nation is free as long as half the population remains oppressed'. But Lamari's model of emancipation was also based on a rejection of western feminism, 'a pretend liberty à la colonialiste', symbolised by the dangers of sisters drinking beer and engaging in other excesses.[90]

The association between the term 'feminism' and a stereotypical, moralistic view of western women seems to have been shared by many Algerian women and even the UNFA, which warned, 'we must avoid feminism'.[91] The official discourse placed women almost entirely within a moral-cultural perspective: through their dedication to the family and the home they were seen as providing a barrier to the ills of modern society, 'the decline in morals', 'the erosion of the family', the 'rise in juvenile delinquency', etc. This ideology served to conceal and block understanding of the social and economic causes of the problems facing post-independence Algeria, as well as the specific political issues facing women, from problems of health and birth-control to training, employment, child-care and housing. If the nation was perceived to be going to the dogs this was singularly the responsibility of women in erring from their allotted function as reproducers, educators and providers. Finally, and most crucially, the dominant discourse could attack the subversive agenda of western 'feminism' since it was all-too-clearly associated with the concerted emancipation drive of French colonialism between 1957 and 1962. This association between the detested oppressor and 'feminism' provided the conservative religious and patriarchal forces in Algerian society almost unlimited powers of marginalising any nascent political women's movement as fundamentally anti-nationalist, a fifth column for cultural imperialism.[92] One of the unseen consequences of the French campaign for emancipation was thus to assist in the creation of a conservative nationalism that was to carry extremely negative consequences for Algerian women for the next twenty years and beyond.

In conclusion, and returning briefly to the key test of legal reform, we have seen how the late colonial state faced considerable difficulty in making any major impact on Algerian social and family structures. The basic administrative means, including a comprehensive *état civil*, were simply too inadequate to guarantee enforcement of the liberal marriage and family law of 1959. However, the newly independent republic maintained a discreet silence on the fact that a law that had been so fiercely attacked as an instrument of colonial subversion was left on the statute books until 1975. One reason why the new state was willing to do this was because the 1959 law was so widely ignored by both the population and the courts. Avoidance of an objectively progressive law suited the purposes of the FLN government since it helped guarantee political tranquillity. Likewise the state constantly stalled on a new code, allowed courts to follow their own devices (mainly leaning to a traditional reliance on *sharia*), and abandoned civil society to an entrenched patriarchy. As Claudine Chaulet notes, 'The function of family solidarities changed: from a method of survival, they changed into a means of establishing an autonomous nucleus working within and against the multifaceted penetration of the State', an interpretation supported by the work of Mounira Charrad.[93] Ben Bella and Boumédienne, in contrast to Bourguiba, abandoned the issue of reform for women because they believed the weight of family structures and ideology were simply too entrenched to be transformed without incurring the risk of a political earthquake. However, while it may in general be true that governments which introduce radical legal change far in advance of the degree of social progress reached by a nation take the risk of generating a political backlash, this is not to say that they have no room for manoeuvre. In the Algerian case the political elites made the costly mistake of formulating an official discourse and policy that reinforced, rather than helping to contain or alter, the most negative features of Arabo-Islamic conservatism, patriarchy and misogyny. In doing so they set Algerian society on course for an eventual catastrophe and the resurrection of Islamic fundamentalism that erupted in bloody civil war, a conflict that was distinguished above all by a vicious, generalised violence which once again targeted women as the symbols of a westernised subversion of Islam.

Notes

1 The term 'neopatriarchy' has been adopted by contemporary Algerian sociologists like Mahfoud Bennoune and Lahouari Addi, mainly from the work of Hisham Sharabi, *Neopatriarchy. A Theory of Distorted Change in Arab Society* (Oxford: Oxford University Press, 1988). Sharabi's thesis (p. 4) is that 'over the last one hundred years the patriarchal structures of Arab society, far from being displaced or truly modernized, have only been strengthened and maintained in deformed, "modernized" forms'.
2 On the economic transformation see especially Bennoune, *The Making of Contemporary Algeria*, Part 3.
3 For an overall, comparative view of such modernisation processes in the Middle East see Valentine M. Moghadam, *Modernizing Women. Gender and Social Change in the Middle East* (Boulder, Colo.: L. Rienner, 1993).
4 Kateb, *École, population*, 74–5.
5 *Ibid.*, 138–9. Data relate here to the ratio of women in employment to total population of women aged fifteen to sixty-five years; Jansen, 'The Economy of Religious Merit', 4.
6 Marnia Lazreg, 'Gender and Politics in Algeria: Unraveling the Religious Paradigm', *Signs: Journal of Women in Culture and Society*, 15: 4 (1990), 770–6.
7 Camille Lacoste-Dujardin, *Un village algérien: structures et évolution récente* (Algiers: SNED, 1976), and *Des mères contre les femmes*. Chaulet,

La Terre, les frères et l'argent; Lahouari Addi, *Les Mutations de la société algérienne. Famille et lien social dans l'Algérie contemporaine* (Paris: La Découverte, 1999). Carlier, *Entre nation et jihad*, 235, notes that pre-1954 nationalism was unable to escape, 'the pressure of the urban quarter, of custom, the tribe. They were constantly reminded of the demands of the family, the needs of the patrimony. The *açabiya*' [clan loyalty] constantly offered a resistance to the party of the people that believed it could defeat it'.

8 Lacoste-Dujardin, *Des mères contre les femmes*, 269–70; see also M'Rabet, *La Femme algérienne*, 52.
9 Claude Chaulet, 'Stratégies familiales et rôles des femmes', in *Femme, famille et société en Algérie. Journées d'étude 2–3 et 4 Juin 1987* (Oran: URASC, 1988), 105–9.
10 Diane Singerman, 'Where Has All the Power Gone? Women and Politics in Popular Quarters of Cairo', in Göçek and Balaghi (eds), *Reconstructing Gender*, 174–200, shows how older women, as heads of households, shared in such informal networks, in particular by arranging marriage alliances that increased the economic and 'political' power of the group.
11 Côte, *L'Algérie*, chapter 2; Pierre Robet Baduel, 'Habitat traditionnel et polarités structurales dans l'aire arabo-musulmane', in P. R. Baduel (ed.), *Habitat, état et société au Maghreb* (Paris: CNRS, 1988), 231–56.
12 Jansen, *Women Without Men*, 18–19. Jansen, p. 97, provides evidence that men suffered anxiety about their masculine identity through an inability to guarantee the seclusion and honour of wives, daughters and mothers.
13 Vandevelde-Daillière, *Femmes algériennes*, 166, 180–1, notes extreme levels of female seclusion in the *bidonvilles* where rural migrants were concentrated. For an excellent anthropological investigation of how extended, Muslim family units adapted to 'western' built forms see Alison Shaw, *A Pakistani Community in Britain* (Oxford: Blackwell, 1988).
14 Vandevelde-Daillière, *Femmes algériennes*, 30–1. Algerian popular discourse often associated the position of secluded Algerian women with the grave, the cemetery and death: as in a saying used by the Minister of Justice, Mohamed Bedjaoui, at a conference in May 1968, 'The woman in her husband's house or in the tomb', *Revue algérienne des sciences juridiques, économiques et politiques*, 5: 4 (December 1968), 1048.
15 *Ibid.*, 160–71, 181.
16 Lacoste-Dujardin, *Des mères contre les femmes*, 81–3.
17 Addi, *Les Mutations*, 105–6, 115–16, 210–12.
18 Vandevelde-Daillière, *Femmes algériennes*, 25.
19 Lazreg, *Eloquence*, 142–50; Zakya Daoud, *Feminisme et politique au Maghreb. Sept décennies de lutte* (Casablanca: Éditions Eddif, 1996), Part 2, 'Algérie'; Addi, *Les Mutations*, 78.
20 On the history of the internal divisions and struggle for power see Harbi, *Le FLN, mirage et réalité*, 355–76; Martin Stone, *The Agony of Algeria* (London: Hurst and Company, 1997), 43–50.

21 See, for example, Ricardo Rene Laremont, *Islam and the Politics of Resistance in Algeria, 1783–1992* (Trenton, N.J.: Africa World Press, 2000).
22 The high point of the intellectual socialist current, represented by Mostefa Lacheraf, Reda Malek and Mohammed Harbi, appears to have been achieved with the Programme of Tripoli of May 1962, but this line was quickly marginalised by Ben Bella who reinforced a conservative religious position. Lacheraf opposed this on two grounds: 'First, Islam carries within it the weight of values that belong to an archaic, rural civilization and its integration into political ideology can work as a brake on the modernisation of the country. Secondly, conservative forces are going to depend on religion in order to perpetuate backward values in relation to the family, the condition of women and social relations': Harbi, *Le FLN, mirage et réalité*, 333–4.
23 Harbi, *L'Algérie et son déstin*, 22. On the populist roots of the nationalist tradition see also Carlier, *Entre nation et jihad*.
24 There is a huge literature on post-independence Algeria: useful background guides can be found in David and Marina Ottaway, *Algeria. The Politics of a Socialist Revolution* (Berkeley and Los Angeles: University of California Press, 1970); Martin Evans and John Philips, *Algeria. Anger of the Dispossessed* (New Haven: Yale University Press, 2007).
25 McDougall, *History*, 136.
26 Harbi, *L'Algérie et son déstin*, 22–33; see also Carlier, 'Nationalisme et populisme', in *Entre nation et jihad*, in which he characterises nationalist ideology as 'vague, catch-all', so lacking in clarity that it could be all things to all people, papering over internal divisions of class and clan.
27 Chilla Bulbeck, *Re-orienting Western Feminism: Women's Diversity in a Postcolonial World* (Cambridge: Cambridge University Press, 1998), 16; see also Lazreg, *Eloquence*.
28 Lazreg, *Eloquence*; Knauss, *The Persistence of Patriarchy*; Monique Gadant, *Le Nationalisme algérien et les femmes* (Paris: l'Harmattan, 1995); Cherifa Bouatta, 'Feminine Militancy: *Moudjahidates* During and After the Algerian War', in Valentine M. Moghadam (ed.), *Gender and National Identity. Women and Politics in Muslim Societies* (London: Zed Books, 1994), 18–39; Doria Cherifati-Merabtine, 'Algeria at a Crossroads: National Liberation, Islamization and Women', also in Moghadam (ed.), *Gender and National Identity*, 40–62. On the centrality of law to contemporary women's movements see Farida Shaheed, 'Controlled or Autonomous: Identity and the Experience of the Network, Women Living under Muslim Laws', *Signs*, 19: 4 (Summer 1994), 997–1019.
29 Pruvost, 'Le Code algérien', 7–21.
30 *Ibid.*, 17–21; and Pruvost, *Femmes d'Algérie*, 265–98.
31 For a sharp analysis of the contradictions and paralysis of Algerian marriage and family law between 1962 and 1984 see 'Perspectives 1991', in Charnay, *La Vie musulmane en Algérie*, 377–90.

32 Vandevelde-Daillière, *Femmes algériennes*, 387, 390; Lazreg, *Eloquence*, 150.
33 Mohand Issad, 'Le Rôle du juge et la volonté des parties dans la rupture du lien conjugal', *Revue algérienne des sciences juridiques, économiques et politiques*, 5: 4 (December 1969), 1082.
34 Borrmans, *Statut personnel*, 537.
35 Addi, *Les Mutations*, 161–2, 204–7. M'Rabet, *La Femme algérienne*, 28–9, excoriates the classic double-standard of Algerian males who, in the street, regarded any women dressed in European style as 'easy' and open to sexual comment or advances.
36 Mir-Hosseini, *Marriage on Trial*, has through her direct observation of Moroccan and Iranian court procedure demonstrated the significant gap between Islamic law and practice, including women's ability to maximise their own interest through flexible negotiation of the rules.
37 Charnay, *La Vie musulmane*, is focused on the colonial period.
38 Fauque, *Stades d'évolution*, 14, noted that urban women were more aware of their legal rights, but often failed to take action through fear of their husband, unless this was managed on their behalf by men of the maternal family group.
39 Borrmans, *Statut personnel*, 515–19.
40 Vandevelde-Daillière, *Femmes algériennes*, 68–9, 176.
41 M'Rabet, *Les Algériennes*, 144–61.
42 *Ibid.*, 185; Borrmans, *Statut personnel*, 517.
43 Harbi and Meynier (eds), *FLN: Documents*, 609–12.
44 *El Moudjahid*, 45 (6 July 1959), quoted in Gadant, *Le Nationalisme*, 85.
45 Fanon, *L'An V*, 31.
46 Borrmans, *Statut personnel*, 538; Lazreg, *Eloquence*, 131–2.
47 Saïd Benabdallah, *La Justice du FLN pendant la guerre de libération* (Algiers: SNED, no date), from an extract in Harbi and Meynier (eds), *FLN: Documents*, 634–5.
48 *Ibid.*, 635.
49 See also Marshall and Stokes, 'Tradition and the Veil'.
50 Borrmans, *Statut personnel*, 521–9, 535–42.
51 Meynier, *Histoire intérieure*, 223–37.
52 Catherine Levy, a teacher and UGTA militant, has provided an eye-witness account. The following day fifty women with marks of physical assault came to the UGTA to seek help after their husbands had repudiated them: 'La Journée du 8 mars 1965 à Alger', *Clio*, 5 (1997), http://clio.revues.org/document415.html?format=print; see also Borrmans, *Statut personnel*, 539.
53 Vandevelde-Daillière, *Femmes algériennes*, 374–5.
54 Lazreg, *Eloquence*, 151.
55 Fanon, *L'An V*, 10, 14.
56 Amrane, *Les Femmes algériennes*, 259–72; Vandevelde-Daillière, *Femmes algériennes*, 89.

57 Amrane-Minne, *Des femmes*, 123, 146; see also M'Rabet, *La Femme algérienne*, 55.

58 Halimi, *Le Lait de l'oranger*, 354–7.

59 Amrane, *Les Femmes algériennes*, 270–1.

60 Saleha Boudefa, 'Image de la femme dans les discours officiels', *Femme, famille et société. Journées d'études 2–3 et 4 juin 1987* (University of Oran: URASC, 1988), 194–5, 199. Boudefa, 191, quotes the position held by Algerian women delegates at the International Congress of the Fédération Démocratique Internationale des Femmes (FDIF) at Copenhagen in 1958: 'It is because of their participation in the liberation struggle that women have acquired a prominent position in society; they will only be able to enjoy their rights in the framework of an independent Algeria completely cleansed of the colonial regime'.

61 Amrane, *Les Femmes algériennes*, 270–2.

62 On the concept of 'state feminism' see Fleischmann, 'The Other "Awakening"', 116–20.

63 Karen Adler, 'No Words to Say It? Women and the Expectation of Liberation', and Hanna Diamond, 'Women's Aspirations, 1943–47: An Oral Enquiry in Toulouse', in Kedward and Wood (eds), *Liberation of France*, 77–89, and 91–101.

64 Diamond, 'Women's Aspirations', 93.

65 See Fleischmann, 'The Other "Awakening"', 107–16, on nationalist movements in Egypt, Turkey, Iran, Syria, Iraq and Palestine as providing the 'honourable door' through which women could participate in public life, but most often a nationalism that failed women after the goals of independence or regime change had been achieved.

66 Baker, *Voices of Resistance*, 10–11, 197.

67 *Ibid.*, 180.

68 *Ibid.*, 11, 273–7.

69 Vandevelde-Daillière, *Femmes algériennes*, 10, 86, 110. In her autobiography, *Malgré la tourmente*, Vandevelde-Daillière, a Catholic militant supporter of the FLN during the war, describes her difficulty as a women carrying out such research, regarded as 'scandalous' in a climate of deepening Islamic conservatism and official authoritarian disapproval.

70 Vandevelde-Daillière, *Femmes algériennes*, 295–6.

71 Amrane, *Les Femmes algériennes*, 265.

72 *Ibid.*, 264. See Ighilahriz, *Algérienne*, 217–23, a leading official in the UNFA from 1974 to 1978, for an inside view of the conservative nature of the UNFA and its tight control by the FLN one-party state.

73 Vandevelde-Daillière, *Femmes algériennes*, 290–4, 303; Shaheed, 'Controlled', 1003.

74 *Ibid.*, 10–12, 223–5.

75 *Ibid.*, 90, 233–41.

76 *Ibid.*, 234.

77 Amrane, *Les Femmes algériennes*, 261–3, and Appendix, 286–92.

78 *Ibid.*, 262.

79 Vandevelde-Daillière, *Femmes algériennes*, 216.

80 Marie-Aimée Helie-Lucas, 'Women, Nationalism and Religion in the Algerian Liberation Struggle', in M. Bodran and M. Cooke (eds), *Opening the Gates* (London: Virago Press, 1990), 104–14.

81 Natalya Vince, 'To Be a Moudjahida in Independent Algeria: Itineraries and Memories of Women Veterans from the Algerian War of Independence, 1954–1962', PhD, University of London, July 2008, appeared too late to be consulted, but should throw further light on this evolution.

82 I am indebted in the following to Saleha Boudefa, 'Image de la femme', which provides a lucid analysis based on official statements, speeches and press.

83 *Ibid.*, 189.

84 *Ibid.*, 189: see also p. 202, a quotation from President Chadli in which he defined the role of women as that of preparing 'the new generation . . . through her labours in the bosom of the family, the fundamental cell of society, where she can achieve that which the State and man cannot'.

85 This over-charged emotional emphasis on the role of the mother was rooted in the extraordinarily intense relationship that Algerian sons invested in the mother, rather than in the spouse: see Lacoste-Dujardin, *Des mères contre les femmes*.

86 *Alger républicain*, 151 (13–14 January 1963).

87 *Ibid.*, 152 (15 January 1963).

88 *Jeune Afrique*, 27 July 1964, quoted in M'Rabet, *La Femme algérienne*, 42.

89 Knauss, *The Persistence of Patriarchy*, 98–9, quotes Mohamed Khider, general secretary of the FLN in Ben Bella's cabinet: 'The way of life of European women is incompatible with our traditions and our culture . . . We can only live by the Islamic morality. European women have no other preoccupations than the twist and Hollywood stars'.

90 *Alger républicain*, 140 (1 January 1963). The more progressive stance of Algerian men in France in relation to women requires further study: this appears to reflect in part their higher level of contact with modern urban society in metropolitan France, with the values and life-style of the French working class, and the fact that many thousands of migrants married or co-habited with European women.

91 Boudefa, 'Image de la femme', 192, quoting from a statement made in May 1976.

92 It is possible that this negative construction was reinforced by the fact that among the very small number of women activists that tried to organise during the difficult years between 1962 and the family code of 1984, most of them from the tiny minority of highly educated and professional women, was a significant number of militants of European origin, some of them married to Algerians, including Monique Gadant, Jacqueline Guerroudj, Hélène Vandevelde-Daillière and Danièle Djamila Amrane-Minne.

93 Quoted in Lacoste-Dujardin, *Des méres contre les femmes*, 287.

Conclusion: the failure of history

Contemporary western concerns about Islamic resurgence, particularly since the Iranian revolution of 1979 and the spread of radicalism post-9/11, has led to a huge revival of academic interest and debate in relation to a much older component of Orientalism, the theory that Muslim societies face an inherent difficulty in making the transition to occidental forms of liberalism or parliamentary democracy. Islam, many have argued, is in essence incompatible with the good or 'open society'.[1] The debate on the modernisation paradigm in Muslim states has invariably centred on gender and the role of women, and has crystallised around certain enduring symbols of perceived Islamic oppression, such as the veil, the harem, seclusion, forced marriage and physical violence. The deep ambiguity of the conservative colonial regime in Algeria, right down until the start of the War of Independence in 1954, was that it condemned the uncivilised and inferior nature of the Muslim family and the treatment of women, but simultaneously had a deep political interest in sustaining such a system of oppression as it provided the key legitimation for maintaining the exclusion of Algerians from full citizenship and power-sharing. Polygamy and child-marriage were viewed by colonial ideologues as incompatible with the republican order. This reactionary position seemed to be all the easier to sustain before 1954, since the colonial governing class entered into a tacit 'gender pact' with conservative Islamic religious clerics and leaders who also had an interest in protecting the family and women from the dangers of secularism and 'westernisation'.

A minority of better-educated, urban Algerian women, along with communist and progressive Catholic activists, began to challenge this conservative block during the turbulent phase of nationalism between the Liberation and 1954. But the outbreak of the War of Independence marked a radical shift in two respects: firstly, the emerging women's organisations were rapidly dissolved and merged under the unitary umbrella of the authoritarian FLN. The most widely shared socialist and liberal internationalist perception of Algerian women at war, one that was later powerfully reinforced through Pontecorvo's *Battle of Algiers* and the works of Franz Fanon, was one of heroic armed fighters that were actively dynamiting all the Orientalist stereotypes of Muslim women as secluded and supine slaves of male domination. But this misperception provided evidence more of the successful nature of FLN propaganda than a meaningful transformation of the role of women. Algerian women did break through some of the constraints of gender, as have women almost universally in modern times under the exceptional conditions of 'total' war in which their labour power and skills became necessary in the desperate struggle for national survival. But the most widely shared male perception of women's active participation in struggle was that this was a purely temporary thing, and that once independence was gained they would revert to their 'natural' domestic function as mothers and wives.

For many historians this particular pattern of war-time 'liberation' of Algerian women, followed by a peacetime reassertion of 'normality' and the status-quo ante, will hold few surprises since it is a pattern that has been witnessed in innumerable global wars, insurrections and patriotic struggles. But what was unusual about the War of Independence was the extent to which this rather typical pattern was further radically distorted by the cross-interference from a French 'emancipation' strategy which was to carry extremely negative long-term consequences for the future women's movement. Algerian nationalism, building on the intellectual traditions of *Ulema* reformism, characterised women's emancipation as an alien, secularising movement orchestrated by military and colonialist interests. This interpretation was quite correct, however, in the post-independence context this nationalist reaction to the subversive germ of an alien and dangerous feminism was deployed to attack the very principle of equality and women's rights, in favour of a highly conservative patriarchal model of society.

Which takes us to the second radical shift precipitated by the war, the U-turn executed by the colonial government after 1954 in relation to Muslim women's rights. Initially it seems surprising or highly contradictory that a huge army of occupation, a largely male-dominated organisation in which the values of the warrior rested on a conservative view of female domesticity and subordination, should have had any interest in the plight of Algerian women. A complex of factors contributed to this innovative shift: faced with significant progressive reform of family law in Tunisia, Morocco and elsewhere, the French government did not want to be seen to fall behind and to give a hostage to those interests that were seeking to pillory French colonialism before the UN and the

court of international opinion. Emancipation was also seen as pre-
empting the dangers of the FLN itself organising women and offering to
liberate them; as the means to win over an oppressed half of the population to support *Algérie française* and as a means of penetrating into the
protected sphere of the Algerian family in order to gain intelligence; and
finally as a way to modernise the overall society and economy, through
civic engagement, education and training.

Overall this strategy failed miserably, a failure that was linked to the
extraordinary inability of European decision-makers to recognise the
enormous weight and complexity of Muslim society and its deep-seated
durability and powers of resistance to colonial attempts to re-shape it in
its own image. The pseudo-revolutionary optimism of '13 May 1958' and
the secretive orchestration of crowd euphoria by psychological warfare
officers convinced many soldiers and settlers that there was indeed mass
Algerian popular support for unveiling and emancipation. But this was
largely an illusion. Also working in the direction of a naive optimism and
over-confidence in the ease with which transformation could be brought
about was the unquestioning Eurocentric belief in the superiority of
western familial values, and the assumption of an inexorable evolution
towards this model that would be readily embraced by all educated and
rational beings. In reality the French, even when backed up by a huge
army of occupation, faced extraordinary difficulty in introducing reforms
or social engineering that attempted to transform the fundamental social
and cultural structures, and in particular of the family, the core building
block of the entire Algerian order and a key site of resistance.

'Post-Marxist' or revisionist historians of the 'classic' revolutions,
especially of the French and Russian Revolutions, have since the
1970s tended to emphasise the limitations of radical movements to
effect a root-and-branch change in the deeper social structures of the
ancien régime, structures which tended to survive underground only to
resurface later. From the 1920s onwards several states engaged in the
authoritarian, 'top-down', modernisation of Muslim societies, and in
particular of the role of women and marriage law. The best conditions
for such 'state feminism', as in the case of Mustapha Kemal in Turkey
and Bourguiba in Tunisia, was where a charismatic leader was able to
benefit from a high level of populist support and nationalist fervour to
effect change. Even under such optimum conditions traditional family
and tribal structures remained deeply entrenched and resilient, but in
the instance of Algeria such a reform agenda was both imported by a
foreign power and attempted under the worst of conditions, during the
political chaos and massive violence that accompanied a particularly
long war of decolonisation.

Any meaningful transformation of the patriarchal family would have required a long time-scale, a sustained reformist endeavour, but time was not on the side of the French government and the generals, who were driven by the instrumental goal of obtaining a rapid or even immediate change in women's lives as part of the ambition to win and terminate an unsustainable and crippling colonial war. Moreover, for all the glowing propaganda surrounding the MSF women's circles, the EMSI medical teams, and schooling of girls, these interventionist organisations were simply too thin on the ground to effect any significant change. The government lacked the economic and qualified human resources to sustain this programme, and the army commanders consistently prioritised budget allocations to counter-guerrilla operations (acquisition of helicopters, weaponry, etc.) and the 'real' war, which left those dedicated on the ground to a strategy of contact with Muslim women desperately short of funds and equipment. Finally, the objective of emancipating Algerian women as a key ingredient of the strategy of revolutionary warfare, the battle for hearts and minds, was fatally contradicted and undermined by the violence and repression of military operations, and in particular by the large-scale destruction, uprooting and displacement of the peasantry into quasi-concentration camp conditions. As Vincent Monteil commented, before quitting Algeria as the Soustelle regime sank into a cycle of deepening repression, 'I am convinced that we are heading for a catastrophe. I persist in my belief that it is not possible to combine both repression and "reform": a choice must be made'.[2]

A comparative perspective shows that the French emancipation agenda in Algeria was not entirely unique and can be related to a much longer tradition of the western 'civilising mission' in the Maghreb, Middle East and Asia. Over the last century the power-games of Orientalism have, in particular, been played out over the representations of Muslim women and their bodies, and especially of veiling, which was strategically deployed as a sign of the very essence of Islamic society, the perception of an 'uncivilised' order that was based on the subjugation of women, despotism, polygamy, the harem and sexual perversion. The French military intervention in Algeria during 1954–62, in its emphasis on un-veiling and the drive to a western style emancipation, derived its force from this Orientalist current in European colonialism, but also seemed to foreshadow the revival of global Islamophobia after 1979 and the eventual moves to 'liberate' Muslim societies by US-led neo-imperialism in Afghanistan and Iraq.

The seismic shift of 9/11 has tended to obscure the fact that the roots of an Islamophobic surge in the USA and Europe can be found much earlier, in particular from the Iranian Revolution in 1979 that was

symbolised by westernised women reverting to the *chador*.[3] The bitter
controversy in France after 1989 over the 'headscarves affair', whether
Muslim girls should be allowed to wear Islamic dress in secular state
schools, was indicative of a shift towards fear of an Islamist threat that
was no longer perceived as only an external enemy, but one that was
now located inside the 'west'. But the closest parallel to the Algerian
War was to come with the US invasion of Afghanistan and Iraq when
the coalition forces attempted, through military conquest, to induce
'regime change' and to export a western model of 'democracy' and of
the good society.

The tone of this 'liberation' was established first in its most evident
'Orientalist' form during the invasion of Afghanistan when President
Bush and the American right discovered a newfound mission to free
Afghan women from the oppression of the 'medieval' Taliban and
the sinister *burqa*. Not unlike the women propagandists of the MSF
during the Algerian War, US 'feminists', funded by Revlon, Clairol,
L'Oréal and various fashion magazines, promised to bring to unveiled
Afghan women, western beauticians and tips on make-up and style.[4]
That George Bush and Donald Rumsfeld should suddenly appear as
the defenders of women's rights might seem anomalous, but was not
without historical precedent. A century earlier Lord Cromer, Governor
of Egypt, had supported the liberation of Egyptian women from the
living incarceration of Islam, while simultaneously opposing the suf-
fragette movement in Britain,[5] while Generals Massu and Salan were
unlikely champions of female emancipation. The common link between
Cromer, Massu and Bush is that all three conservatives deployed a
stereotype of cruel Orientalist oppression so as to legitimate western
intervention, rescue fantasies and the 'civilising mission'.

Susan Faludi notes that the White House concern for Muslim women
stopped as quickly as it had started, once the bombing intervention
had begun in October 2001,[6] but the propaganda image of the *burqa*
set the tone for the later invasion of Iraq in March 2003. In the case of
Iraq the Orientalist stereotyping of a backward Islam, as symbolised
by women, did not serve American propaganda purposes quite as well,
since the coalition confronted a more secular and modernised society in
which women had achieved a high level of education, welfare rights and
employment. If women needed to be 'rescued' from poverty and repression in 2003, this had less to do with the regime of Saddam Hussein
than with the drastic deterioration in living standards due to the ferocious economic sanctions imposed over the previous thirteen years. The
illiteracy rate for women climbed from a low of 8 per cent in 1985 to 45
per cent in 1995.[7]

As the US and British governments pushed towards war through late 2002 and early 2003 numerous experts on Iraq and the Middle East warned of the problems that could be faced in attempting to 'liberate' such a complex society, the difficulty of engaging in post-invasion economic investment and reconstruction, and the dangers of political destabilisation that might undermine 'regime change'. The question was raised as to whether America had an exit strategy that would enable it to hand over power to a stable, 'democratic' Iraqi government. Events on the ground, including the triggering of a civil war and economic meltdown, were quickly to confirm the direst predictions. The catastrophic failure of US decision makers and planners can be significantly linked to an inability or refusal to learn from history, and to understand why it was that similar neo-imperial military interventions into Muslim societies, from the French in Algeria to the Soviet role in Afghanistan, had ended in defeat. This is not to say that the US military showed no interest at all post-9/11 in the Algerian War: indeed the Pentagon, bracing itself for the invasion of Baghdad, began to study Pontecorvo's film, *The Battle of Algiers*, but this was not to learn from the crucial political lessons of French defeat but rather from an interest in the triumphalist claims of Massu's parachutists that they had developed counter-insurgency techniques that had successfully crushed Muslim terrorist networks embedded in an urban society.[8] Media sources claimed that President Bush kept a copy of Alistair Horne's *A Savage War of Peace* as his bedside reading. But US leaders were more interested in anti-guerrilla strategies than taking note of the bigger picture, and examining why France had, despite its military superiority, lost the war.

Underlying the imperial hubris of Bush and Blair was a singular failure to engage in a well-considered evaluation of the history, sociology and politics of the 'enemy' nation. Four months before the invasion of Iraq Blair invited six academics to Downing Street, three specialists on Iraq and three on international security. The Arabacist George Joffe recalled, 'We all pretty much said the same thing. Iraq is a very complicated country, there are tremendous inter-communal resentments, and don't imagine you'll be welcomed'.[9] Blair, added Charles Tripp, showed little interest: 'I felt he wanted us to reinforce his gut instinct that Saddam was a monster. It was a weird mixture of total cynicism and moral fervour'. Even more extraordinary was the fact that fifty-two retired British diplomats, many with a close knowledge of the Middle East, wrote in April 2004 an open letter to Blair deploring the lack of a pre-war analysis of Iraq and the naivety of plans to import a democratic society. A similar disdain for the lessons of the past, a fatal amnesia, was also noted among US leaders by many commentators. Irene Gendzier noted the impoverishment of US analysis of the Middle East which, 'reflects a loss of historical memory, the disappearance from view of the impact of past policies, and an indifference to their human and social as well as political consequences'.[10]

By the early twenty-first century it might have been expected that educated political elites would have been highly attuned to the negative impacts of past colonial empires that had unthinkingly imposed their own values on 'inferior' subject peoples. In the post-colonial age of multiculturalism, anti-racism and universal rights it was widely acknowledged that it was no longer morally or politically right to steamroller the culture of other 'races' or peoples. But since 9/11 there has been a significant revival among academic historians and political commentators of the imperial paradigm, a model which suggests continuity between the contemporary USA and past global empires and the ideological over-determination of international policy. An outstanding characteristic of the 'new imperialism' has been a profound failure by key decision makers to try and understand the political, sociological and cultural structures of Afghan and Iraqi societies. The Bush vision of invasion and the 'quick fix' was a dangerous delusion, a misguided optimism that rather backward oppressed 'Arabs' were bound to gratefully welcome US troops with open arms once 'set free'.

In a scenario that was striking in its similarity to Algeria, the US government failed to investigate or understand family and 'clan' structures; entertained a false and dangerous optimism as to its ability to carry out a rapid transformation of occupied societies; provided inadequate funding and resources for programmes of reform and reconstruction; and rapidly lost any initial support among the population through 'good works' by the descent into violence, anarchy and the collapse of already weakened infrastructures. Iraqi resistance to the coalition rapidly coalesced around Sunni and Shi'i militias that lurched towards conservative forms of radical Islamism that portrayed 'western' intervention, as in Algeria, as a secularist assault on the fundamental religious beliefs and identity of Muslims. The progressive Iraqi personal status laws of 1959 and 1978 that banned forced marriage, restricted polygamy, empowered women to seek divorce, and enforced the intervention of the courts, came under attack in the new Constitution,[11] while Islamist groups unleashed a wave of violence against women, forcing them to wear the *hijab*, or to retreat from education and employment back into the seclusion of the home. The US thus entered into a catastrophic situation that was largely predictable from the earlier history of Algerian decolonisation. The long-term impacts of French emancipation of Algerian women had been equally perverse, and achieved the very opposite results from its proclaimed goals. Through the fatal association between women's liberation and the assault on the Muslim nation, the French succeeded in reinforcing the reactionary elements within the FLN and Islamist currents that blocked reform after independence and consolidated the conservative forces that ultimately resurfaced in the brutal civil war after 1992 and a decade of extreme violence that once again was to centre on reveiling and the bodies of women.

Notes

1 This position is associated, in particular, with the work of Samuel P. Huntington, *The Clash of Civilizations and the Remaking of World Order* (London: Simon and Schuster, 1998). The literature is far too enormous to list here, but for three excellent and balanced over-views see John L. Esposito, *The Islamic Threat. Myth or Reality?* (Oxford: Oxford University Press, 1995 edn); Fred Halliday, *Islam and the Myth of Confrontation. Religion and Politics in the Middle East* (London: I. B. Tauris, 1995), and Halliday, *Two Hours that Shook the World. September 11, 2001: Causes and Consequences* (London: Saqi Books, 2002).

2 Courrière, *La Guerre d'Algérie*, Vol. 2, 135.

3 On the origins of this Islamophobic current in contemporary France see Neil MacMaster, 'Islamophobia in France and the "Algerian Problem"', in Emran Qureshi and Michael A. Sells (eds), *The New Crusades. Constructing the Muslim Enemy* (New York: Columbia University Press, 2003), 288–313.

4 Faludi, *The Terror Dream*, 41.

5 Ahmed, *Women and Gender in Islam*, 151–5.

6 Faludi, *The Terror Dream*, 41–2.

7 Nadj Al-Ali, 'Reconstructing Gender: Iraqi women between dictatorship, war, sanctions and occupation', *Third World Quarterly*, 26: 4–5 (2005), 739–58; and *Iraqi Women. Untold Stories from 1948 to the Present* (London: Zed Books, 2007), 131–46, 171–214.

8 Neil MacMaster, 'Torture: From Algiers to Abu Ghraib', *Race and Class*, 46: 2 (2004), 1–21.

9 Jonathan Steele, 'Guys, I'm Afraid We Haven't Got a Clue', *The Guardian*, 21 January 2008 (extract from his book *Defeat. Why They Lost Iraq* (London: I. B. Tauris, 2008)).

10 Irene L. Gendzier, 'Invisible by Design: US Policy in the Middle East', *Diplomatic History*, 26: 4 (Fall 2002), 618.

11 Al-Ali, *Iraqi Women*, 245–6.

Primary sources and select bibliography

Archive sources

Archives de la Préfecture de police (APP), Paris [subject to dérogation].
APP HA/53, SCINA report, 31 October–2 November, 1959.

Bibliothèque nationale (BN), Paris.
Consulted for Algerian and French press: note especially:
Femmes nouvelles.

British Library, Colindale.
French, Algerian and International Press on micro-film, especially for the events of May to June 1958.
'Fifty Days in French History', M. misc. 39 to 48.
Algerian Press series: M. misc. 49 to 53.

Centre des archives contemporaines (CAC), Fontainebleau.
CAC 19950236, file 7.
CAC 19950236, file 8.
Centre des archives d'outre-mer (CAOM), Aix-en-Provence.
Series: Cabinet of Governor General:
10CAB22; 10CAB155; 10CAB219; 10CAB221; 11CAB28*; 12CAB52*; 12CAB192; 12CAB207; 12CAB230; 12CAB237*; 13CAB7; 13CAB20; 13CAB37*; 13CAB61; 13CAB64; 14CAB9*; 14CAB88; 14CAB162*; 14CAB165–166; 14CAB233; 15CAB118.
Series: Ministère d'État Chargé des Affaires Algériennes:
81F74; 81F88; 81F107; 81F121; 81F367–8; 81F888 ;81F1218; 81F1219; 81F1220; 81F1221; 81F1222; 81F1223; 81F1224;81F1662.
Series: Séction administrative spécialisée (SAS):
SAS4; 2SAS7; 2SAS52; 2SAS53; 2SAS56; 2SAS58; 2SAS59; 2SAS60; 2SAS61–2; 2SAS64; 2SAS67; 2SAS68; 2SAS69; 2SAS71; 2SS72; 3SAS18; 3SAS19; 3SAS29*.

Etablissement de Communication et de Production Audiovisuelle de la Défense (ECPAD), Fort d'Ivry.

The archive includes photographs taken during the Algerian war, mainly by official army photographers: frequently these include valuable typed notes by the journalist on the situation in which these were taken.

Service historique de la Défense, Château de Vincennes (formerly, Service historique l'armée de terre (SHAT)).
Some cartons are subject to permission (*dérogation*), and where granted these are indicated by an asterisk*: however, reorganisation and computerisation of the archives during the research created considerable chaos, and some cartons that were previously open now require permission.
The following have been consulted:
1H1112/3; 1H1117; 1H1147/1; 1H1194/3; 1H1206; 1H1215/3; 1H1216/1; 1H1268/9*; 1H1585/3*; 1H1730/4*; 1H1895; 1H1897/1*; 1H2088/4*; 1H2409; 1H2460/1; 1H2461/1*; 1H2463; 1H2467/2; 1H2476/1; 1H2483; 1H2504; 1H2515; 1H2516; 1H2536/2*; 1H2553/1; 1H2556/1; 1H2566*; 1H2567/1; 1H2569/1* and 2*; 1H2570; 1H2574; 1H2582; 1H3217/4*; 1H3513*; 1H4334*; 1H4395*; 1H4688/4*; 1H4705; 1H4706/2*; Series: 7U20*; 7U21*.

Oral sources/interviews

Monique Hervo, Romilly, 16 October 2005.
Marc Garanger, Paris, 18 October 2005.
Ginette Thévenin-Copin, Montpellier, 2 and 3 November 2006.
Edmée Barbier, Montpellier, 3 November 2006.
Jean-Louis Gérard, Paris, 10 June 2007.
Michel Launay, Paris, 25 June 2008.

Select bibliography

Listed here is a selection of books and articles which relate specifically to Algerian women. Full references to the material used in the book can be found in the endnotes.
Abrous, Dahbia, *L'Honneur face au travail des femmes en Algérie* (Paris: L'Harmattan, 1989).
Addi, Lahouari, *Les Mutations de la société algérienne. Famille et lien social dans l'Algérie contemporaine* (Paris: La Découverte, 1999).
Alloula, Malek, *The Colonial Harem* (Manchester: Manchester University Press, 1987).
Amrane, Djamila, *Les Femmes algériennes dans la guerre* (Paris: Plon, 1991).
Amrane-Minne, Danièle Djamila, *Des femmes dans la guerre d'Algérie* (Paris: Éditions Karthala, 1994).
Arnaud, Georges and Jacques Vergès, *Pour Djamila Bouhired* (Paris: Minuit, 1957).

Beauvoir, Simone de, and Gisèle Halimi, *Djamila Boupacha* (Paris: Gallimard, 1962).

Borrmans, Maurice, *Statut personnel et famille au Maghreb de 1940 à nos jours* (Paris: Mouton, 1977).

Boudefa, Saleha, 'Image de la femme dans les discourse officiels', in *Femme, famille et société. Journées d'études 2–3 et 4 juin 1987* (Oran: URASC, 1988), 178–208.

Brac de la Perrière, Caroline, *Derrière les héros. Les Employées de maison musulmanes en service chez les Européens à Alger pendant la guerre d'Algérie*, 1954–1962 (Paris: L'Harmattan, 1987).

Branche, Raphaëlle, 'Des viols pendant la guerre d'Algérie', *Vingtième siècle. Revue d'histoire*, 75 (July–September, 2002), 123–32.

Charrad, Mounira M., *States and Women's Rights. The Making of Postcolonial Tunisia, Algeria, and Morocco* (Berkeley: University of California Press, 2001).

Daoud, Zakya, *Féminisme et politique au Maghreb. Sept décennies de lutte* (Casablanca: Editions Eddif, 1996).

Dore-Audibert, Andrée, *Des Françaises d'Algérie dans la guerre de libération* (Paris: Karthala, 1995).

Fanon, Frantz, *L'An V de la révolution algérienne* [1959] (Paris: La Découverte, 2001 edn).

Fournier, Christiane, *Les EMSI: des filles comme ça!* (Paris: Arthème Fayard, 1959).

Gadant, Monique, *Le Nationalisme algérien et les femmes* (Paris: L'Harmattan, 1995).

Garanger, Marc, *La Guerre d'Algérie vue par un appelé du contingent* (Paris: Seuil, 1984).

——, *Femmes algériennes 1960* [c. 1989] (Anglet: Atlantica, 2002 edn).

——, *Marc Garanger: Retour en Algérie* (Paris: Atlantica, 2007).

Garanger, Marc, and Leïla Sebbar, *Femmes des Hauts-Plateaux. Algérie 1960* (Paris: La Boîte à Documents, 1990).

Gordon, David C., *Women of Algeria. An Essay on Change* (Cambridge, Mass.: Harvard University Press, 1968).

Guerroudj, Jacqueline, *Des douars et des prisons* (Algiers: Bouchène, 1995).

Ighilahriz, Louisette, *Algérienne* (Paris: Fayard/Calmann-Lévy, 2001).

Jansen, Willy, *Women Without Men: Gender and Marginality in an Algerian Town* (Leiden: E. J. Brill, 1987).

Jauffret, Jean-Charles (ed.), *Des hommes et des femmes en guerre d'Algérie* (Paris: Éditions Autrement, 2003).

Kimble, Sara L., 'Emancipation Through Secularization: French Feminist Views of Muslim Women's Condition in Inter-war Algeria', *French Colonial History*, 7 (2006), 109–28.

Knauss, Peter R., *The Persistence of Patriarchy. Class, Gender, and Ideology in Twentieth Century Algeria* (New York: Praeger, 1987).

Lacoste-Dujardin, Camille, *Des mères contre les femmes. Maternité et patriarcat au Maghreb* (Paris: La Découverte, 1996).

Lazreg, Marnia, *The Eloquence of Silence. Algerian Women in Question* (New York: Routledge, 1994).

Marshall, Susan E. and Randall G. Stokes, 'Tradition and the Veil: Female Status in Tunisia and Algeria', *Journal of Modern African Studies*, 19: 4 (December 1981), 625–46.

M'Rabet, Fadéla, '*La Femme algérienne*', suivi de '*Les Algériennes*' (Paris: Maspero, 1983 edn).

Pruvost, Lucie, *Femmes d'Algérie. Société, famille et citoyenneté* (Algiers: Casbah Éditions, 2002).

Saadia-et-Lakhdar [Rabah Bouaziz], *L'Aliénation colonialiste et la résistance de la famille algérienne* (Lausanne: La Cité, 1961).

Saï, Fatima Zohra, *Mouvement national et question féminine. Des origines à la veille de la guerre de libération nationale* (Oran: Éditions Dar El Gharb, 2002).

Sambron, Diane, 'La Politique d'émancipation du gouvernement français à l'égard des femmes algériennes pendant la guerre d'Algérie', in Jean-Charles Jauffret (ed.), *Des hommes et des femmes en guerre d'Algérie* (Paris: Éditions Autrement, 2003), 226–42.

——, 'L'Evolution du statut juridique de la femme musulmane à l'époque coloniale', in *La Justice en Algérie, 1830–1962* (Paris: La Documentation française, 2005), 123–42.

——, *Femmes musulmanes. Guerre d'Algérie 1954–1962* (Paris: Éditions Autrement, 2007).

Seferdjeli, Ryme, 'French "Reforms" and Muslim Women's Emancipation During the Algerian War', *Journal of North African Studies*, 9: 4 (Winter 2004), 19–61.

——, 'The French Army and Muslim Women During the Algerian War (1954–62) *Hawwa*, 31 (2005), 40–79.

Taraud, Christelle, *La Prostitution coloniale. Algérie, Tunisie, Maroc (1830–1962)* (Paris: Payot, 2003).

Thévenin-Copin, Ginette, *Plaidoyer pour la paix* (Montpellier: Mémoire de Notre Temps, 2001).

Tillion, Germaine, *Le Harem et les cousins* (Paris: Seuil, 1966).

Vandevelde-Daillière, Hélène, *Femmes algériennes à travers la condition féminine dans la Constantinois depuis l'indépendance* (Algiers: Office des Publications Universitaires, 1980).

Whitfield, Lee, 'The French Military Under Female Fire: The Public Opinion Campaign and Justice in the Case of Djamila Boupacha, 1960–62', *Contemporary French Civilization*, 20: 1 (1996), 76–90.

Woodhull, Winifred, *Transfigurations of the Maghreb. Feminism, Decolonization, and Literatures* (Minneapolis: University of Minnesota Press, 1993).

Index

Kemal, Mustapha, reform of Turkish family code 6–9, 16, 22 n.16, 80–1, 169, 375, 396
Khemisti law (1963) 378, 380
Knoertzer, jurist 288
Kock, Hansjoerg, journalist 334
Korean War 153

Laboratoire des science humaines appliqués (LSHR) 155–9, 166, 172
Lacheroy, Colonel Charles 87, 119, 136, 144, 154
Lacoste, Robert, Resident minister policy on women 69, 78, 81–6, 271–2
Operation Pilot 90, 94, 97–8, 100, 302
Lacoste-Dujardin, Camille, anthropologist 221, 370–2
Lacouture, Jean, historian 118
Lakhdar, Si, ALN Commander 224
Lakhdari, Samia, FLN militant 99, 317
Lakhdari, Sheikh Abdelali ben Ahmed 135–6, 169, 287, 298
Laliam, Mustapha, ALN doctor 321
Lalla Aïcha, Moroccan princess 126–7, 148 n.41, 169
Lamari, Areskiou, FLN militant 386
Lamoudi, Lamine, Ulema 272
Laribi, Baya, FLN militant 320, 332
Laribière, Lucette, communist militant 36
Launay, Michel, historian 158, 194
Lazreg, Marnia, historian 213, 380
Lebanon 7, 8, 18, 126, 180, 184
Lefaucheux, Marie-Hélène, deputy and UN diplomat 52–4, 56, 83, 85, 181, 188
adviser to Sid Cara 292, 293–4
Lefébvre, Francine, deputy 85
Lefeuvre, Daniel, historian 78
Léger, Captain Paul-Alain 119, 120–1
Lenoir, Jacques-Guy 280
Lentin, Albert-Paul 121
Léonard, Roger, Governor General 54–6, 72
Lerner, Daniel, political scientist 158

Liberation of France 143, 362, 382
Loi cadre, local government reform 85–6, 94, 302

Macey, David, historian 139, 172
Madagascar, 245
Madani, Ahmed Tawfik al-, Ulema 45, 64 n.96, 79, 374
Madani, Mériem, FLN militant 48
Mafart, M.J. 291
Maison Rouge, Colonel de (later General) 155, 217–18, 225, 230–1, 237 n.21
Mandouze, Mme 35
Mao Tse-Tung 4, 87 n.155, 225
marabouts 42, 92, 194, 263, 287, 303, 356, 358
Mari, Jacques de, administrator 185
Massignon, Louis, historian 75
Massu, General Jacques 90, 99, 102, 123, 182, 222, 279, 398
events of '13 May' 114–17, 129, 136
referendum (1958) 274, 276
Massu, Malika 129, 136
Massu, Suzanne 129, 136, 167–8, 180–7, 292
Maugé, Mme, EMSI 245, 248–9, 251, 253, 262
Mau Mau Revolt (Kenya) 353
'May 13' events (1958)
burning of veils 115, 127
defined 102 n.1, 145 n.5
FLN response 136–7, 141
fraternisation parades 9, 68, 114–44, 396
Gaullist plot 114, 116
loss of impetus 290, 298–9, 352
McDougall, James, historian 45
Menchari, Mrs, Tunisian feminist 126
Mendès-France, Pierre 71–2, 74
Merad, Ali, historian 43
Messali Hadj 32, 37, 43, 46–7, 231, 298, 357, 374
Meurisse, Jean-Paul 223
Meynier, Gilbert, historian 329, 333, 338, 380
Michelet, Edmond, Minister of Justice 291–2
Milliot, Louis, Professor of law 83